GUILD WARS®

PRIMA Official Game Guide

Prima Games
A Division of Random House, Inc.

3000 Lava Ridge Court
Roseville, CA 95661
1-800-733-3000
www.primagames.com

An Incan
Monkey God
Studios
Production

PRIMA OFFICIAL GAME GUIDE

Credits

Editors
David Ladyman, Andrea Silva, Rebecca Chastain

Contributors
Laura "Taera" Genender

Jonathan "Tarinth" Radoff

Bydian

Heather "Orlena" Rothwell

CP "Kittychan" Wilkinson

Jim "Oakleif" Rothwell

Jose Silva

Eric Mylonas

Book Design and Layout
Raini Madden

Maps
Linda "Brasse" Carlson

Game Art
The ArenaNet Team

IMGS Art Assistance
Lynette Alcorn, True Hardt

Many thanks to the folks at Arena.Net, Especially ...
Marti McKenna

Isaiah Cartwright

Steve Hwang

Ben Miller

Stacie Magelssen

Gaile Gray

Tim Jones

Jay Adams

Curtis Johnson

Thanks also to Ethan Kidhardt and our other panelists.

About This Guide

*This guide is a detailed snapshot of **Guild Wars** as it was at the time of release. **Guild Wars** is a living, growing entity, and new content is being added all the time. Use this book as a guide to the initial **Guild Wars** release, then enjoy the new quests, missions, and items as they become available.*

*The material in this guide is both factual and subjective. As **Guild Wars** is a new game with many different character choices and team strategies, players will approach it from many different perspectives. Read through the guide and the opinions of our writers, and then form your own opinions. We haven't eliminated contradictory opinions, as they usually help rather than hurt the reader by providing several different viewpoints to consider. The key is to find a strategy that works best for your play style, and this book will guide you toward that discovery.*

Table of Contents

Read This First

This section is a primer for those who haven't had a lot of online RPG experience. If you're the veteran of many games in this genre, you may want to plunge ahead into the guide; if not, start your adventures here.

Online RPG Frequently Used Terms

The following terms are heavily used in all manner of online RPGs, and *Guild Wars* is no exception. Not only are these terms liberally spread throughout this guide, but you'll hear them more often than not while conversing with online RPG vets:

aggro: When a single monster or group of monsters is attracted to you because you've stumbled into their field of view. Drawing too much aggro can mean a very quick death, so pull one at a time. You can determine which enemies you'll aggro in *Guild Wars* by the small transparent circle surrounding the player's position on the mini-map—if any enemy "trips" over this, they'll be all over you.

AoE: Area of Effect refers to any skill or attack that has an effect (usually a radius of "x" distance from the initial attack/casting point) that will hit more than one enemy. AoEs can take many forms, from offensive spells and attacks to heals, buffs, and everything between.

build: This refers to the type of character you play and the skill set that goes with that character.

buff: Any enchantment that imbues the player or players with a beneficial boost, whether it applies to an attribute, skill, etc. Think of it as temporarily turbocharging your character beyond his or her normal abilities.

combos: Combos or combo'ing refers to using two (or more) complementary skills in rapid succession to inflict more damage or increase the efficacy of a buff or heal.

DD: Direct Damage. This applies to any spell that delivers its full payload of damage in one shot, as opposed to spread out over a span of time (DoT).

de-buff: The opposite of a buff, and is any skill, that removes the beneficial effects of a previously applied buff.

DoT: Damage Over Time refers to any skill attack, etc. with a lingering effect that continues to cause damage after the ability is initiated.

DPS: Damage Per Second is an equation that takes the player character's variables and generates a the amount of "x" damage generated over a "y" span of time. The higher this number is, the better, though; in most cases, this isn't a number that's easy to arrive at.

Grinding: The practice of staying in the same general area killing the same monsters (or doing the same task) over and over to earn EXP rather than participating in quests. It can also refer to exclusively killing monsters to level.

interrupt: Any skill, attack, etc. that disrupts a foe's ability to launch one of his own. This is an advanced skill as it requires knowledge of how long an enemy's skill will take to execute.

kite: Kite or kiting something is a technique whereby you attack a foe from a distance and then, using an ability to slow (or in a Ranger's case, a pet to harass), you attack the foe from afar while constantly moving away from the intended target—like flying a kite, which is where the term derives its name. It can also be done, if the player is fast enough, without any sort of hindrance to a foe.

knockdown: Anything that causes an enemy to be knocked down on the ground, disrupting their offensive moves, and leaving them open for further abuse.

LFG: Looking For Group is the key phrase when looking for other members to group up with. This can be preceded by a class and level to aid those LFM, e.g., "LvL 18 Monk LFG."

LFM: Looking For Member (or More, depending on whom you ask) means that you're looking for a team member. For example: "LFM: LvL 18 Monk or higher" would mean that you're looking for a level 18 Monk. It can also be altered to include multiples such as LF2M (Looking for 2 More/Members).

loot: The spoils that are collected after a fight, and the process of collecting them.

LoS: Line of Sight refers to any skills that require the target to be in view. This means that if the enemy/ally is behind something or over a hill, the attempt will fail.

LvL: This is shorthand for a character's level, which is the basic unit of measuring progression in an online RPG—the higher the better.

mob: The term for any enemy or group of enemies who are tied together via the game's systems. A mob could be a White Mantle Knight or a full squad of them and a boss. The term is shorthand for "mobile."

nerf: To reduce the effectiveness of a certain item, profession, skill, etc. by developer fiat.

newb: Newb or newbie refers to someone who is new to the game (such as a low level character). It's also a pejorative to put someone down.

PST: Please Send Tell means that the person asking for it wants the player to respond with a "whisper" command so that only the two players involved can see the conversation.

pulling: This is a very important concept in *Guild Wars*. As you'll only want to deal with one mob at a time, pulling is a handy skill that you need to hone to a razor's edge. It refers to snagging one enemy and/or mob at a time when many are lurking about so that the player/team has an easier time rather than aggro'ing several mobs at once. However, there is no greater cause of death in an online RPG than a good pull gone bad.

Res: Res or Rez is short for Resurrect, which brings someone back to life after they have been felled by an enemy.

solo: Solo or soloing is the practice of playing an RPG alone (i.e., without a live teammate). While this is fun, most online RPGs are geared at least as much to grouping with teams and, in some cases, soloing is impossible.

spam: Spam or spamming is the practice of using spells over and over again, specifically spells with low Energy cost, low casting time, and low recharge time.

stacking: Denotes how certain skills can be cast on top of one another to increase damage or the potency of attacks or buffs.

tank: Any player character (or NPC Henchmen) who can serve as a primary melee fighter/damage sponge on the team.

WTB: Want To Buy. A player looking to buy something might type this in the main chat window.

WTS: Want To Sell. A player looking to sell something might type this in the main chat window (e.g. "WTS blue dye").

zerg: Zerg or zerg'ing refers to overwhelming a foe with a "death of a thousand cuts." In *Guild Wars*, this refers to a Necromancer's use of minions to swarm and destroy more powerful opponents due to strength of numbers.

zone: Zone or zoning is the act of transitioning from a city or town via the portals scattered about Tyria. Also refers to an area in the world.

XP or **Exp:** Experience points; the basic unit of measurement that leads to character advancement in most online RPGs. XP is rewarded for completing quests, dispatching foes, and loot collected.

Guild Wars FAQ (Frequently Asked Questions)

Q: What is a good profession with which to start?

A: A Warrior with Monk as a secondary is a very effective beginner class. With the Warrior, a player can jump into the heat of action and not be bogged down so much with the nitty-gritty of AoE attacks, kiting, pulling, and all of those other fancy online RPG terms. Just get in there and start hacking and come to grips with the basics of using skills and generating damage via combos. Couple that with the healing abilities of the Monk, and you've got a bloodthirsty blade-wielding barbarian capable of slaying several foes at once with little down time due to premature death.

Q: I'm lost and don't know where to go next—what should I do?

A: Consult your Quest Log by pressing L. Therein is your progress on current quests (if you have any) and what your next step might be. If you click the quest again, it'll give you a general idea of what direction it is you need to go via a green arrow on the mini-map. You can also click M to display a map. Keep an eye out for the zone "vortexes" on the map that signify a portal to a new area.

Q: I'm about to die and I have no healer to pull my fat off the fire—what are some of my options?

A: You have a couple: If you're near a zone's edge, race through it, as enemies can't follow, however, there may be enemies in the next zone to watch for. If you have any speed skills, activate them and run, but make sure it's toward ground you've cleared (it wouldn't do to run blindly into unexplored territory).

Q: I need backup going into a quest or Story mission—what's the best Henchman class to take with me?

A: Bring a healer (a Monk). Monks are a very important class as they are the primary health-givers in the game, and you'd surprised how far you can get with just that one profession at your side. If you're a Monk, bring a Warrior to tank for you.

Q: I'm having a hard time finding items, switches, etc. Am I missing something?

A: If you are having trouble locating interactive objects, etc., hold down Alt to highlight them onscreen, making them easier to pick out against the background.

Q: I keep asking for help while on a quest in the game and nobody replies—can anyone hear me?

A: After you leave the confines of a town or city, you enter your own pocket realm that is only occupied by you and your teammates (only you if you're not on a team) so there won't be anybody (outside of select NPCs) to help. If, however, you want to leave town, you can use the various chat commands to reach out to someone, but you need to meet them outside of the quest zone to recruit them properly. Use the chat window at the bottom left corner of the screen (if it's not there, hit the '~' key). From here you can:

All: Send a message to everyone in your current area (this will NOT work in instances where you are alone, as there is no one else there).

Guild: All members of your guild can see these messages. This is a good window for getting quick help.

Team: Naturally, this is for people in your team/party and only they can see these.

Trade: This is for buying and selling.

Whisper: If you know a player's name, you can message them directly via this window.

Also, as a shortcut, you can type /all, /guild, etc. instead of clicking on the individual chat panes—just make sure you type the players name after a /whisper command like: /whisper Ironbeard Come help me, please!

Q: Are there any tricks to increasing damage without getting better gear, skills, etc.?

A: Yes. Seek the higher ground and attack from above. This imparts a damage and range increase, which is helpful for missile-based classes like the Ranger. Also, if an enemy is fleeing, you can inflict more damage as a Warrior.

Q: Is there a specific order in which I should attack enemy targets?

A: Yes. If there's a mob that contains melee attackers, a caster, and a healer, take down the healer first—this includes mobs that have a nasty habit of self-healing. After that, take out the weakest enemies, then, finally, the strongest—there's nothing worse than taking down an arch-wizard, then getting carved up by his lackeys.

Q: I never have enough room for loot in my bag—what can I do?

A: After every quest, sell excess inventory or salvage it. Anything you don't plan on using is dead weight that's better converted into useful components or gold. As the game progresses, you'll also be able to secure additional bags to carry more loot, and you can bank excess inventory.

Q: This mob is constantly tearing me apart; what can I do to even the odds?

A: While a lot of players go into *Guild Wars* with a "one man against the world" attitude, teams are there for a reason. If you're stuck at one point, head into a town or city and type **LFG:** *name of quest* to collect enough part members to get past a sticking point.

The author would like to thank Isaiah Cartwright for all of his assistance on this guide.

Character Creation

By Heather "Orlena" Rothwell

The first thing you must do in the game is create your character, so now would be a good time to take a look through the profession chapters and determine what type best suits your play style. In general, Warriors are good at melee combat, Rangers are good at ranged weapon damage, Monks are healers, Necromancers are a pet class, Mesmers are a subtle class relying on using others' strengths against them, and Elementalists are damage-dealing spell casters.

The first choice you face after clicking on "Create" at the character selection screen is whether you want a roleplaying character or a PvP Only character.

- A roleplaying character has access to both the cooperative and competitive areas in *Guild Wars*, which means that you get to run cooperative missions and quests, and experience the storyline of the battle against the Charr. This also means that you start at Level 1, although you have complete freedom about the type of character you develop, making you more comfortable with your skill choices for different situations than most PvP Only characters. This is a good choice for players new to *Guild Wars* and RPGs in general.

- A PvP Only character is restricted to the competitive areas in *Guild Wars* where you can participate in player vs. player combat alongside your teammates. If you choose this option, you can choose from provided templates, or customize your character with skills you've unlocked by playing a roleplaying character. Your character starts at the highest level (20). This choice is better for more experienced players, especially those who've already run a character or two through the storyline missions.

Roleplaying Creation

If you choose a roleplaying character, you start by selecting your primary profession. You may also want to gather some ideas for a secondary profession, as well. You can try out different types of secondary skills during the tutorial before settling on which secondary profession you prefer. You also have a chance to customize your character's appearance by selecting gender, hair style, hair color, face, skin color, and body scale. Finally, give your new character a first and last name and you're ready to go.

PvP Creation Templates

If you decide to create a PvP Only character, you can choose from a set of templates.

- **Spell Slasher** is a Mesmer/Warrior designed to take out enemy casters.

- **Flame Slinger** is a Ranger/Elementalist who reduces the Energy cost of attacks and combines natural durability with the Elementalist skills to deal additional damage with every attack.

- **Warrior's Bane** is a Necromancer/Mesmer who relies on stacking Hexes to take out enemy Warriors.

- **Minion Master** is a Necromancer/Mesmer who focuses on raising a pet army.

- **Pyromancer** is an Elementalist/Mesmer focusing on fire attacks that are deadly against tightly packed groups of foes.

- **Ice Blighter** is an Elementalist/Necromancer using Hexes and ice attacks to disrupt enemy movement and provide crowd control.

- **Protection Healer** is a Monk/Warrior who uses stances to keep herself safe from melee attacks while mitigating the damage taken by party members and removing detrimental effects.

- **Fi Boon Healer** is a Monk/Necromancer who combines Divine Favor and Health-sacrifices for powerful healing and nearly endless Energy.

- **Abominable Snowman** is a hammer and ice wielding Warrior/Elementalist who can take out single enemies quickly, or manage groups of foes.

- **Paladin** is a Warrior/Monk who deals damage with one hand while healing herself and her party with the other.

- **IVEX Trapper** is a Ranger who specializes in Traps and uses them to deal massive amounts of damage to enemies who venture near the group's perimeter.

- **DW Healer** is a Monk/Warrior who can heal herself and allies, as well as remove Conditions and Hexes.

Custom Creation

You can also pick a custom character, but you won't have access to many skills unless you've already unlocked them with one of your roleplaying characters. (Whenever any of your roleplaying characters learns a new skill, any PvP Only characters with the same profession also gain access to that skill. That in itself can lead to difficult choices. With only four character slots available, do you create characters with lots of variety, or similar characters who can benefit from the skills your roleplaying character(s) learn?)

Once you've picked a template, you have a basic selection of eight skills and advanced training in two attributes. The next screen in character creation allows you to customize this, depending on what skills you've unlocked, and to modify your attribute point allocation. Then you go through the same appearance customization choices as roleplaying characters have. Next, there's an equipment selection screen where you can outfit your character. Finally, name your character and you're ready to go.

Starting Play

Roleplaying characters start play in the Kingdom of Ascalon (idyllic), in Ascalon City. PvP Only characters start play in the PvP arena of Fort Koga.

My Favorite Character

Name: Curtis Johnson

Title: Game Designer

Character: Wanda Whodat

My Mesmer/Necromancer is an anti-Warrior/Ranger character. She uses Conjure Phantasm, Clumsiness, Ineptitude, Leech Signet, Price of Failure, Arcane Conundrum, Malaise, and Illusion of Weakness.

I built this character to compete directly against the Warriors and Rangers running about in PvP. I call it the "Stab yourself in the face" strategy. Of course, looking as innocent and fragile as possible is important. First rule, always cast Illusion of Weakness well before you see the enemy. Then don't worry about it.

Arcane Conundrum is there to help a bit with casters, and Malaise is for use only when you are not under attack to stop half-Monks from healing.

There's usually an initial stand-off in PvP battles, which is the time to cast Price of Failure on as many Rangers and Warriors as you can, since it lasts quite a while. When the fighting starts, cast Conjure Phantasm on one of your Price of Failure targets. We'll call this character "the victim." Cast Clumsiness and wait for the victim to try an attack and take damage. Cast Ineptitude and wait for the victim to stab himself again. He is now Blinded and taking Price of Failure on every attack for 8 seconds, so let him swing. Watch for the victim to try a heal, and use Leech Signet to stop that. Recast your Conjure Phantasm and finish off with wand attacks and more Clumsiness if the victim isn't already dead.

This character is a little less useful in large groups with healers, such as guild or tournament fights, but is absolutely deadly at taking out enemy NPCs such as Ghostly Heroes and Guild Lords.

Guilds

By Andrea Silva

Guilds are an important part of *Guild Wars*, which should come as a surprise to no one. Being in a guild allows you to participate in Guild vs. Guild PvP battles and to earn status through your guild's performance in these battles. Being a guild member is also a great way to meet other players who share common interests. And one more great feature of guilds — guild chat! Since you always adventure in an instanced area, the only way to talk to anyone outside your party while adventuring is with a whisper to a specific character, or with your guild chat channel. While soloing, guild chat is the best way to keep in touch with your friends even while you're all by yourself.

Note that all characters on an account are always part of the same guild; you can't join different guilds with different characters. The most recent character you've played is the one who is displayed for you in the Guild window. All characters in a guild always wear their cape (if one has been selected).

To create a guild, the player you pick as leader speaks with a Guild Registrar in any major city.

- Type in your guild name. This is the full name of your guild and must be at least two words long.

- Type in your guild tag. This is an abbreviated version of your guild name, is case-sensitive, and must be between two to four characters. Other players will see this tag when viewing your character.

- Pay 100 gold to the registrar.

Growing: Once you've created a guild, you'll be able to add new members! (Well, you will if you're an officer or the leader.) This is as easy as pressing G to open up your guild window and typing the character's name on the Invitations

line. (Your invitee can be anywhere online, anywhere in the game.) Once the invitation is accepted, your new member appears, in your guild window. Use the boxes to the left of each character name to perform guild functions such as promoting or kicking out members and leaving (or in the case of the leader, disbanding) your guild.

Cape: Most guilds opt to design a guild cape so members can stand out from the crowd by proudly wearing their own emblem and colors. As guild leader, speak to the Guild Registrar in any town and click on the Guild Cape tab to create the cape for your guild members to wear. You can alter the Emblem Color, Detail Color, and Background Color by using the color grid and slider bar. Right below the preview pane and above the emblems are a few "Patterns." Click through the arrows to see the many available cuts and background designs available for your guild cape. The final portion of the guild cape creation involves choosing an emblem from the wide selection at the bottom of the window. If you don't want an emblem, there's a blank box to pick from too. You should certainly spend your time carefully reviewing the choices you've made in cape selection as once you've accepted a design for the cape it comes with a price tag of 100 gold!

Celestial Sigil: It is said this Sigil is granted to those brave enough and skillful enough to hold the Hall of Heroes and earn the blessings of the gods. To reach the Hall of Heroes, it is said you must pass through the underworld itself. It is more reliably certain that finding the tombs of ancient kings, in the desert, is the first step toward reaching the Hall of Heroes.

Guild Halls: The epitome of prestige is to own a guild hall. It's difficult to obtain because you won't be allowed to purchase land in either

Ascalon or Kryta. Only the empire of Cantha will allow guilds to build their halls there. However, Canthans are a very religious people and will only allow a guild leader whose reputable guild has been favored by the gods to petition for an island to build their hall upon. Proof of reputation is your guild cape and proof of divine favor is displayed with a Celestial Sigil.

Once you have a Celestial Sigil, head to Lion's Arch and speak with the Canthan Ferry Captain. He shows you around the islands. Speak to the Canthan Ambassador to petition for ownership of the island of your choice once you've viewed them. The Canthan Ambassador takes your Sigil and coin and then swears you in as the new owner of the island. The islands include Burning Isle, Druid's Isle, Frozen Isle, Hunter's Isle, Isle of the Dead, Warrior's Isle, and Wizard's Isle. Each island has its own unique look and you are sure to find one that suits your guild's needs and personal style.

User Interface

By Heather "Orlena" Rothwell

The *Guild Wars* UI is fairly intuitive if you've played online RPGs before, but like most games, there are some differences which can leave you wondering just how to do something in particular. Let's see if we can answer those questions.

Directions

After character creation, your first task is to move to the person standing in front of you with a large exclamation point over his head and speak to him. The default setting for moving allows you to use W, A, S and D, ↑, ←, →, and ↓, or to left-click where you want to go in order to move. The easiest way to speak to Sir Tydus at this point is to simply left-click on him. Left-click on characters in order to speak to them, to open shop windows, and to target them.

Reconfiguring

If you wish to reconfigure movement controls, or any other keyboard commands, click the **Menu** button in the lower left corner and select **Options** to bring up the Options window. Under **Game Options**, select **Control Setup** to reconfigure your keyboard. You will see a list of actions and the current key command for them in this window. At the bottom of this window you can also check the "Disable Mouse Walking" box, "Invert mouse control of camera," and "Double tap forward to auto-run." Auto-run can also be configured to another key by scrolling down the list until you see "Automatic Run."

Guild Wars is configurable from a control standpoint. By accessing the Menu/Options/Control Setup screen, you can re-bind keys at will, allowing more efficient manipulation of various in-game commands.

Simply highlight any of the items in the "Actions" pane, then type in which keyboard (or mouse) button you'd like mapped to that function—this process is known as binding. For example:

1. Left click "Open Fullscreen Map" in the Actions pane—the default is M.

2. Enter a new key (1, for example) for the command in the "Type a new key for this action" field.

3. Finally, press the "Assign" button and you can now call up the map via 1 or M.

You can also remove redundant key commands (as in the above example) by highlighting the command in question and clicking the "Remove" button. This way, there won't be multiple keys performing the same function, thereby freeing them up for other bindings.

You can repeat this process for every command on the "Actions" pane. Manipulating multiple weapon sets can be advantageous for certain professions (especially Rangers, who would frequently switch from ranged to melee combat). Therefore, it is in the player's best interests that those keys are within easy reach during the heat of combat; the same can be said for frequently-used skills.

Main User Interface

It cannot be stressed enough that binding keys will make a huge difference in reaction time and overall smoothness of play. Clustering frequently-used commands around the dominant keyboard hand and binding as many functions to the mouse as possible will make a noticeable difference in higher level play—especially when dealing with very skilled enemies in PvP skirmishes. Experiment with different setups to find the one that works best for you.

Most of the other actions listed are self-explanatory, but as you highlight them by clicking, a brief description of what the action will do is displayed at the bottom of the list. In the Options window you can also set your **default language**, the **chat filter level**, and **Graphics** and **Sound** preferences. If you're experiencing lag while playing, it might be worth going into the **Advanced Graphics** options and setting them to a lower level than the game defaults.

Getting Quests

Now let's get back to talking to Sir Tydus. As with all quest characters, he has a green exclamation point above his head. When you click to him, a dialogue

box opens that ends with selectable lines to respond to him with his text, and response choices for you to click.

Bear in mind that different binding layouts may be advantageous depending on the profession you're playing at that moment. Just because a certain configuration is ideal for the Warrior does not mean it will automatically carry over to Mesmers, for example.

If he has a quest for you, the word "Quest" will appear in parentheses after any of the available quest responses. If you've spoken to someone and already received a quest, but have forgotten what you're supposed to do, you can either open your Quest Log (L) or speak to the quest giver for a brief reminder. Sometimes the information in the Quest Log isn't as detailed as what you can get from a conversation with the quest character, so if you're stuck on a quest you can't complete, talk to the person who gave it to you again and see if you can pick up hints.

Mission Pointer

After you agree to help Sir Tydus out, you will notice that a green triangle shows on your mini-map. This triangle

indicates the direction you must travel to complete your active quest. Highlighting a quest in the Quest Log makes it your currently active quest. Some quests will point you to the portal to a particular area, while others will point you to someone specific within your current area. (Once your next objective is within your mini-map, the arrow is replaced with a glowing green splash.) If you have multiple quests, you can open the Quest Log and highlight each quest to see where it will take you. This will allow you to betterplan what you need to do in a particular area.

Instanced Areas

Sir Tydus sends you into your first instanced area. You begin the game in what is referred to as a town area. Here you can meet and team up with other players, as well as sell and buy equipment. However, outside of town and outpost areas, you are in your own mini-world (called an "instance"). Only those you are grouped with when you leave the town or outpost will be in the same instance as you, and you must remain in the team in order to stay in that instance. If you want to return to the town, you must leave the group unless everyone in the group is going to the town at the same time. Use caution when moving from one instanced area to another, because the whole group will be forced to switch to the new area when you do. However, if you use the maps to "warp" from area to area, it will disband the group completely, so think twice before attempting that shortcut.

Changing Skills

A town or outpost is the only place where you can change which skills equipped in your Skill Bar. At the

> ## ✦ TIP ✦
> *At times, jumping through a portal is the best way to save your party's bacon. When you go through, so do they, pulling them all out of whatever combat you were in the middle of losing. But still, make sure that's what they want before forcing them all to jump. Also be aware that you could be jumping from one problem to the next.*

bottom of your screen is a bar containing eight small icons, each with a number in the lower right corner—this is your Skill Bar. This is where you place the skills that you plan to use while adventuring. At first it won't matter what skills are on the Skill Bar here because you generally won't have more than eight available skills until you complete early missions. But after you've entered the Academy and can purchase more skills from Skill Trainers, you will find that you have to be selective about which skills you equip. Pressing K brings up the Skills menu and allows you to swap skills in and out of your Skill Bar. To increase the effectiveness of skills, allocate your attribute points (you earn five points for each level gained) in the Hero menu (H).

Dragging an unequipped skill on top of an equipped skill replaces the old

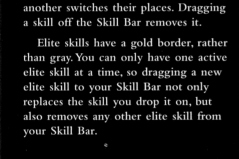

Skills Interface

equipped skill with the new one. Dragging one equipped skill onto another switches their places. Dragging a skill off the Skill Bar removes it.

Elite skills have a gold border, rather than gray. You can only have one active elite skill at a time, so dragging a new elite skill to your Skill Bar not only replaces the skill you drop it on, but also removes any other elite skill from your Skill Bar.

Displaying Friends & Foes

As you leave the safety of Ascalon, one very useful key is left-[Ctrl], which displays all enemies within at least a hundred feet. Similarly, left-[Alt] displays all friendly characters, loot, and area markers. If you hold down either key, you can then click on the highlighted name and your character will run to that location automatically. Note that if you have done this with an enemy, you automatically begin to attack unless you interrupt this action (for example, by moving your character a step or two or by hitting [Esc]). If you selected a non-

combat (green) NPC in this manner, you automatically open up a chat or shop window, depending on the type of NPC.

Maps & Refreshing Areas

As you travel through instanced areas, you will see a red-dot trail on your large map ([M] by default). These dots represent everywhere you have been in the current instance of this area. In most instances, enemies that you kill won't respawn behind you, so if you need to retreat, try to retrace your steps. However, a word of caution: once you leave an instance, all this information clears out so that when you return to it, you have to start over again. On your large map, you will also notice named areas when you are zoomed out (the "+" magnifying glass). These areas are outposts or cities that you can quickly teleport to by clicking on them. You must have visited an area once in order to use this fast mode of travel, but unlike instanced areas, once you have "discovered" a town or an outpost, you can always teleport to it

by way of the large map. In order to scroll around the large map, right-click to bring up the hand icon and drag the mouse. You can also zoom in and out by left-clicking on the map in order to see a map of the whole game world or a close up of your region.

Chat

The chat system is used to communicate with other players throughout *Guild Wars*. At the lower left corner of the screen is the chat window, and atop it are five tabs; you can access these tabs by clicking on them or via shortcut keys:

[!]: Speak to **everyone** in the current town or instance.

[@]: Speak to players in your guild, **only**.

[#]: Speak to everyone on your team, only.

[$]: Advertise trades, buying and selling among PCs only.

["]: Whisper directly to one player.

If the chat window isn't there, simply press [~] to bring it up.

It is very bad etiquette to fill the [!] All channel with communication that should be reserved for any of the other channels—especially for trading, buying, and selling!

Default Controls

The following lists the default commands for most *Guild Wars* functions. You can change many of these settings by going to Menu: Options: Control Setup.

ACTION	DEFAULT	DESCRIPTION
Do It	Spacebar	Performs default action on selected target.
Activate Weapon Set 1	F1	Equip items assigned to weapon set 1.
Activate Weapon Set 2	F2	Equip items assigned to weapon set 2.
Activate Weapon Set 3	F3	Equip items assigned to weapon set 3.
Activate Weapon Set 4	F4	Equip items assigned to weapon set 4.
Close UI	F10	Close any open menus and panels.
Log Out	F12	Display logout confirmation dialog.
Open Chat	Enter	Open chat panel. Also Return on the number pad.
Show Others	Alt (left)	Show ally, NPC, and item names.
Open Attributes	H	Open character attributes panel.
Open Items	I	Open character item inventory.
Open Full Screen Map	M	Open full screen world map.
Open Options Menu	F11	Open the *Guild Wars* Options menu.
Open Log	L	Open character Quest Log.
Open Skills	K	Open character skill inventory.
Reverse Camera	Z	Reverse camera direction while key is held.
Strafe Left	Q	Move left without turning.
Strafe Right	E	Move right without turning.
Target Nearest	C, [	Select nearest target foe (in mission), or player (in towns and outpost).
Show Targets	Ctrl (left)	Show foe names (in mission), or player names (in towns and outposts).
Target Next	], Tab	Select next target foe (in mission), or player (in towns and outpost). Press Shift to select previous target.
Target Previous	↑	Target previous foe (in mission), or player (in towns and outpost). Press Shift to select next target.
Target Priority	T	Select party high priority target.
Target Self	F	Select player character.
Toggle Chat	;	Toggle chat window on or off.
Turn Left	←, A	Turn left.

ACTION	DEFAULT	DESCRIPTION
Turn Right	→, D	Turn right.
Use Skill #	1 – 8	Use skill in that Skill Bar position.
Move Backward	↓, S	Walk backward.
Move Forward	↑, ↑	Jog forward.
Screenshot	Print Screen	Create an image in BMP format of the current screen.
Cancel Action	Cmd 1	Cancels current game action.
Reverse Direction	X	Face character in opposite direction.
Open Backpack	F5	Opens backpack window.
Open Belt Pouch	F6	Opens character belt pouch.
Open Sack 1	F7	Opens character sack 1.
Open Sack 2	F8	Opens character sack 2.
Open Windowed Map	U	Open windowed region map.
Automatic Run	R	Run until another action is taken.
Toggle All Bags	F9	Show or hide all bags.
Open Friends	N	Open friends list.
Open Guild	G	Open guild roster and status.
Language Quick Toggle	Ctrl (right)	Hold this key down to toggle between English and the system default language. IME Key 2 (on Asian language keyboards).
Target Nearest Ally	V	Select nearest ally or NPC.
Open Score Chart	O	Open mission score chart.
Reply	Backspace	Starts a reply to the last player to send you a whisper.

Useful Commands That Cannot be Reassigned

Screenshot, no UI	Shift Print Screen	Take a screenshot that doesn't display any of the UI (User Interface).
Toggle UI	Ctrl Shift H	Turns the UI on or off.

Useful Commands That Don't Have a Default Key

Target Party Member 1-8 — Select party member in party list #1-#8.

Emotes & Special Commands

⚜ TIP ⚜

The various targeting commands (Target Nearest, Target Next, Target Previous, Target Self, and so forth) can be lifesavers. If there's complex combat boiling around you, it can often be hard to click on the opponent or ally you want to select next, and even a couple of seconds of hesitation or searching can mean failure. With Target Nearest, you can work your way through your opponents one at a time; each time one dies, hit it again to find the next one. Or cycle through them with Target Next to select the specific one you want to attack first.

If you use the keyboard for targeting, you almost certainly want to assign keys to your party members. (If you're a healer, it's all but mandatory.) The easiest assignment uses the F-keys (but that eliminates their original functionality) or the numberpad numbers.

One other note: If you fall into an automatic pattern of taking out one opponent at a time (in cooperative play), watch out for monsters who create a Spirit. Unless you want to destroy the Spirit, be careful how rapidly you auto-target a foe—sometimes you can be too trigger happy.

COMMAND	TEXT SHOWN	ANIMATED?
/afk	No text shown.	Y
/agree	\<character> agrees.	Y
/attention	\<character> comes to attention!	Y
/beckon	\<character> beckons.	Y
/beg	\<character> begs.	Y
/boo	\<character> scares you!	Y
/bored	\<character> is bored.	Y
/bow	\<character> bows.	Y
/bowhead	\<character> bows his head.	Y
/catchbreath	\<character> stops to catch his breath.	Y
/clap	\<character> claps.	Y
/cheer	\<character> cheers.	Y
/congrats	\<character> offers congratulations.	Y
/dance	\<character> starts dancing.	Y
/doh	\<character> smacks his head. Doh!	Y
/doubletake	\<character> does a doubletake.	Y
/drum	\<character> plays the drums.	Y
/excited	\<character> is excited!	Y
/fistshake	\<character> shakes a fist angrily.	Y
/flex	\<character> flexes.	Y
/flute	\<character> plays the flute.	Y
/goteam	\<character> cheers wildly, "Go Team!"	Y
/guitar	\<character> plays a mean air guitar.	Y
/help	\<character> requests help!	Y
/highfive	\<character> says, "High Five!"	Y
/jump	\<character> jumps.	Y
/kneel	\<character> kneels.	Y
/laugh	\<character> laughs heartily.	Y
/moan	\<character> moans.	Y
/no	\<character> says, "No."	Y
/paper	\<character> plays paper, rock, scissors.	Y
/pickme	\<character> says, "Pick me!"	Y

COMMAND	TEXT SHOWN	ANIMATED?
/point	\<character> points.	Y
/ponder	\<character> ponders the situation.	Y
/pout	\<character> pouts.	Y
/ready	\<character> is ready for action!	Y
/roar	\<character> roars.	Y
/roll \<#>	\<character> rolls \<x> on a \<#> sided die.	N
/salute	\<character> salutes.	Y
/scratch	\<character> scratches.	Y
/shoo	\<character> shoos you away.	Y
/sigh	\<character> sighs.	Y
/sit	No text shown.	Y
/sorry	\<character> apologizes.	Y
/stand	No text shown.	Y
/taunt	\<character> makes a rude gesture.	Y
/violin	\<character> plays the violin sadly.	Y
/wave	\<character> waves.	Y
/yawn	\<character> yawns.	Y
/yes	\<character> says, "Yes."	Y
/no	\<character> says, "No."	Y
/age	Shows the amount of time you have played character in hours and minutes.	N
/deaths	Shows the number of times that character has died.	N
/health	Shows you your current health and Energy out of your maximum health and Energy.	N

Of course, you'll try out the various emotes next time you're waiting for your last party member to show up, but the dance emotes are worth particular note. They are...astounding. You might even find yourself creating a new character of each profession (and each sex) just to try them out.

Helpers

By Andrea Silva

Henchmen

For the lone adventurer who could use some help exploring new areas or completing tasks, adding a henchman or three can give you just the assistance you need. There are a variety of henchmen to choose from, so it's easy to round out a party no matter what your player character professions are. While not as intelligent or sociable as a party of player characters, henchmen can help get the job done, whatever the job might happen to be. Henchmen are only available to roleplaying characters, and you find them in towns and outposts scattered throughout the world.

You meet your first henchmen when you enter the Ascalon Academy to join the Guard. You won't be able to choose your henchmen at this time, but it'll give you a taste of what grouping with a henchman can be like. While you can't order the henchmen around, he or she does follow you and assists in your battle against the Grawl.

Once you begin playing in the Ruins of Ascalon, you have more choices available for which henchmen join you on your adventures. At lower levels, you only have four henchmen available to choose from, and their levels match the levels of the areas you'll be exploring. In Ascalon City, you meet Orion Elek, Alesia Baptiste, Reyna Sandor, and Stefan Baruch. Choose your henchmen wisely, based on the skills your party is currently lacking. For example, if you don't already have a Monk in the party, Alesia is an excellent choice to bring along. Parties with lots of casters will probably prefer Stefan (the Warrior) to keep your enemies at bay so you can sling your spells. You can ask as many henchmen to join you as the party size limits will allow.

As you travel farther away from Ascalon City, new henchmen are available at the outposts and towns. Eventually you'll be able to invite Little Thom, Valyr Morghulez, Edren Merrick, and more to your party. While henchmen can be extremely useful, there are a few things to keep in mind about them.

- Henchmen will share in party loot, so you'll likely notice fewer item drops if traveling with a lot of henchmen.

- Henchmen stay with you (and even level) until you enter another area with henchmen, such as a town or outpost. Your henchmen's level will then be reset to the level of the other henchmen in the area.

- Henchmen can die and suffer death penalty. Henchmen return to life if you resurrect them, enter a town or outpost, or when you move from one adventure area to another. Death penalties only erase after entering a town or outpost, or by working off the penalty through killing foes.

Pets

Pets are similar to henchmen in that they can't be directly controlled and are subject to gaining experience and dying as they travel with you, but the similarities end there. A character can obtain a pet in one of two ways.

Rangers acquire pets by using the Charm Animal skill. After taming an animal, any time they enter a mission or explorable area with Charm Animal on their Skill Bar, the pet appears beside them and stays with them until death or until the Ranger enters a town or outpost. Animal companions range from Melandru's Stalkers (cats), to moa birds, to wolves and other beasts. Just about any animal that shows green can be tamed. Rangers can also improve their pets through the Beast Mastery attribute and related skills and their pets gain levels much like henchmen do during battles.

Necromancers' pets are more temporary, obtained by animating the corpses of the fallen. These pets eventually expire unless healed or reanimated from a fresh corpse.

Henchmen

HENCHMAN	RESPONSIBILITY	DESCRIPTION
Orion Elek	Mage	Orion specializes in Fire Magic and powerful AoE spells.
Alesia Baptiste	Healer	Alesia is a competent healer who can also resurrect.
Reyna Sandor	Archer	Reyna is a support damage dealer, adept at keeping herself out of harm's way as she shoots from afar.
Stefan Baruch	Fighter	Stefan, a brawny sword fighter, distracts foes by wading right into melee with them.
Little Thom	Brawler	Little Thom does just what the name implies—he brawls! He also wields an axe.
Claude	Cultist	Claude draws on his skills as a Necromancer to raise vanquished foes from the dead to fight as the player's undead army.
Dunham	Enchanter	Dunham has subtle but powerful abilities as a Mesmer that come in handy when you need back-up in the firepower department. Just don't expect him to mix it up, close range.
Lina Esrevni	Protector	Lina is a specialized healer that favors Healing and Protection Prayers. She works in the background, keeping your party healed and shielded.

Elementalist

By Laura "Taera" Genender

Five Reasons to Be an Elementalist

- Damage! Elementalists do a large amount of damage with their highly potent skills. Whichever element you choose, you'll find plenty of spells with which to hurt your target.

- Only Elementalist primaries have the Energy Storage special attribute, which increases your maximum Energy level, as well as improving many spells that help you with Energy renewal. Even if you're concentrating on healing (as a Monk secondary) or another profession's skills, the extra Energy of an Elementalist primary is a blessing.

- Elementalists aren't solely focused on damage dealing. Many of the spells have other effects as well. For instance, Blinding Flash (Air) blinds your opponent, Earthquake (Earth) knocks them down, and Deep Freeze (Water) slows their movement.

- Elementalists can also buff and protect. For example, there are Elementalist spells such as Windborne Speed (Air), which improves an ally's movement (vs. attack), Kinetic Armor (Earth), which improves the Elementalist's armor, or Mist Form (Water), which nullifies physical attacks against the Elementalist.

- Elementalist Attunements improve your Energy-to-damage ratio, and Glyphs improve your efficiency even further.

Mistress of the Elements

 lementalists are amazing damage dealers and are extremely powerful against any foe. While quick to die when targeted, an Elementalist is able to use offense as the best defense: Kill your enemies before they kill you! The Elementalist should be the highest damage profession in the game. On top of that, with more Energy than any other profession, and skills to keep that Energy throughout the battle, they are able to keep dealing damage all combat long.

The key to playing an Elementalist is to keep casting! The incredibly helpful Aura of Restoration restores your Health as you cast spells. If you're an Earth Elementalist, use the skill Kinetic Armor to improve your armor; this spell recharges itself each time you cast. Energy management is very important as an Elementalist; unless your secondary is a Mesmer, make sure to keep your Elemental Attunements on all the time to conserve Energy, and use Glyphs whenever they are ready!

When choosing your element, take a number of factors into account. For example, the Fire element does the most damage but doesn't have any defensive skills. Also, as it is a popular element, more people are prepared to defend against it. Earth is more defensive and less popular, but doesn't do as much damage.

When going into a cooperative player battle, be aware of your surroundings. If you're in an area with lots of lava, Fire spells aren't likely to do you much good (since your enemies will probably be Fire-based). While you aren't likely to focus on more than one element, if you find your element lacking, switch to skills from your secondary profession until you are back in an environment that suits your primary profession better.

Attributes & Skills

Energy Storage
(Primary Elementalists Only)

This is a very useful attribute! Not only does it improve the effects of spells such as Aura of Restoration, but it increases your maximum Energy. Try to max this attribute out! It's only available to characters who choose Elementalist as their primary profession.

Aura of Restoration: The best time to use this skill is when you're spamming low-cost Energy skills because it keeps your Energy levels fairly full and also keeps the caster healthy.

Ether Prodigy (elite): This skill boosts Energy regeneration at the cost of taking serious damage at its cessation. It's best to use when your Health is low. Beware of foes removing it since it will instantly incur the damage penalty and leave the Elementalist in sorry shape.

Ether Renewal (elite): This is effective when stacked with numerous Enchantments, such as Aura of Restoration and Fire/Earth/Air Attunement, and is able to fill the entire Energy bar when it's in effect. The best time to execute it is when Energy levels have ebbed to a very low level.

(No Attribute)

These skills are not tied to any specific Elementalist attribute. They boost your spellcasting abilities in a specific way and some form natural pairs.

Elemental Attunement (elite): When activated, any element-based skills (Fire, Earth, etc.) are essentially free. Combine this with the Attunement skills and they can be repeatedly spammed for free. This is especially impressive given that those skills are anything but cheap, Energy-wise.

Glyph of Concentration: If you have trouble with Daze or are experiencing many interrupts, use this skill to nullify the effects.

Glyph of Elemental Power: This increases the attributes for the spell you cast immediately after casting this spell. It's excellent for getting the most out of higher-powered skills such as Lightning Orb.

Glyph of Energy (elite): This is excellent for use with high Energy spells (25 Energy).

Glyph of Lesser Energy: This is also excellent for use with high Energy spells (15 Energy).

Glyph of Renewal (elite): This Glyph is ideal to drop before skills that take a long time to cast/recharge, as it will accelerate the ability to let you re-use them more often.

Glyph of Sacrifice: Your next spell may be cast instantly, but it takes an additional 120 seconds to recharge. This matches up well with skills that already have a long recharge time, such as Restore Life, so that a party member is instantly returned to battle.

Air Magic

Air Magic doesn't do as much damage as Fire Magic, but the Air element certainly has its advantages! For one, most of the Air Magic spells have 25 percent armor penetration, letting them do more damage even if your target has Air or Elemental resistance. Air Magic also affects the skill Windborne Speed, which improves the speed of an ally by 33 percent. The last advantage to Air Magic is in the spell Whirlwind. Even if your enemy has Air/Lightning

resistance, Whirlwind is the only Air spell that does Cold damage!

Air Attunement: This is excellent to use in combination with high Energy-cost Lightning spells, and is the non-elite version of Elemental Attunement (but only affects Air skills).

Blinding Flash: This is a low recharge skill and is easily spammable. This is especially effective against Warriors and can keep them completely Blind for an entire battle. Due to its high Energy cost, combine this with an Energy recovery skill to keep that Warrior in his place.

Chain Lightning: Like Deathly Swarm for the Necromancer, this spell bounces around, delivering terrific damage to lots of enemies. It is not a skill to waste on a single enemy.

Conjure Lightning: Use this in combination with a lightning wand to do extra damage, or stack it with another weapon that does electrical damage. This is also good to match up with Warrior skills like Frenzy and Flurry.

Enervating Charge: While this skill does less damage than some of your other choices, it inflicts Weakness on a foe. Just make sure the group knows this skill is being used and who your target is before you use it. It combines well with Stoning.

Glimmering Mark (elite): This is fantastic to use against a lot of Warriors when combined with a Lightning wand because it will blind the target and those around him. It's also a good match with Lightning Strike.

Lightning Javelin: This is a fast, spammable Lightning spell that is

excellent for keeping a Warrior in a constant state of interruption. It also has a secondary use against Rangers who, though they have more resistance to Elemental damage, still have to deal with interruptions, albeit on a lesser scale than Warriors.

Lightning Orb: This is one of the highest damage spells in the game, but it can be dodged due to its projectile nature. Combine this with Lightning Surge or Mind Shock so that the target cannot evade its crushing power.

Lightning Strike: This is a cheap, fast, highly spammable spell that can be used to discourage foes that are attempting an ill-planned escape.

Lightning Surge (elite): This is a very short-duration Hex that will knock foes flat on their backs. Combine this with Lightning Orb to inflict massive amounts of damage (often half a foe's lifebar).

Lightning Touch: If you're in a party with a Water Elementalist, communicate with him and work together to use this spell in combination with a water Hex to maximize damage. You could also combine this with Frost Burst and Ice Spikes to really put the deep freeze on an opponent.

Mind Shock (elite): This skill is great on almost any enemy type (save other Elementalists), as your Energy Storage almost guarantees you'll have more Energy than your target. This is a good skill to start an attack with or to combine with Energy-draining skills from a Mesmer, ensuring that you'll always have greater Energy than the target.

Shock: This touch-based spell will knock down a foe, and is helpful against encroaching Warriors. The downside is that it causes Exhaustion, so don't spam this too heavily, or you'll find yourself depleted quickly.

Thunder Clap (elite): As with Glimmering Mark, every time an opponent is struck with Lightning, they are knocked down. Just be wary: Every time an opponent is knocked down, it costs significant Energy.

Earth Magic

Earth Magic is the most defensive of the elements. With skills such as Armor of Earth, Kinetic Armor, and Magnetic Aura, Earth Elementalists are less likely to die than their more aggressive brethren. And while it doesn't have as many damage spells, Earth spells such as Aftershock, Crystal Wave, and Stoning do a good deal of damage to opponents. This is a great, well-rounded attribute to emphasize, and as most Elementalists are Fire or Air, not many people come into battle with skills to defend against Earth.

Aftershock: This is an AoE that does tremendous damage and, if the foe is knocked down, deals a second helping of damage. Combining this with Whirlwind or a Hammer Warrior provides staggering effects.

Armor of Earth: This boosts armor significantly but also slows you down. It is great when trying to stand up against serious damage, provided there is a healer nearby just in case the battle fray gets too intense.

Crystal Wave: This AoE spell ignores all armor, so it's equally effective against all creatures and is combinable with all manner of Conditions.

Earth Attunement: Combine this with high Energy-cost Earth spells.

Eruption: This is a great spell for bogging down a pack of Rangers or an army of Warriors. Combine this with Grasping Earth or Earthquake to really keep them mired until the secondary effect (Blindness) can kick in.

Grasping Earth: This is a point-blank AoE that grants armor but slows the recipient down. Thus, you should consider carefully whether to use it. It is definitely not something to be cast on a group of Warriors.

Iron Mist: This is somewhat tricky to use because it slows your enemy down to a crawl, but leaves them vulnerable only to Lightning attacks. This is also excellent for pinning foes in AoE's such as Maelstrom and Eruption. Finally, it's a great escape spell, granting time to get away.

Kinetic Armor: This armor-boosting spell has a short duration *unless* you keep casting. Use this with builds when you plan to spam a lot of spells, so that your armor boost never wears off.

Magnetic Aura: This is ideal for using against a pack of Warriors because it gives you a 75 percent chance to block for the next ten seconds. It's probably not the best spell to use against heavy casters, however.

Obsidian Flame: This is a very cheap (but high Exhaustion) skill that penetrates armor and does very heavy damage. Try to combine it with other Elementalists casting the same spell for tremendous amounts of damage.

Obsidian Flesh (elite): This prevents any hostile spell from targeting the beneficiary. Combine it with Grasping Earth and Eruption as the foe scrambles to find some way to cope.

Stone Daggers: This cheap, fast, spammable attack hits twice, so it's excellent for nullifying Reversal of Fortune (Monk). Combine this with Kinetic Armor or Ether Renewal for added value.

Stoning: Much like Lightning Orb, this is a high damage, direct attack spell. If, however, it hits a weakened target, it will knock down the target. Combine this with Enfeeble (Necromancer) and Earth Attunement to blunt the Energy drain.

Ward Against Elements: This is a fantastic spell for dealing with Elementalists and Ranger groups that are heavy on Fire-based attacks, since it can mitigate the damage from such sources.

Ward Against Foes: This is great to combine with AoE attacks such as Eruption as it will slow down all foes snared within its reach. It's also excellent for preventing groups of enemies from retreating in swift fashion.

Ward Against Melee: Ideal against packs of Warriors, this is also beneficial because it can't be removed, since it isn't cast on a particular person. Just be wary of having a team group nearby as it will open them up to AoE attacks.

Fire Magic

Fire Magic is the ultimate offensive element. Every Fire spell is offensive and does a lot of damage, which can be somewhat of a disadvantage when the situation calls for defense. Still, spells like Meteor Shower, Mind Burn, Phoenix, and Immolate promote the "offense is the best defense" theory.

Conjure Flame: Combine this with Fire-based weapons such as a fire wand for extra flame damage.

Fire Attunement: This is much like its Attunement brothers in that it returns the Energy lost when cast.

Fireball: This grenade-like spell is terrific for tossing into the midst of a group of enemies. It's a good match for Meteor since foes will be knocked down from Meteor and will be easy prey for the follow-up Fireball.

Flame Burst: This is great to use when you want to rush into groups of enemies and let loose. Use this after Inferno and foes will scramble to get away from the devastating combo.

Flare: This cheap, fast Fire spell combines well with Ether Renewal and Mark of Rodgort for extended Fire damage.

Immolate: This is a good spam attack to keep a foe burning. It is also a good spell to finish off an escaping foe.

Incendiary Bonds: This spell casts a Hex on a target that sets them aflame and does a huge amount of damage. It is also good for throwing down on groups.

Inferno: This is a point-blank AoE spell that is excellent to combine with any spells that slow enemies down, since it will prevent their escape from its deleterious effects.

Lava Font: This AoE spell is a good one to combine with Inferno and Phoenix, or any other skills that keep a foe pinned in one area, so that the lava can work its burning magic.

Mark of Rodgort: Combine this Hex with a fire wand or any other Fire-based attack to keep a foe burning for an extended period of time.

Meteor: This is a cheap, long-lasting AoE spell. It's great for pinning down enemies, then hitting them with another AoE spell such as Inferno to really light them up.

Meteor Shower: This is a very expensive, slow-casting spell and executes three bursts of knockdown. It is very difficult to pull off and its tremendous Energy cost can make using it very tricky.

Mind Burn (elite): Unlike the other Fire spells, this one has an extended period of immolation. The downside is that it will only work if the target has less Energy than the caster, so make sure that requirement is satisfied before letting loose.

Phoenix: This long-casting spell is great for doing serious damage to a single foe, but its slow casting time makes it easy to run from. Combine this with any spell that has a slowing effect to get maximum results.

Rodgort's Invocation: Combine this with Fire Attunement or Glyph of Energy to deliver a devastating, albeit high, Energy-cost, attack.

Searing Heat: This is a very expensive spell that is best used with Fire Attunement (to mitigate Energy loss) and Meteor (to hold foes in place). The damage output on this spell is very high.

Water Magic

Like Earth Magic, Water Magic is more defensive than offensive. Mist Form, Ward Against Harm, Armor of Frost, Armor of Mist, and other defensive skills aid Water Elementalists in staying alive and make the Water Elementalist a good primary profession for a healer. Unfortunately, though, the offensive Water spells tend to do less damage than any of the other elements; their main advantage is that many of them slow your target down.

Armor of Frost: On the one hand, this provides protection against melee attacks, but be wary of Fire-based blows, as this will allow *more* damage to get through.

Armor of Mist: Not only does this strengthen your armor, but it also increases movement speed, making it one of the best spells for escaping a very bad situation.

Blurred Vision: Cast this on Warriors to increase their miss rate to 50 percent and, as it's an AoE spell, use it on large groups that are clumped tightly together.

Conjure Frost: Use this with a frost wand or other Cold-based attack to enhance their efficacy in battle.

Deep Freeze: This is a buffed version of Ice Spikes and is very effective against large groups of foes. Naturally, it is also excellent at preventing large groups from escaping.

Frozen Burst: This spell works well with Inferno and Crystal Wave and is excellent at preventing enemies from escaping.

Ice Prison: Use this to slow enemies down, but do not use it if the team is also hosting a Fire Elementalist since flame spells will cancel out the effects of this spell.

Ice Spear: This is a close-range, fast, spammable, and high damage spell.

Ice Spikes: This is a direct damage spell with a secondary, slow component. Combine this with Maelstrom or Water Trident.

Maelstrom: Use this to disrupt a group of casters as each time it hits, they'll be interrupted. Combine it with other Ice spells to keep the group in place while the shards of Ice rain down on their heads.

Mind Freeze: If your foes have less Energy, this is a good spell to slow them down.

Mist Form (elite): This reduces all damage from any attacks to zero (from Warriors and Rangers, for example). This is not a good spell to use when dealing with caster-heavy groups, though.

Rust: This is a good spell to use on Monks with Bane Signet or Warriors with Healing Signet, as well as any other team heavy in Signet usage.

Shard Storm: Much like Lightning Orb and Stoning, this is a projectile attack that slows down a single enemy. The key to this spell is that it is cheap and spammable, so it's good for preventing a group from escaping.

Swirling Aura: This is excellent protection against a shower of arrows from Ranger-centric groups, as it will allow the caster to evade all incoming projectiles.

Ward Against Harm (elite): This gives a massive boost in armor against any group that's heavy in Fire-based attacks. It's also excellent on your base armor stat.

Water Attunement: This is good for mitigating the cost of high Energy, Cold spells as it replenishes the Energy spent on such spells.

Water Trident (elite): This is a fast, spammable projectile spell that knocks down foes. It's fantastic as a primary damage spell and is also great for pinning down groups of enemies, after which another caster can drop a heavy-damage AoE on them.

Secondary Professions

Elementalist/ Mesmer

The Elementalist/Mesmer is one of the best damage dealers in the game, combining Elementalist attacks with Mesmer Hexes and, most importantly, Arcane Echo. Energy Storage is one of the prime features of this profession combo, a feature not available if you flip into a Mesmer/Elementalist.

As an Elementalist/Mesmer, you have the opportunity to be extremely offensive, so you might as well take it! Concentrate on the Fire and Illusion Magic attributes (and, of course, Energy Storage) to take advantage of some special tricks that only this profession combo can play. The most important skills to have are the elite skill Mind Burn (from your Elementalist half) and Arcane Echo (from your Mesmer half). Fill in the rest of your skill slots with damage-dealing skills such as Flame Burst or Flare, and bring along Aura of Restoration, Fire Attunement, and Glyph of Lesser Energy. When you go into battle, cast Arcane Echo, followed by Mind Burn. You can now cast two Mind Burns on your opponent, and because of your increased Energy due to Energy Storage, you are almost guaranteed to have more Energy than any other enemy, save other Elementalists.

Elementalist/ Monk

Elementalist/Monks are extremely powerful healers and a popular combo. With Energy Storage, an Elementalist/Monk can cast a lot more heals before she runs out of Energy than a Monk primary can. Because of this, many Elementalist/Monks are more like regular monks in disguise!

If you want to be a true Elementalist/Monk, you might concentrate on the Water attribute. Mist Form and Armor of Mist help protect you, as you will be a very popular target. On your Monk side, concentrate on either Healing or Protection Prayers.

You can also choose to follow the Earth Magic attribute, with the extremely useful Kinetic Armor and Magnetic Aura spells. Though the defenses in the Water Magic attribute are more effective, Kinetic Armor is renewed each time you cast a spell, making the effects last for a longer period of time. Earth Magic's offensive skills are also more harmful than Water Magic's, which is another draw.

Elementalist/ Necromancer

Necromancer is a good secondary for any Mesmer, Elementalist, or Monk. As these three professions often get targeted during PvP, a Necromancer secondary specializing in Blood Magic allows you to continue doing damage while maintaining your Health.

Choose your favorite Elementalist element—all work well with a Necromancer—but make sure to put some points into Energy Storage (as always). On your Necromancer side, concentrate on Blood Magic skills such as Vampiric Touch, Vampiric Gaze, or Life Transfer. If there are many enemies attacking you in close quarters at once, Unholy Feast is another good spell to use. If your allies are close to you and you have a corpse at hand (creating a low-level minion is a good way to get a corpse), use Well of Blood or Well of Power.

Elementalist/ Ranger

This is another unusual combination to play. As an Elementalist, you won't get Expertise and you probably won't use Marksmanship, since you'd need to switch to a bow to use most of the skills in that attribute. That leaves Wilderness Survival and Beast Mastery. Beast Mastery is marginally useful with your portable pet tank. Wilderness Survival will give you fair self-healing power with Troll Unguent. If you decide to try this combination, explore your options carefully. Your best bet would be to put most of your points in Elementalist attributes and pick up the few Ranger skills that would complement your play style.

Elementalist/ Warrior

Most Warrior attacks and skills are designed for close combat, meaning you have to wade hip-deep into the fray. A Warrior secondary doesn't have as much armor as a Warrior primary, which makes it a difficult secondary profession no matter what. As an Elementalist primary, your armor isn't very strong, making this an even more difficult combo to play!

The Elementalist/Warrior should put a majority of his points into Tactics. Consider keeping a few battle cries such as "Watch yourself!" and "Shields up!" ready in your arsenal, and most importantly, have Healing Signet close at hand.

One positive aspect to being up close and personal with a Warrior weapon (axe, hammer, sword) is that you can take advantage of some of your area-of-effect (AoE) attacks. If you're a Fire Elementalist, use skills like Flame Burst, Inferno, Lava Font, and Phoenix.

The downside to concentrating on the Fire elemental Magic attribute is your lack of defenses. Make sure to take Warrior defense skills such as Bonetti's Defense.

Cooperative Play

Because of their high damage-dealing abilities and AoE attacks, Elementalists make wonderful cooperative player characters. Whether you are defensive, offensive, or in between, you are an asset to any group.

If you want to play your Elementalist defensively (this is a good idea if your secondary is a Monk), stick with the Water element. Skills such as Mist Form will save your life in sticky situations, and the ability to slow your enemies down while you make a get-

away can be the difference between a failed or successful mission.

On the other hand, if you're going for a more offensive approach, your best bet is a Fire Elementalist. The AoE attacks of Fire Elementalists (Inferno, Fireball, Flame Burst, and so forth) are extremely effective, even if most of them require you to get up close and personal with your enemies. Just make sure you have a good healer as a teammate (or a Necromancer secondary!) and you'll be fine.

The middle routes, of course, would be Earth or Air. While Earth is more medium-defensive and Air is more medium-offensive, either of these elements make great middle-of-the-road choices for a balanced Elementalist.

Player vs. Player

Often, triumph is delivered to those who control mobility on the battlefield. Elementalists have some of the strongest abilities when it comes to impairing the movements of large numbers of enemies. The most talented Elementalists go beyond their brute force damage spells to take advantage of these.

Water Magic offers a good balance of damage combined with movement-impairing effects. Spells like Deep Freeze, Frozen Burst, and Water Trident not only deal damage but slow or knock down your enemies—preventing them from getting to you or getting away.

Earth Magic has Ward Against Foes, which slows down all the enemies that enter its area. While it can be easily avoided, it can't be removed like the slowing effects of Water Magic.

Snaring spells really shine when a team coordinates their tactics so that heavy area damage lands as soon as the snares take effect. Imagine the devasta-

tion if one Elementalist traps a group of enemies with Deep Freeze while another destroys them with a Meteor Shower. Meanwhile, a Ranger could be hammering away with Barrage attacks. Succeeding with these tactics requires good team communication, complementary skills, and excellent timing—and when it all comes together, the results are awesome to behold.

Elementalists have two primary weaknesses. Low armor value is the first, and the other relates to their spellcasting repertoire. Because all of their damage comes from spells, and some of the more powerful spells have longer cast times, Elementalists can be effectively shut down by an anti-caster. Knowing and understanding these weaknesses allows you to find successful tactics for countering them. From Earth Magic skills you can add a hefty amount of all-purpose armor, throw up wards that provide protection against both melee and Elemental damage, or even a ward that will slow all enemies within its range. Ward Against Foes gives opposing Warriors a hard time when they try to reach you or any nearby allies. For some spells, Glyph of Concentration makes a handy addition to your Skill Bar (or Mantra of Resolve if you've got a Mesmer secondary).

The Elementalists' main strengths include their innate ability through Energy Storage to increase their mana Energy pool, and the varied options they have when it comes to dealing damage. They boast some of the most impressive AoE skills in the game. Air and Water Magic skills not only deal significant damage, but they provide bonus effects—for instance, inflicting Conditions or slowing targets.

The better Elementalists will focus on "burst" damage, using their large Energy pool to release a chain of spells to quickly bring down the Health of single or multiple targets. While the Elementalist may have ample time to allow his vast Energy pool to regenerate once his immediate enemies have been defeated in missions and explorable areas, in PvP she will not be afforded that luxury. In PvP play, the Elementalist might want to make a conscious effort to conserve his "burst" damage for when it will actually kill a target. In the meantime, make good use of the more defensive or utility skills (such as blinding with Air Magic, slowing with Water Magic, or raising everyone's melee evasion or Elemental resistances with Earth Magic.

Elementalist Skills

Energy Storage
(Primary Elementalists Only)

Aura of Restoration
Source: Quest, Kingdom of Ascalon/Vendor, Ascalon City (Ruins)
Cost	10	Casting Time	1/4
Duration	60	Recast Time	20

For 60 seconds, you are healed for 152–400% of the Energy cost each time you cast a spell.

Ether Prodigy (elite)
Source: Jyth Sprayburst (Windrider Boss)
Cost	5	Casting Time	1
Duration	10–25	Recast Time	5

Lose all enchantments. For 10–25 seconds, you gain Energy regeneration of 4. When Ether Prodigy ends, you take 2 damage for each point of Energy you have. This spell causes Exhaustion.

Ether Renewal (elite)
Source: Issah Sshay, Vassa Ssiss (Forgotten Bosses)
Cost	10	Casting Time	1
Duration	10	Recast Time	30

For 10 seconds, each time you cast a spell, you gain 1–5 Energy and 5–20 Health for each enchantment on you.

(No Attribute)

Elemental Attunement (elite)
Source: Geckokaru Earthwind (Dragon Boss)
Cost	10	Casting Time	2
Duration	45	Recast Time	60

For 45 seconds, you are attuned to Air, Fire, Water, and Earth. You gain 50% of the Energy cost of the spell each time you use magic associated with any of these elements.

Glyph of Concentration
Source: Vendor, Camp Rankor
Cost	5	Casting Time	1
Duration	15	Recast Time	2

Your next Spell cannot be interrupted and ignores the effects of being Dazed.

Glyph of Elemental Power
Source: Vendor, Port Sledge
Cost	5	Casting Time	1
Duration	15	Recast Time	5

Your elemental attributes are boosted by 2 for your next spell.

Glyph of Energy (elite)
Source: Hyl Thunderwing (Tengu Boss)
Cost	5	Casting Time	1
Duration	15	Recast Time	15

Your next spell costs 20 less Energy to cast.

Glyph of Lesser Energy
Source: Quest, Kingdom of Ascalon/Vendor, Ascalon City (Ruins)
Cost	5	Casting Time	1
Duration	15	Recast Time	30

Your next spell costs 15 less Energy to cast.

Glyph of Renewal (elite)
Source: Clarion Shinypate, Lucid Jewelstone (Earth Elemental Bosses), Nayl Klaw Tuthan (Hydra Boss)
Cost	5	Casting Time	1
Duration	15	Recast Time	15

Your next spell recharges twice as fast as normal.

Glyph of Sacrifice
Source: Vendor, Camp Rankor
Cost	5	Casting Time	1
Duration	15	Recast Time	15

Your next spell may be cast instantly, but takes an additional 120 seconds to recharge.

Air Magic

Air Attunement
Source: Quest, Kryta-The Wilds/Vendor, Amnoon Oasis
Cost	10	Casting Time	2
Duration	36–60	Recast Time	60

For 36–60 seconds, you are attuned to Air. You gain 30% of the Energy cost of the spell whenever you use Air Magic.

Blinding Flash
Source: Quest, Kingdom of Ascalon/Vendor, Ascalon City (Ruins)
Cost	15	Casting Time	3/4
Duration	–	Recast Time	4

Target foe is Blinded for 3–10 seconds.

Chain Lightning
Source: Vendor, Maguuma Stade
Cost	10	Casting Time	2
Duration	–	Recast Time	20

Target foe and up to two other foes near your target are struck for 10–100 Lightning damage. This spell has 25% armor penetration and causes Exhaustion.

Conjure Lightning
Source: Vendor, Camp Rankor
Cost	10	Casting Time	1
Duration	60	Recast Time	60

Lose all enchantments. For 60 seconds, if you're wielding a Lightning weapon, your attacks strike for an additional 1–16 Lightning damage.

Enervating Charge
Source: Vendor, Grendich Courthouse
Cost	10	Casting Time	1
Duration	–	Recast Time	8

Target foe is struck for 5–50 Lightning damage and suffers from Weakness for 5–20 seconds. This spell has 25% armor penetration.

Gale

Source: Quest, Kryta/Henge of Denravi

| Cost | 5 | Casting Time | 1 |
| Duration | 3 | Recast Time | 5 |

Knock down target foe for 3 seconds. This spell causes Exhaustion. (50% failure chance with Air Magic 4 or less.)

Glimmering Mark (elite)

Source: Alana Pekpek (Grawl Boss)

| Cost | 10 | Casting Time | 2 |
| Duration | 1–16 | Recast Time | 15 |

For 1–16 second[s], whenever target foe suffers Lightning damage, that foe and all adjacent foes suffer from Blindness for 3 seconds.

Lightning Javelin

Source: Quest, Kingdom of Ascalon/Vendor, Ascalon City (Ruins)

| Cost | 10 | Casting Time | 1 |
| Duration | – | Recast Time | 5 |

Send out a Lightning Javelin that strikes for 15–50 Lightning damage if it hits. If Lightning Javelin strikes an attacking foe, that foe is interrupted. This spell has 25% armor penetration.

Lightning Orb

Source: Quest, Kryta/Vendor, Henge of Denravi

| Cost | 15 | Casting Time | 2 |
| Duration | – | Recast Time | 5 |

Lightning Orb flies toward target foe and strikes for 10–100 Lightning damage if it hits. This spell has 25% armor penetration.

Lightning Strike

Source: Quest, Shiverpeaks (N)/Vendor, Lion's Arch

| Cost | 5 | Casting Time | 1 |
| Duration | – | Recast Time | 5 |

Strike target foe for 5–50 Lightning damage. This spell has 25% armor penetration.

Lightning Surge (elite)

Source: Oss Wissher (Forgotten Boss)

| Cost | 10 | Casting Time | 2 |
| Duration | 3 | Recast Time | 10 |

After 3 seconds, target foe is knocked down and struck for 14–100 Lightning damage. This spell causes Exhaustion.

Lightning Touch

Source: Vendor, Beetletun

| Cost | 15 | Casting Time | 3/4 |
| Duration | – | Recast Time | 10 |

Target-touched foe and all adjacent foes are struck for 10–40 Lightning damage. Foes suffering from a Water Magic Hex are struck for an additional 10–40 Lightning damage. This spell has 25% armor penetration.

Mind Shock (elite)

Source: Old Red Claw (Griffon Boss)

| Cost | 10 | Casting Time | 1 |
| Duration | – | Recast Time | 20 |

Target foe suffers 10–50 Lightning damage. If you have more Energy than target foe, that foe suffers 10–50 additional Lightning damage and is knocked down. This spell has 25% armor penetration and causes Exhaustion.

Shock

Source: Vendor, Fishermen's Haven

| Cost | 10 | Casting Time | 3/4 |
| Duration | – | Recast Time | 10 |

Target-touched foe is struck for 10–60 Lightning damage and is knocked down. This spell has 25% armor penetration.

Thunderclap (elite)

Source: Chrysos the Magnetic (Mursaat Boss)

| Cost | 10 | Casting Time | 2 |
| Duration | 8–20 | Recast Time | 15 |

For 8–20 seconds, the next time target foe is struck for Lightning damage, that foe and adjacent foes are knocked down, and you lose 15–7 Energy or Thunderclap ends.

Whirlwind

Source: Quest, Shiverpeaks (N)/Vendor, Lion's Arch

| Cost | 10 | Casting Time | 3/4 |
| Duration | 2 | Recast Time | 20 |

All adjacent foes take 15–60 Cold damage. Attacking foes struck by Whirlwind are knocked down.

Windborne Speed

Source: Quest, Crystal Desert/Vendor, Droknar's Forge

| Cost | 10 | Casting Time | 1 |
| Duration | 5–9 | Recast Time | 5 |

For 5–9 seconds, target ally moves 33% faster.

Earth Magic

Aftershock

Source: Vendor, Marhan's Grotto

| Cost | 10 | Casting Time | 3/4 |
| Duration | – | Recast Time | 10 |

Nearby foes are struck for 26–100 damage. Knocked down foes are struck for 10–68 additional damage.

Armor of Earth

Source: Quest, Ruins of Ascalon/Vendor, Yak's Bend

| Cost | 10 | Casting Time | 3/4 |
| Duration | 30 | Recast Time | 15 |

For 30 seconds, you gain 24–60 armor, but move 50–14% slower than normal.

Crystal Wave

Source: Vendor, Maguuma Stade

| Cost | 15 | Casting Time | 3/4 |
| Duration | – | Recast Time | 20 |

Foes near you are struck for 10–100 damage, but are cured of any negative Conditions. This spell ignores armor and magic resistance.

Earth Attunement

Source: Quest, Ruins of Ascalon/Vendor, Yak's Bend

| Cost | 10 | Casting Time | 2 |
| Duration | 36–60 | Recast Time | 60 |

For 36–60 seconds, you are attuned to Earth. You gain 30% of the Energy cost of the spell each time you use Earth Magic.

Earthquake

Source: Quest, Kryta-The Wilds/Vendor, Droknar's Forge

Cost	25	Casting Time	3
Duration	–	Recast Time	15

You invoke an Earthquake at target foe's location. All foes near this location are knocked down and are struck for 26–100 Earth damage. This spell causes Exhaustion.

Eruption

Source: Quest, Ruins of Ascalon/Vendor, Yak's Bend

Cost	25	Casting Time	3
Duration	5	Recast Time	30

Cause an Eruption at target foe's location. For 5 seconds, foes near this location are struck for 5–34 Earth damage each second. When Eruption ends, foes in the area of effect are Blinded.

Grasping Earth

Source: Quest, Kryta/Vendor, Henge of Denravi

Cost	5	Casting Time	3/4
Duration	8–20	Recast Time	30

For 8–20 seconds, all nearby foes move 50% slower but have +24 armor against physical damage.

Iron Mist

Source: Quest, Kryta-The Wilds/Vendor, Amnoon Oasis

Cost	10	Casting Time	2
Duration	5–17	Recast Time	30

For 5–17 seconds, target foe moves 90% slower than normal. That foe gains immunity to damage from all sources except Lightning.

Kinetic Armor

Source: Vendor, Fishermen's Haven

Cost	15	Casting Time	3
Duration	8	Recast Time	60

For 8 seconds, you gain +10–40 armor. Whenever you cast a spell, Kinetic Armor is renewed for 8 seconds.

Magnetic Aura

Source: Quest, Ruins of Ascalon/Vendor, Yak's Bend

Cost	10	Casting Time	1
Duration	5–11	Recast Time	60

For 5–11 seconds, Magnetic Aura has a 75% chance to block melee attacks.

Obsidian Flame

Source: Quest, Crystal Desert/Vendor, Droknar's Forge

Cost	5	Casting Time	2
Duration	–	Recast Time	5

Deal 22–112 damage to target foe. This spell ignores armor but causes Exhaustion.

Obsidian Flesh (elite)

Source: Obsidian Guardian (Behemoth Boss), Harn Coldstone (Forgotten Enchanted Boss)

Cost	10	Casting Time	1
Duration	8–20	Recast Time	30

For 8–20 seconds, you gain +20 armor and cannot be the target of enemy spells, but move 50% slower.

Stone Daggers

Source: Quest, Kryta-The Wilds/Vendor, Amnoon Oasis

Cost	5	Casting Time	1
Duration	–	Recast Time	–

You send out two Stone Daggers. If it hits, each Stone Dagger strikes for 3–24 Earth damage.

Stoning

Source: Vendor, Ice Tooth Cave

Cost	15	Casting Time	1
Duration	–	Recast Time	5

You send a flurry of stones at target foe. If they hit, the stones strike for 20–90 Earth damage. If target foe is suffering from Weakness, that foe is knocked down.

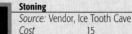

Ward Against Elements

Source: Quest, Ruins of Ascalon/Vendor, Yak's Bend

Cost	15	Casting Time	1
Duration	8–20	Recast Time	20

For 8–20 seconds, nearby allies gain +24 armor against Elemental damage.

Ward Against Foes

Source: Quest, Shiverpeaks (N)/Vendor, Lion's Arch

Cost	10	Casting Time	1
Duration	8–20	Recast Time	20

You create a Ward Against Foes at your current location. For 8–20 seconds, foes in this area move 50% slower.

Ward Against Melee

Source: Vendor, North Kryta Province

Cost	10	Casting Time	1
Duration	8–20	Recast Time	20

You create a Ward Against Melee at your current location. For 8–20 seconds, allies in this area have a 50% chance to evade melee attacks.

Fire Magic

Conjure Flame

Source: Quest, Shiverpeaks (N)/Vendor, Lion's Arch

Cost	10	Casting Time	1
Duration	60	Recast Time	60

Lose all enchantments. For 60 seconds, if you're wielding a Fire weapon, your attacks strike for an additional 1–16 Fire damage.

Fire Attunement

Source: Quest, Kryta-The Wilds/Vendor, Droknar's Forge

Cost	10	Casting Time	2
Duration	36–60	Recast Time	60

For 36–60 seconds, you are attuned to Fire. You gain 30% of the Energy cost of the spell each time you use Fire Magic.

Fire Storm

Source: Quest, Kingdom of Ascalon/Vendor, Ascalon City (Ruins)

Cost	15	Casting Time	4
Duration	10	Recast Time	30

For 10 seconds, the area around target foe is bombarded with a rain of fire that strikes for 5–29 Fire damage each second.

Fireball

Source: Quest, Ruins of Ascalon/Vendor, Yak's Bend

Cost	15	*Casting Time*	2
Duration	–	*Recast Time*	10

Fireball flies toward target foe and explodes on impact, striking for 7–112 Fire damage in an area.

Flame Burst

Source: Quest, Crystal Desert/Vendor, Droknar's Forge

Cost	15	*Casting Time*	3/4
Duration	–	*Recast Time*	5

All nearby foes are struck by jets of flame for 7–112 Fire damage.

Flare

Source: Quest, Kingdom of Ascalon/Vendor, Ascalon City (Ruins)

Cost	5	*Casting Time*	1
Duration	–	*Recast Time*	–

Flare flies toward target foe, striking for 16–46 Fire damage if it hits.

Immolate

Source: Vendor, Grendich Courthouse

Cost	10	*Casting Time*	1
Duration	–	*Recast Time*	5

Target foe is struck for 5–50 Fire damage and is set on fire for 1–3 second[s].

Incendiary Bonds

Source: Quest, Crystal Desert/Vendor, Droknar's Forge

Cost	15	*Casting Time*	2
Duration	3	*Recast Time*	15

After 3 seconds, target foe and nearby foes are struck for 10–60 Fire damage and are set on fire for 1–3 second[s].

Inferno

Source: Quest, Kryta/Vendor, Henge of Denravi

Cost	10	*Casting Time*	3/4
Duration	–	*Recast Time*	20

All adjacent foes are struck for 15–120 Fire damage.

Lava Font

Source: Quest, Ruins of Ascalon/Vendor, Yak's Bend

Cost	10	*Casting Time*	2
Duration	5	*Recast Time*	4

For 5 seconds, foes adjacent to the location where this spell was cast are struck for 5–29 Fire damage.

Mark of Rodgort

Source: Vendor, Copperhammer Mines

Cost	25	*Casting Time*	2
Duration	8–20	*Recast Time*	20

For 8–20 seconds, whenever target foe is struck for Fire damage, that foe is set on fire for 1–3 second(s).

Meteor

Source: Quest, Kryta-The Wilds/Vendor, Amnoon Oasis

Cost	10	*Casting Time*	3
Duration	–	*Recast Time*	30

Call down a fiery meteor on your target foe. The meteor explodes, striking for 7–112 damage and knocking down anyone it hits. This spell causes Exhaustion.

Meteor Shower

Source: Vendor, North Kryta Province

Cost	25	*Casting Time*	5
Duration	9	*Recast Time*	60

Exploding meteors strike the area near your target. Each strikes for 7–112 damage and knocks down anyone it hits. This spell causes Exhaustion.

Mind Burn (elite)

Source: Scelus Prosum (Titan Boss)

Cost	15	*Casting Time*	1
Duration	–	*Recast Time*	20

Target foe takes 15–60 Fire damage. If you have more Energy than target foe, that foe takes an additional 15–60 Fire damage and is set on fire for 1–7 second(s). This spell causes Exhaustion.

Phoenix

Source: Vendor, Grendich Courthouse

Cost	15	*Casting Time*	3
Duration	–	*Recast Time*	25

A fiery phoenix rises at your location, striking nearby foes for 7–112 Fire damage, and flies out to your target, exploding on impact. This explosion strikes for an additional 15–90 Fire damage.

Rodgort's Invocation

Source: Vendor, Marhan's Grotto

Cost	25	*Casting Time*	5
Duration	–	*Recast Time*	15

You invoke the power of Rodgort at target foe's location. All foes near this location are struck for 7–112 Fire damage and are set on fire for 1–3 second(s).

Searing Heat

Source: Vendor, Copperhammer Mines

Cost	25	*Casting Time*	3
Duration	5	*Recast Time*	30

Cause Searing Heat at target foe's location. For 5 seconds, foes near this location are struck for 5–29 Fire damage each second. When Searing Heat ends, foes in the area of effect are set on fire for 3 seconds. This spell causes Exhaustion.

Water Magic

Armor of Frost

Source: Vendor, Beetletun

Cost	5	*Casting Time*	1
Duration	10–34	*Recast Time*	45

For 10–34 seconds, you gain +40 armor against physical damage, but -24 armor against Fire damage. Armor of Frost ends if you use any Fire Magic.

Armor of Mist

Source: Vendor, North Kryta Province

Cost	10	*Casting Time*	2
Duration	8–20	*Recast Time*	30

For 8–20 seconds, you gain +10–40 armor and move 33% faster.

Blurred Vision

Source: Vendor, Ice Tooth Cave

Cost	15	Casting Time	1
Duration	8–20	Recast Time	20

For 8–20 seconds, target foe and nearby foes are Hexed with Blurred Vision. While Hexed, those foes have a 50% chance to miss with attacks.

Conjure Frost

Source: Quest, Kryta-The Wilds/Vendor, Amnoon Oasis

Cost	10	Casting Time	1
Duration	60	Recast Time	60

Lose all enchantments. For 60 seconds, if you're wielding a Cold weapon, your attacks strike for an additional 1–16 Cold damage.

Deep Freeze

Source: Quest, Kryta-The Wilds/Vendor, Droknar's Forge

Cost	25	Casting Time	3
Duration	10	Recast Time	15

You cause a Deep Freeze at target foe's location. All foes near this location are struck for 10–85 Cold damage. For 10 seconds, all foes move 50% slower than normal.

Frozen Burst

Source: Quest, Ruins of Ascalon/Vendor, Yak's Bend

Cost	15	Casting Time	3/4
Duration	5–11	Recast Time	30

Foes adjacent to you are struck for 20–80 Cold damage and are slowed for 5–11 seconds.

Ice Prison

Source: Quest, Shiverpeaks (N)/Vendor, Lion's Arch

Cost	10	Casting Time	2
Duration	8–20	Recast Time	30

For 8–20 seconds, target foe's legs are encased in ice, causing the foe to move 66% slower than normal. This effect ends if target takes Fire damage.

Ice Spear

Source: Quest, Shiverpeaks (N)/Vendor, Lion's Arch

Cost	5	Casting Time	1
Duration	–	Recast Time	–

Ice Spear flies toward target foe, striking for 10–55 Cold damage if it hits. Ice Spear has half the normal spell range.

Ice Spikes

Source: Quest, Ruins of Ascalon/Vendor, Yak's Bend

Cost	15	Casting Time	2
Duration	2–6	Recast Time	15

Target and nearby foes are struck for 20–80 Cold damage and are slowed for 2–6 seconds.

Maelstrom

Source: Vendor, Maguuma Stade

Cost	25	Casting Time	4
Duration	10	Recast Time	30

Create a Maelstrom at target foe's location. For 10 seconds, foes in that area are struck for 10–25 Cold damage each second. Maelstrom interrupts spell-casting when it hits. This spell causes Exhaustion.

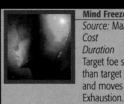

Mind Freeze (elite)

Source: Maak Frostfriend (Imp Boss)

Cost	10	Casting Time	1
Duration	2–6	Recast Time	20

Target foe suffers 10–40 Cold damage. If you have more Energy than target foe, that foe suffers an additional 10–40 Cold damage and moves 50% slower for 2–6 seconds. This spell causes Exhaustion.

Mist Form (elite)

Source: Brrrr Windburn (Nightmare Boss), Frash the Cold (Skale Boss), Ice Beast (Ghost Boss)

Cost	10	Casting Time	2
Duration	8–20	Recast Time	30

For 8–20 seconds, you cannot take or deal damage from attacks.

Rust

Source: Vendor, Port Sledge

Cost	5	Casting Time	2
Duration	6–42	Recast Time	45

For 6–42 seconds, target foe and all adjacent foes take 3 times as long to activate Signet rings.

Shard Storm

Source: Quest, Ruins of Ascalon/Vendor, Yak's Bend

Cost	10	Casting Time	1
Duration	2–6	Recast Time	10

This projectile strikes for 10–65 damage and slows the target's movement for 2–6 seconds.

Swirling Aura

Source: Quest, Crystal Desert/Vendor, Droknar's Forge

Cost	10	Casting Time	1
Duration	8–20	Recast Time	60

For 8–20 seconds, Swirling Aura has a 75% chance to block arrows and magical projectiles.

Ward Against Harm (elite)

Source: Obsidian Guardian (Behemoth Boss), Arkhel Havenwood (Plant Boss)

Cost	15	Casting Time	1
Duration	8–20	Recast Time	20

Create a Ward here. For 8–20 seconds, nearby allies have 12–60 armor against Fire damage and 12–24 armor against other damage.

Water Attunement

Source: Quest, Kryta/Vendor, Henge of Denravi

Cost	10	Casting Time	2
Duration	36–60	Recast Time	60

For 36–60 seconds, you are attuned to Water. You gain 30% of the Energy cost of the spell each time you use Water Magic.

Water Trident (elite)

Source: The Judge (L24; Golem Boss)

Cost	5	Casting Time	1
Duration	–	Recast Time	3

Send out a Water Trident at target foe. Water Trident strikes for 10–70 Cold damage if it hits. If it hits a moving foe, that foe is knocked down.

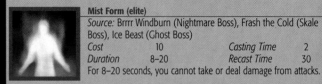

Mesmer

The Powers of the Mind

To play a Mesmer takes preparation, thought, and awareness. If you're constantly casting Backfire against melee creatures, you're useless to your group. But if you remember a few key rules, you are sure to be a popular party member in and out of PvP.

Never underestimate any skill in your arsenal. While you may have trouble understanding the worth of some skills, a wise Mesmer can use everything she has to her advantage. With spells like Shatter Hex or Shatter Delusion, even a "pointless" Hex becomes deadly in your hands.

Know what you're up against. Many of your skills are less useful if you don't know what kind of creature/profession you will be fighting. If you go into battle against melee creatures with Elemental Resistance, you've wasted a spell slot. But if you know that you're going to be coming up against an enemy that casts lots of fire spells, you'll be well prepared—and protected!

When going into battle, consult with other group members. Do they have lots of Hexes that they'll be casting? If so, bring Shatter Hex. Is one of them a high-damage Elementalist? If so, concentrate more heavily on Hexes. Is one a Hex-casting Necromancer? If so, put some damage-dealing skills on your list.

Specialization is the key. Many of your spells depend on other spells that you can cast, or other spells that your enemy/ally casts. If you have a mishmash of spells from different attributes for different targets, you're not as

Five Reasons to Be a Mesmer

- With Fast Casting and Energy-stealing spells, you seldom find yourself out of Energy.
- While not as much of a damage dealer as an Elementalist, Mesmers have some pretty powerful damage spells. Spells such as Phantom Pain and Conjure Phantasm can burn away at your enemy's Health, and Shatter Hex and Shatter Enchantment work on any profession.
- Mesmers aren't all about PvP! When hunting and fighting monsters, you're an invaluable party member against magic-using monsters. Mesmers are also self-sufficient with spells such as Ether Feast.
- Your Mantras and Illusions allow you to make quick escapes from dangerous situations.

effective as, for example, a Mesmer who specializes in Domination spells against casters.

And very importantly, remember that a popular party member is also a popular target. When the other team figures out who is doing all the damage, you are sure to get targeted with some heavy spells. Be ready to defend with Mantras, slow down the opposition with Ethereal Burden, disable them with Power Block, Blackout, and similar spells, or make a run for it with Illusion of Haste!

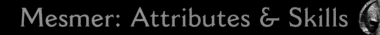

Attributes & Skills

Fast Casting
(Primary Mesmers Only)

The Fast Casting attribute is a good one to put your extra points in. As the name suggests, Fast Casting improves your spellcasting speed. Fast Casting also improves the spell Mantra of Recovery (elite). This attribute is only available to Mesmer primaries.

(No Attribute)

Arcane Mimicry (elite): For 20 seconds, Arcane Mimicry becomes the elite spell from the ally that you target. This is a fun way to double your teams' best spells against your foes.

Epidemic: All negative Conditions that your target suffers from are spread from him to nearby foes. This skill is a great way to affect a whole group of enemies with one spell. It's even more useful in a group with other players helping to load on the Hexes.

Domination Magic

Putting your points in Domination Magic increases the duration and effectiveness of your Domination skills, such as Backfire or Blackout. Most of the skills based on this attribute focus on manipulating your target's Energy and/or skill use.

Backfire: This skill is far more useful on NPCs than it is on PCs. A good PC will figure out not to use any skills until Backfire runs out, but NPCs are not able to make this connection. Use this skill more in cooperative play, or against henchmen in PvP.

Blackout: This skill is a good example of "taking one for the team." While both your skills and your target's skills are disabled, it gives the rest of your party a chance to kill the enemy before he can fully fight back. Just make sure you have backup, and communicate with your team so they know who to target!

Chaos Storm: This AoE is very effective against groups of casters and is especially effective when combined with skills that slow enemies. For example, you can keep them mired in place, then hit them with Chaos Storm.

Cry of Frustration: Interruption skills like Cry of Frustration or Power Spike work well when your enemy is casting a spell that you know has a long cast time.

Diversion: This skill is extremely useful for disabling healing Monks. If you're having a hard time finding a counter to a particular skill, this is a good default choice.

Empathy: This is primarily effective against fast Warriors, as it deals damage with every swing.

Energy Burn. This skill is very effective against anyone with Energy, so the more the better. Combine this with Mindwrack to really inflict maximum damage.

Guilt: This is an effective shutdown against any offensive-based caster, as well as a good Energy-stealing skill for a domination caster.

Hex Breaker: Use this when fighting Necromancers or Hex-heavy Mesmers.

Ignorance: The primary use for this skill is to disrupt Warriors spamming Healing Signet during a fierce battle.

Mind Wrack: Using this skill in conjunction with Energy-draining skills can really do a lot of damage to your opposition. A very good combination is Panic followed by Mind Wrack. With this combination, your enemy will continually lose Energy (for 2 to 20 seconds) and possibly take plenty of damage. Note: Because of Energy Storage, this skill is less useful against Elementalists.

Power Block (elite): Another very useful skill when fighting Monks, this can block off all of their healing abilities if timed right. This spell can win you the battle.

Power Leak: This interrupt drains a large amount of Energy, making it very effective against a Monk. It also combines well with Arcane Conundrum.

Power Spike: An interrupt skill, Power Spike is best used against enemy casters, as it also deals damage, especially against Elementalists and Monks.

Shatter Delusions: This skill is tricky to apply, but can be fantastic once the timing is down. Simply wait for the Hex on a foe to almost deplete, cast Shatter Delusions, so that the Hex extracts as much pain as possible, then drop it to do even more damage.

Shatter Enchantment: This skill is useful when fighting a group with a Monk who specializes in Enchantments.

Signet of Weariness: Foes often know better than to cluster together, but use Signet of Weariness as well as other area-of-effect (AoE) spells to take advantage of clustered enemies.

Wastrel's Worry: Use this in combination with skills like Backfire or Power Block.

Illusion Magic

As the name suggests, Illusion Magic skills create illusions affecting the target's abilities. These illusions can either be helpful to the target, such as Illusion of Haste, or harmful, such as Ethereal Burden. Putting your points in this attribute will increase the effect and duration of Illusion skills.

Arcane Conundrum: Use this spell on a foe that you plan to interrupt (with spells like Power Block, Power Spike, and so forth).

Conjure Phantasm: This is a highly spammable skill that will gradually drain enemies of precious Health. This stacks well with Shatter Delusions.

Crippling Anguish (elite): This not only drains Health, it also slows enemies down. Excellent for kiting enemies or slowing down foes that are attempting to flee the battlefield.

Distortion: This stance allows you to evade, but it also steals Energy. If, however, there is a large band of Warriors, it's not the best skill to use, as it'll suck your Energy dry in short order.

Echo (elite): Echo and Arcane Echo allow you to have more than one of a skill. This is very useful if you are fighting an intelligent enemy; they won't be expecting you to be able to cast back-to-back Backfires.

Ethereal Burden: Use this skill when you're convinced that your enemy will live at least another 10 seconds, or when your enemy does not have a Hex-shattering Mesmer on his team.

Fevered Dreams (elite): This is an elite version of Epidemic and it's very effective for Condition-based builds. It's especially useful in large groups as it will quickly spread those Conditions.

Fragility: This is very effective with any Condition, as it will deal extra damage across the board, even if the victim attempts to remove it.

Illusion of Haste: So long as you have at least one attribute rank in Illusion Magic, this spell lasts longer than its recast time. Use this when you need to flee to survive, and not before.

Illusion of Weaponry (elite): Low melee attack and high Illusion Magic score? This allows you to do a lot more damage to your target without casting multiple spells.

Ineptitude (elite): Even if your enemy notices that you've cast this spell on him, it puts him out of the picture for 4 to 10 seconds.

Migraine (elite): This is a buffed version of Arcane Conundrum and is effective when stacked with Arcane Conundrum to significantly slow down a foe's ability to cast.

Phantom Pain: The real gold in this spell is not the DoT, but rather the Deep Wound that afflicts your target afterward. Even if you don't have ranks in Illusion Magic, consider using this spell.

Sympathetic Visage: This a very good anti-Warrior skill because it saps adrenaline, though it's important to be aware of where on the battlefield the most enemies congregate.

Inspiration Magic

Inspiration Magic focuses on aiding the caster and allies in battle with such skills as Mantra of Signets or Power Drain, though some skills (for example, Spirit of Failure) are offensive. Like the other attributes, putting your points in Inspiration Magic will improve the skills.

Channeling: Combine this with fast-casting Monk or Elementalist skills and position yourself amidst a knot of enemies for massive Energy gain. More effective in large groups than with single enemies.

Drain Enchantment: Good for removing enchantments that are hindering you and, at the same time, grants you a boost in Energy. Especially effective on heavy enchantment characters.

Elemental Resistance: This spell is great if you're going up against casters, especially Elementalists. On the other hand, it's also a perfect example of why you should know your enemy. If you find yourself up against a bunch of fighters, Elemental Resistance is a wasted spell slot and a potential handicap.

Energy Drain (elite): A more powerful version of Energy Tap, it recharges faster, casts faster, and steals more Energy than its lesser sibling.

Energy Tap: A great spell for any inspiration Mesmers to take into battle. If you wait until the right time to cast it, it'll strip an opponent's crucial Energy core at just the wrong time—for him.

Ether Feast: One of the only ways to heal yourself as a Mesmer, it's worth putting a few points into Inspiration Magic to use this skill.

Ether Lord: This skill is most effective when the Mesmer is at low Energy, since it shuts down your enemy for a short period of time.

Inspired Enchantment: Inspired Enchantment and Inspired Hex are excellent ways to take care of enemy enchantments/ally Hexes, as well as gain an extra skill for you.

Keystone Signet: If you use a lot of Signets, keep this skill handy—it instantly recharges all Signets. However, if you're Signet-light, this skill is not for you, as it will block access to your other skills.

Mantra of Earth: Mantra of Earth, Flame, Frost, and Lightning are great skills to take into battle if you know what your enemy's element is. These skills are often more valuable in cooperative play encounters, when you know what element most of the monsters in a given area are.

Mantra of Inscriptions: This reduces the recharge of any Signet and is really effective when used with Signet of Judgment and other, long-recharge Signets.

Mantra of Persistence: Increases the duration on Illusion-based Hexes, such as Conjure Phantasm, which will increase the amount of damage dealt.

Mantra of Recall (elite): Combine this with self-Enchantment skills and it acts as a stealth buff, granting a massive Energy boost when a foe attempts to remove other, beneficial enchantments.

Spirit of Failure: This Hex is most effective when applied to Warriors and Rangers. It combines well with Blind and Price of Failure.

Secondary Professions

Mesmer/ Elementalist

The Mesmer/Elementalist combination is a powerful damage dealer and a scary sight to any PvP or cooperative play opponent. The Elementalist's high damage spells, coupled with Mesmer Fast Casting, make this a popular and deadly build.

As with the Monk combo, make sure to put at least 10 ranks into Fast Casting, then follow your favorite Attribute lines from there. Any of the elements (Water, Fire, Earth, Air) coupled with Inspiration Magic on your Mesmer side, allows you to deal a lot of damage and keep your Energy from running out. First of all, make sure to have your chosen element's Attunement spell in your arsenal. Use a high-damage Elemental spell such as Aftershock (Earth) or Rodgort's Invocation (Fire) after casting your Mesmer skill Arcane Echo to achieve double the spell power, and when you're low on Energy, use spells like Power Drain and Energy Tap.

If you are fighting Warrior or Ranger primaries, bring along an Elementalist spell such as Mind Burn (Fire), Mind Shock (Air), or Mind Freeze (Water). Couple this with your Arcane Echo spell to devastate enemies in two hits.

If you want to be a more aggressive Mesmer/Elementalist, concentrate your Mesmer side on Domination magic rather than Inspiration. Due to the Elementalist's high damage output, the Illusion line of Mesmers is less useful, but Domination interrupts and skill disablers are still extremely useful in combat.

Mesmer/Monk

A Mesmer/Monk is a great profession choice if you want to be a healer. While you don't get Divine Favor, Fast Casting more than makes up for it. Also, as a Mesmer primary, you are likely to last a bit longer than a Monk primary, who will get targeted at the beginning of a fight.

Make sure to put a fair amount of your points in Fast Casting, then follow your favorite attribute lines from there. One suggestion is to concentrate on Healing/Protection on your Monk side and Inspiration on your Mesmer side. Though this is a more defensive build than most Mesmers, you're unlikely to run out of Energy with spells such as Energy Tap or Power Drain. The trick is juggling between enemy targets to interrupt and ally targets to heal. Another advantage to this build is your access to the Mantras, which can come in handy defense-wise!

If you want to be more offensive, stick with a smiting Monk and an illusion Mesmer. Use the Bane and Holy Strike combo to lay your target flat, and use Illusion Spells such as Summon Phantasm to inflict damage over time on your target.

Of course, you can always mix and match the different elements of Monk and Mesmer to find a balance between the offensive and defensive builds. For example, a Healing and Illusion build would be great for cooperative play, or a Smiting and Inspiration build would be a powerful damage dealer with lots of Energy.

Mesmer/Ranger

This isn't too common of a combination, but it does bring a unique blend of skills to a group. Using Epidemic or Fevered Dreams with Poison or Pin Down works really well. Depending on whether you choose to specialize in Domination or Illusion, you can either be an anti-caster, or you can pretty much slow everything in sight with

Imagined Burden and Pin Down. The Mesmer/Ranger provides enough damage and anti-caster power to annihilate enemy spellslingers in large fights.

Mesmer/ Necromancer

If you're looking for Hexes, a Mesmer/Necromancer is the way to go. This powerful combo is great for taking down Warriors, or if you want to concentrate on your Mesmer skills and just use the Necromancer's Blood Magic, that works, too!

The more aggressive way to play a Mesmer/Necromancer is to concentrate your attribute points on Curses and Domination magic, with extra points in Fast Casting or Blood Magic. In this build you'll specialize in killing Warriors and Rangers rather than magic types, so pick up Curses such as Enfeeble, Insidious Parasite, Faintheartedness, Price of Failure, Spiteful Spirit, Suffering, and Weaken Armor. On your Mesmer side, use anti-Warrior skills such as Empathy, Soothing Images, and Ignorance.

Of course, the above build example leans more to Necromancer than Mesmer. If you want to use Necromancer as more of a support profession, put your attribute points into Blood Magic, Fast Casting, and your favorite Mesmer skill line (Domination or Illusion Magic; Inspiration is not suggested). Use Blood Magic spells to keep Health up when pesky enemies decide to target you.

Mesmer/Warrior

Most Warrior attacks and skills are designed for close combat, meaning you have to wade hip-deep into the fray. A Warrior secondary doesn't have as much armor as a Warrior primary, which makes it a difficult secondary profession no matter what. As a Mesmer primary, you're a favorite target in PvP, which makes this an even more difficult combo to play!

The Mesmer/Warrior should put a great deal of his points into Tactics. Consider keeping a few battle cries such as "Watch Yourself!" and "Shields Up!" ready in your arsenal, and most importantly, have Healing Signet close at hand.

If you choose to use one of the Warrior weapons (axe, hammer, sword) instead of a ranged Mesmer wand, be very careful about regulating your Health. A defensive skill such as Bonetti's Defense is a must-have. These defensive skills are still useful even if you take the ranged route instead of the melee route. As most Warrior skills use adrenaline instead of Energy, a Mesmer/Warrior is better off following the Domination or Illusion lines instead of the Inspiration line. Bonetti's Defense is a good way to get Energy while protecting yourself, and Energy Tap, even without ranks in the Inspiration attribute, can be helpful.

Cooperative Play

While the Mesmer is generally thought of as a PvP character, it is still an amazing character in cooperative play, and in some cases, some of its spells actually work better on NPCs than PCs.

When going into cooperative play battles, focus more on spells that do damage or Hex opponents than the spells that regenerate your Energy. While it is good to take Energy Tap or Power Drain along with you, your main focus should be spells like Backfire, Power Spike, or Conjure Phantasm. Perhaps the most beneficial aspect of fighting NPCs is that they aren't smart enough to interrupt your casting, or even to stop casting after you have Backfired them!

As cooperative play often provides a more diverse group of targets than PvP, be sure not to specialize too much. If you are a Mesmer/

Necromancer with the majority of your spells focused on killing melee characters, bring a spell such as Power Spike or Backfire to damage magical opponents. Likewise, if your build character is made to kill magic users, consider taking along a pure damage dealing spell such as Conjure Phantasm. If you are an illusion Mesmer, Illusionary Weaponry is a very good spell to take with you into cooperative play. PvP is often fast-paced and constant casting, but in cooperative play you are likely to be using regular attacks a bit more often. Unless your secondary is a Ranger or a Warrior and you are using one of their specialty weapons, Illusionary Weaponry is going to improve your damage by a lot.

Player vs. Player

Mesmers are amazing PvP characters. Because of their spells, you can specialize in taking down a specific type of character. Want to kill Warriors or Rangers? Get set up with Ignorance, Empathy, Panic, Soothing Images, and some damage spells. Want to take down Elementalists, Monks, Necromancers, or other Mesmers? Use Backfire, Power Block, Power Spike, and similar spells.

Mesmers with Domination Magic are a key component in almost any winning team. Without them, it is very hard to kill enemy casters. With them, things can sometimes seem all too easy. The top weapons in the Domination arsenal are Backfire and Shatter Enchantment. These two skills alone are enough to destroy any sloppy caster. Against a skilled opponent, a domination Mesmer may not single-handedly defeat them, but she'll delay them enough so that the other damage dealers can finish them off.

What's the downside of a domination Mesmer? You'll be identified as a primary threat, hated almost as much as the Monks you are designed to kill.

You'll need to learn how to duck in and out of range and avoid direct confrontations. Good team coordination is also important.

If Domination sounds appealing, then you may want to complement it with the skills of another profession. The good news is that it combines well with almost anything else—regardless of whether Mesmer is chosen as primary or secondary. The interruption-attacks from either Ranger or Warrior are a good combination. Monks can combine self-healing and Smiting abilities (Scourge Healing is a great supplement for aspiring Monk-slayers). Elementalists can offer a larger Energy pool and direct damage. Necromancers can stack other deadly Hexes atop the Mesmer's.

When playing 8v8, become a caster-hunter. Seek out enemy Monks and offensive casters and shut them down for your team. You can choose disruption (skills like Power Leak, Power Block, Migraine, and Guilt) or destruction (Backfire, Power Leak, and DoTs). Control their actions, drain their Energy, or make their healers heal your decoy target, while your damagers easily tear apart your team's real target.

In 4v4, Ignorance and Backfire are staples. Removing a Warrior's ability to use Healing Signet makes the battle much easier; making casters take damage when they cast will throttle back their casters' output, or (if they're as foolish as you are lucky) they may even kill themselves. DoTs also shine in these arenas, as Hex removal is less common.

If you're going anti-Warrior, take Ineptitude, Clumsiness, Mantra of Persistence, Conjure Phantasm, and Phantom Pain. Throw in Illusion of Weakness for a free 200-Health heal, or Illusion of Haste for constant-run that'll keep you away from those pesky Warriors with their nasty melee attacks.

If you're going anti-Elementalist/Monk, take Migraine, Mantra of Persistence, Conjure Phantasm, Phantom Pain, Power Drain, and Leech Signet. You can also choose Backfire, Blackout, or Wastrel's Worry if you want to make a splash in Domination.

Try to concentrate on control rather than kills. Let your Warriors, Elementalists, and Rangers polish off targets, while you keep them safe from casters or melee fighters with shutdowns. Be an opportunist—wait for the best time to use long cooldown skills like shatters and interrupts to get maximum effectiveness out of your heavy-cost skills.

Try to be subtle. Mesmers are at their best when they can go about doing their little mischievous deeds unnoticed. A definite weakness of Mesmers is the fact that a lot of the skills rely on your enemies' actions rather than your own. Wait for the right opportunities before striking! Keep back; most enemies in PvP won't consider you a target until later. Show them how wrong they are by keeping the entire enemy team busy with DoTs, Migraine, or Inept. In addition, Mesmers are the only class that can counter a nature ritual (with Unnatural Signet).

Mesmer Skills

Look for new skills to be added to *Guild Wars* over time.

Fast Casting
(Primary Mesmers Only)

Mantra of Recovery (elite)
Source: Ayassah Hess, Goss Aleessh, Tiss Danssir (Forgotten Bosses)

Cost	15	Casting Time	–
Duration	30–90	Recast Time	30

For 5–20 seconds, spells you cast recharge 50% faster.

(No Attribute)

Arcane Mimicry
Source: Vendor, Maguuma Stade

Cost	15	Casting Time	2
Duration	20	Recast Time	60

For 20 seconds, Arcane Mimicry becomes the elite spell from target other ally.

Epidemic
Source: Vendor, Grendich Courthouse

Cost	15	Casting Time	2
Duration	–	Recast Time	15

All negative Conditions target foe suffers from are spread from target foe to nearby foes.

Signet of Humility
Source: Vendor, Fishermen's Haven

Cost	–	Casting Time	2
Duration	–	Recast Time	20

Target foe's elite skill is disabled for 15 seconds.

Signet of Midnight (elite)
Source: Malus Phasmatis (Ghost Boss)

Cost	–	Casting Time	3/4
Duration	15	Recast Time	15

You and target touched foe become Blinded for 15 seconds.

Domination Magic

Arcane Thievery
Source: Quest, Kryta-The Wilds/Vendor, Amnoon Oasis

Cost	10	Casting Time	1
Duration	5–35	Recast Time	10

For 5–35 seconds, one random spell is disabled for target foe, and Arcane Thievery is replaced by that spell.

Backfire
Source: Quest, Kingdom of Ascalon/Vendor, Ascalon City (Ruins)

Cost	15	Casting Time	3
Duration	10	Recast Time	20

For 10 seconds, whenever target foe casts a spell, that foe takes 35–140 damage.

Blackout
Source: Quest, Kryta-The Wilds/Vendor, Droknar's Forge

Cost	10	Casting Time	1
Duration	10	Recast Time	10

For 2–7 seconds, all of target foe's skills are disabled, and all of your skills are disabled for 5 seconds.

Chaos Storm
Source: Quest, Ruins of Ascalon/Vendor, Yak's Bend

Cost	15	Casting Time	2
Duration	10	Recast Time	30

Create a Chaos Storm at target foe's location. For 10 seconds, foes near this location suffer 5–14 damage each second. Chaos Storm drains 1–7 Energy whenever it strikes a foe casting a spell.

Cry of Frustration
Source: Vendor, Beetletun

Cost	15	Casting Time	3/4
Duration	–	Recast Time	20

If target foe is using a skill, that foe and nearby foes are interrupted and suffer 10–44 damage.

Diversion
Source: Quest, Ruins of Ascalon

Cost	10	Casting Time	2
Duration	6	Recast Time	5

For 6 seconds, The next time target foe uses a skill, that skill takes an additional 10–56 seconds to recharge.

Empathy
Source: Quest, Kingdom of Ascalon/Vendor, Ascalon City (Ruins)

Cost	10	Casting Time	2
Duration	8–20	Recast Time	20

For 8–20 seconds, whenever target foe attacks, that foe takes 3–30 damage.

Energy Burn
Source: Vendor, Ruins of Ascalon/Vendor, Yak's Bend

Cost	10	Casting Time	2
Duration	–	Recast Time	20

Target foe loses 4–10 Energy and takes 8 damage for each point of Energy lost.

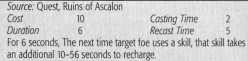

Energy Surge (elite)
Source: Pantheras the Deceiver (Mursaat Boss)

Cost	10	Casting Time	2
Duration	–	Recast Time	20

Target foe loses 4–10 Energy. For each point of Energy lost, that foe and all foes in the area take 8 damage.

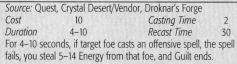

Guilt
Source: Quest, Crystal Desert/Vendor, Droknar's Forge

Cost	10	Casting Time	2
Duration	4–10	Recast Time	30

For 4–10 seconds, if target foe casts an offensive spell, the spell fails, you steal 5–14 Energy from that foe, and Guilt ends.

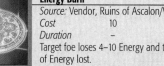

Hex Breaker

Source: Quest, Kryta-The Wilds/Vendor, Amnoon Oasis

Cost	10	*Casting Time*	–
Duration	60–180	*Recast Time*	20

For 60–180 seconds, the next time you are the target of a Hex, that Hex fails, the caster takes 10–46 damage, and Hex Breaker ends.

Ignorance

Source: Vendor, Port Sledge

Cost	15	*Casting Time*	2
Duration	8–20	*Recast Time*	10

For 8–20 seconds, target foe cannot use Signet rings.

Mind Wrack

Source: Quest, Kryta-The Wilds/Vendor, Droknar's Forge

Cost	5	*Casting Time*	1
Duration	20	*Recast Time*	5

If (within the 20-second duration) target foe's Energy is zero, that foe takes 15–90 damage and Mind Wrack ends.

Panic (elite)

Source: Moles Quibus (Titan Boss)

Cost	25	*Casting Time*	2
Duration	8–20	*Recast Time*	10

Target foe and all adjacent foes are Hexed with Panic for 8–20 seconds. While Hexed, they suffer Energy degeneration of 2 and take 10–82 damage whenever they use a Signet ring.

Power Block (elite)

Source: Lyssa's Cursed (Golem Boss)

Cost	15	*Casting Time*	1/4
Duration	–	*Recast Time*	30

If target foe is casting a spell, that spell is interrupted. The interrupted spell and all spells of the same attribute are disabled for 3–15 seconds for that foe.

Power Leak

Source: Quest, Ruins of Ascalon/Vendor, Yak's Bend

Cost	10	*Casting Time*	1/4
Duration	–	*Recast Time*	20

If target foe is casting a spell, the spell is interrupted and target foe loses 10–25 Energy.

Power Spike

Source: Quest, Shiverpeaks (N)/Vendor, Lion's Arch

Cost	10	*Casting Time*	1/4
Duration	–	*Recast Time*	15

If target foe is casting a spell, the spell is interrupted and target foe takes 20–102 damage.

Shame

Source: Vendor, North Kryta Province

Cost	10	*Casting Time*	2
Duration	4–10	*Recast Time*	30

For 4–10 seconds, the next time target foe casts a spell on an ally, the spell fails and you steal 5–14 Energy from that foe and Shame ends.

Shatter Delusions

Source: Quest, Kingdom of Ascalon/Vendor, Ascalon City (Ruins)

Cost	5	*Casting Time*	1
Duration	–	*Recast Time*	20

Remove all Mesmer Hexes from target foe. For each Hex removed, that foe takes 15–75 damage.

Shatter Enchantment

Source: Quest, Shiverpeaks (N)/Vendor, Lion's Arch

Cost	15	*Casting Time*	1
Duration	–	*Recast Time*	25

Remove an enchantment from target foe. If an enchantment is removed, that foe takes 14–100 damage.

Shatter Hex

Source: Quest, Ruins of Ascalon/Vendor, Yak's Bend

Cost	15	*Casting Time*	1
Duration	–	*Recast Time*	10

Remove a Hex from target ally. If a Hex is removed, foes near that ally take 22–140 damage.

Signet of Weariness

Source: Vendor, Camp Rankor

Cost	–	*Casting Time*	1
Duration	–	*Recast Time*	30

Target foe and all nearby foes lose 3–10 Energy.

Wastrel's Worry

Source: Quest, Kryta/Vendor, Henge of Denravi

Cost	5	*Casting Time*	1/4
Duration	3	*Recast Time*	1

After 3 seconds, target foe takes 8–64 damage. Wastrel's Worry ends prematurely if that foe uses a skill.

Illusion Magic

Arcane Conundrum

Source: Quest, Crystal Desert/Vendor, Droknar's Forge

Cost	10	*Casting Time*	2
Duration	6–30	*Recast Time*	20

For 6–30 seconds, spells cast by target foe take twice as long to cast.

Arcane Echo

Source: Vendor, Beetletun

Cost	15	*Casting Time*	2
Duration	10–30	*Recast Time*	30

If you cast a spell in the next 10–30 seconds, Arcane Echo is replaced with that spell for 20 seconds. Arcane Echo ends prematurely if you use a non-spell skill.

Clumsiness

Source: Vendor, Copperhammer Mines

Cost	10	*Casting Time*	1
Duration	4–8	*Recast Time*	10

For 4–8 seconds, if target foe attempts to attack, the attack is interrupted, target foe suffers 10–92 damage, and Clumsiness ends.

Conjure Phantasm

Source: Quest, Kingdom of Ascalon/Vendor, Ascalon City (Ruins)

Cost	10	Casting Time	1
Duration	2–14	Recast Time	5

For 2–14 seconds, target foe experiences Health degeneration of 5.

Crippling Anguish (elite)

Source: Fuury Stonewrath (Summit Dwarf Boss)

Cost	15	Casting Time	1
Duration	8–20	Recast Time	20

For 8–20 seconds, target moves 50% slower and suffers Health degeneration of 1–3.

Distortion

Source: Quest, Ruins of Ascalon/Vendor, Yak's Bend

Cost	5	Casting Time	–
Duration	5	Recast Time	5

For 5 seconds, you have a 75% chance to evade attacks. Whenever you evade an attack this way, you lose 1–3 Energy or Distortion ends.

Echo (elite)

Source: Rwek Khawl Mawl (Hydra Boss)

Cost	5	Casting Time	1
Duration	10–30	Recast Time	30

For 10–30 seconds, Echo is replaced with the next skill you use. Echo acts as this skill for 20 seconds.

Ethereal Burden

Source: Quest, Kryta-The Wilds/Vendor, Amnoon Oasis

Cost	15	Casting Time	3
Duration	10	Recast Time	45

For 10 seconds, target foe moves 50% slower than normal. When Ethereal Burden ends, you gain 10–22 Energy.

Fevered Dreams (elite)

Source: Plexus Shadowhook (Dryder Boss)

Cost	10	Casting Time	2
Duration	4–16	Recast Time	10

For 4–16 seconds, whenever target foe suffers from a new Condition, all nearby foes suffer from that Condition as well.

Fragility

Source: Quest, Shiverpeaks (N)/Vendor, Lion's Arch

Cost	15	Casting Time	1
Duration	8–20	Recast Time	15

For 8–20 seconds, target foe takes 5–34 damage each time that foe suffers or recovers from a new Condition.

Illusion of Haste

Source: Quest, Ruins of Ascalon/Vendor, Yak's Bend

Cost	10	Casting Time	1
Duration	5–11	Recast Time	5

For 5–11 seconds you move 33% faster than normal, and the effects of the Crippled Condition are removed. When Illusion of Haste ends, you become Crippled.

Illusion of Weakness

Source: Quest, Kryta/Vendor, Henge of Denravi

Cost	10	Casting Time	2
Duration	until broken	Recast Time	30

You lose 50–240 Health. Illusion of Weakness ends if damage drops your Health below 25% of your maximum. When Illusion of Weakness ends, you gain 50–240 Health.

Illusionary Weaponry (elite)

Source: Gack the Mindwrecker (Skale Boss), Seear Windlash (Nightmare Boss)

Cost	15	Casting Time	1
Duration	30	Recast Time	40

For 30 seconds, you deal no damage in melee, but whenever you attack in melee, target foe takes 8–40 damage.

Imagined Burden

Source: Quest, Kingdom of Ascalon/Vendor, Ascalon City (Ruins)

Cost	15	Casting Time	1
Duration	8–20	Recast Time	30

For 8–20 seconds, target foe moves 50% slower than normal.

Ineptitude (elite)

Source: Wyt Sharpfeather (Tengu Boss), Tachi Forvent (Human Boss)

Cost	10	Casting Time	1
Duration	4–10	Recast Time	20

For 4–10 seconds, if target foe attacks, that foe takes 10–82 damage and becomes Blinded, and Ineptitude ends.

Migraine (elite)

Source: Pytt Spitespew (Windrider Boss)

Cost	10	Casting Time	2
Duration	6–30	Recast Time	15

For 6–30 seconds, target foe suffers Health degeneration of 1–3 and takes 100% longer to cast spells.

Phantom Pain

Source: Quest, Ruins of Ascalon/Vendor, Yak's Bend

Cost	10	Casting Time	2
Duration	10	Recast Time	15

For 10 seconds, target foe suffers Health degeneration of 1–3. When Phantom Pain ends, that foe suffers a Deep Wound, lowering that foe's maximum Health by 20% for 5–20 seconds.

Soothing Images

Source: Vendor, Marhan's Grotto

Cost	10	Casting Time	2
Duration	8–20	Recast Time	5

For 8–20 seconds, target foe cannot gain adrenaline.

Sympathetic Visage

Source: Vendor, Fishermen's Haven

Cost	10	Casting Time	1
Duration	8–20	Recast Time	30

For 8–20 seconds, whenever target ally is hit by a melee attack, all nearby foes lose all adrenaline and 3 Energy.

Inspiration Magic

Channeling
Source: Quest, Shiverpeaks (N)/Vendor, Lion's Arch

Cost	5	*Casting Time*	1
Duration	8–56	*Recast Time*	15

For 8–56 seconds, whenever you cast a spell, you steal 1 Energy from each nearby foe.

Drain Enchantment
Source: Vendor, Ice Tooth Cave

Cost	10	*Casting Time*	1
Duration	–	*Recast Time*	25

Remove an enchantment from target foe. If an enchantment is removed, you gain 10–22 Energy.

Elemental Resistance
Source: Quest, Crystal Desert/Vendor, Droknar's Forge

Cost	10	*Casting Time*	–
Duration	30–90	*Recast Time*	20

For 30–90 seconds, you gain +40 armor against Elemental damage, but you lose 24–12 AL against physical damage.

Energy Drain (elite)
Source: Sniik Hungrymind (Imp Boss)

Cost	5	*Casting Time*	1
Duration	–	*Recast Time*	20

Steal 8–20 Energy from target foe.

Energy Tap
Source: Quest, Ruins of Ascalon/Vendor, Yak's Bend

Cost	5	*Casting Time*	3
Duration	–	*Recast Time*	20

Steal 8–14 Energy from target foe.

Ether Feast
Source: Quest, Kingdom of Ascalon/Vendor, Ascalon City (Ruins)

Cost	5	*Casting Time*	2
Duration	–	*Recast Time*	8

Target foe loses 5 Energy. You are healed 8–28 for each point of Energy lost.

Ether Lord
Source: Quest, Crystal Desert/Vendor, Droknar's Forge

Cost	5	*Casting Time*	2
Duration	5–10	*Recast Time*	20

You lose all Energy. For 5–10 sec, target foe suffers Energy degeneration of 1–3, and you experience Energy regeneration of 1–3.

Inspired Enchantment
Source: Quest, Kryta/Vendor, Henge of Denravi

Cost	10	*Casting Time*	1
Duration	20	*Recast Time*	–

Remove an enchantment from target foe and gain 3–15 Energy. For 20 seconds, Inspired enchantment is replaced with the enchantment removed from target foe.

Inspired Hex
Source: Quest, Shiverpeaks (N)/Vendor, Lion's Arch

Cost	5	*Casting Time*	1
Duration	20	*Recast Time*	–

Remove a Hex from target ally and gain 3–15 Energy. For 20 seconds, Inspired Hex is replaced with the Hex that was removed.

Keystone Signet (elite)
Source: Rune Ethercrash (Ice Elemental Boss)

Cost	–	*Casting Time*	2
Duration	–	*Recast Time*	30

All of your other Signet rings are recharged. All of your non-Signet skills are disabled for 5-17 seconds.

Leech Signet
Source: Quest, Kryta/Vendor, Henge of Denravi

Cost	–	*Casting Time*	1/4
Duration	–	*Recast Time*	45

Interrupt target foe's action. If that action was a spell, you gain 3–15 Energy.

Mantra of Concentration
Source: Vendor, North Kryta Province

Cost	5	*Casting Time*	–
Duration	60–180	*Recast Time*	20

For 60–180 seconds, the next time you would be interrupted while performing a skill, you are not interrupted, and Mantra of Concentration ends.

Mantra of Earth
Source: Quest, Kryta-The WIlds/Vendor, Droknar's Forge

Cost	15	*Casting Time*	–
Duration	30–90	*Recast Time*	20

For 30–90 seconds, whenever you take Earth damage, the damage is reduced by 26–50% and you gain 1 Energy.

Mantra of Flame
Source: Quest, Ruins of Ascalon/Vendor, Yak's Bend

Cost	15	*Casting Time*	–
Duration	30–90	*Recast Time*	20

For 30–90 seconds, whenever you take Fire damage, the damage is reduced by 26–50% and you gain 1 Energy.

Mantra of Frost
Source: Quest, Shiverpeaks (N)/Vendor, Lion's Arch

Cost	15	*Casting Time*	–
Duration	30–90	*Recast Time*	20

For 30–90 seconds, whenever you take Cold damage, the damage is reduced by 26–50% and you gain 1 Energy.

Mantra of Inscriptions
Source: Vendor, Camp Rankor

Cost	10	*Casting Time*	–
Duration	30–90	*Recast Time*	20

For 30–90 seconds, your Signet rings recharge 25–50% faster.

Mantra of Lightning

Source: Vendor, Port Sledge

Cost	15	Casting Time	–
Duration	30–90	Recast Time	20

For 30–90 seconds, whenever you take Lightning damage, the damage is reduced by 26–50% and you gain 1 Energy.

Mantra of Persistence

Source: Quest, Crystal Desert/Vendor, Droknar's Forge

Cost	15	Casting Time	–
Duration	30–90	Recast Time	20

For 30–90 seconds, any Illusion Magic Hex you cast lasts 20–100% longer.

Mantra of Recall (elite)

Source: Massou Blyss (Forgotten Boss), Featherclaw (Griffon Boss)

Cost	15	Casting Time	1
Duration	20	Recast Time	20

For 20 seconds, you gain no benefit from it. You gain 20–32 Energy when Mantra of Recall ends.

Mantra of Resolve

Source: Vendor, Marhan's Grotto

Cost	10	Casting Time	–
Duration	30–90	Recast Time	20

For 30–90 seconds, you cannot be interrupted, but each time you would have been interrupted, you lose 2–7 Energy, or Mantra of Resolve ends.

Mantra of Signets

Source: Vendor, Copperhammer Mines

Cost	15	Casting Time	–
Duration	10–25	Recast Time	30

For 10–25 seconds, the next time you use a Signet ring, it recharges immediately, and Mantra of Signets ends.

Physical Resistance

Source: Vendor, Grendich Courthouse

Cost	10	Casting Time	–
Duration	30–90	Recast Time	20

For 30–90 seconds, you gain +40 armor against physical damage, but you lose 12–24 AL against Elemental damage.

Power Drain

Source: Vendor, Maguuma Stade

Cost	5	Casting Time	1/4
Duration	–	Recast Time	25

If target foe is casting a spell, the spell is interrupted and you gain 1–31 Energy.

Spirit of Failure

Source: Quest, Kryta-The Wilds/Vendor, Amnoon Oasis

Cost	10	Casting Time	3
Duration	30	Recast Time	10

For 30 seconds, target foe has a 25% chance to miss with attacks. You gain 1–5 Energy whenever that foe misses in combat.

Spirit Shackles

Source: Quest, Kryta-The Wilds/Vendor, Amnoon Oasis

Cost	10	Casting Time	3
Duration	8–28	Recast Time	5

For 8–28 seconds, target foe loses 5 Energy whenever that foe attacks.

Monk

By Jonathan "Tarinth" Radoff

All Things in Balance

layers are always looking for Monks to join their teams. Monks keep their teams alive, and the success or failure of a battle often comes down to the healing and protective skills of the Monk. It is a challenging, high-pressure, essential job.

Monks are healers with the ability to cure damage on themselves and their allies; they have protective spells to prevent damage, mend Conditions, and stop enemies from attacking; and they have access to offensive capabilities in the form of their Smiting Prayers. Any of these skills are helpful, whether Monk is your primary or secondary profession. However, when Monk is your primary profession, your healing capabilities excel.

What makes a Monk primary the strongest healer in the game? It comes down to Divine Favor. The gods show their favor by empowering Monk primaries with the ability to dish out extra healing. If you have chosen a different primary profession, but you just want some healing to supplement your

other skills, Monk makes and excellent secondary profession.

Aside from being a healer, the Monk's skills and attributes as a primary (specifically, Smiting Prayers, the ability to retain higher Energy, and the regeneration skills) complement the fighting skills of a Warrior or Ranger. The downside to the Monk's healing prowess is that he is the PvP primary target. If you choose Monk primary, you must master more than healing. A wise Monk practices his maneuvering and defensive skills, and learns quickly to utilize the skills of his secondary profession to stay alive.

Attributes and Skills

Divine Favor

(Primary Monks Only)

For every rank you acquire in Divine Favor, every spell you cast on your allies heals them +3. This works for healing and non-healing spells. Only primary Monks can put points into Divine Favor, and that's what makes them such strong healers. In addition to this passive benefit, Monks can also cast a number of spells that draw from the Divine Favor attribute.

Aura of Faith (elite): This is a worthy alternative to Word of Healing because it strengthens your healing spells. This is a good choice in cooperative play when you focus your healing on a particular person. However, this attribute can be stripped or shattered like any enchantment.

Blessed Signet: When you activate this signet, you will get bonus Energy for every enchantment you have on yourself. If you have an enchantment-heavy build, this is worth considering. Otherwise, it is not enough of a boost to justify a space on your Skill Bar.

Divine Boon: This enchantment boosts the inherent effect of Divine Favor, providing a bit of extra healing with every Monk spell you cast on an ally. Each time you take advantage of this, you'll be charged 2 Energy, and you also need to maintain the enchantment. If you use this spell, stick to cheap heals, like Orison of Healing and Word of Healing, to maximize your efficiency.

Divine Healing: This is a stronger alternative to Heal Party, and has the additional benefit of only helping your allies (unlike Heal Area). You can only use it once per minute.

Peace and Harmony (elite): This enchantment's negative drain is nullified by the enchantment itself—one extra point of Energy regeneration is commonly underestimated, but over the course of this enchantment, it adds up to a lot of extra Energy. It's the equivalent of maintaining another enchantment for free. As long as you don't plan to attack anyone, consider taking this skill.

Signet of Devotion: Use this once every five seconds for a free heal. If you only choose one skill from Divine Favor, choose this one!

Spell Breaker (elite): The key here is timing. The duration of Spell Breaker isn't long, but when you know a caster is about to throw everything he has at you, it renders him harmless for a bit. As an elite skill, it requires practice to use it well. If you're not up to this, find an easier skill for your Skill Bar.

Watchful Spirit: While this enchantment is on a target, he or she gains Health regeneration. However, the benefitial aspect of this enchantment is that you can instantly heal the target simply by ending it.

(No Attribute)

A number of Monk skills are not tied to any attribute. These are useful for a primary or secondary Monk, regardless of the points you put into the other Monk attributes.

Essence Bond: Gain 1 Energy every time the target takes damage. This is useful when you are spending Energy to heal someone who is surrounded by enemies, but do not want to expose them to a Shatter Enchantment.

Holy Veil: This skill shields allies from Hexes, so enemies are less likely to cast them. Your enemies can easily remove this enchantment.

Martyr (elite): If you're running into a lot of opponents who cast Conditions, this is helpful, and you can also combine it with Plague Sending (Necro skill) or Purge Condition (Monk skill) for a party-wide cleansing.

Purge Signet: This removes all Hexes and Conditions from a target, but at an onerous cost: 10 Energy each. However, it is a signet, so you can use this to remove a Backfire without taking damage.

Remove Hex: Hex Monks should set aside a spot for this on their Skill Bars because Hexes are often dangerous. In team situations with multiple Monks, assign one Monk this duty to avoid duplication of effort.

Healing Prayers

Each rank in Healing Prayers increases the power of your healing spells. Any Monk who intends to heal people should plan on a minimum of 10 ranks in this attribute. Many healing spells can only be used on other people.

Dwayna's Kiss: This costs the same as Orison of Healing, has the same casting time, and a slightly longer recharge. However, it heals for an extra +15 for each enchantment or Hex on your target. Use this when you face many Necromancers and Mesmers, or when you enchant others in your group. Unlike Orison of Healing, this spell can only be cast on other people.

Heal Area: This is a group heal that is stronger and more Energy-efficient than Heal Party. Its disadvantage is that it will heal any nearby enemies as well as your friends. It is helpful in situations where you support a group of ranged attackers who are exchanging fire with another ranged group, but its usefulness is negated when enemies wade into close range.

Heal Other: At first glance, this is more efficient than Orison of Healing, but that is only when you forget the benefits of Divine Favor. Still, it is a decent emergency heal alternative to Word of Healing in those builds that include a different elite skill. Don't use this in a build with Word of Healing, because Word or Orison is a better option.

Heal Party: Unlike Heal Area, this is safe to use near your enemies. Because there is no recharge time, you can cast it in quick succession, but the 15 Energy cost is high.

Healing Breeze: This is a strong HoT effect and can be used for self-healing. Use it immediately before someone starts taking damage. Because this is an enchantment, it couples well with Dwayna's Kiss.

Healing Hands (elite): This is a solid choice for your elite skill, particularly if you are the frequent target of melee attacks. During the 10-second duration, this enchantment makes the target able to ignore any number of low damage melee attackers.

Healing Seed: This is a top skill that belongs in any healer's repertoire. Like Healing Hands, it is an enchantment that heals the target whenever he takes damage. Unlike Healing Hands, it can't be self-cast, but it is not elite, has a longer duration, and heals anyone else who is near the person this enchantment is used on (including the caster).

Healing Touch: This heal doubles Divine Favor's effect. Because it requires you to touch your target, it's a great self-heal when Orison isn't adequate.

Infuse Health: This is the strongest heal, but potentially dangerous. Because you are left with half of your Health, you could become an easy target. Save this for emergencies.

Live Vicariously: Enchant your fastest attackers with this to get a steady stream of self-healing. You can cast this on yourself if you plan to attack, but Vigorous Spirit is a better choice for Monks who intend to fight a lot on their own.

Orison of Healing: This is the healing workhorse. If you have ranks in Healing Prayers, you should have this skill on your Skill Bar. Its versatility comes from the fact that it is cheap, fast casting, and fast recharging. It is also one of the few targeted healing spells you can cast on yourself.

Restore Life: This is preferred to the simpler Resurrect skill because it restores your target to life with more Health and Energy. Because this involves standing in a dangerous spot, leave this job to Warrior/Monks rather than to the primary healers.

Vigorous Spirit: This is similar to Live Vicariously, except that it heals the target instead of the caster, and it also works when spells are cast. It has a limited duration, but does not require any upkeep. Monks can cast this on themselves, so it works well in melee-oriented Monk/Warrior builds.

Word of Healing (elite): This is another top skill, and the best Monk skill for those in the "pure healer" role. It has fast activation and costs the same as Orison of Healing, yet it includes a significant boost to the amount of healing your target receives when his Health is below 50 percent. The low Energy cost makes it a better emergency heal than Heal Other. You can't use this on yourself, so you'll still need Orison of Healing.

Protection Prayers

Each rank in Protection Prayers increases the power of a group of spells that prevent damage, stop attacks, and remove Conditions. "Pure healers" (those with ranks in Healing Prayers, Protection Prayers, and Divine Favor only) should also take a couple of skills from this attribute. Protection skills are good for secondary Monks who are looking for added defense as well.

Aegis: This has a similar effect to the Elementalist Ward Against Melee skill except it is less effective. It has a shorter duration, longer recharge, and can be destroyed by Shatter Enchantment.

Amity (elite): This is the best crowd control spell in the game—it prevents adjacent enemies from attacking you. However, it takes excellent team coordination, because its benefit is erased when one of your allies (PC or NPC) unwittingly attacks the wrong person.

Draw Conditions: Removes Conditions (Bleeding, Crippled, etc.) from an ally and gives them to you. This is best used when you're not under attack. It also combines well with the Ranger elite skill Melandru's Resilience.

Life Attunement: If you're playing on a team with a decoy/tank character—someone who wades into the midst of the enemy to absorb their attacks—this helps. The target ally will do less damage when enchanted by this spell, but the ally will receive greater healing benefits.

Life Barrier (elite): If you aren't being attacked and someone else is, this works marvelously. It is best used in well-oiled teams with multiple Monks who can maintain a high level of healing. Teams with two Monks who cast this on each other are hard to kill.

Mark of Protection (elite): Throw this on an ally taking large amounts of damage and combine it with Protective Spirit to make the target invulnerable for 10 seconds.

Mend Ailment: The low Energy cost makes this a decent skill even for Monks who have no ranks in Protection.

Mend Condition: This is an excellent skill for Protection Monks because it combines Condition removal with healing. The downside is that Monks cannot cast it on themselves. However, for a Monk who is looking for a general purpose Condition remover, and who lacks ranks in Protection Prayers, Mend Ailment is a better option.

Pacifism: Got an annoying Warrior who is swinging at you, and no time to heal yourself? Cast this at him, and he'll be twiddling his thumbs for a while. This is a strong skill, but good teamwork is required—it takes only one attack on the enchanted Warrior to break the spell.

Protective Spirit: This enchantment is one of the Protection Monk's signature abilities. Because many attacks (particularly from Elementalists) can hit hard, this helps take the bite out of their assaults.

Rebirth: This resurrects a party member from a distance, making it safer to use than Restore Life.

Restore Condition (elite): If the target ally is laden with many Conditions, this spell removes them and gives him a lot of healing. This is an effective spell against Condition-centric enemies.

Shield of Deflection (elite): This spell offers an impressive amount of defense

against melee and ranged attacks, so it is effective against heavy Warrior and Ranger builds.

Shield of Regeneration (elite): This is most useful to people who choose Monk as a secondary profession to obtain access to Protection Prayers. For primary Monks, there are better elite skills for healing and defense.

Shielding Hands: This is good for fighting fast-attacking opponents (such as sword wielders). It doesn't provide enough damage prevention on its own, so combine it with another HoT effect, such as Healing Seed or Healing Hands. If you want defense against powerful attacks, choose Protective Spirit instead.

Vital Blessing: This is most useful in cooperative play situations where you need to give an ally an extra buffer against hard-hitting opponents.

Smiting Prayers

Smiting is the advanced section of the Monk skill selection. These skills are strong when your goal is damage-dealing, but they don't integrate well with the primary healer role. Monk/Rangers and Monk/Warriors with Smiting skills are tough offensive fighters and effective cooperative play soloists. These skills are also useful when Monk is the secondary profession.

Balthazar's Aura: One nice thing about this spell is that it is hard to escape—the target of this spell can move to keep the enemies in range of the damage. For best results, use it as part of a team strategy.

Balthazar's Spirit: In offensive Warrior/Monk and Monk/Warrior builds, this is a powerful enchantment that can ensure ample adrenaline and Energy.

Bane Signet: Good for interrupting an attack; it works well when followed with an ability like Holy Strike. Because it is a signet, it has the advantage of costing no Energy.

Holy Strike: Another direct-damage spell, this one has a faster casting time than Banish. Because it does bonus damage when the target is knocked down, combine it with Bane Signet or other knockdown attacks.

Judge's Insight: Because this makes your attacks Holy and adds armor penetration, you will deal more damage to anything. Few opponents are protected against Holy damage.

Retribution: This reflects melee damage to your opponent. The amount of reflection isn't as high as with Holy Wrath, but you aren't charged Energy when the reflection occurs.

Scourge Healing: This is an outstanding skill to include in a Mesmer/Monk anti-healer build. Spam this to multiple enemy party members to destroy their healer(s) in short order.

Scourge Sacrifice: This spell is most effective against Necromancers highly specialized in Sacrifice spells. Because it is an AoE spell, use it against groups.

Shield of Judgment (elite): This is a potent enchantment, but it is best used in knockdown-oriented builds. For example, Elementalist/Monks could use this with Aftershock to dish out terrifying amounts of damage to anyone crazy enough to engage them in melee.

Signet of Judgment (elite): It's free and it's a knockdown. Combine it with a team that has a lot of knockdowns (perhaps other Monks with Signet of Judgment) to lay waste to many opponents.

Smite Hex: For Monks with ranks in Smiting Prayers, this is a good alternative to Remove Hex. Use this when there are enemies surrounding a Hexed ally; it ends the Hex and hits everyone nearby with damage—at a cost of only 5 Energy.

Zealot's Fire: To exploit this skill, toss it on an ally (or yourself) who is going to be surrounded by enemies, then cast your cheapest, fastest spell over and over. Orison of Healing is a good choice. The target is healed, and everything near him will takes damage.

Secondary Professions

When you play a Monk as a group healer, every secondary profession has something to offer—your choice of secondary profession is more a matter of your experience, play style, and what you'd like to offer your group.

Monk/Elementalist

The spells within Earth and Water Magic pair well with healers. Both of these schools offer a number of effective defenses, and should you choose, some powerful offenses.

If you select Elementalist as your secondary profession, choose skills that won't run you out of Energy. There's nothing worse than being a healer who doesn't have the Energy to keep the group alive! Fortunately, one of the skills that you'll gain access to as an Elementalist is the Glyph of Lesser Energy. If you're running into Energy problems, add this to your Skill Bar to reduce the cost of your next spell by 15.

Avoid diluting your effectiveness. Make sure you choose either Earth or Water and spend points in only one of them. If you're playing as part of a team, base part of your decision on what the other Elementalists are using—many of these spells are not useful when duplicated.

Monk/Elementalists with Earth Magic have access to some potent defensive spells. Ward Against Melee blocks 50 percent of the melee attacks in its AoE. More importantly, this spell is cast on the ground and not on a person, which makes it impossible to shatter or remove. It will help you avoid melee attacks while you continue to heal, and it helps your teammates while they remain nearby. Kinetic Armor enchants you with additional armor. It expires in eight seconds, but renews automatically if you cast another spell. If a Warrior is attacking you, this, along with the

frequent use of Orison of Healing, can keep you alive for a long time. One of the most powerful elite defense skills, Obsidian Flesh, gives you armor and makes it impossible for enemy spell casters to target you.

You must give up some of your healing power with this skill, but it's a good trade-off.

If you prefer Water Magic, choose defensive skills, such as Swirling Aura and Armor of Mist. Water also has a number of good snaring spells, such as Frozen Burst. Point-blank area attacks like this are a good damage-dealing option for healers because it means you won't have to select an enemy target in the middle of your healing regimen.

For a strong self-defense build, use Healing Prayers (11), Divine Favor (10), and Earth Magic (10). Take Orison of Healing, Signet of Devotion, Healing Touch, Heal Other, Mend Ailment, Glyph of Lesser Energy, Obsidian Flesh, and Ward Against Melee. For a build that uses Water Magic, put 10 ranks into that attribute and take Word of Healing, Orison of Healing, Signet of Devotion, Healing Touch, Mend Ailment, Glyph of Lesser Energy, Swirling Aura, and Frozen Burst.

Monk/Mesmer

In the right hands, a Monk/Mesmer can be the strongest overall healer in the game. Using the Mesmer's Inspiration Magic, a Monk/Mesmer can steal Enchantments and Energy from other casters, allowing him to enhance his group and maintain a steady stream of healing.

Inspired Enchantment is an excellent choice, because it removes an Enchantment from an opponent and puts it on your Skill Bar for 20 seconds. Because many of the best Enchantment skills come from Healing Prayers, you can cast them at full strength. See a Warrior/Monk charging you with a glowing white aura? He is using Healing Hands—steal it from him and give it to yourself!

A Monk/Mesmer who focuses on healing should consider the following build: Inspiration Magic (10), Divine Favor (10), and Healing Prayers (11). Add in Word of Healing, Orison of Healing, Healing Touch, Signet of Devotion, and Mend Ailments to your Mesmer skills, and you'll be a healing powerhouse. The challenge with a Monk/Mesmer is to juggle the healing of your group with the offensive use of Inspired Enchantment and Energy Tap. You'll have fewer defenses than other builds, but you can swap in Healing Hands if you're taking too much melee damage.

Monk/Necromancer

The Necromancer's minions are good supplements to the Monk's healing capabilities. The advantage is that you can assist in offense without needing to manage it. Your minions can also act as a Health reservoir when you're under physical attack.

For a strong Monk/Necromancer, consider the following build: Healing Prayers (10), Divine Favor (8), Death Magic (12), and Blood Magic (2). For skills, take Dark Bond, Animate Bone Fiend, Animate Bone Horror, Word of

Healing, Signet of Devotion, Orison of Healing, Healing Touch, and Mend Ailment. You'll have strong healing, combined with the ability to raise minions from your fallen enemies. In an emergency, use Dark Bond to divert 75 percent of your physical damage to a minion (even though this is a Blood Magic skill, the 34-second duration you get from the two ranks is long enough to help). Alternately, you can swap out one of the Animate spells for a direct-damage spell like Deathly Swarm, but do not overuse your Energy when others need healing.

Monk/Ranger

Like Warriors, Rangers can stick to a primary healing role or go for a Smiting build. They are good at either.

When assigned the role of healing Conditions, the Monk/Ranger shines. Invest in Healing Prayers (10), Protection Prayers (5), Divine Favor (10), and Wilderness Survival (10). Use Draw Conditions to transfer Conditions from other party members, then use Melandru's Resilience (an elite Ranger skill) to give yourself a big Health and Energy regeneration boost for each of the Conditions with which you become afflicted. For a stronger character, add in a couple of other Wilderness Survival skills, such as Troll Unguent, a powerful self-heal, and Dryder's Defenses, which grants 75 percent evasion from attacks and a large amount of armor against elemental damage. To round out a character who will keep your group free of annoying Hexes while offering self-defense and effective healing capabilities, include Orison of Healing, Heal Other, Healing Seed, and Remove Hex.

If you'd rather play offense, your build will look like a ranged version of a Smiting Monk/Warrior. Invest in Healing Prayers (10), Divine Favor (5), Smiting Prayers (10), and Marksmanship (10). Take Orison of Healing, Healing Touch, Live Vicariously, Balthazar's Spirit, Judge's Insight, Favorable Winds,

Barrage, and Pin Down. Barrage will hit the enemies near your target, and with Live Vicariously active, you'll be healed for everything you hit. Pin Down gives you the ability to snare an opponent if something gets too close. When attacking multiple enemies, this build can do more damage than its Warrior counterpart. However, it can use more Energy if you need to self-heal frequently, so team up with a Warrior who will tank for you.

Monk/Warrior

This is a solid secondary profession for both new and experienced players. There are three degrees of investment you could make in the Warrior skills:

1. Spend no points on the Warrior attributes, yet utilize the Warrior's Sprint skill. Sprint uses the Strength attribute (which is restricted to primary Warriors), but even at its minimum duration of eight seconds, it is useful. You will have times when you need to flee or to catch up to a member of your group, and having the Sprint skill equipped can be a lifesaver. This also works well for players who want to be "pure healers," focusing their attribute points on Monk skills—Healing Prayers (11), Divine Favor (10), and Protection Prayers (10). For this build, equip Word of Healing (for an elite skill), Orison of Healing, Signet of Devotion, Dwayna's Kiss, Mend Condition, Protective Spirit, Pacifism, and Sprint.

2. Tap into the Warrior's Tactics attribute. With Healing Prayers (11), Tactics (10), and Divine Favor (10), you'll be a strong healer with access to some of the Warrior's defensive Stances. You should experiment with some of the different Stances to determine which ones work best for your play style. Some of the Warrior Stances require adrenaline, and some will end if you use a skill—avoid those. Disciplined Stance is a good option, as well as Shield Stance, but

have a shield equipped before you use it. If you use Shield Stance, it is better to switch to a shield rather than equip one all the time, or else you will drain your Energy. Another option is Gladiator's Defense, an elite skill that gives 75 percent blocking and damages your melee attackers.

In addition to the use of two defensive Stances and Sprint, the Warrior can also utilize Healing Signet—it's a free self-heal that takes a mere two seconds to cast. With a four second recharge time and up to 115 points in healing, it's an invaluable part of a Warrior's arsenal. This also helps keep you alive without a heavy Energy expenditure. One disadvantage of Healing Signet is that you take double damage while activating it, so only use it when you're not being attacked. If you're only facing melee attackers, activate a Stance first.

A good Skill Bar for a tactics-oriented Monk/Warrior should include Word of Healing, Orison of Healing, Signet of Devotion, Infuse Health, Mend Ailment, Healing Signet, Disciplined Stance, and Sprint. You can swap out Disciplined Stance for Shield Stance if you prefer to play with a shield. If you want to try Gladiator's Stance, replace Word of Healing with Healing Seed. One strong feature of this build is that, as long as you're not under attack, you can use Infuse Health for a huge target ally heal, then cast Healing Signet to repair the damage to yourself for free.

3. Change the Monk from a healer to a powerful holy Warrior. You won't be as strong a healer, but you'll possess impressive offensive capabilities. Allocate your attribute points so that you have Swordsmanship (10), Healing Prayers (10), Smiting Prayers

(10), and Divine Favor (6). Limit your sword attacks to adrenaline-based skills so that your Energy pool is reserved for Smiting and Enchantment spells. Sever Artery, Gash, and Final Thrust are three attacks that work well together. Add in Judge's Insight, Balthazar's Spirit, and Zealot's Fire from your Smiting Prayers and round out your Skill Bar with Orison of Healing and Healing Touch. Because of the Monk's high Energy regeneration, you can maintain these enchantments while regaining more Energy from Balthazar's Spirit. You also can rely on cheap self-heals and simultaneously smite nearby foes. Avoid Mesmers and Necromancers, however, because their enchantment-removal abilities will compromise your effectiveness.

Cooperative Play

If you wish to solo play, Monk/Warriors with a focus on Smiting Prayers are effective. However, most people play Monks as group-support characters, which means the majority of your time will be spent with others.

Playing a Monk involves more than pressing the healing button: It involves smart use of your secondary skills and expert Energy management; it means understanding your enemies, recognizing the worst threats, and understanding how to deal with them; and it requires you to know your limits and make sure your teammates know them as well.

Unlike PvP, where the role of resurrecting a fallen party member is best left to a Warrior/Monk (due to their high survivability), in cooperative play, it falls upon the Monk to perform this service. It helps to have an understanding of the maps you're exploring so that you can choose what spell to throw out for Restore Life. For example, if you're not going to face many nasty poisons, you don't need Mend Condition. On other maps, Restore Hex is important. Whenever possible equip skills based on the needs of a particular area.

When you play with groups, have hotkeys set up to target each member of your group. Otherwise, you'll always be clicking on the screen, which is time consuming and keeps your eyes off the battlefield.

Click on Options, select Control Setup at the bottom of the dialog box, and scroll down to the actions that start with "Target Party Member."

Player vs. Player

When it comes to PvP, the question isn't whether you need a Monk, it's how many Monks do you need?

For a four-person arena team, one Monk is often sufficient. Things get more complicated when you graduate to the eight-person Tombs or a Guild-vs.-Guild battle. There, teams relying on a single Monk are doomed. The opposition will target the Monk, and after he is down, the rest of his teammates will fall like dominoes.

With two Monks, your team is tougher. If your opponent focuses on one of your Monks, the other can help keep him alive. In addition, having two Monks means they can diversify their skill set. For example, one could be a "pure healer" with skills in both Healing and Protection, while the other could have Healing complemented by defensive Earth Magic.

However, most experienced eight-person teams have found that two Monks aren't enough, either. Because Monks don't have good heals for themselves, self-healing and the heals of one other Monk are not enough to stop a concentrated focus-firing effort. Three is the magic number. It's difficult to focus-fire a Monk who is being focus-healed by two others. And if one gets killed, the two remaining Monks can remain an effective combination for quite some time—often long enough for the fallen Monk to be revived.

Get three Monks for your eight-person team. Any more, and you'll compromise your damage output. Any less, and you'll risk a quick defeat. And no, people with Monk as their secondary don't count toward the three. This gives an excellent balance.

Look for new skills to be added to *Guild Wars* over time.

Monk Skills

Divine Favor
(Primary Monks Only)

Aura of Faith (elite)
Source: Demetrios the Enduring (Mursaat Boss)

Cost	10	Casting Time	1
Duration	60	Recast Time	20

For 60 seconds, target ally gains 24–50% more Health when healed.

Blessed Aura
Source: Quest, Crystal Desert/Vendor, Droknar's Forge

Cost	10	Casting Time	2
Duration	upkeep	Recast Time	2

While you maintain this enchantment, Monk enchantments you cast last 10–35% longer than normal.

Blessed Signet
Source: Quest, Kryta-The Wilds/Vendor, Droknar's Forge

Cost	–	Casting Time	2
Duration	–	Recast Time	10

For each enchantment you are maintaining, you gain 3 Energy, maximum 3–24.

Contemplation of Purity
Source: Quest, The Wilds/Vendor, Amnoon Oasis

Cost	10	Casting Time	1/4
Duration	–	Recast Time	5

Lose all enchantments. For each one lost, you gain 6–80 Health, lose one Hex, and lose one Condition.

Divine Boon
Source: Quest, Shiverpeaks (N)/Vendor, Lion's Arch

Cost	5	Casting Time	1/4
Duration	upkeep	Recast Time	–

While you maintain this enchantment, whenever you cast a Monk spell on an ally, that ally is healed for 25–70 points, and you lose 2 Energy.

Divine Healing
Source: Vendor, Port Sledge

Cost	10	Casting Time	2
Duration	–	Recast Time	60

Heal yourself and nearby party members for 10–260 points.

Divine Intervention
Source: Vendor, Copperhammer Mines

Cost	10	Casting Time	1/4
Duration	10	Recast Time	30

For 10 seconds, if target ally receives damage that would be fatal, the damage is negated and that ally is healed for 26–240 points.

Divine Spirit
Source: Quest, Shiverpeaks (N)/Vendor, Lion's Arch

Cost	10	Casting Time	1/4
Duration	1–16	Recast Time	60

For 1–16 seconds, Monk spells cost you 5 less Energy to cast. (Minimum cost: 1 Energy.)

Peace and Harmony (elite)
Source: Marnta Doomspeaker (Human Boss)

Cost	5	Casting Time	1
Duration	30–90	Recast Time	45

For 30–90 seconds, target ally gains +1 Energy regeneration. Peace and Harmony ends if that ally attacks or casts a spell that does not target an ally.

Signet of Devotion
Source: Vendor, North Kryta Province

Cost	–	Casting Time	2
Duration	–	Recast Time	5

Heal target ally for 14–100 points.

Spell Breaker (elite)
Source: Raptorhawk (Griffon Boss)

Cost	15	Casting Time	1
Duration	5–17	Recast Time	45

For 5–17 seconds, enemy spells targeted against target ally fail.

Unyielding Aura (elite)
Source: Ipillo Wupwup (Grawl Boss)

Cost	3	Casting Time	4
Duration	upkeep	Recast Time	45

Bring dead target ally back to life at full Health and full Energy. If you stop maintaining this enchantment or if this enchantment is removed, that ally dies. Deaths while enchanted with Unyielding Aura do not incur a death penalty. (50% failure chance with Divine Favor 4 or less.)

Watchful Spirit
Source: Vendor, Maguuma Stade

Cost	15	Casting Time	2
Duration	upkeep	Recast Time	10

While you maintain this enchantment, target ally gains Health regeneration of 2. That ally is healed for 30–180 points when Watchful Spirit ends.

(No Attribute)

Essence Bond
Source: Vendor, Beetletun

Cost	10	Casting Time	2
Duration	upkeep	Recast Time	–

While you maintain this enchantment, whenever target ally takes physical damage, you gain 1 Energy.

Holy Veil
Source: Quest, Kryta/Vendor, Henge of Denravi

Cost	10	Casting Time	2
Duration	upkeep	Recast Time	–

While you maintain this enchantment, any Hex cast on target creature take twice as long to cast.

Light of Dwayna
Source: Vendor, Marhan's Grotto

Cost	25	Casting Time	4
Duration	–	Recast Time	30

Resurrect all nearby dead allies.

Martyr (elite)

Source: Dwayna's Cursed (Golem Boss)

Cost	5	*Casting Time*	1/4
Duration	–	*Recast Time*	10

All Conditions on party members are transferred to you.

Purge Conditions

Source: Quest, Ruins of Ascalon/Vendor, Yak's Bend

Cost	5	*Casting Time*	1/4
Duration	–	*Recast Time*	30

Remove all Conditions (Poison, Disease, Blindness, Dazed, Bleeding, Crippled, and Deep Wound) from target ally.

Purge Signet

Source: Vendor, Fishermen's Haven

Cost	–	*Casting Time*	3
Duration	–	*Recast Time*	30

Remove all Hexes and Conditions from target ally. You lose 10 Energy for each Hex and each Condition removed.

Remove Hex

Source: Quest, Shiverpeaks (N)/Vendor, Lion's Arch

Cost	5	*Casting Time*	2
Duration	–	*Recast Time*	5

Remove a Hex from the target ally.

Resurrect

Source: Quest, Ruins of Ascalon/Vendor, Yak's Bend

Cost	10	*Casting Time*	8
Duration	–	*Recast Time*	–

Resurrect target party member.

Succor

Source: Vendor, Ice Tooth Cave

Cost	10	*Casting Time*	1
Duration	upkeep	*Recast Time*	10

While you maintain this enchantment, target other ally gains Health and Energy regeneration of 1, but you lose 1 Energy each time that ally casts a spell.

Vengeance

Source: Quest, Crystal Desert/Vendor, Droknar's Forge

Cost	10	*Casting Time*	4
Duration	30	*Recast Time*	60

Bring dead target ally back to life at full Health and full Energy. After 30 seconds, or if this enchantment is removed, the enchanted ally dies. Deaths while enchanted with Vengeance do not incur a death penalty.

Healing Prayers

Dwayna's Kiss

Source: Quest, Kryta/Vendor, Henge of Denravi

Cost	5	*Casting Time*	1
Duration	–	*Recast Time*	3

Heal target other ally for 15–60 points and an additional 5–20 points for each enchantment or Hex on that ally.

Heal Area

Source: Quest, Ruins of Ascalon/Vendor, Yak's Bend

Cost	10	*Casting Time*	1
Duration	–	*Recast Time*	5

Heal yourself and all nearby creatures for 30–180 points.

Heal Other

Source: Quest, Kryta/Vendor, Henge of Denravi

Cost	10	*Casting Time*	3/4
Duration	–	*Recast Time*	3

Heal target ally for 35–180 points.

Heal Party

Source: Quest, Ruins of Ascalon/Vendor, Yak's Bend

Cost	15	*Casting Time*	2
Duration	–	*Recast Time*	–

Heal entire party for 16–80 points.

Healing Breeze

Source: Quest, Kingdom of Ascalon/Vendor, Ascalon City (Ruins)

Cost	10	*Casting Time*	1
Duration	10	*Recast Time*	2

For 10 seconds, target ally gains Health regeneration of 3–9.

Healing Hands (elite)

Source: Muga Riptide (Gargoyle Boss), Rull Browbeater (Ettin Boss)

Cost	5	*Casting Time*	1/4
Duration	10	*Recast Time*	25

For 10 seconds, whenever target ally is struck by an attack, that ally is healed for 5–25 points.

Healing Seed

Source: Quest, Kryta-The Wilds/Vendor, Amnoon Oasis

Cost	15	*Casting Time*	2
Duration	8–20	*Recast Time*	25

For 8–20 seconds, whenever target ally takes damage, that ally and all adjacent allies gain 3–30 Health.

Healing Touch

Source: Quest, Crystal Desert/Vendor, Droknar's Forge

Cost	5	*Casting Time*	3/4
Duration	–	*Recast Time*	5

Heal touched target ally for 16–60 points. Health gain from Divine Favor is doubled for this spell.

Infuse Health

Source: Quest, Ruins of Ascalon/Vendor, Yak's Bend

Cost	10	Casting Time	1/4
Duration	–	Recast Time	–

Lose half your current Health. Target ally is healed for 100–136% of the amount you lost.

Live Vicariously

Source: Quest, Ruins of Ascalon/Vendor, Yak's Bend

Cost	10	Casting Time	2
Duration	upkeep	Recast Time	–

While you maintain this enchantment, whenever target ally hits a foe, you gain 1–14 Health.

Mending

Source: Quest, Ruins of Ascalon/Vendor, Yak's Bend

Cost	10	Casting Time	2
Duration	upkeep	Recast Time	–

While you maintain this enchantment, target ally gains Health regeneration of +1–4.

Orison of Healing

Source: Quest, Kingdom of Ascalon/Vendor, Ascalon City (Ruins)

Cost	5	Casting Time	1
Duration	–	Recast Time	2

Heal target ally for 20–70 points.

Restore Life

Source: Vendor, Grendich Courthouse

Cost	10	Casting Time	8
Duration	–	Recast Time	–

Touch the body of a fallen ally member. Target ally is returned to life with 26–50% Health and 42–90% Energy.

Vigorous Spirit

Source: Quest, Shiverpeaks (N)/Vendor, Lion's Arch

Cost	5	Casting Time	1
Duration	30	Recast Time	4

For 30 seconds, each time target ally attacks or casts a spell, that ally is healed for 1–14 points.

Word of Healing (elite)

Source: Dassk Arossyss, Josso Essher, Wissper Inssani (Forgotten Bosses)

Cost	5	Casting Time	3/4
Duration	–	Recast Time	4

Heal target ally for 16–80 points. Heal for an additional 15–100 points if that ally is below 50% Health.

Protection Prayers

Aegis

Source: Vendor, Fishermen's Haven

Cost	15	Casting Time	1
Duration	5–11	Recast Time	30

For 5–11 seconds, all party members have a 50% chance to block attacks.

Amity (elite)

Source: Pravus Obsideo (Ghost Boss)

Cost	5	Casting Time	1/4
Duration	8–20	Recast Time	60

For 8–20 seconds, adjacent foes cannot attack. For each foe, Amity ends if that foe takes damage.

Convert Hexes

Source: Vendor, Camp Rankor

Cost	15	Casting Time	2
Duration	8–20	Recast Time	20

Remove all Hexes from target other ally. For 8–20 seconds, that ally gains +10 armor for each Necromancer Hex that was removed.

Draw Conditions

Source: Vendor, Copperhammer Mines

Cost	5	Casting Time	1/4
Duration	–	Recast Time	–

All negative Conditions are transferred from target ally to yourself. For each Condition acquired, you gain 6–26 Health.

Guardian

Source: Vendor, Ascalon City (Ruins)

Cost	5	Casting Time	1
Duration	5	Recast Time	2

For 5 seconds, target ally has a 20–50% chance to block attacks and magical projectiles.

Life Attunement

Source: Quest, Kryta/Vendor, Henge of Denravi

Cost	10	Casting Time	2
Duration	upkeep	Recast Time	–

While you maintain this Enchantment, target ally deals less damage in combat, but gains 14–50% more Health when healed.

Life Barrier (elite)

Source: Esnhal Hardwood (Plant Boss)

Cost	15	Casting Time	2
Duration	upkeep	Recast Time	5

While you maintain this enchantment, damage dealt to target ally is halved. If your Health is below 40–70% when that ally takes damage, Life Barrier ends.

Life Bond

Source: Vendor, Beetletun

Cost	10	Casting Time	2
Duration	upkeep	Recast Time	–

While you maintain this enchantment, whenever target ally takes damage from an attack, half the damage is redirected to you. The damage you receive this way is reduced by 3–30 points.

Mark of Protection (elite)

Source: Bolis Hillshaker (Dolyak Boss)

Cost	15	Casting Time	1
Duration	10	Recast Time	45

For 10 seconds, whenever target ally would take damage, that ally is healed for that amount instead, maximum 6–60. All your Protection Prayers are disabled for 10 seconds.

Mend Ailment

Source: Quest, Kryta/Vendor, Henge of Denravi

Cost	5	Casting Time	3/4
Duration	–	Recast Time	2

Remove one Condition (Poison, Disease, Blindness, Dazed, Bleeding, Crippled, or Deep Wound) from target ally. That ally is healed for 5–70 points for each remaining Condition.

Mend Condition

Source: Quest, Crystal Desert/Vendor, Droknar's Forge

Cost	5	Casting Time	3/4
Duration	–	Recast Time	2

Remove one Condition (Poison, Disease, Blindness, Dazed, Bleeding, Crippled, or Deep Wound) from target ally. That ally is healed for 5–70 points.

Pacifism

Source: Quest, Shiverpeaks (N)/Vendor, Lion's Arch

Cost	10	Casting Time	3
Duration	8–20	Recast Time	30

For 8–20 seconds, target foe cannot attack. This effect ends if the target takes damage.

Protective Bond

Source: Vendor, Maguuma Stade

Cost	10	Casting Time	2
Duration	upkeep	Recast Time	–

While you maintain this enchantment, target ally cannot take more than 5% damage at one time. When Protective Bond prevents damage, you lose 2–6 Energy or the spell ends.

Protective Spirit

Source: Quest, Kryta-The Wilds/Vendor, Amnoon Oasis

Cost	10	Casting Time	1/4
Duration	5–23	Recast Time	5

For 5–23 seconds, target ally cannot lose more than 10% Health due to damage from a single attack or spell.

Rebirth

Source: Quest, Kryta-The Wilds/Vendor, Amnoon Oasis

Cost	10	Casting Time	6
Duration	–	Recast Time	–

Resurrect target party member, teleporting him to your current location. All of target's skills are disabled for 5–20 seconds. This spell consumes all of your remaining Energy.

Restore Condition (elite)

Source: Spindle Agonyvein (Dryder Boss)

Cost	10	Casting Time	3/4
Duration	–	Recast Time	2

Remove all Conditions (Poison, Disease, Blindness, Dazed, Bleeding, Crippled, and Deep Wound) from target ally. That ally is healed 10–100 points for each Condition removed.

Reversal of Fortune

Source: Quest, Kingdom of Ascalon/Vendor, Ascalon City (Ruins)

Cost	5	Casting Time	1/4
Duration	8	Recast Time	2

The next time target ally would take damage, that ally gains that amount of Health instead, maximum 15–80.

Shield of Deflection (elite)

Source: Grun Galesurge (Windrider Boss)

Cost	15	Casting Time	2
Duration	5–11	Recast Time	5

For 5–11 seconds, target ally has a 50–75% chance to evade attacks and gains 12–24 armor.

Shield of Regeneration (elite)

Source: Pessh Missk (Forgotten Boss)

Cost	15	Casting Time	1
Duration	5–11	Recast Time	20

For 5–11 seconds, target ally gains 3–10 Health regeneration and 40 armor.

Shielding Hands

Source: Quest, Kingdom of Ascalon/Vendor, Ascalon City (Ruins)

Cost	5	Casting Time	3/4
Duration	10	Recast Time	25

For 10 seconds, damage received by target ally is reduced by 3–18.

Vital Blessing

Source: Quest, Ruins of Ascalon/Vendor, Yak's Bend

Cost	10	Casting Time	2
Duration	upkeep	Recast Time	–

While you maintain this enchantment, target ally has +40–200 maximum Health.

My Favorite Arena

Name: Brian Porter

Title: Level Artist

Character: Funky Monkey

I really enjoy the Ascalon Arena. I love the quick satisfaction you get out of the speed of the battles and the camaraderie you gain after winning a few battles with some new people. Often, I end up going through missions with some of these people later because we had such a great time playing together and have put each other on our respective Friends lists. One of the best things about playing in the Arena is that if things don't work out with the first group and you get beaten, you just go back to the start and you get a new random group that might work together a little better. As far as tactics go, you need to work together and focus your efforts. If one of your teammates goes down, you need to resurrect that character quickly so that you get back to a 4-versus-4, or better yet, put the odds in your favor if you've already taken someone down.

Smiting Prayers

Balthazar's Aura
Source: Quest, Kryta-The Wilds/Vendor, Droknar's Forge

Cost	25	Casting Time	1
Duration	10	Recast Time	15

For 10 seconds, foes adjacent to target ally take 10–25 Holy damage each second.

Balthazar's Spirit
Source: Quest, Shiverpeaks (N)/Vendor, Lion's Arch

Cost	10	Casting Time	2
Duration	upkeep	Recast Time	–

While you maintain this enchantment, target ally gains adrenaline and Energy after taking damage.

Bane Signet
Source: Quest, Kingdom of Ascalon/Vendor, Ascalon City (Ruins)

Cost	–	Casting Time	2
Duration		Recast Time	25

Target foe takes 26–56 Holy damage. If that foe was attacking, he is knocked down.

Banish
Source: Quest, Kingdom of Ascalon/Vendor, Ascalon City (Ruins)

Cost	5	Casting Time	1
Duration	–	Recast Time	10

Target foe takes 20–56 Holy damage.

Holy Strike
Source: Vendor, Ice Tooth Cave

Cost	5	Casting Time	3/4
Duration	–	Recast Time	8

Touched target foe takes 10–55 Holy damage. If knocked down, your target takes an additional 10–25 Holy damage.

Holy Wrath
Source: Vendor, North Kryta Province

Cost	10	Casting Time	2
Duration	upkeep	Recast Time	–

While you maintain this enchantment, whenever target ally takes melee damage, this spell deals 25–67% of the damage back to the source, and you lose 10 Energy.

Judge's Insight
Source: Vendor, Grendich Courthouse

Cost	10	Casting Time	2
Duration	8–20	Recast Time	10

For 8–20 seconds, target ally's attacks deal Holy damage and have +20% armor penetration.

Retribution
Source: Quest, Kingdom of Ascalon/Vendor, Ascalon City (Ruins)

Cost	10	Casting Time	2
Duration	upkeep	Recast Time	–

While you maintain this Enchantment, whenever target ally takes melee damage, this spell deals 19–34% of the damage back to the source.

Scourge Healing
Source: Quest, Kryta-The Wilds/Vendor, Droknar's Forge

Cost	10	Casting Time	2
Duration	30	Recast Time	5

For 30 seconds, every time target foe is healed, the healer takes 15–80 Holy damage.

Scourge Sacrifice
Source: Vendor, Copperhammer Mines

Cost	10	Casting Time	2
Duration	8–20	Recast Time	5

For 8–20 seconds, every time target foe sacrifices life, he sacrifices twice the normal amount.

Shield of Judgment (elite)
Source: Myd Springclaw (Tengu Boss)

Cost	15	Casting Time	1
Duration	8–20	Recast Time	45

For 8–20 seconds, anyone striking target ally with an attack is knocked down and suffers 5–50 damage.

Signet of Judgment (elite)
Source: Frostbite (Nightmare Boss), Tree of Judgment (Plant Boss)

Cost	–	Casting Time	2
Duration		Recast Time	30

Target foe is knocked down. That foe and all adjacent foes take 15–75 Holy damage.

Smite
Source: Quest, Ruins of Ascalon/Vendor, Yak's Bend

Cost	10	Casting Time	1
Duration	–	Recast Time	10

This attack deals 10–55 Holy damage. If attacking, your target takes an additional 10–25 Holy damage.

Smite Hex
Source: Quest, Kryta-The Wilds/Vendor, Amnoon Oasis

Cost	5	Casting Time	1
Duration	–	Recast Time	15

Remove a Hex from target ally. Foes near that ally suffer 10–85 damage.

Strength of Honor
Source: Quest, Ruins of Ascalon/Vendor, Yak's Bend

Cost	10	Casting Time	2
Duration	upkeep	Recast Time	–

While you maintain this enchantment, target ally deals 1–10 more damage in melee.

Symbol of Wrath
Source: Quest, Kingdom of Ascalon/Vendor, Ascalon City (Ruins)

Cost	5	Casting Time	2
Duration	5	Recast Time	30

For 5 seconds, foes in this location take 8–32 Holy damage each second.

Zealot's Fire
Source: Quest, Crystal Desert/Vendor, Droknar's Forge

Cost	10	Casting Time	1
Duration	60	Recast Time	30

For 60 seconds, whenever you use a skill on an ally, all foes adjacent to your target are struck for 5–45 Fire damage.

Necromancer

By Kitty Chan

The Power of Death

The Necromancer is a versatile and powerful profession. He can become the strongest member of a party and will often be the last player standing. As a Necromancer, you might be the only thing standing between your party and an untimely demise.

The right combination of skills grants you and your party a long life. For example, Verata's Gaze in combination with Taste of Death allows you to take control of an undead creature, then claim its life for your own. A Necromancer is also able to help a group with spells like Well of Power and Well of Blood.

Every skill you have available to you is invaluable to your success. There are many ways to specialize your Necromancer; both a good defense and a good offense are available to you when you take the Necromancer's path. Though your skills are useful, it's important to know when you expect to be in a group and when you're going to stand alone.

Who are your teammates going to be? If you have a good Monk in the party, focus on damage spells and beefing up the party, with skills like Putrid Explosion and Barbs. If you're going to have a Mesmer in the party, focus on skills that work with his enchantments, like Soul Barbs and Virulence.

Though you can do well with a wide range of skills, some specific combinations of skill sets give you a greater chance of success. Equip skills that complement each other. For example, there's little sense in having Taste of Death (stealing Health from an undead ally) without also including something like Animate Bone Horror (which creates undead allies).

Lastly, if you are doing your job well, you will be a primary target for the enemy. Keep at least one skill like Vampiric Touch or Parasitic Bond to help you keep up your Health.

Five Reasons to Be a Necromancer

- Necromancers are well-balanced, with a good mix of both offensive and defensive skills that allows them to perform well on their own.

- Necromancers can fill out a party by increasing the overall effectiveness of allies or decreasing the effectiveness of enemies.

- As the battle wanes, the Necromancer's power only increases as her reservoir of potential minions waxes.

- A Necromancer can wield the dead as weapons by bringing back allies or raising vanquished foes to fight on her side.

- Necromancers can simulate an army with the ability to raise minions from the corpses of their fallen foes.

Attributes & Skills

Soul Reaping
(Primary Necromancers Only)

Soul Reaping: This allows the Necromancer to draw upon the spirits of dead corpses, restoring small portions of Energy for each dead body on the field. For each creature (ally, enemy, minion, pet, or anyone else) who dies close to you, you will gain Energy equal to your ranks in Soul Reaping. It's a handy attribute for any Necromancer style.

(No Attribute)

These Necromancer skills are not affected by an attribute.

Grenth's Balance (elite): The point of this skill is to vampirize a foe's Health. Only use this when you're at low ebb because the effect is magnified. Preceed this with a skill that sacrifices Health (like Dark Pact) to destroy your life bar, then combo with this skill to nail an unsuspecting foe.

Plague Touch: This is a great way to turn your foe's Energy into Hexes on themselves. Use this against Warriors to give them the Conditions they've inflicted on you (for example, Bleeding), thereby freeing you from their ill effects.

Blood Magic

Blood Magic increases the effectiveness of skills that deal damage and steal life from your enemies. This is a good choice for a primary attribute if you're interested in PvP or solo missions.

Awaken the Blood: This trades Health for Blood Magic and Curse buffs. To use this spell, combo it with things that do more damage, but do not have a heavy penalty in sacrificing your Health to make the most of them.

Barbed Signet: This sacrifices Health to steal more Health from a foe. This is a good match for Dark Aura or if you're a Necro/Mesmer with Signet recharging skills.

Blood Renewal: This sacrifices Health to heal faster. When the spell wears off, you gain the amount sacrificed. Use this before a battle so you're always gaining Health during the fight.

Blood Ritual: Sacrifice Health with this spell to give your ally increased regeneration. This is the first of several spells by which a Necromancer can heal in her own way. This is key for boosting an Elementalist or Monk's natural (or augmented) Energy regen abilities.

Blood is Power (elite): This sacrifices Health so that the target ally may regenerate Energy faster. This is a buffed-up version of Blood Ritual and allows for faster regen and longer range, and is one of the best buffs in the game.

Dark Bond: When you receive physical damage, your closest minion suffers 75 percent of the damage for you. This is a useful skill to keep you alive. Combine with Death Nova, Taste of Death, and various minion heal skills so that your cattle absorb most of your pain.

Dark Fury: This sacrifices Health so that attacking party members get a hit of adrenaline. Use this to boost the Warriors in your party (or to give yourself more adrenaline if you're playing either side of a Necro/Warrior combo). This is best for teams heavy in Warriors.

Dark Pact: Use this to sacrifice Health and deal that much damage to an enemy. Follow this up with Life Siphon to replenish some of your Health while taking more Health from your enemy. This is a fast, efficient way to take out foes who are low in Health—it combines well with Dark Aura and Grenth's Balance to ruin someone's day.

Demonic Flesh: This sacrifices temporary Health to increase maximum Health, which is useful if you're about to be healed beyond full and head into battle. This is good for tanks and those who take the fight up-close and personal, such as Smiting Monks.

Life Siphon: Use this to steal Health from your target foe. This is valuable, especially in solo situations where nobody is around to heal you. Spam this on mutliple foes to get your Health regeneration cranking—it's not useful against a single foe, however.

Life Transfer (elite): This steals Health from your target foe over time. This is a great skill to keep on the Skill Bar to replenish Health lost in battle and from sacrifices. Toss this on a boss or a strong Warrior or Monk to strip away 3x the Health, as the lesser version of this skill (Life Siphon) would. You can only use this on one foe at a time.

Mark of Subversion: Use this when your target foe casts a spell on an ally, the spell fails, and you gain Health from the caster. This is more effective in cooperative play, as other players will catch on to this tactic. This is a good spell to hit bosses with because it'll interrupt their cast and give you a boost.

Offering of Blood (elite): This sacrifices Health to gain Energy. This is good when you're in a safe place casting as backup for a party. Necro/Monks can use this to quick-charge their Energy then heal themselves. Repeat until your Energy bar is full.

Order of Pain: A powerful spell when used with a group that is heavy in Warriors, it elevates their melee damage to terrific levels. Use this against bosses, and they'll fall before you know it.

Order of the Vampire (elite): This sacrifices Health so when a party member attacks, that ally steals Health. Use this on allies who use physical attacks frequently, such as Warriors, to grant them extra Health cover in the heat of a fight.

Shadow Strike: This strikes a foe for damage; if the enemy is mostly healed, you gain Health. This is a great spell for opening a battle, as it vampirizes a portion of the foe's life bar and passes it to you. If they have less than 50 percent Health, this is not the best skill upon which to rely.

Signet of Agony: To rid yourself of the Bleeding it inflicts, use Plague Touch to pass it to a nearby foe. It stacks well with Dark Aura.

Soul Leech (elite): Whenever your target foe casts a spell on anyone, you steal Health from him. This is a fun skill to use on spellcasting foes. It's also a great way to deter enemy casters from efficiently casting their spells, as they notice the damage they're taking. Tack this onto a fast-casting character such as a Mesmer, Monk, or cooperative play enemies who are spamming spells to inflict massive damage.

Strip Enchantment: Your target foe loses an enchantment, and you gain Health. This is another win-win skill, a great skill to use when your enemy's party is casting a lot of enchantments. This is an especially key skill for countering powerful Monk enchantments, leaving them less able to effectively contribute to a battle.

Touch of Agony: As with Plague Touch, you're betting that your foe will run out of Health before you do. This is like Dark Pact, but combos well with Plague Touch and Vampiric Touch, as all of them are touch-based in range.

Unholy Feast: This steals Health from each nearby enemy. This is a useful skill, and is helpful in large groups. It's maximally effective when you're surrounded by large swarms of enemies who re-invigorate your character.

Vampiric Gaze: This steals Health from target foes. It's a good basic spell; get it early, and keep it unless you're sure you're replacing it with something better. As it's a ranged version of Vampiric Touch, it's perfect after Dark Pact or when your party is focusing fire on one foe.

Vampiric Touch: Touch a target to steal Energy from him. Like Vampiric Gaze, this is a staple for Necromancers, especially when you face powerful enemy casters. As it's a touch-based

attack, combo this with Touch of Agony and Plague Touch and get maximum bang for your Necromantic buck.

Well of Blood: This is a great mid-battle heal, and can be used in a sly way at a fight's beginning. Have one of your team members sacrifice himself at the battle's beginning, cast this on the resultant corpse, reap the benefits during the fight, then resurrect the ally afterward.

Well of Power (elite): This is like Well of Blood except that it does both Health and Energy regeneration, making it a valuable skill.

Curses

This skill set affects the Strength of your enemies by reducing their overall effectiveness via reducing their resiliency, making them easier to kill. It's complimentary to Warriors and Rangers and other melee-oriented characters. This is a good skill set for the target caller in a team.

Defile Flesh: You sacrifice Health so that your target foe doesn't heal effectively. Use this spell to annoy enemy Monks! It's also a great finisher when a foe is weak, as it blunts the Healing effect of spells.

Desecrate Enchantments: Your target and nearby enemies take basic damage, as well as additional damage for each enchantment they have. This is another good spell for facing an enchantment-heavy group of foes. This is a terrific AoE skill to use on large groups.

Enfeeble: Your target foe suffers from Weakness; use this against an enemy Warrior. It's fast and easily spammable on multiple enemies. The net effect is that it brings damage-dealing down 66 percent.

Enfeebling Blood: Your target foe and nearby foes suffer from Weakness. This is good against a Warrior group in cooperative play. Like Enfeeble, only it costs you Health and is best against groups.

Faintheartedness: Your target foe attacks more slowly and loses Health over time. This is a good skill to use against any Profession.

Feast of Corruption (elite): Your target and nearby foes take Shadow damage (against which there is little protection), plus each of those foes who is suffering from a Hex takes even more damage. This is one of the biggest and best attacks in the game.

Insidious Parasite: When your target foe makes an attack, you steal Health from him. This is a great skill to use on fast-attacking enemy Warriors or any other speedy foe who gets by on quantity rather than quality of attacks.

Lingering Curse (elite): This sacrifices Health so your target loses all enchantments and only gains half of normal Health when being healed. Focus your allies' fire on a target. Cast this on the enemy target, then let your allies finish him off in his vulnerable state. This is an improved version of Defile Flesh.

Malaise: This is a good skill to match up against Life Siphon, as it negates its life-draining aspect and makes it spammable. If you don't have Life Siphon or a nearby healer, this isn't the best skill to use.

Parasitic Bond: Your target is damaged each round. When the spell wears off, you gain Health. This is a useful skill to spam on many foes, as it'll keep you going at your foe's expense.

Plague Signet (elite): This takes all Conditions currently ascribed to you and passes them to a target. This is a good combo for the Monk skill Draw Conditions. Use this combo to hurl a giant ball of Conditions at a very unlucky foe.

Price of Failure: This increases the chance an enemy spell will miss, and causes the enemy damage each time he does so. Mix this with your spells that drain Health and Energy from your foes, and with Oppressive Failure and Blinding skills, so that they'll miss 100 percent of the time. Stack that with Spirit of Failure, and someone will have a bad day.

Rend Enchantments: Your target loses a number of enchantments; for each of those enchantments a Monk cast, you lose Health, so be careful with this one!

Rigor Mortis: Your target cannot defend or evade. This is another great skill to use when focusing your allies' attacks on a single target; it's useful against enemy Warriors and good for countering heavy evasion groups.

Shadow of Fear: Your target foe and all nearby foes attack more slowly. This is good against large groups and is an AoE version of Faintheartedness.

Soul Barbs: This causes your target foe to take damage for each enchantment cast on it. This is helpful when an enemy Monk is beefing up his party. Combo this with fast-casting Hex spells (this also goes for ice skills).

Spinal Shivers: Whenever you strike your target foe for cold damage, that foe's skills are interrupted. At the same time, you lose Energy until Spinal Shivers ends. Use this in conjunction with cold-based Death Magic or Elemental spells to interrupt enemy spellcasters.

Spiteful Spirit (elite): When your target foe attacks or uses any skill, that foe and any nearby foes receive damage. This is a useful skill in any situation where there are tight enemy groups, especially large Warrior groups.

Suffering: Your target and surrounding foes suffer from Health degeneration. Combo this with Soul Barbs or Feast of Corruption. It is also good for masking other Hexes you've thrown on someone.

Weaken Armor: Your target foe has weakened armor for a period of time—yet one more weapon in your anti-Warrior arsenal. Combo this with Order of Pain for more pain.

Wither (elite): Your target foe loses Health and Energy until he runs out of Energy (max 35 seconds). This is a double-whammy of a spell that is especially crippling to casters. It's a good pick for your elite skill, if it's available to you.

Death Magic

Death Magic increases the effectiveness of skills that animate and control corpses and deal cold damage. This is a good choice as a primary attribute when you are interested in party missions and group PvP. This is also the suggested secondary attribute if you prefer solo missions, because it helps you beef up your group without relying on other players.

Animate Bone Fiend: This creates a Bone Fiend under your control; it can attack at range. This is a good spell to add support to a melee fighter group.

Animate Bone Horror: This creates a Bone Horror under your control. This is a good spell to bolster small groups and/or someone soloing, as the corpses are resilient.

Animate Bone Minions: This also brings a corpse to life as two lower-level minions under your control. This is great for making cannon fodder for a group under heavy attack and/or when using the corpses to zerg (overwhelm) larger enemies.

Aura of the Lich (elite): Use this to halve your max Health, as well as halve damage against you. It doubles your healing ability.

Blood of the Master: This sacrifices Health so that a nearby undead ally may gain Health. Use this spell to get more mileage out of your minions. Combo this with Verata's Sacrifice and Summon Bone Minion for an army that is feared far and wide.

Consume Corpse: Teleport to and steal Energy from your target corpse. This is a combination of Soul Feast and Necrotic Traversal. Two-for-one skills save space on your Skill Bar. Don't wait until you have to both teleport and "eat"—cast this any time you're wanting either one.

Dark Aura: This targets an enemy; each time the enemy sacrifices Health, his allies near him lose Health. Use this skill against enemy Monks and Necromancers. This is a great skill to use heavily as long as you have someone handy to keep you alive.

Death Nova: This enchants an ally; if he falls in combat, he causes damage to everything around him. If you know an ally is about to fall, it is a good way to exact revenge for the death! A good spell to combo on a group of Bone Minions with Taste of Death—this creates a small army of living bombs whom you can detonate at will.

Deathly Chill: This is a cold-based attack you should use on a foe with over 50 percent Health, as you'll lose half of its effectiveness on someone who has less than 50 percent Health.

Deathly Swarm: This strikes your target foe(s) with cold damage. Combine

this with Spinal Shivers to interrupt enemy casters. It does solid damage against massed groups of enemies.

Infuse Condition: Whenever you receive a Condition, it is passed to your closest minion instead.

Malign Intervention: If your target dies while under the influence of this spell, a masterless undead is raised from its corpse to attack anyone nearby. Raising a masterless undead is helpful when your target dies near other foes, not near you. However, if you use Vampiric Gaze in combination, you can take control of the newly-created creature.

Necrotic Traversal: Teleport to the location of your target corpse. Use it with a combination of ranged attacks to make your movement quicker and safer. Use it when teleporting into a large group to inflict poison upon it.

Putrid Explosion: This turns a corpse into a bomb, damaging all nearby. Keep yourself and your party away from its vicinity. Spam in a domino-like fashion: As each enemy goes down, re-cast the spell to wreak havoc.

Soul Feast: This steals life from any available corpse. This will keep you near full Health from battle to battle.

Tainted Flesh (elite): This makes a target ally immune to Disease, which is helpful when the enemy has a strong Necromancer. Anyone infected with Tainted Flesh will infect anyone they strike with Disease. Spam this on your team to infect your foes in short order.

Taste of Death: Steal Health from an undead ally with this spell. This is good when you are low on life and have minions to spare, and when combo'ed up with Death Nova. Use Vampiric Gaze to steal an enemy's minion and devour him for a Health boost.

Verata's Aura: Take control of all undead minions in the area at a great cost. Use this skill in areas with a lot of minions, especially where they outnumber you. Be wary, however: after it expires, they'll turn on you once more.

Verata's Gaze: Take control of or break the master-minion bond of your target undead creature. This is helpful if you can't find any corpses.

Verata's Sacrifice: This sacrifices Health to heal all undead allies and take any Condition of theirs onto yourself. This skill is most useful when running a solo mission and using a great number of minions; it will keep them alive for a much longer span of time.

Vile Touch: Touch your target to cause damage with Vile Touch. It is good for Warrior combinations and others who fight up close. The best benefit is the excellent casting speed.

Virulence (elite): If a target suffers from a Condition, he will also suffer from Weakness, Disease, and Poisoning. This is useful when you are grouped with a second Necromancer or a Mesmer.

Well of Suffering: Turns a corpse into the location of a Well of Suffering (which inflicts damage); this skill is useful when tight groups of enemies outnumber you.

Well of the Profane: This turns a corpse into the location of a Well of the Profane (which strips enchantments). Use this skill when the enemy has a good Monk on his side.

Secondary Professions
Necromancer/ Elementalist

Necromancer/Elementalist is not a common combination; most who want this pairing choose Elementalist/ Necromancer instead. However, that doesn't mean this combo shouldn't be considered. There are a few compatible skills, and even without the most compatible, a combination of the Necrotic and Elemental damage spells is a force to be reckoned with.

This profession combo is most effective for solo work because the Necromancer is a more capable self-healer than a healer for others. While the Elementalist side has strong offensive attributes, it is less capable of healing. The Elementalist provides raw damage and a few more debuffs, as well as glyphs, which help offset those high-Energy spells.

Necromancer/ Mesmer

With its combination of Hexes and Illusion Magic, the Necromancer/ Mesmer combo is one of the strongest offensive characters in the game.

Use the Illusion Magic of the Mesmer (such as Fragility) in combination with the Necromancer's Curses to make a strong, feared character in PvP play. The Channeling skill allows you to steal Energy from nearby foes, which is a great addition to the other Energy-stealing skills of the Necromancer. Grab Epidemic, which is the most useful crossover skill for a Necromancer/Mesmer. Cast any negative Conditions on a foe, then hit him with Epidemic, and he spreads it through his party.

Mesmers add shutdowns, reactive damage, and Hex removal to the Necromancer's arsenal. These are usually a good choice for offensive support.

The Necromancer/Mesmer is great in cooperative play and group PvP situations. Expect to be in high demand when you play this combination.

Necromancer/Monk

The Necromancer/Monk is another strong combination. Use both the Healing and Smiting aspects of the Monk profession to make solid, interesting characters.

The healing abilities of the Monk mixed with the dark arts of the Necromancer make an effective combo. Though the Necromancer has a lot of ways to keep himself alive, he could never be as effective at survival as a Monk. Adding skills like Resurrect and Light of Dwayna makes you a strong teammate. Though you can't heal as much as a Monk primary, you will be capable of healing your allies, as well as taking Health from your enemies.

This combination makes a well-balanced character and can allow even greater achievements for the solo Necromancer.

The other combination Necromancer/Monk is based on Smiting Prayers. Use the damage-dealing skills of the Monk alongside the Dark and cold skills of the Necromancer. This combination is not as well-balanced, but it can be very strong and a PvP player should fear and avoid the results. Though mostly offensive, pick up a few defensive skills, perhaps some of the Vampiric Touch spells or the Monk's Healing, to make sure you live long enough to make full use of the damage you can inflict.

Necromancer/ Ranger

The Necromancer/Ranger combination is similar to the Necromancer/Warrior. The skills of the Necromancer complement the abilities of any offensive physical attack profession. The Necromancer is not physically weak, but could never carry the weight a tank can carry. The Ranger profession differs from that of the Warrior in that its main attacks are ranged. Because the Necromancer spends most of the time in ranged combat, this is a good match.

This combination is strong for both PvP and cooperative play. The combination of ranged weapons and spells makes you one of the most formidable back-up characters ever. Any experienced group knows that having a strong ranged player standing back and softening opposing

groups before they reach the party is a great way to win battles.

Necromancer/ Warrior

The Necromancer/Warrior combination is well-rounded. If you play it right, this combo is amazing.

The Necromancer is a strong profession with the ability to take care of your Health and Energy and do significant damage. When coupled with a Warrior's melee skills, you are formidable. Pick up a few good melee attacks and choose a weapon in which to specialize. Sticking to the simple general Necromancer skills (like a Health-draining skill and an Energy-draining skill) complements the Warrior. Grab some Hexes to increase the effectiveness of your melee skills.

Even if a particular combination is not the norm, Necromancers are some of the most flexible characters in the game. They play well offensively and defensively, especially solo. This means that you have more choices in how to play your character than for any other primary class. Try new combinations and see where they lead.

Cooperative Play

Necromancers are well-suited for cooperative play. One good combination to consider if you'd like a strong offensive character is a Necromancer/Mesmer. If you're going to be mostly in groups with other PCs, pick up Order of the Vampire. When playing mostly solo, there are a great number of skills to keep you alive. The best way for a Necromancer to survive in cooperative play is to go more offensive—kill your foes before they have a chance to kill you. It helps that many of your offensive skills, such as Vampiric Touch, also help keep you alive.

One strong tactic for Necromancers includes building a group out of undead. Equip skills like Animate Bone Horror and Animate Bone Minions to build up your group; include defensive skills like Dark Bond and Infuse Condition, which is your lifeline. The key to progress isn't just with those skills, but also in some of the higher damage skills available. Price of Failure, Shadow Strike, and Dark Pact are great skills to take along, too.

The fallen corpses of your enemy are your best allies.

Player vs. Player

Necromancers are good at turning the tide of battle late in the game when there are plenty of bodies lying around. Their weaknesses are slow casting time and the inability to act in the absence of corpses. Patience is the name of the Necromancer's game. With Hex spells that can last 40 seconds, the damage a Necromancer can inflict over time if heavy Hex removal is absent is incredible. Alternately, Blood Wells can keep a team alive in a "king of the hill" match where one team has to hold a position.

Necromancers are one of the strongest anti-Warrior professions. With the right combination of Curses, a Necromancer/Warrior without the heavy armor of a primary Warrior can go toe-to-toe with a Warrior.

For only five Energy, the Enfeeble curse takes the punch out of a Warrior's

attacks, and Weaken Armor removes the usefulness of his armor. Spiteful Spirit punishes a Warrior for trying to attack, and Faintheartedness slows his attack and burdens him with Health degeneration.

With a Necromancer/ Warrior build, combine these anti-Warrior Curses with adrenaline-based sword or axe skills. Avoid hammers and shields so you can hold a focus item in your off-hand for extra Energy.

Need healing? Round out your skills with Blood Magic. Vampiric Touch and Life Siphon will hurt your foe while healing you, and because your opponent will be cursed with your damage-impairing Hex spells, you won't need much healing.

Inexperienced Warriors will run straight for Necromancers, assuming they'll be easy prey. A Curse-oriented Necromancer/Warrior will turn the tables on them.

My Favorite Character

Name: Tami Foote

Title: Level Artist

Character: Charlie F

I like the Necromancer/Monk the best. For that combo, I typically use Vampiric Gaze, Deathly Swarm, Life Siphon, Rotting Flesh, and Dark Pact for my primary profession.

Often, I'll use Rotting Flesh to begin with. It weakens the foe degeneratively, which I find makes them easier to kill. Next I use Deathly Swarm and Dark Bond for some good hits. At this point, my Health is usually half gone, and that's when I cast Life Siphon and Vampiric Gaze because I get Health regeneration from both. Of course, if my Health has suffered too greatly, I won't even use those two skills—I'll run for my life or die trying.

For my secondary profession, I generally use Heal Party, Reversal of Fortune, and Resurrect. With a PvP character, I use Necromancer skills while keeping an eye on my party members. As for the Monk skills, I use Resurrect, obviously, when a character dies. I use the other two Monk skills when my group's Health is getting low.

Necromancer Skills

Look for new skills to be added to *Guild Wars* over time.

Soul Reaping

(Primary Necromancers Only; No Skills)

(No Attribute)

Grenth's Balance (elite)

Source: Nash Cusstuss (Forgotten Boss)

Cost	15	Casting Time	1/4
Duration	–	Recast Time	60

If target foe has more Health than you, you gain half the difference (up to your maximum Health), and that foe loses an equal amount.

Plague Touch

Source: Quest, Kryta/Vendor, Henge of Denravi

Cost	5	Casting Time	3/4
Duration	–	Recast Time	

Transfer a negative Condition from yourself to target-touched foe.

Blood Magic

Awaken the Blood

Source: Vendor, Fishermen's Haven

Cost	10	Casting Time	1
Duration	20–44	Recast Time	45

For 20–44 seconds, you gain +2 Blood Magic and +2 Curses, but whenever you sacrifice Health, you sacrifice 50% more than the normal amount.

Barbed Signet

Source: Quest, Kryta-The Wilds/Vendor, Amnoon Oasis

Cost	–	Casting Time	2
Duration	–	Recast Time	30

Sacrifice 10% max Health. You steal 18–60 Health from target foe.

Blood is Power (elite)

Source: Cry Darkday (Nightmare Boss)

Cost	5	Casting Time	1/4
Duration	10	Recast Time	–

Sacrifice 33% max Health. For 10 seconds, target ally gains +3–6 Energy regeneration.

Blood Renewal

Source: Quest, Kingdom of Ascalon/Vendor, Ascalon City (Ruins)

Cost	5	Casting Time	1
Duration	–	Recast Time	10

Sacrifice 33% max Health. For 10 seconds, you gain Health regeneration of 3. When Blood Renewal ends, you gain 20–160 Health.

Blood Ritual

Source: Quest, Kryta/Vendor, Henge of Denravi

Cost	10	Casting Time	2
Duration	8–14	Recast Time	2

Sacrifice 17% max Health. For 8–14 seconds, target ally gains Energy regeneration of 3.

Dark Bond

Source: Quest, Kryta-The Wilds/Vendor, Amnoon Oasis

Cost	10	Casting Time	2
Duration	30–60	Recast Time	60

For the next 30–60 seconds, whenever you receive physical damage, your closest minion suffers 75% of that damage for you.

Dark Fury

Source: Vendor, Marhan's Grotto

Cost	10	Casting Time	3/4
Duration	5	Recast Time	5

Sacrifice up to 17% max Health. For 5 seconds, the next time any nearby party member attacks, that party member gains one hit of adrenaline.

Dark Pact

Source: Quest, Ruins of Ascalon/Vendor, Yak's Bend

Cost	5	Casting Time	1
Duration	–	Recast Time	2

Sacrifice up to 10% Health and deal 10–48 shadow damage to target foe.

Demonic Flesh

Source: Quest, Kryta-The Wilds/Vendor, Droknar's Forge

Cost	5	Casting Time	1
Duration	30–60	Recast Time	60

Sacrifice 20% max Health. For 30–60 seconds, your maximum Health is increased by 80–200.

Life Siphon

Source: Quest, Kingdom of Ascalon/Vendor, Ascalon City (Ruins)

Cost	10	Casting Time	2
Duration	12–24	Recast Time	2

For 12–24 seconds, target suffers Health degeneration of 1–3, and you gain Health regeneration of 1–3.

Life Transfer (elite)

Source: Shadow of Death, Murk Darkshriek (Nightmare Bosses), Agyris the Scoundrel (Mursaat Boss)

Cost	10	Casting Time	2
Duration	6–12	Recast Time	30

For 6–12 seconds, target foe suffers Health degeneration of 3–8, which you gain as Health regeneration.

Mark of Subversion

Source: Vendor, Grendich Courthouse

Cost	10	Casting Time	1
Duration	4–10	Recast Time	20

For 4–10 seconds, the next time target foe casts a spell on an ally, the spell fails and you steal 10–92 Health from that foe.

Offering of Blood (elite)

Source: Riine Windrot (Summit Dwarf Boss)

Cost	5	Casting Time	1/4
Duration	–	Recast Time	15

Sacrifice 10% maximum Health. You gain 8–20 Energy.

Order of Pain

Source: Vendor, Port Sledge

Cost	10	*Casting Time*	2
Duration	5	*Recast Time*	–

Sacrifice 17% Health. For 5 seconds, whenever a party member hits a foe with physical damage, that party member does an additional 3–16 damage.

Order of the Vampire (elite)

Source: Byssha Hisst, Hessper Sasso, Uussh Visshta (Forgotten Bosses)

Cost	10	*Casting Time*	2
Duration	5	*Recast Time*	5

Sacrifice 17% max Health. For 5 seconds, whenever a party member hits a foe with physical damage, that party member steals 3–16 Health.

Shadow Strike

Source: Quest, Ruins of Ascalon/Vendor, Yak's Bend

Cost	10	*Casting Time*	2
Duration		*Recast Time*	8

Target foe takes 12–48 shadow damage. If that foe's Health is above 50%, you steal 12–48 Health.

Signet of Agony

Source: Quest, Crystal Desert/Vendor, Droknar's Forge

Cost	–	*Casting Time*	3/4
Duration	–	*Recast Time*	15

Sacrifice 10% max Health and suffer from Bleeding. All nearby foes take 10–44 damage.

Soul Leech (elite)

Source: Goss Darkweb (Dryder Boss)

Cost	10	*Casting Time*	2
Duration	10	*Recast Time*	15

For 10 seconds, whenever target foe casts a spell, you steal 16–80 Health from that foe.

Strip Enchantment

Source: Quest, Shiverpeaks (N)/Vendor, Lion's Arch

Cost	10	*Casting Time*	1
Duration	–	*Recast Time*	20

Target foe loses one enchantment, and you gain 30–120 Health.

Touch of Agony

Source: Vendor, Beetletun

Cost	5	*Casting Time*	3/4
Duration	–	*Recast Time*	3

Sacrifice 10% max Health. Target-touched foe takes 20–58 shadow damage.

Unholy Feast

Source: Vendor, Maguuma Stade

Cost	15	*Casting Time*	1
Duration	–	*Recast Time*	30

Steal 8–40 Health from each nearby foe.

Vampiric Gaze

Source: Quest, Kingdom of Ascalon/Vendor, Ascalon City (Ruins)

Cost	10	*Casting Time*	1
Duration	–	*Recast Time*	5

Steal 18–60 Health from target foe.

Vampiric Touch

Source: Quest, Kingdom of Ascalon/Vendor, Ascalon City (Ruins)

Cost	15	*Casting Time*	3/4
Duration	–	*Recast Time*	5

Touch target foe to steal up to 29–74 Health.

Well of Blood

Source: Quest, Shiverpeaks (N)/Vendor, Lion's Arch

Cost	15	*Casting Time*	2
Duration	8–20	*Recast Time*	2

Exploit nearest corpse to create a Well of Blood at its location. For 8–20 seconds, allies in that area receive Health regeneration of 1–6.

Well of Power (elite)

Source: Nhy Darkclaw (Tengu Boss)

Cost	15	*Casting Time*	3
Duration	8–20	*Recast Time*	15

Exploit nearest corpse to create a Well of Power at that location. For 8–20 seconds, allies within 39' of the Well of Power gain Health regeneration of 1–6 and Energy regeneration of 2.

Curses

Barbs

Source: Vendor, Camp Rankor

Cost	10	*Casting Time*	2
Duration	30	*Recast Time*	30

For 30 seconds, target foe takes 1–10 more damage when hit by physical damage.

Chilblains

Source: Quest, Crystal Desert/Vendor, Droknar's Forge

Cost	25	*Casting Time*	3/4
Duration	–	*Recast Time*	15

You become poisoned for 3–15 seconds. Nearby foes are struck for 10–44 Cold damage and lose one enchantment.

Defile Flesh

Source: Quest, Shiverpeaks (N)/Vendor, Lion's Arch

Cost	10	*Casting Time*	1
Duration	8–20	*Recast Time*	10

Sacrifice 20% max Health. For 8–20 seconds, target foe receives only 2/3 benefit from healing.

Desecrate Enchantments

Source: Vendor, Marhan's Grotto

Cost	15	*Casting Time*	2
Duration	–	*Recast Time*	15

Target foe and all nearby foes take 6–60 shadow damage and 4–20 shadow damage for each enchantment on them.

Enfeeble
Source: Quest, Kryta/Vendor, Henge of Denravi

Cost	5	Casting Time	1
Duration	–	Recast Time	5

Target suffers from Weakness for 5–20 seconds.

Enfeebling Blood
Source: Vendor, Grendich Courthouse

Cost	10	Casting Time	2
Duration	–	Recast Time	10

Sacrifice 17% max Health. Target foe and all nearby foes suffer from Weakness for 5–20 seconds.

Faintheartedness
Source: Quest, Kingdom of Ascalon/Vendor, Ascalon City (Ruins)

Cost	10	Casting Time	1
Duration	8–44	Recast Time	5

For the next 8–44 seconds, target foe's attack speed is reduced and that foe suffers Health degeneration of 1–3.

Feast of Corruption (elite)
Source: Maw The Mountain Heart (Worm Boss)

Cost	10	Casting Time	2
Duration	–	Recast Time	20

Target foe and all adjacent foes are struck for 16–80 Shadow damage. You steal 8–40 Health from each struck foe who is suffering from a Hex.

Insidious Parasite
Source: Quest, Ruins of Ascalon/Vendor, Yak's Bend

Cost	15	Casting Time	2
Duration	8–20	Recast Time	20

For 8–20 seconds, whenever target foe hits with an attack, you steal 5–20 Health from that foe.

Lingering Curse (elite)
Source: Griffon (Griffon Boss), Grenth's Cursed (Golem Boss)

Cost	25	Casting Time	3
Duration	8–20	Recast Time	10

Sacrifice 10% max Health. Target foe loses all enchantments. For 8–20 seconds, target foe gains only half Health from healing spells.

Malaise
Source: Quest, Crystal Desert/Vendor, Droknar's Forge

Cost	5	Casting Time	2
Duration	5–35	Recast Time	2

For 5–35 seconds, target foe suffers Energy degeneration of 2 and you suffer Health degeneration of 2.

Mark of Pain
Source: Quest, Ruins of Ascalon/Vendor, Yak's Bend

Cost	10	Casting Time	2
Duration	30	Recast Time	30

For 30 seconds, whenever target foe takes physical damage, Mark of Pain deals 10–40 shadow damage to adjacent foes.

Parasitic Bond
Source: Quest, Ruins of Ascalon/Vendor, Yak's Bend

Cost	5	Casting Time	1
Duration	20	Recast Time	2

For 20 seconds, target foe suffers Health degeneration of 1. You are healed for 30–120 when Parasitic Bond ends.

Plague Sending
Source: Vendor, North Kryta Province

Cost	10	Casting Time	2
Duration	–	Recast Time	–

Sacrifice 10% max Health. Transfer one negative Condition from yourself to target foe and all adjacent foes.

Plague Signet (elite)
Source: Karobo Dimdim (Grawl Boss)

Cost	–	Casting Time	2
Duration	–	Recast Time	20

Transfer all negative Conditions from yourself to target foe. (50% failure chance with Curses 4 or less.)

Price of Failure
Source: Quest, Kryta-The Wilds/Vendor, Droknar's Forge

Cost	10	Casting Time	3
Duration	30	Recast Time	10

For 30 seconds, target foe has a 25% chance to miss with attacks and takes 6–30 damage whenever that foe misses in combat.

Rend Enchantments
Source: Quest, Kryta-The Wilds/Vendor, Amnoon Oasis

Cost	10	Casting Time	3
Duration	–	Recast Time	30

Target foe loses 2–9 enchantments. For each Monk Enchantment removed, you take 40 damage.

Rigor Mortis
Source: Vendor, Beetletun

Cost	10	Casting Time	2
Duration	8–20	Recast Time	30

For 8–20 seconds, target foe cannot block or evade.

Shadow of Fear
Source: Quest, Ruins of Ascalon/Vendor, Yak's Bend

Cost	10	Casting Time	2
Duration	20–44	Recast Time	10

Target foe and all adjacent foes attack slower than normal for the next 20–44 seconds.

Soul Barbs
Source: Quest, Kingdom of Ascalon/Vendor, Ascalon City (Ruins)

Cost	10	Casting Time	2
Duration	30	Recast Time	20

For 30 seconds, target foe takes 15–30 damage when an enchantment or Hex is cast on that target.

Spinal Shivers
Source: Vendor, Fishermen's Haven

Cost	10	*Casting Time*	2
Duration	12–30	*Recast Time*	15

For 12–30 seconds, whenever target foe is struck for Cold damage, that foe is interrupted and you lose 10–5 Energy or Spinal Shivers ends.

Spiteful Spirit (elite)
Source: Nighh SpineChill (Nightmare Boss)

Cost	15	*Casting Time*	2
Duration	8–20	*Recast Time*	10

For 8–20 seconds, whenever target foe attacks or uses a skill, Spiteful Spirit deals 5–35 shadow damage to that foe and all adjacent foes.

Suffering
Source: Quest, Shiverpeaks (N)/Vendor, Lion's Arch

Cost	15	*Casting Time*	2
Duration	6–30	*Recast Time*	20

For 6–30 seconds, target foe and all nearby foes suffer Health degeneration of 2.

Weaken Armor
Source: Quest, Ruins of Ascalon/Vendor, Yak's Bend

Cost	10	*Casting Time*	3
Duration	30	*Recast Time*	30

For 10–40 seconds, target foe has an armor penalty of -20 against physical damage.

Wither (elite)
Source: Ignis Effigia (Ghost Boss)

Cost	10	*Casting Time*	2
Duration	5–35	*Recast Time*	10

For 5–35 seconds, target foe suffers Health degeneration of 2 and Energy degeneration of 2. Wither ends if target foe's Energy reaches 0.

Death Magic

Animate Bone Fiend
Source: Quest, Crystal Desert/Vendor, Droknar's Forge

Cost	25	*Casting Time*	3
Duration	–	*Recast Time*	5

Exploit nearest corpse to animate a level 1–17 Bone Fiend. Bone Fiends can attack at range.

Animate Bone Horror
Source: Quest, Kingdom of Ascalon/Vendor, Ascalon City (Ruins)

Cost	15	*Casting Time*	3
Duration	–	*Recast Time*	5

Exploit nearest corpse to animate a level 1–17 Bone Horror.

Animate Bone Minions
Source: Quest, Kryta-The Wilds/Vendor, Droknar's Forge

Cost	25	*Casting Time*	3
Duration	–	*Recast Time*	5

Exploit nearest corpse to animate two level 0–12 Bone Minions.

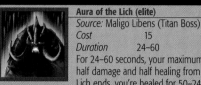

Aura of the Lich (elite)
Source: Maligo Libens (Titan Boss)

Cost	15	*Casting Time*	3
Duration	24–60	*Recast Time*	30

For 24–60 seconds, your maximum Health is halved, but you take half damage and half healing from all sources. When Aura of the Lich ends, you're healed for 50–240 Health.

Blood of the Master
Source: Quest, Kryta/Vendor, Henge of Denravi

Cost	10	*Casting Time*	1
Duration	–	*Recast Time*	5

Sacrifice 10% max Health. All adjacent undead allies are healed for 30–116.

Consume Corpse
Source: Vendor, Camp Rankor

Cost	10	*Casting Time*	2
Duration	–	*Recast Time*	–

Exploit a random target, teleport to that corpse's location, and gain 25–100 Health and 3–8 Energy.

Dark Aura
Source: Quest, Kryta/Vendor, Henge of Denravi

Cost	10	*Casting Time*	1
Duration	30	*Recast Time*	10

For 30 seconds, whenever target ally sacrifices Health, Dark Aura deals 5–50 Shadow damage to adjacent foes, and you lose 5–20 Health.

Death Nova
Source: Quest, Kryta-The Wilds/Vendor, Amnoon Oasis

Cost	5	*Casting Time*	2
Duration	30	*Recast Time*	–

For 30 seconds, if target ally dies, Death Nova deals 26–100 damage to all nearby creatures.

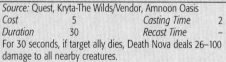

Deathly Chill
Source: Vendor, Maguuma Stade

Cost	10	*Casting Time*	1
Duration		*Recast Time*	5

Target foe is struck for 5–34 Cold damage (before armor). If that foe's Health is above 50%, you deal an additional 5–34 Shadow damage.

Deathly Swarm
Source: Quest, Kingdom of Ascalon/Vendor, Ascalon City (Ruins)

Cost	10	*Casting Time*	3
Duration	10	*Recast Time*	3

Deathly Swarm flies out slowly and strikes for 15–80 Cold damage (before armor) on up to three targets.

Infuse Condition
Source: Vendor, Port Sledge

Cost	10	*Casting Time*	1
Duration	15–60	*Recast Time*	60

For the next 15–60 seconds, whenever you receive a Condition, that Condition is transferred to your closest minion instead.

Malign Intervention

Source: Vendor, Beetletun

Cost	10	Casting Time	1
Duration	5–20	Recast Time	20

For 5–20 seconds, target foe receives 20% less benefit from healing. If target foe dies while Hexed with Malign Intervention, a level 1–17 masterless Bone Horror is summoned.

Necrotic Traversal

Source: Quest, Shiverpeaks (N)/Vendor, Lion's Arch

Cost	5	Casting Time	3/4
Duration	–	Recast Time	–

Exploit a random corpse; you teleport to that corpse's location and all nearby foes become poisoned for 5–20 seconds.

Putrid Explosion

Source: Quest, Ruins of Ascalon/Vendor, Yak's Bend

Cost	10	Casting Time	1
Duration	–	Recast Time	–

The corpse nearest your target explodes, sending out a shockwave that deals 24–120 damage to each nearby creature.

Rotting Flesh

Source: Quest, Shiverpeaks (N)/Vendor, Lion's Arch

Cost	15	Casting Time	3
Duration	–	Recast Time	3

Target fleshy creature becomes Diseased for 10–25 seconds and slowly loses Health.

Soul Feast

Source: Quest, Ruins of Ascalon/Vendor, Yak's Bend

Cost	10	Casting Time	1
Duration	–	Recast Time	–

Exploit nearest corpse to steal 50–280 Health.

Tainted Flesh (elite)

Source: Dosakaru Fevertouch (Dragon Boss)

Cost	5	Casting Time	1
Duration	20–44	Recast Time	5

For 20–44 seconds, target ally is immune to Disease, and anyone striking that ally in melee becomes Diseased for 3–15 seconds.

Taste of Death

Source: Vendor, North Kryta Province

Cost	5	Casting Time	1/4
Duration	–	Recast Time	–

Steal 100–400 Health from target animated undead ally.

Verata's Aura

Source: Vendor, Copperhammer Mines

Cost	15	Casting Time	3/4
Duration	120–300	Recast Time	30

Sacrifice 33% maximum Health. All hostile animated undead in the area become bound to you. Verata's Aura ends after 120–300 seconds. When Verata's Aura ends, you lose your bond with any undead bound to you. (50% failure chance with Death Magic 4 or less.)

Verata's Gaze

Source: Vendor, Copperhammer Mines

Cost	5	Casting Time	1
Duration	–	Recast Time	5

If target hostile animated undead has a master, its bond to its master is broken, making it hostile to all other creatures. If it had no master, you become its master. (50% failure chance with Death Magic 4 or less.)

Verata's Sacrifice

Source: Vendor, Copperhammer Mines

Cost	10	Casting Time	2
Duration	8–20	Recast Time	30

Sacrifice 15% max Health. For 8–20 seconds, all undead allies gain 10 Health regeneration. All Conditions are removed from those allies and transferred to you.

Vile Touch

Source: Quest, Ruins of Ascalon/Vendor, Yak's Bend

Cost	10	Casting Time	3/4
Duration	–	Recast Time	4

Touch target foe to deal 18–60 damage.

Virulence (elite)

Source: Mossk Rottail (Devourer Boss), Unthet Rotwood (Plant Boss)

Cost	5	Casting Time	1
Duration	–	Recast Time	10

If target foe was already suffering from a Condition, that foe suffers from Disease and Weakness for 3–15 seconds.

Well of Suffering

Source: Quest, Kryta-The Wilds/Vendor, Amnoon Oasis

Cost	15	Casting Time	2
Duration	8–20	Recast Time	10

Exploit nearest corpse to create a Well of Suffering at its location. For 8–20 seconds, foes in that area suffer Health degeneration of -1–5.

Well of the Profane

Source: Quest, Crystal Desert/Vendor, Droknar's Forge

Cost	25	Casting Time	3
Duration	8–20	Recast Time	10

Exploit nearest corpse to create a Well of the Profane at its location. For 8–20 seconds, foes in that area are stripped of all enchantments and cannot be the target of further enchantments. (50% failure chance with Death Magic 4 or less.)

Ranger

By Heather "Orlena" Rothwell

One with Nature

angers in *Guild Wars* are a hybrid profession, similar to what most games would classify as a druid and ranger. With moderate melee ability, strong ranged attacks with bows, and the ability to charm and command a pet, Rangers make even better solo players than they do group-support characters. A Ranger's primary weakness is melee combat with multiple enemies. Their inability to command pets to help manage damage can lead to Ranger deaths. Counter this weakness by using your skills intelligently. For example, always use preparations before engaging multiple enemies.

Rangers are limited to leather-type armor and use two-handed bows as their primary weapons. Because of this, they are at a disadvantage compared to other professions who can carry focuses or shields. A Ranger can equip either of these only if he unequips the bow first. With Poison, bursts of multiple arrows, and a hardy pet by your side, you can solo as a Ranger more readily than with most other characters.

Five Reasons to Be a Ranger

- Rangers are the masters of interrupting enemy spell casters.
- Having a pet act as a tank for you decreases the likelihood that you'll die in a mission. If you become overwhelmed with foes, your pet can distract them while you run.
- Preparation skills like Troll Unguent are unique to Rangers, giving them a pre-battle advantage.
- Rangers can provide ranged crowd control on enemies, using skills from a variety of attributes.
- Traps, Poisons, and Stances enable you to prepare in advance for really difficult combats, often turning the tide of an upcoming battle in your favor.

Pets

The only class capable of recruiting wild fauna to its side is the Ranger. These animals (moa bird, bear, lynx, dune lizard, etc.) are helpful, allowing a Ranger to double up on attacks and deliver more damage over a given time span. This requires a trade-off in the number of skills he can utilize at once due to the Skill Bar's limitations 8-skill cap. But the extra damage pets provide can be well worth the sacrifice.

Pets draw their power from the amount of focus a Ranger places on the Beast Mastery attribute. The skills derived from Beast Mastery are also the basis for the pets' attacks. Skills such as Feral Lunge, Maiming Strike, and others are invaluable to a talented pet handler.

Though not necessary to play a successful Ranger, having pets adds additional flavor to the profession.

❧ CAUTION ❧

If a pet dies during combat, the Ranger's skills are reset, locking them down till they recharge. Thus, your pet's death could lead to your death; plan ahead to save your life.

Attributes & Skills

Expertise
(Primary Rangers Only)

The Expertise Attribute reduces the Energy cost of Attack, Preparation, and Trap skills by 4 percent; 10 ranks in Expertise can almost double your effective Energy for these skills.

Distracting Shot: One of the most useful skills when facing a caster or healer foes, Distracting Shot disables them from casting long enough to finish the combat.

Dodge: If another Ranger attacks you and you must flee, Dodge allows you to run faster than Escape, and it increases your evasion of incoming arrows. The elite skill Escape is more useful for getting clear of the combat skill if you're not trying to avoid arrows.

Escape (elite): This skill helps you to run away from combat; this stance costs little Energy to cast and can save you from an unexpected attack.

Lightning Reflexes: This reduces the damage amount you take in combat while increasing your attack speed.

Marksman's Wager (elite): This is a risky skill to use, especially against enemies who have a Dodge, Evade, or Block skills. However, the payoff is worth it—it grants high amounts of Energy with every attack.

Oath Shot (elite): Although this is a risky shot to use because of a higher chance of missing, use it to recharge skills that have long reuse timers.

Point Blank Shot: This skill recharges fast enough that it is available every other attack.

(No Attribute)

Specific attributes do not affect these skills.

Called Shot: This is a fast way to finish off an enemy, especially when your party is grouped and has to attack different targets. Called Shot is an almost guaranteed hit, but it does only normal damage.

Debilitating Shot: This is an effective Energy shutdown: Spam it on healers and elemental-based attackers to keep their reserves low.

Dual Shot: Combine this with Preparation skills like Kindle or Ignite Arrow. It also works well with other profession skills, including various conjures and Order of Pain.

Quick Shot (elite): Spamming this increases damage output. Combined with Preparation skills, it allows easier destruction of multiple enemies.

Beast Mastery

Beast Mastery skills allow you to tame and control pets, augmenting the animals' attacks at higher ranks.

Bestial Pounce: Use this to interrupt casters. Not only will it disrupt them, it will also knock them down.

Brutal Strike: This is a brilliant finishing move for any pet-owning Ranger. While the damage is extreme, it will only work on a foe with less than 50 percent Health.

Charm Animal: Add this skill to your Skill Bar if you want to travel with

Beast Mastery Pros and Cons

Pro: It's nice to have someone to draw attacks and distribute damage while you eliminate your foes.

Con: This one attribute requires one to three slots, if not more. If you choose to take a pet, you must fill at least one slot with Charm Animal. You also should add Comfort Animal, to revive your pet if it's hurt, and Resurrect, to heal it if it dies. If you want your pet to have any special attacks or defenses, these require at least one more slot.

your pet. If you don't have a pet, use this skill to capture one.

Call of Protection: Use this when multiple enemies are attacking your pet. This reduces the damage amount the pet sustains, allowing it to live much longer (which also avoids a dreaded skill reset).

Disrupting Lunge: This is a spell-disruption attack that locks out an enemy caster in the midst of launching a spell.

Feral Lunge: This attack applies Bleeding to any foe who is attacking. This is excellent against Warriors and Rangers, as they are melee-driven.

Ferocious Strike (elite): This is a good move to combine with a Warrior—it boosts adrenaline to staggering levels.

Maiming Strike: This Cripples a moving target, which makes it perfect to slow a running enemy, allowing the pet to have a snack.

Melandru's Assault: This is a pet AoE and is good to inflict damage on a group rather than a single opponent.

Predator Pounce: This skill is a solid choice if a pet is flagging and needs a Health boost. It also inflicts damage.

Scavenger Strike: Combine this with Maiming Strike or Feral Lunge to increase the amount of damage a pet inflicts on a Bleeding foe.

Spirits: You can specialize in Beast Mastery and never tame a pet. There are several Spirit skills that boost Health, drain Health, save Energy, or create other effects for creatures and characters in its range.

These spirits can last over two minutes, but they are fixed in place—they don't follow their targets, and they don't follow you. Thus, they're more useful in a pitched battle than in a running engagement.

Marksmanship

Marksmanship reflects the Ranger's extensive training with a bow, giving him the ability to make a variety of special bow attacks.

Barrage (elite): This focuses on a boss mob that is surrounded by other mobs. However, it negates anything you cast before it, such as Poison or Stance. But by focusing your target on the boss and using Barrage, most minions fall with the boss mob or quickly thereafter.

Concussion Shot: Though it doesn't deal much damage, this skill is a must-have when fighting healers. Anticipating the enemy attack pays off when using this skill. Its expensive Energy cost means you should combine it with Expertise skills.

Crippling Shot (elite): Because it cannot be blocked or evaded, this skill is useful for putting distance between you and the enemy if you plan to run.

Determined Shot: When up against foes with high evasion, this recharges other attack skills when a foe evades it.

Hunter's Shot: This skill is useful after you pull back and the enemy closes with you, because the damage increases when the enemy is moving.

Pin Down: Use this skill on Warriors to slow them, making it easier to escape their attacks.

Power Shot: Combine this damage-add skill with Kindle Arrow or Ignite Arrow for a solid bloodletting increase.

Precision Shot: Use this when you're not being attacked. It's cheaper than Power Shot, but is easily evaded.

Punishing Shot (elite): This is a more powerful version of Power Shot; it interrupts the target. Use this against healers and other casters to disrupt their spells and deal high damage.

Read the Wind: One of the most useful preparations you can have, this skill increases your bow damage during combat.

Savage Shot: Combine this with Read the Wind for an interrupt and huge damage.

Wilderness Survival

Wilderness Survival represents the Ranger's experience with surviving harsh outdoor climates. This includes laying Traps for enemies and augmenting bow attacks.

Apply Poison: This DoT Poison can turn a battle from a loss to a win, due to its ability to constantly diminish a foe's Health. If it's not cured, it's near-certain death for a weaker enemy.

Barbed Trap: Traps are a great way to add fast damage in combat. Barbed Trap is useful when fighting groups of enemies in an enclosed area. This is efficacious against Warriors because it prevents them from withdrawing.

Flame Trap: Set this Trap before starting combat. You don't have to maneuver your enemies onto the Trap, just near it.

Healing Spring: This skill is useful if you're working with others. Healing Spring restores your group to health. It is useful against enemies with AoE attacks.

Kindle Arrows: Combine this with other Ranger Attack skills like Dual Shot or Power Shot for high damage boosts, and with the Elementalist spell Conjure Flame for burning damage.

Poison Arrow: This is a useful DoT skill that can add damage, especially when you are highly trained in Wilderness Survival. Spam it over multiple enemies.

Secondary Professions

Ranger skills combine well with most other secondary professions. Your play style affects how successful the combination is.

Ranger/ Elementalist

The Elementalist secondary profession combines to make a character who is a ranged combat powerhouse. For a Ranger who specializes in Fire Magic, this combination is adept at handling multiple enemies at a time. Air Magic also works well with a Ranger's abilities—it allows the Ranger to momentarily knock down a foe or add extra damage over time. The disadvantage with many Air Magic skills is that they can cause exhaustion, which reduces the Ranger's Energy pool, and Energy management is critical.

Earth Magic isn't as useful to a solo Ranger as Air or Fire Magic, but it works well for a Ranger who is the only Elementalist in a group (due to its AoE armor boosts). For any Ranger who plans to use his Elementalist skills frequently, though, Glyph of Lesser Energy and Glyph of Energy are must-haves. These Glyphs allow you to cast your spells without cost, especially when you activate the Glyph before starting a battle. Because Rangers need to watch their Energy use more closely than an Elementalist, low-cost skills that combine well with Marksmanship skills are recommended.

Ranger/Elementalists are effective damage dealers; their pet(s) are secondary to their abilities. Because of this, spending attribute points in Beast Mastery isn't as useful as it is for other profession combinations. Choosing one attribute to specialize in from the Elementalist profession will allow you to have enough points to put in your Ranger attributes. A well-rounded character includes: Fire or Air Magic (8), Beast Mastery (4), Expertise (10), Wilderness Survival (7), and Marksmanship (10). With this Ranger, your Skill Bar should include Charm Animal, Barrage, Distracting Shot, Lightning Reflexes, Troll Unguent, a Trap to fill out your Ranger skills, plus high-damage AoE skills from the Elementalist profession.

Use one of the Conjure Frost/Flame/Lightning sets. If you can find a weapon that also does Fire or Cold damage, the corresponding Elementalist skills will increase the total damage output.

Ranger/Mesmer

The Ranger/Mesmer is one of the strongest anti-caster combinations. Under Domination Magic, Mesmers have great anti-caster skills, such as Backfire and Shatter Enchantment. Rangers have excellent interruption skills, such as Concussion Shot, Punishing Shot, and Savage Shot. Bring these two halves together for a powerful and effective shutdown of enemy spellcasters.

A Ranger/Mesmer uses skills to disable an enemy from attacking before going in for the kill. Use Mesmer skills such as Arcane Conundrum, Drain Enchantment, Energy Tap, and Ether Feast to disable an enemy's casting ability, often helping the Ranger in the process. Because a Ranger can become low on Energy, using Mesmer skills to give added Energy or Health also helps win combats. Use Mesmer skills to drain an enemy before attacking with bow skills.

My Favorite Characters

Name: Marti McKenna

Title: Editor, Writer

Characters: Coyote Girl, Tiger Lily

I have two favorite characters, depending on whether I'm playing PvP or cooperative play.

For cooperative play, I love my Ranger. Right now I'm training up a new one and have opted to concentrate on just the Ranger profession for now. Coyote Girl uses Ignite Arrows stacked with Dual Shot first and foremost, and follows up with Power Shot and Point Blank Shot when they're needed to finish off a foe. Her pet, a Melandru's Stalker, keeps most foes at range so she can stick with her bow most of the time. When she's up close she uses a sword, so she might end up taking Warrior as a secondary profession so she can beef up her Swordsmanship and deal more damage at close range. She keeps Comfort Animal on hand to heal her Stalker, and Troll Unguent to heal herself.

For PvP, I like to play the healer, so I have a Monk primary named Tiger Lily. She uses Smiting Prayers like Bane Signet, Banish, and Symbol of Wrath to deal damage to foes, and Healing Prayers like Orison of Healing, Heal Other, and Heal Party to keep her team alive. She's a Ranger secondary, and her pet warthog, Babe, accompanies her wherever her adventures take her, so Comfort Animal is also at the ready.

Focus on Ranger skills when spending attribute points, though. Raising the Mesmer attribute Inspiration increases the amount of Energy drained, thus making it easier to use other skills. Marksmanship and Expertise should be raised to at least 10, with Inspiration at around 8. To use all possible attribute points, distribute the remaining in a 6:4:4 or 8:4:2 ratio between Domination, Beast Mastery, and Wilderness Survival.

An animal companion isn't as important to a Ranger/Mesmer as it is to other professions—the Mesmer skills enable this character to disable an enemy before he does much damage to the Ranger. It's possible that you won't even keep Charm Animal on your Skill Bar, using the space instead to keep more Mesmer skills. Keep Troll Unguent equipped, however, because it is your primary heal. Include high-damage attacks as well, and if you've raised Wilderness Survival, add Preparation

skills to use before combat starts. The Mesmer skills allow you to recover the Energy expended on Preparation skills at the start of a combat.

Ranger/Monk

A Ranger (especially one with a pet) has few attribute points left, so a Monk secondary should concentrate on a single attribute (at most). If you plan to group, choose Resurrect or Restore if you concentrate on Healing Prayers, or Rebirth if you specialize in Protection Prayers. Either way, be prepared if you're in a party without a few others who can Resurrect.

If you have difficulty keeping an eye on your group members' well-being while you pour on the offense, avoid Healing or Protection. If you become the monster pack's focus, skills that take a couple of seconds to cast—especially those that are easily interrupted—aren't

going to do you much good. Skills that transfer Hexes to you, or heal others at your expense, aren't the best choices, either—you need to be out there striking as rapidly as possible, not absorbing your teammates' problems. When you're the focus of attack, using skills that remove Hexes from you is a waste of time and Energy. If you can juggle both offense and defense, put attribute points into Healing or Protection Prayers. Even without being able to juggle, there's an elite skill—Mark of Protection—that is worth 5 or 10 levels of Protection Prayers. For 10 seconds, it converts any damage against you into healing. If you're near death and six monsters are surrounding you, Mark of Protection is the quickest route to a full heal. You can also cast it on a target ally.

If you're looking for add-ons to your offensive Energy, focus your points on Smiting Prayers. Consider the skills that deal Holy damage because your Poison is worthless against bloodless Undead, while Holy damage is doubled against them.

If you're soloing most of the time, putting attribute points into Healing Prayers or Smiting Prayers (though not both) is your best option, depending on whether you want to increase your offense or defense. Choose Orison of Healing, Troll Unguent, and Healing Breeze if you focus on Healing Prayers. If you focus on Smiting Prayers, Scourge Healing or Judge's Insight are both good support skills. Rangers perform well as long-range damage dealers or as an anti-caster profession, and Smiting Prayers skills fit in nicely with that role.

Ranger/Necromancer

A Ranger who takes Necromancer as a secondary profession is one who is better prepared for PvP than cooperative play. Because Necromancers specialize in debuffs and

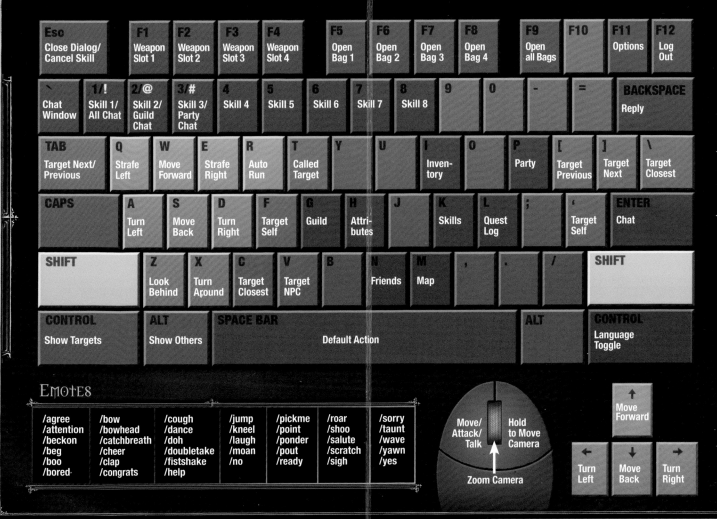

KEYBOARD COMMANDS

Menu Items & Windows — Movement
Targeting — Combat

Esc	Close Dialog/ Cancel Skill
F1	Weapon Slot 1
F2	Weapon Slot 2
F3	Weapon Slot 3
F4	Weapon Slot 4
F5	Open Bag 1
F6	Open Bag 2
F7	Open Bag 3
F8	Open Bag 4
F9	Open all Bags
F10	
F11	Options
F12	Log Out

`	Chat Window
1/!	Skill 1/ All Chat
2/@	Skill 2/ Guild Chat
3/#	Skill 3/ Party Chat
4	Skill 4
5	Skill 5
6	Skill 6
7	Skill 7
8	Skill 8
9	
0	
-	
=	
BACKSPACE	Reply

TAB	Target Next/ Previous
Q	Strafe Left
W	Move Forward
E	Strafe Right
R	Auto Run
T	Called Target
Y	
U	
I	Inventory
O	
P	Party
[	Target Previous
]	Target Next
\	Target Closest

CAPS	
A	Turn Left
S	Move Back
D	Turn Right
F	Target Self
G	Guild
H	Attributes
J	
K	Skills
L	Quest Log
;	
'	Target Self
ENTER	Chat

SHIFT	
Z	Look Behind
X	Turn Around
C	Target Closest
V	Target NPC
B	
N	Friends
M	Map
,	
.	
/	
SHIFT	

CONTROL	Show Targets
ALT	Show Others
SPACE BAR	Default Action
ALT	
CONTROL	Language Toggle

EMOTES

/agree	/bow	/cough	/jump	/pickme	/roar	/sorry
/attention	/bowhead	/dance	/kneel	/point	/shoo	/taunt
/beckon	/catchbreath	/doh	/laugh	/ponder	/salute	/wave
/beg	/cheer	/doubletake	/moan	/pout	/scratch	/yawn
/boo	/clap	/fistshake	/no	/ready	/sigh	/yes
/bored	/congrats	/help				

Move/ Attack/ Talk — Hold to Move Camera
Zoom Camera

Move Forward
Turn Left — Move Back — Turn Right

Attribute Point Allocation

Attribute Level	Point Cost	Total Cost
1	1	1
2	2	3
3	3	6
4	4	10
5	5	15
6	6	21
7	7	28
8	9	37
9	11	48
10	13	61
11	16	77
12	20	97

Guild Wars Online Manual

The *Guild Wars* online manual contains detailed information and instructions to help you get the most out of the game. Visit http://www.guildwars.com/manual for more information.

Guild Wars Support

Our support staff is standing by to answer your questions. Visit http://www.guildwars.com/support to find answers to frequently asked questions or to contact a support representative.

ARENANET

NCSOFT

GUILDWARS QUICK REFERENCE

SKILL TYPES

ATTACK	An enhanced melee or projectile attack.
SPELL	A skill that results in a one-time effect, such as damage, healing, Energy loss or gain.
ENCHANTMENT SPELL	A spell that causes a positive effect for a period of time (e.g., speed, increased armor, increased Energy).
HEX SPELL	A spell that causes a negative effect for a period of time (e.g., movement/attack speed reduction, Health or Energy degeneration).
SIGNET	A skill that costs no Energy to use.
PREPARATION	A skill that enhances your attacks for the next few seconds.
TRAP	Creates a trap that you set and leave for your enemy to trigger.
SHOUT	A motivational phrase that benefits you and nearby allies, or hinders nearby enemies.
STANCE	A posture that provides an advantage in battle, either by protecting against attacks or improving your offensive abilities.
GLYPH	A skill that enhances the next spell you cast.
NATURE RITUAL	Creates a totem that emits an environmental enchantment affecting allies and foes alike.

life taps, this character is more suited to attacking other characters than to taking on your average mob.

In cooperative play, the Ranger/ Necromancer has a better skill set for facing boss mobs and caster-type mobs than any other secondary professions. One thing to be cautious of when playing this profession combination is how many sacrifice skills you use. Rangers do not have high Health and Energy to begin with, and many of the Necromancer skills require both Energy and a Health sacrifice, making them less than ideal for Rangers to use. On the other hand, skills that allow you to steal Health from corpses, or animate corpses briefly, can help a Ranger win difficult combats. Because the number of animated corpses you can have is only limited by how long the corpse animation exists, you can focus on being the leader of an army of undead and pets. Animating multiple targets takes a good deal of Energy, however, so you won't have much left over for when the battle starts. Make sure you have enough Energy left to use Soul Feast (or a similar skill) when the first enemy falls, and you can get back to full Health halfway through a battle.

A Ranger/ Necromancer who builds up Marksmanship, Expertise, plus Death Magic will be balanced well enough to face most situations. Increasing Beast Mastery gives you a more effective animal companion who can kill an enemy quickly, providing a corpse you can animate early in a battle group of enemies. A well-rounded group of attributes includes: Marksmanship (10), Expertise (10), Death Magic (8), and Beast Mastery (7). Spread the remaining points between the other attributes. If you plan to use Poison and Traps, put some points into Wilderness Survival; otherwise leave this attribute untrained so more points can go to Blood Magic and Curses. Useful Necromancer skills with this Ranger include Well of Blood, Soul Feast, and Consume Corpse, all of which allow you to heal.

Including the Animate Bone Horror line of skills allows you to have additional pets so you can form your own army from dead foes. Because of the Necromancer skills, you won't need to include Troll Unguent on your Skill Bar, but having Comfort Animal lets you heal your pet in an emergency. Filling out your Skill Bar with Ranger skills that help you fight against casting enemies and enemy groups leaves you prepared for most combat situations.

Ranger/Warrior

The Warrior secondary profession enables Rangers to survive well in close combat due to melee weapon styles. Rangers in this combination are restricted to armor based on their primary profession, so they cannot wear armor as thick as a Warrior/Ranger would. For this reason, if you plan to combine with Warrior for your second profession and to go for pure damage absorption, begin as a Warrior and add Ranger skills. You will sacrifice the Expertise skill, which means that your Energy costs for ranged skills will remain high. However, because many Warrior skills rely on adrenaline instead of Energy, the sacrifice is not as significant as sacrificing the better armor. A Ranger/ Warrior is still a strong combination. While the armor rating may not be as high, Ranger armor has a good rating and is effective at absorbing elemental damage.

Ranger/Warriors should focus on abilities that allow them to kill quickly when spending attribute points. This will mean picking a weapon and sticking with it throughout most of your career. (See the

"Warrior" section for a comparison of weapon masteries.) Raise your weapon mastery of choice to eight, and if you plan to group, your Tactics to seven. If you travel solo, forgo spending points in Tactics and put more into your Ranger skills. Raising Beast Mastery to a six makes your pet a better damage dealer. Split the remaining points between Marksmanship, Expertise, and Wilderness Survival. Your Skill Bar will vary depending on which weapon style you choose, but good choices from the Ranger profession include Charm Animal and Comfort Animal to keep your pet alive and helpful, Troll Unguent for healing yourself, and a variety of high-damage skills from the Marksmanship and Expertise attributes. Include at least one skill that can disrupt casters, or you will find yourself in a never ending combat when faced with an enemy who can heal. Depending on how high you raised Wilderness Survival, using Traps and Poisoned arrows is also be an easy way to increase your damage potential before combat begins.

Another direction to take when creating a strong melee Ranger/Warrior is to place attribute points in Expertise and Wilderness Survival on the Ranger side, then Swordsmanship on the Warrior side. You can also raise Wilderness Survival and pick up Apply Poison, which works on melee and ranged weapons. Lightning Reflexes from the Expertise attribute is another good Skill Bar addition for its

evasion and fast attack speed. Add in Throw Mud from the Expertise attribute and a few Sword skills from the Warrior set, and you'll have a skill combination that deals melee damage while avoiding return damage.

Cooperative Play

Use your bow for long-range attacks. Good options to begin with are Precision Shot, which has increased damage and cannot be blocked or evaded, or Penetrating Attack, which has 20 percent armor penetration. Follow up with a Power Shot or Quick Shot as the enemy closes in, and you are prepared for melee-range combat.

If you use your skills to hold aggro on you, it isn't as necessary to keep Beast Mastery skills beyond Charm Animal in your available skill set. Your pet becomes a secondary damage dealer rather than your primary tank. If you plan to have your pet hold aggro, however, train in Beast Mastery and have Comfort Animal on your Skill Bar.

If your secondary profession does not include a healing ability, Troll Unguent is a must-have. This skill costs little Energy to cast and, depending on your Wilderness Survival skill can provide a great deal of healing.

Regardless of your build, have at least one way of disrupting casting enemies, especially healers. While an enemy equal to your level with healing skills won't likely defeat you, you also won't defeat him without some way to stop his healing.

Your group role as a Ranger changes little from what it is during solo play. However, you may wish to forego having animal companions in a group because they are difficult to control.

Player vs. Player

In PvP, Rangers are masters at interrupting their opponents' actions. Interruption is important in PvP because it helps define a battle on your own terms: You decide which spells and abilities an opponent can use by putting a stop to his most dangerous spells and letting him waste his time with lesser abilities.

Savage Shot is a great skill for shutting down an enemy spellcaster, especially a Monk. Using this skill effectively takes experience. Familiarize yourself with the names of common spells and their casting times. Because it's easier to interrupt a spell that takes a long time to cast, target it with Savage Shot. Watch your target, wait for him to begin casting the spell, then loose the arrow. If the spell is something important (like a big heal) it can spell his doom.

If you want to master interruption, Rangers have a number of skills beyond Savage Shot. Concussion Shot is expensive, but dazes a target in addition to the spell-interruption effect. Punishing Shot is an elite skill which can interrupt any ability.

Rangers who know how to interrupt the most dangerous spells are a welcome addition to any PvP team!

Ranger Skills

Look for new skills to be added to *Guild Wars* over time.

Expertise

(Primary Rangers Only)

Distracting Shot
Source: Quest, Ruins of Ascalon/Vendor, Yak's Bend

Cost	10	Casting Time	3/4
Duration	–	Recast Time	10

If Distracting Shot hits, it interrupts target foe's action but deals only 1–16 damage. If the interrupted action was a skill, that skill is disabled for an additional 20 seconds.

Dodge
Source: Quest, Ruins of Ascalon/Vendor, Yak's Bend

Cost	5	Casting Time	–
Duration	5	Recast Time	30

For 5 seconds, you move 33% faster than normal and have a 27–75% chance to evade incoming arrows. Dodge ends if you attack.

Escape (elite)
Source: Whuup Buumbuul (Troll Boss)

Cost	5	Casting Time	–
Duration	5–17	Recast Time	60

For 5–17 seconds, you move 25% faster than normal and have a 75% chance to evade attacks.

Lightning Reflexes
Source: Quest, Ruins of Ascalon/Vendor, Yak's Bend

Cost	10	Casting Time	–
Duration	5–11	Recast Time	60

For 5–11 seconds, you have a 75% chance to evade melee and arrow attacks, and you attack 33% faster.

Marksman's Wager (elite)
Source: Garris Nightwatch, Ulhar Stonehound (Summit Dw. Bosses), Custodians Jenus, Kora, Phebus (Forgotten Enchanted Bosses)

Cost	5	Casting Time	2
Duration	12	Recast Time	24

For 12 seconds, you gain 5–10 Energy whenever your arrows hit, but lose 10 Energy whenever your arrows fail to strike.

Oath Shot (elite)
Source: Perfected Cloak (Mursaat Boss)

Cost	10	Casting Time	–
Duration	–	Recast Time	20

If Oath Shot hits, all your other skills are recharged. If it misses, all your skills are disabled for 10 seconds. (50% miss chance with Marksmanship 7 or less.)

Point Blank Shot
Source: Quest, Kingdom of Ascalon/Vendor, Ascalon City (Ruins)

Cost	10	Casting Time	–
Duration	–	Recast Time	3

Shoot an arrow that has half the normal range, but strikes for +10–20 damage.

Practiced Stance (elite)
Source: Ryk Arrowwing (Tengu Boss)

Cost	5	Casting Time	–
Duration	20–35	Recast Time	15

For 20–35 seconds, your Preparations are ready 50% faster and last 24–50% longer.

Throw Dirt
Source: Quest, Kryta/Vendor, Henge of Denravi

Cost	5	Casting Time	1
Duration	3–10	Recast Time	45

Target-touched foe and foes adjacent to your target become Blinded for 3–15 seconds.

Whirling Defense
Source: Quest, Shiverpeaks (N)/Vendor, Lion's Arch

Cost	10	Casting Time	–
Duration	8–20	Recast Time	60

For 8–20 seconds, you have 75% chance to block attacks. Whenever you block an arrow this way, adjacent foes take 5–11 piercing damage.

(No Attribute)

Antidote Signet
Source: Quest, Kryta-The Wilds/Vendor, Amnoon Oasis

Cost	–	Casting Time	2
Duration	–	Recast Time	8

Cleanse yourself of Poison, Disease, and Blindness.

Called Shot
Source: Quest, Ruins of Ascalon/Vendor, Yak's Bend

Cost	10	Casting Time	–
Duration	–	Recast Time	4

Shoot an arrow that moves 3 times faster than normal and cannot be blocked or evaded.

Debilitating Shot
Source: Quest, Shiverpeaks (N)/Vendor, Lion's Arch

Cost	10	Casting Time	–
Duration	–	Recast Time	5

If Debilitating Shot hits, your target loses 10 Energy.

Dual Shot
Source: Quest, Kingdom of Ascalon/Vendor, Ascalon City (Ruins)

Cost	10	Casting Time	–
Duration	–	Recast Time	5

Shoot two arrows simultaneously at target foe. These arrows deal 25% less damage than normal.

Quick Shot (elite)
Source: Henge Guardian (Behemoth Boss), Igg Fecpelter (Devourer Boss), Maxine Coldstone (Human Boss)

Cost	5	Casting Time	1
Duration	–	Recast Time	3

Shoot an arrow 3 times faster than normal. All your attack skills are disabled for 2 seconds.

Beast Mastery

Bestial Pounce

Source: Quest, Kryta/Vendor, Henge of Denravi

Cost	5	Casting Time	–
Duration	10	Recast Time	15

Your animal companion attempts a Bestial Pounce that deals +5–20 damage. If the attack strikes a foe who is casting a spell, that foe is knocked down.

Brutal Strike

Source: Vendor, Fishermen's Haven

Cost	10	Casting Time	–
Duration	10	Recast Time	5

Your animal companion attempts a Brutal Strike that deals +5–20 damage. If that attack strikes a foe who's Health is below 50%, that foe takes an additional +5–20 damage.

Call of Haste

Source: Quest, Ruins of Ascalon/Vendor, Yak's Bend

Cost	10	Casting Time	–
Duration	30	Recast Time	25

For 30 seconds, your animal companions have a 25% faster attack speed and move 33% faster than normal.

Call of Protection

Source: Quest, Shiverpeaks (N)/Vendor, Lion's Arch

Cost	5	Casting Time	–
Duration	120	Recast Time	115

For 120 seconds, your animal companions have a 1–14 base damage reduction.

Charm Animal

Source: Quest, Kingdom of Ascalon/Vendor, Ascalon City (Ruins)

Cost	10	Casting Time	10
Duration	–	Recast Time	–

Charm target animal. Once charmed, your animal companion will travel with you whenever you have Charm Animal equipped.

Comfort Animal

Source: Quest, Kingdom of Ascalon/Vendor, Ascalon City (Ruins)

Cost	10	Casting Time	1
Duration	–	Recast Time	1

You heal your animal companion for 20–104 points. If your companion is dead, it is resurrected with 10–58% Health and all your skills are disabled for 8 seconds.

Disrupting Lunge

Source: Vendor, Port Sledge

Cost	5	Casting Time	–
Duration	10	Recast Time	5

Your animal companion attempts a Disrupting Lunge that deals +1–12 damage. If that attack strikes a foe using a skill, that skill is interrupted and is disabled for an additional 20 seconds.

Edge of Extinction

Source: Quest, Kryta-The Wilds/Vendor, Droknar's Forge

Cost	5	Casting Time	5
Duration	30–150	Recast Time	60

Create a level 1–10 Spirit. For creatures within its range, whenever any creature dies, Edge of Extinction deals 14–50 damage to all nearby creatures of the same type. This Spirit dies after 30–150 seconds.

Energizing Wind

Source: Vendor, Port Sledge

Cost	5	Casting Time	5
Duration	30–150	Recast Time	60

Create a level 1–10 Spirit. For creatures within its range, all skills cost 15 less Energy (minimum cost 10 Energy), and skills recharge 25% slower than normal. This Spirit dies after 30–150 seconds.

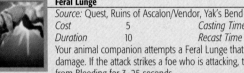

Feral Lunge

Source: Quest, Ruins of Ascalon/Vendor, Yak's Bend

Cost	5	Casting Time	–
Duration	10	Recast Time	10

Your animal companion attempts a Feral Lunge that deals +5–20 damage. If the attack strikes a foe who is attacking, that foe suffers from Bleeding for 3–25 seconds.

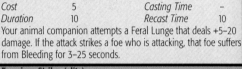

Ferocious Strike (elite)

Source: Thul The Bull (Summit Dwarf Boss)

Cost	5	Casting Time	–
Duration	10	Recast Time	8

Your animal companion attempts a Ferocious Strike that deals +13–28 damage. If that attack hits, you gain adrenaline and 3–10 Energy.

Fertile Season

Source: Vendor, Fishermen's Haven

Cost	5	Casting Time	5
Duration	30–90	Recast Time	30

Create a level 1–10 Spirit. For creatures within its range, every creature's maximum Health is increased by 50–580 and they gain +24 armor. This Spirit dies after 30–90 seconds.

Maiming Strike

Source: Vendor, Maguuma Stade

Cost	10	Casting Time	–
Duration	10	Recast Time	10

Your animal companion attempts a Maiming Strike that deals +5–20 damage. If that attack hits a moving foe that foe becomes Crippled for 3–15 seconds.

Melandru's Assault

Source: Vendor, Ice Tooth Cave

Cost	10	Casting Time	–
Duration	10	Recast Time	10

Your animal companion attempts a Melandru's Assault that deals +5–20 damage. If that attack strikes a foe enchantment, that foe and all adjacent foes takes additional +5–20 damage.

Otyugh's Cry

Source: Quest, Kryta/Vender, Henge of Denravi

Cost	5	Casting Time	–
Duration	30	Recast Time	30

All animals in the area become hostile to your target and gain +20 armor for 30 seconds. Otyugh's Cry cannot turn charmed animals against their masters or their masters' allies. (50% failure chance with Beast Mastery 4 or less.)

Predator's Pounce

Source: Vendor, Grendich Courthouse

Cost	5	Casting Time	–
Duration	10	Recast Time	5

Your animal companion attempts a Predator's Pounce that deals +5–20 damage. If that attack hits, your animal companion gains 5–50 Health.

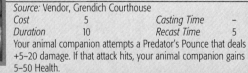

Predatory Season

Source: Quest, Kryta-The Wilds/Vendor, Amnoon Oasis

Cost	5	Casting Time	5
Duration	30–150	Recast Time	60

Create a level 1–10 Spirit. For creatures within its range, all healing is reduced by 20%. If any of your attacks hit, you gain 5 Health. This Spirit dies after 30–150 seconds.

Primal Echoes

Source: Vendor, Copperhammer Mines

Cost	5	Casting Time	5
Duration	30–150	Recast Time	60

Create a level 1–10 Spirit. For creatures within its range, Signet rings cost 10 Energy to use. This Spirit dies after 30–150 seconds.

Scavenger Strike

Source: Vendor, Maguuma Stade

Cost	10	Casting Time	–
Duration	10	Recast Time	5

Your animal companion attempts a Scavenger Strike that deals +5–20 damage. If the attack strikes a foe who is suffering a Condition, that foe takes an additional +1–15 damage.

Symbiosis

Source: Vendor, Marhan's Grotto

Cost	5	Casting Time	5
Duration	30–150	Recast Time	60

Create a level 1–10 Spirit. For creatures within its range, for each enchantment on a creature, that creature's maximum Health is increased by 27–150. This Spirit dies after 30–150 seconds.

Tiger's Fury

Source: Quest, Crystal Desert/Vendor, Droknar's Forge

Cost	10	Casting Time	–
Duration	5–11	Recast Time	5

All your non-attack skills are disabled for 5 seconds. For 5–11 seconds, you attack 33% faster than normal.

Marksmanship

Barrage (elite)

Source: Vatlaaw Doomtooth (Charr Boss), Snyk the Hundred Tongue (Behemoth Boss)

Cost	5	Casting Time	–
Duration	–	Recast Time	1

All your Preparations are removed. Shoot arrows at up to 5 foes near your target. These arrows strike for +1–16 damage if they hit.

Concussion Shot

Source: Quest, Kryta-The Wilds/Vendor, Droknar's Forge

Cost	25	Casting Time	3/4
Duration	10	Recast Time	10

If Concussion Shot hits while target foe is casting a spell, the spell is interrupted and your target is Dazed for 5–20 seconds. This attack deals only 1–16 damage.

Crippling Shot (elite)

Source: Melandru's Cursed (Golem Boss)

Cost	10	Casting Time	–
Duration	–	Recast Time	10

If Crippling Shot hits, your target becomes Crippled for 15 seconds. This attack cannot be blocked or evaded.

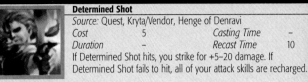

Determined Shot

Source: Quest, Kryta/Vendor, Henge of Denravi

Cost	5	Casting Time	–
Duration	–	Recast Time	10

If Determined Shot hits, you strike for +5–20 damage. If Determined Shot fails to hit, all of your attack skills are recharged.

Favorable Winds

Source: Quest, Ruins of Ascalon/Vendor, Yak's Bend

Cost	5	Casting Time	5
Duration	30–150	Recast Time	60

Create a level 1–10 Spirit. For creatures within its range, arrows move twice as fast as normal and strike for +3 damage. This Spirit dies after 30–150 seconds.

Hunter's Shot

Source: Quest, Ruins of Ascalon/Vendor, Yak's Bend

Cost	5	Casting Time	–
Duration	–	Recast Time	5

If Hunter's Shot hits, you strike for +3–18 damage. If this attack hits a foe that is moving or knocked down, that foe begins Bleeding for 3–25 seconds.

Penetrating Attack

Source: Quest, Ruins of Ascalon/Vendor, Yak's Bend

Cost	10	Casting Time	–
Duration	–	Recast Time	3

If Penetrating Attack hits, you strike for +10–20 damage and this attack has 20% armor penetration.

Pin Down

Source: Quest, Shiverpeaks (N)/Vendor, Lion's Arch

Cost	15	Casting Time	–
Duration	–	Recast Time	15

If Pin Down hits, your target is Crippled for 3–15 seconds.

Power Shot

Source: Quest, Kingdom of Ascalon/Vendor, Ascalon City (Ruins)

Cost	10	Casting Time	–
Duration	–	Recast Time	6

If Power Shot hits, you strike for +10–20 damage.

Precision Shot

Source: Quest, Crystal Desert/Vendor, Droknar's Forge

Cost	10	Casting Time	–
Duration	–	Recast Time	6

If Precision Shot hits, you strike for +13–28 damage. Precision Shot cannot be blocked or evaded. This action is easily interrupted.

Punishing Shot (elite)

Source: Thul Boulderrain (Giant Boss)

Cost	10	Casting Time	–
Duration	–	Recast Time	6

If Punishing Shot hits, you strike for +10–20 damage and your target is interrupted.

Read the Wind

Source: Quest, Kingdom of Ascalon/Vendor, Ascalon City (Ruins)

Cost	5	*Casting Time*	2
Duration	12	*Recast Time*	12

For 12 seconds, your arrows move twice as fast and deal 3–10 extra damage.

Savage Shot

Source: Quest, Kryta-The Wilds/Vendor, Amnoon Oasis

Cost	10	*Casting Time*	–
Duration	–	*Recast Time*	5

If Savage Shot hits, your target's action is interrupted. If that action was a spell, you strike for 13–28 damage.

Wilderness Survival

Apply Poison

Source: Vendor, North Kryta Province

Cost	15	*Casting Time*	2
Duration	24	*Recast Time*	12

For 24 seconds, foes struck by your physical attacks become Poisoned for 3–15 seconds.

Barbed Trap

Source: Quest, Kryta-The Wilds/Vendor, Amnoon Oasis

Cost	15	*Casting Time*	2
Duration	90	*Recast Time*	20

When Barbed Trap is triggered, all foes in the area take 20–65 piercing damage, become Crippled, and begin Bleeding for 3–25 seconds. Barbed Trap ends after 90 seconds. While activating this skill, you are easily interrupted.

Choking Gas

Source: Quest, Kryta-The Wilds/Vendor, Droknar's Forge

Cost	15	*Casting Time*	2
Duration	1–12	*Recast Time*	24

For 1–12 seconds, your arrows deal 1–8 more damage and spread Choking Gas on impact. Choking Gas interrupts foes attempting to cast spells.

Dryder's Defenses

Source: Vendor, Marhan's Grotto

Cost	5	*Casting Time*	–
Duration	5–11	*Recast Time*	60

For 5–11 seconds, you gain 75% chance to evade attacks and 34–60 armor against Elemental damage.

Dust Trap

Source: Quest, Crystal Desert/Vendor, Droknar's Forge

Cost	25	*Casting Time*	2
Duration	90	*Recast Time*	30

When Dust Trap is triggered, all foes in the area are Blinded for 3–10 seconds and take 10–68 Earth damage. While activating this skill, you are easily interrupted. Dust Trap ends after 90 seconds.

Flame Trap

Source: Quest, Crystal Desert/Vendor, Droknar's Forge

Cost	10	*Casting Time*	2
Duration	90	*Recast Time*	20

When Flame Trap is triggered, for 3 seconds all foes in the area are struck for 15–30 Fire damage and set on fire for 1–3 second(s). Flame Trap automatically triggers after 90 seconds. While activating this skill, you are easily interrupted.

Frozen Soil

Source: Vendor, Marhan's Grotto

Cost	5	*Casting Time*	5
Duration	30–90	*Recast Time*	30

Create a level 1–10 Spirit. For creatures within its range, dead creatures cannot be resurrected. This Spirit dies after 30–90 sec.

Greater Conflagration (elite)

Source: Valetudo Rubor (Titan Boss)

Cost	5	*Casting Time*	5
Duration	30–150	*Recast Time*	60

Create a level 1–10 Spirit. For creatures within its range, all physical damage is Fire damage instead. This Spirit dies after 30–150 seconds.

Healing Spring

Source: Vendor, North Kryta Province

Cost	10	*Casting Time*	2
Duration	10	*Recast Time*	20

For 10 seconds, all allies in the area are healed for 15–60 every 2 seconds. While activating this skill, you are easily interrupted.

Ignite Arrows

Source: Quest, Kingdom of Ascalon/Vendor, Ascalon City (Ruins)

Cost	10	*Casting Time*	2
Duration	24	*Recast Time*	12

For 24 seconds, your arrows explode on contact, dealing 3–18 Fire damage.

Incendiary Arrows (elite)

Source: Casses Flameweb (Arachnid Boss)

Cost	5	*Casting Time*	2
Duration	8	*Recast Time*	24

For 8 seconds, targets struck by your arrows are interrupted and set on fire for 1–3 second(s).

Kindle Arrows

Source: Vendor, Grendich Courthouse

Cost	5	*Casting Time*	2
Duration	24	*Recast Time*	12

For 24 seconds, your arrows deal an additional 3–24 Fire damage.

Melandru's Arrows (elite)

Source: Ulhar Stonehound (L24; Summit Dwarf Boss)

Cost	5	*Casting Time*	2
Duration	18	*Recast Time*	12

For 18 seconds, whenever your arrows hit, they cause Bleeding for 3–25 seconds and do +8–28 damage if they hit a target who is under an enchantment.

Melandru's Resilience (elite)

Source: Ssyl Feshah (Forgotten Boss)

Cost	5	*Casting Time*	–
Duration	8–20	*Recast Time*	15

For 8–20 seconds, you gain Health regeneration of 2 and Energy regeneration of 1 for each Condition and Hex you are suffering.

Muddy Terrain
Source: Vendor, Copperhammer Mines

Cost	5	Casting Time	5
Duration	30–90	Recast Time	30

Create a level 1–10 Spirit. For creatures within its range, all creatures move 10% slower than normal and speed boosts have no effect. This Spirit dies after 30–90 seconds.

Nature's Renewal
Source: Vendor, Camp Rankor

Cost	5	Casting Time	5
Duration	30–150	Recast Time	60

Create a level 1–10 Spirit. For creatures within its range, all enchantments and Hexes are removed. For 30–150 seconds, enchantments and Hexes take twice as long to cast. This Spirit dies after 30–150 seconds.

Poison Arrow (elite)
Source: Salani Pippip (Grawl Boss)

Cost	5	Casting Time	–
Duration	–	Recast Time	1

If Poison Arrow hits, your target becomes Poisoned for 5–20 seconds.

Quickening Zephyr
Source: Quest, Ruins of Ascalon/Vendor, Yak's Bend

Cost	5	Casting Time	5
Duration	30–150	Recast Time	60

Create a level 1–10 Spirit. For creatures within its range, all skills recharge twice as fast as normal and cost 30% more Energy to cast. This Spirit dies after 30–150 seconds.

Serpent's Quickness
Source: Quest, Shiverpeaks (N)/Vendor, Lion's Arch

Cost	5	Casting Time	–
Duration	15–30	Recast Time	45

For 15–30 seconds, recharge times for your skills are reduced by 33%. Serpent's Quickness ends if your Health drops below 50%.

Spike Trap (elite)
Source: Vulg Painbrain (Ettin Boss), Cella the Hooded (Skale Boss)

Cost	10	Casting Time	2
Duration	90	Recast Time	20

When Spike Trap is triggered, all foes in the area take 10–68 piercing damage, become Crippled for 3–15 seconds, and are knocked down. Spike Trap ends after 90 seconds. While activating this skill, you are easily interrupted.

Storm Chaser
Source: Quest, Kryta-The Wilds/Vendor, Amnoon Oasis

Cost	10	Casting Time	–
Duration	8–20	Recast Time	30

For 8–20 seconds, you move 25% faster, and you gain 1–5 Energy whenever you take Elemental damage.

Troll Unguent
Source: Quest, Kingdom of Ascalon/Vendor, Ascalon City (Ruins)

Cost	5	Casting Time	3
Duration	10	Recast Time	10

For 10 seconds, you gain Health regeneration +3–10.

Winnowing
Source: Quest, Crystal Desert/Vendor, Droknar's Forge

Cost	5	Casting Time	5
Duration	30–150	Recast Time	60

Create a level 1–10 Spirit. For creatures within its range, creatures take 4 additional damage whenever they take physical damage. This Spirit dies after 30–150 seconds.

Winter
Source: Quest, Shiverpeaks (N)/Vendor, Lion's Arch

Cost	5	Casting Time	5
Duration	30–150	Recast Time	60

Create a level 1–10 Spirit. For creatures within its range, all Elemental damage is Cold damage instead. This Spirit dies after 30–150 seconds.

Warrior

By Bydian

Live by the Sword... or Axe... or Hammer

he Warrior profession in *Guild Wars* is not what you may expect. Anyone who has ever played an MMORPG would agree that the traditional notion of a Warrior (or "tank," as they have come to be known) is a character that is designed to absorb massive amounts of abuse while other characters/ professions dish out the damage. *Guild Wars* has broken this longstanding mold by giving Warriors not only traditional damage-mitigating abilities through heavy armor and shields, but also the power to deliver reasonable damage with additional skills.

Warrior-specific abilities are based on adrenaline, which is a separate pool of power from Energy. Several skills, however, require Energy to activate them, especially those based on the Sword attribute. This doesn't present a problem for the Warrior, but Warriors have a smaller base Energy pool and regeneration rate than caster-oriented classes. Since you don't have a large reserve of Energy, and depending on the secondary profession you have chosen, you might find yourself constantly waiting on Energy to regenerate. The good news is that you

> ## Five Reasons to Be a Warrior
>
> - You want to be the master of Guild Wars *melee combat.*
> - You are looking for a durable and solo-able cooperative play profession.
> - It's a good starting class as you get used to the wilds of Tyria.
> - You like to be the center of the offensive assault in PvP and cooperative play.
> - It's an excellent base profession to match up with other secondary professions.

can continue to dish out damage even if you are completely tapped on Energy. Warriors have the ability to draw from two active pools, allowing you to use more skills than may be apparent at first glance.

Adrenaline is gained one point at a time, each time you land a hit on an opponent or take damage yourself. Each adrenaline-based ability has a specific adrenaline cost. As you build adrenaline, you will see each of your adrenaline-based abilities light up after you build up enough adrenaline to activate it.

One of your biggest advantages in PvP combat is the natural hierarchy of target selection. This hierarchy is alive and well in *Guild Wars*. This game element is a traditional system of choosing a target based on priority. The following list indicates the order of priority usually followed in PvP combat.

1. Kill the healers first. As long as your opponent has healers, targets take a

long time to eliminate. The longer an enemy lives, the longer he is distributing damage to your team.

2. High damage-output professions are targeted next. They can dish out massive punishment, but without healing, they also go down fast.

3. Tanks or Warrior-type professions are left for last. The Warrior types are the hardest (or take the longest) to kill and dish out the least amount of damage.

Knowing the hierarchy, you can exploit targeting priority to your advantage. In most cases, you will not be the primary focus of fire. Use this knowledge wisely and make sure your Warrior unloads maximum damage on your unsuspecting opponents.

Weapon Selection

Warriors in *Guild Wars* have three viable choices for weapons: axes, hammers, and swords. The abilities for each category will be discussed in detail further on in this section, but here are the basics of your weapon choices:

- **Swords:** This is a one-handed weapon (which allows you to hold something in your other hand) with a 1.33-second attack speed. Sword skills focus on Bleeding and situational use of abilities. Also, swords offer more Energy-based abilities, in addition to the more standard adrenaline-based abilities.

- **Axes:** Another one-handed weapon with a 1.33-second attack speed, its powers are concentrated in damage boosts, with a few Bleeding abilities thrown in. Axes have a higher damage potential than swords, but also have a lower base damage. This gives you a greater damage capability on the top end, which is tempered by having a lower guaranteed damage base. Axes also receive a bonus percentage to land critical hits.

- **Hammers:** A two-handed weapon with a 1.75-second attack speed, hammers have powers concentrated in knockdowns and snares. Hammers also have a higher damage range on both the low and high ends. They are slow weapons, but they pack a bigger punch. Hammers are the ultimate choice if you want to get in close to your enemy to put him on his back. Knockdowns and interrupts are a crucial PvP element in *Guild Wars*, so hammers are the best weapon for anti-caster builds.

Armor Selection

Each armor set has its advantages; learn to evaluate the situation to choose the best set for you. If you are dying from Elemental spell damage, reduce your death frequency by equipping a Warrior with armor that protects against Elemental damage. Go with one armor theme or another; mixing and matching armor leads to uncertainty as to whether or not you're getting the type of reduction you wanted.

Most of the endgame helms offer a bonus to a primary stat, such as +1 to Strength or Tactics, +1 to Sword/Axe/Hammer Mastery, and so forth.

Attributes & Skills

Strength
(Primary Warriors Only)

Ranks in this attribute increase the armor penetration of your attack skills by one percent per attribute rank. Strength also improves the effectiveness of skills that keep you alive, as well as those that inflict damage on your opponents. Only characters who take Warrior as their primary profession can benefit from this attribute.

Battle Rage (elite): Useful when you need to boost your movement speed or generate a lot of adrenaline in a hurry,

this combos well with Executioner's Strike and Galrath Slash, which are both low-cost, direct damage skills. Do not use non-attack skills with Battle Rage, as non-attack skills cancel it out and drain all adrenaline.

Berserker Stance: This is a useful skill for boosting attack speed over a short duration, with little to no drawback. The recast is considerable, but this is a nice way to generate quick adrenaline for high adrenaline-cost skills.

Bull's Charge (elite): This is a handy skill to have for neutralizing runners, as it knocks down anyone you hit who is running away from you.

Bull's Strike: This skill is similar to Bull's Charge, but this one is a one-shot deal. It might be a preferable alternative in skill choice if you don't want to burn your elite skill slot on Bull's Charge.

Defy Pain (elite): This is a more powerful version of Endure Pain and increases your armor resiliency. To further increase your role as team juggernaut, choose this.

Dwarven Battle Stance (elite): Specific to Hammer Warriors, this skill is great for shutting down casters so you can take them down without interruption—it's also great for dealing with annoying Mesmers.

Endure Pain: This skill is useful in those situations when you are almost out of Health and your heals aren't coming. This commonly used skill is recommended for most builds.

Griffon's Sweep: Useful against evasion builds, even if your target doesn't evade, you still get the small damage boost with this skill.

Power Attack: The Energy cost for this skill is low, as is the recycle time. It also inflicts decent damage and is well-suited for most builds. If you have the room, pick this up.

Protector's Strike: This is a more impressive version of Power Attack, but is only effective against a moving target. It is an excellent skill for

dealing with PvP enemies as they try to make an escape.

Rush: As an adrenaline-based sprint with no recast time and a reasonable adrenaline cost, this is a good pick. If you have no problems generating adrenaline, or need to move quickly and often, pick this up.

Shield Bash: This is useful for the Sword and Axe Warriors who fight other Warriors.

Sprint: This skill has a reasonable Energy cost, but the 20-second recast is something to consider. Sprint, or a similar skill, is required on most Warriors to chase down runners or get out of trouble because of melee range limitations.

Warrior's Cunning: The considerable Energy cost and recast make this skill less attractive, but it is a good skill when you want your blows to land.

Warrior's Endurance (elite): This is a good skill for Warriors who have taken a secondary profession with high Energy consumption. This skill allows you to regenerate that Energy in a hurry.

(No Attribute)

"For Great Justice": This is a handy skill for quickly charging adrenaline skills.

Distracting Blow: This is a good skill to use on casters.

Flurry: This skill for is useful for building adrenaline or for combining with damage-increasing skills.

Frenzy: This is useful for finishing off an opponent, or when your opponent is attacking another target.

Skull Crack: This is good to use on a caster, especially a Monk. It's also one of the best suppression skills in the game. It's tricky to execute, but worth it when dealing with skills that take a long time to execute.

Axe Mastery

Ranks in this attribute increase basic

axe damage and damage dealt by axe skills.

Axe Rake: This essential skill is costly adrenaline-wise, but is fantastic to use on someone with a Deep Wound. The crippling effect makes this a popular skill.

Cleave (elite): With a moderate damage boost and a low adrenaline cost, this adds to your damage output, but don't combo it with too many adrenaline skills, as they'll be wasted.

Cyclone Axe: This is a great skill for building adrenaline, but it takes careful positioning, as it works best when surrounded by foes.

Dismember: A skill that puts a Deep Wound on your target, Dismember is a great intro to Axe Rake. The adrenaline cost is high, but the results are worth it.

Disrupting Chop: This is a great interrupt skill—use it to disable enemy skills with a long duration or for a Monk heal with a long casting time.

Eviscerate (elite): As a more powerful version of Dismember, it also increases overall damage while inflicting a Deep Wound. Combo this with Axe Rake or Axe Twist for greater carnage.

Executioner's Strike: This is a simple, straightforward damage add spell which, when combined with adrenaline-increasing skills (Battle Rage, Berserker Stance, etc.), is very effective.

Swift Chop: This is a good skill to use on characters who have a high chance of blocking an attack.

Hammer Mastery

While you lose the ability to carry a shield, this allows you to do more damage than Axe or Sword Mastery, though attacks are slower.

Backbreaker (elite): This has a long duration knockdown with a high adrenaline cost. Shutting down a target for four seconds, especially a caster, is a recipe for success. Combo this with skills that require knockdowns, like

Holy Strike and Aftershock.

Belly Smash: This is a good skill to use as a follow-up for any knockdown skill.

Counter Blow: Use this for a cheap knockdown on an opponent engaging in melee. It's handy to use repeatedly to keep a foe flat on his back.

Crushing Blow: Another great skill to use on a knocked-down opponent, this doesn't require making your opponent Bleed. It immediately reduces his maximum hit points and the effect of heals thrown on him.

Devastating Hammer (elite): Use this for a terrific knockdown skill that combos well with Heavy Blow, as it also inflicts Weaken on the target.

Earth Shaker (elite): This knocks down all adjacent foes. If you can get into the middle of a group of enemies, this can be very effective. However, consider its high adrenaline cost and elite status when deciding whether to include it in your Skill Bar.

Hammer Bash: This low-adrenaline knockdown is useful, but it drains all

adrenaline, making it good to use as a final blow.

Heavy Blow: This is the prime follow-up skill to Devastating Hammer. It's also good if you have Weaken equipped.

Mighty Blow: As a basic hammer attack skill, it combos well with adrenaline-increasing skills (Battle Rage, Berserker Stance, etc.) for large amounts of damage.

Staggering Blow: This is a great way to set up a target for Heavy Blow or reduce the damage of an enemy Warrior.

Swordsmanship

The damage inflicted with a sword is more predictable when compared to damage inflicted by an axe. It's also reliant on various Conditions, such as Bleeding, for full benefits.

Final Thrust: This is one of the highest damage Warrior skills. This causes massive pain when the target has below 50 percent hit points. This is a great finishing move to use in combinations, such as the Sever Artery, Gash, and Final Thrust combination.

Gash: The follow-up attack to Sever Artery, it is a must-have for a Sword Warrior who also has Sever Artery on his Skill Bar.

Hamstring: This is a standard snare. When you land this attack, your target is crippled for a short period of time. This is a great, high-impact skill to use on runners.

Hundred Blades (elite): A great adrenaline-building skill, as it strikes multiple enemies, this also combos well with any damage-adding skill (the various "Order" skills, etc.).

Pure Strike: This is a good skill to have on your Skill Bar if you need that last bit of damage output, you're sitting on unused Energy, or you're waiting on adrenaline to build for your other skills.

Savage Slash: This is a fantastic skill to

use against casters, especially busy Monks. If this skill lands on a target who is casting a spell, the target takes extra damage.

Sever Artery: This makes your target Bleed. It is great not only because it's highly effective, but also because it is the beginning of an impressive, three-step attack chain: Sever Artery, Gash, and Final Thrust.

Tactics

Ranks in this attribute improve Shouts and Stances and give you and your party an advantage in battle. Tactics are also required to use some high-end shields—usually 6–9 ranks.

"Charge!", (elite): This makes the group run buff. This stacks well with skills like Sprint, as it increases a party member's run speed up to 50 percent.

"Shields Up!": This is useful for defending against Ranger-heavy groups; you may find it less effective in other situations.

"To the Limit!": This is a good skill if you are in the middle of enemy groups and you need a quick way to make your adrenaline soar. The Energy cost is right, but the recast is lengthy.

"Victory Is Mine!" (elite): This is a very effective Health and Energy regeneration skill to use mid-battle especially, if you're in a party that spreads Conditions.

"Watch Yourself!": This is a good low cost skill to pack if you fight Warrior-heavy groups. The added armor is especially useful for assisting other professions when they come under melee attack.

Balanced Stance: For Warrior/Monks who don't like the idea of being knocked down in the middle of a rez-cast, this is a good skill choice. Removing the enemy's ability to knock you down can be very useful for casting Warriors.

Bonetti's Defense: This is an effective dodge spell if the Warrior is under heavy attack. It is also excellent when combo'd with a profession (Monk or Elementalist) that requires a lot of Energy.

Deadly Riposte: For Tactics-based Warriors, this is a good damage-dealing skill.

Desperation Blow: When matched with Balanced Stance or Dolyak's Signet, this is a solid spell in desparate circumstances.

Disciplined Stance: This is a great evasion buff for a Warrior who is not using adrenaline-based skills.

Gladiator's Defense (elite): This awesome skill is used when physical damage is directed at you. Each time you block an enemy's attack, you deal out respectable damage. This skill is useful against Warrior-heavy groups.

Healing Signet: This is highly effective heal, use this, but keep in mind that it puts you in a vulnerable state. It is best used after a battle or when under the effects of a heavy defensive enchantment.

Riposte: This is a lesser version of Deadly Riposte. It requires the use of adrenaline to fuel its counterstrike properties.

Wary Stance: This is great when combo'd with a high adrenaline Warrior. When under heavy attack and maxed out, unleash this one.

Secondary Professions

Guild Wars offers a rich and detailed character creation process where hundreds of builds are viable. There is no right or wrong combination of professions in this game, so don't take any of the comments or suggestions here as the final answer on how to create a character. The best advice is to experiment with character builds, read template forums, and make sure you

understand the game's skills and how they work. The more you know about the game, the easier it is for you to piece together a character you will enjoy playing.

Warrior/ Elementalist

The Warrior/Elementalist is an offensive powerhouse and is suitable for all three weapon lines. A Hammer Warrior might focus on Hammer Mastery, Strength, and Earth Magic, and seek to repeatedly knock a target, then follow with Aftershock for big damage. Conjure (Element) enchantments work well with the fast attack speed of swords and axes. A Sword, Tactic, and Air Warrior/Elementalist can use Conjure Lightning for added swinging damage, Gale for ranged knockdowns, and Shock to knock the target down again after he has closed to melee range.

The Water spells feature a Conjure and the valuable elite spell Water Trident, which is superb for knocking down and damaging fleeing targets. It also offers lots of snares and surprise spells like Blurred Vision, an AoE Blindness for use in the thick of battle.

Fire boasts not only a Conjure, but offers quick-casting damage spells like Immolate and the point-blank area-of-effect (PBAoE) damager Inferno, which, at the cost of 10 Energy each, are within the Warrior's available Energy pool. An example build would be to take Sprint, Sever Artery, Gash, and Final Thrust (Warrior), and Water Trident, Conjure Frost, Glyph of Elemental Power, and Shard Storm (Water Elementalist). Water Trident and Shard Storm help you deal with fleeing enemies and give you quick, cheap, ranged attacks. Conjure Frost adds 1–13 more damage to your attacks. Finally, Glyph of Elemental Power boosts the attribute rating of your next spell by two and allows you to toss out

damage like an Elementalist until your power runs out. A variation would be to become an Air Elementalist instead take Battle Rage, Sever Artery, Gash, Final Thrust, and Hamstring (Warrior), and Shock, Whirlwind, and Conjure Lightning (Air Elementalist). Shock is a PBAoE spell that does moderate damage and knocks targets down. Whirlwind is also a PBAoE spell with moderate damage, but knocks down foes that attack when you cast this spell. Finally, Conjure Lightning adds 1–13 Lightning damage to your attacks.

Warrior/Mesmer

The Warrior/Mesmer is a unique blend of damage dealing and disruption. You may not be able to tank as well as some of the other Warriors (assuming you make armor selections that augment your casting abilities in lieu of damage reduction), but you can incapacitate your target as you pound him into the dirt. A Warrior/Mesmer is able to mix skills that use adrenaline and Energy and put constant pressure on his foes. Direct disruption spells like Power Block and Power Spike can interrupt crucial actions, and when the Warrior is within touch range, skills like Blackout can deny an opponent the means to act. Shatter Hex can turn the Warrior/Mesmer into a running bomb, and Shatter Enchantment serves the dual purpose of mitigating a target's defense while applying damage. Using adrenaline attack skills like Dismember damages and inflicts a Deep Wound to reduce healing. Follow with an Axe Rake to inflict Cripple and prevent flight. As the Warrior/Mesmer's role is less about being a heavy tank, he is able to use an offhand Energy focus and buffed armor to achieve an Energy pool in the mid 30s. An example build would be to take Sword and Strength skills primarily, and select Inspiration from your secondary profession.

Recommended skills are Battle Rage, Sever Artery, Gash, Final Thrust, and Hamstring (Warrior), and Ether Feast, Leech Signet, and Power Drain (Mesmer). Ether Feast is a low-cost heal that powers itself with your opponent's Energy. Leech Signet is a no-cost skill that interrupts your opponent's spellcasting and transfers their Energy to you, which is useful for interrupting an elite skill of any type. Finally, Power Drain (Inspiration) is a low-cost spellcasting interrupt that drains off Energy for a low investment, which, when used in the right circumstances, keeps your Energy pool overflowing. A variation is to select Signet of Humility instead of the Leech Signet. This is a touch-activated skill that shuts down an opponent's elite skill for 15 seconds, with a 20-second recast timer, for no Energy cost. If an opponent tries to use an elite spell within that five-second window, you have Power Drain ready for him. Both of these variations are good for shutting down an enemy and keeping your Energy pool full while you go about your business of applying damage, snares, and wounds.

Warrior/Monk

The Warrior/Monk is a great character to learn the game with, as it is one of the most defensive and self-sufficient builds in the game. Most often, a Warrior/Monk opts to augment her already high survivability with either Healing or Protection skills. Skills commonly on the Skill Bar are Endure Pain, Sprint, Wary Stance, Sever Artery, Gash, Final Thrust, and Healing Breeze. Healing Breeze is a handy skill to have, as its heal-over-time allows you to get back to fighting and also mitigates future damage. A variation is to remove Wary Stance and replace it with Restore Life, a powerful healing resurrection spell that requires you to touch your fallen teammate. Warrior/Monks are excellent for resurrecting fallen teammates due to their low priority on target lists. If a Monk sneaks off to try to resurrect a comrade, most people notice, and

precious time is wasted when the Monk could be keeping someone else alive. If a Warrior/Monk wanders off to try to heal someone, there's a good chance that the enemy will leave him alone to concentrate on the rest of the party. Even if you don't have the Energy pool to be a party healer, you can augment your character with enough healing capabilities to ensure that you're not a constant drain on your party's primary healing resources.

Another build option is to focus on the Hammer and Smite attributes, which work well together, adding a more offensive punch to the package. Take Staggering Blow, Heavy Blow, Hammer Bash, Bull's Strike, and Sprint (Warrior), and Shield of Judgment, Bane Signet, and Restore Life (Monk). In addition to the three knockdowns you have as a Warrior, Bane Signet damages and knocks down, for no Energy cost. Shield of Judgment is the real twist on the build, as for up to 18 seconds this skill knocks down anyone attacking you, be it melee or ranged attack, including caster wand attacks. Combining this with five other knockdowns accessible together, you can ruin an opposing group's day as you keep most of them on their backs and out of the fight. Finally, Restore Life adds a nice high-restoration resurrection spell to bring back fallen allies.

Warrior/ Necromancer

The Warrior/Necromancer has skills that add to his Health pool, at the expense of his opponent's Health. This build also is more offensive and might feature an axe and shield. From the Necromancer line, Blood Magic is a logical choice, as many of the skills allow you to drain Health from your opponent and add it to your own. Skills commonly on the Skill Bar would be Sprint, Battle Rage, Dismember, Axe Rake, Executioner's Strike, Vampiric Gaze, Life Siphon, and Demonic Flesh. Vampiric Gaze is a ranged life tap, while

Life Siphon is a life drain (removing Health over time from your target and adding it to your own Health pool). Demonic Flesh temporarily boosts your maximum Health, something a Warrior always needs.

An alternative build, based on Necromancer Curse skills, would be Battle Rage, Dismember, Axe Rake, and Executioner's Strike again, plus Parasitic Bond, Rigor Mortis, Barbs, and Weaken Armor. This build focuses a bit more on applying quick damage to targets that have more armor and may evade or block more often. It features Parasitic Bond as the healing spell. Choose one Necromancer attribute in which to invest. If you try to spread points around to two or three attributes, you're going to end up with a watered-down character. Pick one thing that your Necromancer will do well, and meld that with what Warriors do best. Due to your tiny Energy pool, select skills that have a low Energy cost and a shorter cast time.

Warrior/Ranger

The Ranger profession brings a wealth of options to the primary Warrior. Without spending any attribute points, a Warrior/Ranger can wade into the fray with a trusted animal companion, thanks to Charm Animal. Wilderness Survival offers not only valuable stances, but also Troll Unguent, a self-regeneration skill that works well with your Warrior's heavy armor. Apply Poison works as well on blades as it does on arrows, and Melandru's Resilience can turn a downtrodden Warrior into a fortress. Beast Mastery offers the Warrior a plethora of ways to boost her pet's abilities and some surprisingly useful nature rituals. Frozen Soil can keep the dead from resurrecting, while Predatory Season dampens healing and gives the Warrior Health for each blow she inflicts. The Ranger is a nice secondary profession because it offers a lot of variety to the Warrior builds. If you're looking to augment speed, lay AoE traps, summon

an animal pet to fight by your side, or add to your defense or Health-regeneration capabilities—you can get it as a Ranger. An example is to select Battle Rage, Dismember, Axe Rake, and Executioner's Strike (Warrior), and Troll Unguent, Storm Chaser, Apply Poison, and Barbed Trap (Ranger). Storm Chaser is a Sprint skill that recharges your Energy if Elemental damage hits you. Barbed Trap can add to your strategic options, especially when defending an area, as not only does it cause AoE damage, but it also Cripples and Bleeds your targets as well, all for the cost of 15 Energy. Another build option is to go with Sever Artery, Gash, and Final Thrust (Warrior), and Troll Unguent, Storm Chaser, Spike Trap, Charm Animal, and Comfort Animal (Ranger). Spike Trap is an elite version of Barbed Trap that costs less Energy and adds a knockdown. Charm Animal allows you to tame, then bring an animal into any mission you enter. The Ranger pet must be leveled up alongside you in missions and is a handy addition. Comfort Animal is a must-have if you elect to use an animal, as it both heals your pet when it becomes damaged and resurrects the animal if dead.

Cooperative Play

Warriors are most comfortable fighting NPCs. Here they can show off their ability to soak up damage and protect their teammates, using mob AI and collision detection to their advantage. NPCs attack the targets that come into range and damage them first, so a good Warrior will charge ahead of his teammates (using Sprint) and engage the enemy, throwing down an AoE skill to gain the targets' attention. Using a damage-over-time, snare, or knockdown skill as your first or second attack helps to ensure that the target stays on you— exactly where you and the rest of your team want it to be. Be careful not to accidentally aggro more than the healer can handle, as mobs are more

aggressive against healers than against damagers. Running up until a target attacks, then falling back to separate it from other targets in the area, distances your foes and makes them easier to deal with. This is also good practice for PvP arenas.

Additionally, in cooperative play the Warrior is the best target caller, hitting [Ctrl] + double-click to announce what target they're attacking so their teammates can hit [T] and assist them. A Warrior has an up-close look at which targets are engaging the party and can see skill animations that players farther in the rear may miss out on seeing. This helps you to identify the true professions of your opponents. When the party stays on the same target, this allows the Warrior to hold aggro more easily and helps to take down the selected target more quickly. Target healers, then damage dealers, then tanks.

An underestimated tool in managing aggro is collision detection. Collision detection takes the place of taunting, as just your intimidating presence next to a target may be enough to make it attack you instead of your more vulnerable teammates. Trapping your target against an object will keep its attention, as will blocking off a pathway of advance. Also, "pick plays" works well in taking aggro off of teammates—when the endangered PC runs the mob around you, step in front of it, while simultaneously damaging it, especially with a snare or knockdown. This makes the target unhappy with you and may gain its attention, saving your teammate's life. Take pleasure in stepping in front of an embattled teammate and taking the cruel attentions of the NPC. Block the advance of the enemy, putting your armored body and strong right arm on the line. Be creative, throw yourself into the fray, and enjoy playing a tank.

Soloing quests is a great way to build up experience, items, and cash. Not having to rely on other players is a big benefit, especially if you have a

limited amount of time and don't want to wait around, trying to form a group. A Warrior can defeat most quests with the addition of a healer henchman who does a good, if automated, job of keeping you alive. You can gain more speed by adding a damage dealer, most likely the Elementalist henchman.

Given the way the AI and collision detection work, a live Warrior is almost a necessity for cooperative play. Also, equip your Resurrection Signet skill, as your healer henchmen will often go down before you do. If this happens, retreat and let the NPCs return to their original locations, then go back and bring your healer back to life. Otherwise, you will find yourself mapping to the beginning of the quest, or dying.

Finally, this is the perfect place for you to become popular with other players who are seeking out a Warrior to help them. Wait in the staging area before entering cooperative missions and join someone forming a group, or grab a healer henchman and start one. Use your social skills, do a good job in the mission, and make friends for the PvP and Guild vs. Guild areas, where playing with friends is vital to your success. With a healer henchman, there is little personal risk in joining random player characters to run a cooperative mission. A good reputation, and cool-looking equipment, will make you a standout character in cooperative play missions, and is your ticket to meeting players from many guilds.

Player vs. Player

Wise men advise their students to "know thine enemy." For Warriors, this might be revised to "choose thine enemy." The most successful offensive Warriors are those that pick a type of opponent and excel at killing that type of opponent above all others. If you are the type of Warrior who is less interested in tanking and more

My Favorite Guild

Name: Andrew Patrick

Title: Community Relations Assistant

Character: Quag Frostraven

My favorite guild, naturally, is my guild, the Zealots of Shiverpeak [ZoS]. We differ from many other guilds in that we concentrate much more on cooperative missions and creating a friendly community than we do on creating dominating builds for PvP play. All of our members take an active roll in the community, and many of the ZoS members work on fansites. Perhaps we spend a bit too much time socializing and running missions until we find the right amount of a certain dye ... but we have fun doing it! I think Isaiah put it best when he said: "You know, we always beat your guild in Tombs, but you guys sure are the best-dressed characters in the game!"

Conditions

Bleeding: While Bleeding, you suffer -3 Health degeneration.

Blind: While Blind, your melee and missile attacks have a 90% chance to miss. Your projectiles also have a greater chance to stray from their intended target.

Burning: While Burning, you lose 7 Health regularly (DoT).

Crippled: While Crippled, you move at half speed.

Dazed: While Dazed, you take twice as long to cast spells, and all your spells are easily interrupted.

Deep Wound: While suffering from a Deep Wound, your maximum Health is reduced by 10% and you only heal for 80% of the normal amount.

Disease: While Diseased, you suffer -4 Health degeneration. Disease is contagious between creatures of the same kind.

Exhaustion: Max Energy drops by 10. It returns to normal at 1 Energy every 3 seconds.

Poison: While poisoned, you suffer -4 Health degeneration.

Weakness: While suffering from Weakness, you inflict 1/3 your normal damage with a bow or melee weapon.

interested in slaughter, read on.

Anti-caster Warriors have the job of taking on enemy Monks, Mesmers, and Elementalists. For this job, you need the ability to stop your opponent from casting spells. Each type of weapon has attacks that can do this. Several hammer attacks are capable of knocking down your opponent (thus stopping whatever action he was performing). These cost adrenaline, so you might not be able to interrupt your target's casting early in a battle. Likewise, axes have Disrupting Chop, which interrupts and disables the skill in use for 20 seconds. This also costs adrenaline, although it costs less than most hammer skills. Swords can use Savage Slash, which costs Energy, so you can use it earlier in a fight. However, be wary of draining yourself. The sword's Hamstring attack is also good against casters because it forces them to run.

Anti-tank Warriors have the job of killing other Warriors with high melee defenses. To do so, you need ways to bypass their armor. Find a method for dealing something other than physical damage. One method that works with almost any build is to obtain a weapon that deals Elemental damage (for example, a hammer with a Shocking Hammer Haft strikes for Lightning damage). If you wanted to take it a

step further, you could build a Warrior whose main damage output is Elemental damage. For example, a Warrior/Elementalist with a fiery weapon could take Conjure Flame to further increase his damage.

Another method for bypassing armor is to become a Warrior/Mesmer with the elite Illusionary Weaponry skill. When you attack with this skill, you'll do Illusion-based damage that armor won't reduce. Use a sword so you strike as fast as possible.

If you don't want to depend on enchantments or special weapons, hammers provide the best offense against other tanks. Hammers hit hardest, so more of their damage will get through. In addition, players who use Healing Hands to tank other Warriors find that it can't keep up with a hammer's high damage.

Warrior Skills

Look for new skills to be added to *Guild Wars* over time.

Strength

(Primary Warriors Only)

"I Will Avenge You!"

Source: Vendor, North Kryta Province

Cost	5E	Casting Time	–
Duration	10	Recast Time	45

For each dead ally in the area you gain 10 seconds of increased attack speed and Health regeneration +3–7.

"I Will Survive!"

Source: Quest, Kryta-The Wilds/Vendor, Amnoon Oasis

Cost	5E	Casting Time	–
Duration	5–11	Recast Time	60

You gain Health regeneration of 3 for each injury (Bleeding, Deep Wound, Crippled, and Weakness) you are suffering. This regeneration expires after 5–11 seconds.

Battle Rage (elite)

Source: Krogg Shmush (Troll Boss)

Cost	3A	Casting Time	–
Duration	5–20	Recast Time	–

For 5–20 seconds, you move 25% faster and gain double adrenaline from attacks. Battle Rage ends if you use any non-attack skills. When Battle Rage ends, you lose all adrenaline.

Berserker Stance

Source: Vendor, Port Sledge

Cost	5E	Casting Time	–
Duration	5–11	Recast Time	30

For 5–11 seconds, you attack 33% faster than normal and gain 20% more adrenaline each time you hit in melee. Berserker Stance ends if you use a skill.

Bull's Charge (elite)

Source: Skintekaru Manshredder (Dragon Boss), Rage Maulhoof (Minotaur Boss)

Cost	5E	Casting Time	–
Duration	5–11	Recast Time	20

For 5–11 seconds, you move 25% faster than normal and if you strike a fleeing foe in melee, that foe is knocked down. Bull's Charge ends if you use a skill.

Bull's Strike

Source: Quest, Crystal Desert / Vendor, Droknar's Forge

Cost	5E	Casting Time	–
Duration	2	Recast Time	8

If this attack hits a fleeing foe, you strike for +5–30 damage, and your target is knocked down.

Defy Pain (elite)

Source: Obrhit Barkwood (Plant Boss)

Cost	6A	Casting Time	–
Duration	8	Recast Time	–

For 8 seconds you have an additional 90–300 Health and an additional 20 armor.

Dolyak Signet

Source: Vendor, Ice Tooth Cave

Cost	–	Casting Time	–
Duration	8–20	Recast Time	20

For 8–20 seconds, you have +10–20 armor and cannot be knocked down, but your movement is slowed by 75%.

Dwarven Battle Stance (elite)

Source: Marika Granitehand (Summit Dwarf Boss)

Cost	10E	Casting Time	–
Duration	3–9	Recast Time	30

For 3–9 seconds, if they hit, your hammer attacks interrupt your target. Dwarven Battle Stance ends if you use a skill.

Endure Pain

Source: Quest, Ruins of Ascalon/Vendor, Yak's Bend

Cost	5E	Casting Time	–
Duration	7–13	Recast Time	30

For 7–13 seconds you have an additional 90–300 Health.

Flourish (elite)

Source: Syr Honorcrest (Tengu Boss)

Cost	5E	Casting Time	1
Duration	–	Recast Time	10

All of your attack skills become recharged. You gain 1–7 Energy for each skill recharged by Flourish.

Griffon's Sweep

Source: Quest, Kryta/Vendor, Henge of Denravi

Cost	5E	Casting Time	–
Duration	–	Recast Time	5

If this attack hits, you strike for +1–10 damage. If this attack is evaded, your target is knocked down and suffers 10–34 damage.

Power Attack

Source: Quest, Ruins of Ascalon/Vendor, Yak's Bend

Cost	5E	Casting Time	–
Duration	–	Recast Time	4

If this attack hits, you strike for +10–30 damage.

Protector's Strike

Source: Quest, Shiverpeaks (N)/Vendor, Lion's Arch

Cost	5E	Casting Time	–
Duration	–	Recast Time	2

If this attack strikes a moving foe, you strike for 5–30 more damage.

Rush

Source: Vendor, Copperhammer Mines

Cost	3A	Casting Time	–
Duration	8–20	Recast Time	–

For 8–20 seconds, you move 25% faster.

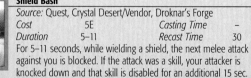

Shield Bash

Source: Quest, Crystal Desert/Vendor, Droknar's Forge

Cost	5E	Casting Time	–
Duration	5–11	Recast Time	30

For 5–11 seconds, while wielding a shield, the next melee attack against you is blocked. If the attack was a skill, your attacker is knocked down and that skill is disabled for an additional 15 sec.

Sprint

Source: Quest, Ruins of Ascalon/Vendor, Yak's Bend

Cost	5E	Casting Time	–
Duration	8–14	Recast Time	20

For 8–14 seconds, you move 25% faster.

Warrior's Cunning

Source: Vendor, Marhan's Grotto

Cost	10E	Casting Time	–
Duration	5–11	Recast Time	60

For 5–11 sec, your melee attacks cannot be blocked or evaded.

Warrior's Endurance (elite)

Source: Custodians Dellus, Fidius, Hulgar (Forgotten Enchanted Bosses)

Cost	5E	Casting Time	–
Duration	5–23	Recast Time	30

For 5–23 seconds, you gain 3 Energy each time you hit with a melee attack. Warrior's Endurance cannot raise your Energy above 5–17.

(No Attribute)

"For great justice!"

Source: Quest, Ruins of Ascalon/Vendor, Yak's Bend

Cost	10E	Casting Time	–
Duration	20	Recast Time	45

For 15 seconds, your adrenaline skills charge twice as fast.

Counter Blow

Source: Quest, Kryta/Vendor, Henge of Denravi

Cost	4A	Casting Time	–
Duration	2	Recast Time	–

If this attack hits an attacking foe, that foe is knocked down.

Disrupting Chop

Source: Vendor, Grendich Courthouse

Cost	6A	Casting Time	–
Duration	–	Recast Time	–

If it hits, this attack interrupts the target's current action. If that action was a skill, that skill is disabled for an additional 20 seconds.

Distracting Blow

Source: Vendor, Ice Tooth Cave

Cost	5E	Casting Time	0.5
Duration	–	Recast Time	10

Swipe your weapon at the target, dealing no damage but disrupting the target's current action (and the actions of foes adjacent to your target).

Flurry

Source: Quest, Shiverpeaks (N)/Vendor, Lion's Arch

Cost	5E	Casting Time	–
Duration	5	Recast Time	5

For 5 seconds, your attack rate is increased, but you deal less damage.

Frenzy

Source: Quest, Kingdom of Ascalon/Vendor, Ascalon City (Ruins)

Cost	5E	Casting Time	–
Duration	8	Recast Time	4

For 8 seconds, you attack 33% faster but take double damage.

Hundred Blades (elite)

Source: Gorgaan Hatemonger, Lumps Ruinator, Spar the Ravager (Charr Bosses), Bonetti (Human Boss), Prince Rurik (Zombie Boss)

Cost	5E	Casting Time	–
Duration	–	Recast Time	8

Swing twice at target foe and foes adjacent to your target.

Skull Crack (elite)

Source: Hail Blackice (Ice Elemental Boss), Thorgrim Beastlasher (Giant Boss)

Cost	10A	Casting Time	–
Duration	–	Recast Time	–

If this attack hits while target foe is casting a spell, that foe is Dazed for 15 seconds.

Wild Blow

Source: Quest, Ruins of Ascalon/Vendor, Yak's Bend

Cost	5E	Casting Time	–
Duration	–	Recast Time	5

Lose all adrenaline. If it hits, this attack will be a critical hit. If blocked or evaded, any Stance being used by your target ends.

Axe Mastery

Axe Rake

Source: Quest, Kryta-The Wilds/Vendor, Amnoon Oasis

Cost	6A	Casting Time	–
Duration	–	Recast Time	–

If this attack hits a foe suffering from a Deep Wound, you strike for +1–10 damage, and that foe becomes Crippled.

Axe Twist

Source: Quest, Kryta/Vendor, Henge of Denravi

Cost	8A	Casting Time	–
Duration	–	Recast Time	–

If this attack hits a foe suffering from a Deep Wound, you strike for 1–20 more damage and that foe suffers from Weakness.

Cleave (elite)

Source: Gornar Bellybreaker (Summit Dwarf Boss)

Cost	3A	Casting Time	–
Duration	–	Recast Time	–

If this attack hits, you strike for +10–30 damage.

Cyclone Axe

Source: Quest, Kingdom of Ascalon/Vendor, Ascalon City (Ruins)

Cost	5E	Casting Time	–
Duration	–	Recast Time	4

Perform a spinning axe attack striking for +4–12 damage to all adjacent opponents.

Dismember

Source: Quest, Ruins of Ascalon/Vendor, Yak's Bend

Cost	6A	Casting Time	–
Duration	–	Recast Time	–

If it hits, this axe blow will inflict a Deep Wound on the target foe, lowering that foe's maximum Health by 20% for 5–20 seconds.

Eviscerate (elite)

Source: Tortitudo Probo (Titan Boss)

Cost	6A	Casting Time	–
Duration	–	Recast Time	–

If Eviscerate hits, you strike +1–30 damage and inflict a Deep Wound, lowering your target's maximum Health by 20% for 5–20 seconds.

Executioner's Strike

Source: Quest, Kingdom of Ascalon/Vendor, Ascalon City (Ruins)

Cost	8A	Casting Time	–
Duration	–	Recast Time	–

If this attack hits, you strike +10–40 damage.

Penetrating Blow

Source: Quest, Ruins of Ascalon/Vendor, Yak's Bend

Cost	5A	Casting Time	–
Duration	–	Recast Time	–

This axe attack has 50% armor penetration.

Swift Chop

Source: Quest, Shiverpeaks (N)/Vendor, Lion's Arch

Cost	5E	Casting Time	–
Duration	–	Recast Time	4

If this attack hits, you strike +1–20 damage. If Swift Chop is blocked, your target suffers a Deep Wound and takes an additional 1–20 damage. Swift Chop cannot be evaded.

Hammer Mastery

Backbreaker (elite)

Source: Ferk Mallet (Ettin Boss)

Cost	10A	Casting Time	–
Duration	4	Recast Time	–

If Backbreaker hits, you strike +1–20 damage and your target is knocked down for 4 seconds.

Belly Smash

Source: Vendor, Beetletun

Cost	5E	Casting Time	–
Duration	–	Recast Time	30

If this attack strikes a foe who is on the ground, the resulting dust cloud will blind nearby foes 3–10 seconds.

Crude Swing

Source: Vendor, Marhan's Grotto

Cost	5E	Casting Time	–
Duration	–	Recast Time	5

Attack all adjacent foes. Each foe you hit is struck +1–10 damage. This action is easily interrupted.

Crushing Blow

Source: Quest, Kryta-The Wilds/Vendor, Amnoon Oasis

Cost	5E	Casting Time	–
Duration	–	Recast Time	10

If this attack hits, you strike +1–20 damage. If you hit a knocked-down foe you inflict a Deep Wound, lowering your target's maximum Health by 20% for 5–20 seconds.

Devastating Hammer (elite)

Source: Perfected Armor (Mursaat Boss)

Cost	6A	Casting Time	–
Duration	–	Recast Time	–

If Devastating Hammer hits, your target is knocked down and suffers from Weakness for 5–20 seconds.

Earth Shaker (elite)

Source: Kor Stonewrath (Giant Boss)

Cost	10A	Casting Time	–
Duration	2	Recast Time	–

All adjacent foes are knocked down. (50% failure chance with Hammer Mastery 4 or less.)

Hammer Bash

Source: Quest, Kingdom of Ascalon/Vendor, Ascalon City (Ruins)

Cost	5A	Casting Time	–
Duration	2	Recast Time	–

Lose all adrenaline. If Hammer Bash hits, target is knocked down.

Heavy Blow

Source: Vendor, Maguuma Stade

Cost	5A	Casting Time	–
Duration	–	Recast Time	–

Lose all adrenaline. If this attack hits a foe suffering from Weakness, that foe is knocked down and you strike +1–30 damage.

Irresistible Blow

Source: Quest, Shiverpeaks (N)/Vendor, Lion's Arch

Cost	5E	Casting Time	–
Duration	–	Recast Time	4

If Irresistible Blow is blocked, your target is knocked down and takes 1–30 damage. Irresistible Blow cannot be blocked or evaded.

Mighty Blow

Source: Quest, Ruins of Ascalon/Vendor, Yak's Bend

Cost	6A	Casting Time	–
Duration	–	Recast Time	–

If this attack hits, you strike +1–30 damage.

Staggering Blow

Source: Quest, Kryta/Vendor, Henge of Denravi

Cost	5A	Casting Time	–
Duration	–	Recast Time	–

If this hammer blow hits, your target will suffer from Weakness for 5–15 seconds.

Swordsmanship

Final Thrust
Source: Quest, Kryta/Vendor, Henge of Denravi

Cost	10A	Casting Time	–
Duration	–	Recast Time	–

Lose all adrenaline. If Final Thrust hits, you deal 1–40 more damage. This damage is doubled if your target was below 50% Health. This skill requires adrenaline.

Galrath Slash
Source: Vendor, Beetletun

Cost	8A	Casting Time	–
Duration	–	Recast Time	–

This attack strikes +1–40 damage if it hits.

Gash
Source: Quest, Kingdom of Ascalon/Vendor, Ascalon City (Ruins)

Cost	6A	Casting Time	–
Duration	–	Recast Time	–

If this attack hits a Bleeding foe, you strike 5–10 more damage and that foe suffers a Deep Wound, lowering that foe's maximum Health by 20% for 5–20 seconds.

Hamstring
Source: Quest, Ruins of Ascalon/Vendor, Yak's Bend

Cost	10E	Casting Time	–
Duration	–	Recast Time	15

If this attack hits, your target is Crippled for 3–15 seconds, slowing his movement.

Pure Strike
Source: Quest, Kryta-The Wilds/Vendor, Amnoon Oasis

Cost	5E	Casting Time	–
Duration	–	Recast Time	8

If Pure Strike hits, you strike +1–30 damage. If you are not using a Stance, Pure Strike cannot be blocked or evaded.

Savage Slash
Source: Quest, Kryta-The Wilds/Vendor, Droknar's Forge

Cost	5E	Casting Time	–
Duration	–	Recast Time	10

If this attack hits, it interrupts the target foe's action. If that action was a spell, you deal 1–40 extra damage.

Seeking Blade
Source: Quest, Shiverpeaks (N)/Vendor, Lion's Arch

Cost	5E	Casting Time	–
Duration	–	Recast Time	4

If this attack hits you strike +1–20 damage. If Seeking Blade is evaded, your target begins Bleeding and takes 1–20 damage. Seeking Blade cannot be blocked.

Sever Artery
Source: Quest, Kingdom of Ascalon/Vendor, Ascalon City (Ruins)

Cost	4A	Casting Time	–
Duration	–	Recast Time	–

If this attack hits, the opponent begins Bleeding for 5–25 seconds, losing Health over time.

Tactics

"Charge!" (elite)
Source: Balthazaar's Cursed (Golem Boss)

Cost	5E	Casting Time	–
Duration	5–11	Recast Time	20

For 5–11 seconds, all allies in the area move 25% faster.

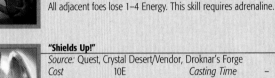
"Fear me!"
Source: Quest, Crystal Desert/Vendor, Droknar's Forge

Cost	3A	Casting Time	–
Duration	–	Recast Time	–

All adjacent foes lose 1–4 Energy. This skill requires adrenaline.

"Shields Up!"
Source: Quest, Crystal Desert/Vendor, Droknar's Forge

Cost	10E	Casting Time	–
Duration	8–20	Recast Time	30

For 8–20 seconds, you and nearby allies gain 50 armor against piercing damage and 10–40% chance to block incoming projectile attacks.

"To the Limit!"
Source: Quest, Kryta-The Wilds/Vendor, Droknar's Forge

Cost	5E	Casting Time	–
Duration	–	Recast Time	20

For each adjacent foe (maximum 1–6), you gain one strike of adrenaline.

"Victory is Mine!" (elite)
Source: Sakalo Yawpyawl (Grawl Boss)

Cost	5E	Casting Time	–
Duration	–	Recast Time	15

You gain 10–68 Health and 5 Energy for each Condition suffered by adjacent foes.

"Watch yourself!"
Source: Quest, Ruins of Ascalon/Vendor, Yak's Bend

Cost	3A	Casting Time	–
Duration	5–11	Recast Time	–

Party members near you gain +20 armor for 5–11 seconds.

Balanced Stance
Source: Quest, Kryta-The Wilds/Vendor, Droknar's Forge

Cost	5E	Casting Time	–
Duration	8–20	Recast Time	30

For 8–20 seconds, you cannot be knocked down and you do not suffer extra damage from a critical attack.

Bonetti's Defense
Source: Quest, Shiverpeaks (N)/Vendor, Lion's Arch

Cost	8A	Casting Time	–
Duration	5–11	Recast Time	–

For 5–11 seconds, you have a 75% chance to block incoming melee attacks and arrows. You gain 5 Energy for each successful melee attack blocked. Bonetti's Defense ends if you use a skill.

Deadly Riposte

Source: Vendor, Fishermen's Haven

Cost	5E	Casting Time	–
Duration	8	Recast Time	10

For 8 seconds, while you have a sword equipped, you block the next attack against you, and your attacker takes 1–30 damage and begins Bleeding for 3–25 seconds.

Defensive Stance

Source: Quest, Crystal Desert/Vendor, Droknar's Forge

Cost	5E	Casting Time	–
Duration	5–11	Recast Time	45

For 10 seconds, you have a 75% chance to evade melee attacks and arrows. Defensive Stance ends if you use a skill.

Deflect Arrows

Source: Vendor, Port Sledge

Cost	5E	Casting Time	–
Duration	8–20	Recast Time	30

For 8–20 seconds, you have a 75% chance to block arrows. This effect ends if you attack.

Desperation Blow

Source: Vendor, North Kryta Province

Cost	5E	Casting Time	–
Duration	2	Recast Time	7

If this attack hits, you strike +10–40 damage, and your target either suffers a Deep Wound, begins Bleeding, or becomes Crippled. After making a Desperation Blow, you fall down.

Disciplined Stance

Source: Vendor, Maguuma Stade

Cost	10E	Casting Time	–
Duration	5–11	Recast Time	60

For 5–11 seconds, you gain +24 armor and have a 75% chance to block attacks. Disciplined Stance ends if you use an adrenal skill.

Gladiator's Defense (elite)

Source: Resso Biiss (Forgotten Boss)

Cost	5E	Casting Time	–
Duration	5–11	Recast Time	30

For 5–11 seconds, you have a 75% chance to block incoming attacks. Whenever you block a melee attack this way, the attacker suffers 5–35 damage.

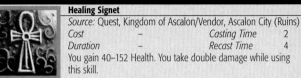

Healing Signet

Source: Quest, Kingdom of Ascalon/Vendor, Ascalon City (Ruins)

Cost	–	Casting Time	2
Duration	–	Recast Time	4

You gain 40–152 Health. You take double damage while using this skill.

Riposte

Source: Vendor, Copperhammer Mines

Cost	3A	Casting Time	–
Duration	8	Recast Time	–

For 8 seconds, while you have a sword equipped, you block the next attack against you, and your attacker takes 1–40 damage.

Shield Stance

Source: Quest, Kryta-The Wilds/Vendor, Amnoon Oasis

Cost	5E	Casting Time	–
Duration	8–20	Recast Time	60

For 8–20 seconds, while wielding a shield, you have a 75% chance to block incoming attacks, but you move 33% slower.

Thrill of Victory

Source: Vendor, Fishermen's Haven

Cost	5E	Casting Time	–
Duration	–	Recast Time	10

If this blow hits, and you have more Health than target foe you strike +10–40 damage.

Wary Stance

Source: Vendor, Grendich Courthouse

Cost	10E	Casting Time	–
Duration	5–11	Recast Time	60

For 5–11 seconds, you block any attack skills used against you. For each successful block, you gain adrenaline and 5 Energy. Wary Stance ends if you use a skill.

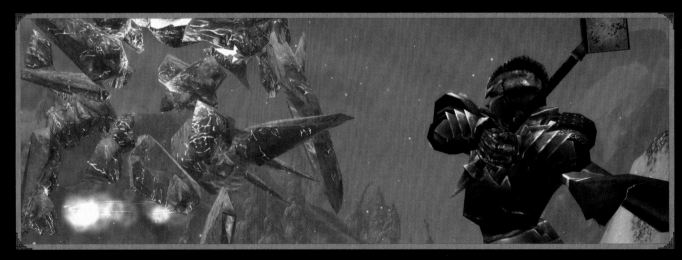

Kingdom of Ascalon

By Andrea Silva

Pre-Searing

Roleplaying characters have the enjoyment of exploring Ascalon City and the surrounding countryside prior to the Charr invasion that destroys the kingdom. Once you've created your character, you'll find yourself standing near Sir Tydus in Ascalon City. Speak with Sir Tydus to begin preparation for your career as a new recruit in Ascalon's army.

> ### ✂ TIP ✂
> *Speak with a Town Crier before talking to Sir Tydus when you enter the game to receive the quest "Message from a Friend." If you do, you'll score a bonus 100 EXP and 10 gold when you talk to Tydus! If you talk to Sir Tydus first, this quest won't be available.*

Leave Ascalon City through the portal to Lakeside County and you'll see your initial class trainer for your primary profession. Depending on your chosen profession, you'll encounter:

- Howland the Elementalist
- Sebedoh the Mesmer
- Ciglo the Monk
- Verata the Necromancer
- Artemis the Ranger
- Van the Warrior

Speak with your trainer to get started on a quest to unlock new skills!

After completing your initial training quest, you'll be directed to speak with Haversdan, who will point you toward your next profession trainer. It's a good idea to speak with and complete the tasks appointed to you by your profession trainers in order to unlock additional skills.

With the initial quests out of the way, it's time to consider a secondary profession. If you already know which secondary profession you want to select, go straight to that profession's trainer and complete his initial task. Once you complete the task given to you by the trainer, you'll be given an opportunity to accept or decline further training in that profession. If you accept, your character immediately gains access to that profession's starting skills. If you're undecided, you can decline the profession (even after completing the quest) and seek out another trainer instead. You can even come back at a future time to accept the profession. For the truly undecided in this manner, you can speak with each profession trainer and try out all of your options before deciding on which profession to take as your secondary. It is a good way to discover which profession's skills will best mesh with your primary choice and your play style. Once you've picked a secondary profession, seek out the other trainers in both your primary and secondary professions, and undertake their missions so that you can unlock the skills they give as a reward.

> ### ✂ TIP ✂
> *Rangers (primary or secondary) who want a pet should complete "The Ranger's Companion" quest and keep Charm Animal on their Skill Bar so their pet can level up with them as they explore and fight in the Kingdom of Ascalon.*

The Kingdom of Ascalon includes the following explorable areas and outposts: Ascalon City, Lakeside County (and Ashford Abbey), the Catacombs, Green Hills County (and Barradin Estate), Regent Valley (and Fort Ranik and King's Watch), and Wizard's Folly (and Foible's Fair).

Profession Trainers

ELEMENTALIST	Howland the Elementalist
	Elementalist Aziure
	Ralena Stormbringer
MESMER	Sebedoh the Mesmer
	Lady Althea
	Vassar
MONK	Ciglo the Monk
	Brother Mhenlo
	Grazden the Protector
NECROMANCER	Verata the Necromancer
	Necromancer Munne
	Kasha Blackblood
	Oberan the Reviled
RANGER	Artemis the Ranger
	Master Ranger Nente
	Ivor Trueshot
	Aidan
WARRIOR	Aidan Van the Warrior
	Warmaster Grast
	Duke Barradin
	Little Thom

> ### ✂ TIP ✂
> *Farmer Dirk in Ashford will start complaining that his prize-winning hogs have escaped. Round up all five of the aggravating porkers by running behind them to shoo them into their pen for a reward of 25 EXP!*

GUILD WARS
PRIMA OFFICIAL GAME GUIDE

> ### ❧ TIP ❧
>
> *Gwen is exceptionally perky (which can be a little annoying to anyone who doesn't do perky well), but if you allow her to follow you, she'll offer assistance during battles in the form of an occasional 20-point heal. Be sure to listen to her cues as to what she's interested in and thinking about. For starters, Gwen's flute is broken. She'd love to have a shiny new one, and you can purchase one from a merchant for 4 gold. (In fact, that's the flute she uses to heal you. No new flute, no heals.) If you're doing well for funds, you might also want to purchase the small red cape for 200 gold. Gwen loves to skip around in a pretty red cape and owning one makes her really happy! The last thing that Gwen enjoys—what is sure to make you Gwen's favorite person—is a Red Iris Flower. Or two. Or a dozen or more. You'll find these scattered about as you explore, so pick them up and give them to Gwen. (That's assuming you don't mind passing up the merchant's offer for them; he must be sweet on someone.) Eventually, she might decide to give you something in return as well!*

Collectors

If you're receiving oddball loot from your adventures in explorable areas, chances are there's a collector out there who might trade useful items for a few of those objects. After the Searing, other survivors have also started looking to trade items they can no longer use to those who are fighting the Charr.

In Lakeside County, one of the first collectors you'll likely encounter is Collector Brownlow, who stands next to the resurrection shrine right outside the gate from Ascalon City. If you bring him five skale fins, he'll give you a belt pouch that adds five spaces to your inventory. As the skale fins drop

off of the various types of river skale all along the river, you can quickly accumulate the five skale fins you need. If you run out of river skale to hunt before you accumulate five skale fins, just pop back into Ascalon City and back out again (resetting all of the Lakeside monsters) and resume your hunting. Collector Humphreys in Ashford also gives out belt pouches, but you need to kill bandits to collect them. As the bandits are more challenging than the river skale, and you can only wear one belt pouch at a time, completing the collection for Collector Humphreys is not necessary unless you wish to sell the extra belt pouch(es) for coin.

The four armor upgrades that each profession can get from collectors in the Kingdom of Ascalon are also worth spending the time to acquire. Check the maps for the locations of these collectors.

The other items from Kingdom of Ascalon collectors tend to be of more questionable worth (but collectors change what they offer from time to time, so check out the current selection every once in a while). The different

staves, wands, swords, axes, and hammers from collectors in the kingdom are all equivalent to starting gear, so those usually aren't worth picking up unless you haven't gotten a better item as loot and want to change your damage type. All of the artifacts, chakrams, idols, scrolls, and other off-hand items in the Kingdom of Ascalon generally give +3 Energy, so once you have one it's not really worth getting more.

Once the Searing has taken place, you can get decent armor, weapon, and gear upgrades from different collectors.

Collectors

PROFESSION	CHEST	HANDS	LEGS	FEET
ELEMENTALIST	Vaughn Smoldering Hearts Regent Valley	Mindle Enchanted Lodestones Wizard's Folly	Savich Icy Lodestones Wizard's Folly	Rownan Dull Carapaces Regent Valley
MESMER	Savich Icy Lodestones Wizard's Folly	— — —	Varis Spider Legs Regent Valley, Ft. Ranik	Jacobs Baked Husks Lakeside County
MONK	Walden Unnatural Seeds Ashford Village	Mindle Enchanted Lodestones Wizard's Folly	Rownan Dull Carapaces Regent Valley	Savich Icy Lodestones Wizard's Folly
NECROMANCER	Findley Colossal Jawbones Regent Valley	Gwynn Skeletal Limbs Catacombs	Varis Spider Legs Ft. Ranik	Hatcher Wardens Trophies Regent Valley
RANGER	Walden/Kaylee Unnatural Seeds/Grawl Necklaces Ashford Village	Walden Unnatural Seeds Ashford Village	Gwynn Skeletal Limbs Catacombs	Jacobs Baked Husks Lakeside County
WARRIOR	Kaylee Grawl Necklaces Lakeside County	Jacobs Baked Husks Lakeside County	Rownan Dull Carapaces Regent Valley	Rownan Dull Carapaces Regent Valley

Kingdom of Ascalon

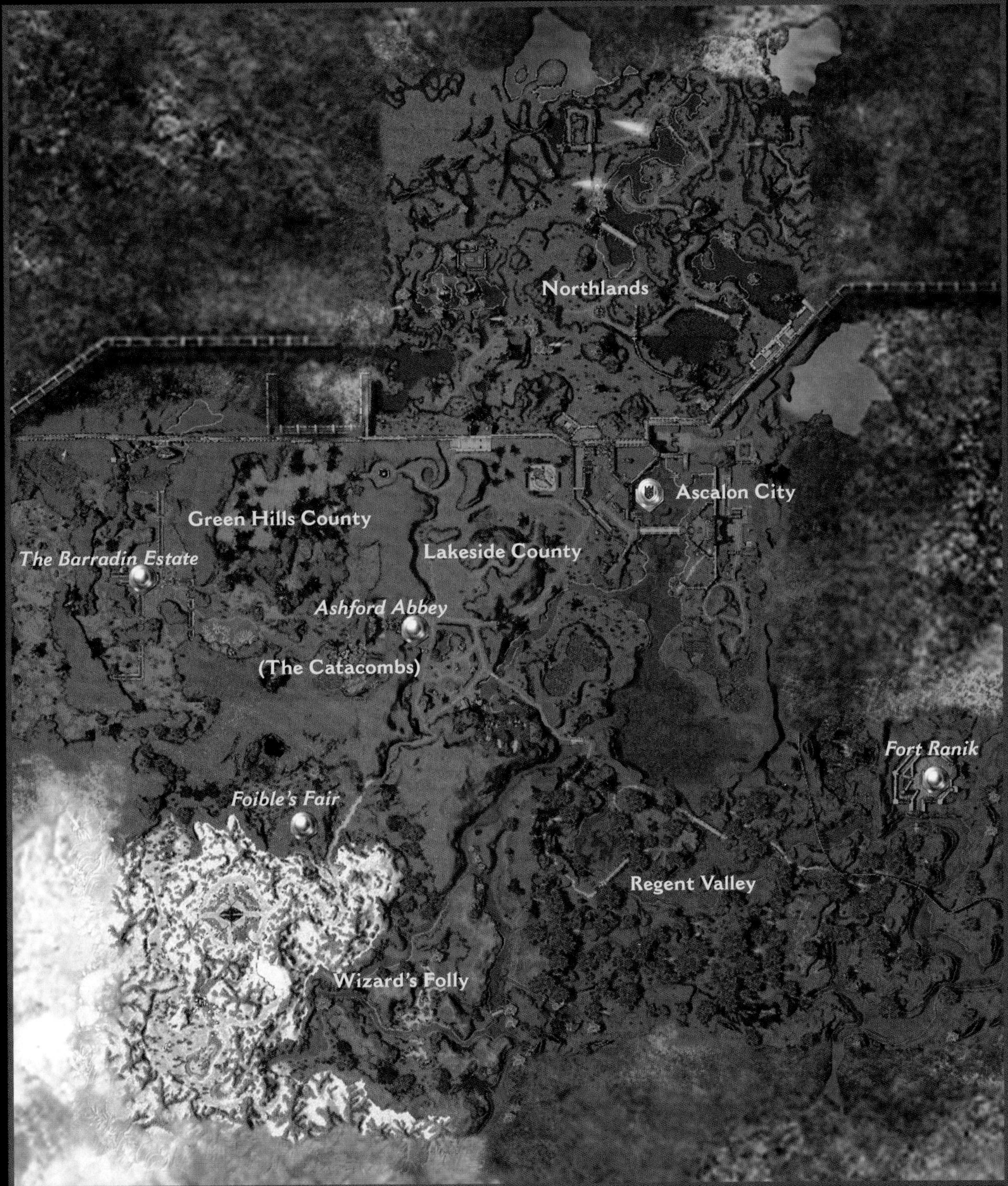

Northlands

Ascalon City

Green Hills County

The Barradin Estate

Lakeside County

Ashford Abbey

(The Catacombs)

Fort Ranik

Foible's Fair

Regent Valley

Wizard's Folly

> ASCALON CITY: The largest city in the kingdom, Ascalon City is known for its beautiful architecture, numerous libraries, and bountiful shops. Because it is where many noble families make their homes, it tends to receive a large number of visitors and has become the cultural center of Ascalon.

KINGDOM OF ASCALON -
Ascalon City

3 1 W
7 6
2 4
8
5

M
9
Lakeside
County

Ascalon
Academy

(Academy
accessed
via quest)

3 4
2
5
1
2
2
2
2
2

=>> DANSSE <<=
DWARVEN CARTOGRAPHER

Ascalon City

1 Crafter (2)
2 Baron Egan (2)
3 Cynn (5)
4 Guild Registrar (2)
5 King Adelbern (10)
6 Namar (1)
7 Prince Rurik (10)
8 Sandre Elek (1)
9 Sir Tydus (2)
M Merchant (2)
W Weaponsmith (2)

Ascalon Academy

1 Corporal Timlin (2)
2 Academy Monk (5)
3 Corporal Timlin (2)
4 Drill Sergeant Mahoney (2)
5 Lieutenant Fisk (2)

1 Vatlaaw Doomtooth
   (Boss R; 2)
2 Grawl (1)
   Grawl (4)
   Grawl Longspear (3)
   Grawl Shaman (2)

Quests to Get Started

More quests are listed later in this section; these are the four that make the rest of them available.

Message from a Friend

• Speak with the Town Crier in Ascalon City.

• Go to the town square in Ascalon City and speak with Sir Tydus.

Reward: 100 EXP, 10 gold

War Preparations

• Speak with Sir Tydus.

• Go out the gate to Lakeside County to find a trainer.

• Talk to your trainer to learn basic skills by completing a test.

• Return to Sir Tydus for your reward.

Reward: 250 EXP

A Second Profession

• Speak to Armin Saberlin, Ascalon City.

• Ask Armin Saberlin for directions to the profession trainer of your choice.

• Speak with the trainer for your chosen secondary profession and complete that trainer's initial task. Accept the new profession once the task is complete.

• Return to Armin Saberlin in Ascalon City to receive your reward.

Reward: 250 EXP

Further Adventures

- Speak to Haversdan by the Ascalon City gate in Lakeside County.
- Follow the road from Ascalon to the southwest and speak to Devona in Ashford.

Reward: 250 EXP

Gwen's Flute

Strictly speaking, this isn't a preparation quest. However, once you've found the broken flute and replaced it with a new one, you have a constant companion whenever you want her, who is good for healing you when you need it.

- Speak to Gwen as she runs up to you in Lakeside County when you leave Ascalon City the first time.
- Find her broken flute on the other side of the river.
- Return the flute to Gwen for your reward.

Reward: 250 EXP

Leaving the Kingdom of Ascalon Behind

When you're ready to formally enter the Ascalon Academy (you must be at least Level 3), complete The Path to Glory quest (talk to any Ascalon Guard and then to Sir Tydus). Once you've done that, talk to Sir Tydus one more time and accept his offer to enter the Ascalon Academy. Any incomplete quests will be purged from your quest log after accepting Sir Tydus's offer to enter the Academy. Upon entering the Academy, you'll be teamed up with another random player and a few henchmen for a quick PvP battle with another team of Academy recruits. There isn't much time to prepare before the battle starts, and the fighting is fast and furious for those not used to PvP play. But don't worry—if you die, you'll be resurrected almost immediately. Once the battle is over, Prince Rurik will follow you to an old bunker that has become occupied by some Grawl and a nasty Charr by the name of Vatlaaw Doomtooth, all of whom you must defeat. Completing this task will start a cinematic sequence.

If there aren't enough players to form the teams for the PvP battle, you skip this section and head directly to the bunker to kill Vatlaaw and the Grawl.

Ascalon City and the outlying areas as you've known them are destroyed. When you enter the game again, you stand amidst the Ruins of Ascalon. The greater war to reclaim a kingdom has just begun.

Once you reach Level 3, every Ascalon Guard you see will sprout a green exclamation point. However, they all have the same single message—an invitation to join the army. You don't need to stop and talk to any of them unless you're ready to sign up.

- KINGDOM OF ASCALON -
Lakeside County

1	Collector Brownlow (Collector)
2	Collector Humphreys (Collector)
3	Collector Jacobs (Collector)
4	Collector Kaylee (Collector)
5	Collector Walden (Collector)
6	Alison the Tanner (1)
7	Annette Landru (1)
8	Captain Osric (20)
9	Chantalle the Troubadour (1)
10	Ciglo the Monk (2)
11	Devona (5)
12	Fadden Hathorn (1)
13	Farmer Dirk (1)
14	Farrah Cappo (2)
15	Gate Guard Torin (2)
16	Gwen (1)
17	Harner (2)
18	Haversdan (2)
19	Howland the Elementalist (2)
20	Lina the Healer (5)
21	Miller Upton (1)
22	Odette (2)
23	Old Mack (1)
24	Pitney (1)
25	Reginald (2)
26	Sarah (1)
27	Sebedoh the Mesmer (2)
28	Van the Warrior (2)
29	Verata the Necromancer (2)
30	Warmaster Riga (20)
31	Lady Althea (Trainer Ms; 5)
32	Warmaster Grast (Trainer W; 5)
33	Prize-Winning Hog (1)
34	Rabbit (1)
35	Rogue Bull (5)
36	Strider (Pet; 1)
37	Swarm of Bees (0)
38	Wolf (Pet; 2)
39	Brother Mhenlo (Trainer Mk; 5)
M	Merchant (2)

1	Bandit Blood Sworn (3)	
	Bandit Firestarter (1)	
	Bandit Raider (2)	
2	Charr Mind Spark (5)	
	Vatlaaw Doomtooth (Boss R; 2)	
3	Carrion Devourer (1)	
	Diseased Devourer (0)	
	Lash Devourer (1)	
	Plague Devourer (2)	
4	River Drake (5)	
5	Haunting Spectre (0)	
6	Grawl (1)	
	Grawl Longspear (3)	
7	Alain (3)	
8	Aloe Seed (0)	
9	River Skale (1)	
	River Skale Brood (4)	
	River Skale Queen (0)	
	River Skale Tad (0)	
	Skale Broodcaller (2)	
10	Skeleton Raider (1)	
11	Plague Worm (0)	
	Worm (0)	

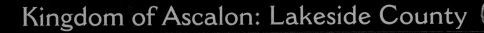

Profession-Specific Quests

All of these quests start in Lakeside County unless otherwise indicated.

Elementalist Quests

Elementalist Test

- Speak to Howland the Elementalist by the Ascalon City gate in Lakeside County.
- Kill skale to the southwest along the road to Ashford. Acquire a Shimmering Scale.
- Return to Howland the Elementalist for your reward.

Reward: 500 EXP

Skill Unlock: Aura of Restoration, Flare

A New Elementalist Trainer

Wizard's Folly

- Speak to Haversdan by the Ascalon City gate in Lakeside County.
- Follow the road southwest from town and continue past Ashford to find Wizard's Folly. Continue through Wizard's Folly to the tower. Speak to Elementalist Aziure.

Reward: 250 EXP

The Elementalist Experiment

Wizard's Folly

- Speak to Elementalist Aziure near the tower in Wizard's Folly.
- Use your Fire Storm spell to defeat the waves of ice beasts that attack Aziure.
- Talk to Elementalist Aziure for your reward.

Reward: 250 EXP

Skill Unlock: Fire Storm, Glyph of Lesser Energy

The Supremacy of Air

Wizard's Folly

- Speak to Ralena Stormbringer in Foible's Fair.
- Follow the road up to the wizard tower. Destroy the tower golem.
- See Elementalist Aziure near the tower in Wizard's Folly for your reward.

Reward: 250 EXP

Skill Unlock: Blinding Flash, Lightning Javelin

Mesmer Quests

Mesmer Test

- Speak to Sebedoh the Mesmer by the Ascalon City gate in Lakeside County.
- Follow the road southwest until you find skale. Clear the road of skale.
- Return to Sebedoh the Mesmer for your reward.

Reward: 500 EXP

Skill Unlock: Empathy, Ether Feast

A New Mesmer Trainer

- Speak to Haversdan by the Ascalon City gate in Lakeside County.
- Follow the road northwest from town. Talk to Lady Althea at the Actor's Stage.

Reward: 250 EXP

A Mesmer's Burden

- Speak to Lady Althea in Lakeside County at the Actor's Stage.
- Kill the rogue bull near the watering hole that is threatening Althea's theatre.
- Return to Lady Althea for your reward.

Reward: 250 EXP, Starter Cane

Skill Unlock: Conjure Phantasm, Ether Feast, Imagined Burden

Domination Magic

Wizard's Folly

- Speak to Vassar in Foible's Fair.
- Head east from Foible's Fair to the woods. Destroy the Skale Brood.
- Return to Vassar in Foible's Fair for your reward.

Reward: 250 EXP

Skill Unlock: Backfire, Shattered Delusions

Monk Quests

Monk Test

- Speak to Ciglo the Monk by the Ascalon City gate in Lakeside County.
- Follow the road until you find skale. Cross the river and find the missing girl, Gwen.
- Lead Gwen back to Ciglo the Monk. Gwen will not follow you until the skale are out of the way.
- Speak with Ciglo again to claim your reward.

Reward: 500 EXP

Skill Unlock: Healing Breeze, Banish

A New Monk Trainer

- Speak to Haversdan by the Ascalon City gate in Lakeside County.
- Follow the road southwest toward Ashford Abbey. Enter Ashford Abbey and talk to Brother Mhenlo.

Reward: 250 EXP

A Monk's Mission

Catacombs

- Speak to Brother Mhenlo in Ashford Abbey.
- Meet Paulus inside the Catacombs and follow him as he retrieves the relic. Keep Paulus alive by using your healing skill.
- Talk to Brother Mhenlo in Ashford Abbey to receive your reward.

Reward: 250 EXP, Starter Holy Rod

Skill Unlock: Bane Signet, Orison of Healing

The Blessings of Balthazar

- Speak to Brother Mhenlo in Ashford Abbey.
- Travel to the fields North of Ashford and dispatch the skeletons there.
- Talk to Brother Mhenlo in Ashford Abbey to receive your reward.

Reward: 250 EXP

Skill Unlock: Retribution, Symbol of Wrath

Protection Prayers

Green Hills and Lakeside Counties

- Speak to Grazden the Protector in Green Hills County.
- Meet Farrah Cappo, Lakeside Cnty.
- Keep Farrah alive while she hunts down the infamous Alain.
- Return to Grazden the Protector in Green Hills County for reward.

Reward: 250 EXP

Skill Unlock: Reversal of Fortune, Shielding Hands

Necromancer Quests

Necromancer Test

- Speak to Verata the Necromancer by the Ascalon City gate in Lakeside County.
- Go south of the river and kill a skale so Verata can animate a bone horror.
- Speak with Verata the Necromancer to receive your reward.

Reward: 500 EXP

Skill Unlock: Deathly Swarm, Vampiric Gaze

A New Necromancer Trainer

Catacombs

- Speak to Haversdan by the Ascalon City gate in Lakeside County.

- Follow the road southwest from town. Enter Ashford Abbey and proceed to the Catacombs. Talk to Necromancer Munne to receive further training tasks.

Reward: 250 EXP

The Necromancer's Novice

Catacombs

- Speak to Necromancer Munne in the Catacombs.
- Follow Necromancer Munne to the trial area. Use bone horrors to get

past the fire traps. The traps will glow green when they've been deactivated.
- Return to Necromancer Munne for your reward.

Reward: 250 EXP

Skill Unlock: Animate Bone Horror, Life Siphon

Rites of Remembrance

Catacombs

- Speak to Necromancer Munne in the Catacombs.
- Light the Votive Candles in all four Remembrance Braziers in the Catacombs to appease the angry spirits.
- Return to Necromancer Munne for your reward.

Reward: 250 EXP

The Power of Blood

Catacombs

- Speak to Kasha Blackblood in Green Hills County.
- Enter the Catacombs and destroy the four Blood Fanatics.
- Return to Kasha Blackblood in Green Hills County for your reward.

Reward: 250 EXP

Skill Unlock: Blood Renewal, Vampiric Touch

The Accursed Path

Catacombs

- Speak to Oberan the Reviled in the Catacombs.
  - Clear the Crypt Fiends from the tunnel north of Oberan.
    - Return to Oberan the Reviled for your reward.

Reward: 500 EXP

Skill Unlock: Faintheartedness, Soul Barbs

Ranger Quests

Ranger Test

- Speak to Artemis the Ranger by the Ascalon City gate in Lakeside County.
- Find River Skale Queen across the river to the southwest and kill it.
- Return to Artemis the Ranger for your reward.

Reward: 500 EXP

Skill Unlock: Power Shot, Troll Unguent

A New Ranger Trainer

- Speak to Haversdan by the Ascalon City gate in Lakeside County.
- Follow the road southwest from town. Turn south on the bridge near Ashford Village and enter Regent Valley. Follow the road until you find Master Ranger Nente and then speak with him.

Reward: 250 EXP

The Ranger's Companion

Regent Valley

- Speak to Master Ranger Nente in Regent Valley.
- Find the statue of Melandru along the path in the woods. Just take the dusty path (shored up with wood buttresses) directly southwest of Master Ranger Nente and you'll quickly stumble across it. Once there, kill one of the Stalkers lurking about.

- Use the Charm Animal skill on one of Melandru's Stalkers when it appears.
- Return to Nente to receive your reward.

Reward: 250 EXP

Skill Unlock: Charm Animal, Comfort Animal

A Test of Marksmanship

Regent Valley

- Speak to Ivor Trueshot on a ridge in eastern Regent Valley.
- Kill all the plague worms (located just below Ivor to the east) in the allotted time (1 minute, 30 seconds).
- Speak with Ivor Trueshot again to receive your reward.

Reward: 250 EXP

Skill Unlock: Point Blank Shot, Read the Wind

Unnatural Growths

Wizard's Folly

- Talk to Aidan in Wizard's Folly near the fishing village.
- Go to the falls to the west. Destroy the aloe husks until you find an aloe root.
- Return to Aidan with the aloe root to receive your reward.

Reward: 250 EXP

Skill Unlock: Dual Shot, Ignite Arrows

Warrior Quests

Warrior Test

- Speak to Van the Warrior by the Ascalon City gate in Lakeside County.
- Follow the road southwest until you find the skale. Clear the river of skale.
- Return to Van the Warrior for your reward.

Reward: 500 EXP

Skill Unlock: Frenzy, Healing Signet

A New Warrior Trainer

Green Hills County

- Speak to Haversdan by the Ascalon City gate in Lakeside County.
- Follow the road northwest from town. Follow the signs to Green Hills County. Talk to Warmaster Grast.

Reward: 250 EXP

Grawl Invasion

Green Hills County

- Speak to Warmaster Grast in Green Hills County.
- Look for Grawl invaders along the road. Eliminate all six invaders.
- Return to Warmaster Grast for your reward.

Reward: 250 EXP, Starter Sword

Skill Unlock: Gash, Healing Signet, Sever Artery

Warrior's Challenge

Green Hills County

- Go to Barradin's Estate in Green Hills County and speak with Duke Barradin.
- Go out to the vineyard in Green Hills County and defeat Agnar the Foot. Use Hamer Bash to interrupt his Rage skill.
- Return to Duke Barradin for your reward.

Reward: 250 EXP, Starter Hammer

Skill Unlock: Hammer Bash

The Vineyard Problem

Green Hills County

- Speak to Little Thom at Barradin's Estate.
- Go out to the vineyard in Green Hills County and kill all the aloe seeds.
- Return to Little Thom for your reward.

Reward: 250 EXP, Starter Axe

Skill Unlock: Cyclone Axe, Executioner's Strike

(See map, p. 90.)

LAKESIDE COUNTY: Lakeside County is home to the village of Ashford and the adjacent Ashford Abbey. Following the roads in Lakeside County will take you to Regent Valley, Wizard's Folly, Green Hills County, or even to the Northlands if you travel past the gate protecting Ascalon.

Adventure with an Ally

- Speak with Lina the Healer in Lakeside County.
- Return to Ascalon City and form a party with another player.
- Go back to Lakeside County and speak with Lina the Healer again.

Reward: 100 EXP
Skill Unlock: Resurrection Signet

A Gift for Althea

- Watch Prince Rurik and Captain Osric discussing the upcoming wedding and Althea's birthday. Once Prince Rurik leaves, speak to Captain Osric. (You don't actually have to watch the conversation, although it's interesting; just speak to Osric afterward.)
- Find the perfect gift for Lady Althea. It must be something beautiful.
- Find the Beautiful Feather in Ashford and give it to Captain Osric.
- Find the Beautiful Pearl inside the Beautiful Shell near the watermill in Ashford and give it to Captain Osric.
- Find the Beautiful Pendant inside the Chest near the bandits in Lakeside County and give it to Captain Osric.
- Speak with either Lady Althea or Captain Osric.

Reward: 250 EXP

Bandit Raid

- Speak to Baron Egan, Ascalon City.
- Recover the Ashford Strongbox from the bandits in Lakeside County.
- Return the Ashford Strongbox to Devona in Ashford.

Reward: 250 EXP

Charr at the Gate

- Speak to Prince Rurik, Ascalon City.
- Follow Prince Rurik to the gate in Lakeside County and help him defeat the Charr.
- Speak with Prince Rurik again.

Reward: 200 EXP

Poor Tenant

- Speak with Namar in Ascalon City.
- Follow the road southwest from town to Ashford. Find Miller Upton and ask him to help Namar.
- Use the Massive Honeycomb to lure the three bee swarms across the bridge.
- Return to Miller Upton.

Reward: 500 EXP

The Charr Threat

- Speak with Devona in Ashford.
- Talk to Brother Mhenlo in Ashford Abbey and receive a Message for Sir Tydus.
- Deliver the message to Sir Tydus in Ascalon City. Use your map to travel there quickly.

Reward: 250 EXP

The Poison Devourer

- Speak to Baron Egan, Ascalon City.
- Cross the river and destroy the Plague Devourer to get a Poisonous Stinger.
- Deliver the Poisonous Stinger to Brother Mhenlo in Ashford Abbey.

Reward: 250 EXP

The Rogue's Replacement

- Speak to Old Mack in Lakeside County after completing "A Mesmer's Burden" quest.
- Collect a Devourer Egg for Old Mack by talking to and then escorting Duke Gaban through the devourer cave in Lakeside County.
- Speak to Old Mack again and give him the Devourer Egg.

Reward: 250 EXP

The Worm Problem

- Speak to Pitney in Ashford.
- Talk to Duke Gaban outside the devourer cave in Lakeside County.
- Lead Fadden through the devourer cave, killing all the devourers while he collects the eggs.
- Receive the Devourer Egg from Fadden and return to Ashford. Give the Devourer Egg to Pitney in Ashford.
- Follow Pitney and kill the Worm Queen in the field. Speak to Pitney again.

Reward: 250 EXP

Trouble in the Woods

- Speak to the Town Crier.
- Go to Lakeside County and follow the road to Ashford. Talk to Devona about the Grawl threat.
- Follow Devona and destroy the Grawl threatening Ashford.
- Speak with Devona again.

Reward: 500 EXP

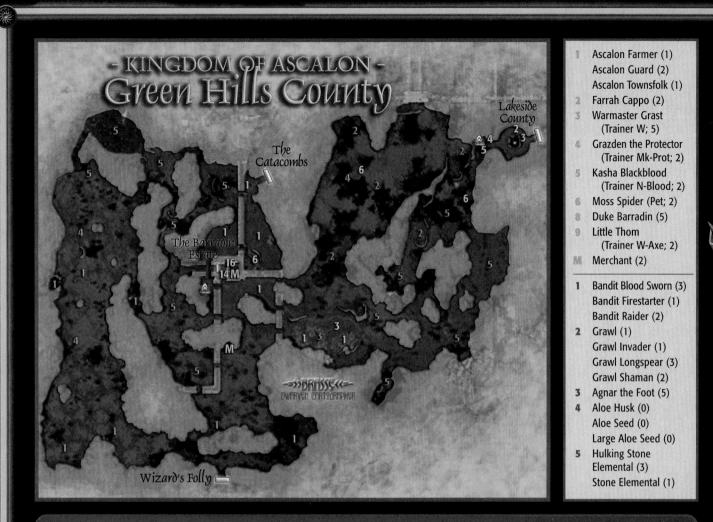

- KINGDOM OF ASCALON -
Green Hills County

Lakeside County

The Catacombs

The Barradin Estate

Wizard's Folly

DRNSSE
DWARVEN CARTOGRAPHER

1	Ascalon Farmer (1)
	Ascalon Guard (2)
	Ascalon Townsfolk (1)
2	Farrah Cappo (2)
3	Warmaster Grast (Trainer W; 5)
4	Grazden the Protector (Trainer Mk-Prot; 2)
5	Kasha Blackblood (Trainer N-Blood; 2)
6	Moss Spider (Pet; 2)
8	Duke Barradin (5)
9	Little Thom (Trainer W-Axe; 2)
M	Merchant (2)

1	Bandit Blood Sworn (3)
	Bandit Firestarter (1)
	Bandit Raider (2)
2	Grawl (1)
	Grawl Invader (1)
	Grawl Longspear (3)
	Grawl Shaman (2)
3	Agnar the Foot (5)
4	Aloe Husk (0)
	Aloe Seed (0)
	Large Aloe Seed (0)
5	Hulking Stone Elemental (3)
	Stone Elemental (1)

THE BARRADIN ESTATE: *Duke Barradin's family estate covers nearly two hundred hectares of Green Hills County. The Duke's vineyard is known throughout Ascalon for the exquisite grapes it produces, which are used to make Amethyst, the most coveted wine in the kingdom.*

Opposition to the King

- Speak with Devona in Ashford.
- Go north from Ashford to find the road to Green Hills County. Once in Green Hills County, question at least three locals about opposition to the king.
- Talk to Farrah Cappo, Grazden the Protector, and Kasha Blackblood.
- Return to Devona for your reward.

Reward: 500 EXP

The True King

- Speak to Duke Barradin at Barradin's Estate.

- Travel east from the Barradin Estate to Lakeside County. Head south to Ashford. Take the southeast bridge to Regent Valley. Once in Regent Valley, follow the road to Fort Ranik.
- Deliver the message from Barradin to Lord Darrin.

Reward: 750 EXP

Tithe for Ashford Abbey

- Speak with Devona in Ashford.
- Head due north from Ashford until you find the road to Green Hills County. Go to Green Hills County and talk to Grazden the Protector.

- Receive Barradin's Tithe and deliver it to Devona in Ashford.

Reward: 250 EXP, 1 Skill Point

Profession-Specific Quests (pp. 91-93)

Protection Prayers (Monk)

A New Warrior Trainer

Grawl Invasion (Warrior)

Warrior's Challenge

The Vineyard Problem (Warrior)

- Kingdom of Ascalon -
Regent Valley

Lakeside County

Fort Ranik

Wizard's Folly

Little Thom's Big Cloak

- Speak to Alison the Tanner in Ashford.
- Head to Wizard's Folly and hunt bears until you acquire a bear pelt.
- Bring the pelt to Alison the Tanner and receive Little Thom's cloak.
- Go to Barradin's Estate in Green Hills County and deliver the cloak to Little Thom.

Reward: 250 EXP

The Hunter's Horn

- Speak to Chantalle the Troubadour in Ashford.
- Purify the Hunter's Horn in the healing spring in Regent Valley.
- Go to the fishing village in Wizard's Folly and deliver the horn to Aidan.

Reward: 500 EXP

The Orchard

- Speak to Mary Malone in Regent Valley.
- Head to the orchard (south of Fort Ranik) and retrieve the Basket of Apples.
- Return the Basket of Apples to Mary Malone in Regent Valley.

Reward: 250 EXP

The True King

- Speak to Duke Barradin at his Estate.
- Travel east from the Barradin Estate to Lakeside County, then south to Ashford. Take the southeast bridge to Regent Valley. Once in Regent Valley, follow the road to Fort Ranik.
- Deliver the message from Barradin to Lord Darrin.

Reward: 750 EXP

FORT RANIK: Used as a training facility for the Ascalon army, Fort Ranik houses new recruits. Here, soldiers learn what it takes to be one of Ascalon's finest and bravest, and how to use their talents to defeat the enemy. Fort Ranik is one of the best-equipped strongholds in the kingdom.

1	Jarrel the Tamer (Animal Trader)	1	Giant Needle Spider (2)
2	Collector Karleen (Collector)		Giant Tree Spider (3)
3	Collector Rownan (Collector)	2	Bandit Blood Sworn (3)
4	Hunters		Bandit Firestarter (1)
5	Academy Monk (5)	3	Carrion Devourer (1)
6	Gwen (1)		Lash Devourer (1)
7	Mary Malone (1)	4	Grawl (1)
8	Mast. Ranger Nente (Trainer R; 5)		Grawl Longspear (3)
9	Ivor Trueshot (Trainer R-Marks; 5)		Grawl Shaman (2)
10	Melandru's Stalker (Pet: 3)	5	Aloe Husk (0)
11	Moss Spider (Pet; 2)		Aloe Seed (0)
12	Wolf (Pet; 2)		Oakheart (5)
13	Black Bear (Pet; 3)	6	River Skale (1)
14	Collector Hatcher (Collector)		Skale Broodcaller (2)
15	Collector Varis (Collector)	7	Plague Worm (1)
16	Lord Darrin (Trainer R; 5)		
M	Merchant (2)		

KINGDOM OF ASCALON - The Catacombs

Green Hills County

Ashford Abbey (Lakeside County)

Wizard's Folly

DANSSE
DWARVEN CARTOGRAPHER

1 Collector Gwynn (Collector)
2 Collector Karleen (Collector)
3 Academy Monk (5)
4 Paulus the Abbot (3)
5 Necromancer Munne (Trainer N; 5)
6 Oberan the Reviled (Trainer N-Curse; 2)
7 Prize Bull (5)

1 Deadly Crypt Spider (2)
2 Vatlaaw Doomtooth (Boss R; 2)
3 Carrion Devourer (1)
4 Gargoyle (1)
  Shatter Gargoyle (3)
5 Restless Spirit (10)
6 Crypt Fiend (3)
  Tomb Nightmare (4)
7 Blood Fanatic (2)
  Restless Corpse (1)

THE CATACOMBS: The Catacombs connect nearly all of the nearby areas of the Kingdom of Ascalon together. This extensive network of underground tunnels is home to many undead souls, animated gargoyles, and some very large spiders. The dark rituals of Necromancers seem natural here, and those brave enough to travel to the depths of the Catacombs may be rewarded with the view of a statue of Grenth.

Profession-Specific Quests
(pp. 91-93)

A New Ranger Trainer
The Ranger's Companion
A Test of Marksmanship (Ranger)

Charr in the Catacombs

- Speak to Prince Rurik in Ascalon City.
- Find out if the Charr Ranger is using the Catacombs. Speak to Brother Mhenlo in Ashford Abbey.
- Ask Necromancer Munne if she has any information on the Charr.
- Seek out Oberan the Reviled deep within the Catacombs. Ask him about the Charr Ranger.
- Return to Rurik in Ascalon City and show him the sharp Charr tooth.

Reward: 250 EXP, 100 Gold

The Prize Moa Bird

- Speak to Pitney in Ashford.
- Go to the Catacombs and search for his Prize Moa Bird.
- Return to Ashford and tell Pitney the news of his Prize Moa Bird.

Reward: 250 EXP

Profession-Specific Quests (pp. 91-93)

A Monk's Mission
A New Necromancer Trainer
The Necromancer's Novice
Rites of Remembrance (Necromancer)
The Power of Blood (Necromancer)
The Accursed Path (Necromancer)

The Wayward Wizard

- Speak to Sandre Elek in Ascalon City.
- Travel to Foible's Fair and speak to Ralena Stormbringer to learn Orion's whereabouts.
- Find Orion in Wizard's Folly and convince him to come home.
- Return to Sandre Elek.

Reward: 250 EXP

Profession-Specific Quests (pp. 91–93)

A New Elementalist Trainer
The Elementalist Experiment
The Supremacy of Air (Elementalist)
Domination Magic (Mesmer)
Unnatural Growths (Ranger)

KINGDOM OF ASCALON
Wizard's Folly

Green Hills County
Lakeside County
The Catacombs
DRAKSS DWARVEN CARTOGRAPHER
Foible's Fair
Regent Valley

1	Collector Mindle (Collector)	**1**	Giant Needle Spider (2)
2	Collector Savich (Collector)	**2**	Bandit Blood Sworn (3)
3	Academy Monk (5)		Bandit Firestarter (1)
4	Gwen (1)	**3**	Tower Golem (3)
5	Orion Elek (2)	**4**	Ice Elemental (3)
6	Elementalist Aziure (Trainer E; 5)		Ice Elemental Shard (1)
7	Aidan (Trainer R; 5)	**5**	Aloe Seed (0)
8	Wolf (Pet; 2)		Large Aloe Seed (3)
9	Black Bear (Pet; 3)	**6**	River Skale (1)
10	Ralena Stormbringer (Trainer E-Air; 2)		River Skale Brood (4)
11	Vassar (Trainer Ms Domin; 2)		Skale Broodcaller (2)
M	Merchant (2)	**7**	Hulking Stone Elemental (3)
			Stone Elemental (1)m

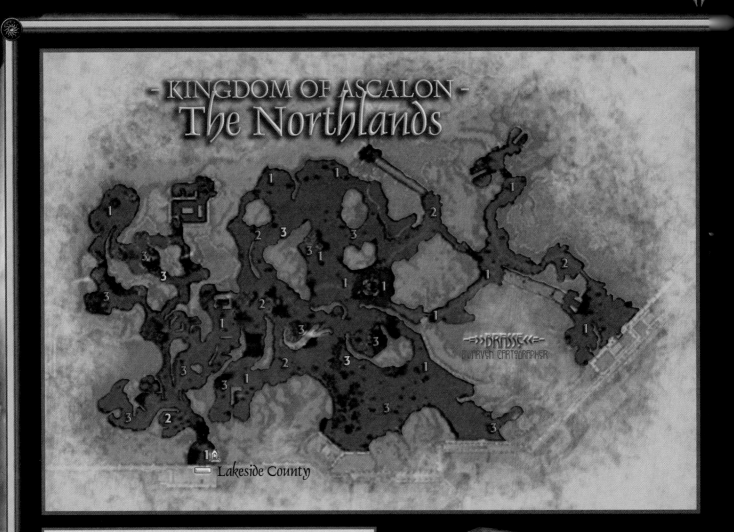

- KINGDOM OF ASCALON -
The Northlands

Lakeside County

1	Academy Monk (5)	1	Charr Blade Storm (8)
2	Ben Wolfson (Trainer R; 5)		Charr Hunter (8)
3	Fern Lizard (Pet; 1)		Jaw Smokeskin (Boss E; 6)
			Red Eye the Unholy (Boss N; 6)
		2	Grawl Longspear (3)
		3	Oakheart (5)

Across the Wall

- Speak to Gate Guard Torin near the Great Northern Wall's gate in Lakeside County.

- Have a friend pull the lever on top of the gate while you run through once the portal is opened.

- Locate Ben Wolfson along the road to Piken Square and lead him back to the gate.

Reward: 250 EXP

Storyline Missions

An RPG in an RPG....

nce you arrive in the Ruins of Ascalon, role-playing characters have the opportunity to pursue a massive, multi-part adventure that will take you across the world. In each of the following 24 mission areas (plus one smaller boss area), you take further steps on the path to making things right in the world again. The only part of each of these areas you can reach without undertaking the associated mission is a small staging area.

These story missions set **Guild Wars** *apart from every other online RPG to date; they make the game a story-driven quest with a definite beginning, middle, and end. Essentially, the Story Missions of* **Guild Wars** *are a lengthy, traditional RPG that you can play through with your friends! If you skip this part of the adventure, you will also miss all the diverse history and exciting lore of Tyria.*

These missions are significantly different from the other roleplaying quests in the game:

- Each mission is several times longer than any other quest, and there is no partial success; you either succeed or you don't. However, you can complete the primary and bonus missions at separate times.

- There are no resurrection shrines; if you don't survive, you return to the staging area (where you can try again if you wish).

- These missions are emphatically not solo adventures. Even with a full team of henchmen and a pet, you have very little chance of surviving all the way through to the end without the help of other players.

- Start this series of missions by talking to Warmaster Tydus in Ascalon City (Ruins). Sometimes you need to talk to someone to start a new mission; sometimes the Enter Mission option

is available as soon as you reach a new staging area.

- While they aren't required, certain Story Missions have an intermediary link quest that can be completed before embarking on the next chapter in the over-arching story. These quests help link certain larger chapters in the overall story by pointing you in the correct direction. These are noted at the very beginning of each story mission.

- The actual maps themselves have a route traced out on them, denoting the optimal path throughout the mission. Use these in conjunction with the text-based walkthrough to find the most efficient way through each level—they'll also help a great deal to prevent you from becoming hopelessly lost in some of the larger maps.

- The reward for primary mission completion is 1,000 EXP and one skill point. Each mission also has a secondary/bonus mission with a completion reward of another 1,000 EXP. (When you complete the primary mission, a sword appears from the upper left of the area's map shield icon; when you complete the bonus mission, a sword is added from the upper right. You can tell at a glance which missions you have completed and which ones you haven't.)

- Bear in mind that, in some cases, you may want to play through a mission more than once (perhaps to kill enemies for experience.) Also if you do not complete all the bonus missions on the first pass, it behooves you to go back and beat them all for experience and loot.

- The only way to get elite skills is to confront bosses and grab these skills

with a Signet of Capture when the bosses use them. There are about 75 elite skills (15 for each profession) used by the bosses throughout the game. Some bosses only appear from time to time—it's not unusual for a scheduled boss to vary among four or more professions—which means it's a good idea to run through an area more than once to ensure that you pick up any elite skills hidden therein.

Carrying Large Items: *With only a few exceptions (such as explosives), you can safely drop any quest item you're carrying if you need to fight, then pick it up again. While carrying an item, there's a small "Drop Item" button at the bottom of your screen.*

The author would like to thank Ben Miller and Steve Hwang for their invaluable assistance on this section.

A	Path
1	Ascalon Veteran (5)
2	Captain Calhaan (6)
3	Kilnn Testibrie (15)
4	Squire Zachery (5)
H	Henchmen (3)
M	Merchant (5)

1	Charr Axe Fiend (8)
	Charr Axe Warrior (6)
	Charr Blade Storm (8)
	Charr Blade Warrior (6)
	Charr Shaman (7)
	Charr Stalker (6)
	Marr Burnhorn (Boss Ms; 3)
2	Carrion Devourer (4)
	Fleck Grokspit (Boss N; 2)
	Plague Devourer (3)
	Whiptail Devourer (4)
3	Shatter Gargoyle (4)
	Gargoyle Boss (Boss Ms; 2)
4	Grawl (4)
	Grawl Ulodyte (3)
	Grawl Boss (Boss Mk; 2)

DRASSE
DWARVEN CARTOGRAPHER

(outpost)

Old Ascalon

- RUINS OF ASCALON -
The Great Northern Wall

Primary Mission

General Map Direction: Northwest

Captain Calhaan has requested your help! He believes that the Charr are planning something big, but isn't quite sure what....

- Talk to Captain Calhaan; he is northwest of your starting point.

❧ TIP ❧

When you come upon the gargoyle/Grawl battle, take out the gargoyles first.

❧ CAUTION ❧

During this battle, you will also be menaced by a gargoyle boss, so keep an eye out for him as he descends from above.

- On the northwest side of the map (A) is a square-shaped loop in the path; head down this loop to trigger a cinematic. Make sure you're ready to finish up, as there's no turning back!

- Once the cinematic is over, RUN! Follow the path south. Only one member of the party needs to live, so have the rest run interference while one player gets safely away.

- Talk to Calhaan. Even if only one member of your party makes it there alive, the entire party will still be sucessful.

Bonus Mission

The ghost of Kilnn Testibrie is a shadow of his past self. In life, he was a great warrior—but in death, he is a lonely spirit, unable to return to his grave until his quest is done.

- Talk to Kilnn Testibrie; he is in front of a large tomb.

- Examine wreckage piles until you find all four pieces of Kilnn's armor: the Cuisse, Greaves, Pauldron, and Crest. Note that sometimes you have to search this area several times before finding all four items.

- Return to Kilnn.

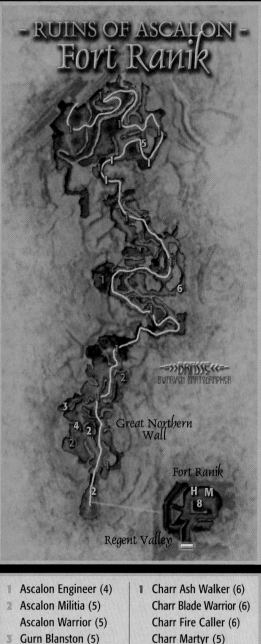

- RUINS OF ASCALON -
Fort Ranik

Great Northern Wall

Fort Ranik

Regent Valley

=»DRESSE«=
DWARVEN CARTOGRAPHER

1	Ascalon Engineer (4)	1	Charr Ash Walker (6)
2	Ascalon Militia (5)		Charr Blade Warrior (6)
	Ascalon Warrior (5)		Charr Fire Caller (6)
3	Gurn Blanston (5)		Charr Martyr (5)
4	Master Armin Saberlin (5)		Charr Mind Spark (6)
5	Siegemaster Lormar (4)		Charr Overseer (6)
6	Trooper Deeter		Charr Stalker (6)
	Saberlin (4)		Charr Warrior (5, 6)
7	Lord Darrin (7)		Charr Boss (Boss Ms; 4)
H	Henchmen (6)	2	Carrion Devourer (4)
M	Merchant (5)		Plague Devourer (3)

Primary Mission

General Mission Direction: North

The Great Northern Wall has been lost, and Ascalon could soon follow. It is your duty to help retake the Wall and secure temporary safety for your home.

- As the mission begins, be sure to stick with the Ascalon warriors to help them fend off the Charr.
- Head beneath the fallen column to attain the high ground and wipe out the foes below. If you skip this, you'll only increase the difficulty later.
- At a shallow ravine flanked by archers, a Charr boss rushes you—let it come to you to meet its doom.
- After defeating the boss, wipe out each group of archers.
- Find and talk to Siegemaster Lormar.
- Search Wrecked Catapults to find the three pieces that Lormar requires to fix the trebuchet: a release lever, a restraining bolt, and an arming crank. Note that you can only carry one piece at a time and you cannot use a weapon or shield while carrying an item. It's best to clear the immediate area of Charr before you even start trying to fix the trebuchet.

You will not get the cinematic without killing the final group of Charr.

- Once you've brought all three pieces back to Lormar, pull the firing lever near him twice to load and fire the trebuchet.
- To the west is a flaming structure; head toward it and a number of Charr will crowd around it.
- Head northwest of the first trebuchet to find a second one; operate it in the same fashion as the first.
- Make your way into the fortress and drive out the last of the invasion force.

> **TIP**
> One player can lure the Charr into the impact zone, while a second operates the trebuchet to make short work of your enemies.

Bonus Mission

Master Armin Saberlin is a hardened Warrior fighting for the freedom of Ascalon. His son, Deeter Saberlin, was carried off by the Charr forces that overtook the wall, and Armin would give anything to have his son back.

- Escort Master Armin Saberlin to the ruins.
- Talk to Saberlin.
- On a hill to the north you find two Overseers guarding a cage. Kill the Overseers and the cage will open.

> **TIP**
> Using skills that interrupt your enemies' attacks will make this battle much less frustrating.

- Talk to Trooper Deeter Saberlin.

"Deliver This Message to My Wife"

Gurn Blanston is a soldier protecting the Wall. He has not been home for three months, and though he has lived until now, he fears for his life in the near future. He requests that you pass on a message to his beloved wife just outside of Ascalon City.

- Talk to Gurn Blanston; he is on the east side of the Fort Ranik area.
- Enter Old Ascalon from the Ascalon City gate. Just west of you is Melka Blanston.
- Talk to Melka.

Reward: 500 EXP

Prisoners of War

Victory always comes with a price. While you saved the Wall and the city, you were too late to save many soldiers from death or capture. Prince Rurik refuses to allow his men to remain prisoner to the barbaric Charr, and thus you must help avenge the dead and free the living.

- You receive a quest upon completing the primary mission.
- Battle through the enemies blocking your path, then talk to Warmaster Riga at the Frontier Gate.

Reward: 500 EXP

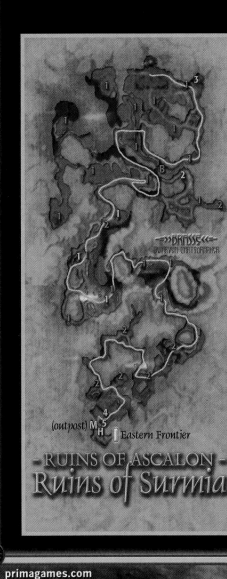

(outpost) M 4 5 H Eastern Frontier

- RUINS OF ASCALON -
Ruins of Surmia

*Speak with Warmaster Riga at the Frontier Gate and take the **Ruins of Surmia Quest**. This will lead you into the Fort Ranik Story Mission.*

Primary Mission

General Map Direction: North

Along with Prince Rurik, you need to rescue the soldiers taken prisoner by the Charr.

- Approach Prince Rurik; he is southeast of your starting point.
- Rurik is ready to start immediately. Go with him along the paths, helping him fight any foes along the way.

� TIP ✍

While Rurik is quite hardy, preceding him into battle will help ensure his survival.

- Rurik stops to free three huts full of Ascalon prisoners. In the last hut (3rd 1) you find Erol, an Elementalist. Erol triggers a cinematic.
- Go with Prince Rurik until you reach a drawbridge (B). Rurik and Erol wait on this side of the bridge while you make your way down and then northeast to open the bridge.

✍ CAUTION ✍

Stay as far away as possible from the flaming effigy in the distance. The horde of foes down there will lay waste to your party at this point in the game.

- Follow Prince Rurik until you come upon three mages.
- Approach the mages so they will follow you, then follow Rurik through the gate.

- Pull the two levers to close the gate after everyone is inside.
- Lead the three mages to the obelisks.

The mages are invaluable to you, raining fiery death (among other things) down upon the unwitting heads of your foes, so be sure to keep them healthy!

- Defend your position until Rurik succeeds in getting the door open.
- Take the portal to the next mission.

Bonus Mission

Breena Stavinson has been a "guest" of the Charr for many years, and she has seen them come and go carrying a flame in a ritualistic procession.

- Talk to Breena Stavinson; she is near the drawbridge.
- Backtrack, then take the northern path instead of the route Rurik took. Follow this route until you loop south and find the Flame Temple (A).

✍ CAUTION ✍

Do not kill the Ember Bears until they open the gate. If you do kill them beforehand, you will fail the mission.

- Kill all the Flame Keepers.

A	Flame Temple	H	Henchmen (6)		Charr Shaman (7)
B	Drawbridge	M	Merchant (5)		Charr Boss (Boss Mk; 5)
					Flame Carrier (7)
1	Ascalon Prisoner (7)	1	Charr Ashen Claw (8)		Flame Keeper (7)
2	Breena Stavinson (10)		Charr Axe Fiend (8)	2	Gnash Underfoot (5)
3	Mage (7)		Charr Chaot (8)		Whiptail Devourer (7)
4	Prince Rurik (10)		Charr Flame Wielder (8)		
5	Captain Miken (4)		Charr Hunter (8)		

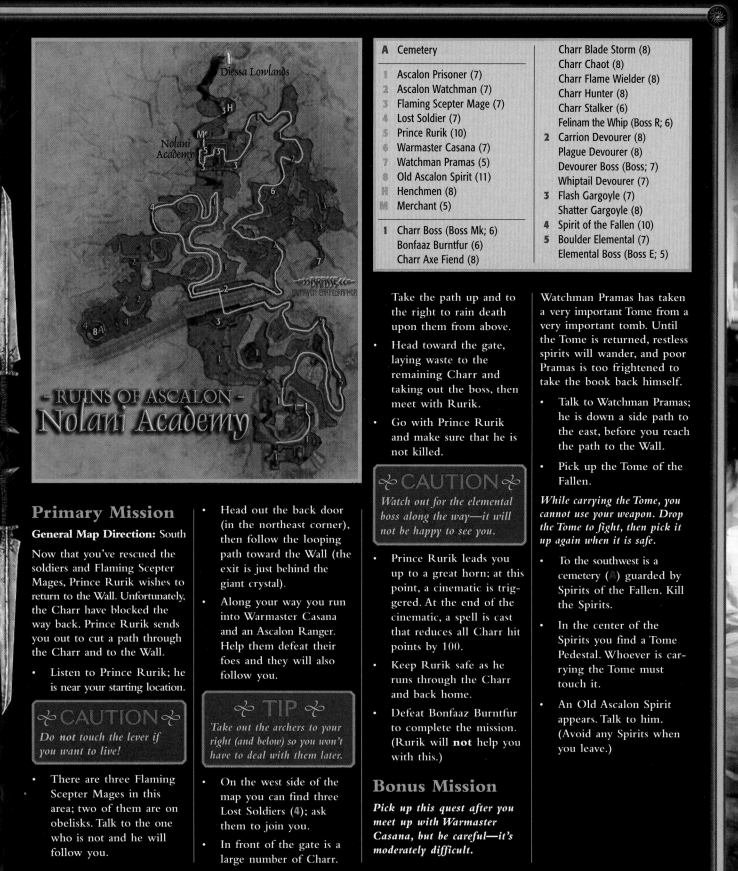

- RUINS OF ASCALON -
Nolani Academy

A	Cemetery		Charr Blade Storm (8)
			Charr Chaot (8)
1	Ascalon Prisoner (7)		Charr Flame Wielder (8)
2	Ascalon Watchman (7)		Charr Hunter (8)
3	Flaming Scepter Mage (7)		Charr Stalker (6)
4	Lost Soldier (7)		Felinam the Whip (Boss R; 6)
5	Prince Rurik (10)	2	Carrion Devourer (8)
6	Warmaster Casana (7)		Plague Devourer (8)
7	Watchman Pramas (5)		Devourer Boss (Boss; 7)
8	Old Ascalon Spirit (11)		Whiptail Devourer (7)
H	Henchmen (8)	3	Flash Gargoyle (7)
M	Merchant (5)		Shatter Gargoyle (8)
		4	Spirit of the Fallen (10)
1	Charr Boss (Boss Mk; 6)	5	Boulder Elemental (7)
	Bonfaaz Burntfur (6)		Elemental Boss (Boss E; 5)
	Charr Axe Fiend (8)		

Primary Mission

General Map Direction: South

Now that you've rescued the soldiers and Flaming Scepter Mages, Prince Rurik wishes to return to the Wall. Unfortunately, the Charr have blocked the way back. Prince Rurik sends you out to cut a path through the Charr and to the Wall.

- Listen to Prince Rurik; he is near your starting location.

> **CAUTION**
> *Do not touch the lever if you want to live!*

- There are three Flaming Scepter Mages in this area; two of them are on obelisks. Talk to the one who is not and he will follow you.

- Head out the back door (in the northeast corner), then follow the looping path toward the Wall (the exit is just behind the giant crystal).

- Along your way you run into Warmaster Casana and an Ascalon Ranger. Help them defeat their foes and they will also follow you.

> **TIP**
> *Take out the archers to your right (and below) so you won't have to deal with them later.*

- On the west side of the map you can find three Lost Soldiers (4); ask them to join you.

- In front of the gate is a large number of Charr.

Take the path up and to the right to rain death upon them from above.

- Head toward the gate, laying waste to the remaining Charr and taking out the boss, then meet with Rurik.

- Go with Prince Rurik and make sure that he is not killed.

> **CAUTION**
> *Watch out for the elemental boss along the way—it will not be happy to see you.*

- Prince Rurik leads you up to a great horn; at this point, a cinematic is triggered. At the end of the cinematic, a spell is cast that reduces all Charr hit points by 100.

- Keep Rurik safe as he runs through the Charr and back home.

- Defeat Bonfaaz Burntfur to complete the mission. (Rurik will **not** help you with this.)

Bonus Mission

Pick up this quest after you meet up with Warmaster Casana, but be careful—it's moderately difficult.

Watchman Pramas has taken a very important Tome from a very important tomb. Until the Tome is returned, restless spirits will wander, and poor Pramas is too frightened to take the book back himself.

- Talk to Watchman Pramas; he is down a side path to the east, before you reach the path to the Wall.

- Pick up the Tome of the Fallen.

While carrying the Tome, you cannot use your weapon. Drop the Tome to fight, then pick it up again when it is safe.

- To the southwest is a cemetery (A) guarded by Spirits of the Fallen. Kill the Spirits.

- In the center of the Spirits you find a Tome Pedestal. Whoever is carrying the Tome must touch it.

- An Old Ascalon Spirit appears. Talk to him. (Avoid any Spirits when you leave.)

- SHIVERPEAK MOUNTAINS -
Borlis Pass

Traveler's Vale

(outpost)

-=»BRASSE«=-
DWARVEN CARTOGRAPHER

A	Gate 1
B	Gate 2
C	Gate 3
D	Snow Wall
E	Stone Summit Engineers
F	3 Torches
K1	Dwarven Powder Keg Station
K3	Pile of Dwarven Powder Kegs

1	King Jalis Ironhammer (24)
2	Rornak Stonesledge (10)
3	Ascalon Guard Hayden (7)
4	Ascalon Guard Tolis (7)
5	Prince Rurik (10)
6	Lore Keeper Beccum (1)
H	Henchmen (8)
M	Merchant (5)

1	Shiverpeak Longbow (8)
	Shiverpeak Protector (Boss Ms; 7)
	Shiverpeak Warrior (8)
2	Dolyak Rider (11)
	Priest of Dagnar (9)
3	Whiskar Featherstorm (Boss E; 10)
4	Frostfire Dryder (10)
5	Summit Beastmaster (13)
6	Ice Golem (10)
7	Dwarf Boss (Boss Ms; 8)
	Stone Summit Crusher (10)
	Stone Summit Engineer (9)
	Stone Summit Howler (10)
	Stone Summit Scout (9)
	Summit Axe Wielder (9)

You find yourself in Yak's Bend. Search out Captain Osric to pick up The Way is Blocked *Quest, which will lead you to Borlis Pass.*

Primary Mission

General Map Direction: West

You've led the Ascalon refugees into the teeth of a fierce storm, and now you must find them shelter within Grooble's Gulch lest they perish at the icy hands of fate.

- Talk to Ascalon Guard Hayden. Whoever talks to him receives a torch.

You need the torch to light the seven Storm Beacons. If you wish, you can drop the torch and let another group member pick it up.

- The first Storm Beacon is just behind Hayden. Light it, then continue following the path and lighting beacons. You can temporarily drop the torch to fight.

❧ TIP ❧

As you come across patrolling bands of Centaurs, be sure to destroy the Spirit of Winter totems that they drop first.

- Talk to Ascalon Guard Tolis; he is west of the final beacon.
- Have the torch holder talk to Tolis to give him the torch.
- Head through the gate that opens behind Tolis.

This is the first time you encounter Dwarves. Armor-piercing skills are useful.

- Find the Dwarven Powder Keg Station (K1). Take a Powder Keg.
- Drop the keg next to the gate (A) to knock the gate down. (If you have to drop it earlier to fight, you can go back for another keg.) Remember that you can also use the kegs against enemies.

❧ CAUTION ❧

Proceed cautiously at this point as there are a myriad of mobs lurking about that are looking to do you serious harm.

- Head inside and kill the Stone Summit Engineers at (E). You gain a 2 percent morale boost for each, and the siege equipment will be broken.
- Follow the path onward through the next gate (use the lever to open it) and destroy the other Summit Engineers just beyond (E).
- Once you kill the second set of Engineers and the monsters around the gate, you can go through the gate.

❧ CAUTION ❧

Be careful in the next area and try to focus on one mob at a time or you'll be in a world of hurt.

- Talk to Prince Rurik.
- Follow the road west to engage the Dwarf boss, then continue on to light the three final torches.

Bonus Mission

Rornak Stonesledge requests that you dispatch of a certain Ice Drake.

- Blow up the gate (C) using a Dwarven Powder Keg. You can find a pile of them at (K3).
- Talk to Ronark Stonesledge; he is behind the gate.
- Get another Powder Keg and place it at (D) to blow away the snow wall.

❧ TIP ❧

Be prepared to perform healing and Hex-removal against the Frostfire Dryders.

- Head down the newly opened path into a cave of Drdyers. Continue through the cave until you find Whiskar Featherstorm.

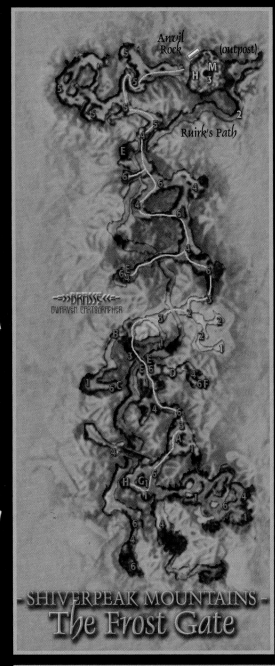

Anvil Rock
(outpost)
H M 3
Ruirk's Path
E

≈≫DRASSE≪≈
DWARVEN CARTOGRAPHER

B
E
D
C F
H G I

- SHIVERPEAK MOUNTAINS -
The Frost Gate

Primary Mission

General Map Direction: South

On the final leg of your journey, make your way over the mountains. Prince Rurik needs you to take out the ballista along the way so that his people can move beyond the Frost Gate and on to Kryta.

- Follow the path through the area as the minotaurs come charging down—let them come to you!

- Follow the path through the area. Destroy Engineers as you come to them. As you do, you receive morale boosts, gates open before you, and Prince Rurik is able to continue on his safe path. There are four Engineers in total, one at each (E).

✂ TIP ✂

After the first Engineer, wait for the patrolling bands of Ice Golems to come to you before proceeding.

✂ CAUTION ✂

After defeating each Engineer, you battle a Dwarf boss, so be on your toes.

- Once you slay the final Engineer, head into the next area and kill the monsters within.

- Pick up the gear lever and use it to activate the first gear (A). Note that the lever will drop and you must pick it up again.

- After a moment, the large door opens. Head inside and clear out the monsters.

- Send one party member back to a safe area, preferably a character who can resurrect. This is a dangerous part of the mission, and should you turn all three gears and then die, you'll be happy you still have a live group member hanging back!

- Use the gear lever to activate the three remaining gears (G), (H), and (I). Note that each gear opens a gate that releases a Stone Summit force to attack you, so you must move fast!

Bonus Mission

This mission takes place after you defeat the second Engineer in the Primary Mission.

Rornak Stonesledge needs you to take him to the correct ballista so that he can shoot down a door.

- Talk to Rornak Stonesledge; he is in a cave.

- Head down hidden path (B).

✂ CAUTION ✂

If Rornak dies, you won't be able to complete the mission.

- Take Rornak to the ballista (C). Once he speaks, fire the ballista by pulling the lever.

✂ TIP ✂

After shattering the gate, send some party members down to draw out enemies. Continue to shell them with the ballista to make life much easier for everyone.

- Head back down the hidden path and along the regular road. You find a broken gate (D)—the one you blasted with the ballista. Continue through it.

- Follow the path until you find a chest (F). Open the chest to reveal...the secret plans! Better get those back to Rornak on the double.

- Return to Rornak.

A	First Gear	H	Henchmen (8)	5	Minotaur (10)
B	Hidden Path	M	Merchant (5)		Minotaur (Boss W; 9)
C	Ballista			6	Dwarf Boss (Boss Ms; 9)
D	Broken Gate	1	Dolyak Rider (11)		Stone Summit Engineer (10)
E	Engineers		Shalis Ironmantle (Boss Mk; 9)		Stone Summit Howler (10)
F	Chest	2	Frostfire Dryder (10)		Stone Summit Sage (10)
G|H|I	Remaining Gears	3	Snow Ettin (11)		Stone Summit Scout (9)
		4	Bucknar Runeguard (Boss E; 9)		Summit Axe Wielder (9)
1	Rornak Stonesledge (10)		Ice Golem (10)		
2	Prince Rurik (10)		Stone Summit Crusher (10)		
3	Lore Keeper Larthan (10)				

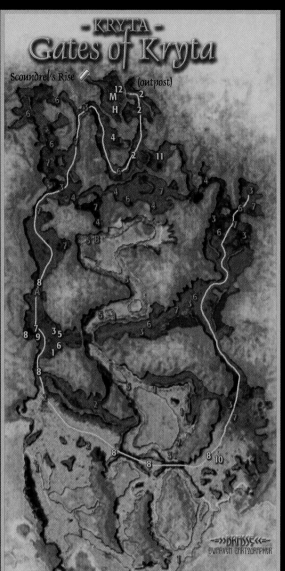

Primary Mission

General Map Direction: South

In order to reach the Gates of Kryta, you'll need to complete the following quests:

1. **To Kryta: The Refugees** *via Master Saberlin in Beacon's Perch*
2. **To Kryta: The Ice Cave** *via Master Seeker Nathaniel in Griffon's Mouth*
3. **To Kryta: Journey's End** *via Aidan in Griffon's Mouth*

With the passing of Prince Rurik, the duty of finding a permanent home for the refugees of Ascalon falls to you. Your first step is to clear the Undead-infested realm of the Gates of Kryta.

THE DEAD LIVE!

As this is the first time you face Undead foes, bear in mind a few things:

1. Smiting Prayers to double damage to Undead foes, so you might want to re-spec your healing monks to focus on Smiting (you can always change back later).
2. Condition Removal skills such as Purge Condition, Antidote Signet, and Mend Ailment will come in handy when combating the effects of poison.

- As the mission begins, a group of villagers approach quickly with a band of monsters hot on their heels—slay the monsters and save the villagers.
- Next, you come upon some Warlocks—slay them first, then kill any minions they've summoned.
- As you approach the bridge, let the squad of Undead trundle past before heading across (watch out for the trailing group as well).
- Follow the road through the Undead until you come to a gate (**A**) being defended by White Mantle Knights. Defeat the monsters in the area to open the gate.

- Talk to Justiciar Torimo; he is near a large set of gates.
- Heading along the bridge after speaking with Torimo, you encounter some Sorcerers and a Warlock. This is a tough battle, so make sure you're prepared before engaging them.

⚜ TIP ⚜

If you make your way down to the beach from this area, you find there are drakes you can hunt to gain some huge EXP and great loot.

- Head south and follow the beaches until you come to Justiciar Hablion.
- Talk to Hablion, then follow him. Help him and his cohorts fight the Undead in the swamp.

⚜ CAUTION ⚜

The swamp is poisonous, so watch your step. Try to stick to dry land whenever possible.

- If you aid Hablion's men, they help you move deeper into the swamp, where you find the boss you need to slay.

Bonus Mission

This mission takes place just to the left of the start point, next to a small, abandoned farm.

Find a little lost Oink and return it to its master, Cheswick. In thanks, his father, Orrian Historian McClain, offers to translate the Orrian Text you found along the way.

- Click on Oink. It follows you.
- Head out the south gate and to the bridge. Go under the bridge and along the river bank until you come to a chest (**B**).
- Open the chest and pick up the Orrian Text.
- Take Oink to Cheswick (**1**).
- Cheswick's father, Orrian Historian McClain, who is right next to Cheswick in town will translate the text for you.

A Gate	**12** Lore Keeper Casori (15)
B Chest	**H** Henchmen (10)
	M Merchant (12)
1 Cheswick (10)	
2 Farmer (10)	**1** Lightning Drake (18)
3 Josephine (10)	**2** Mergoyle (14)
4 Kryta Male (8)	**3** Grasping Ghoul (11)
5 Merchant (10)	Undead Boss
6 Orrian Historian McClain (10)	(Boss W; 11)
7 Recruit (10)	**4** Hellhound (16)
Veteran (10)	**5** Smoke Phantom (17)
8 Lion's Arch Guard (15)	**6** Undead Boss
9 Justiciar Toriimo (15)	(Boss Ms; 11)
10 Justiciar Hablion (18)	Skeleton Mesmer (13)
White Mantle Abbot (15)	Skeleton Ranger (13)
White Mantle Knight (15)	Skeleton Sorcerer (13)
White Mantle Seeker (12)	**7** Undead Boss (Boss N; 11)
11 Oink (8)	Zombie Warlock (14)

- KRYTA -
D'Alessio Seaboard

A	First Altar
B	Second Altar
1	Benji Makala (10)
2	Dinas (20)
3	Kryta Male (8)
4	Villager (10)
	Villager (10)
5	Gate Guard (15)
	White Mantle Guard (15)
	White Mantle Seeker (12)
6	Confessor Dorian (20)
7	Gate Guard Makala (15)
8	Justiciar Isaiah (12)
9	Lynx (Pet; 10)
10	Krytan Herald (Crafter; 15)
11	Mantle Knight Karriya (15)
H	Henchmen (10)
M	Merchant (12)

1	Ettin Boss (Boss W; 13)
	Gypsie Ettin (15)
2	Mergoyle (14)
	Mergoyle Boss (Boss Ms; 13)
3	Grasping Ghoul (11)
4	Ancient Oakheart (17)
	Treant Boss (Boss R; 13)
5	Bog Skale (11)
	Bog Skale Boss (Boss N; 13)
6	Skeleton Mesmer (13)
	Skeleton Monk (12)
	Skeleton Ranger (13)
	Skeleton Sorcerer (13)
	Undead Boss (Boss Ms; 12)
7	Undead Boss (Boss N; 12)
	Zombie Warlock (14)

Primary Mission

General Map Direction: West

To reach this story mission, find the Armanthe Guide in Lion's Arch and pick up the quest Report to the White Mantle.

The Undead are laying siege to Lion's Arch and the White Mantle need you to help Confessor Dorian repel the unholy assault.

- Talk to Justiciar Isaiah. He leads you onward until you come to a bridge.
- Isaiah decides you need more help; he returns to find White Mantle Knights to assist you. You must continue on yourself.
- Follow the path until you come to a village under attack.

> ### ⚜ TIP ⚜
> *If you approach from the beach, you only activate part of the area, giving you more time to deal with the mobs (not to mention more breathing room).*

- Save every villager; each villager saved gives you a +2% morale boost. You should end up with +10%.

You can actually let the raised Undead die on their own but you will not get the morale boost, nor will you be able to tackle the bonus mission.

- Talk to the Gate Guard (the first **5**). He opens the gate.
- Head through the gate.
- Proceed through the swamp, combating ghouls, and various other Undead.
- Help the White Mantle Knight defeat the ghouls, and he helps you as you progress.
- Stay as close to the Shrine of Mending as you can—it heals you. Fend off attackers until they stop coming.
- Talk to Confessor Dorian.
- Head southwest down the path to fight another group of foes and take on the boss.
- Speak to Dinas to complete this chapter of the story.

Bonus Mission

Deliver the village's offering to the statue of Melandru.

- When you get to the village, make sure to save all of the villagers along with Benji Makala; he's fighting a boss. His brother guards the northern gate and won't let you through if Benji dies.
- Go through the northern gate and then head northeast.
- In the northeast, right before you turn south toward the fort, you find a pot on an altar (**A**). Take the pot.

Note that you cannot use a weapon while holding the pot and, even more importantly, if you drop it, it will disappear. However, you can go back and restart the bonus mission.

- Transfer the pot to the other altar (**B**). To find it, head south through the gate, west past the Shrine of Mending and Confessor Dorian, then north through the Oakhearts.

A	Fountain of Truth
B	Town & Villagers
C	Bridge, Second Villager
D	Third Villager
E	Fourth Villager
F	Path to Loamhurst
J	Eye of Janthir

1	Merchant (10)
2	Villager (10)
3	Coastal Keep Guard (12)
4	Justiciar Hablion (18)
5	Justiciar Lashona (12)
6	Lion's Guard Minah (15)
7	Shaemoor Gate Guard (15)
8	White Mantle Abbot (15)
	White Mantle Knight (15)
9	Lynx (Pet; 10)
10	Lore Keeper Franklin (15)
H	Henchmen (12)
M	Merchant (12)

1	Grand Drake (20)
	Lightning Drake (18)
2	Gypsie Ettin (15)
3	Mergoyle Boss (Boss Ms; 14)
	Mergoyle Wavebreaker (12)
4	Grasping Ghoul (11)
5	Hellhound (16)
6	Inferno Imp (13)
7	Spined Aloe (11)
8	Bog Skale (11)
9	Undead Boss (Boss Ms; 13)
	Skeleton Ranger (13)
	Skeleton Sorcerer (13)
10	Caromi Tengu Brave (13)
	Tengu Boss (Boss N; 14)
11	Zombie Warlock (14)
	Zukra Cadava (Boss N; 13)

Primary Mission

General Map Direction: West

Now that you are a member of the White Mantle Knights, they entrust to you the administration of the Test of the Chosen.

- Talk to Justiciar Hablion; to find him, follow the long path north to the village.
- Head east of town to the Fountain of Truth (A); bathe in it to advance the quest.
- Return to Justiciar Hablion and get the Eye of Janthir.
- Talk to the villagers around the town; some of them, the Chosen, begin following you.
- Go through the gate west of town.
- Follow the path to Loamhurst (F); there you see a glowing pedestal. Take the Eye of Janthir to the pedestal.

> **TIP**
>
> *The Eye makes an excellent weapon and will knock down or interrupt most of the enemies with which its eldritch energy comes in contact with (ettins, however, aren't as susceptible to this).*

Bonus Mission

A caravan of five villagers have been attacked and are now split up. Some of them are the Chosen, so it is your duty to rescue them!

> **CAUTION**
>
> *The Chosen aren't very smart, so give any poison water a wide berth to make sure that the Chosen ensure that they don't perish within in its confines.*

- Talk to the villagers around the town (B); some of them, the Chosen, begin following you. Note that you must have the Eye before any Chosen will follow you.

- Once you cross the large bridge (C), you see a villager under attack. Rescue him.
- Talk to the villager. He begins to follow you.
- Talk to the second villager (in the southwest (D).
- Talk to the third villager (near a group of villagers (E); follow the path onward to find him).
- To complete this mission, you must lead the Chosen to Loamhurst. You receive a bonus in gold for each Chosen villager who survives.

=»»BRASSE«=
DWARVEN CARTOGRAPHER

- THE WILDS -
The Wilds

(outpost)

M
H

Sage Lands

Primary Mission

General Map Direction: West

Starting in Druid's Overlook, speak to Trader Versailles and pick up the quest A Brother's Fury to reach this Story Mission.

The Shining Blade have forced the Chosen into the Wilds of the Maguuma Jungle. You must venture into this treacherous and confusing place and save the Chosen.

- Follow the White Mantle Guides till you come upon the entangling roots.
- Defeat the various lifepods, scarabs, etc. before attacking the entangling roots.

✂ CAUTION ✂
After the roots die, watch out for the scarabs that unlurk from the ground!

- Proceeding to the next area, pull one scarab mob at a time and use Fire-based AoE skills (Fire Storm, Immolate, etc.).
- Before long, the White Mantle give up—shortly thereafter a cinematic is triggered that instructs you in how to create the vine bridges.
- Move forward to catch sight of a fleeing Shining Blade. Give chase (up the path to the left).

- Proceed into the gorge and deal with the myriad of spiders. Stay in the water to mitigate the effects of their poison attacks.
- Soon you're treated to another cinematic, after which you must deal with Kurza Spindleweb and her coterie of Spider minions.

Bonus Mission

You overhear two Centaurs talking in the wood about a meeting of the Centaur leaders. Slay the leaders and protect the people of Tyria from the Centaur menace.

- At A there are two Centaurs. Stop and listen to them talk. Hear them out to receive the bonus mission.
- Kill the Centaurs and take the seed. You cannot wield a weapon while holding the seed, so a spell caster should take it.
- At B is a vine bridge that needs activating. Drop your seed on the glowing area to activate the bridge, then cross it.
- There are two Centaur chieftains southwest of the large lake in the north at C. Careful—they have lots of friends!

A	Centaurs
B	Vine Bridge
C	Centaur Chieftains
1	White Mantle Knight (15)
2	Witness Giselle (15)
H	Henchmen (12)
M	Merchant (12)
1	Kurza Spindleweb (16)
2	Centaur Scout (16)
	Centaur Boss (Boss E; 15)
	Maguuma Avenger (16)
	Maguuma Enchanter (16)
	Maguuma Hunter (16)
	Maguuma Protector (16)
	Maguuma Warlock (16)
	Maguuma Warrior (16)
	Centaur Boss (Boss Ms; 14)
	Centaur Boss (Boss E; 14)
3	Saidra (15)
4	Shining Blade Scout (15)
5	Entangling Roots (18)
	Life Pod (15)
	Treant Boss (Boss Mk; 14)
6	Wind Rider Boss (Boss Ms; 14)
	Wind Rider (12)
7	Moss Scarab Boss (Boss N; 14)
	Moss Scarab (12)
8	Troll Boss (Boss W; 14)
	Jungle Troll (14)

Primary Mission

General Map Direction: West, then East

The White Mantle are spiriting the Chosen to Bloodstone Fen. Give chase to ascertain whether the Shining Blade are being forthright with the truth as the web grows increasingly complex.

> ❧ **CAUTION** ❧
>
> *Melee classes (Warriors) should steer clear of the Thron Stalkers to avoid their AoE knockdown attacks.*

- Talk to Saidra; she is northwest of where you start. She gives you a seed.
- Drop the seed on the glowing circle to build a bridge; cross it after it is up, and continue following the path.
- Along the path are trees growing seeds. Harvest the seeds as you find them; you will need them to open more bridges.

> ❧ **TIP** ❧
>
> *Drop the vine seeds to entangle foes.*

- There are many paths to take, but your final destination is (**2**). Here is Blade Scout Ryder.
- Talk to Ryder.
- Across a few more bridges are White Mantle. If you do not see them, you are going the wrong way.
- Follow the path and fight the Mantle.
- After you make it to the large stone platform, be careful; as Ryder told you, resurrections take a long time here.
- As you approach the Bloodstone, knock off the two White Mantle mobs patrolling it before heading in for Justicar Hablion.
- To deal with Hablion, send one person to lead him on a chase. Use your healer to keep that group member alive. Have the rest of the group focus on knocking off Hablion's healer, then descend on Hablion like a pack of ravenous wolves.

Bonus Mission

The Elder Druid must be awakened. Awaken all the Druids of the forest to awaken their elder.

- Find one of the many seed trees in the jungle and get a seed. Do not hit the Jungle Guardians. If they die, game over.

> ❧ **CAUTION** ❧
>
> *If you kill a Guardian, Ravagers will attack you, so watch yourself!*

- Take the seed to the platform at **A**. This awakens the first Druid and starts the quest.
- Awaken the other three Druids using the same method (seed on platform). They are at **B**, **C**, and **D**.
- The four Druids converge at **E** and awaken the Elder Druid.
- Talk to the Elder Druid.

A	Platform
B|C|D	Druids
E	Elder Druid
F	Justiciar Hablion
G	Seeds

1	Druid (20)
	Elder Druid (20)
2	Blade Scout Ryder (15)
3	Chosen Villager (10)
4	Saidra (15)
5	Lore Keeper Braden (15)
H	Henchmen (15)
M	Merchant (12)

1	Root Behemoth (19)
2	Maguuma Protector (16)
	Maguuma Warrior (16)
3	Fevered Devourer (17)
	Devourer Boss (Boss N; 16)
	Thorn Devourer (17)
4	Ravager (20)
5	Jungle Guardian (19)
	Thorn Stalker (17)
	Thorn Stalker Boss (Boss E; 16)
	Tree of Life (Boss Mk; 16)
	Tree of Winds (Boss R; 16)
6	Hepp Bilespitter (Boss Ms; 16)
	Wind Rider (12)
7	Moss Scarab (12)
8	Jungle Troll (18)
9	White Mantle Boss (Boss Ms; 16)
	White Mantle Abbot (18)
	White Mantle Knight (16)
	White Mantle Seeker (16)

A	First Druid
B	Second Druid
C	Pool
D	Demagogue

1	Druid (20)
2	Less Longbow (15)
3	Lore Keeper Gretchen (15)
H	Henchmen (15)
M	Merchant (12)

1	Spider Boss (Boss R; 14)
	Maguuma Spider (16)
2	Behemoth (19)
	Henge Guardian (16)
3	Thorn Devourer (17)
4	Thorn Stalker (17)
	Treant Boss (Boss Mk; 14)
5	Wind Rider Boss (Boss Ms; 14)
	Wind Rider (12)
6	Moss Scarab (12)
7	Troll Boss (Boss W; 14)
	Jungle Troll (18)
8	Demagogue (16)
	Lars the Obeisant (Boss Ms; 16)
	White Mantle Knight (16)
	White Mantle Savant (16)
	White Mantle Seeker (16)

Primary Mission

General Map Direction: East

In Quarrel Falls, pick up the quest series **White Mantle's Wrath**:

1. *White Mantle's Wrath: Demagogue's Vanguard via Gareth Quickblade in Quarrel Falls*

2. *White Mantle's Wrath: A Helping Hand via Councilor Vaylor in Ettin's Back*

3. *White Mantle's Wrath: Urgent Warning via Councilor Vaylor in Ettin's Back*

These will lead you into the Story Mission.

The White Mantle—enraged over the untimely demise of Justiciar Hablion—attempt to deny you access to the ancient Druidic portal to Denravi while waging war on the Shining Blade.

- Go through the jungle until you come to a Druid (A).

- Talk to the Druid.

- Take the crystal near him to the thorn pedestal west of him.

- Go along the previously blocked path.

- When you come to the second Druid (B), kill all the White Mantle you can reach; you'll need to move as quickly as possible after you activate both pedestals.

- Use both crystals to activate the two pedestals ahead. Have someone ready at the gate to run in.

- Have your first runner talk to the Druid to get a crystal, then head toward the white pedestal. The NPCs turn pedestals red and you turn them blue—your goal is to capture and hold all three.

> ⚜ **CAUTION** ⚜
>
> *Do not kill the White Mantle here—hold them at bay, or you'll get more than you bargained for.*

- After all three pedestals are blue, you are teleported to another area.

- Follow the jungle path and kill the Henge Guardian. He is in a pool at C. To tackle him, take out the Wind Riders, then the Behemoths around him. With his troops down, swarm in and take him out, but do not use Signets against him!

Bonus Mission

Your target is the Demagogue who is leading this operation. Speak to Less Longbow for the details and find out why you must put an untimely end to this monster.

- Talk to Less Longbow.

- Kill the Demagogue at D. Be careful—he is in the pedestal war area; it takes planning to reach him without losing your pedestal! (In order to earn this mission, you must complete it before you capture all three pedestals and are teleported to another area. Alternatively, you can come back and run it again.)

- KRYTA -
Riverside Province

Primary Mission

General Map Direction: East

You're in Denravi. Speak to shining Blade Shadow to pick up the quest Passage Through the Dark River to reach the Riverside Province Story Mission.

You must steal the Scepter of Orr from the White Mantle.

- Head south until you come to the first watchtower (A). Sneak around and pick off the White Mantle slowly or you might get ambushed!

- Head through the tunnel to the southwest, and a squad of Undead will attack you.

- Approach the Tower at (C), and the White Mantle moves to this Tower. Sneak through the gate.

- Take out the small patrol, then head northwest to fight some more Undead.

- Avoid the remaining Towers and go to the temple.

> ✤ **TIP** ✤
> *Destroy the White Mantle Zealots and Priests to capture some great loot.*

- Once inside, talk to Dinas; he gives you the Scepter of Orr. You cannot use weapons while holding this item;

have a caster carry it, as it gives +1 Energy regeneration. If you drop it, anyone near it, including you, gets +10 max Energy.

- Go northeast to a bridge guarded by a boss at 8.

- Kill the boss by rushing him to avoid the wrath of the two Towers, then cross the bridge with the Scepter in tow.

Bonus Mission

Saidra, the Shining Blade, is disguised and waiting to help take a load of smuggled weapons to the Blade. She needs you to take out the Towers so she doesn't get searched.

- Take out the Tower at A.

- Talk to Saidra; she is west of the first Tower. She tells you that you must kill the guards at the Towers. They are at the following locations: A, B, C, D, E, F, G, H, and I.

- Kill the guards at the second Tower southwest of Saidra.

- Turn around and head back the way you came, then turn southeast. Follow the path and kill the Tower Guards. When you see the temple, turn east and continue on that path to find more Towers.

A - I	Towers
1	Dinas (20)
2	Grimnalt (10)
3	Jonas (10)
4	Saidra (10)
5	Lore Keeper Derikk (15)
H	Henchmen (15)
M	Merchant (12)

1	Undead Boss (Boss Ms; 17)
	Wraith (17)
2	Grasping Ghoul (11)
3	Hill Giant (20)
4	Hellhound (16)
5	Fog Nightmare (20)
6	Smoke Phantom (17)
	Undead Boss (Boss E; 17)
7	Skeleton Bowmaster (17)
	Skeleton Ranger (13)
8	White Mantle Boss (Boss Ms; 16)
	Watchtower Guard (20)
	White Mantle Abbot (18)
	White Mantle Justiciar (18)
	White Mantle Ritualist (16)
	White Mantle Savant (16)
	White Mantle Seeker (16)
	White Mantle Sycophant (16)
	White Mantle Zealot (24)
9	Bone Dragon (18)
	Undead Boss (Boss N; 17)
	Damned Cleric (17)
	Executioner (18)
	Necrid Horseman (18)

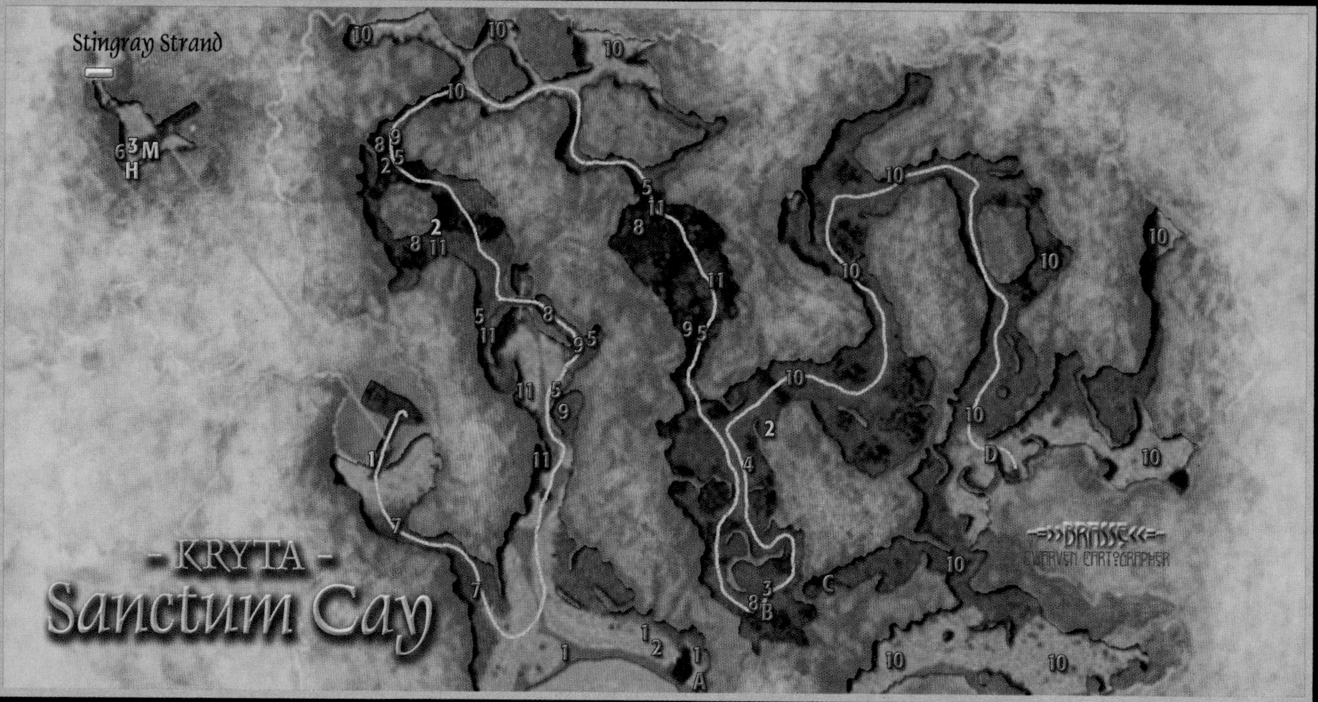
Stingray Strand
- KRYTA -
Sanctum Cay

Primary Mission

General Map Direction: East

You are tasked with taking the Scepter of Orr to the Vizier. The bad news is that the way to his post is fraught with peril of the Undead persuasion.

Evannia is on the dock. Talk to her, and she gives you the Scepter of Orr.

> **TIP**
>
> *Use the terrain in this area to your advantage: anytime you can, take the high road to shell foes from above.*

Make your way across the area, laying waste to Undead, till you come upon the dragon Rotscale.

The best bet to defeat Rotscale is to simply wade in and destroy him, but be aware that his Choking Gas attack will interrupt casters, and Condition Removal Skills are a must to negate the effects of poison.

Southeast of that battle is a large temple-like structure (B) guarded by Giants. Take it easy and eliminate them one at a time, then go to the front of the structure.

Vizier Khilbron appears. Talk to him.

The Vizier summons a large number of Undead—fear not, though, for they help you!

- Follow the Undead and help them head off the first onslaught of White Mantle. Don't be too upset if they all die; just continue on the path.
- At the end of the path (D), the Vizier appears once again and tells you that the White Mantle are too strong and you must escape. Protect him while he summons a ship from its grave at the bottom of the sea. Use the dock to your advantage and force foes to come to its edge where they are easy prey when bottlenecked.
- Quickly board the ship before the White Mantle overwhelm you! This triggers the end cinematic.

Bonus Mission

Help the Restless Spirit find his final resting place.

- Talk to the Restless Spirit at A so he follows you.
- Lead the Restless Spirit to Vizier Khilbron.
- Talk to the Restless Spirit again after the cinematic with Vizier Khilbron.
- Lead the Restless Spirit to his family's grave site.
- Talk to the Restless Spirit after he thanks you to receive the bonus reward.

A	Restless Spirit
B	Vizier Khilbron
C	Spirit's Family Grave
D	End of Path
1	Evennia (15)
2	Lore Keeper Silas (15)
H	Henchmen (15)
M	Merchant (12)
1	Lightning Drake (18)
2	Undead Boss (Boss Ms; 17)
3	Grasping Ghoul (11)
4	Hill Giant (20)
5	Hellhound (16)
6	Vizier Khilbron (20)
7	Inferno Imp (13)
8	Undead Boss (Boss E; 17)
	Smoke Phantom (17)
	Smoke Phantom (18)
9	Skeleton Ranger (13)
10	Undead Boss (Boss Ms; 16)
	White Mantle Knight (16)
	White Mantle Savant (16)
	White Mantle Seeker (16)
11	Bone Dragon (18)
	Damned Cleric (17)
	Executioner (18)
	Undead Boss (Boss N; 17)
	Necrid Horseman (18)
	Rotscale (Boss R; 17)

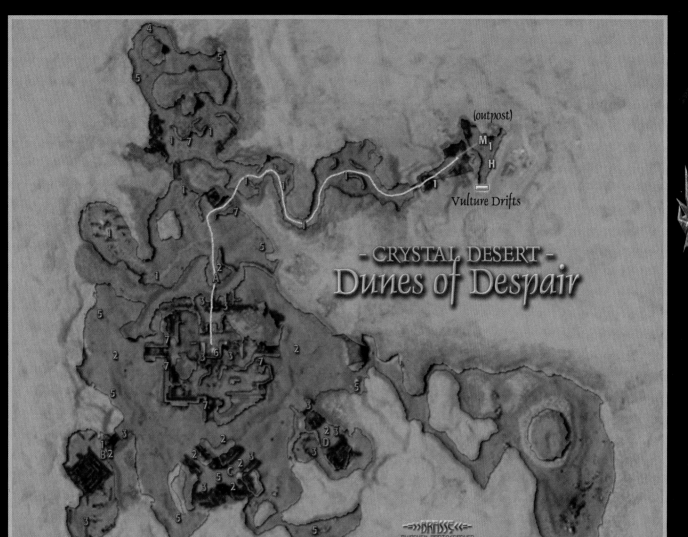

- CRYSTAL DESERT -
Dunes of Despair

(outpost)

Vulture Drifts

-»»BRASSE««-
DWARVEN CARTOGRAPHER

A	Forgotten Boss
B|C|D	Forts
I	Ghostly Hero (24)
H	Henchmen (17)
M	Merchant (12)
1	Losaru Bladehand (20)
	Losaru Bowmaster (20)
	Losaru Lifeband (20)
2	Ayassah Hess (Boss Ms; 20)

	Forgotten Arcanist (20)
	Forgotten Cursebearer (20)
	Forgotten Illusionist (20)
3	Eldriss Blesst (Boss W; 20)
	Enchanted Bow (20)
	Enchanted Sword (20)
4	Storm Kin (20)
5	Jade Scarab (20)
6	Enemy Ghostly Hero (24)
7	Siege Wurm (20)

✣ TIP ✣

To use the teleporters in the Crystal Desert, watch the stones that flash directly across from the teleporters and hit the switches in the order in which they blink.

This mission is very similar to King of the Hill in PvP.

The following three story missions can be tackled in any order you choose and there is no best path to take.

Start in the Amnoon Oasis and pick up the Sand of Souls Quest from the Ghostly Hero. From there, head east into Prophet's Path to Augury Rock by following the tall, stone pillars. There you find Great Ritual Priest Zahmut. Launch your assault on the Crystal Desert from here. You can also take a trip down to the nearby Oasis for Intel on the three missions you must undertake in the desert.

Primary Mission

To reach the Dunes of Despair, exit Augury Rock, then head south into Vulture Drifts, which will take you to the Dunes themselves.

General Map Direction: Southwest

The Temple of Ascension is where the gods focus their gaze when they look upon Tyria. In order to draw their holy gaze, you must aid the Ghostly Hero in an attempt to reclaim the Temple from the usurper, the Enemy Ghostly Hero.

- Talk to the Ghostly Hero; he is near your starting location.
- Head over the southwest bridge. The Hero follows you. Escort the Ghostly Hero to the Temple of Ascension by going west, then south over the bridge.

> ❧ **TIP** ❧
>
> *As you begin to head south, you need to have a gameplan to deal with the Siege Wurm, even though it's mainly a giant pest. Your safest bet is to simply ignore it and keep running. If you want to kill it, make sure you have lots of armor.*

After you cross the Siege Wurm bridge, you can go to an area to the west where the Slow Totem is located. The Slow Totem will place the Imagined Burden skill on any enemies that pass within its AoE. This is, however, optional.

- Go to **A** and kill the Forgotten boss and its cohorts. Their destruction triggers a cinematic.
- Now approach the drawbridge slowly, taking out the archers as you approach (if you don't, you will have more trouble later).
- Approach the Temple of Ascension, and the drawbridge lowers. If you picked up the Slow Totem, drop it in the doorway to give the onrushing foes some trouble. From there, just pick them off as they come to you.
- Defeat the Enemy Ghostly Hero by rushing in and taking him down with whatever means you have at your disposal.

- Protect the Ghostly Hero as he performs his ritual (this takes 10 minutes). If you have the Slow Totem, it's a good idea to use it here, as well.

> ❧ **TIP** ❧
>
> *If you're having trouble, be sure to buff the Ghostly Hero so that he can last the entire 10 minute countdown. Have the Monks mind his health and keep a keen eye on the radar to track where foes are coming from.*

Bonus Mission

Defeat the three Forgotten generals in the fort just south of the Temple of Ascension at **C**, to gain more prestige. Get the bonus mission when the Ghostly Hero claims the throne.

> ❧ **CAUTION** ❧
>
> *You have to do this mission while the Ghostly Hero is claiming the throne, so it requires splitting up your team.*

- Head through the south exit of the Temple of Ascension to reach the forts.
- Defeat the generals in the forts surrounding the Temple of Ascension at **B**, **C**, and **C** to gain more prestige.

- After you kill each general, an additional wave of Forgotten accosts the remainder of your team defending the Ghostly Hero, so be prepared.

If this is the last of the three Crystal Desert Missions for you, teleport to the mesa to enter the rune circle. Once aflame, ignite the three nearby stones and the mesa itself will open for the final trial of Ascension, which involves a battle against your mirror self.

Diviner's Ascent

(outpost)

A	Second Crystal Shard
B	Final Crystal Shard
C	Ritual Priest Kahdat
D	Ritual Priest Nahtem
E	Ritual Priest Hehmnut

1	Ghostly Hero (24)
2	Ghostly Priest (24)
H	Henchmen (17)
M	Merchant (12)

1	Dune Burrower (22)
2	Forgotten Arcanist (20)
	Forgotten Cursebearer (20)
	Forgotten Boss (Boss Ms; 20)
3	Enchanted Sword (20)
	Forgotten Boss (Boss W; 20)
4	Minotaur (20)

Primary Mission

To get to the Elona Reach, head northeast into Skyward Reach and on to Diviner's Ascent.

General Map Direction: West

The Ghostly Hero needs your help with a ritual that will combine the three shards of the Vision Crystal. With this Crystal, he will be able to help focus the gods' gaze on the rune circle. You must find the shards while he conducts the ritual.

- As the mission begins, keep an eye out for the charging minotaur so that you don't get caught between more groups of foes than you're ready for.

> ### ❧ TIP ❧
> *The Splinter Mines make handy "tire spikes" for foes—rush in and grab them (you'll have to deal with Bleeding and Cripple conditions, so make sure you choose a stout soul for this task), then drop them to inflict damage on your enemies.*

- Talk to the Ghostly Priest. He gives you the first shard of the Vision Crystal. Remember: You cannot wield weapons while holding the shard.

> ### ❧ CAUTION ❧
> *Once you have the shard(s) in your possession, a lot more enemies spawn to menace you.*

- Talk to the Ghostly Hero. After turning over the first shard, a 30-minute timer is activated.

> ### ❧ TIP ❧
> *The shards are kept in the giant Sail Towers, so keep an eye out for the Towers if you're having trouble orienting yourself!*

- Retrieve the second crystal shard and return to the Ghostly Hero.

> ### ❧ TIP ❧
> *The easiest way to reach each Tower is to hug the canyon walls to the east and west, cutting a path to each Tower so that the way is clear on the return trip.*

- Take the final crystal shard to the Ghostly Hero to complete the mission.

Bonus Mission

Awaken the Ritual Priests using the Vision Crystal.

> ### ❧ CAUTION ❧
> *In this bonus mission, you need one of the shards, so you must complete this mission before turning in the final shard to the Ghostly Hero. Also, keep an eye on the clock!*

- Go to C with a crystal shard in your hands; awaken the spirit of Ritual Priest Kahdat.
- Talk to Kahdat and he follows you.
- Take Khadat with you when you go to talk to the Ghostly Hero for the first time; this activates the quest.
- Awaken Ritual Priest Nahtern with the crystal shard.
- Awaken the last Ritual Priest, Hehmnut.

If this is the last of the three Crystal Desert Missions for you, teleport to the mesa to enter the rune circle. Once aflame, ignite the three nearby stones and the mesa itself will open for the final trial of Ascension, which involves a battle against your mirror self.

GUILD WARS
PRIMA OFFICIAL GAME GUIDE

A Ghostly Hero

1	King Khimaar (2)
2	Ghostly Hero (20)
	Ghostly Hero (24)
H	Henchmen (17)
M	Merchant (12)

1	Blighted Devourer (20)
2	Enemy Priest (20)
	Forgotten Arcanist (20)
	Forgotten Cursebearer (20)
	Forgotten Illusionist (20)
	Goss Aleessh (Boss Ms; 20)
	Hessper Sasso (Boss N; 20)
	Issah Sshay (Boss E; 20)
	Josso Essher (Boss Mk; 20)
3	Forgotten Avenger (20)
	Forgotten Champion (20)
	Forgotten Boss (Boss W; 20)
	Forgotten Boss (Boss R; 20)
4	Sand Giant (22)

This Mission mirrors the Annihilation mode in PvP.

Primary Mission

Head out of Augury Rock and make your way northeast to Skyward Reach, then continue northeast to Destiny's Gorge. From there, make your way to the Scar, moving southeast to Thirsty River.

General Map Direction: South

In order to be worthy of Ascension, you must cleanse yourself in the rune circle located in Thirsty River. However, to reach it, you must first defeat the Forgotten leaders, while still defending the Ghostly Hero.

- Make sure to kill all the Sand Giants you find; they give you 2% morale boost each (10% max).
- At (A), talk to the Ghostly Hero.

This Mission is extremely hard to complete with henchmen, so make sure to tackle it with other players.

- The Ghostly Hero leads you through several arenas where you must fight opposing teams.

❧ TIP ❧

Your spells are not impeded by obstructions in your path, so if the Priests are staying out of sight, shell them through the walls.

- As you defeat each group of monsters, you gain access to the next group. The battles happen in three stages, starting with a battle against an opposing team lead by Goss Aleesh. Next are the two combined teams of Issah Sshay and Hessper Sasso. Finally, you meet the three combined teams of

Josso Essher, Lyssha Suss, and Kesskah Shissh. Defeat them all to win.

- To make life a lot easier on you and your cohorts, lead the second and third arena teams toward each other.

❧ CAUTION ❧

As long as the enemy Priests survive, they resurrect your enemy every two minutes. Try to kill the Priests as quickly as possible!

Bonus Mission

King Khimaar's spirit lingers uneasily in this realm, wanting to see the blasphemous invaders banished before he rests in peace. But sadly, he cannot wait long.

- Defeat each enemy force in under 9:45 minutes or King Khimaar will disappear. The timer pauses as you defeat all the teams in one stage, then resets to 0:00 when you start the next stage.

If this is the last of the three Crystal Desert Missions for you, teleport to the mesa to enter the rune circle. Once aflame, ignite the three nearby stones and the mesa itself will open for the final trial of Ascension, which involves a battle against your mirror self.

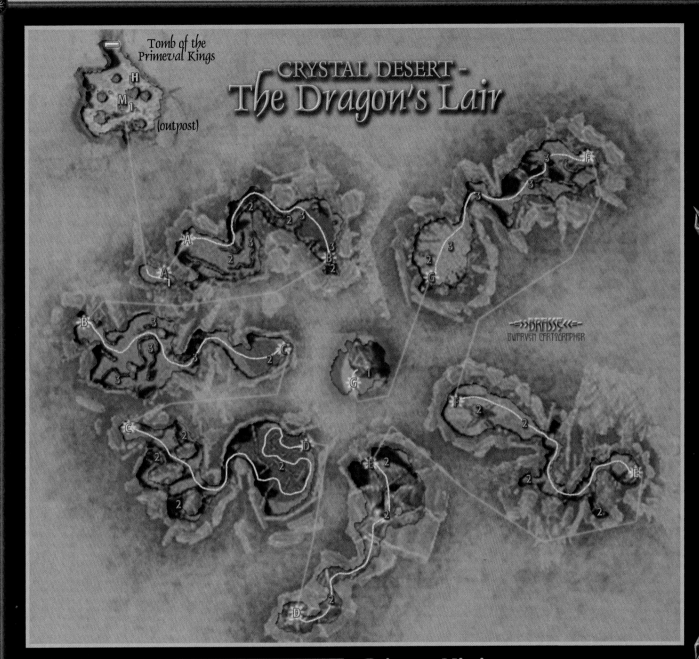

A Facet of Light
B Facet of Nature
C Facet of Chaos
D Facet of Darkness
E Facet of Elements
F Facet of Strength
G Glint

1 Forgotten Gate Keeper (20)
H Henchmen (18)
M Merchant (12)

1 Glint (31)

2 Facet of Chaos (Boss Ms; 22)
Facet of Darkness (Boss N; 22)
Facet of Elements (Boss E; 22)
Facet of Light (Boss Mk; 22)
Facet of Nature (Boss R; 22)
Facet of Strength (Boss W; 22)
Forgotten Arcanist (20)
Forgotten Cursebearer (20)
Forgotten Illusionist (20)
Forgotten Sage (20)
3 Enchanted Bow (20)
Enchanted Sword (20)

Primary Mission

General Map Direction: NA

Now that you've Ascended, you have earned the opportunity for an audience with Glint (a dragon), but it isn't quite that simple. First you'll have to battle your way to your audience with the mighty wurm through a series of trials.

- Talk to the Forgotten Gate Keeper. He opens a portal to A.

Key references here are to the island with the first occurrence of each key; pairs of keys—A, A, and so forth—indicate linked teleportals.

- Defeat the Facet of Light guarding the portal to B. (Domain of Health Draining—Energy degeneration.)

> ✂ TIP ✂
>
> *Health Skills (Troll Unguent, Mending, Healing Breeze, etc.) are key during this battle to negate the health drain you will suffer.*

- Defeat the Facet of Nature guarding the portal to C. (Domain of Slow—movement is slowed.)

> ✂ TIP ✂
>
> *Movement skills are key here (Dodge, Sprint, Illusion of Haste, etc.) due to the movement-sapping nature of the area.*

- Defeat the Facet of Chaos guarding the portal to D. (Domain of Chaos—using skills will do a bit of backfire damage to you.)

> ✂ TIP ✂
>
> *The best strategy here is to simply hack away at your foe and rely less on skills that take time to recharge. Also be sure to time your Skills in between the enemy's use of Diversion (which will cause your skill to recharge slowly) and/or burn a cheap skill to force them to use Diversion.*

- Defeat the Facet of Darkness guarding the portal to E. (Domain of Energy Draining—Energy degeneration.)

> ✂ TIP ✂
>
> *The Necro skill Blood is Power and skills that cause Bleeding (Sever Artery, Hunter's Shot, etc.) are key here. Also try to stay in open areas to avoid clumping up and falling prey to Death Nova when enemies die.*

- Defeat the Facet of Elements guarding the portal to F.

> ✂ TIP ✂
>
> *For this battle, stay out of range of the elemental effects (Fire Storm, Maelstrom, Eruption, and Chain Lightning) and use skills that negate elemental damage (Ward Against Elements).*

- Defeat the Facet of Strength guarding the portal to G and Glint.

> ✂ TIP ✂
>
> *During this battle you'll constantly be knocked down, so make sure to execute skills after you get up.*

- Speak to Glint.

Bonus Mission

You must do this Mission after you complete the Primary Mission.

There's nothing to excite rage like messing with a creature's child, and if you touch Glint's eggs, you are sure to make an enemy.

- Pick up one of Glint's Dragon Eggs near 1, but be careful! This makes Glint aggressive, and she's no easy fight.

- Defeat Glint.

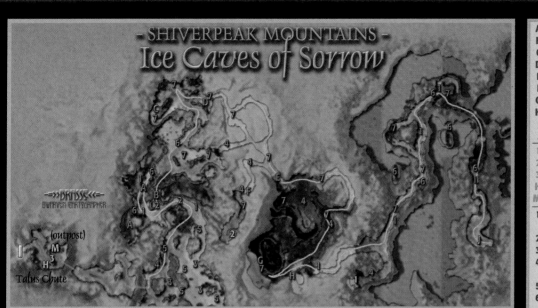

A	Catapult
B	Bridge
C	Dwarven Powder Keg Station
D	Door to Blow Up
E	Opening
F	Second Door to Blow Up
G	Dwarven Powder Keg Station
H	Prison
I	Third Door to Blow Up
J	Ship

1	Hamdor Grandaxe (10)
2	Rornak Stonesledge (10)
3	Blade Scout Shelby (15)
H	Henchmen (18)
M	Merchant (12)

1	Dolyak Master (24)
	Stone Summit Arcanist (24)
2	Summit Beastmaster (13)
3	Ice Imp (22)
4	Jade Armor (24)
	Mursaat Elementalist (24)
5	Pinesoul (24)
6	Dwarf Boss (Boss Ms; 8)
	Stone Summit Carver (24)
	Stone Summit Engineer (10, 24)
	Stone Summit Ranger (24)
7	White Mantle Engineer (20)
	White Mantle Savant (16)
	White Mantle Seeker (16)
	White Mantle Zealot (24)

Primary Mission

Prior to embarking upon the next Story Mission, you will want to complete the Seeking the Seer Quest given to you by Captain Hugo Bronzebeard in Droknar's Forge.

General Map Direction: East

The Shining Blade have fled to the Shiverpeaks, but unfortunately Evennia and Saidra have been taken captive by the White Mantle due to the treachery of Markis. Your job is to recover them from the Ice Caves of Sorrow.

- Make your way down the path avoiding the Mursaat at all costs.

✂ CAUTION ✂

Don't bother trying to fight the Mursaat. Their Spectral Agony Skill is extremely deadly and impossible to counter.

- Fight the Stone Summit on your way to the Stone Summit Icebreaker on the frozen lake.
- Fire the Stone Summit Icebreaker (A). This triggers a cinematic.
- Before crossing the bridge, be sure you've taken out any trouble with the Icebreaker so that you don't get crushed trying to cross.
- After this point, the trebuchets are knocked down and you can proceed across the bridge (B).
- Remember those good old Dwarven

Powder Keg Stations? You find another one (C). Pick up a few kegs; it's time to blow up some doors!

- There's a door at D. Blow it up using a Powder Keg.
- Go through the opening (E).

Keep an eye out for more Mursaat patrols at this point; they'll be lurking about just looking to put a premature end to your adventure.

✂ TIP ✂

If you want to save some time, be sure you have two Powder Kegs with you when you go into the next sequence.

- Evennia and Saidra are in a prison (H). Use what you find at the Dwarven Powder Keg Station (G) to break in.
- Watch the cinematic, then quickly escort Evennia to the waiting ship (J). As you're rushing into the teeth of the Stone Summit, keep in mind the Mursaat giving chase; don't dawdle.

✂ CAUTION ✂

You must save Evennia for the Mission to be successful, so make sure your Monks have her covered.

- Complete the Mission by boarding the ice ship.

Bonus Mission

The best way to complete this mission is

1) wait till you complete the following Story Mission, then 2) have someone hang back at the final sequence of Evennia's escape, sacrificing him or herself to speak to Hamdor Grandaxe.

Rornak Stonesledge was sent by King Jallis to spy on the White Mantle's activities and look for signs of the Ancient Seer. Not suprisingly, he managed to get himself captured once more, and now it's up to you to inform Hamdor Grandaxe of his current whereabouts.

- After going through the door (D), return to get another keg.
- At F you find another door. Blow it up!
- Talk to Rornak Stonesledge; he is in a prison (2).
- There is another Dwarven Powder Keg Station (G). Use a Powder Keg to blow up the door (I).
- Hamdor Grandaxe (2) is guarded by a bunch of scary Mursaat Elementalists; be careful!
- Once you've killed the Elementalists, head back and get another keg. Take out the ice wall between you and Hamdor.
- Talk to Hamdor to finish the Bonus Mission.

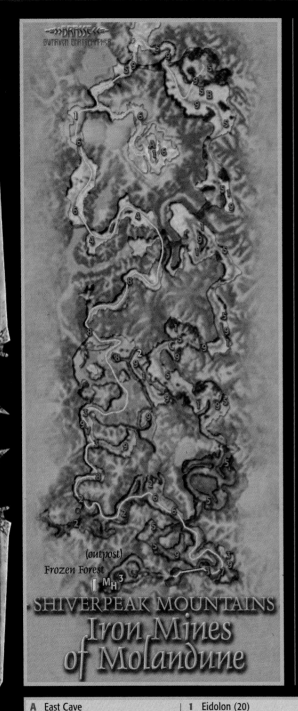

SHIVERPEAK MOUNTAINS
Iron Mines
of Molandune

Primary Mission

General Map Direction: North

You need the Ancient Seer's aid in defeating the Mursaat, so you must journey far to the north to find him. It also turns out that the traitorous wretch, Markis, is also somewhere in the frozen wastes, which should make you extra eager to spill some blood.

- Head north and cross a small bridge which is the site of a skirmish between the White Mantle and the Stone Summit.

- Beyond this battle, follow the ice river north, beneath the large arching bridge.

> ⚜ TIP ⚜
>
> *Once you reach the basin being shelled by ballistae, do not make the mistake of stopping once you've started to run—the ice will slow you down if you come to a halt.*

- Just beyond the griffons, proceed carefully. This area is full of Azure Shadows (they won't be visible, so don't alert them inadvertently).

- Talk to the Seer; he is in a cave far to the north.

- The Seer sends you to kill the Eidolon in a cave to the east (A), but keep an eye out for the Azure Shadows wandering about—kill them first!

> ⚜ TIP ⚜
>
> *Armor and skills that protect against cold damage are good to bring along in the battle against the Eidolon.*

- Bring the Ancient Essence of the Eidolon back to the Seer to have your armor imbued.

- Head north to engage the Mursaat in combat for the first time due to the protection of your striking new armor. Be wary, however; dying now means you have to start from scratch.

> ⚜ TIP ⚜
>
> *To defeat the Mursaat, send one player in to absorb their initial volley of Spectral Agony, then wade in and lay waste to the Mursaat, starting with the Monks and White Mantle.*

- Head north to B to kill Markis by rushing him and ignoring all other foes. The Mission ends with his well-earned demise.

Bonus Mission

The (Mursaat) Inquisitor has interrogated his last victim—in this case a Shining Blade Scout by the name of Ryder. It's time to put an end to the Inquisitor's malevolent ways by showing him the business end of your most handy weapon.

- Talk to Shining Blade Scout Ryder (2).

- Defeat the Inquisitor (C) before he leaves with the information about the Shining Blade.

If the Inquisitor manages to leave the map, you will fail this Mission. You can repeat this Mission up to five times to earn additional Infusions from the Eidolon which will bulk up your armor to aid you in your battles against the Mursaat. These Infusions can be carried over to new armor as well, though each succeeding piece of Infusion is less effective than the previous.

A East Cave	1 Eidolon (20)	6 Azure Shadow (22)
B Markis	2 Summit Giant Herder (24)	7 Stone Summit Carver (24)
C Inquisitor	Tundra Giant (24)	8 Mountain Troll (24)
	3 Siege Ice Golem (24)	9 Markis (20)
1 Seer (Crafter; 30)	4 Blessed Griffon (24)	White Mantle Engineer (16)
2 Shining Blade Scout Ryder (15)	5 Jade Armor (24)	White Mantle Knight (16)
3 Evennia (20)	Mursaat Elementalist (24)	White Mantle Priest (24)
H Henchmen (18)	Mursaat Mesmer (24)	White Mantle Ritualist (16)
M Merchant (12)	Mursaat Monk (24)	White Mantle Seeker (16)
	The Inquisitor (24)	White Mantle Zealot (24)

SHIVERPEAK MOUNTAINS
Thunderhead Keep

(outpost)

←→BRIDGE←→
DWARVEN CARTOGRAPHER

Ice Floe

Primary Mission

General Map Direction: North

Having been driven from their native territory, the Stone Summit have taken up residence in the Deldrimor Dwarves' capital of Thunderhead Keep. Since you are one who always pays your debts, you have agreed to help the Deldrimor Dwarves reclaim their ancestral home from their malicious cousins—it's time to make the Summit re-pay their debt...in blood.

- Talk to King Jalis Ironhammer (1); he is near your starting location.
- Head through the city around A. Defeat the seven groups of enemies within by sticking to the wall to the left and tackling them one at a time.
- Take Jalis to the door located at D, pass through, and continue onward.

> ### ⚜ CAUTION ⚜
> Do not let Jalis die or the Mission comes to an abrupt end.

- Make your way forward to retake the fort (B).
- Kill Dagnar Stonepate and the Dwarves within the fort (C).
- Help King Jalis Ironhammer defend the fort from the Mursaat forces! When he shouts out that a wave of enemies is coming to an end, use that time to rest and heal any fallen allies.

- Since foes come from both directions, skills that impart increased speed are handy when racing to and fro to cover the field.
- The enemy force will be formidable, so you need to be prepared for a long, drawn-out fight with a total of four waves:
  1. Dwarves and Giants with a Stone Summit boss.
  2. Jade Armor and Jade Bow with a Mursatt boss.
  3. Jade Armor and Jade Bow with a Mursatt boss.
  4. Mursaat Casters with Confessor Dorian.
- Eventually, Confessor Dorian arrives—slay him to complete the mission.

> ### ⚜ TIP ⚜
> Use the ballistae to wreak havoc on approaching enemies, thus making it that much easier to keep them at bay. Also, use the wall to see where incoming enemy forces are coming from and attack them from above.

Bonus Mission

Light the beacons to distract the Mursaat forces from laying waste to the two small Dwarven villages they currently menace.

- Pick up the Enchanted Torch and light the storm beacons along the wall of the fort—you need two players to light the beacons within 30 seconds or the villages will be razed.

A Village	1 Stone Summit Boss (Boss Mk; 24)	6 Jade Bow (24)
B Fort	Dolyak Master (24)	Mursaat Elementalist (24)
C Dagnar Stonepate	Stone Summit Arcanist (24)	7 Dagnar Stonepate (Boss W; 24)
D Door	2 Enslaved Frost Giant (24)	Dwarf Boss (Boss Ms; 24)
	Summit Giant Herder (24)	Stone Summit Carver (24)
1 King Jalis Ironhammer (24)	3 Siege Ice Golem (24)	Stone Summit Gnasher (24)
2 Grambol Stonebook (10)	The Judge (24)	Stone Summit Ranger (24)
H Henchmen (20)	4 Blessed Griffon (24)	8 Avicara Brave (24)
M Merchant (12)	5 Vizier Khilbron (20)	Avicara Fierce (24)
		9 Confessor Dorian (20)

- KOMALIE'S REST -
Ring of Fire

A	Eidolon
B	Citadel Guardhouse Gate Lever
C	Guardhouse of Mursaat

1	Brechnar Ironhammer (24)
2	Dwarven Soldier (10)
3	Ancient Seer (Crafter; 30)
4	Fogard Axemighty (10)
H	Henchmen (20)
M	Merchant (12)

1	Lava Spitter (22)
2	Drake (20)
3	Igneous Ettin (20)
4	Eidolon (20)
	Phantom (20)
5	Vizier Khilbron (20)
6	Lava Imp (20)
7	Jade Armor (24)
	Jade Bow (24)
	Mursaat Elementalist (24)
	Mursaat Monk (24)
	Ether Seal (24)
8	Nightmare (24)
9	Breeze Keeper (24)

Primary Mission

General Map Direction: West

*Before reaching the Ring of Fire, pick up the **Final Blow** Quest from Shining Blade Shadow in Ember Light Camp.*

The Flameseeker Prophecies have foreseen that you will open the Door of Komalie, which you reach after you pass through the Ring of Fire. The Mursaat greatly fear the achievement of this goal and stand ready to prevent it at any cost.

- Gain access to the Citadel Guardhouse by destroying the Ether Seals (one per tower) and any other enemies in your way.
- Take it slowly as you go since you have to contend with party after party of Mursaat and their awakened Jade Armors. If you can take them three at a time, this makes life much more bearable.
- You have to destroy numerous towers along the way, as well. Send a quick character in to draw the enemies away and deal with them first. Then

you can concentrate on avoiding the debilitating effects of the towers.

- After you kill the guards, you can destroy the Ether Seal, which will take out the tower, *or* simply run right on by. Ranged attacks might be a good idea for taking out the Seals.

⚜ CAUTION ⚜

If you decide to run, only let one person go at a time: the tower will attack more rapidly if it can siphon off the Energy of multiple characters at one time.

- After you get by the first tower, you happen upon a pool of lava—destroy the ettins lurking nearby from the safety of either side of the pool, but do not try to engage them while standing *in* the pool.
- After the cinema, you come upon the Guardhouse (C)—avoid it for the time being and start making your way to the rear.

⚜ CAUTION ⚜

The multiple streams of lava you pass over will hurt...a lot. Make sure you're fully healed, have speed skills equipped, and don't dawdle.

- You finally come upon the rear, less heavily guarded doorway, which is also bound by an Ether Seal. Destroy it to head inside the Guardhouse.
- Open the main gate to the Citadel Guardhouse by pulling the lever (B).
- Clear the Guardhouse of Mursaat (C).

Bonus Mission

Defeat the Eidolon.

- Talk to the Ancient Seer.
- Expose the Eidolon by destroying the Ether Seals that protect the magical towers around the island, primarily the ones surrounding the Guardhouse. The Eidolon appears at the four mursaat towers.
- Destroy the Eidolon (A).
- Take the ancient essence back to the Ancient Seer.

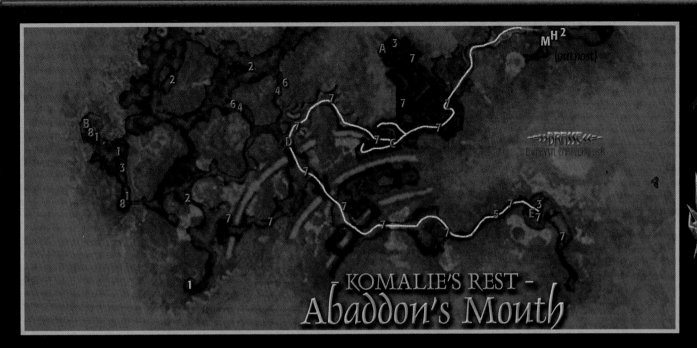

KOMALIE'S REST –
Abaddon's Mouth

Primary Mission

General Map Direction: West, then East up the Volcano

Fulfill the prophecy by throwing open the Door of Komalie! Keep in mind, however, this is the last bastion of the Mursaat, and they have no intention of standing idly by.

- Head out and speak to the Vizier, and he'll grant you two buffs (Shimmer of Intensity and Quickening Zephyr).

- Slowly approach the wall and draw off individual mobs along the wall starting from the right or left, then working your way in the opposite direction.

- After you clear out the mobs, take out the Ether Seal to open the doorway and enter the Mursaat stronghold.

- Work your way through the stronghold, hacking and slashing, till you reach another doorway with two Ether Seals and two Mursaat bosses. Whittle down the weaker mobs before taking out the bosses.

- Disable the Seals (C) to power down the Onyx Gate.

- Through the Gate and over the bridge is a Monk making a run for it. If you can catch and kill him, he won't bring reinforcements. If he gets away, though, be ready.

- Climb the path into Abaddon's Mouth (D). Head east, shattering Ether Seals and foes as you go.

- You come upon the shimmering Soul Bridge, and past that is Optimus Caliph and a secondary, weaker, Mursaat boss.

- Afterward, you run into the Vizier once more. He'll relate to you how to unlock the Door.

- Break the six magical seals (E) holding closed the Door of Komalie by attacking them one at a time. Also, each time you shatter one, three Seal Guards accost you—take them out before moving on to the next seal.

- In addition to the seals and the Seal Guards, watch for random Mursaat to join the fray. Take things slowly, and you'll come out relatively unscathed.

- Treachery! The Vizier turns out to be a vile lich. He summons a mighty Titan to destroy you and your party! Focus fire and hammer pound on him till he drops.

Bonus Mission

Follow the spirit of Leah Stone to its final resting place, making sure she makes it there "alive."

- Free Leah Stone's spirit by destroying the Ether Seal (A).

- Escort Leah Stone's spirit to its final resting place (B).

A	Leah Stone's Spirit
B	Leah Stone's Final Resting Place
C	Seals for Onyx Gate
D	Path Into Abaddon's Mouth
E	Six Magical Seals, Door of Komalie

1	Ancient Seer (Crafter; 30)
2	Lore Keeper (15)
H	Henchmen (20)
M	Merchant (12)

1	Burrower (24)
2	Dark Flame Dryder (24)
3	Eidolon (20)
	Leah Stone (10)
	Seal Guard (10)
4	Flesh Golem (20)
5	Vizier Khilbron (20)
6	Mahgo Hydra (24)
7	Mursaat Boss (Boss N; 24)
	Mursaat Boss (Boss E; 24)
	Mursaat Boss (Boss Mk; 24)
	Jade Armor (24)
	Jade Bow (24)
	Mursaat Elementalist (24)
	Mursaat Guardian (24)
	Mursaat Monk (24)
	Mursaat Boss (Boss Ms; 24)
	Perfected Armor (Boss W; 24)
	Ether Seal (24)
	Optimus Caliph (Boss E; 24)
8	Volcanic Wurm

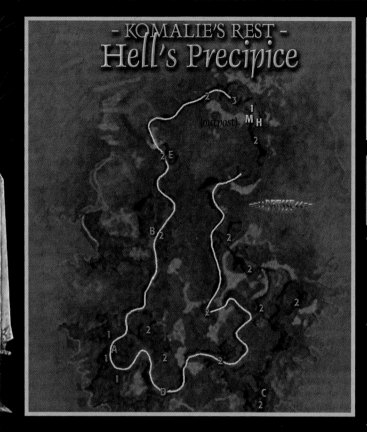

- KOMALIE'S REST -
Hell's Precipice

A	Portal Wraiths	1	Portal Wraith (17)
B	Undead Rurik	2	Burning Titan (24)
C	Ancient Seer		Spark of the Titans (24)
D	Armageddon Lords		Ancient Seer (30)
E	Vizier Khilbron		Armageddon Lord (24)
			Titan (Boss W; 24)
I	Lore Keeper (10)	3	The Lich (24)
H	Henchmen (20)		
M	Merchant (12)		

Primary Mission

General Map Direction: South, then North

Prevent the Lich from sending his Titan hordes across the world to subjugate it to his twisted nefarious will. It's time for some payback!

- You need to fight your way through a legion of Titans (hopefully one at a time) as you go through Hell's Precipice.

Titan Toppling

Titans are tricky for a number of reasons:

1. They start out as Burning Titans. Defeat that and an...

2. Ashen Hulk rises from its husk. Defeat that and a...

3. Hands of the Titan and Fists of the Titan appear from its remains.

To take out the Titan's primary form, use anti-melee skills; to take out the Ashen Hulk, use the Mesmer skill Strip Enchantment (or other anti-enchantment skills) to remove Aura of the Lich; to destroy its final form, go to anti-melee.

When dealing with Titans, as long as you can strip away the Ashen Hulk's Aura of the Lich, keep them in that form if you get caught up with other mobs, in the Ashen Hulk's aura-free state, it's the weakest of the three.

❦ CAUTION ❦

Titans burn with each melee strike, so you're going to take damage with each hit.

- As you make your way through Hell's Precipice, the Lich appears regularly to taunt you. Don't waste your time attacking him right now.
- Disable the Titan portals by defeating the Portal Wraiths at A. You'll want to use ranged attacks and keep the group dispersed so as to avoid their vicious Chain Lightning strikes.
- As you're taking out the portals, watch out for the patrolling bands—tangling with one of these while dealing with the Wraiths, etc., is a headache.
- After condemning the portals, a cinematic plays. After it ends, be on your toes!
- Destroy the Hands and Fists swarming you, then proceed to battle an unwilling, undead Rurik (B).
- While Rurik isn't easy, he is merely a powered up melee character, so get in there, focus fire, and take him down.

❦ TIP ❦

Using a Signet of Capture, snare the Elite Skill Hundred Blades from Rurik when he attempts to use it.

- With Rurik down, it's time to finish off that repellant Lich...for the last time.

The Lich

Defeating the Lich is no simple task. He relies on the skill Soul Vortex to teleport you into the lava as he teleports to either side of the area, across two lava rivers. You can race across the lava if you have someone repeatedly casting condition removal skills on you, but make sure you're on the same page if you're going to risk it. You'll have to "kill" the Lich three times to finish him off. Each time you take out one of his forms, a Hand and Fist appear, so take them down.

The key here is to have a good, well-balanced team, and have your Warriors steer clear of the Lich's Soul Vortex, as they are more susceptible to it due to their general range limitations.

Your team has sufficient damage output, so the battle won't drag on, and the Lich will never have the upper hand.

❦ CAUTION ❦

If you die on the Bloodstone, any resurrection spells take four times as long to cast!

Bonus Mission

Destroy all three Armageddon Lords.

- Rescue the Ancient Seer at C from a group of Titans.
- Destroy the three Armageddon Lords at D quickly due to their nasty habit of generating massive spikes in damage.

Ruins of Ascalon

By Andrea and Jose Silva

Ascalon City

(See map on next page.)

Defend the Wall

- Speak with Warmaster Tydus in Ascalon City.
- Talk to Squire Zachery at the Great Northern Wall.

The King's Message

- Speak with Warmaster Tydus in Ascalon City to receive the Royal Message.
- Go to Old Ascalon. Deliver the Royal Message to Ambassador Zain.
- Return to Warmaster Tydus in Ascalon City for your reward.

Recruits for Hollis

- Speak with Warmaster Tydus in Ascalon City.
- Go from town to Old Ascalon and find the Army Recruits.
- Lead all three recruits west along the wall to the far gate and present them to Gate Guard Hollis.
- Speak with Gate Guard Hollis for your reward.

Scavengers in Old Ascalon

- Speak with Warmaster Tydus in Ascalon City.
- Go southwest in Old Ascalon to the ruins. Clear out any scavengers.
- Speak to Thaddiel in the ruins and send him away.

- Return to Warmaster Tydus for your reward.

Cities of Ascalon

- Speak to Symon the Scribe in Ascalon City.
- Find the historical monument in Surmia.
- Find the historical monument in Nolani.
- Find the historical monument in King's Watch.
- Return to Symon the Scribe in Ascalon City to receive your reward.

Counting the Fallen

- Speak to Symon the Scribe in Ascalon City.
- Find the Ascalon census in the ruins of Old Ascalon.
- Return to Symon the Scribe in Ascalon City for your reward.

Vanguard Equipment

- Speak to Captain Arne in Ascalon City.
- Go to Regent Valley. Acquire the Vanguard equipment from Gelsan.
- Recover Gelsan's stolen goods from the bandits.
- Take the stolen goods to Gelsan.
- Deliver the Vanguard equipment to Captain Arne in Ascalon City to claim your reward.

The Troublesome Artifact

- Speak to Warmaster Tydus in Ascalon City.
- Starting at the Frontier Gate, follow the road south through the Eastern Frontier and into Pockmark Flats.
- Enter Serenity Temple and speak to Priestess Rashenna.
- Return to Warmaster Tydus for your reward.

Old Ascalon

(See map on next page.)

Supplies for the Duke

- Speak to Gate Guard Hollis by the far west gate in Old Ascalon.
- Find out what happened to the missing supply column along the road to Piken Square.
- Escort the supply column to Piken Square.
- See Quartermaster Aada to receive your reward.

Skill Unlock: Purge Conditions (Mk), Called Shot (R), Distortion (Ms), Ice Spikes (E), Weaken Armor (N), "Watch yourself!" (W)

The Charr Patrol

Requirement: Ranger

- Speak to Master Ranger Nente in Old Ascalon.
- Hunt down the Charr patrol by following Master Ranger Nente as he follows the patrol's tracks through Old Ascalon.

- Destroy the Charr patrol across the wooden bridge, then speak to Master Ranger Nente for your reward.

Skill Unlock: Feral Lunge (R), Favorable Winds (R)

The Charr Staging Area

Requirement: Ranger

- Speak to Master Ranger Nente in Old Ascalon after completing The Charr Patrol quest.
- Head to the Breach and kill Gorgaan Hatemonger.
- Return to Master Ranger Nente for your reward.

Skill Unlock: Dodge (R), Quickening Zephyr (R)

Helping the People of Ascalon

Requirement: Monk or Ranger

- Speak to Ambassador Zain in Old Ascalon.
- Deliver the supplies to Ellie Rigby, in Ascalon City.
- Return to Ambassador Zain for your reward.

Skill Unlock: Mending (Mk), Penetrating Attack (R)

Ambassador's Quandary

- Speak to Ambassador Zain in Old Ascalon.
- Go to Regent Valley. Hunt down the bandit Torin.
- Return to Ambassador Zain to receive your reward.

Old Ascalon

1	Jarrel the Tamer (Animal Trader)
2	Fadden Hathorn (Collector)
3	Innis the White (Collector)
4	Palben Tunne (Collector)
5	Penelope Hoode (Collector)
6	Saba Blackstone (Collector)
7	Parchment Maker Daved (Crafter; 1)
8	Ambassador Zain (15)
9	Army Recruit (10)
10	Farmer Hamnet (10)
11	Gate Guard Hollis (4)
12	Gate Guard Sebastein (4)
13	Gate Guard Wendell (4)
14	Melka Blanston (10)
15	Rogenn (5)
16	Sergeant Clark (2)
17	Shalev the Hermit (8)

18	Thaddiel (10)
19	Witness Rastin (2)
20	Elementalist Aziure (Trainer E; 5)
21	Grazden the Protector (Trainer Mk; 2)
22	Necromancer Munne (Trainer N; 5)
23	Master Ranger Nente (Trainer R; 5)
24	Warmaster Grast (Trainer W; 5)
25	Melandru's Stalker (Pet; 3)
26	Moa Bird (Pet; 3)
27	Horace (Crafter; 1)
28	Fadden Hathorn (10)
29	Warmaster Tharan (4)
30	Vassar (Trainer Ms; 2)
31	Necromancer Munne (Trainer N; 5)
32	Kasha Blackblood (Trainer N-Blood; 2)
H	Henchmen (3)
M	Merchant (5)

1	Charr Axe Warrior (6)
	Charr Stalker (6)
2	Carrion Devourer (4)
	Plague Devourer (3, 8)
	Stig Plopgush (Boss N; 2)
	Whiptail Devourer (4)
3	Flash Gargoyle (3)
	Ignis Phanaura (Boss Ms; 2)
	Shatter Gargoyle (4, 8)
4	Gougi Gakula (Boss Ms; 2)
	Grawl (4)
	Grawl Ulodyte (3)
5	Oberan's Minion (4)
6	Crown of Thorns (5)
7	Bonetti (Boss W; 2)
	Oberan the Reviled (6)
8	Flint Touchstone (Boss E; 2)
	Grit Slingstone (Boss R; 3)
	Hulking Stone Elemental (3)

Mission of Peace

- Speak to Ambassador Zain in Old Ascalon after completing The Ambassador's Quandary.
- Find Gate Guard Hollis at the eastern gate in Old Ascalon. Give him Zain's strongbox.
- Return to Ambassador Zain for your reward.

Scorched Earth

Requirement: Elementalist

- Speak to Elementalist Aziure in Old Ascalon.
- Slay five Hulking Stone Elementals.
- Return to Elementalist Aziure for your reward.

Skill Unlock: Ward Against Elements

Elemental Knowledge

Requirement: Elementalist

- Speak to Elementalist Aziure in Old Ascalon.
- Find Shalev the Hermit

for your reward.

Skill Unlock: Armor of Earth (E), Frozen Burst (E)

Shalev's Task

Requirement: Elementalist

- Speak to Shalev the Hermit in Old Ascalon.
- Go to the Breach and kill Charr Fire Callers to obtain a bottle of fiery unguent.
- Give the fiery unguent to Shalev for reward.

Skill Unlock: Eruption (E), Shard Storm (E)

Sowing Seeds

Requirement: Monk

- Speak to Grazden the Protector by the ruins in Old Ascalon.
- Escort Farmer Hamnet to Ascalon City.
- Return to Grazden the Protector for your reward.

Skill Unlock: Heal Party

Protecting Ascalon

Requirement: Monk

- Speak to Grazden the Protector by the ruins in Old Ascalon.
- Find Paulus the Monk in Regent Valley.
- Search Paulus's body for any personal effects.
- Return the holy symbol to Grazden the Protector.

Skill Unlock: Heal Area (Mk), Vital Blessing (Mk)

In Memory of Paulus

Requirement: Monk

- Speak to Grazden the Protector in Old Ascalon

after completing the Protecting Ascalon quest.

- Find Melka Blanston, outside of Ascalon City. Give her Paula's holy symbol and tell her of his death.

Skill Unlock: Resurrect (Mk), Live Vicariously (Mk)

Endangered Species

Requirement: Ranger

- Speak to Master Ranger Nente in Old Ascalon.
- Find and tame a Melandru's Stalker.
- Return to Master Ranger Nente for your reward.

Skill Unlock: Hunter's Shot

Gargoyle Trouble

Requirement: Warrior

- Speak to Warmaster Grast in Old Ascalon.
- Kill six gargoyles.
- Return to Warmaster Grast for your reward.

Skill Unlock: Wild Blow

Military Matters

Requirement: Warrior

- Speak to Warmaster Grast in Old Ascalon.
- Speak to Sergeant Clark in Regent Valley.
- Escort Sergeant Clark back to Warmaster Grast in Old Ascalon.
- Speak to Warmaster Grast in Old Ascalon to receive your reward.

Skill Unlock: Power Attack (W), Sprint (W)

Into the Breach

Requirement: Warrior

- Speak to Warmaster Grast in Old Ascalon.
- Head to the Breach and

repel the Charr attacks.

- Speak to Warmaster Grast in Old Ascalon to receive your reward.

Skill Unlock. Penetrating Blow (W), Endure Pain (W)

Sardelac Sanitarium

Mesmerizing the Enemy

Requirement: Mesmer

- Speak to Vassar in Sardelac.
- Go south of the Sanitarium to the ruins of Ashford and defeat Ignis Phanaura.
- Return to Vassar for a reward.

Skill Unlock: Power Leak

Trying Times

Requirement: Mesmer

- Speak to Vassar in Sardelac Sanitarium.
- Find and retrieve a Mossy Rock from the cave near the ruins of Ashford.
- Return to Vassar with the Mossy Rock for your reward.

Skill Unlock. Chaos Storm (Ms), Mantra of Flame (Ms)

The Stolen Artifact

Requirement: Necromancer

- Speak to Necromancer Munne in Sardelac Sanitarium.
- Find the grawl that have stolen the relic. Look for them in the fields just north of the Sanitarium.
- Escort Necromancer Munne and the relic back to Sardelac Sanitarium.

Skill Unlock: Insidious Parasite

A Cure for Ralena

Requirement: Mesmer

- Speak to Vassar in Sardelac.

- Find Master Ranger Nente in Old Ascalon.

- Return with the cure to Vassar in Sardelac Sanitarium for reward.

Skill Unlock: Illusion of Haste (Ms), Energy Burn (Ms)

Death in the Ruins

Requirement: Necromancer

- Speak to Kasha Blackblood in Sardelac Sanitarium.

- Slay six of Oberan's Minions south of the Sardelac Sanitarium.

- Return to Kasha Blackblood in Sardelac Sanitarium.

Skill Unlock: Dark Pact (N), Mark of Pain (N)

Oberan's Rage

- Speak to Kasha Blackblood in Sardelac Sanitarium.

- Slay Oberan the Reviled, Old Ascalon.

- Return to Kasha Blackblood in Sardelac Sanitarium for your reward.

Skill Unlock: Parasitic Bond (N), Putrid Explosion (N)

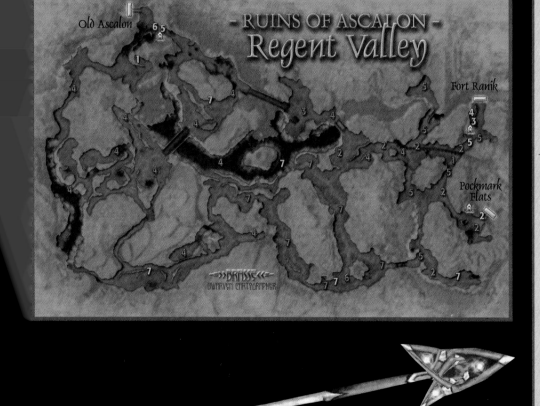

1. Corwin Luceinne (Collector)
2. Sir Nyman (Collector)
3. Valeria Benes (Collector)
4. Gelsan (Crafter; 1)
5. Ascalon Guard (5)
   Ascalon Warrior (5)
6. Sergeant Clark (2)
7. Moa Bird (Pet; 3)

---

1. Charr Ash Walker (6)
2. Carrion Devourer (8)
   Plague Devourer (3)
   Whiptail Devourer (7)
3. Flash Gargoyle (3)
   Shatter Gargoyle (8)
4. Grawl Heretic (4)
   Grawl High Priest (3)
   Grawl Petitioner (4)
   Grawl Ulodyte (3)
5. Renegade (3)
   Renegade Elementalist (3)
   Bandit (3)
   Torin (4)
6. Storm Rider (7)
7. Hulking Stone Elemental (3)

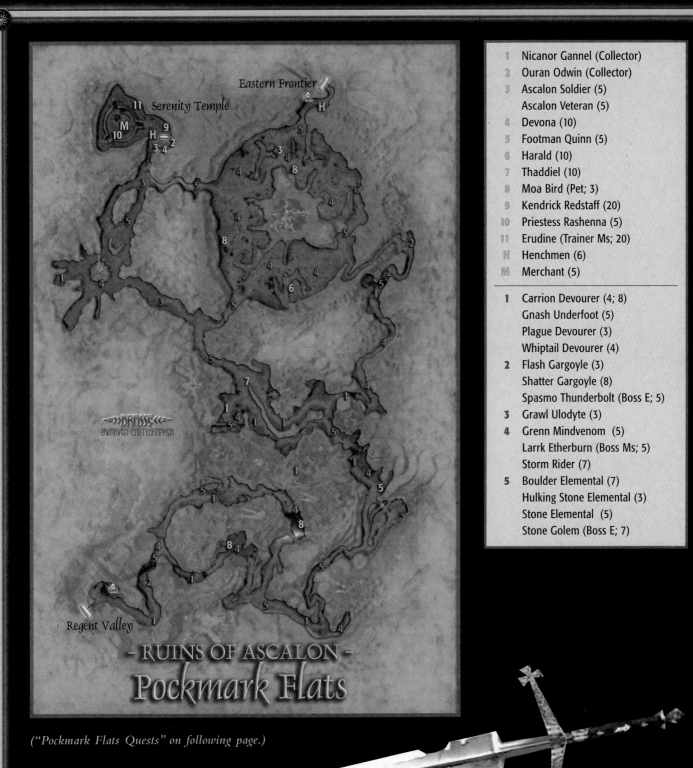

Eastern Frontier

Serenity Temple

11

M
10

H 9
3 4 2

RUINS OF ASCALON
Pockmark Flats

Regent Valley

("Pockmark Flats Quests" on following page.)

1	Nicanor Gannel (Collector)
2	Ouran Odwin (Collector)
3	Ascalon Soldier (5)
	Ascalon Veteran (5)
4	Devona (10)
5	Footman Quinn (5)
6	Harald (10)
7	Thaddiel (10)
8	Moa Bird (Pet; 3)
9	Kendrick Redstaff (20)
10	Priestess Rashenna (5)
11	Erudine (Trainer Ms; 20)
H	Henchmen (6)
M	Merchant (5)

1	Carrion Devourer (4; 8)
	Gnash Underfoot (5)
	Plague Devourer (3)
	Whiptail Devourer (4)
2	Flash Gargoyle (3)
	Shatter Gargoyle (8)
	Spasmo Thunderbolt (Boss E; 5)
3	Grawl Ulodyte (3)
4	Grenn Mindvenom (5)
	Larrk Etherburn (Boss Ms; 5)
	Storm Rider (7)
5	Boulder Elemental (7)
	Hulking Stone Elemental (3)
	Stone Elemental (5)
	Stone Golem (Boss E; 7)

Pockmark Flats Quests

Replacement Healers

Requirement: Monk

- Speak to Priestess Rashenna in Serenity Temple.
- Meet Devona in Pockmark Flats.
- Lead Devona to the Eastern Frontier.
- Help Devona defeat the Charr warband in the Eastern Frontier.
- Return to Priestess Rashenna for your reward.

Skill Unlock: Infuse Health (Mk), Strength of Honor (Mk)

Unnatural Creatures

Requirement: Mesmer

- Speak to Erudine in Serenity Temple.
- Slay Gren Mindvenom near the large crystal in Pockmark Flats.
- Pick up the Beholder Tissue Sample and return to Erudine in Serenity Temple for your reward.

Skill Unlock: Diversion (M)

Experimental Elixir

Requirement: Mesmer

- Speak to Erudine in Serenity Temple.
- Give the elixir to Fadden Hathorn in Sardelac Sanitarium.
- Report your findings to Vassar at Sardelac Santitarium to receive your reward.

Skill Unlock: Shatter Hex (M)

The Way of the Geomancer

Requirement: Elementalist

- Speak to Kendrick Redstaff in Serenity Temple.
- Kill 10 hulking stone elementals in Pockmark Flats.
- Return to Kendrick Redstaff for your reward.

The Geomancer's Test

Requirement: Elementalist

- Speak to Kendrick Redstaff in Serenity Temple.
- Activate all three earth shrines in Pockmark Flats by placing enchanted lodestones upon them.
- Return to Kendrick Redstaff in Serenity Temple for your reward.

Skill Unlock: Magnetic Aura (E), Earth Attunement (E)

The Breach Quests

(See map on next page.)

Fires in the North

- Speak to Duke Barradin in Piken Square.
- Find the Charr fires along the southern edge of the Diessa Lowlands. Kill the Flame Keepers and extinguish the flames.
- Return to Duke Barradin for your reward.

The Siege of Piken Square

- Speak to Duke Barradin in Piken Square.
- Destroy the Charr forces besieging Piken Square in the Breach.
- Return to Duke Barradin in Piken Square for your reward.

Charr Reinforcements

- Speak to Ivor Trueshot in Piken Square.
- Meet Aidan just outside of Piken Square.
- Ambush the Charr reinforcements.
- Pillage the Charr supply depot.
- Kill Kaargoth Bloodclaw.
- Return to Ivor Trueshot for your reward.

Skill Unlock: Distracting Shot (R), Call of Haste (R)

The Duke's Daughter

- Speak to Viggo in Piken Square.
- Search of signs of Duke Barradin's lost daughter, Althea, in the Diessa Lowlands.
- Tell Duke Barradin about Althea's ghost.

Casualty Report

- Speak to Undertaker Cortis in Piken Square.
- Deliver the Casualty Report to Warmaster Tydus in Ascalon City.
- Return to Undertaker Cortis in Piken Square to receive your reward.

Skill Unlock: Shadow Strike (N)

The Red-Cloaked Deserter

- Speak to Farrah Cappo in Piken Square.
- Deliver Farrah's message to Little Thom in Regent Valley.
- Return to Piken Square.

- RUINS OF ASCALON -
The Breach

Piken Square

Diessa Lowlands

Old Ascalon

>>BRASSE<<
DWARVEN CARTOGRAPHER

1	Sally Kaugie (Collector)
2	Aidan (7)
3	Ascalon Militia (5)
	Ascalon Warrior (5)
4	Captain West (6)
5	Old Mac (7)
6	Supply Bearer (4)
7	Louise Haup (Collector)
8	Crafter (Crafter; 1)
9	Armsman Pitney (7)
10	Duke Barradin (7)
11	Farrah Cappo (2)
12	Quartermaster Aada (5)
13	Viggo (4)
14	Undertaker Cortis (Trainer N; 20)
15	Ivor Trueshot (Trainer R; 5)
H	Henchmen (6)
M	Merchant (5)

1	Tar Behemoth (6)
2	Charr Ash Walker (5, 6)
	Charr Ashen Claw (8)
	Charr Axe Warrior (6)
	Charr Blade Warrior (5, 6)
	Charr Captain (Boss W; 6)
	Charr Fire Caller (5, 6)
	Charr Flame Wielder (8)
	Charr Martyr (5)
	Charr Mind Spark (5)
	Charr Overseer (6)
	Charr Stalker (5, 6)
	Gorgaan Hatemonger (Boss W; 3)
	Grimm Sharpfang (Boss R; 3)
	Kaargoth Bloodclaw (Boss N; 6)
	Mirash Dreambreaker (Boss Ms; 3)
3	Carrion Devourer (8)
	Joe (5)
4	Flash Gargoyle (3)
5	Crown of Thorns (5)

Hammer and Anvil

- Speak to Duke Barradin in Piken Square after completing The Siege of Piken Square quest.

- Ambush the Charr in the tar pits south of Piken Square. Strike down Grimm Sharpfang.

- Return to Duke Barradin for your reward.

Garfazz Bloodfang

- Speak to Viggo in Piken Square after completing The Siege of Piken Square quest.

- Go to the Diessa Lowlands. Kill Garfazz Bloodfang.

- Return to Viggo for your reward.

Althea's Ashes

- Speak to Duke Barradin in Piken Square after completing The Duke's Daughter quest.

- Find the temple where Althea was killed and gather her ashes.

- Bring Althea's Ashes to Duke Barradin in Piken Square.

Army Life

- Speak to Armsman Pitney in Piken Square.

- Find Old Mac's body out the in Breach.

- Lead Old Mac back to Piken Square.

- Talk to Armsman Pitney to receive your reward.

Skill Unlock: Mighty Blow (W)

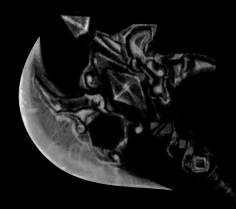

1	Fytch (Collector)
2	Guardsman Noell (Collector)
3	Paige Osbourne (Collector)
4	Raymon Elsworth (Collector)
5	Devona (10)
6	Footman Tate (5)
7	Thaddiel (10)
8	Moa Bird (Pet; 3)
9	Meerak the Shouter (Crafter; 1)
10	Warmaster Riga (20)
H	Henchmen (6)

1	Charr Axe Fiend (8)
	Charr Hunter (8)
	Charr Shaman (7)
	Charr Stalker (6)
	Flame Keeper (7)
	Rrrack Whitefire (Boss Mk; 4)
2	Carrion Devourer (4)
	Gnash Underfoot (5)
3	Grawl (4)
	Murg (3)

- RUINS OF ASCALON -
Eastern Frontier

Pockmark Flats

Ruins of Surmia

- Speak to Warmaster Riga in Frontier Gate.
- Go north of the Wall in the Eastern Frontier and follow the road to Surmia.
- Talk to Captain Miken to receive reward.

Frontier Gate Fugitives

- Speak to Warmaster Riga in Frontier Gate.
- Search the Eastern Frontier and Pockmark Flats for Footman Tate and Footman Quinn. Bring them to justice.
- Speak with Footman Tate in the Eastern Frontier. Footman Tate surrenders. Lead him back to Frontier Gate.
- Kill Footman Quinn in Pockmark Flats.
- Return to Warmaster Riga for reward.

Flame Temple Corridor

Ascalon Foothills

8 M H
7 2

>>BRISSE<<
DWARVEN CARTOGRAPHER

Nolani
Academy

- RUINS OF ASCALON -
Diessa Lowlands

The Breach

- RUINS OF ASCALON -
Ascalon Foothills

Traveler's
Vale

>>BRISSE<<
DWARVEN CARTOGRAPHER

Diessa
Lowlands

Diessa Lowlands

1 Gil Moriddan (Collector)
2 Lenerd Aberold (Collector)
3 Martel Bastions (Collector)
4 Wain Hughes (Collector)
5 Moa Bird (Pet; 3)
6 Ghost of Althea (5)
7 Graine Hathorn (Collector)
8 Warmaster Labofski (4)
H Henchmen (8)
M Merchant (5)

1 Charr Axe Fiend (8)
 Charr Flame Wielder (8)
 Charr Hunter (8)
 Charr Shaman (7)
 Cruc the Reborn (Boss Mk; 5)
 Flame Keeper (7)
 Garfazz Bloodfang (Boss N; 6)
 Maim Deathrain (Boss R; 5)

2 Whiptail Devourer (7)
3 Flash Gargoyle (7)
 Shatter Gargoyle (8)
 Spasmo Thunderbolt
  (Boss E; 5)
4 Hydra (11)
5 Storm Rider (7)
6 Boulder Elemental (7)
 Pulv Rubblegrinder
  (Boss W; 7)
 Stone Fury (8)

Ascalon Foothills

1 Voice of Grenth (24)
2 Dael (Collector)

1 Oswalt Alston (10)
2 Hydra (11)
3 Singed Oak (10)
4 Boulder Elemental (7)
 Stone Fury (8)

- RUINS OF ASCALON -
Dragon's Gullet

Flame
Temple
Shrine

Diessa Lowlands

>>DANSSE<<
DWARVEN CARTOGRAPHER

Dragon's Gullet

1	Ashram Fenn (Collector)
2	Nazag Fenn (Collector)

1	Tar Behemoth (6)
2	Charr Axe Fiend (8)
3	Abomination (11)
4	Hydra (11)

Flame Temple Corridor

1	Ascalon Striker (7)

1	Charr Ashen Claw (8)
	Charr Axe Fiend (8)
	Charr Blade Storm (8)
	Charr Chaot (8)
	Charr Flame Wielder (8)
	Charr Hunter (8)
	Charr Shaman (7)
2	Hydra (11)
3	Plague Worm (1)

Shiverpeaks

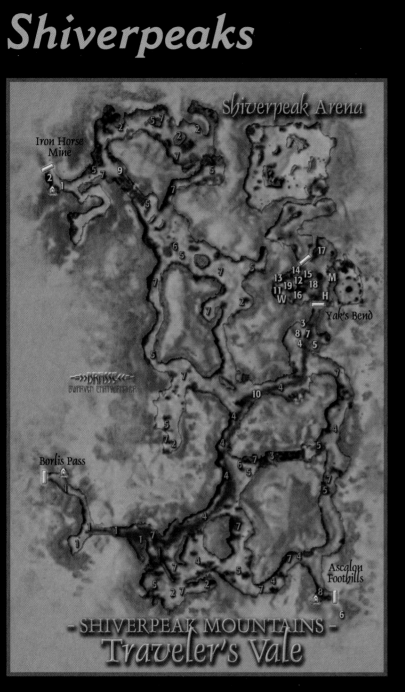

Shiverpeak Arena

Iron Horse Mine

Dwarven Craftworker

Borlis Pass

Yak's Bend

Ascalon Foothills

– SHIVERPEAK MOUNTAINS –
Traveler's Vale

Traveler's Vale

1	Rangil Ironbow (10)
2	Asgrim Brightaxe (Collector)
3	Pyrs Harven (Collector)
4	Ascalon Guard (7)
	Ascalon Refugee (10)
	Caravan Guard (7)
5	Cynn (13)
6	Devona (13)
7	Elsa Alston (10)
8	Guard Markus (7)
9	Artemis the Ranger (Trainer R; 2)
10	Snow Wolf (Pet; 5)
11	Grand Mason Stonecleaver (10)
12	Sadira Powell (Collector)
13	Crafter (Crafter; 1)
14	Gladiator's Arena Gate Guard (2)
15	Howland the Elementalist (Trainer E; 2)
16	Sebedoh the Mesmer (Trainer Ms; 2)
17	Necromancer Morgan (Trainer N; 2)
18	Captain Osric (Trainer W; 20)
19	Van the Warrior (Trainer W; 20)
H	Henchmen (8)
M	Merchant (2)
W	Weaponsmith (2)

1	Shiverpeak Longbow (8)
	Shiverpeak Protector (8)
	Shiverpeak Warrior (8)
2	Hussar Ironfeast (Boss Mk; 8)
3	Greplak Froststaff (8)
4	Snow Ettin (11)
5	Ice Golem (10)
	The Judge (8)
6	Juniper Bark (7)
7	Inar Frostbite (Boss Ms; 8)
	Saris Headstaver (Boss Ms; 8)
	Stone Summit Brute (10)
	Stone Summit Sage (10)
	Summit Axe Wielder (9)
	Ulrik the Undefeated (Boss Ms; 9)
8	Verata the Necromancer (Boss N; 20)
	Verata's Fiend (6)
	Verata's Horror (6)

Stone Summit Beastmasters

Requirement: Ranger

- Speak to Artemis the Ranger in Traveler's Vale.
- Track down and destroy Thorgrim Beastlasher in Iron Horse Mine.
- Return to Artemis for your reward.

Skill Unlock: Whirling Defense (R), Winter (R), Call of Protection (R)

Minaar's Trouble

- Speak to Rangil Ironbow in Traveler's Vale.
- Find Minaar Stonesledge in Iron Horse Mine.
- Escort Minaar back to Traveler's Vale.
- Return to Rangil Ironbow for your reward.

Minaar's Worry

- Speak to Rangil Ironbow in Traveler's Vale after completing the Minaar's Trouble quest.
- Go to Iron Horse Mine and kill Ore Darkwhip. Pick up War Machine Plans.
- Bring the War Machine Plans to Rangil Ironbow to receive your reward.

(Quests continued on next page.)

Yak's Bend

The Road to Borlis Pass

- Speak to Captain Osric.
- Follow the road from Yak's Bend to Borlis Pass. Defeat all Stone Summit raiders along the road.
- Return to Captain Osric to receive your reward.

Shiverpeak Stragglers

- Speak to Captain Osric.
- Search road to Ascalon for refugees.
- Rush to the aid of the refugees when you hear their shouts.
- Speak to Elsa Alston.
- Lead Elsa and the refugees back.
- Speak to Captain Osric in Yak's Bend to receive your reward.

The Way is Blocked

- Speak to Captain Osric.
- Clear the Stone Summit blocking the entrance to Borlis Pass.
- See Beccum Reedly in Borlis Pass for your reward.

The Wayward Monk

Requirement: Monk

- Speak to Van the Warrior.
- Talk to Cynn in Traveler's Vale.
- Talk to Cynn upon entering Iron Horse Mine.
- Find Mhenlo and speak with him to receive your reward.

Skill Unlock: Vigorous Spirit (Mk), Pacifism (Mk), Divine Boon (Mk)

Helping the Dwarves

- Speak to Grand Mason Stonecleaver.
- Find and speak to Rangil Ironbow in Traveler's Vale to receive reward.

Skill Unlock: Remove Hex (Mk), Debilitating Shot (R), Protector's Strike (W), Suffering (N), Mantra of Frost (Ms), Gale (E)

Stone Summit Champion

Requirement: Mesmer

- Talk to Sebedoh the Mesmer.
- Defeat Ulrik the Undefeated in Traveler's Vale.
- Return to Sebedoh the Mesmer in Yak's Bend for your reward.

Skill Unlock: Fragility (Ms), Power Spike (Ms), Channeling (Ms)

Iron Horse Mine		
1 Minaar Stonesledge (10)	1 Dolyak Rider (11)	5 Ice Golem (10)
2 Norin Stonegrimm (Collector)	Shalis Ironmantle (Boss Mk; 9)	6 Minotaur (10)
3 Aidan (13)	2 Frostfire Dryder (10)	7 Fendar Stonestance (Boss W; 9)
4 Cynn (13)	Frostfire Dryder (Boss Ms; 8)	Stone Summit Crusher (10)
5 Mhenlo (13)	3 Snow Ettin (11)	Stone Summit Howler (10)
6 Snow Wolf (Pet; 5)	4 Ore Darkwhip (8)	Stone Summit Sage (10)
	Summit Beastmaster (13)	Stone Summit Scout (9)
	Thorgrim Beastlasher (24)	Summit Axe Wielder (9)

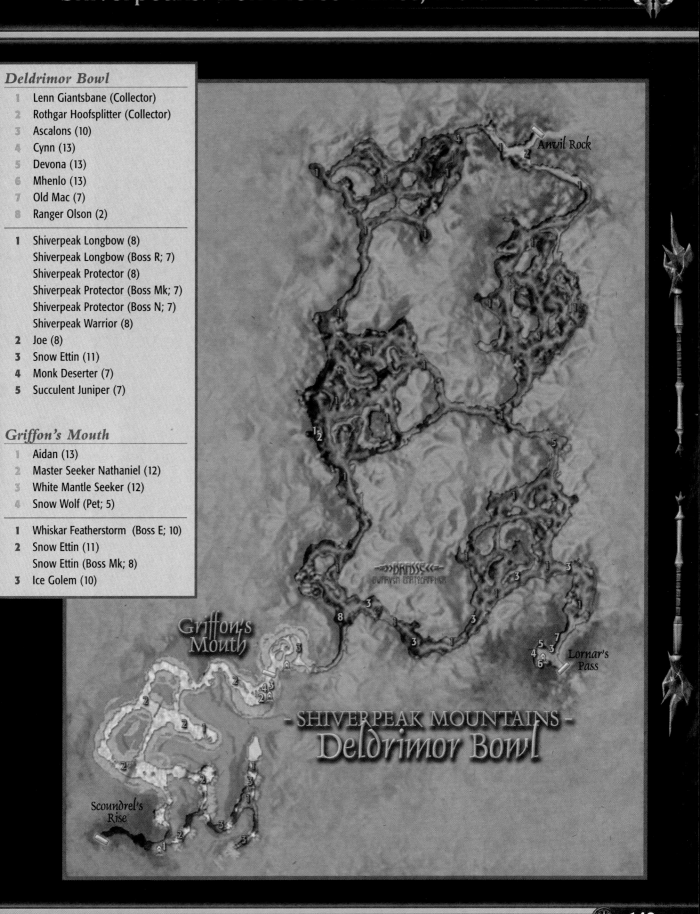

Deldrimor Bowl

1. Lenn Giantsbane (Collector)
2. Rothgar Hoofsplitter (Collector)
3. Ascalons (10)
4. Cynn (13)
5. Devona (13)
6. Mhenlo (13)
7. Old Mac (7)
8. Ranger Olson (2)

1. Shiverpeak Longbow (8)
   Shiverpeak Longbow (Boss R; 7)
   Shiverpeak Protector (8)
   Shiverpeak Protector (Boss Mk; 7)
   Shiverpeak Protector (Boss N; 7)
   Shiverpeak Warrior (8)
2. Joe (8)
3. Snow Ettin (11)
4. Monk Deserter (7)
5. Succulent Juniper (7)

Griffon's Mouth

1. Aidan (13)
2. Master Seeker Nathaniel (12)
3. White Mantle Seeker (12)
4. Snow Wolf (Pet; 5)

1. Whiskar Featherstorm (Boss E; 10)
2. Snow Ettin (11)
   Snow Ettin (Boss Mk; 8)
3. Ice Golem (10)

Anvil Rock

Griffon's Mouth

-SHIVERPEAK MOUNTAINS-
Deldrimor Bowl

Lornar's Pass

Scoundrel's Rise

Iron Horse Mine

Ice Tooth Cave

BRISE
DWARVEN CARTOGRAPHER

The Frost Gate

Deldrimor Bowl

– SHIVERPEAK MOUNTAINS –
Anvil Rock

Anvil Rock

1	Maccus Ironjaw (Collector)
2	Sander the Gray (Collector)
3	Snow Wolf (Pet; 5)
H	Henchmen (8)
M	Merchant (5)

1	Shiverpeak Longbow (8)
	Shiverpeak Protector (Boss Mk; 7)
	Shiverpeak Warrior (8)
2	Dolyak Rider (11)
3	Frostfire Dryder (10)
	Frostfire Dryder (Boss Ms; 8)
4	Minotaur (10)
	Minotaur (Boss W; 9)
5	Riine Windrot (Boss N; 8)
	Stone Summit Howler (10)

SHIVERPEAK MOUNTAINS
Lornar's Pass

Deldrimor Bowl

Beacon's Perch

=»»BRASSE««
DWARVEN CARTOGRAPHER

Dreadnought's Drift

Snake Dance

Lornar's Pass

1	Voice of Grenth (24)
2	Nord Stonegrimm (Collector)
3	Master Saberlin (4)
4	Vault Keeper (2)
H	Henchmen (10)
M	Merchant (5)

1	Shiverpeak Protector (8)
2	Dolyak Master (24)
	Dolyak Rider (11)
	Stone Summit Arcanist (24)
3	Frostfire Dryder (10)
4	Grawl (22)
5	Minotaur (10)
6	Stone Summit Carver (24)
	Stone Summit Gnasher (24)
	Stone Summit Ranger (24)
7	Mountain Troll (24)
8	Frost Wurm

Dreadnought's Drift

1	Avatar of Dwayna (24)

1	Dolyak Master (24)
	Stone Summit Arcanist (24)
2	Summit Giant Herder (24)
	Tundra Giant (24)
3	Siege Ice Golem (24)
4	Blessed Griffon (24)
5	Azure Shadow (22)
6	Stone Summit Carver (24)
	Stone Summit Gnasher (24)
	Stone Summit Ranger (24)

Hungry Devourer

Requirement: Monk, Necromancer, Ranger, or Warrior

- Speak to Master Saberlin in Beacon's Perch.
- Speak to Old Mac in Deldrimor's Bowl.
- Feed Joe 10 succulent juniper meats.
- Return Joe to Old Mac in Deldrimor's Bowl and speak with Old Mac again.
- Enter Beacon's Perch and speak with Master Saberlin to receive your reward.

Skill Unlock: Divine Spirit (Mk), Pin Down (R), Flurry (W), Rotting Flesh (N)

To Kryta: Refugees

- Speak to Master Saberlin in Beacon's Perch.
- Eliminate the centaur patrols along the main road.
- Speak to Ranger Olson to receive your reward.

The Deserters

Requirement: Monk or Ranger

- Speak to Master Saberlin in Beacon's Perch.
- Find the deserters in Deldrimor's Bowl.
- Bring word to Master Saberlin in Beacon's Perch that the supplies have been recovered.

Skill Unlock: Balthazar's Spirit (Mk), Serpent's Quickness (R)

SHIVERPEAK MOUNTAINS
Snake Dance

Dreadnought's Drift

=»DRNSE«=
DWARVEN CARTOGRAPHER

Camp Rankor

Talus Chute

Snake Dance

1 Hagnon Warblade (Collector)
2 Hoknil the Lesser (Collector)
3 Merin Trollsbane (Collector)
4 Radamon (Collector)
5 Lynx (Pet; 10)
H Henchmen (18)
M Merchant (12)

1 Bolis Hillshaker (Boss Mk; 24)
   Dolyak Master (24)
   Stone Summit Arcanist (24)

2 Summit Giant Herder (24)
   Tundra Giant (24)
3 The Judge (24)
4 Blessed Griffon (24)
5 Azure Shadow (22)
6 Fuury Stonewrath (Boss Ms; 24)
   Riine Windrot (Boss N; 24)
   Stone Summit Ranger (24)
7 Mountain Troll (24)

My Favorite Character

Name: Gaile Gray

Title: Community Relations Manager

Character: Gaile Gray, Stormy Weathor

Mine is a Ranger/Monk or Beastmaster Ranger/Monk. I place in my Skill Bar, left to right, Troll Unguent, Healing Breeze, Orison of Healing, Resurrect, Apply Poison, Kindle Arrow (sometimes swapped with Exploding Arrow or another fire arrow skill), Comfort Animal and Charm Animal. Alternative Monk Set: Troll Unguent, Infuse Health, Heal Area, and Resurrect. Alternative Ranger Set: Some combination of Apply Poison, Kindle Arrow, Dual Shot, Barrage, and Escape.

My choices do not reflect the most sterling or complex of strategical options, but they're ones that work well for a player like me who enjoys a sort of randomly dual role. I can't stand to see my teammates die! I love keeping the team healthy. It's great fun to be able to bring the team back from the edge of extinction by remaining alive and resurrecting the rest of the party. With the alternative Monk skills, I layer Resurrect with Infuse Health and Heal Area to get a fallen comrade back into the battle quickly. I'm greatly fond of the bow, and love having a huge variety of types of bows and arrow skills. I am most excited that my traditional favorite character class, the Ranger, is also able to charm animals— it's a combination made in heaven. I have a special relationship with my charmed lynx, George XVI, and I probably spend more time healing him than I should. On the other hand, I don't often equip a full list of pet skills because I do enjoy dealing damage, too. I prefer splashy bow effects rather than evasive skills or those that halt the damage of others. My next build will be a single-profession Ranger, if I can tear myself away from playing a Monk secondary.

SHIVERPEAK MOUNTAINS
Talus Chute

Snake Dance

Icedome

Ice Caves of Sorrow

Deldrimor Arena

»DAGESS«
BUTRVEN CHROEROPHER

Droknar's Forge

Talus Chute

1	Korg Snowfoot (10)
2	Onar Ironblood (10)
3	Cember Goreaxe (Collector)
4	Hoknil the Greater (Collector)
5	Volsung Stoneketil (Collector)
6	Lynx (Pet; 10)

1	Stone Summit Arcanist (24)
2	Tundra Giant (24)
3	Ice Golem (10)
	Siege Ice Golem (24)
4	Grawl (22)
	Grawl Ulodyte (22)
5	Blessed Griffon (24)
6	Ice Imp (22)
7	Azure Shadow (22)
8	Stone Summit Crusher (10)
	Stone Summit Gnasher (24)
9	Avicara Brave (24)
	Avicara Fierce (24)
	Avicara Wise (24)
10	Mountain Troll (24)

Droknar's Forge

1	Champion of Balthazar (24)
2	Voice of Grenth (24)
3	Captain Hugo Bronzebeard (20)
4	Ornhelm Brightaxe (20)
5	Crafter (Crafter; 10)
6	Gladiator's Arena Gate Guard (2)
H	Henchmen (18)
M	Merchant (12)

Seeking the Seer

- Speak to Captain Hugo Bronzebeard in Droknar's Forge.
- Speak with Korg the Scout in Talus Chute.
- Speak with Onar Ironblood in Talus Chute.
- See Blade Scout Shelby in the Ice Caves of Sorrow for your reward.

Droknar's Forge

6
6
6
6
2
1
1
6
6
1
1
6
1
1
1
1
1
1
2
3
5
5
2
1
4
5
3
4
5
3

=»BRASSE«=
DWARVEN CARTOGRAPHER

Port Sledge

M H

– SHIVERPEAK MOUNTAINS –
Witman's Folly

Witman's Folly

1	Mag Ironwall (Collector)
2	Vania Sewell (Collector)
H	Henchmen (18)
M	Merchant (12)

1	Grawl (22)
	Grawl Ulodyte (22)
2	Ice Imp (22)
3	Mursaat Mesmer (24)
4	Azure Shadow (22)
5	White Mantle Priest (24)
	White Mantle Sycophant (16)
	White Mantle Zealot (24)
6	Frost Wurm

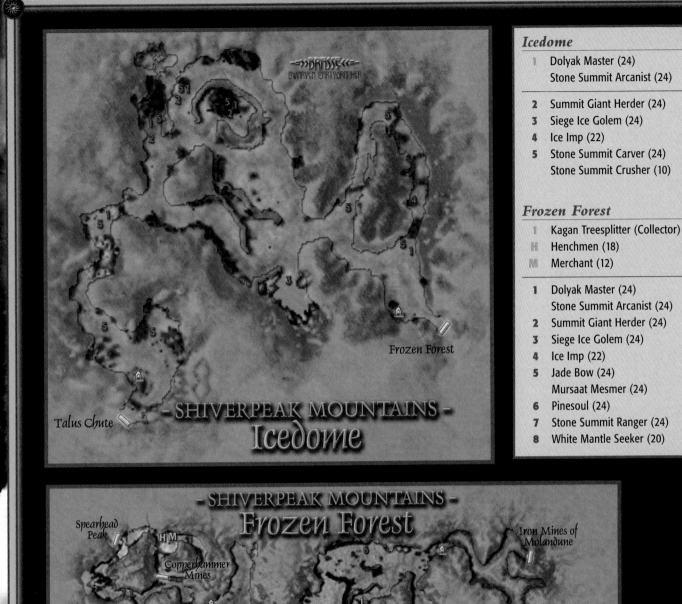

Icedome

1 Dolyak Master (24)
  Stone Summit Arcanist (24)

2 Summit Giant Herder (24)
3 Siege Ice Golem (24)
4 Ice Imp (22)
5 Stone Summit Carver (24)
  Stone Summit Crusher (10)

Frozen Forest

1 Kagan Treesplitter (Collector)
H Henchmen (18)
M Merchant (12)

1 Dolyak Master (24)
  Stone Summit Arcanist (24)
2 Summit Giant Herder (24)
3 Siege Ice Golem (24)
4 Ice Imp (22)
5 Jade Bow (24)
  Mursaat Mesmer (24)
6 Pinesoul (24)
7 Stone Summit Ranger (24)
8 White Mantle Seeker (20)

Frozen Forest

Talus Chute

- SHIVERPEAK MOUNTAINS -
Icedome

- SHIVERPEAK MOUNTAINS -
Frozen Forest

Spearhead Peak

Copperhammer Mines

Iron Mines of Molandune

Ice Dome

Ice Floe

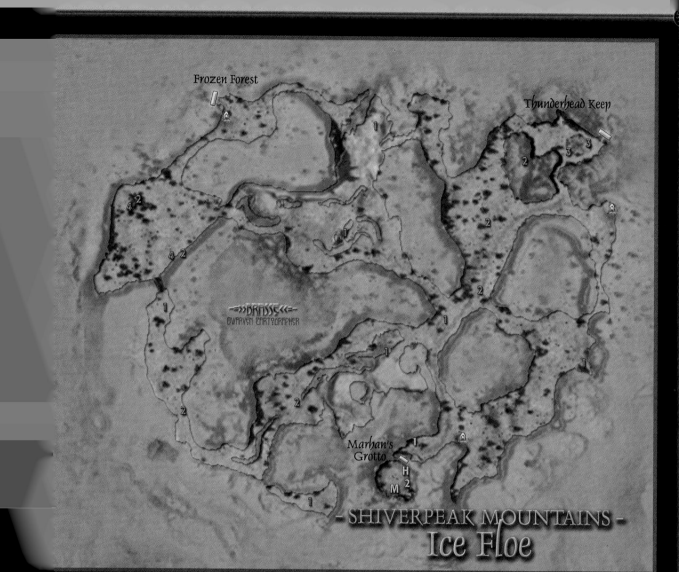

Frozen Forest

Thunderhead Keep

DANSE
DWARVEN CARTOGRAPHER

Marhan's Grotto

— SHIVERPEAK MOUNTAINS —
Ice Floe

Ice Floe

1	Turlo Oakenspear (Collector)
2	Crafter (Crafter; 10)
H	Henchmen (18)
M	Merchant (12)

1	Ice Imp (22)
2	Jade Armor (24)
	Jade Bow (24)
	Mursaat Elementalist (24)
	Mursaat Mesmer (24)
	Mursaat Necromancer (24)
3	Azure Shadow (22)
	Frostbite (Boss Mk; 24)
4	White Mantle Seeker (20)
	White Mantle Zealot (24)

My Favorite Guild

Name: Horia Dociu

Title: Artist

Character: Ragnar X

We started a guild called the Scorpion Lords of Doom (SLOD). The best thing about playing with SLOD is the people. Everyone is out to have a good time, and no matter how serious the tournament, the SLOD guys and gals are always up for a good laugh. It's not about winning, but having fun, and there's nothing like playing with some of your raddest friends. But be warned: We will "SLOD-er" any guild that gets in our way!

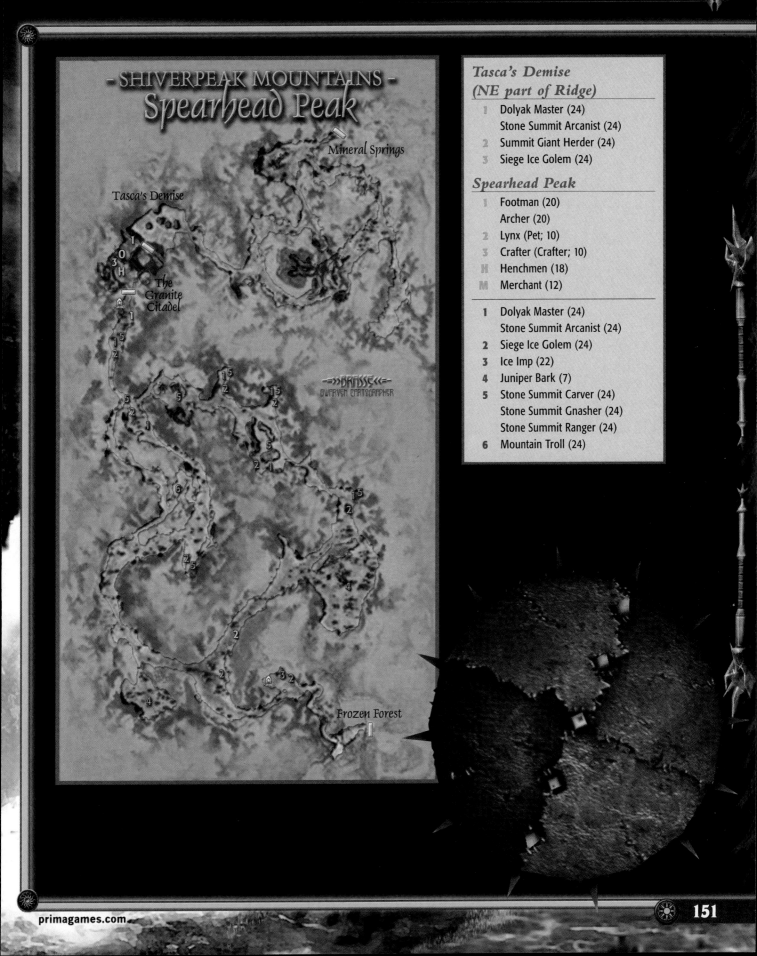

- SHIVERPEAK MOUNTAINS -
Spearhead Peak

Mineral Springs

Tasca's Demise

The Granite Citadel

>>BRASSE<<
DWARVEN CARTOGRAPHER

Frozen Forest

**Tasca's Demise
(NE part of Ridge)**

1 Dolyak Master (24)
  Stone Summit Arcanist (24)
2 Summit Giant Herder (24)
3 Siege Ice Golem (24)

Spearhead Peak

1 Footman (20)
  Archer (20)
2 Lynx (Pet; 10)
3 Crafter (Crafter; 10)
H Henchmen (18)
M Merchant (12)

1 Dolyak Master (24)
  Stone Summit Arcanist (24)
2 Siege Ice Golem (24)
3 Ice Imp (22)
4 Juniper Bark (7)
5 Stone Summit Carver (24)
  Stone Summit Gnasher (24)
  Stone Summit Ranger (24)
6 Mountain Troll (24)

Tasca's Demise

- SHIVERPEAK MOUNTAINS -
Mineral Springs

— DATSSE —
DWARVEN CARTOGRAPHER

Mineral Springs

1   Lyssa's Muse (24)
2   Bariel Darkroot (Collector)
3   Goran Grimyak (Collector)
4   Trego Stonebreaker (Collector)

1   Ice Beast (20)
2   Tundra Giant (24)
3   Ice Golem (10)
4   Ice Imp (22)
5   Azure Shadow (22)
6   Juniper Bark (7)
7   Avicara Ardent (24)
    Avicara Brave (24)
    Avicara Fierce (24)
    Avicara Wise (24)
8   Mountain Troll (24)
9   Frost Wurm

Kryta

North Kryta Province

Griffon's Mouth

DRAKKE
DWARVEN EARTGRAPHER

— KRYTA —
Scoundrel's Rise

Gates of Kryta

N. Kryta Province
Duties of a Lionguard

- Speak to Lionguard Riddik (NKP).
- Look for Lionguard Orrin at Miraba's farm.
- Speak to Miraba (NKP) to receive your reward.

Bandit Trouble

- Speak to Miraba (NKP).
- Tell Mantle Knight Karriya in D'Alessio Seaboard of Miraba's bandit problem.
- Deliver Token of Janthir to Miraba (NKP) to receive reward.

Blankets for Settlers

- Speak to Captain Greywind at the settlement in North Kryta Province.
- Go to Nebo Village with the militia weapons. Talk to Weaver Danzar and trade the weapons for blankets.
- Bring the blankets to Captain Greywind in North Kryta Province to receive your reward.

Lion's Arch
Report to White Mantle

- Speak to Armen the Guide in Lion's Arch.
- Go to North Kryta Province and follow the road to the fort in the D'Alessio Seaboard. Once there, report your presence to Mantle Knight Karriya.
- Speak to Mantle Knight Karriya.

Merchant's Plea

- Speak to Bodrus the Merchant in Lion's Arch.
- Head out the northwest gate and follow the road to the Ascalon Settlement. Deliver the Settlement's Strongbox to Captain Greywind.
- Talk to Captain Greywind at the settlement in North Kryta Province to receive your reward.

(North Kryta Province map on following page.)

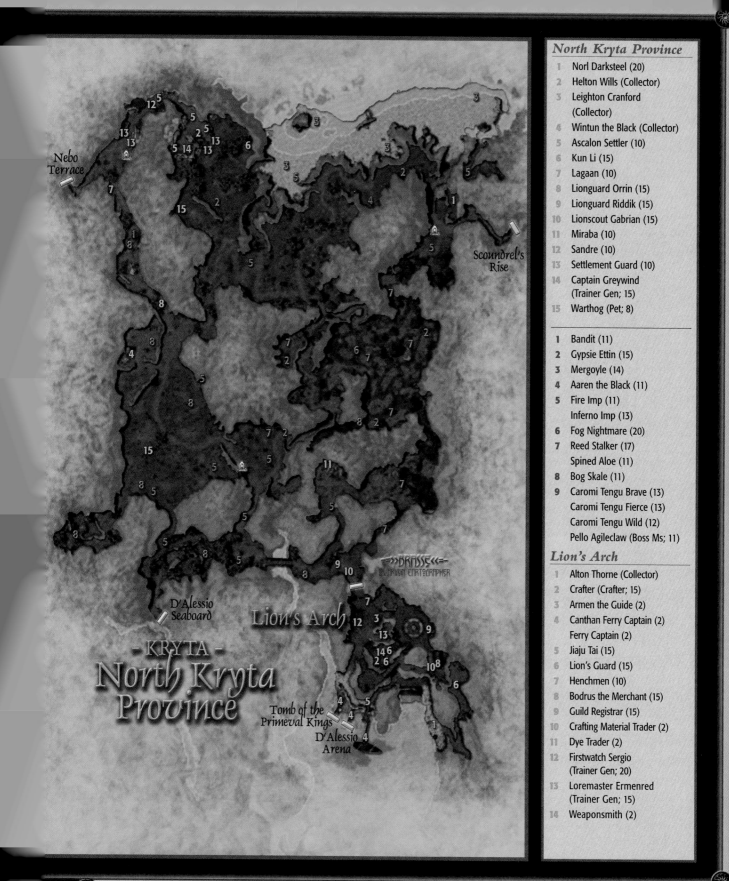

North Kryta Province

1. Norl Darksteel (20)
2. Helton Wills (Collector)
3. Leighton Cranford (Collector)
4. Wintun the Black (Collector)
5. Ascalon Settler (10)
6. Kun Li (15)
7. Lagaan (10)
8. Lionguard Orrin (15)
9. Lionguard Riddik (15)
10. Lionscout Gabrian (15)
11. Miraba (10)
12. Sandre (10)
13. Settlement Guard (10)
14. Captain Greywind (Trainer Gen; 15)
15. Warthog (Pet; 8)

1. Bandit (11)
2. Gypsie Ettin (15)
3. Mergoyle (14)
4. Aaren the Black (11)
5. Fire Imp (11)
   Inferno Imp (13)
6. Fog Nightmare (20)
7. Reed Stalker (17)
   Spined Aloe (11)
8. Bog Skale (11)
9. Caromi Tengu Brave (13)
   Caromi Tengu Fierce (13)
   Caromi Tengu Wild (12)
   Pello Agileclaw (Boss Ms; 11)

Lion's Arch

1. Alton Thorne (Collector)
2. Crafter (Crafter; 15)
3. Armen the Guide (2)
4. Canthan Ferry Captain (2)
   Ferry Captain (2)
5. Jiaju Tai (15)
6. Lion's Guard (15)
7. Henchmen (10)
8. Bodrus the Merchant (15)
9. Guild Registrar (15)
10. Crafting Material Trader (2)
11. Dye Trader (2)
12. Firstwatch Sergio (Trainer Gen; 20)
13. Loremaster Ermenred (Trainer Gen; 15)
14. Weaponsmith (2)

Nebo Terrace

Scoundrel's Rise

D'Alessio Seaboard

Lion's Arch

- KRYTA -

North Kryta Province

Tomb of the Primeval Kings

D'Alessio Arena

Watchtower Coast

The Black
Curtain

The Black
Curtain

Cursed Lands

North
Kryta
Province

~BRASSE~
DWARVEN CARTOGRAPHY

- KRYTA -
Nebo Terrace

Bergen
Hot Springs

Nebo Terrace

1 Avatar of Dwayna (24)
2 Beldon the Blade (Collector)
3 Kira Thorne (Collector)
4 Milny Samhammil (Collector)
5 Crafter (Crafter; 15)
6 Krytan Herald (Crafter; 15)
7 Weaver Danzar (Crafter; 10)
8 Elder Sobel (10)
9 Kun Li (15)
10 Warthog (Pet; 8)
H Henchmen (12)
M Merchant (12)

1 Gypsie Ettin (15)
2 Mergoyle (14)
    Mergoyle Wavebreaker (12)

3 Wraith (17)
4 Grasping Ghoul (11)
5 Hellhound (16)
6 Inferno Imp (13)
7 Spined Aloe (11)
    Tree of Renewal (Boss R; 13)
8 Bog Skale (11)
    Bog Skale Blighter (18)
9 Abijah the Decayed (Boss R; 12)
    Skeleton Mesmer (13)
    Skeleton Ranger (13)
    Skeleton Sorcerer (13)
10 Caromi Tengu Wild (12)
    Rawr Wildeye (Boss N; 11)
11 Damned Cleric (17)
    Necrid Horseman (18)
    Nizza the Sickle (Boss W; 12)
    Zombie Warlock (14)

Cursed Lands
(SW corner of Farm)

1 Kun Li (15)

1 Wraith (17)
2 Grasping Ghoul (11)
3 Hellhound (16)
4 Smoke Phantom (17)
5 Skeleton Mesmer (13)
    Skeleton Ranger (13)
    Skeleton Sorcerer (13)
6 Damned Cleric (17)
    Executioner (18)
    Zombie Warlock (14)

KRYTA
Watchtower Coast

=»>BRASSE<<=
DWARVEN CARTOGRAPHER

Divinity Coast

Beetletun

Nebo Terrace

Watchtower Coast

1	Ian Sturmme (Collector)
2	Tenlach Silverhand (Collector)
3	Farmer Fanella (2)
4	Warthog (Pet; 8)
5	Crafter (Crafter; 15)
H	Henchmen (12)
M	Merchant (12)

1	Mergoyle (14)
	Mergoyle Wavebreaker (12)
2	Ancient Oakheart (17)
	Spined Aloe (11)
3	Bog Skale (11)
4	Caromi Tengu Brave (13)
	Caromi Tengu Fierce (13)
	Caromi Tengu Wild (12)

The Black Curtain

1 Ian Borish (Collector)
2 Liris the Sage (Collector)
3 Sir Robert (Collector)
4 Kun Li (15)
5 Avatar of Dwayna (24)
6 Champion of Balthazar (24)
7 Lyssa's Muse (24)
8 Melandru's Watcher (24)
9 Voice of Grenth (24)
10 Kolleen Redstone (Collector)
11 Krytan Herald (Crafter; 15)
12 Brother Theophilus (2)

13 Skill Trainer (Trainer Gen; 2)
H Henchmen (15)
M Merchant (12)

1 Wraith (17)
2 Hellhound (16)
3 Inferno Imp (13)
4 Forest Minotaur (19)
   Rage Maulhoof (Boss W; 24)
5 Fog Nightmare (20)
   Shadow of Death (Boss N; 24)
6 Smoke Phantom (17)
7 Reed Stalker (17)

   Spined Aloe (11)
   Tree of Judgment (Boss Mk; 24)
8 Bog Skale Blighter (18)
   Frash the Cold (Boss E; 24)
   Gack the Mindwrecker (Boss Ms; 24)
9 Skeleton Bowmaster (17)
   Skeleton Mesmer (13)
10 Caromi Tengu Elite (18)
   Winglord Caromi (Boss R; 24)
11 Bone Dragon (18)
   Damned Cleric (17)
   Necrid Horseman (18)

Kessex Peak

1. Brion Elston (Collector)
2. Brynden Cromwell (Collector)
3. William Pennington (Collector)
4. Lion Guard Gariol (15)
5. Lynx (Pet; 10)
   Playful Lynx (Pet; 12)

1. Bandit (11)
2. Hill Giant (20)
3. Forest Minotaur (19)
4. Fog Nightmare (20)
5. Ancient Oakheart (17)
   Reed Stalker (17)
   Spined Aloe (11)
6. Fen Troll (20)
7. Apprentice of Verata (20)
   Eyes of Verata (20)
   Sage of Verata (20)
   Shepherd of Verata (20)
   Verata (20)
8. Galrath (Boss W; 16)

- KRYTA -
Kessex Peak

The Black Curtain

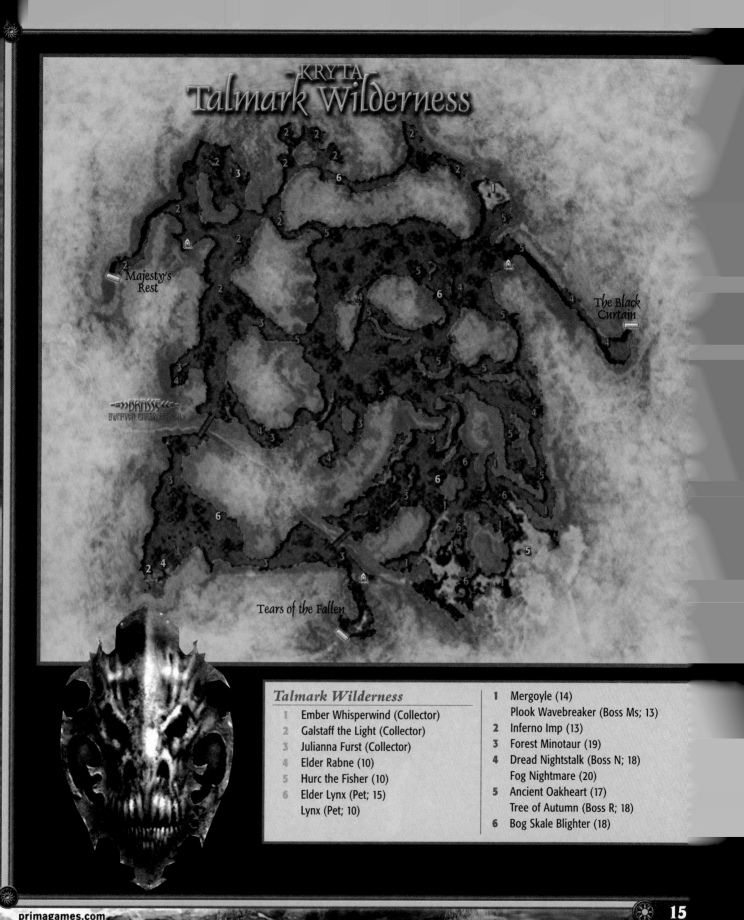

KRYTA
Talmark Wilderness

Majesty's Rest

The Black Curtain

BRASSE
DWARVEN CARTOGRAPHER

Tears of the Fallen

Talmark Wilderness

1 Ember Whisperwind (Collector)
2 Galstaff the Light (Collector)
3 Julianna Furst (Collector)
4 Elder Rabne (10)
5 Hurc the Fisher (10)
6 Elder Lynx (Pet; 15)
   Lynx (Pet; 10)

1 Mergoyle (14)
   Plook Wavebreaker (Boss Ms; 13)
2 Inferno Imp (13)
3 Forest Minotaur (19)
4 Dread Nightstalk (Boss N; 18)
   Fog Nightmare (20)
5 Ancient Oakheart (17)
   Tree of Autumn (Boss R; 18)
6 Bog Skale Blighter (18)

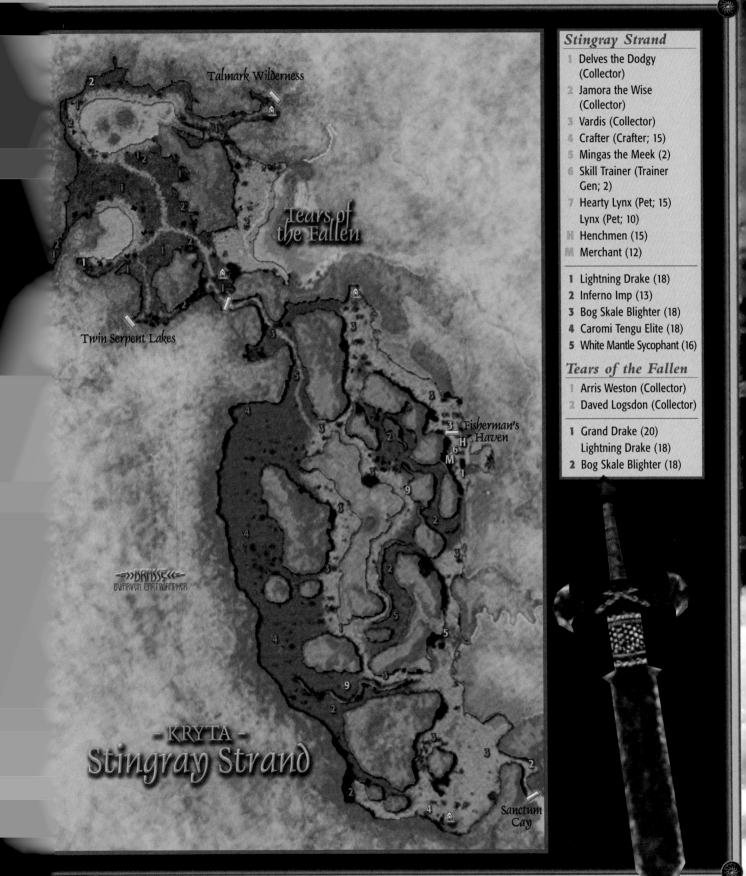

Talmark Wilderness

Tears of
the Fallen

Twin Serpent Lakes

Fisherman's
Haven

>>>BRASSE<<<
DWARVEN CARTOGRAPHER

- KRYTA -
Stingray Strand

Sanctum
Cay

- KRYTA -
Twin Serpent Lakes

Tears of the Fallen

Riverside Province

=>>BRASSE<<=
DWARVEN CARTOGRAPHER

Twin Serpent Lakes

1. Melandru's Watcher (24)
2. Falhurst (Collector)
3. Gruhn the Fisher (Collector)
4. Kournis the Tracker (10)
5. Dire Lynx (Pet; 15)
   Lynx (Pet; 10)

1. Lightning Drake (18)
2. Mergoyle (14)
3. Ancient Oakheart (17)
4. Bog Skale Blighter (18)
5. Caromi Tengu Elite (18)

- KRYTA -
Majesty's Rest

Sage Lands

≈≫BRASSE≪≈
DWARVEN CARTOGRAPHER

Talmark
Wilderness

Majesty's Rest

1 Champion of Balthazar (24)
2 Isabaeux Navarre (Collector)
3 Robin Neils (Collector)

1 Maguuma Spider (16)
2 Fevered Devourer (17)
  Thorn Devourer (17)
3 Haja Bloodwail (Boss W; 11)
4 Hellhound (16)
5 Fog Nightmare (20)
6 Smoke Phantom (17)
7 Ancient Oakheart (17)
  Entangling Root (18)
  Reed Stalker (17)
8 Skeleton Monk (12)
9 Fen Troll (20)
10 Bone Dragon (18)
  Damned Cleric (17)
  Necrid Horseman (18)
  Rotscale (24)

The Wilds

Sage Lands

1	Lyssa's Muse (24)
2	Aaron Fletcher (Collector)
3	Elwynn Kirby (Collector)
4	Crafter (Crafter; 15)
5	Chosen Villager (10)
6	House Ranger Amon (12)
7	House Ranger Lanalt (12)
8	House Ranger Marco (12)
9	House Ranger Rionel (12)
10	Justiciar Thommis (15)
11	Warthog (Pet; 12)
12	Mosreh the Exile (Collector)
13	Trader Versai (Merchant; 12)
14	Skill Trainer (Trainer Gen; 2)
H	Henchmen (12)
M	Merchant (12)

1	Maguuma Spider (16)
2	Fevered Devourer (17)
	Thorn Devourer (17)
3	Redwood Shepherd (19)
	Thorn Stalker (17)
4	Wind Rider (12)
	Wind Rider (17)
5	Moss Scarab (12)

Mamnoon Lagoon

1	Vargil the White (Collector)
1	Root Behemoth (19)
2	Life Pod (15)
3	Wind Rider (17)

Druid's Overlook
(Sage Lands)

A Brother's Fury

- Speak to Trader Versai at the Druid's Overlook.
- Speak with Justiciar Thommis.
- Speak with House Ranger Amon.
- Speak with House Ranger Lanalt.
- Speak with House Ranger Rionel.
- See Witness Giselle in The Wilds for reward.

Bloodstone Fen

THE WILDS
Silverwood

Mamnoon Lagoon

Quarrel Falls

≈≫DRASSE≪≈
DWARVEN CARTOGRAPHER

Ettin's Back

Silverwood

1 Crispin Bryllis (Collector)
2 Farmer Conklin (Collector)
3 Lady Engelram (Collector)
4 Warthog (Pet; 12)
5 Seris the Red (Collector)
6 Gareth Quickblade (15)
7 Crafter (Trainer Gen; 2)
8 Skill Trainer (Trainer Gen; 2)
H Henchmen (15)
M Merchant (12)

1 Maguuma Hunter (16)
   Maguuma Protector (16)
   Maguuma Warrior (16)
2 Wind Rider (12)
3 Moss Scarab (12)
   Moss Scarab (16)
4 Jungle Troll (14)
5 White Mantle Knight (16)

Silverwood

Aurora Glade

Ventari's Refuge

9
10 11 M
8
H

=»»DADSS«=
DWARVEN CARTOGRAPHER

Dry Top

— THE WILDS —
Ettin's Back

Reed Bog

Ettin's Back

1 Hember (Collector)
2 Horton Longsnout (Collector)
3 Lord Engelram (Collector)
4 Councilor Vaylor (15)
5 Shining Blade Mesmer (15)
6 Snakebite (15)
7 Warthog (Pet; 12)
8 Jaden Fletcher (Collector)
9 Crafter (Crafter; 2)
10 Ventari (Crafter; 15)
11 Skill Trainer (Trainer Gen; 2)
H Henchmen (15)
M Merchant (2)

1 Maguuma Hunter (16)
2 Fevered Devourer (17)
3 Thorn Stalker (17)
4 Moss Scarab (12)
5 White Mantle Knight (16)

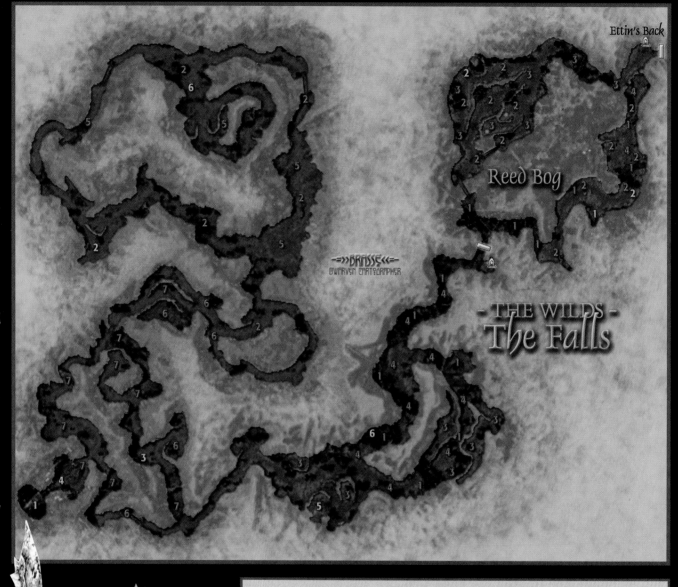

Ettin's Back

Reed Bog

=»»BRASSE«=
DWARVEN CARTOGRAPHER

- THE WILDS -
The Falls

Reed Bog

1   Elene the Vigilant (Collector)
2   Warthog (Pet; 12)

1   Maguuma Spider (16)
2   Life Pod (15)
    Redwood Shepherd (19)
3   Moss Scarab (16)
4   Jungle Troll (14)

The Falls

1   Champion of Balthazar (24)
2   Agrippa Stonehands (Collector)

3   Llourdes the Arcane (Collector)
4   Meghan the Bright (Collector)
5   Slayton Redblade (Collector)
6   Warthog (Pet; 12)

1   Maguuma Spider (16)
2   Root Behemoth (19)
3   Maguuma Hunter (16)
4   Life Pod (15)
    Redwood Shepherd (19)
5   Wind Rider (17)
6   Jungle Skale (19)
7   Jungle Troll (14)
    Jungle Troll (18)

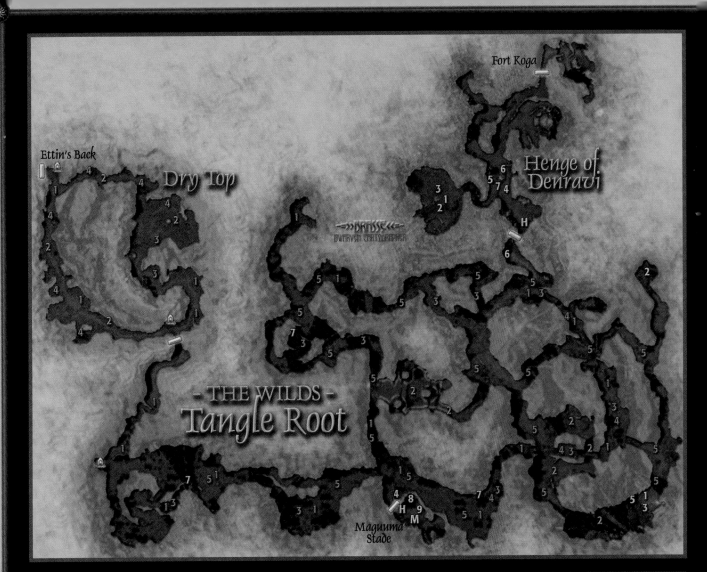

Fort Koga

Ettin's Back

Dry Top

Henge of Denravi

⊲⊲BRASSE⊲⊲
ВИҐRVSE CRRTISLRR3PR

- THE WILDS -
Tangle Root

Maguuma
Stade

Henge of Denravi

Passage Through The Dark River

- Talk to Shadow in Henge of Denravi.

- Talk to Old Joness in Tangle Root to gain passage down the Ullen River.

- See Blade Warrior Derikk in Riverside Province for your reward.

Tangle Root

1	Melandru's Watcher (24)
2	Orson Cooper (Collector)
3	Serah Shaes (Collector)
4	Tully Blackvine (Collector)
5	Old Joness (10)
6	Carlotta (2)
7	Warthog (Pet; 12)
8	Ingrid Larson (Collector)
9	Skill Trainer (Trainer GEn; 2)
H	Henchmen (15)
M	Merchant (12)

1	Life Pod (15)
	Redwood Shepherd (19)
	Thorn Stalker (17)
2	Wind Rider (17)
3	Moss Scarab (16)
4	Jungle Skale (19)

5	Jungle Troll (14)
	Jungle Troll (18)

Dry Top

1	Root Behemoth (19)
2	Maguuma Hunter (16)
	Maguuma Protector (16)
3	Fevered Devourer (17)
	Thorn Devourer (17)
4	Thorn Stalker (17)

Henge of Denravi

1	Adam Solstrum (Collector)
2	Loreen Cranford (Collector)
3	Thyfir Greenleaf (Collector)
4	Crafter (Crafter; 15)
5	Master Scout Kiera (15)
6	Shadow (15)
7	Moss Spider (Pet; 2)
H	Henchmen (15)

The Crystal Desert

Amnoon Oasis

Sands of Souls

- Speak to the Ghostly Hero in Amnoon Oasis.

- Speak to Great Ritual Priest Zahmut in Augury Rock to the east to receive your reward.

The Amnoon Oasis	
1	Ardenoth Oakenshield (Collector)
2	Ekimeel Trueshot (Collector)
3	Crafter (Crafter; 10)
4	Ghostly Hero (24)
5	Gladiator's Arena Gate Guard (2)
H	Henchmen (17)
M	Merchant (12)

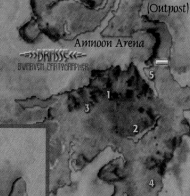

- CRYSTAL DESERT -
Amnoon Oasis

(Outpost)

Amnoon Arena

>>DANSSE<<
DWARVEN CARTOGRAPHER

Prophet's Path

The Amnoon Oasis

Salt Flats

>>DANSSE<<
DWARVEN CARTOGRAPHER

Skyward Reach

Hero's Audience

Vulture Drifts

- CRYSTAL DESERT
Prophet's Path

(Key on next page.)

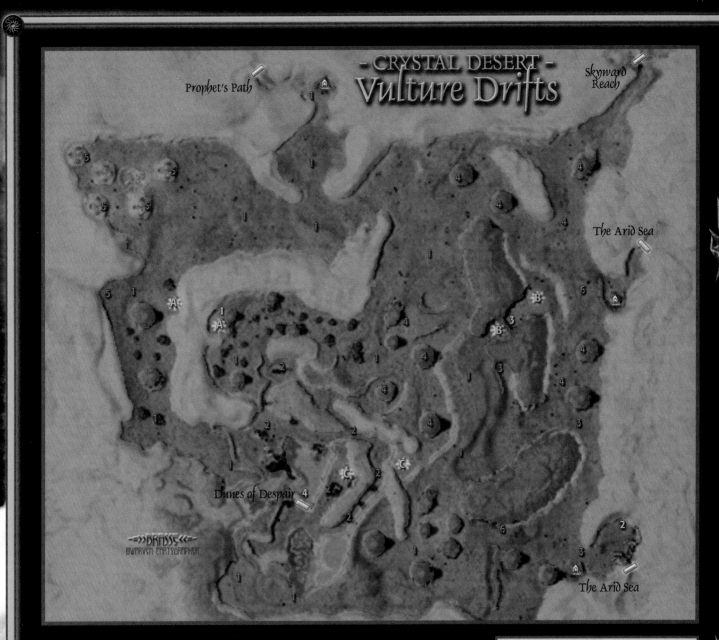

Prophet's Path

Skyward Reach

- CRYSTAL DESERT -
Vulture Drifts

The Arid Sea

Dunes of Despair

=>DRASSE<<=
DWARVEN CARTOGRAPHER

The Arid Sea

Prophet's Path

1	Fenster the Golden (Collector)
2	Gustov the Silent (Collector)
3	Kyle the Rich (Collector)
4	Winfield Michelson (Collector)
H	Henchmen (17)
M	Merchant (12)

1	Rockshot Devourer (20)
2	Sand Elemental (20)
3	Tortured Spirit (10)
4	Desert Griffon (21)
5	Minotaur (20)
6	Salving Cactus (20)
7	Storm Kin (20)
8	Jade Scarab (20)
9	Crystal Wurm

Vulture Drifts

1	Brandon Harlin (Collector)
2	Karl Jakobs (Collector)
3	Kraviec the Cursed (Collector)
4	Uderit Ignis (Collector)

1	Sand Elemental (20)
2	Enchanted Bow (20)
	Enchanted Hammer (20)
3	Sand Giant (22)
4	Desert Griffon (21)
5	Jade Scarab (20)
6	Crystal Wurm

GuildWars

PRIMA OFFICIAL GAME GUIDE

Diviner's Ascent

- CRYSTAL DESERT -
Salt Flats

Prophet's Path

Seeker's Passage

Skyward Reach

=»»»BRASSE«=
DWARVEN CARTOGRAPHER

Salt Flats

1	Kelsay Pradist (Collector)
2	Sir Norrington (Collector)
H	Henchmen (17)
M	Merchant (12)

1	Blighted Devourer (20)
2	Storm Kin (20)
3	Jade Scarab (20)

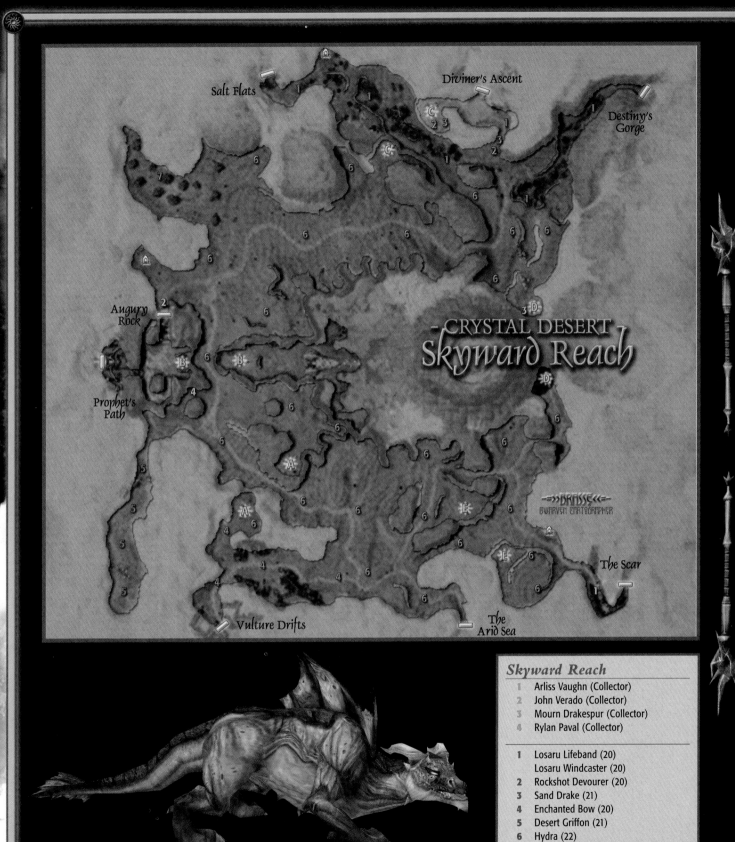

Salt Flats

Diviner's Ascent

Destiny's Gorge

CRYSTAL DESERT
Skyward Reach

Augury Rock

Prophet's Path

>>BRASSE<<
DWARVEN CARTOGRAPHER

The Scar

Vulture Drifts

The Arid Sea

Skyward Reach

1 Arliss Vaughn (Collector)
2 John Verado (Collector)
3 Mourn Drakespur (Collector)
4 Rylan Paval (Collector)

1 Losaru Lifeband (20)
   Losaru Windcaster (20)
2 Rockshot Devourer (20)
3 Sand Drake (21)
4 Enchanted Bow (20)
5 Desert Griffon (21)
6 Hydra (22)
7 Storm Kin (20)

GUILD WARS
PRIMA OFFICIAL GAME GUIDE

Skyward Reach

CRYSTAL DESERT
The Arid Sea

Vulture
Drifts

Vulture
Drifts

DRASS
DWARVEN CARTOGRAPHER

The Arid Sea

1 Sir Kaufman (Collector)
2 Sir Pohl Sanbert (Collector)

1 Dune Burrower (22)
2 Enchanted Hammer (20)
3 Sand Giant (22)
4 Salving Cactus (20)
5 Jade Scarab (20)
6 Crystal Wurm

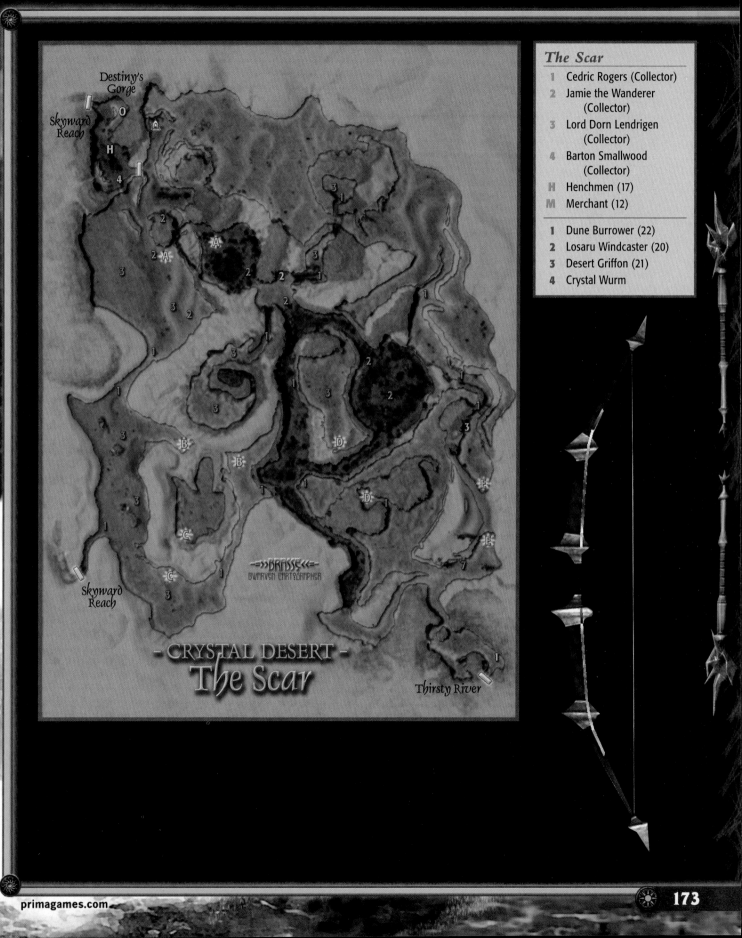

The Scar

1	Cedric Rogers (Collector)
2	Jamie the Wanderer (Collector)
3	Lord Dorn Lendrigen (Collector)
4	Barton Smallwood (Collector)
H	Henchmen (17)
M	Merchant (12)

1	Dune Burrower (22)
2	Losaru Windcaster (20)
3	Desert Griffon (21)
4	Crystal Wurm

Destiny's Gorge

Skyward Reach

Skyward Reach

BRASSE
DWARVEN CARTOGRAPHER

- CRYSTAL DESERT -
The Scar

Thirsty River

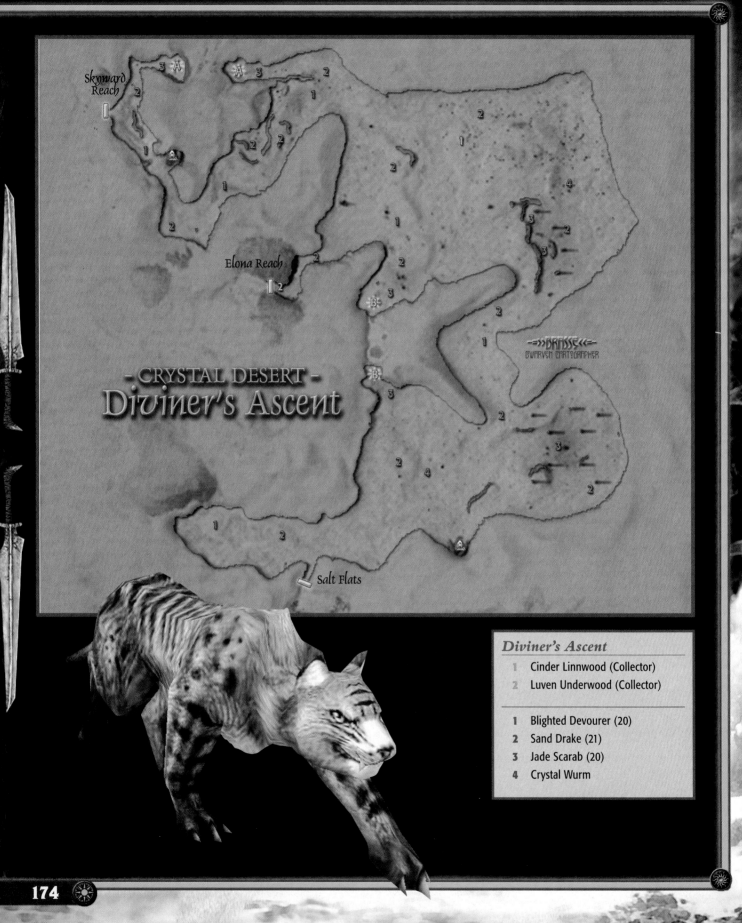

Skyward
Reach

Elona Reach

- CRYSTAL DESERT -
Diviner's Ascent

→⇒BRASSE⇐←
DWARVEN CARTOGRAPHER

Salt Flats

Diviner's Ascent

1	Cinder Linnwood (Collector)
2	Luven Underwood (Collector)

1	Blighted Devourer (20)
2	Sand Drake (21)
3	Jade Scarab (20)
4	Crystal Wurm

Komalie's Rest

KOMALIE'S REST
Perdition Rock

Ember Light Camp

Thunderhead Keep

Perdition Rock	
1	Captain Grumby (2)
2	Lavadome Gate Guard (2)
3	Shadow (15)
4	Moss Spider (Pet; 2)
H	Henchmen (20)
M	Merchant (12)
1	Drake (20)
2	Dark Flame Dryder (24)
3	Phantom (20)
4	Flesh Golem (20)
5	Mahgo Hydra (24)
6	Jade Bow (24)
	Ether Seal (24)
7	Breeze Keeper (24)
8	Inner Council Member Argyle (Boss Ms; 16)
	Inner Council Member Bolivar (Boss W; 16)
	Inner Council Member Cuthbert (Boss Ms; 16)
	White Mantle Knight (16)
	White Mantle Savant (16)
9	Volcanic Wurm

Numbers & Mechanics

Guild Wars *is a living, growing entity, and new content is being added all the time. Use this section as a guide to the initial* **Guild Wars** *release, then enjoy the new content as it becomes available.*

Point Progressions

Experience

The experience needed to gain each new level is not nearly as steep in *Guild Wars* as it is in other games—the designers do not intend to make it supremely difficult to reach new levels. Here is the experience needed to reach each level:

LEVEL	EXP	HEALTH
1	–	100
2	2000	120
3	2600	140
4	3200	160
5	3800	180
6	4400	200
7	5000	220
8	5600	240
9	6200	260
10	6800	280
11	7400	300
12	8000	320
13	8600	340
14	9200	360
15	9800	380
16	10,400	400
17	11,000	420
18	11,600	440
19	12,200	460
20	12,800	480

After level 20, you gain a new skill point (but no new levels or attribute points) each time you "cycle" your level.

Attributes

LEVEL	LVL COST	TOTAL COST
1	1	1
2	2	3
3	3	6
4	4	10
5	5	15
6	6	21
7	7	28
8	9	37
9	11	48
10	13	61
11	16	77
12	20	97

Equipment

How Damage Is Applied

Each weapon and damage skill has a specific base damage (or a range of damage). However, that doesn't always indicate how much damage is applied.

Each attack can be modified by a number of factors:

- Character level
- Attribute level
- Difference between the player's level and an enemy's level
- Weapon's attribute level
- Enemy's armor level

Example 1: Damage Range Across Armor Levels

A Warrior at Level 20 with a 12 in Swordsmanship, fighting a Level 20 monster with 60 armor, does the base damage of the weapon. This also assumes that the foe is completely free of buffs and isn't currently under any Conditions, Hexes, Enchantments, etc.

Now take the preceding example and increase the foe's armor to Level 20 and damage will *increase* to double the weapon's base level.

As a final example, increase the foe's armor to Level 100 and damage will *reduce* to half of the weapon's base level.

Example 2: Damage Range Across Armor Levels

A Warrior at Level 20 with a 4 in Swordsmanship, fighting a Level 20 monster with 60 armor, does half the base damage of the weapon. This also assumes that the foe is completely free of buffs and isn't currently under any Conditions, Hexes, Enchantments, etc.

Now take the preceding example and increase the Warrior's Swordsmanship to 16 and damage will *increase* to the base damage level plus 15 percent.

Ignore the percent of the armor when determining damage reduction due to armor penetration. For example, if an attack has Armor Penetration 20 percent, then the target's base armor is reduced by 20 percent.

Damage reduction is applied once the final damage total has been calculated. Subtract the damage reduction from that total before applying the damage.

Damage Types

There are ten types of damage. Three are Physical:

Blunt   Piercing   Slashing

Four are Elemental:

Cold   Fire   Earth   Lightning

The remaining three don't take armor into account. No attack or defense modifiers are calculated; damage is simply the basic damage. (But wands of these sorts do take armor into account.)

Chaos   Shadow   Holy (x2 vs. Undead)

Weapon Speeds

The time for each strike is as follows:

Weapon	Speed
Axe	1.33 sec.
Sword	1.33 sec.
Hammer	1.75 sec.
Rod, Staff	1.75 sec.
Bow	
Short	~2 sec.
Long	~2.5 sec.
Flat	~2 sec.
Recurve	~2.5 sec.
Horn	~2.7 sec.

Note: Half Moon is a Short Bow.

Bow Comparisons

Bow Type	Attack Speed	Range	Accuracy	Armor Penetration
Short	Good	Poor	Good	–
Long	Fair	Good	Fair	–
Flat	Good	Good	Poor	–
Recurve	Fair	Fair	Good	–
Horn	Poor	Fair	Fair	10%

Crafter (Materials)

Product	Item Materials
Clay Brick	1 Brick of Clay, 1 Pile of Glittering Dust, 20g
Tempered Glass Vial	5 Piles of Glittering Dust, 20g
Leather Square	5 Tanned Hide Squares, 50g
Vial of Ink	4 Plant Fibers, 1 Tempered Glass Vial, 20g
Lump of Charcoal	10 Wood Planks, 200g
Spiritwood Plank	5 Wood Planks, 10 Piles of Glittering Dust, 100g
Steel Ingot	10 Iron Ingots, 1 Lump of Charcoal, 200g

Ranges

All spellcasting has a range of 88 feet (the same as the small circle that appears around you on your "radar").

A spell's AoE is indicated by how it is described. For example, "adjacent" spells affect everyone within 13 feet.

AoE Description	Range
Melee, Touch	2 feet
Adjacent	13 feet
Nearby, Near the Target	20 feet
In the Location, In the Area	26 feet
Any Shout	39 feet
Bow Ranges	
Short	112 feet
Long	167 feet
Flat	67 feet
Recurve	142 feet
Horn	142 feet

Crafters & Other Vendors

Abbreviations

Only a few abbreviations are used in this section. They include 2H (2-Handed), Dmg (Damage), En (Energy), ER (Energy regeneration rate), Phy (Physical), Prc (Pierce), and Sla (Slash). In addition, crafting materials have been shortened, so that Cloth stands for Bolt of Cloth, Dust for Pile of Glittering Dust, and so forth.

City Codes

Most items available for sale or through crafting are only found in certain towns. When that's the case, the following town abbreviations are used:

AC	Ascalon City	QF	Quarrel Falls
Be	Beetletun	SL	Sage Lands
BHS	Bergen Hot Springs	SS	Stingray Strand
HD	Henge of Denravi	VR	Ventari's Refuge
LA	Lion's Arch	YB	Yak's Bend
		PS	Piken Square

Merchant

Equipment	Cost
Identification Kit	100g
Salvage Kit	100g
Expert Salvage Kit	400g
Dye Remover	50g
Tempered Glass Vial	60g
Bag (5 slots) (LA)	100g
Rune of Holding (BHS, Be)	500g
(bag slots go from 5 to 10)	

Dye Trader

Equipment	Cost
Blue	200g
Purple	240g
Orange	270g
Red	365g
Green	240g
Yellow	275g
Silver	380g

Vault Keeper

Equipment	Cost
20-Item Bank Vault	50g

Guild Registrar

Equipment	Cost
Guild Creation	100g
Guild Cape	100g

Weaponsmith

Equipment	Damage	Cost
Weapon Customization	+20% damage	10g

Crafter (Weapon, Defense)

BATTLE AXE (req. 5 Axe Mastery) (YB)
Dmg 3-6 (Sla), +2 vs. Dwarves
8 Iron Ingot, 2 Wood Planks, 200g

BATTLE AXE (req. 6 Axe Mastery) (LA)
Dmg 4-10 (Sla), +3 vs. Undead
12 Iron Ingot, 3 Wood Planks, 1 Steel Ingot, 750g

DIVINE SYMBOL (req. 6 Divine Favor) (LA)
Energy +8 | AL +5 vs. Undead
15 Granite Slabs, 5 Scales, 750g

FROST ARTIFACT (req. 6 Water Magic) (LA)
Energy +8 | AL +5 vs. Giants
15 Granite Slabs, 5 Scales, 750g

GRIM CESTA (req. 5 Death Magic) (YB)
Energy +6 | Health +10
10 Granite Slabs, 200g

HEALING ANKH (req. 5 Healing Prayers) (YB)
Energy +6 | Health +10
10 Granite Slabs, 200g

INSCRIBED CHAKRAM (req. 6 Domin. Magic) (LA)
Energy +8 | AL +5 vs. Undead
15 Granite Slabs, 5 Scales, 750g

IDOL (req. 6 Curses) (LA)
Energy +8 | AL +5 vs. Undead
15 Granite Slabs, 5 Scales, 750g

JEWELED CHALICE (req. 5 Illusion Magic) (YB)
Energy +6 | Health +10
10 Granite Slabs, 200g

LONGBOW (req. 5 Marksmanship) (YB)
Dmg 11-18 (Prc) | AL +8 vs. Dwarves
10 Wood Planks, 200g

LONGBOW (req. 6 Marksmanship) (LA)
Dmg 10-19 (Prc), +3 vs. Undead
15 Wood Planks, 5 Feathers, 750g

LONG SWORD (req. 5 Swordsmanship) (YB)
Dmg 10-14 (Sla) | AL +8 vs. Dwarves
10 Iron Ingots, 200g

LONG SWORD (req. 7 Swordsmanship) (LA)
Dmg 13-19 (Sla), +3 vs. Giants
15 Iron Ingots, 1 Steel Ingot, 750g

SCROLL (req. 5 Earth Magic) (YB)
Energy +6 | Health +10
10 Granite Slabs, 200g

WAR HAMMER (2H; req. 4 Hammer Mast.) (YB)
Dmg 9-12 (Blt) | AL +8 vs. Dwarves
6 Iron Ingots, 4 Wood Planks, 200g

WAR HAMMER (2H; req. 7 Hammer Mast.) (LA)
Dmg 15-24 (Blt), +4 vs. Undead
9 Iron Ingots, 6 Wood Planks, 1 Steel Ingot, 750g

Crafter (Armor)

Elementalist Armor

ADEPT'S ARMOR (Cloth/Silk)
AL 60 (VR)

Adept's Gloves	En +5, AL +5 (Elem)
Adept's Robes	En +5, AL +5 (Elem)
Master's Leggings	ER +1, AL +5 (Elem)
Adept's Shoes	ER +1, AL +5 (Elem)

AEROMANCER'S ARMOR (Cloth/Linen, Dust/Iron)

AL	30	39	45	51	60
	AC/YB/LA	BHS/QF/VR	HD	SL	VR
Storm's Eye					Air Magic +1
Aeromancer's Gloves		En +5, AL +15 (Ltng)			
Aeromancer's Robes		En +5, AL +15 (Ltng)			
Aeromancer's Leggings		ER +1, AL +15 (Ltng)			
Aeromancer's Shoes		ER +1, AL +15 (Ltng)			

ELEMENTALIST'S ARMOR (Cloth, Dust)

AL	15	30	39	45	57	60
	AC/PS	AC/YB/LA	BHS/QF/VR	HD	SS	VR
Third Eye						(no mods)
Elementalist's Gloves						En +5
Elementalist's Robes						En +5
Elementalist's Leggings						ER +1
Elementalist's Shoes						ER +1

GEOMANCER'S ARMOR (Cloth/Granite, Dust/Granite)

AL	30	39	45	57	60
	AC/YB/LA	BHS/QF/VR	HD	SS	VR
Stone's Eye					Earth Magic +1
Geomancer's Gloves		En +5, AL +15 (Earth)			
Geomancer's Robes		En +5, AL +15 (Earth)			
Geomancer's Leggings		ER +1, AL +15 (Earth)			
Geomancer's Shoes		ER +1, AL +15 (Earth)			

HYDROMANCER'S ARMOR (Cloth/Shell, Dust/Iron)

AL	30	39	45	51	60
	AC/YB/LA	BHS/Be/QF/VR	HD	SL	VR
Glacier's Eye					+1 Water Magic
Hydromancer's Gloves		En +5, AL +15 (Cold)			
Hydromancer's Robes		En +5, AL +15 (Cold)			
Hydromancer's Leggings		ER +1, AL +15 (Cold)			
Hydromancer's Shoes		ER +1, AL +15 (Cold)			

PYROMANCER'S ARMOR (Cloth/Scale, Dust/Iron)

AL	15	30	39	45	57	60
	AC/PS	AC/YB/LA	BHS/Be/QF/VR	HD	SS	VR
Flame's Eye						+1 Fire Magic
Pyromancer's Gloves			En +5, AL +15 (Fire)			
Pyromancer's Robes			En +5, AL +15 (Fire)			
Pyromancer's Leggings			ER +1, AL +15 (Fire)			
Pyromancer's Shoes			ER +1, AL +15 (Fire)			

ADDITIONAL HEADPIECES (Dust, Iron, and/or Granite)

AL	30	39	45	51	60
AC/YB/LA/BHS	QF/VR	HD	Be	VR	
All Seeing Eye				+1 Energy Storage	
Stone's Eye (AL 51 Only)				+1 Earth Magic	
Flame's Eye (AL 51 Only)				+1 Fire Magic	
Third Eye (AL 51 Only)				(no mods)	

Mesmer Armor

COURTLY ARMOR (Cloth, Linen)

AL	15	30	39	45	57	60
	PS	AC/YB/LA	BHS/Be/QF/VR	HD	SS	VR
Courtly Gloves		En +5, AL +15 (while casting spells)				
Courtly Attire		En +5, AL +15 (while casting spells)				
Courtly Hose		ER +1, AL +15 (while casting spells)				
Courtly Footwear		ER +1, AL +15 (while casting spells)				

ENCHANTER'S ARMOR (Cloth, Dust)

AL	30	45	60
	AC/YB/LA	BHS/QF/VR	HD	VR
Enchanter's Gloves			En +6
Enchanter's Attire			En +8
Enchanter's Hose			En +2, ER +1
Enchanter's Footwear			En +1, ER +1

PERFORMER'S ARMOR (Cloth, Silk)

AL	30	39	45	60
	AC/YB/LA	BHS/QF/VR	HD	VR
Performer's Gloves	En +5, AL +15 (while casting spells)			
Performer's Attire	En +5, AL +15 (while casting spells)			
Performer's Hose	ER +1, AL +15 (while casting spells)			
Performer's Foot.	ER +1, AL +15 (while casting spells)			

REGAL ARMOR (Cloth, Silk)

AL	35	44	50	65
	AC/YB/LA	BHS/QF/VR	HD	VR
Regal Gloves			En +5, AL -5 (Earth)
Regal Attire			En +5, AL -5 (Earth)
Regal Hose			ER +1, AL -5 (Earth)
Regal Footwear			ER +1, AL -5 (Earth)

ROGUE'S ARMOR (Cloth, Leather Squares)

AL	15	30	39	45	60
	AC/PS	AC/YB/LA	BHS/Be/QF/VR	HD	VR
Rogue's Gloves			En +4, AL +10 (Phy)		
Rogue's Attire			En +4, AL +10 (Phy)		
Rogue's Hose			En – 1, ER +1, AL +10 (Phy)		
Rogue's Footwear			En – 1, ER +1, AL +10 (Phy)		

STYLISH ARMOR (Cloth, Dust)

AL	15	30	39	45	60
	AC/PS	AC/YB/LA	BHS/QF/VR	HD	VR
Discreet Mask					(no mods)
Stylish Gloves					En +5
Stylish Attire					En +5
Stylish Hose					ER +1
Stylish Footwear					ER +1

MASKS (Cloth, Dust, Tanned Hide, Feathers, Steel, Linen)

AL	30	39	45	51	60
	AC/YB/LA	BHS/QF/VR	HD	Be	VR
Animal Mask					Inspiration Magic +1
Costume Mask					Illusion Magic +1
Discreet Mask (AL 51 Only)					(no mods)
Imposing Mask					Domination Magic +1
Sleek Mask					Fast Casting +1

Monk Armor

ASCETIC'S ARMOR – DRAGON/STAR PATTERN (Parchment, Ink)

AL	30	39	45	57	60
	AC/YB/LA	BHS/QF/VR	HD	SS	VR
Scalp Design					En +1
Ascetic's Arm Design					En +6
Ascetic's Chest Design					En +8
Ascetic's Leg Design					En +2, ER +1
Ascetic's Foot Design					En +1, ER +1

CENSOR'S ARMOR (Cloth, Steel)

AL	30	39	45	51	60
	AC/YB/LA	BHS/Be/QF/VR	HD	SL	VR
Censor's Handwraps			En +4, AL +10 (Phy)		
Censor's Vestments			En +4, AL +10 (Phy)		
Censor's Pants			En -1, ER +1, AL +10 (Phy)		
Censor's Sandals			En -1, ER +1, AL +10 (Phy)		

MONK'S ARMOR (Cloth, Parchment)

AL	15	30	39	45	57	60
	AC/PS	AC/YB/LA	BHS/QF/VR	HD	SS	VR
Believer's Scalp Design						(no mods)
Monk Handwraps						En +5
Monk Raiment						En +5
Monk Pants						ER +1
Monk Sandals						ER +1

SACRED ARMOR (Cloth, Linen)

AL	30	39	45	57	60
	AC/YB/LA	BHS/QF/VR	HD	SS	VR
Sacred Handwraps			En +5, AL +5 (Elem)		
Sacred Raiment			En +5, AL +5 (Elem)		
Sacred Pants			ER +1, AL +5 (Elem)		
Sacred Sandals			ER +1, AL +5 (Elem)		

SILK ARMOR (Cloth, Silk)

AL	35	44	50	65
	AC/YB/LA	BHS/QF/VR	HD	VR
Silk Handwraps			En +5, AL -5 (Cold)
Silk Raiment			En +5, AL -5 (Cold)
Silk Pants			ER +1, AL -5 (Cold)
Silk-laced Sandals			ER +1, AL -5 (Cold)

WANDERER'S ARMOR (Cloth, Tanned Hide)

AL	15	30	39	45	60
	AC/PS	AC/YB/LA	BHS/Be/QF/VR	HD	VR
Wanderer's Handwraps			En +5, AL +5 (Elem)		
Wanderer's Vestments			En +5, AL +5 (Elem)		
Wanderer's Pants			ER +1, AL +5 (Elem)		
Wanderer's Sandals			ER +1, AL +5 (Elem)		

SCALP DESIGNS (Parchment, Ink)

AL	30	39	45	51	60
	AC/YB/LA	BHS/QF/VR	HD	Be	VR
Prophet's Scalp Design					Divine Favor +1
Servant's Scalp Design					Healing Prayers +1
Defender's Scalp Design					Protection Prayers +1
Defender's Scalp Design					Smiting Prayers +1
Believer's Scalp Design (AL 51 Only)					(no mods)

Necromancer Armor

BONELACE ARMOR (Tanned Hide, Bones)

AL	15	30	39	45	60
	AC/PS	AC/YB/LA	BHS/Be/QF/VR	HD	VR

Bonelace Gloves	En +5, AL +15 (Piercing)
Bonelace Tunic	En +5, AL +15 (Piercing)
Bonelace Leggings	ER +1, AL +15 (Piercing)
Bonelace Boots	ER +1, AL +15 (Piercing)

FANATIC'S ARMOR (Tanned Hide, Leather)

AL	30	39	45	60
	AC/YB/LA	BHS/QF/VR	HD	VR

Fanatic's Gloves	En +5, AL +15 (Piercing)
Fanatic's Tunic	En +5, AL +15 (Piercing)
Fanatic's Leggings	ER +1, AL +15 (Piercing)
Fanatic's Boots	ER +1, AL +15 (Piercing)

NECROMANCER'S ARMOR (Tanned Hide, Parchment)

AL	15	30	39	45	57	60
	AC/PS	AC/YB/LA	BHS/QF/VR	HD	SS	VR

Crude Scar Pattern	(no mods)
Necromancer's Gloves	En +5
Necromancer's Tunic	En +5
Necromancer's Leggings	ER +1
Necromancer's Boots	ER +1

NECROTIC ARMOR (Tanned Hide, Shells)

AL	40	49	55	70
	AC/YB/LA	BHS/Be/QF/VR	HD	VR

Necrotic Gloves	En +5, Debuffs Holy AL
Necrotic Tunic	En +5, Debuffs Holy AL
Necrotic Leggings	ER +1, Debuffs Holy AL
Necrotic Boots	ER +1, Debuffs Holy AL

PAGAN ARMOR (Tanned Hide, Granite)

AL	40	49	55	70
	AC/YB/LA	BHS/QF/VR	HD	VR

Pagan Gloves	En +5, Debuffs Holy AL
Pagan Tunic	En +5, Debuffs Holy AL
Pagan Leggings	ER +1, Debuffs Holy AL
Pagan Boots	ER +1, Debuffs Holy AL

SCAR PATTERN ARMOR (Parchment, Ink)

AL	30	39	45	60
	AC/YB/LA	BHS/QF/VR	HD	VR

Arm Scar Pattern	En +6
Chest Scar Pattern	En +8
Leg Scar Pattern	En +2, ER +1
Foot Scar Pattern	En +1, ER +1

TORMENTOR'S ARMOR (Tanned Hide, Steel)

AL	40	49	55	70
	AC/YB/LA	BHS/QF/VR	HD	VR

Tormentor's Gloves	En +5, Debuffs Holy AL
Tormentor's Tunic	En +5, Debuffs Holy AL
Tormentor's Leggings	ER +1, Debuffs Holy AL
Tormentor's Boots	ER +1, Debuffs Holy AL

SCAR PATTERNS (Parchment, Ink)

AL	30	39	45	51	60
	AC/YB/LA	BHS/QF/VR	HD	SL	VR

Devilish Scar Pattern	Soul Reaping +1
Ragged Scar Pattern	Blood Magic +1
Vile Scar Pattern	Death Magic +1
Wicked Scar Pattern	Curses +1
Crude Scar Pattern (AL 51 Only)	(no mods)

MISCELLANEOUS (Tanned Hide, Scales)

AL	45	51
	HD	VR

Bloodstained Boots	ER +1, Speeds corpse-targeted spells

Ranger Armor

DRAKESCALE ARMOR (Tanned Hide, Scales)

AL	40	49	55	70
	AC/YB/LA	BHS/Be/QF/VR	HD	VR

Drakescale Gloves	AL +30 (Elem), AL +15 (Fire)
Drakescale Vest	En +5, AL +30 (Elem), AL +15 (Fire)
Drakescale Leg.	ER +1, AL +30 (Elem), AL +15 (Fire)
Drakescale Boots	AL +30 (Elem), AL +15 (Fire)

DRUID'S ARMOR (Tanned Hide, Wood)

AL	40	49	60	70
	AC/YB/LA	BHS/QF/VR	HD	VR

Druid's Gloves	En +1, AL +30 (Elem)
Rawhide Vest	En +8, AL +30 (Elem)
Druid's Leggings	En +1, ER +1, AL +30 (Elem)
Druid's Boots	En +1, AL +30 (Elem)

FUR-LINED ARMOR (Tanned Hide, Fur)

AL	25	40	49	55	70
	AC/PS	AC/YB/LA	BHS/Be/QF/VR	HD	VR

Fur-lined Gloves	AL +30 (Elem), AL +15 (Cold)
Fur-lined Vest	En +5, AL +30 (Elem), AL +15 (Cold)
Fur-lined Leggings	ER +1, AL +30 (Elem), AL +15 (Cold)
Fur-lined Boots	AL +30 (Elem), AL +15 (Cold)

HUNTER'S ARMOR (Tanned Hide, Bones)

AL	40	49	60	70
	AC/YB/LA	BHS/QF/VR	HD	VR

Hunter's Gloves	AL +30 (Elem), AL +15 (Piercing)
Rawhide Vest	En +5, AL +30 (Elem), AL +15 (Prc)
Hunter's Leggings	ER +1, AL +30 (Elem), AL +15 (Prc)
Hunter's Boots	AL +30 (Elem), AL +15 (Prc)

LEATHER ARMOR (Tanned Hide, Cloth)

AL	25	40	49	55	61	70
	AC/PS	AC/YB/LA	BHS/QF/VR	HD	SL	VR

Simple Mask	AL +30 (Elem)
Leather Gloves	AL +30 (Elem)
Rawhide Vest	En +5, AL +30 (Elem)
Leather Leggings	ER +1, AL +30 (Elem)
Leather Boots	AL +30 (Elem)

STUDDED LEATHER ARMOR (Tanned Hide, Steel)

AL	40	49	55	70
	AC/YB/LA	BHS/QF/VR	HD	VR

Studded L. Gloves	AL +30 (Elem), AL +15 (Ltng)
Studded L. Vest	En +5, AL +30 (Elem), AL +15 (Ltng)
Studded L. Leg.	ER +1, AL +30 (Elem), AL +15 (Ltng)
Studded L. Boots	AL +30 (Elem), AL +15 (Ltng)

MASKS (Cloth, Linen, Silk, Scale, Fur)

AL	40	49	55	61	70
	AC/YB/LA	BHS/QF/VR	HD	SL	VR

Tamer's Mask	AL +30 (Elem), Beast Mastery +1
Traveler's Mask	AL +30 (Elem), Wilderness Survival +1
Hunter's Mask (Excl. AL 61)	AL +30 (Elem), Expertise +1
Hunter's Mask (Excl. AL 61)	AL +30 (Elem), Marks. +1

Warrior Armor

ASCALON ARMOR (Iron, Fur)

AL	35	50	59	65	80
	AC/PS	AC/YB/LA	BHS/QF/VR	HD	VR

Ascalon Helm	AL +20 (Phy)
Ascalon Gauntlets	AL +10 (Phy)
Ascalon Cuirass	AL +10 (Phy)
Ascalon Leggings	AL +10 (Phy)
Ascalon Boots	AL +10 (Phy)

GLADIATOR'S ARMOR (Iron, Tanned Hide)

AL	50	59	65	80
	AC/YB/LA	BHS/Be/QF/VR	HD	VR

Gladiator's Helm	En +1
Gladiator's Gauntlets	En +1, AL +20 (Phy)
Gladiator's Hauberk	En +3
Gladiator's Leggings	En +2, AL +20 (Phy)
Gladiator's Boots	En +1, AL +20 (Phy)

RINGMAIL ARMOR (Iron)

AL	35	50	59
	AC/PS	AC/YB/LA	BHS/QF/VF

Recruit's Cap	AL +20 (Phy)
Ringmail Gauntlets	AL +20 (Phy)
Ringmail Hauberk	AL +20 (Phy)
Ringmail Leggings	AL +20 (Phy)
Ringmail Boots	AL +20 (Phy)

WYVERN ARMOR (Iron, Scales)

AL	55	61	64	70	85
	AC/YB/LA	BHS/QF/VR	Be	HD	VR

Wyvern Helm	AL +10 (Phy)
Wyvern Gauntlets	+10 (Phy)
Wyvern Hauberk	+10 (Phy)
Wyvern Leggings	+10 (Phy)
Wyvern Boots	+10 (Phy)

HELMS (Iron, Steel)

AL	50	59	65	80
	AC/YB/LA	BHS/QF/VR	HD	VR

Captain's Helm	AL +20 (Phy), Axe Mastery +1
Captain's Helm	AL +20 (Phy), Hammer Mastery +1
Captain's Helm	AL +20 (Phy), Swordsmanship +1
Captain's Helm	AL +20 (Phy), Strength +1
Captain's Helm	AL +20 (Phy), Tactics +1

MISCELLANEOUS (Iron, Granite)

AL	60	75
	HD	VR

Stonefist Gauntlets	AL +20 (Phy), Target's knockdown increased
Lieutenant's Helm (AL 60 Only)	AL +20 (Phy), Reduces hex duration on you

KNIGHT'S ARMOR (Iron, Leather)

AL 80 (VR)

Knight's Helm	AL +20 (Phy)
Knight's Gauntlets	AL +10 (Phy)
Knight's Cuirass	AL +10 (Phy)
Knight's Leggings	AL +10 (Phy)
Knight's Boots	AL +10 (Phy)

PLATEMAIL ARMOR (Iron, Steel)

AL 80 (VR)

Platemail Helm	AL +20 (Phy)
Platemail Gauntlets	AL +10 (Phy)
Platemail Cuirass	AL +10 (Phy)
Platemail Leggings	AL +20 (Phy)
Platemail Boots	AL +20 (Phy)

Drops

Drops are classified in the game as common (white or blue text), uncommon (purple text), or rare (gold text). If a common drop is enhanced, it will have blue text; otherwise, its description will be white.

Some drops are unidentified, with only basic stats available. Using an identification kit on an unidentified item will tell you more about it. Sometimes, identification points out a significant increase in effect or value.

New drops are being added regularly.

Identification and Salvage

Identification and salvage both cost money, and both are a risk. Will the identification and the salvage make the item more valuable? Probably. Will the increase in value offset the cost of the identification or salvage charge? Not always.

Guild Wars prices aren't fixed, so you have to determine when to identify or salvage an item. With a limit on inventory slots, it is sometimes useful to salvage an item just so you can carry more (since salvaged components stack).

Still, there's every possibility that you may find more loot than you can carry. Accept that fact, and be picky about what you take.

Also, your bags can get full quickly, and there will be times that you want to grab a special drop and run before a bad situation gets worse. Of course, the best drops can sometimes happen in the worst situation. In that instance, you don't want to have to stop to unload or salvage an item just to make room for the better loot. Be aware of what you're carrying, and always try to save an empty slot for a prime drop.

A regular salvage kit can only extract these components (use an expert kit for uncommon salvage items):

Bolts of Raw Cloth	Bones	Bricks of Mud
Feathers	Granite Slabs	Hides
Iron Ingots	Plant Fibers	Scales
Shells	Wood Planks	Piles of Glittering Dust

Random Loot

Most drops are random loot, but they do follow a few patterns. A creature's level is the major factor in determing what it drops; the higher the level, the better the loot. The following table lists the damage, defense, and value of nearly all loot, based on the level of the creature that dropped it. To find what you can expect a creature to drop, look at the line for its level, plus the line above and below it. Nearly all creatures drop items within those ranges.

If a creature drops an uncommon or rare item, that item's damage, armor, and Energy bonus are better than common. For uncommon items, use the stats for items two or three levels higher. For rare items, go three or four levels higher to find the stats you can expect.

Salvage vs. Expert Salvage

In the following lists, each item is listed with its basic component—what you'll get with a regular salvage kit. At the beginning of each category are the components that you can get with an expert kit (sometimes, however, an expert salvage yields nothing better than a regular salvage). If there are two expert salvage components, you're more likely to get the first.

To match an item with its expert salvage results, find the basic component in the list of items. Match that item at the top of the section with a list of expert salvage possibilities. For example, Abbot's Robes (at the beginning of the Armor section) yields Bolts of Raw Cloth as basic salvage. Looking above that a few lines, you can see that Bolts of Raw Cloth (basic salvage) matches Bolts of Linen and Bolts of Silk (expert salvage). So an expert salvage of Abbot's Robes will give you bolts of Raw Cloth, Linen, or Silk.

Keep in mind that more items are being added to *Guild Wars* all the time!

Lvl	Axes (dam.)	Sword (dam.)	Hammer (dam.)	Bow (dam.)	Rod, Staff (dam.)	Shield (armor)	Focus (energy)	Common (gold)	Uncommon (gold)	Rare (gold)
1	3-5	3-4	4-6	4-6	2-4	4	3	5	10	20
2	3-5	4-5	5-7	5-7	3-5	5	3	8	15	30
3	4-6	4-6	6-8	6-8	4-5	5	4	10	20	40
4	4-7	5-7	7-9	6-8	4-6	6	4	13	25	51
5	4-8	5-7	7-10	7-9	5-7	6	5	16	31	62
6	5-9	6-8	8-11	7-10	5-7	7	5	19	37	74
7	5-10	7-9	9-13	8-11	5-8	7	5	22	44	87
8	5-11	7-10	10-14	8-12	6-9	8	6	25	51	101
9	6-12	8-10	10-15	9-13	6-10	8	6	29	58	116
10	6-13	8-11	11-16	9-14	7-10	9	7	33	66	132
11	6-14	9-12	12-18	10-15	7-11	9	7	37	74	149
12	6-15	9-13	13-19	10-16	8-12	10	7	42	83	167
13	6-16	10-13	13-20	11-17	8-13	10	8	47	93	187
14	6-17	11-14	14-22	11-18	8-13	11	8	52	104	208
15	6-18	11-15	14-23	12-19	9-14	11	8	58	116	231
16	6-19	12-16	15-24	12-20	9-15	12	9	64	128	256
17	6-20	12-17	15-26	12-21	9-16	12	9	71	142	284
18	6-21	13-17	16-27	13-22	10-17	13	10	78	157	313
19	6-22	13-18	17-28	13-23	10-18	13	10	86	173	346
20	6-23	14-19	17-30	13-24	10-18	14	10	95	191	381
21	6-24	14-20	17-31	14-25	10-19	14	11	105	210	420
22	6-26	14-21	18-32	14-26	11-20	15	11	116	231	463
23	6-27	15-21	18-34	14-27	11-21	15	12	127	255	509
24	6-28	15-22	19-35	15-28	11-22	16	12	140	280	560

Armor

Profession abbreviations for armor are only to help you identify what type of monster drops that item, since you can't wear it yourself.

Basic Salvage	Expert S.
Bolts of Raw Cloth	Bolts of Linen, Silk
Bolts of Raw Cloth*	Piles of Glitter, Globs of Ectoplasm
Hides	Leather Squares
Iron Ingots	Steel Ingots

Item	Basic Salvage
Abbot's Robes (Mk)	Bolts of Raw Cloth
Avicara Ardent Robes (Mk)	Bolts of Raw Cl.
Avicara Brave Armor (W)	Iron Ingots
Avicara Element. Robes	Bolts of Raw Cloth
Avicara Fierce Vest (R)	Hides
Avicara Guile Tunic (N)	Hides
Avicara Wise Attire (Ms)	Bolts of Raw Cl.
Beastmaster Harness	Iron Ingots
Bloodstained Jerkin (R)	Hides
Broken Armor (W)	Iron Ingots
Centaur Harn. (E,Mk,Ms,N)	Bolts of Raw Cl.
Centaur Harness (R)	Hides
Centaur Harness (W)	Iron Ingots
Corrupt. Orr Collar (Ms)	Bolts of Raw Cloth
Corrupted Orr Vest. (Mk)	Bolts of Raw Cloth
Decayed Orr Armor (R)	Hides
Decayed Orr Robes (E)	Bolts of Raw Cloth
Dolyak Cladding	Hides
Dwarven Armor	Iron Ingots
Dwarven Healer Outfit	Bolts of Raw Cloth
Dwarven Howler Outfit	Bolts of Raw Cloth
Dwarven Robes (Ms, N)	Bolts of Raw Cloth
Dwarven Sage Outfit	Bolts of Raw Cloth
Dwarven Scout Armor	Hides
Dwarven Warrior Armor	Iron Ingots
Executioner's Breastplate	Iron Ingots
Ghoul's Collar	Bolts of Raw Cloth
Giant's Boots	Iron Ingots
Grawl Element. Gear	Bolts of Raw Cloth
Grawl Gear (W)	Iron Ingots
Grawl Longspear Gear (R)	Hides
Grawl Mesmer Gear	Bolts of Raw Cloth
Grawl Necromancer Gear	Hides
Grawl Sham. Gear (Mk)	Bolts of Raw Cloth
Jade Gorget (R)	Piles of Glittering Dust
Jade Pauldron (W)	Piles of Glittering Dust
Justiciar's Armor (W)	Iron Ingots
Knight's Armor (W)	Iron Ingots
Mursaat Garments	Bolts of Raw Cloth
Necrid Robes	Bolts of Raw Cloth
Phantasmal Armor	Bolts of Raw Cloth*
Priest's Robes (Mk)	Bolts of Raw Cloth
Ritualist's Tunic (N)	Bolts of Raw Cloth
Savant's Robes (E)	Bolts of Raw Cloth
Seeker's Vest (R)	Hides
Shiverpk. Bladehand Armor (W)	Iron Ingots
Shiverpeak Bowmaster Vest (R)	Hides
Shiverpk. Element. Robes	Bolts of Raw Cl.
Shiverpk. Lifeb. Robes (Mk)	Bolts of Raw Cl.
Shiverpeak Necromancer Tunic	Hides
Shiverpk. Windc. Robes (Ms)	Bolts of Raw Cl.
Sycophant's Robes (Ms)	Bolts of Raw Cl.
Titan Armor	Iron Ingots
Warlock's Robes	Bolts of Raw Cloth
Zealot's Armor (W)	Iron Ingots

Axe

Basic Salvage	Expert S.
Iron Ingots	Wood Planks, Steel Ingots
Granite Slabs	Wood Planks

Item	Basic Salvage
Battle Axe	Iron Ingots
Battlepick	Iron Ingots
Chaos Axe (Ms)	Iron Ingots
Charr Axe	Iron Ingots
Cleaver	Granite Slabs
Double-bladed Axe	Iron Ingots
Dwarven Axe	Iron Ingots
Great Axe	Iron Ingots
Greater Summit Axe	Iron Ingots
Hand Axe	Iron Ingots
Hatchet	Granite Slabs
Krytan Axe	Iron Ingots
Piercing Axe	Iron Ingots
Sephis Axe	Iron Ingots
Serpent Axe	Iron Ingots
Sickle	Iron Ingots
Spiked Axe	Iron Ingots
Summit Axe	Iron Ingots
Titans Axe	Iron Ingots
Tribal Axe	Iron Ingots
War Axe	Iron Ingots
White Scythe	Iron Ingots

Hammer

Basic Salvage	Expert S.
Granite Slabs	Wood Planks, Steel Ingots
Iron Ingots	Wood Planks, Steel Ingots

Item	Basic Salvage
Ball Hammer	Iron Ingots
Break Hammer	Iron Ingots
Dwarven Hammer	Iron Ingots
Edron Hammer	Iron Ingots
Ettin Hammer	Granite Slabs
Foehammer	Iron Ingots
Giant Slayers Hammer	Iron Ingots
Greater Summit Hammer	Iron Ingots
Magmas Arm	Iron Ingots
Mursaat Hammer	Iron Ingots
Rams Hammer	Iron Ingots
Righteous Maul	Iron Ingots
Runic Hammer	Iron Ingots
Shining Maul	Iron Ingots
Summit Hammer	Iron Ingots
Swamp Club	Iron Ingots
Twin Hammer	Iron Ingots
War Hammer	Iron Ingots

Sword

Steel Ingots are the only expert salvage possible for a sword.

Item	Basic Salvage
Brute Sword	Iron Ingots
Butterfly Sword	Iron Ingots
Canthan Blade	Iron Ingots
Canthan Machete	Iron Ingots
Canthan Saber	Iron Ingots
Canthan Shortsword	Iron Ingots
Crusader's Sword	Iron Ingots
Crystalline Sword	Piles of Glittering Dust
Dragon Sword	Iron Ingots
Falchion	Iron Ingots
Fellblade	Iron Ingots
Flamberge	Iron Ingots
Forked Sword	Iron Ingots
Gladius	Iron Ingots
Krytan Sword	Iron Ingots
Long Sword	Iron Ingots
Longclaw	Iron Ingots
Rekki Blade	Iron Ingots
Rinblade	Iron Ingots
Scimitar	Iron Ingots
Sephis Sword	Iron Ingots
Shadow Blade	Iron Ingots
Shining Gladius	Iron Ingots
Short Sword	Iron Ingots
Spatha	Iron Ingots
Tribal Blade	Granite Slabs
Tribal Blade	Iron Ingots
Wingblade Sword	Iron Ingots
Wyvern Blade	Iron Ingots

Bow

Basic Salvage	Expert S.
Wood Planks	(none)
Wood Planks*	Bones

Item	Basic Salvage
Composite Bow	Wood Planks
Dead Bow	Wood Planks
Eternal Bow	Wood Planks
Flatbow	Wood Planks
Half Moon	Wood Planks
Horn Bow	Wood Planks
Ivory Bow	Wood Planks
Longbow	Wood Planks
Recurve Bow	Wood Planks
Shadow Bow	Wood Planks
Short Bow	Wood Planks
Storm Bow	Wood Planks

Focus

Basic Salvage	Expert S.
Bones	(none)
Granite Slabs	(none)
Iron Ingots	Steel Ingots
Piles of Glittering Dust	Iron Ingots
Rolls of Parchment	Bolts of Raw Cloth
Wood Planks	Sections of Ivory

Item	Basic Salvage
Ankh	Granite Slabs
Divine Symbol (Mk - Divine)	Wood Planks
Dwarven Cesta	Granite Slabs
Flame Artifact (E - Fire)	Rolls of Parchment
Frost Artifact (E - Water)	Rolls of Parchm.
Grim Cesta (N - Curse)	Granite Slabs
Grim Cesta (N - Death)	Bones
Healing Ankh (Mk - Healing)	Granite Slabs
Idol (N - Blood)	Bones
Inscribed Chakram (Ms - Dom.)	Iron Ingots
Jeweled Chakram (Ms - Illus.)	Iron Ingots
Jeweled Chalice (Ms - Insp.)	Piles of Gl. Dust
Protective Icon (Mk - Prot.)	Granite Slabs
Scroll (E - Earth)	Rolls of Parchment
Storm Artifact (E - Air)	Rolls of Parchment

Rod

Basic Salvage	Expert S.
Iron Ingots	Steel Ingots

Item	Basic Salvage
Air Wand (E - Air)	Iron Ingots
Cane (Ms - Domination)	Iron Ingots
Cane (Ms - Illusion)	Iron Ingots
Deadly Cesta (N - Death)	Iron Ingots
Earth Wand (E - Earth)	Iron Ingots
Fire Wand (E - Fire)	Iron Ingots
Holy Rod (Mk - Divine)	Iron Ingots
Smiting Rod (Mk - Smiting)	Iron Ingots
Truncheon (N - Blood)	Iron Ingots
Water Wand (E - Water)	Iron Ingots

Staff

Only the Wrathful Staff can give expert salvage: Steel Ingots.

Item	Basic Salvage
Accursed Staff (N - Curse)	Wood Planks
Air Staff (E - Air)	Wood Planks
Bone Staff (N - Death)	Bones
Dead Staff	Bones
Earth Staff (E - Earth)	Wood Planks
Fire Staff (E - Fire)	Wood Planks
Ghostly Staff	Wood Planks
Holy Staff (Mk - Divine)	Wood Planks
Inscribed Staff (Ms - Dom.)	Wood Planks
Jeweled Staff (Ms - Illusion)	Wood Planks
Raven Staff	Wood Planks
Sacred Staff (Mk - Divine)	Wood Planks
Serpentine Wand	Wood Planks
Shadow Staff	Wood Planks
Smiting Staff (Mk - Smiting)	Wood Planks
Smiting Staff (Mk - Smiting)	Wood Planks
Water Staff (E - Water)	Wood Planks
Wrathful Staff (Mk - Smiting)	Iron Ingots

Shield

Basic Salvage	Expert S.
Iron Ingots	Steel Ingots
Wood Planks	Steel Ingots

Item	Basic Salvage
Aegis	Iron Ingots
Bladed Buckler	Iron Ingots
Charr Shield	Iron Ingots
Crude Shield	Wood Planks
Defender	Iron Ingots
Eternal Shield	Iron Ingots
Magmas Shield	Iron Ingots
Militia Shield	Wood Planks
Ornate Buckler	Iron Ingots
Reinforced Buckler	Iron Ingots
Round Shield	Iron Ingots
Shadow Shield	Iron Ingots
Shield of the Dead	Iron Ingots
Shield of the Wing	Iron Ingots
Skeleton Shield	Iron Ingots
Skull Shield	Iron Ingots
Spider Shield	Iron Ingots
Spiked Targe	Iron Ingots
Stone Summit Shield	Iron Ingots
Summit Warlord Shield	Iron Ingots
Tall Shield	Iron Ingots
Tower Shield	Iron Ingots
Wooden Buckler	Wood Planks

---

* Collectibles can yield a different result with expert salvage. See page 182 for more details.

Raw Materials

Basic Salvage	Expert S.
Bolts of Raw Cloth	Bolts of Linen, Silk
Bones	Hides
Hides	Leather Squares
Hides*	Pelts
Hides**	Bones
Piles of Glittering Dust	Bolts of Silk

Item	Basic Salvage
Animal Hides	Hides*
Centaur Hides	Hides*
Charr Hides	Hides*
Dolyak Hides	Hides*
Ebon Spider Webs	Piles of Gl. Dust
Ettin Hides	Hides
Forest Minotaur Hide	Hides
Half-Chewed Masses	Bones
Half-Digested Masses	Hides**
Half-Eaten Blobs	Hides**
Half-Eaten Masses	Bolts of Raw Cloth
Hill Giant's Bracers	Bolts of Raw Cloth
Igneous Ettin Hides	Hides
Losaru Hides	Hides*
Maguuma Animal Hides	Hides
Maguuma Spider Webs	Piles of Gl. Dust
Minotaur Hide	Hides
Mountain Minotaur Hides	Hides
Pristine Animal Hides	Hides
Sand Giant's Bracers	Bolts of Raw Cloth
Singed Animal Hides	Hides
Snowy Animal Hides	Hides*
Snowy Centaur Hides	Hides
Snowy Ettin Hides	Hides
Spider Webs	Piles of Glittering Dust
Tundra Giant's Bracers	B. of Raw Cloth

Component Drops

Some creatures drop items that are directly usable for crafting. In this list, the closer the item is to the top of the list, the likelier it is to drop.

Burrower	Shells	Monstrous Claws	–	–
Devourer	Shells	Monstrous Claws	–	–
Drake	Scales	Bones	Monstrous Claws	Monstrous Fangs
Elemental	Granite Slabs	Lumps of Charcoal	Ruby	Sapphires
Forgotten	Scales	Bones	Monstrous Claws	Monstrous Fangs
Gargoyle	Granite Slabs	Lumps of Charcoal	Ruby	Sapphires
Ghost	Bones	Piles of Glittering Dust	–	–
Ghoul	Bones	Piles of Glittering Dust	–	–
Griffon	Feathers	Bones	Monstrous Claws	Monstrous Eyes
Hellhound	Bones	Piles of Glittering Dust	–	–
Imp	Scales	Lumps of Charcoal	Ruby	Sapphires
Nightmare	P. of Gl. Dust	Globs of Ectoplasm	–	–
Plants	Plant Fibers	Wood Planks	Monstrous Eyes	–
Scarab	Shells	Monstrous Claws	–	–
Skale	Scales	Bones	Monstrous Claws	Monstrous Fangs
Skeleton	Bones	Piles of Glittering Dust	–	–
Spider	Shells	Monstrous Claws	–	–
Spirit	P. of Gl. Dust	Globs of Ectoplasm	–	–
Tengu	Feathers	Bones	Monstrous Eyes	Monstrous Eyes
Treant	Plant Fibers	Wood Planks	Monstrous Eyes	–
Troll	Scales	Bones	Monstrous Claws	Monstrous Fangs
Undead	Bones	Piles of Glittering Dust	–	–

Collectibles

Only collectibles with an "*" can yield a different result with expert salvage:

Bones*	Sections of Ivory
Granite Slabs*	Lumps of Charcoal
Hides*	Bones
Hides**	Leather Squares
Piles of Glitter. Dust*	Globs of Ectoplasm

Enhanced Items can have enhanced parts and they can have bonuses. An expert salvage kit can extract an enhanced part. It can never extract a bonus. (A regular salvage kit can only extract basic crafting components.)

Dropped materials (scales, husks, seeds, and so forth) can be sold or they can be traded to a Collector for equipment.

Dropped armor can never be equipped by a PC. It can only be sold or salvaged.

Dropped weapons, focuses, and wands can be used directly, or they can be salvaged or sold.

Collectible Drop	Monster	Basic Salvage
Abnormal Seeds	Krytan Plant	Plant Fibers
Ancient Eyes	Wilds Beholder	P. of Gl. Dust*
Baked Husks	Worm (standard)	Shells
Behemoth Jaws	Wilds Burrower	Shells
Bleached Carapaces	Crystal Desert Devourer	Shells
Bleached Shells	Crystal Desert Wurm	Shells
Bog Skale Fins	Krytan Skale	Scales
Charr Carvings	Charr (standard)	Wood Planks
Demonic Fangs	Rift Dryder	P. of Gl. Dust
Demonic Remains	Rift Nightmare	P. of Gl. Dust*
Dessicated Hydra Claws	Crystal Desert Hydra	Scales
Dull Carapaces	Devourer (standard)	Shells
Dune Burrower Jaws	Crystal Desert Burrower	Scales
Ebon Spider Legs	Wilds Arachnid	Shells
Enchanted Lodestones	Stone (standard)	Granite Slabs
Encrusted Lodestones	Crystal Desert Earth	Granite Slabs
Explorer's Trophies	Wilds Animal	Hides*
Feathered Caromi Scalps	Krytan Tengu	Feathers
Fetid Carapaces	Ruins of Ascalon Devourer	Shells
Forest Minotaur Horns	Krytan Minotaur	Hides*
Forgotten Seals	Forgotten (standard)	Wood Planks
Gargantuan Jawbones	Krytan Giant	Bones
Gargoyle Skulls	Gargoyle (standard)	Bones
Ghostly Remains	Ruins of Ascalon Ghost	P. of Gl. Dust*
Glowing Hearts	Krytan Imp	Granite Slabs*
Grawl Necklaces	Grawl (standard)	Plant Fibers
Gruesome Ribcages	Ruins of Ascalon Golem	Bones
Gruesome Sternums	Rift Golem	Bones
Hardened Humps	Krytan Ettin	Hides*
Hunter's Keepsakes	Krytan Animal	Hides*
Hunter's Trophies	Ruins of Ascalon Animal	Hides*
Icy Hunter's Trophies	Shiverpeaks Animal	Hides*
Icy Lodestones	Cold (standard)	Granite Slabs
Iridescent Griffin Wings	Crystal Desert Griffon	Feathers
Ivory Troll Tusks	Krytan Troll	Scales
Jade Mandibles	Crystal Desert Scarab	Shells
Jungle Skale Fins	Wilds Skale	Scales
Jungle Troll Tusks	Wilds Troll	Bones
Leather Belts	Krytan Human	Hides**
Leathery Claws	Ruins of Ascalon Hydra	Scales
Losaru Manes	Crystal Desert Centaur	Hides*
Maguuma Manes	Wilds Centaur	P. of Gl. Dust
Massive Jawbones	Crystal Desert Giant	Bones
Mergoyle Skulls	Krytan Gargoyle	Bones
Minotaur Horns	Crystal Desert Minotaur	Bones*
Mossy Mandibles	Wilds Scarab	Shells
Mursaat Tokens	Mursaat (standard)	P. of Gl. Dust
Obsidian Burrower Jaws	Rift Burrower	Shells
Ornate Grawl Necklaces	Ruins of Ascalon Grawl	Plant Fibers
Phantom Residues	Rift Ghost	P. of Gl. Dust*
Scar Behemoth Jaws	Ruins of Ascalon Burrower	Shells
Scorched Seeds	Ruins of Ascalon Plant	Plant Fibers
Shadowy Remnants	Krytan Nightmare	P. of Gl. Dust*
Shiverpeak Manes	Shiverpeaks Centaur	P. of Gl. Dust
Shriveled Eyes	Crystal Desert Beholder	P. of Gl. Dust*
Singed Gargoyle Skulls	Ruins of Ascalon Gargoyle	Bones
Skale Fins	Skale (standard)	Scales
Skeletal Limbs	Skeleton (standard)	Bones
Spider Legs	Arachnid (standard)	Shells
Spiked Crests	Krytan Dragon	Scales
Spiny Seeds	Crystal Desert Plant	Plant Fibers
Stormy Eyes	Ruins of Ascalon Beholder	P. of Gl. Dust*
Tangled Seeds	Wilds Plant	Plant Fibers
Thorny Carapaces	Wilds Devourer	Shells
Topaz Crests	Crystal Desert Dragon	Scales
Unnatural Seeds	Plant (standard)	Plant Fibers
Warden's Trophies	Animal (standard)	Hides*
White Mantle Badges	Shining Mantle (Officer)	B. of Raw Cloth
White Mantle Emblems	Shining Mantle (standard)	B. of Raw Cloth
Worn Belts	Human (standard)	Hides**

Drop Enhancements & Bonuses

Most dropped equipment is basic. It functions like any basic equipment, with no enhancements or bonuses. However, a few items have extra features.

Enhanced Parts

Every weapon can have up to two enhanced parts. What these parts are varies by weapon (hilts for swords, strings for bows, and so forth), but they all fall into one of two groups—prefixes and suffixes. Why "prefixes" and "suffixes"? Because the enhanced item's name describes its enhancements with either a prefix or a suffix. For example, some swords have enhanced hilts, which are described by an adjective at the beginning of the sword's name: an Icy Sword has a hilt that changes the sword's damage from Slashing to Cold. A Fiery Sword has a hilt that changes damage to Fire.

Meanwhile, some swords have enhanced pommels (the pommel is the part at the very base of the sword that holds it all together). Swords with enhanced pommels have an additional description at the end of their names (called a suffix here): a Sword of Defense adds to your armor. A Sword of Charr Slaying boosts your damage against Charr.

You get these parts by using an expert salvage kit on enhanced equipment. (A basic kit will only yield basic crafting components.) However, even an expert kit will only yield one part per item, even if the original item has two enhanced parts. Sometimes it's better to start using the dropped item, rather than trying to salvage it.

A very few weapons have both types of enhancements: prefix and suffix. Using our example above, they would be named the Icy Sword of Charr Slaying, or the Fiery Sword of Defense.

Bonuses

Equipment can also have bonuses (extra armor, boosted Energy, and so forth). Unfortunately, bonuses can never be salvaged—the only way to get the bonus is to equip the original item. Sometimes that's your best option, sometimes it's not.

Types of Drops

Common (white) drops occur all over an area. A few common items have an enhanced prefix part or a bonus. Those items will have blue text, not white.

Uncommon (purple) items can also drop all over the area, but the higher the monster level, the likelier an uncommon drop will be. Uncommon drops can have a prefix, a suffix, and a bonus (but rarely have all three).

Rare (gold) drops...well, you weren't expecting them to fall off the easiest monsters in the area, were you? There are one to three rare drops in an area, and if you want to find them, go after the highest monsters (think "boss" and "far end of the area" and you'll be right more often than wrong). Rare drops aren't always on the same monster each time you enter the area, and even when a rare drop is assigned to a monster, it won't always drop it.

Rare drops can have a prefix, a suffix, and up to two bonuses.

Weapon Bonuses & Enhancements

Possible Axe, Hammer, Sword Damage Bonuses

Increases damage by +10-15% but reduces armor by X while attacking
Increases damage by +10-15% but gives you -1 Health regeneration
Increases damage by +10-15% but gives you -1 Energy regeneration
Increases damage by +10-15% but gives you -X max Energy
Increases damage by +10-15% while you're enchanted
Increases damage by +10-15% against a hexed foe
Increases damage by +10-15% while your Health is above 50%
Increases damage by +15-20% while your Health is below 50%
Increases damage by +15-20% while you're suffering from a Hex
Increases damage by +10-15% while you're in a Stance

Possible Axe, Hammer, Sword Prefixes

X Axe Haft, X Hammer Haft, X Sword Hilt

Icy	Changes damage to Cold
Ebon	Changes damage to Earth
Shocking	Changes damage to Lightning
Fiery	Changes damage to Fire
Barbed (not Hammer)	Increases Bleed duration by 33%
Crippling (not Hammer)	Increases Cripple duration by 33%
Cruel (not Sword)	Increases Deep Wound duration by 33%
Furious	Doubles your Adrenaline gain, X% of the time
Poisoner's	Increases Poison duration by 33%
Heavy (not Sword)	Increases Weaken duration by 33%
Zealous	Each hit gives you 1 Energy, but you have -1 Energy regen
Vampiric	Each hit steals 1-3 target Health, but you have -1 Health regen
Sundering	X% of the time; your hit has 10% armor penetration

Possible Axe, Hammer, Sword Suffixes

Axe Grip of X, Hammer Grip of X, Sword Pommel of X

Defense	+4-5 Armor
Shelter	+4-7 Armor vs Physical Attacks
Warding	+4-7 Armor vs Elemental Attacks
X Slaying	+15-30% damage vs. a creature type
Fortitude	+20-30 max Health
Enchanting	Enchantments you cast last 10-20% longer
Appropriate Attribute*	10-20% chance of +1 attribute each time you use one of that attribute's skills

* Axe Mastery, Hammer Mastery or Swordsmanship

Possible Staff Bonuses

Shorten Condition Dur.	Reduces the duration of X Condition by 33%
Impr. Skill Recharge	5-10% chance to reduce your skills' recharge by 20%
Impr. Skill Recharge	10-20% chance to reduce (X attribute) skills' recharge by 20%
Impr. Casting Speed	5-10% chance to improve your skills' casting speed by 20%
Impr. Casting Speed	10-20% chance to cut (X attribute) skills' casting time by 20%

Possible Staff Prefixes (Heads)

Defensive	+4-5 Armor
Insightful	+1-5 max Energy
Hale	+20-30 max Health

Possible Staff Suffixes (Wrappings)

Defense	+4-5 Armor
Shelter	+4-7 Armor vs. physical attacks
Warding	+4-7 Armor vs. Elemental attacks
X Slaying	+15-30% damage vs. a creature type
Fortitude	+20-30 max Health
Enchanting	Enchantments you cast last 10-20% longer

Possible Rod Bonuses

Energy Bonus	+1-5 Energy while you are enchanted
Energy Bonus	+10-15 Energy; -1 Energy regeneration
Energy Bonus	+1-5 Energy while Health is greater then 50%
Energy Bonus	+1-5 Energy while Health is less then 50%
Energy Bonus	+1-5 Energy while Hexed
Impr. Skill Recharge	5-10% chance to reduce your skills' recharge by 20%
Impr. Skill Recharge	10-20% chance to reduce (X Attribute) skills' recharge by 20%
Impr. Casting Speed	5-10% chance to improve your skills' casting speed by 20%
Impr. Casting Speed	10-20% chance to improve (X attribute) skills' casting speed by 20%

Possible Focus Bonuses

+1 Attribute if using skills	10-20% chance to cut (X attributes) skills' casting time by 20%
Shorten Condition Dur.	Reduces the duration of X condition by 33%
Energy Bonus	+10-15 Energy -1 Energy Regeneration
Impr. Skill Recharge	5-10% chance to reduce your skills' recharge by 20%
Impr. Skill Recharge	10-20% chance to reduce (X attribute) skills' recharge by 20%
Improved Armor	+3 Armor
Improved Armor	+4-8 Armor for X damage type
Improved Armor	+4-5 Armor vs. Elemental damage
Improved Armor	+4-8 Armor vs. X creature type
Improved Armor	+4-5 Armor vs. physical damage
Improved Armor	+4-5 Armor while casting
Improved Armor	+4-5 Armor while attacking
Improved Armor	+4-5 Armor while enchanted
Improved Armor	+4-8 Armor while Health is less than 50%
Improved Armor	+4-5 Armor while Health is greater than 50%
Improved Armor	+4-8 Armor while Hexed
Health Bonus	+20-30 max Health
Health Bonus	+15-45 Health while enchanted
Health Bonus	+15-45 Health while Hexed

Possible Shield Bonuses

+1 Attribute if using skills	10-20% chance to cut (X attribute's) skills' casting time by 20%
Shorten Condition Dur.	Reduces the duration of X condition by 33%
Health Bonus	+20-30 max Health
Health Bonus	+15-45 Health while enchanted
Health Bonus	+15-45 Health while hexed
Improved Armor	+4-8 Armor for X damage type
Improved Armor	+4-8 Armor vs. X creature type
Damage Reduction	10-20% chance to reduce damage by 1-3
Damage Reduction	-1-2 Damage while enchanted
Damage Reduction	-1-3 Damage while Hexed
Damage Reduction	-1-2 Damage while in a Stance
Health Bonus	+15-45 Health while in a Stance

Runes

There are minor, major, and superior runes for all attributes (except Soul Reaping). A minor rune boosts your attribute by +1, a major rune by +2, and a superior rune by +3. Runes don't "stack," that is to say, you can only gain the effect of a single rune type at any time, so a rune of Minor Fast Casting (on your boots) and a Rune of Major Fast Casting (on your gloves) would only give you +2 Fast Casting.

Collectors

There are collectors throughout the realms of Guild Wars, happy to give you something for the various monster bits and pieces that remain after combat. Most of them want three to five items (scales, fins, or whatever). Some collectors were still deciding what they would give as a reward for your collection as this guide went to press, and others will change their minds from time to time, but here is the current list:

Abbreviations: E=Elementalist, Mk=Monk, N=Necromancer, M=Mesmer, W=Warrior, R=Ranger

Kingdom of Ascalon Collectors

Collector	Collectible	How Many	Ms Reward	N Reward	E Reward	Mk Reward	W Reward	R Reward
Hatcher	Unnatural Seeds	3	—	—	—	—	—	—
Walden	Unnatural Seeds	3	Leather Vest	Truncheon	Scroll	Mk Raiment	Battle Axe	Leather Gloves
Varis	Spider Legs	3	Stylish Hose	N's Leggings	Water Staff	Smiting Staff	Earth Wand	Fire Wand
Almi	Charr Carvings	5	—	—	—	—	—	—
Savich	Icy Lodestones	3	Stylish Attire	Bone Staff	E's Leggings	Mk Sandals	Battle Axe	Ascalon Bow
Rownan	Dull Carapaces	3	Devourer Egg	Grim Cesta	E's Shoes	Mk Pants	Ringmail Leggings	Ascalon Bow
Karleen	Gargoyle Skulls	5	Ringmail Boots	N's Boots	Storm Artifact	Holy Rod	Crimson Carapace Shield	Inscribed Staff
Humphreys	Worn Belts	5	Belt Pouch	—	—	—	—	—
Brownlow	Skale Fins	5	Belt Pouch	Devourer Egg	—	—	—	—
Gwynn	Skeletal Limbs	3	Cane	N's Gloves	Frost Artifact	Holy Staff	War Hammer	Leather Leggings
Mindle	Enchanted Lodestones	3	Cane	Grim Cesta	E's Gloves	Mk Handwraps	War Hammer	Ascalon Bow
Kaylee	Grawl Necklaces	3	Jeweled Chakram	Grim Cesta	Scroll	Divine Symbol	Ringmail Hauberk	Leather Vest
Jacobs	Baked Husks	3	Stylish Footwear	Idol	Flame Artifact	Healing Ankh	Ringmail Gauntlets	Leather Boots

Ruins of Ascalon Collectors

Collector	Collectible	How Many	Ms Reward	N Reward	E Reward	Mk Reward	W Reward	R Reward
Valeria Benes	Singed Gargoyle Skulls	3	Cane	Grim Cesta	Storm Artifact	Fire Staff	Bulwark of Balthazar	Longbow
Sir Nyman	Rawhide Belts	3	Belt Pouch	—	—	—	—	—
Corwin Luceinne	Ornate Grawl Necklaces	3	Cane	Truncheon	Flame Artifact	Healing Ankh	Runic Hammer	Air Staff
Louise Haup	Charr Carvings	3	Cane	Grim Cesta	Storm Artifact	Air Wand	Ascalon Razor	Ascalon Bow
Sally Kaugie	Scorched Seeds	3	Jeweled Chalice	Truncheon	Scroll	Divine Symbol	Holy Staff	Ascalon Bow
Dael	Leathery Claws	3	Bag	—	—	—	—	—
Ouran Odwin	Stormy Eyes	3	Cane	Idol	Water Wand	Smiting Staff	Ascalon Axe	Diessa Flatbow
Nicanor Gannel	Enchanted Lodestones	3	Inscribed Chakram	Idol	Earth Wand	Smiting Staff	Flame Spitter	Ascalon Bow
Ashram Fenn	Scar Behemoth Jaws	3	Inscribed Chakram	Grim Cesta	Scroll	Plasma Blade	Grim Cesta	Ascalon Bow
Nazag Fenn	Gruesome Ribcages	9	Bag	—	—	—	—	—
Wain Hughes	Charr Carvings	3	Jeweled Chakram	Cruel Staff	Fire Wand	Ascalon Battle Staff	Earth Staff	Ascalon Bow
Graine Hathorn	Fetid Carapaces	4	Stylish Footwear	N's Boots	E's Shoes	Mk Sandals	Ringmail Boots	Leather Boots
Lenerd Aberold	Singed Gargoyle Skulls	3	Belt Pouch	—	—	—	—	—

Collector	Collectible	How Many	Ms Reward	N Reward	E Reward	Mk Reward	W Reward	R Reward
Gil Moriddan	Leathery Claws	4	Stylish Attire	N's Tunic	E's Robes	Mk Raiment	Ringmail Hauberk	Leather Vest
Martel Bastions	Enchanted Lodestones	3	Jeweled Chalice	Wicked Staff	Scroll	Protective Icon	Grim Cesta	Ascalon Bow
Raymon Elsworth	Stormy Eyes	3	Jeweled Staff	Cruel Staff	Frost Artifact	Healing Ankh	War Hammer	Earth Wand
Paige Osbourne	Charr Carvings	3	Inscribed Staff	Bone Staff	Water Staff	Protective Icon	Ascalon Maul	Fire Wand
Fytch	Fetid Carapaces	3	Jeweled Chakram	Truncheon	Flame Artifact	Divine Symbol	Runic Shield	Water Wand
Guardsman Noell	Ornate Grawl Necklaces	3	Inscribed Staff	Cruel Staff	Earth Staff	Wicked Staff	Crimson Carapace Shield	Air Wand
Calissa Sedgwick	Charr Hides	4	Belt Pouch	Fur Squares				
Dreaz Bowem	Fetid Carapaces	3	Inscribed Chakram	Truncheon	E's Gloves	Mk Handwraps	Ringmail Gauntlets	Leather Gloves
Innis the White	Singed Gargoyle Skulls	3	Stylish Gloves	N's Gloves	Fire Staff	Diessa Icon	War Hammer	Air Staff
Penelope Hoode	Scorched Seeds	3	Inscribed Chakram	Bone Staff	Frost Artifact	Holy Staff	Rinblade	Ascalon Bow
Saba Blackstone	Enchanted Lodestones	3	Jeweled Staff	Grim Cesta	Scroll	Holy Staff	Ascalon Aegis	Diessa Flatbow
Palben Tunne	Ornate Grawl Necklaces	4	Stylish Hose	N's Leggings	E's Leggings	[proper] Mk Pants	Ringmail Leggings	Leather Leggings

Shiverpeaks Collectors

Collector	Collectible	How Many	Ms Reward	N Reward	E Reward	Mk Reward	W Reward	R Reward
Hoknil the Greater	Huge Jawbones	7	Stylish Attire	N's Tunic	E's Robes	Mk Raiment	Ringmail Hauberk	Leather Vest
Cember Goreaxe	Frigid Hearts	5	–	–	Fire Staff	Divine Symbol	–	Earth Wand
Volsung Stoneketil	Feathered Avicara Scalps	5	–	Grim Cesta	Air Wand	–	Grim Cesta	–
Norin Stonegrimm	Frostfire Fangs	5	Imposing Mask	Ragged Scar Pattern	Storm's Eye	Defender's Scalp Design	Executioner's Helm	Tamer's Mask
Sander the Gray	Frostfire Fangs	5	Stylish Hose	N's Leggings	Glacier's Eye	Mk Pants	Tactician's Helm	Leather Leggings
Maccus Ironjaw	Curved Minotaur Horns	5	Stylish Attire	N's Tunic	E's Robes	Mk Raiment	Ringmail Hauberk	Leather Vest
Nord Stonegrimm	Frozen Shells	5	–	Truncheon	–	Smiting Staff	Battle Axe	Ascalon Bow
Radamon	Huge Jawbones	5	Cane	Truncheon	Fire Wand	Healing Ankh	War Hammer	–
Hagnon Warblade	Frosted Griffin Wings	5	Cane	–	Frost Artifact	Defender's Scalp Design	Crimson Carapace Shield	Air Staff
Hoknil the Lesser	Azure Remains	5	Inscribed Staff	Wicked Staff	–	Holy Rod	–	Ascalon Bow
Merin Trollsbane	Mountain Troll Tusks	5	Jeweled Staff	Bone Staff	Water Staff	–	Long Sword	–
Turlo Oakenspear	Frigid Hearts	7	Stylish Hose	N's Leggings	E's Leggings	Mk Pants	Ringmail Leggings	Leather Leggings
Vania Sewell	Azure Remains	7	Stylish Footwear	N's Boots	E's Shoes	Mk Sandals	Ringmail Boots	Leather Boots
Mag Ironwall	Intricate Grawl Necklaces	5	–	Cruel Staff	Scroll	Holy Staff	–	Ascalon Bow
Bariel Darkroot	Alpine Seeds	5	Jeweled Chakram	–	Earth Staff	Jeweled Chalice	Scroll	Ascalon Bow
Goran Grimyak	Feathered Avicara Scalps	5	Inscribed Chakram	Idol	Flame Artifact	–	Water Wand	–
Trego Stonebreaker	Mountain Troll Tusks	5	Inscribed Chakram	Deadly Cesta	Flame's Eye	–	Protective Icon	Ascalon Bow
Ornhelm Brightaxe	Stone Summit Badges	5	–	Grim Cesta	Storm Artifact	Smiting Rod	–	–
Kagan Treesplitter	Alpine Seeds	7	Stylish Gloves	N's Gloves	E's Gloves	Mk Handwraps	Ringmail Gauntlets	Leather Gloves
Sadira Powell	Alpine Seeds	5	Stylish Footwear	N's Boots	E's Shoes	Mk Sandals	Ringmail Boots	Leather Boots
Pyrs Harven	Shiverpeak Manes	5	Sleek Mask	Devilish Scar Pattern	All-Seeing Eye	Prophet's Scalp Design	Brute's Helm	Hunter's Mask
Asgrim Brightaxe	Stone Summit Badges	5	Stylish Gloves	N's Gloves	E's Gloves	Mk Handwraps	Ringmail Gauntlets	Leather Gloves
Rothgar Hoofsplitter	Shiverpeak Manes	5	Costume Mask	Vile Scar Pattern	Stone's Eye	Servant's Scalp Design	Dwarven Helm	Traveler's Mask
Lenn Giantsbane	Icy Humps	5	Animal Mask	Wicked Scar Pattern	–	–	Duelist's Helm	Archer's Mask

Kryta Collectors

Collector	Collectible	How Many	Ms Reward	N Reward	E Reward	Mk Reward	W Reward	R Reward
Arris Weston	Spiked Crests	4	Inscribed Chakram	Bone Staff	Air Staff	Deadly Cesta	Battle Axe	Scroll
Daved Logsdon	Abnormal Seeds	4	Cane	Grim Cesta	Water Wand	Protective Icon	Fire Staff	Ascalon Bow
Helton Wills	Hardened Humps	4	Jeweled Staff	Idol	Scroll	Holy Rod	Storm Artifact	Ascalon Bow
Leighton Cranford	Bog Skale Fins	4	Cane	Bone Staff	Fire Wand	Smiting Staff	Battle Axe	–
Wintun the Black	Feathered Caromi Scalps	4	Inscribed Chakram	Grim Cesta	Scroll	Protective Icon	Fire Staff	–
Camryn Jamison	Decayed Orr Emblems	4	Cane	Truncheon	Air Staff	Holy Staff	Cruel Staff	Flame Artifact
Milny Samhammil	Mergoyle Skulls	4	Jeweled Chalice	Grim Cesta	Water Wand	Holy Rod	Crimson Carapace Shield	Air Wand
Beldon the Blade	Mergoyle Skulls	4	Inscribed Staff	Wicked Staff	Frost Artifact	Storm Artifact	Grim Cesta	Ascalon Bow
Kira Thorne	Glowing Hearts	4	Inscribed Chakram	Deadly Cesta	Earth Staff	Healing Ankh	Wicked Staff	Air Wand
Galstaff the Light	Mergoyle Skulls	5	Stylish Footwear	N's Boots	E's Shoes	Mk Sandals	Ringmail Boots	Leather Boots
Julianna Furst	Glowing Hearts	5	Stylish Footwear	N's Boots	E's Shoes	Mk Sandals	Ringmail Boots	Leather Boots
Ember Whisperwind	Forest Minotaur Horns	5	Stylish Attire	N's Tunic	E's Robes	Mk Raiment	Ringmail Hauberk	Leather Vest
Robin Neils	Shadowy Remnants	5	Stylish Attire	N's Tunic	E's Robes	Mk Raiment	Ringmail Hauberk	Leather Vest
Falhurst	Mergoyle Skulls	5	Stylish Gloves	N's Gloves	E's Gloves	Mk Handwraps	Ringmail Gauntlets	Leather Gloves
Gruhn the Fisher	Bog Skale Fins	5	Stylish Gloves	Gloves	E's Gloves	Mk Handwraps	Ringmail Gauntlets	Leather Gloves
Tenlach Silverhand	Abnormal Seeds	5	Imposing Mask	Ragged Scar Pattern	Storm's Eye	Prophet's Scalp Design	Executioner's Helm	Tamer's Mask
Ian Sturmme	Feathered Caromi Scalps	5	Sleek Mask	Wicked Scar Pattern	Stone's Eye	Servant's Scalp Design	Dwarven Helm	Archer's Mask
Vardis	Spiked Crests	5	Costume Mask	Vile Scar Pattern	All-Seeing Eye	Defender's Scalp Design	Duelist's Helm	Hunter's Mask
Delves the Dodgy	Gargantuan Jawbones	5	Animal Mask	Devilish Scar Pattern	Flame's Eye	Defender's Scalp Design	Brute's Helm	Traveler's Mask
Jamora the Wise	Glowing Hearts	5	Stylish Hose	N's Leggings	E's Leggings	Mk Pants	Ringmail Leggings	Leather Leggings
Ian Borish	Shadowy Remnants	5	Stylish Hose	N's Leggings	E's Leggings	Mk Pants	Ringmail Leggings	Leather Leggings
Sir Robert	Abnormal Seeds	4	Jeweled Staff	Grim Cesta	Earth Wand	Healing Ankh	Long Sword	Flame Artifact
Liris the Sage	Bog Skale Fins	4	Jeweled Chakram	Cruel Staff	Water Staff	Smiting Rod	Truncheon	Ascalon Bow
Kolleen Redstone	Decayed Orr Emblems	4	Inscribed Chakram	Truncheon	Scroll	Divine Symbol	War Hammer	–
Alton Thorne	Leather Belts	4	Jeweled Chalice	Grim Cesta	Fire Wand	Smiting Staff	Crimson Carapace Shield	–
Brynden Cromwell	Gargantuan Jawbones	4	Inscribed Staff	Idol	Earth Staff	Holy Staff	Water Staff	Ascalon Bow
Brion Elston	Forest Minotaur Horns	4	Cane	Truncheon	Frost Artifact	Smiting Rod	War Hammer	–
William Pennington	Ivory Troll Tusks	4	Jeweled Chakram	Cruel Staff	Earth Wand	Divine Symbol	Long Sword	–

The Wilds Collectors

Collector	Collectible	How Many	Ms Reward	N Reward	E Reward	Mk Reward	W Reward	R Reward
Jaden Fletcher	Ancient Eyes	5	Stylish Footwear	N's Boots	E's Shoes	Mk Sandals	Ringmail Boots	Leather Boots
Lord Engelram	Maguuma Manes	5	Stylish Footwear	N's Boots	E's Shoes	Mk Sandals	Ringmail Boots	Leather Boots
Hember	Thorny Carapaces	5	Stylish Attire	N's Tunic	E's Robes	Mk Raiment	Ringmail Hauberk	Leather Vest
Horton Longsnout	White Mantle Emblems	5	Stylish Attire	N's Tunic	E's Robes	Mk Raiment	Ringmail Hauberk	Leather Vest
Elene the Vigilant	Ebon Spider Legs	5	Stylish Gloves	N's Gloves	E's Gloves	Mk Handwraps	Ringmail Gauntlets	Leather Gloves
Mosreh the Exile	Ebon Spider Legs	5	Stylish Gloves	N's Gloves	E's Gloves	Mk Handwraps	Ringmail Gauntlets	Leather Gloves
Aaron Fletcher	Ancient Eyes	5	Imposing Mask	Ragged Scar Pattern	Storm's Eye	Prophet's Scalp Design	Executioner's Helm	Tamer's Mask
Elwynn Kirby	Tangled Seeds	5	Sleek Mask	Wicked Scar Pattern	Stone's Eye	Servant's Scalp Design	Dwarven Helm	Archer's Mask
Agrippa Stonehands	Behemoth Jaws	5	Costume Mask	Vile Scar Pattern	All-Seeing Eye	Defender's Scalp Design	Duelist's Helm	Hunter's Mask
Slayton Redblade	Tangled Seeds	5	Animal Mask	Devilish Scar Pattern	Flame's Eye	Defender's Scalp Design	Brute's Helm	Traveler's Mask
Llourdes the Arcane	Jungle Skale Fins	5	Stylish Hose	N's Leggings	Glacier's Eye	Mk Pants	Tactician's Helm	Leather Leggings
Meghan the Bright	Jungle Troll Tusks	5	Stylish Hose	N's Leggings	E's Leggings	Mk Pants	Ringmail Leggings	Leather Leggings
Isabaeux Navarre	Thorny Carapaces	5	Jeweled Chalice	Truncheon	Water Wand	Holy Staff	Battle Axe	

Collector	Collectible	How Many	Ms Reward	N Reward	E Reward	Mk Reward	W Reward	R Reward
Vargil the White	Ancient Eyes	5	Cane	Grim Cesta	Storm Artifact	Healing Ankh	Crimson Carapace Shield	Ascalon Bow
Orson Cooper	Ancient Eyes	5	Jeweled Chakram	Idol	Water Staff	Holy Rod	War Hammer	–
Tully Blackvine	Tangled Seeds	5	Jeweled Staff	Cruel Staff	Scroll	Divine Symbol	–	Ascalon Bow
Ingrid Larson	Mossy Mandibles	5	Inscribed Staff	Grim Cesta	Fire Wand	Healing Ankh	Long Sword	–
Serah Shaes	Jungle Skale Fins	5	Inscribed Chakram	Grim Cesta	Storm Artifact	Divine Symbol	War Hammer	–
Seris the Red	Behemoth Jaws	5	Inscribed Staff	Wicked Staff	Air Staff	Smiting Rod	–	Ascalon Bow
Lady Engelram	Maguuma Manes	5	Cane	Grim Cesta	Flame Artifact	Holy Rod	Long Sword	–
Farmer Conklin	Mossy Mandibles	5	Jeweled Chakram	Idol	Earth Wand	Smiting Staff	–	Ascalon Bow
Crispin Bryllis	Jungle Troll Tusks	5	Inscribed Chakram	Deadly Cesta	Frost Artifact	Protective Icon	Battle Axe	–
Adam Solstrum	White Mantle Emblems	5	Cane	Grim Cesta	Fire Staff	Smiting Staff	Crimson Carapace Shield	–
Thyfir Greenleaf	White Mantle Emblems	5	Inscribed Chakram	Truncheon	Air Wand	Holy Staff	–	Ascalon Bow
Loreen Cranford	Jungle Troll Tusks	5	Jeweled Chalice	Bone Staff	Earth Staff	Protective Icon	–	–

The Crystal Desert Collectors

Collector	Collectible	How Many	Ms Reward	N Reward	E Reward	Mk Reward	W Reward	R Reward
Cinder Linnwood	Bleached Carapaces	5	Jeweled Staff	Idol	Storm Artifact	Divine Symbol	Long Sword	–
Luven Underwood	Minotaur Horns	5	Cane	Bone Staff	Fire Wand	Smiting Staff	War Hammer	Ascalon Bow
Brandon Harlin	Encrusted Lodestones	5	Jeweled Chalice	Grim Cesta	Scroll	Protective Icon	Battle Axe	–
Karl Jakobs	Massive Jawbones	5	Inscribed Staff	Deadly Cesta	Fire Staff	Holy Rod	Crimson Carapace Shield	Ascalon Bow
Kraviec the Cursed	Iridescent Griffin Wings	5	Jeweled Chakram	Grim Cesta	Scroll	Healing Ankh	War Hammer	–
Uderit Ignis	Jade Mandibles	5	Inscribed Chakram	Truncheon	Water Wand	Smiting Staff	Long Sword	–
Sir Pohl Sanbert	Dune Burrower Jaws	5	Cane	Grim Cesta	Flame Artifact	Divine Symbol	Battle Axe	Ascalon Bow
Sir Kaufman	Massive Jawbones	5	Stylish Footwear	N's Boots	E's Shoes	Mk Sandals	Ringmail Boots	Leather Boots
Gustov the Silent	Dune Burrower Jaws	5	Stylish Footwear	N's Boots	E's Shoes	Mk Sandals	Ringmail Boots	Leather Boots
Kyle the Rich	Losaru Manes	5	Stylish Attire	N's Tunic	E's Robes	Mk Raiment	Ringmail Hauberk	Leather Vest
Winfield Michelson	Bleached Carapaces	5	Stylish Attire	N's Tunic	E's Robes	Mk Raiment	Ringmail Hauberk	Leather Vest
Fenster the Golden	Minotaur Horns	5	Stylish Gloves	N's Gloves	E's Gloves	Mk Handwraps	Ringmail Gauntlets	Leather Gloves
Sir Norrington	Shriveled Eyes	5	Stylish Gloves	N's Gloves	E's Gloves	Mk Handwraps	Ringmail Gauntlets	Leather Gloves
Kelsay Pradist	Jade Mandibles	5	Imposing Mask	Ragged Scar Pattern	Storm's Eye	Prophet's Scalp Design	Executioner's Helm	Tamer's Mask
Ekimeel Trueshot	Forgotten Seals	5	Sleek Mask	Wicked Scar Pattern	Stone's Eye	Servant's Scalp Design	Dwarven Helm	Archer's Mask
Ardenoth Oakenshield	Bleached Shells	5	Costume Mask	Vile Scar Pattern	All-Seeing Eye	Defender's Scalp Design	Duelist's Helm	Hunter's Mask
Barton Smallwood	Shriveled Eyes	5	Animal Mask	Devilish Scar Pattern	Flame's Eye	Defender's Scalp Design	Brute's Helm	Traveler's Mask
Jamie the Wanderer	Dune Burrower Jaws	5	Stylish Hose	N's Leggings	E's Leggings	Mk Pants	Ringmail Leggings	Leather Leggings
Cedric Rogers	Losaru Manes	5	Stylish Hose	N's Leggings	E's Leggings	Mk Pants	Ringmail Leggings	Leather Leggings
Lord Dorn Lendrigen	Bleached Shells	5	Cane	Idol	Air Staff	Holy Rod	Crimson Carapace Shield	–
John Verado	Topaz Crests	5	Inscribed Staff	Cruel Staff	Earth Wand	Protective Icon	–	Ascalon Bow
Arliss Vaughn	Iridescent Griffin Wings	5	Jeweled Chalice	Truncheon	Frost Artifact	Smiting Rod	–	–
Mourn Drakespur	Dessicated Hydra Claws	5	Jeweled Chakram	Wicked Staff	Air Wand	Healing Ankh	–	Ascalon Bow
Rylan Paval	Spiny Seeds	5	Inscribed Chakram	Grim Cesta	Water Staff	Holy Staff	–	–

Henchmen

Henchmen stats and abbreviations are the same as those for Foes (p. 188).

Roleplaying Henchmen

Stefan Baruch (W-Fighter)

Healing Signet	Power Attack
Griffon's Sweep	Balanced Stance
Sprint (3-17)	"Charge!" (20)
Resurrection Signet	

L3	AL30	Dmg 3–6 (M-Sla)
L6	AL38 (Phy +20)	Dmg 3–6 (M-Sla)
L8	AL42 (Phy +20)	Dmg 6–8 (M-Sla)
L10	AL50 (Phy +20)	Dmg 7–10 (M-Sla)
L12	AL56 (Phy +20)	Dmg 7–10 (M-Sla)
L15	AL65	Dmg 9–14 (M-Sla)
L17	AL71 (Phy +20)	Dmg 12–17 (M-Sla)
L20	AL80	Dmg 12–17 (M-Sla)

Orion Elek (E-Mage)

Fire Storm	Fireball
Incendiary Bonds (8-20)	Fire Attunement
Aura of Restoration	Resurrection Signet
Mind Burn (20)	

L3	AL10 (Phy +20)	Dmg 3–5 (R-Lgt)
L6	AL15	Dmg 4–7 (R-Lgt)
L8	AL24	Dmg 4–7 (R-Lgt)
L10	AL30	Dmg 5–10 (R-Fire)
L12	AL36	Dmg 5–10 (R-Fire)
L15	AL45	Dmg 5–12 (R-Fire)
L17	AL51	Dmg 10–16 (R-Fire)
L20	AL60	Dmg 11–22 (R-Dark)

Alesia Baptiste (Mk-Healer)

Orison of Healing	Healing Breeze
Heal Other (8-17)	Word of Healing (20)
Healing Touch (15-20)	Restore Life

L3	AL10 (Elem +30)	Dmg 3–5 (R-Fire)
L6	AL15	Dmg 4–7 (R-Fire)
L8	AL24	Dmg 4–7 (R-Fire)
L10	AL30	Dmg 5–10 (R-Fire)
L12	AL36	Dmg 5–10 (R-Fire)
L15	AL45	Dmg 5–12 (R-Fire)
L17	AL51	Dmg 10–16 (R-Fire)
L20	AL60 (Elem +30)	Dmg 10–16 (R-Lgt)

Reyna Sandor (R-Archer)

Kindle Arrows	Power Shot
Dual Shot	Troll Unguent
Resurrection Signet	Practiced Stance (20)

L3	AL20	Dmg 5–9 (R-Prc)
L6	AL28 (Phy +20)	Dmg 7–12 (R-Prc)
L8	AL34 (Phy +20)	Dmg 7–12 (R-Prc)
L10	AL40 (Phy +20)	Dmg 9–15 (R-Prc)
L12	AL46 (Phy +20)	Dmg 9–15 (R-Prc)
L15	AL55	Dmg 12–29 (R-Prc)
L17	AL61 (Phy +20)	Dmg 14–24 (R-Prc)
L20	AL70	Dmg 14–24 (R-Prc)

Dunham (Ms-Enchanter)

Imagined Burden (8-17)	Crippling Anguish (20)
Shatter Hex	Drain Enchantment

Empathy	Distortion
Resurrection Signet	

L8	AL24 (Elem +30)	Dmg 4–7 (R-Dark)
L10	AL30 (Elem +30)	Dmg 5–10 (R-Dark)
L12	AL36 (Elem +30)	Dmg 5–10 (R-Fire)
L15	AL45 (Elem +30)	Dmg 5–12 (R-Fire)
L17	AL51	Dmg 10–16 (R-Fire)
L20	AL60 (Phy +20)	Dmg 11–22 (R-Dark)

Little Thom (W-Brawler)

Healing Signet	Wild Blow	Swift Chop
Executioner's Strike	Sprint (8-17)	"Charge!" (20)
Resurrection Signet		

L8	AL42	Dmg 2–13 (M-Sla)
L10	AL50	Dmg 4–15 (M-Sla)
L12	AL56	Dmg 4–17 (M-Sla)
L15	AL65	Dmg 4–20 (M-Sla)
L17	AL71 (Phy +20)	Dmg 4–22 (M-Sla)
L20	AL80 (Fire +100)	Dmg 5–24 (M-Sla)

Claude (N-Cultist)

Shadow Strike	Vampiric Gaze
Deathly Swarm	Blood Ritual
Resurrection Signet	Grenth's Balance (20)

L8	AL24	Dmg 4–7 (R-Dark)
L10	AL30	Dmg 5–10 (R-Dark)
L12	AL36	Dmg 5–10 (R-Fire)
L15	AL45	Dmg 5–12 (R-Fire)
L17	AL51	Dmg 10–16 (R-Fire)
L20	AL60 (Elem +30)	Dmg 11–22 (R-Dark)

Final Mission Henchmen

Aidan (R-Archer)

L20
Dmg 15–28 (R-Prc)
Power Shot
Troll Unguent
Practiced Stance

AL70
Kindle Arrows
Dual Shot
Resurrection Signet

Cynn (E-Mage)

L20
Dmg 11–22 (R-Fire)
Fireball
Fire Attunement
Resurrection Signet

AL60 (Phy +20)
Fire Storm
Incendiary Bonds
Aura of Restoration
Mind Burn

Devona (W-Fighter)

L20
Dmg 15–30 (M-Blt)
Mighty Blow
Counter Blow
Resurrection Signet

AL95
Healing Signet
Irresistible Blow
"Charge!"

Eve (N-Blood Mage)

L20
Dmg 11–22 (R-Dark)
Vampiric Gaze
Blood Ritual
Grenth's Balance

AL60
Shadow Strike
Deathly Swarm
Resurrection Signet

Lina Esrevni (Mk-Protector)

L20
Dmg 10–16 (R-Lgt)
Protective Spirit
Shield of Regeneration

AL51
Reversal of Fortune
Aegis
Restore Life

Mhenlo (Mk-Healer)

L20
Dmg 11–22 (R-Lgt)
Healing Breeze
Healing Touch

AL60
Orison of Healing
Word of Healing
Restore Life

PvP Henchmen

Archer Henchman (R)

L20
Dmg 15–28 (R-Prc)
Power Shot
Troll Unguent
Practiced Stance

AL70
Kindle Arrows
Dual Shot
Resurrection Signet

Fighter Henchman (W)

L20
Dmg 15–22 (M-Sla)
Power Attack
Balanced Stance
Resurrection Signet

AL80
Healing Signet
Griffon's Sweep
"Charge!"

Healer Henchman (Mk)

L20
Dmg 11–22 (R-Lgt)
Healing Breeze
Healing Touch

AL60
Orison of Healing
Word of Healing
Restore Life

Mage Henchman (E)

L20
Dmg 11–22 (R-Fire)
Fireball
Fire Attunement
Resurrection Signet

AL60
Fire Storm
Incendiary Bonds
Aura of Restoration
Mind Burn

Pets

Both Rangers and Necromancers can acquire pets. For the Ranger, it's an animal companion of one sort or another; for the Necromancer, it's the temporary, undead remains of someone, or something, that should really be buried.

The following table shows the initial level for each possible Ranger pet, but note that these pets grow with you—as long as they adventure by your side, they are basically earning as much experience as you are. As they grow, their attacks get better and they gain more Health. (Pet Health, like most other Health in the game, is determined by level—see the chart on p. 176.) Check the maps for where you can find each type of pet, but you might find that some potential pets (particularly bears) will resist your best efforts to charm them.

Animal	Lvl	Dmg	Armor
Strider	1	Prc 3-5	AC 3
Wolf	2	Sla 4-6	AC6
Warthog	2	Blunt 4-6	AC6
Moa Bird	3	Sla 5-8	AC 9
Melandru's Stalkers	5	Sla 6-10	AC 15
Snow Wolf	5	Sla 6-10	AC 15
Lynx	5	Sla 6-10	AC 15
Warthog	5	Blunt 6-10	AC 15
Dune Lizard	5	Prc 6-10	AC 15
Black Bear	5	Sla 6-10	AC 15
Elder Black Widow	20	Prc 17-29	AC 60

Pets may experience "evolutions" as they level and are granted stronger or weaker attacks and defenses. Which evolution occurs depends on your play style and how you utilize your pet.

Necromancer Pet	Lvl	AL	Damage
Bone Minion	–	1	Dmg 1–20 (M-Blt)
Bone Fiend	–	3	Dmg 1–30 (M-Prc)
Bone Horror	–	5	Dmg 1–30 (M-Blt)

Foes

A foe's level determines its Health, with a few exceptions (noted each time). In fact, foes at a given level have the same base Health as PCs. (Level 0 foes have a varying amount of Health, but it's usually very low.) If the entry covers two different levels for the same creature, both levels are listed on the following pages in the Foe Stats table.

Foe Stats table guidelines:

• AL lists each foe's armor level. If the entry covers two different ALs for the same creature, both ALs are listed.

• AL's can be modified based on the type of damage an enemy is strong or weak against. In those cases, a + (strong) or weak - (weak) will be noted before the damage type. The types of damage include: **Blt** (Blunt), **Elem** (Elemental), **Ltng** (Lightning), **Phy** (Physical), **Prc** (Piercing), and **Sla** (Slash).

• Any non-standard Health is listed in the description.

• If the foe has a physical attack, first the base damage range is listed, then whether it's a melee (**M**) or ranged (**R**) attack, and finally what type of damage is inflicted.

• After attack stats, skills are listed. If the entry describes multiple types of foes, and only certain foes have that particular skill, either that skill will be in parentheses or the level of foe that uses it will immediately follow the skill. For example, "(Flare)" means that this foe *might* have the skill Flare; Flare (18) means that only the Level 18 version of this foe has this skill.

• The final abbreviated listing gives probable types of loot for the foe. Types of loot include: **Ar** (Armor), **Ax** (Axe), **B** (Bow), **D** (Dye), **F** (Focus), **G** (Gold), **H** (Hammer), **R** (Rod), **Sh** (Shield), **St** (Staff), and **Sw** (Sword).

• Bosses are marked with "•B•."

Player vs. Player

(outside columns)

By Jonathan "Tarinth" Radoff

Guild Wars is a competitive roleplaying game, which means that much of the content is focused on battling other players. Unlike most online roleplaying games, the PvP in *Guild Wars* features real objectives that go beyond randomly killing other characters.

There are several ways to get involved in PvP. Your roleplaying character can enter competitive missions as early as Level 1—there are special arenas that don't allow high-level characters. The more advanced missions require a lot more strategy and coordination, and are generally the domain of Level 20 characters. Fortunately, you don't have to wait for your roleplaying character to get that high. You can create a PvP Only character, which starts at Level 20. You may choose from a number of pre-made builds, or you may customize a character with any skills or equipment you've gotten while adventuring with your roleplaying character. Your PvP Only character cannot play in any of the cooperative missions or visit any of the cities, but you can jump into the PvP action right away.

Competitive missions are marked on your map by a red icon. When you play in these areas, you'll be playing against other players.

Competitive Areas for All Characters

- Fort Koga
- Tomb of the Primeval Kings
- D'Alessio Arena
- Guild vs. Guild Battle

Competitive Missions for Roleplaying Characters

Explore the map to locate these arenas (they are only available to roleplaying characters). Some of the areas are also intended for lower levels.

- Ascalon Arena
- Shiverpeak Arena
- Deldrimor Arena
- The Crag
- Amnoon Arena

Foe Stats (inside columns)

Foe	Prof	Lvl	AL	Description
Unrelated				
Deadly Crypt Spider	R	2	9	Dmg 1-2 (R-Prc) | D
Ghostly Hero	W	24	90	Dmg 7-20 (M-Sla) | Cyclone Axe
Ghostly Mage	E	24	60	Flare
Helmed Horror	W	8	46	Phy +20, Ltng -40 | H.G.Ar
Arachnid				
Armored Cave Spider	R	24	–	Elem +30 | Apply Poison | Called Shot | Savage Shot | Melandru's Resilience | Healing Spring
Casses Flameweb •B•	R	24	–	Incendiary Arrows | Dryder's Defenses | Penetrating Attack | Troll Unguent
Giant Needle Spider	R	2	9	Dmg 1-2 (R-Prc) | D
Giant Tree Spider	R	3	13	Dmg 6-9 (R-Prc) | D
Kezra Spindleweb •B•	R	14	63	Dmg 17-30 (R-Blt) | Apply Poison | Penetrating Attack | Favor. Winds | Troll Ung. | D
Lava Spitter	R	22	–	Incendiary Arrows | Dryder's Defenses | Penetrating Attack
Maguuma Spider	R	16	64	Dmg 14-24 (R-Prc) | Apply Poison | Pin Down | Storm Chaser | G.D
Behemoth				
Burrower	R	24	–	Blt +20, Prc +40, Cold -25 | Barrage | Apply Poison | Healing Spring
Dune Burrower	R	22	96	Dmg 24-46 (R-Blt) | Muddy Terrain | Apply Poison | Healing Spring | St.G.D.
Henge Guardian •B•	R	16	69	Dmg 13-36 (M-Blt) | Serpent's Quickness | Primal Echoes | Quick Shot | Healing Spring | Distracting Shot | St.G.D.
Obsidian Behemoth	R	22	80	Dmg 12-46 (R-Blt) | Blt +20, Cold -25 | Whirling Defense | Nature's Renewal | Healing Spring | Flame Trap | Barbed Trap | Throw Dirt | G.D.
Obsidian Guardian •B•	E	22	70	Dmg 12-46 (R-Blt) | Blt +20, Prc +20, Cold -25 | Ward Against Melee | Ward Against Foes | Ward Against Elements | Ward Against Harm | Obsidian Flesh | G.D.
Root Behemoth	W	19	77	Dmg 13-45 (M-Blt) | Phy +20 | Wild Blow | Deflect Arrows | "I Will Survive!" | G.D.
Snyk the Hundr. Tongue •B•R		24	–	Barrage | Serpent's Quickness | Savage Shot | Troll Unguent
Tar Behemoth	W	6	40	Dmg 6-13 (M-Blt) | Phy +20 | Wild Blow | Deflect Arrows | "I Will Survive!" | G.D.
Centaur				
Fawa Torncalf •B•	E	14	43	Ice Prison | Rust | Shard Storm | Aura of Restoration | R.F.G.Ar.D
Horm Frostrider •B•	E	15	46	Earth Attune. | Ward Against Foes | Magn. Aura | Aura of Restor. | Ice Spear | R.F.G.D
Kara Bloodtail •B•	N	14	43	Well of Blood | Order of Pain | Signet of Agony | Life Siphon | R.F.G.Ar.D
Losaru Bladehand	W	20	80	Phy +20 | Sw.Sh.Ar.D
Losaru Bowmaster	R	20	70	Elem +30 | B.Ar.D
Losaru Lifeband	Mk	20	60	Heal Other | R.St.F.Ar.D
Losaru Windcaster	Ms	20	60	R.St.F.Ar.D
Maguuma Avenger	E	16	48	Ice Prison | Rust | Shard Storm | R.F.St.G.D
Maguuma Enchanter	Ms	16	48	Mantra of Earth | Energy Burn | Leech Signet | R.F.St.G.D
Maguuma Hunter	R	16	69	Symbiosis | Flame Trap | Hunter's Shot | B.G.D
Maguuma Protector	Mk	16	48	Watchful Spirit | Succor | Life Bond | Heal Other | R.F.St.G.D
Maguuma Warlock	N	16	48	Well of Blood | Order of Pain | Signet of Agony | R.F.St.G.D
Maguuma Warrior	W	16	69	Phy +20 | Swift Chop | ("I Will Avenge You!") | (Executioner's Strike) | (Seeking Blade) | (Warrior's Cunning) | Ax.Sw.Sh.G.D
Malla Arrowmane •B•	R	14	63	Symbiosis | Flame Trap | Hunter's Shot | Healing Spring | B.G.Ar.D
Paka Blackhoof •B•	Ms	14	43	Mantra of Earth | Energy Burn | Leech Signet | Ether Feast | R.F.G.Ar.D
Rapa Ironhaunch •B•	W	14	63	Phy +20 | Executioner's Strike | Galrath Slash | Healing Signet | Ax.Sw.Sh.Ar.D
Shiverpeak Longbow	R	8	46	Distracting Shot | Winter | Serpent's Quickness | B.G.D
Shiverpeak Longbow •B•	R	7	43	Distracting Shot | Winter | Serpent's Quickness | B.G.D
Shiverpk Protector (E) •B•	E	7	23	Earth Attune. | Ward Against Foes | Magn. Aura | Aura of Restor. | Ice Spear | R.F.G.D
Shiverpk Protect. (Mk) •B•	Mk	7	23	Vigorous Spirit | Healing Breeze | Purge Conditions | Mend Ailment | R.F.G.D
Shiverpk Protect (Ms) •B•	Ms	7	23	R.F.G.D
Shiverpk Protect (N) •B•	N	7	23	R.F.G.D
Shiverpeak Warrior •B•	W	7	23	Phy +20 | Dismember | Sever Artery | Shield Stance | Ax.Sw.Sh.G.D
Tama Blessedhoof •B•	Mk	14	43	Watchful Spirit | Succor | Life Bond | Orison of Healing | Restore Life | R.F.G.Ar.D
Ventari	R	15	150	–
Charr				
Blaze Bloodbane •B•	Mk	6	20	Infuse Health | Bane Signet | Banish | Heal Area | St.R.Ar.D
Bonfaaz Burntfur •B•	E	6	20	Flare | Lava Font | Conjure Flame | Aura of Restoration | St.Ar.D
Brand the Brawler •B•	W	6	40	Phy +20 | Penetr. Blow | Cyclone Axe | Shield Stance | Healing Signet | Ax.Sh.G.Ar
Burr Mankiller •B•	N	5	17	Faintheartedness | Life Siphon | Mark of Pain | St.R.Ar.D
Cess Corpselighter •B•	N	3	12	Faintheartedness | Life Siphon | Mark of Pain | St.R.Ar.D
Charr Ash Walker	N	5/6	17/20	Faintheartedness | Life Siphon | St.R.Ar.D
Charr Ashen Claw	N	8	26	Faintheartedness | Life Siphon | Mark of Pain | St.R.Ar.D
Charr Axe Fiend	W	7/8	43/46	Phy +20 | Cyclone Axe | Frenzy | Ax.Sh.G.D.Ar
Charr Axe Warrior	W	6	40	Phy +20 | Cyclone Axe | Ax.Sh.G.D.Ar
Charr Blade Storm	W	8	46	Phy +20 | Wild Blow | Frenzy | Sw.Sh.G.D.Ar
Charr Blade Warrior	W	5/6	37/40	Phy +20 | Wild Blow | Frenzy (5) | Sw.Sh.G.D.Ar
Charr Chaot	Ms	8	26	Energy Burn | Shatter Hex | Shatter Enchantment | St.R.Ar.D
Charr Fire Caller	E	5/6	17/20	Flare | Lava Font | Conjure Flame | St.R.Ar.D
Charr Flame Keeper	E	7	23	Lava Font | Fire Storm | St.R.Ar.D
Charr Flame Wielder	E	6/8	20/26	Flare | Lava Font | Conjure Flame | St.R.Ar.D
Charr Hunter	R	8	41	Ignite Arrows | Penetrating Attack | B.G.D.Ar
Charr Martyr	Mk	4/5	14/17	Infuse Health | St.R.Ar.D
Charr Mind Spark	Ms	5/6	17/20	Energy Burn | Shatter Hex (6) | St.R.Ar.D
Charr Overseer	Mk	6	20	Heal Area | Infuse Health | Bane Signet | St.R.Ar.D

See page 187 for table guidelines.

Foe	Prof	Lvl	AL	Description
Charr Shaman	Mk	7	23	Heal Area | Infuse Health | Bane Signet | Banish | St.R.Ar.D
Charr Stalker	R	5/6	31	Ignite Arrows | Penetrating Attack | B.G.D.Ar
Craze the Unforgiving •B•	Ms	4	14	Mantra of Flame | Energy Burn | Illusion of Haste | Ether Feast | St.R.Ar.D
Cruc the Reborn •B•	Mk	5	17	Infuse Health | Bane Signet | Banish | Heal Area | St.R.Ar.D
Drim Cindershot •B•	R	3	32	Ignite Arrows | Penetrating Attack | Favorable Winds | Troll Unguent | B.G.D.Ar
Drub Gorefang •B•	W	3	32	Phy +20 | Penetr. Blow | Cyclone Axe | Shield Stance | Healing Signet | Ax.Sh.G.Ar
Felinam the Whip •B•	R	6	40	Ignite Arrows | Penetrating Attack | Favorable Winds | Troll Unguent | B.G.Ar
Fling Bloodpelt •B•	R	3	32	Ignite Arrows | Penetrating Attack | Favorable Winds | Troll Unguent | B.G.Ar
Fume Kindleflail	E	3	12	Flare | Lava Font | Conjure Flame | Aura of Restoration | St.R.Ar.D
Ghast Ashpyre •B•	Ms	6	20	Mantra of Flame | Energy Burn | Illusion of Haste | Ether Feast | St.R.Ar.D
Gorgaan Hatemonger •B•	W	3	32	Phy +20 | Hundred Blades | Frenzy | Shield Stance | Healing Signet | Sw.Sh.G.Ar
Jaw Smokeskin •B•	E	6	20	Flare | Lava Font | Conjure Flame | Aura of Restoration | St.R.Ar.D
Klawd FeatherStorm •B•	R	4	34	Ignite Arrows | Penetrating Attack | Favorable Winds | Troll Unguent | G.Ar
Lumps Ruinator •B•	W	5	37	Phy +20 | Hundred Blades | Frenzy | Shield Stance | Healing Signet | Sw.Sh.G.Ar
Maim Deathrain •B•	R	5	37	Ignite Arrows | Penetrating Attack | Favorable Winds | Troll Unguent | B.G.D.Ar
Marr Burnhorn •B•	Ms	3	12	Mantra of Flame | Energy Burn | Illusion of Haste | Ether Feast | St.R.Ar.D
Maul Riptear •B•	N	3	12	Faintheartedness | Life Siphon | Mark of Pain | St.R.Ar.D
Mirash Dreambreaker •B•	Ms	3	12	Mantra of Flame | Energy Burn | Illusion of Haste | Ether Feast | St.R.Ar.D
Phang the Deceiver •B•	Ms	5	17	Mantra of Flame | Energy Burn | Illusion of Haste | Ether Feast | St.R.Ar.D
Puugh the Slasher •B•	W	5	37	Phy +20 | Penetr. Blow | Cyclone Axe | Shield Stance | Healing Signet | Ax.Sh.G.Ar
Red Eye the Unholy •B•	N	6	20	Faintheartedness | Life Siphon | Mark of Pain | St.R.Ar.D
Roarst One Eye •B•	N	4	14	Faintheartedness | Life Siphon | Mark of Pain | St.R.Ar.D
Rrrack Whitefire	Mk	4	14	Infuse Health | Bane Signet | Banish | Heal Area | St.R.Ar.D
Scaar Sternclaw •B•	Mk	5	17	Infuse Health | Bane Signet | Banish | Heal Area | St.R.Ar.D
Scint The Malign •B•	Ms	5	17	Mantra of Flame | Energy Burn | Illusion of Haste | Ether Feast | St.R.Ar.D
Slaug Firehide •B•	E	5	17	Flare | Lava Font | Conjure Flame | Aura of Restoration | St.R.Ar.D
Slur Scarchest •B•	R	3	32	Ignite Arrows | Penetrating Attack | Favorable Winds | Troll Unguent | B.G.Ar
Smoke Kindlefist •B•	E	5	17	Fireball | Lava Font | Conjure Flame | Aura of Restoration | St.R.Ar.D
Smuuz the Unfeeling •B•	N	5	17	Faintheartedness | Life Siphon | Mark of Pain | St.R.Ar.D
Spar the Ravager •B•	W	4	34	Phy +20 | Hundred Blades | Frenzy | Shield Stance | Healing Signet | Sw.Sh.G.Ar
Suurg the Hateful •B•	E	3	12	Flare | Lava Font | Conjure Flame | Aura of Restoration | St.R.Ar.D
Swag the Lasher •B•	Mk	3	12	Infuse Health | Bane Signet | Banish | Heal Area | St.R.Ar.D
Taag Relicbinder •B•	Mk	3	12	Infuse Health | Bane Signet | Banish | Heal Area | St.R.Ar.D
Torch Spitfur •B•	E	4	14	Flare | Lava Font | Conjure Flame | Aura of Restoration | St.R.Ar.D
Vatlaaw Doomtooth •B•	R	2	19	Elem +30 | Ignite Arrows | Favorable Winds | Barrage | D
Charr Flame Artifact	E	8	150	Dmg 2-10 (M-Prc)

Devourer

Foe	Prof	Lvl	AL	Description
Blighted Devourer	N	20	66	Dmg 7-20 (M-Prc) | Malaise | Consume Corpse | Unholy Feast | G.D
Carrion Devourer	W	1/4/8	10/25/40	Dmg 1/3-4/4-5 (M-Prc) | Cold -20 (4,8) | Flurry | Endure Pain (4,8) | G.D
Crimson Devourer	R	1	10	Dmg 1 (R-Prc) | Cold -20 | Quick Shot | Lightning Reflexes | G.D
Diseased Devourer	R	0	10	Dmg 1 (M-Prc) | G.D
Fester Fang •B•	N	5	80	Dmg 9-23 (M-Prc) | Fire -20 | Putrid Explosion | Weaken Armor | Parasitic Bond | Life Siphon | G.D
Fevered Devourer	N	17	54	Dmg 6-18 (M-Prc) | Enfeebling Blood | Deathly Chill | G.D
Fleck Grokspit •B•	N	2	21	Dmg 6-10 (M-Prc) | Fire -20 | Putrid Explosion | Weaken Armor | Parasitic Bond | Life Siphon | G.D
Gnash Underfoot •B•	W	5	80	Dmg 9-23 (M-Prc) | Fire -20 | G.D
Hurl Foulspine •B•	R	5	80	Dmg 9-23 (M-Prc) | Fire -20 | G.D
Igg Fecpelter •B•	R	2	35	Dmg 6-12 (R-Prc) | Fire -20 | Quickening Zephyr | Quick Shot | Lightning Reflexes | Troll Ung. | G.D
Joe	W	8	46	Dmg 6-9 (M-Prc) | G.D
Joe the Devourer	W	5	37	Dmg 2-5 (M-Prc) | G.D
Lash Devourer	R	1	10	Dmg 1 (R-Prc) | Health 80 | G.D
Mossk Rottail •B•	N	16	49	Dmg 6-17 (M-Prc) | Enfeebling Blood | Deathly Chill | Virulence | Life Siphon | G.D
Plague Devourer	N	3/7/8	1/18/18	Dmg 3-5/7-16/7-16 (M-Prc) | Cold -20 | Putrid Explosion | Weaken Armor | Parasitic Bond (7,8) | G.D
Rockshot Devourer	R	20	80	Dmg 7-20 (M-Prc) | G.D
Rot Chuchau •B•	R	2	41	Dmg 10-13 (R-Prc) | Fire -20 | Called Shot | Quickening Zephyr | Lightning Reflexes | Troll Unguent | G.D
Scrag Nettleclaw •B•	W	16	69	Dmg 13-33 (M-Blt) | Phy +20 | Flurry | Distracting Blow | Rush | "I Will Survive!" | D
Skuzz Sudgereaper •B•	N	5	80	Dmg 12-22 (M-Prc) | Fire -20 | Putrid Explosion | Weaken Armor | Parasitic Bond | Life Siphon | G.D
Snapping Devourer	R	2	10	Dmg 1 (R-Prc) | Cold -20 | G.D
Stank Reekfoul •B•	W	7	70	Dmg 13-18 (M-Prc) | Fire -20 | G.D
Stig Plopgush •B•	N	2	21	Dmg 6-10 (M-Prc) | Fire -20 | Putrid Explosion | Weaken Armor | Parasitic Bond | Life Siphon | G.D
Thorn Devourer	R	17	71	Dmg 13-33 (R-Prc) | G.D
Thorn Devourer Drone	R	14	63	Dmg 13-33 (R-Prc) | G.D
Whep Dungflinger •B•	R	5	80	Dmg 12-22 (M-Prc) | Fire -20 | G.D
Whiptail Devourer	R	2/4/7	10/20/33	Dmg 1/5-7/9-15 (R-Prc) | Cold -20 | Quick Shot | Lightn. Reflexes (4,7) | G.D

Dolyak

Foe	Prof	Lvl	AL	Description
Bolis Hillshaker •B•	Mk	24	–	Mark of Protection | Mend Ailment | Life Attunement | Orison of Healing
Dolyak Master	Mk	24	–	Mark of Protection | Strength of Honor | Shielding Hands | Heal Other
Dolyak Rider	Mk	11	–	Remove Hex | Strength of Honor | Shielding Hands | Heal Other
Hussar Ironfeast •B•	Mk	8	26	Remove Hex | Strength of Honor | Shielding Hands | Heal Other | R.F.G.D.Ar
Priest of Dagnar •B•	E	9	29	–
Shalis Ironmantle •B•	Mk	9	–	Remove Hex | Strength of Honor | Shielding Hands | Heal Other
Stone Summit Arcanist	Ms	24	–	Crippling Anguish | Shatter Enchantment | Empathy | Illusion of Haste

See page 187 for table guidelines.

Fort Koga and D'Alessio Arena

These are the most basic type of PvP arenas. Two teams fight until one is eliminated and the surviving team advances to battle again. You do not get to choose your teammates, so luck plays a major role in whether you survive or not. On the other hand, it's easy to jump into the fray, and this is a good way to test your skills. Players here tend to be Level 20 (especially in D'Alessio), although some players that are Level 15 or above may also visit Koga.

Tomb of the Primeval Kings

This is an area for more advanced players with good team strategy, good communication, and good coordination. Each team consists of eight players. Initially, your team enters a waiting area where you battle various Necromancers and undead horrors until another team is ready. During this phase, you can kill Rift Wardens to gain morale boosts, which will carry over to the following competitions. Once another team is ready, you are moved to a random battlefield. Some battlefields are simple elimination, while others require that you kill a specific NPC. Some allow only two teams, while others have a king-of-the-hill format where multiple teams vie for domination. Most players who enter the Tombs are Level 20, and many teams are organized by specific guilds. If you are patient, Level 20, and have skills that are in demand (the world can never have enough Monks) you can find a team here even if you aren't there with a guild.

Guild vs. Guild Battle

This is only for players who are members of a guild.

Build your team from inside your guild hall. Victories and losses are recorded, and affect the placement of your guild in the ladder—so don't start one of these battles until your team is fully prepared!

In Guild vs. Guild battles, fighting can occur in the wilderness area separating the guild halls and inside the respective guild halls. Each guild hall is guarded by a variety of NPC archers and footmen, and each guild hall contains an NPC known as the Guild Lord. The first team to eliminate the enemy Guild Lord wins.

Each guild hall features locked gates. To gain access, you have to kill the enemy guards while keeping another NPC—your Guild Thief—alive long enough to pick the locks.

A resurrection shrine is located in each guild hall, so if you die and nobody is able to revive you, you automatically rejoin the battle after one or two minutes.

The wilderness area between the guild halls has features that can grant you various advantages. For example, you can plant your team's flag in the center of the map to gain a morale boost. Another advantage is the catapults that can devastate characters who are standing inside their guild hall—which is especially effective when fighting "base campers."

FOE	PROF	LVL	AL	DESCRIPTION
Drake/Dragon				
Dosakaru Fevertouch •B•	N	24	–	Tainted Flesh	Malign Intervention	Defile Flesh	Parasitic Bond	Life Siphon
Drake	E	20	–	Elemental Attunement	Flare	Aftershock	Earth Attunement
Geckokaru Earthwind •B•	E	24	–	Elemental Attun.	Mark of Rodgort	Flame Burst	Lava Font	Aura of Restoration
Glint •B•	Ms	25	80	Dmg 110-130 (M-Sla)	D
Grand Drake	E	20	80	Dmg 7-20 (M-Ltng)	Lightning Orb	Obsidian Flesh	G.D
Lightning Drake	E	18	64	Dmg 7-19 (M-Ltng)	Lightning Orb	G.D
Obsidian Furnace Drake	E	20	–	Mark of Rodgort	Flare	Ward Against Foes	Obsidian Flesh	Aura of Restoration
River Drake	E	5	35	Dmg 6-9 (M-Cold)	Cold +20, Ltng -40	Blurred Vision	G.D
Sand Drake	E	21	83	Dmg 7-20 (M-Ltng)	Phy +20	Ward ag. Mel.	Earthqk.	Aftersh.	Earth Attune.	G.D
Scale Fleshrend •B•	E	18	54	Dmg 15-42 (M-Sla)	Frozen Burst	Maelstrom	Blurred Vision	Aura of Restoration	Glyph of Concentration	G.D
Skintekaru Manshredder •B•	W	24	–	Bull's Charge	Distracting Blow	Wild Blow
Summit Drake	E	18	–	Frozen Burst	Maelstrom	Blurred Vision	Aura of Restor.	Glyph of Concentrat.
Whiskar Featherstorm •B•	E	10	32	Dmg 10-16 (M-Sla)	Ice Prison	Enervating Charge	Whirlwind	Aura of Restoration	Glyph of Concentration	G.D
Dryder				
Spindle Agonyvein •B•	Mk	24	–	Restore Condition	Light of Dwayna	Smite Hex	Judge's Insight	Rev. of Fortune
Dark Flame Dryder	N	24	–	Soul Leech	Animate Bone Minions	Rend Enchantments
Doubters Dryder	Ms	24	–	Shame	Guilt	Drain Enchantment	Shatter Enchantment	Wastrel's Worry
Frostfire Dryder	N	10	31	Dmg 9-13 (R-Dark)	Defile Flesh	Suffering	Faintheartedness	Shadow Strike	D
Frostfire Dryder (E) •B•	E	8	26	Dmg 6-10 (R-Dark)	G.D
Frostfire Dryder (Ms) •B•	Ms	8	26	Dmg 6-10 (R-Dark)	G.D
Frostfire Dryder (N) •B•	N	8	26	Dmg 6-10 (R-Dark)	Defile Flesh	Suffering	Vampiric Touch	G.D
Goss Darkweb •B•	N	24	–	Soul Leech	Strip Enchantment	Shadow Strike	Life Siphon
Keeper of Souls	Ms	24	71	Dmg 14-28 (R-Dark)	Lingering Curse	G.D
Plexus Shadowhook •B•	Ms	24	–	Fevered Dreams	Phantom Pain	Mantra of Persistence	Conjure Phantasm
Terrorweb Dryder	E	24	71	Dmg 14-28 (R-Dark)	Meteor Shower	Mark of Rodgort	Fireball	Immolate	Lava Font	Aura of Restoration	G.D
Terrorweb Queen •B•	E	24	71	Dmg 30-56 (R-Dark)	Meteor Shower	Mark of Rodgort	Fireball	Immolate	Lava Font	Aura of Restoration	G.D
Dwarf (Summit)				
Cronis Bonebreaker •B•	Ms	9	–	Channeling	Shatter Enchantment	Empathy	Ether Feast	Illusion of Haste
Dagnar Stonepate (E) •B•	E	24	–	Ice Spikes	Water Attunement	Frozen Burst	Aura of Restoration
Dagnar Stonepate (W) •B•	W	24	–	Disrupting Chop	Penetrating Blow	"For Great Justice!"	Healing Signet
Durnar Skullcracker •B•	N	9	–	Vile Touch	Strip Enchantment	Vampiric Touch	Soul Feast	Plague Touch
Fendar Stonestance •B•	W	9	–	Phy +20	Disrupting Chop	Penetrat. Blow	"For Great Justice!"	Healing Signet
Fuury Stonewrath •B•	Ms	24	–	Crippling Anguish	Conjure Phantasm	Shatter Enchantment	Ether Feast
Garris Nightwatch •B•	R	9	–	Marksman's Wager	Pin Down	Fertile Season	Troll Unguent
Gornar Bellybreaker •B•	W	24	–	Phy +20	Cleave	Disrupting Chop	"For Great Justice!"	Healing Signet
Marika Granitehand •B•	W	24	–	Phy +20	Dwarven Battle Stance	Counter Blow	Rush	Healing Signet
Riine Windrot •B•	N	8	26	Offer. of Blood	Strip Enchant.	Vamp. Touch	Soul Feast	Plague Touch	R.F.G.D.Ar
Saris Headstaver •B•	Ms	8	26	Illusion of Haste	Shatter Enchantment	Empathy	Ether Feast	R.F.G.D.Ar
Stone Summit Carver	W	24	–	Phy +20	Cleave	Penetrating Blow	"For Great Justice!"
Stone Summit Crusher	W	10	–	Phy +20	Protector's Strike	Griffon's Sweep	"For Great Justice!"
Stone Summit Gnasher	N	24	–	Offering of Blood	Strip Enchantment	Vamp. Touch	Soul Feast	Plague Touch
Stone Summit Howler	N	10	–	Vile Touch	Strip Enchantment	Vampiric Touch	Soul Feast	Plague Touch
Stone Summit Ranger	R	24	–	Melandru's Arrows	Pin Down	Called Shot
Stone Summit Rebel	Ms	8	–	–
Stone Summit Sage	Ms	10	–	Channeling	Shatter Enchantment	Empathy	Illusion of Haste
Stone Summit Scout	R	9	–	Marksman's Wager	Pin Down	Called Shot
Summit Axe Wielder	W	9	–	Phy +20	Disrupting Chop	Penetrating Blow	"For Great Justice!"
Thul The Bull •B•	R	24	–	Ferocious Strike	Tiger's Fury	Melandru's Assault	Troll Ung.	Charm Animal
Toris Stonehammer •B•	W	8	46	Phy +20	Mighty Blow	Bull's Strike	Dolyak Signet	Healing Signet	H.G.Ar
Ulhar Stonehound •B•	R	24	–	Melandru's Arrows	Tiger's Fury	Precision Shot	Troll Unguent
Ulhar Stonehound •B•	R	8	46	Dmg 10-23 (R-Prc)	Marksman's Wager	Pin Down	Fertile Seas.	Troll Ung.	B.G.Ar
Ulrik the Undefeated •B•	E	9	–	Health 410	Kinetic Armor	Armor of Earth	Stone Daggers	Aura of Restoration	Ward Against Melee
Earth Elemental				
Boulder Elemental	W	7	58	Dmg 7-16 (M-Blt)	Blt -40	G.D
Buhr Skullstone •B•	N	3	12	Dmg 10-20 (M-Blt)	Blt -40, Cold -20	G.D
Clarion Shinypate •B•	E	20	70	Dmg 13-19 (R-Blt)	Eruption	Shock	Aftershock	Glyph of Renewal	R.St.G.D.Ar.
Clob Stonearch •B•	Mk	7	36	Dmg 12-22 (M-Blt)	Blt -40, Cold -20	G.D
Cobble Poundstone •B•	W	2	60	Dmg 5-11 (M-Blt)	Blt -40, Cold -20	Endure Pain	Shield Stance	Heal. Signet	G.D
Cobble Poundstone •B•	W	3	32	Dmg 7-17 (M-Blt)	Phy +20, Blt -40, Cold -20	Wild Blow	Healing Signet	G.D
Crush Kill •B•	W	5	76	Dmg 12-22 (M-Blt)	Blt -40, Cold -20	Distracting Blow	G.D
Crystal Guardian	E	22	18	Dmg 10-19 (R-Blt)	Ltng +40	Ward Against Melee	Eruption	Earthquake	G.D
Crystal Spider	E	20	60	Dmg 12-46 (R-Fire)	Ward Against Melee	Eruption	D
Drub Slingstone •B•	R	7	56	Dmg 14-18 (R-Blt)	Blt -40, Cold -20	G.D
Flint Touchstone (L2) •B•	E	2	24	Dmg 5-11 (M-Blt)	Blt -40, Cold -20	Eruption	Whirlwind	Ward Against Melee	Aura of Restoration	G.D
Flint Touchstone (L3) •B•	E	3	12	Dmg 7-17 (M-Blt)	Blt -40, Cold -20	Eruption	Stoning	Armor of Earth	Aura of Restoration	G.D
Grit Slingstone •B•	R	3	32	Dmg 10-20 (R-Blt)	Blt -40, Cold -20	G.D
Hulking Stone Elemental	E	3	10	Dmg 2-5 (M-Blt)	Ward Against Melee	D
Hulking Stone Elemental	W	3	43	Dmg 4-7 (M-Blt)	Blt -40	Ward Against Melee	G.D
Hulking Stone Elemental	E	7	18	Dmg 10-19 (R-Blt)	Ltng +40	Ward Against Melee	Eruption	G.D
Igmon Quivcaver •B•	Ms	7	46	Dmg 12-22 (M-Blt)	Blt -40, Cold -20	Mantra of Earth	G.D

See page 187 for table guidelines.

Foe	Prof	Lvl	AL	Description
Lucid Jewelstone •B•	R	20	70	Dmg 13-19 (R-Blt) | Eruption | Shock | Aftershock | Glyph of Renewal
Mallet Runecolumn •B•	E	7	36	Dmg 12-22 (M-Blt) | Blt -40, Cold -20 | Grasping Earth | Aura of Restoration | G.D
Pulv Rubblegrinder •B•	W	7	76	Dmg 12-22 (M-Blt) | Blt -40, Cold -20 | G.D
Rock Fist •B•	W	5	76	Dmg 12-22 (M-Blt) | Blt -40, Cold -20 | Endure Pain | G.D
Sand Elemental	E	20	18	Dmg 10-19 (R-Blt) | Eruption | G.D
Slate Addlestone •B•	Ms	3	12	Dmg 7-17 (M-Blt) | Blt -40, Cold -20 | Mind Wrack | G.D
Slog Bloodsplatter •B•	N	7	36	Dmg 12-22 (M-Blt) | Blt -40, Cold -20 | Dark Aura | G.D
Stone Elemental	E	1	4	Dmg 2-5 (M-Blt) | Health 80 | D
Stone Elemental	E	5	18	Dmg 10-19 (R-Blt) | Ltng +40 | Ward Against Melee | Eruption | G.D
Stone Fury	E	8	18	Dmg 10-19 (R-Blt) | Ltng +40 | Ward Against Melee | Eruption | G.D
Tufa Holystone •B•	Mk	3	12	Dmg 10-20 (R-Blt) | Blt -40, Cold -20 | Orison of Healing | G.D

Ettin

Foe	Prof	Lvl	AL	Description
Droog Stoneclub •B•	W	13	60	Dmg 8-22 (M-Blt) | Phy +20 | Endure Pain | Balanced Stance | Irresistible Blow | Healing Signet | G.D.Ar
Ferk Mallet •B•	W	24	–	Backbreaker | "To the Limit!" | Berserker Stance | Staggering Blow | Healing Signet
Gypsie Ettin	W	15	66	Dmg 12-21 (M-Blt) | Phy +20 | End. Pain | Bal. Stance | Irr. Blow | Heal. Signet | G.D.Ar
Igneous Ettin	W	20	–	Backbreaker | "To the Limit!" | Berserker Stance | Staggering Blow
Rull Browbeater •B•	Mk	24	–	Healing Hands | Restore Life | Purge Signet | Signet of Devotion
Smuush Fatfist •B•	W	11	54	Dmg 8-19 (M-Blt) | Phy +20 | Endure Pain | Balanc. Stance | Irresist. Blow | G.D.Ar
Snow Ettin	W	11	54	Dmg 9-16 (M-Blunt) | Phy +20 | Power Attack | Balanc. Stance | Stagger. Blow | G D
Snow Ettin (Mk) •B•	Mk	8	46	Dmg 11-19 (M-Blt) | Phy +20 | G.D
Snow Ettin (W) •B•	W	8	46	Dmg 11-19 (M-Blt) | Phy +20 | Power Atk | Bal. Stance | Stag. Blow | Heal. Signet | G.D
Vulg Painbrain •B•	R	24	–	Spike Trap | Primal Echoes | Troll Unguent

Forgotten

Foe	Prof	Lvl	AL	Description
Ayassah Hess •B•	Ms	20	60	Energy Burn | Chaos Storm | Mantra of Recovery | Ether Feast | R.St.F.Ar.D
Byssha Hisst •B•	N	20	60	Order of the Vampire | Consume Corpse | Deathly Chill | Life Siphon | R.St.F.Ar.D
Cyss Gresshla •B•	E	20	60	Stoning | Earthquake | Ether Renewal | Aura of Restor. | Kinetic Armor | R.St.F.Ar.D
Dassk Arossyss •B•	Mk	20	60	Dmg 14-19 (R-Holy) | Word of Heal. | Vigor. Spirit | Aegis | Orison of Heal. | R.St.F.Ar.D
Forgotten Arcanist	E	20	60	Stoning | Earthquake | Ether Renewal | Kinetic Armor | R.St.G.D.Ar
Forgotten Cursebearer	N	20	60	Order of the Vampire | Consume Corpse | Deathly Chill | R.St.G.D.Ar
Forgotten Guide	E	20	80	Dmg 15-42 (M-Ltng) | Aftershock | Ward Against Melee | Ward Against Foes | Meteor Shower | Aura of Restoration
Forgotten Illusionist	Ms	20	60	Energy Burn | Chaos Storm | (Mantra of Recovery) | (Energy Burn) | Shatter Hex | R.St.G.D.Ar
Forgotten Sage	Mk	20	60	Dmg 14-19 (R-Holy) | Word of Healing | Vigorous Spirit | Aegis | (Orison of Healing) | R.St.G.D.Ar
Goss Aleessh •B•	Ms	20	60	Energy Burn | Chaos Storm | Mantra of Recovery | Ether Feast | R.St.F.Ar.D
Hessper Sasso •B•	N	20	60	Order of the Vampire | Consume Corpse | Deathly Chill | Life Siphon | R.St.F.Ar.D
Issah Sshay •B•	E	20	60	Stoning | Earthquake | Ether Renewal | Aura of Restor. | Kinetic Armor | R.St.F.Ar.D
Josso Essher •B•	Mk	20	60	Word of Healing | Vigorous Spirit | Aegis | Orison of Healing | R.St.F.Ar.D
Massou Blyss •B•	Ms	22	66	Dmg 30-42 (M-Blt) | Mantra of Recall | Diversion | Shatter Hex | Ether Feast | D
Nassh Cusstuss •B•	N	22	66	Dmg 30-42 (M-Blt) | Grenth's Balance | Blood Ren. | Paras. Bond | Unholy Feast | D
Oss Wissher •B•	E	22	66	Dmg 30-42 (M-Blt) | Lightning Surge | Crystal Wave | Shock | Aftershock | Aura of Restoration | D
Pessh Missk •B•	Mk	22	66	Dmg 30-42 (R-Fire) | Shield of Regeneration | Guardian | Signet of Devotion | D
Resso Biiss •B•	W	22	86	Dmg 30-42 (M-Blt) | Phy +20 | Gladiator's Defense | Wild Blow | Power Attack | Healing Signet | D
Ssyl Feshah •B•	R	22	86	Dmg 30-42 (R-Fire) | Health 1020 | Melandru's Resilience | Concussion Shot | Pin Down | Hunter's Shot | D
Tiss Danssir •B•	Ms	20	60	Energy Burn | Chaos Storm | Mantra of Recovery | Ether Feast | R.St.F.Ar.D
Uussh Visshta •B•	N	20	60	Order of the Vampire | Consume Corpse | Deathly Chill | Life Siphon | R.St.F.Ar.D
Vassa Ssiss •B•	E	20	60	Stoning | Earthquake | Ether Renewal | Aura of Restor. | Kinetic Armor | R.St.F.Ar.D
Wissper Inssani •B•	Mk	20	60	Word of Healing | Vigorous Spirit | Aegis | Orison of Healing | R.St.F.Ar.D

Forgotten Enchanted

Foe	Prof	Lvl	AL	Description
Custodian Dellus •B•	W	20	80	Warrior's Endurance | Thrill of Victory | Hamstring | Endure Pain
Custodian Fidius •B•	W	20	80	Phy +20 | Warrior's Endurance | Thrill of Victory | Hamstring | Endure Pain
Custodian Hulgar •B•	W	20	80	Phy +20 | Warrior's Endurance | Thrill of Victory | Hamstring | Endure Pain
Custodian Jenus •B•	R	20	–	Marksman's Wager | Concussion Shot | Penetrating Attack | Throw Dirt | Troll Ung.
Custodian Kora •B•	R	20	80	Phy +20 | Marksman's Wager | Concus. Shot | Penet. Attack | Throw Dirt | Troll Ung.
Custodian Phebus •B•	R	20	80	Elem +30 | Marksman's Wager | Concus. Shot | Penet. Attack | Throw Dirt | Troll Ung.
Drifting Cloak	R	22	92	Pin Down | Debilitating Shot | Read the Wind | Throw Dirt | B.G.D.Ar
Eldriss Blesst •B•	W	20	80	Phy +20 | Warrior's Endur. | Thrill of Victory | Hamstring | Endure Pain | Ax.Sh.Ar.D
Enchanted Armor	W	22	112	Staggering Blow | Heavy Blow | Counter Blow | Defensive Stance | H.G.D.Ar
Enchanted Bow	R	20	92	Marksman's Wager | Concussion Shot | Penetrating Attack | Throw Dirt | B.G.D.Ar
Enchanted Hammer	W	20	112	Staggering Blow | Heavy Blow | Counter Blow | Defensive Stance | H.G.D.Ar
Enchanted Sword	W	20	112	Warrior's Endurance | Thrill of Victory | Hamstring | Endure Pain | Sw.G.D.Ar
Fahessh Sseel •B•	R	20	80	Marksman's Wager | Concuss. Shot | Penetrat. Attack | Throw Dirt | Troll Ung. | B.Ar.D
Forgotten Avenger	R	20	80	Marksman's Wager | Concussion Shot | Penetrating Attack | Throw Dirt | B.G.D.Ar
Forgotten Champion	W	20	80	Phy +20 | Warrior's Endur. | Thrill of Victory | Hamstring | Endure Pain | Sw.Sh.G.D.Ar
Harn Coldstone •B•	E	20	–	Obsidian Flesh | Armor of Frost | Conjure Frost | Crystal Wave | Aura of Restoration
Kesskah Shissh •B•	W	20	80	Phy +20 | Warrior's Endur. | Thrill of Victory | Hamstring | Endure Pain | Sw.Sh.Ar.D
Lysshal Suss •B•	R	20	80	Marksman's Wager | Concuss. Shot | Penetrat. Attack | Throw Dirt | Troll Ung. | B.Ar.D
Obsidian Hound	E	20	–	Mark of Rodgort | Flare | Ward Against Foes | Obsidian Flesh | Aura of Restoration
Tower Golem	E	3	33	Dmg 8-12 (M-Blt) | Ltng -80 | D
Yossha Ess •B•	W	20	80	Phy +20 | Warrior's Endur. | Thrill of Victory | Hamstring | Endure Pain | Ax.Sh.Ar.D
Zass Dousso •B•	R	20	80	Marksman's Wager | Concuss. Shot | Penetrat. Attack | Throw Dirt | Troll Ung. | B.Ar.D

See page 187 for table guidelines.

Ascalon Arena

This is an arena for players Level 10 and under. It is near Ascalon City. Teams are selected randomly.

Shiverpeak Arena

Located near Borlis Pass, this is another arena for random teams. The max level here is Level 15.

Deldrimor Arena

You can find this near Droknar's Forge. It is a more sophisticated arena with pre-selected teams and a resurrection shrine for each team. You need to eliminate the enemy team as well as the enemy priest to ensure they aren't revived. The center of the map features an icy lake that will slow you down if you stop moving on it. The max level here is Level 20.

The Crag

This is a 4v4 arena with predetermined teams. It is located near the Ring of Fire. The max level here is Level 20.

Amnoon Arena

This is another 4v4 arena with predetermined teams. It is located near the Amnoon Oasis. The max level here is Level 20.

- GUILD ARENA -
Arcane

Team Strategy

In *Guild Wars,* teams win when they master the three Cs: composition, coordination, and communication.

Composition

Victories will be rare unless your team complements and supports each other. Characters generally fall into one of three categories: healers (Monks) who keep your team alive, killers who attack the opponent's weak points, and those who impede mobility and interfere with the opponent's plans. Each team needs a good mix of these to succeed.

Basic Team Composition

The basic eight-person team consists of two or three healers, one or two meddlers, and the remainder killers. Here is an outline for a strong team that is capable of succeeding in a number of situations:

- **Frontline healer:** Monk/Elementalist with Healing Prayers, Divine Favor, and Earth Magic. This character heals the team and uses spells like Obsidian Flesh and Ward Against Melee to survive difficult situations.

- **Middle-field healer:** Monk/Mesmer with Healing Prayers, Divine Favor, and Inspiration Magic. He uses healing skills to keep the team alive, generally staying off the frontline. This character runs in and out of the battle to drain Energy and enchantments from the enemy with Inspiration skills.

- **Rear healer:** Monk/Warrior with high Healing Prayers, Protection Prayers, and Divine Favor. This

Foe	Prof	Lvl	AL	Description
Gargoyle				
Claw Fleshfixer •B•	E	2	21	Dmg 6-9 (R-Blt) | Ltng +40 | Whirlwind | Ltng Strike | Ltng Orb | Aura of Restor. | G.D
Flash Gargoyle	E	2/3/7	3/3/18	Lightning Strike | Lightning Orb (7)
Fluum Banzo •B•	Mk	14	43	Dmg 12-17 (R-Holy) | Blessed Signet | Guardian | Protective Bond | Orison of Healing | Restore Life | G.Ar
Frak Undertow •B•	E	14	43	Dmg 12-17 (R-Holy) | Deep Fr. | Gly. of Less. En. | Grasp. Earth | Aura of Restor. | G.Ar
Gargoyle	Ms	1	4	Dmg 2-3 (R-Cold) | Health 80 | G.D
Gargoyle	E	2	3	Dmg 3-5 (R-Fire) | Ltng +40 | G.D
Gren Wavelslosh •B•	Ms	14	43	Dmg 12-17 (R-Holy) | Mind Wrack | Spirit Shackl. | Mantra of Ltng | Ether Feast | G.Ar
Ignis Phanaura (L2) •B•	Ms	2	27	Dmg 7-11 (R-Blt) | Ltng +40 | Empathy | Ch. Storm | Ether Lord | Ether Feast | G.D
Ignis Phanaura (L5) •B•	Ms	5	36	Dmg 8-13 (R-Blt) | Ltng +40 | Hex Breaker | G.D
Leaps Thunderclap •B•	Mk	11	34	Dmg 12-17 (R-Dark) | Blessed Signet | Guardian | Protective Bond | Orison of Healing | Restore Life | G.D
Mergoyle	Ms	14	29	Dmg 9-14 (R-Cold) | Cold +40 | Mind Wrack | Spirit Shack. | Mantra of Ltng | G.D
Mergoyle Wavebreaker	E	12	25	Dmg 7-12 (R-Cold) | Cold +40 | Deep Freeze | Glyph of Lesser Energy | Grasping Earth | Aura of Restoration | G.D
Muga Riptide •B•	Mk	13	40	Dmg 12-17 (R-Holy) | Life Attunement | Healing Hands | Protective Spirit | Blessed Signet | Mend Condition | G.D
Plook Wavebreaker •B•	Ms	13	40	Dmg 12-17 (R-Chaos) | Mind Wrack | Spirit Shack. | Mantra of Ltng | Ether Feast | G.D
Resurrect Gargoyle	Mk	2	3	Dmg 3-5 (R-Fire) | Ltng +40 | Resurrect | G.D
Rif Telourau (L2) •B•	Mk	2	27	Dmg 7-11 (R-Blt) | Ltng +40 | Orison of Heal. | Symbol of Wrath | Mending | G.D
Rif Telourau (L5) •B•	Mk	5	36	Dmg 8-13 (R-Blt) | Ltng +40 | Draw Conditions | Blessed Signet | G.D
Shatter Gargoyle	Ms	3	8	Dmg 2-3 (R-Cold) | Cold +40 | Energy Tap | G.D
Shatter Gargoyle	Ms	4	3	Dmg 3-5 (R-Fire) | Ltng +40 | Energy Tap | Imagined Burden | G.D
Shatter Gargoyle	Ms	8	18	Dmg 4-8 (R-Ltng) | Ltng +40 | Energy Tap | Conjure Phant. | Imag. Burden | G.D
Slikk Sandhopper •B•	Ms	11	34	Dmg 12-17 (R-Dark) | Mind Wrack | Spirit Shack. | Mantra of Ltng | Ether Feast | G.D
Spasmo Thunderbolt •B•	E	5	36	Dmg 8-13 (R-Blt) | Ltng +40 | Whirlwind | G.D
Spazz Mindrender •B•	Ms	2	21	Dmg 6-9 (R-Blt) | Ltng +40 | Empathy | Ch. Storm | Ether Lord | Ether Feast | G.D
Ghost				
Angry Spirit	W	10	52	Dmg 6-10 (M-Sla) | Phy +40 | Hamstring | Final Thrust | G.D
Banished Dream Rider	Ms	24	71	Shatter Enchantment | Power Spike | Empathy | Energy Drain | Cry of Frustration | Power Drain | St.R.F.Ar.D
Dream Knight	Ms	24	71	Shatter Enchantment | Power Block | Diversion | Signet of Humility | Wastrel's Worry | Cry of Frustration | Drain Enchantment | St.R.F.Ar.D
Eternal Elementalist	E	24	–	Flare | Fire Storm | Fireball | Incendiary Bonds | Aura of Restor. | Resurrection Signet
Eternal Forge Lord	W	24	–	–
Eternal Mesmer	Ms	24	–	Channeling | Shatter Enchantment | Empathy | Illusion of Haste
Eternal Monk	Mk	24	–	Orison of Healing | Heal Other | Healing Breeze | Heal Area | Restore Life
Eternal Necromancer	N	24	–	Vile Touch | Strip Enchantment | Vampiric Touch | Soul Feast | Plague Touch
Eternal Ranger	R	24	–	Elem +30 | Kindle Arrows | Dual Shot | Troll Ung. | Resurrect. Signet
Eternal Warrior	W	24	–	Phy +20 | Healing Signet | Power Attack | Griffon's Sweep | Frenzy | Sprint | Resurrection Signet
Gaiza Deadeye •B•	Ms	17	–	Phy +40 | Empathy | Signet of Weariness | Mantra of Inscriptions | Ether Feast | Chaos Storm
Ghost of Bob	E	15	90	Dmg 6-16 (M-Prc) | Ward Against Melee | Lightning Orb
Haunting Spectre	Mk	0	150	D.Ar
Ice Beast •B•	W	20	80	Dmg 13-36 (M-Blt) | Blt +20, Cold +40, Fire -15 | Mist Form | D
Ignis Effigia •B•	M	24	–	Wither | Malaise | Strip Enchantment | Life Siphon
Malus Phasmatis •B•	M	24	–	Signet of Midnight | Ether Lord | Spirit Shackles | Mind Wrack
Mindblade Spectre	Ms	23	57	Dmg 68-100 (M-Blt) | Phy +40 | Conjure Phantasm | Migraine | Clumsiness | Energy Tap | Ignorance | Power Drain | G.D
Misery's Company	Ms	20	50	Dmg 13-36 (M-Sla) | Phy +40 | Conjure Phantasm | Migraine | Drain Enchantment | Ether Feast
Phantom	Ms	20	–	Phy +40 | Signet of Midnight | Soothing Images | Shatter Enchantment
Pravus Obsideo •B•	Ms	24	–	Amity | Holy Strike | Pacifism | Scourge Healing | Reversal of Fortune
Rift Spirit	Mk	24	120	Dmg 7-20 (M-Prc) | Fire, Cold, Ltng -120 | Double damage vs Monk
Smite Crawler	Mk	24	60	Dmg 24-45 (M-Prc) | Zealot's Fire | Reversal of Fortune | Mend Condition | Smite Hex | Shield of Judgment | Divine Intervention | G.D
Spirit Elementalist	E	24	60	Inferno | (Lightning Strike) | (Gale) | (Lava Font) | (Fire Storm)
Temporal Vortex	N	8	–	Vampiric Touch
Tortured Spirit	Mk	10	32	Dmg 3-5 (M-Blt) | Illusion of Weakness
Veteran Spirit	W	11	54	Dmg 6-11 (M-Sla) | Phy +40 | Healing Signet | G.D
Wailing Lord	Ms	24	71	Dmg 7-20 (M-Prc) | Phy +40 | G.D
Wings of Illusion	Ms	24	–	–
Wraith	Ms	17	–	Phy +40 | Epidemic | Signet of Weariness | Chaos Storm
Wraith	Ms	18	–	Phy +40 | Epidemic | Signet of Weariness | Mantra of Inscriptions
Zaim Grimeclaw •B•	Ms	17	–	Phy +40 | Epidemic | Signet of Weariness | Mantra of Inscriptions | Ether Feast
Ghoul				
Fallen Ghoul	W	20	80	Dmg 7-20 (M-Prc) | Phy +20 | Power Attack | Bull's Strike
Grasping Ghoul	W	11	–	Phy +20
Grasping Ghoul	W	11	–	Health 200
Haja Bloodwail •B•	W	11	–	Phy +20 | Sever Artery | Hamstring | Deflect Arrows | Healing Signet
Giant				
Hill Giant	W	20	80	Dmg 13-36 (M-Blt) | Blt +20, Fire -20 | Ar.G.D
Kor Stonewrath •B•	W	24	80	Dmg 21-39 (M-Blt) | Blt +20, Cold +40, Fire -15 | Earth Shaker | Berserker Stance | Crushing Blow | Healing Signet | H.G.D
Ore Darkwhip •B•	W	8	–	Phy +20 | Bull's Strike | Dolyak Signet | "For Great Justice!" | Healing Signet
Sand Giant	N	22	80	Dmg 15-42 (M-Blt) | Blt +20, Fire -20 | H.G.D
Summit Beastmaster	W	13	–	Phy +20 | Bull's Strike
Summit Giant Herder	W	24	–	Phy +20 | Bull's Strike | "Charge!"

See page 187 for table guidelines.

Foe	Prof	Lvl	AL	Description
Thorgrim Beastlasher	W	24	–	Phy +20	Galrath Slash	Skull Crack	"Shields Up!"	Healing Signet
Thul Boulderrain •B•	W	24	80	Dmg 21-39 (M-Blt)	Blt +20, Cold +40, Fire -15	Punishing Shot	Frozen Soil	Troll Unguent	H.G.D
Tundra Giant	W	24	80	Dmg 22-35 (M-Blt)	Blt +20, Cold +40, Fire -15	Berser. Stance	Crush. Blow	H.G.D

Golem

Foe	Prof	Lvl	AL	Description
Abomination	N	11	34	Dmg 10-17 (M-Blt)	Animate Bone Horror	Shadow Strike	Soul Feast	G.D
Balthazaar's Cursed •B•	W	24	–	"Charge!"	Endure Pain	Counter Blow	Healing Signet
Bucknar Runeguard •B•	E	9	–	Ice Spikes	Water Attunement	Frozen Burst	Aura of Restoration
Dead Collector	N	23	69	Dmg 10-17 (M-Blt)	Animate Bone Horror	Shadow Strike	Well of Power	Life Siphon	G.D
Dead Thresher	N	23	100	Dmg 13-36 (R-Blt)	Feast of Corruption	Suffering	Mark of Pain	Parasitic Bond	Faintheartedness	G.D
Dwayna's Cursed •B•	Mk	24	–	Martyr	Contemplation of Purity	Watchful Spirit	Rebirth	Reversal of Fortune
Flesh Golem	W	20	–	Lingering Curse
Grenth's Cursed •B•	N	24	–	Lingering Curse	Animate Bone Minions	Faintheartedness	Life Siphon
Ice Golem	E	10	–	Fire -40	Ice Spikes	Water Attunement	Frozen Burst
Lyssa's Cursed •B•	Ms	24	–	Power Block	Diversion	Signet of Humility	Wastrel's Worry
Melandru's Cursed •B•	R	24	–	Crippling Shot	Apply Poison	Barbed Trap	Troll Unguent
Siege Ice Golem	E	24	–	Fire -40	Water Trident	Water Attunement	Frozen Burst
The Judge •B•	E	24	–	Water Trident	Rust	Deep Freeze	Aura of Restoration
The Judge •B•	E	8	–	Ice Spikes	Water Attunement	Frozen Burst	Aura of Restoration

Grawl

Foe	Prof	Lvl	AL	Description
Alana Pekpek •B•	E	24	71	Ltng -20	Glimmering Mark	Lightning Javelin	Lightning Strike	R.F.D.Ar
Anani Mokmok •B•	R	2	29	Dmg 8-15 (R-Prc)	Dual Shot	Penetr. Attack	Favorable Winds	Troll Ung.	B.G.Ar
Burzag	N	3	12	Deathly Swarm	Shadow of Fear	Soul Feast	Life Siphon
Gougi Gakula •B•	Ms	2	9	Blt -40, Cold -20	Mantra of Flame	Energy Burn	Ill. of Haste	Ether Feast	G.Ar
Grawl	R	1	26	Health 80	"Victory is Mine!"	B.G.D.Ar
Grawl	W	4	34	Phy +20	"Victory is Mine!"	Mighty Blow	H.G.D.Ar
Grawl	W	22	86	Phy +20, Ltng -20	"Victory is Mine!"	Belly Smash	Hammer Bash	H.D.Ar
Grawl Longspear	R	3/4	32/34	B.G.D.Ar
Grawl Shaman	Mk	2	6	Infuse Health	G.D.Ar
Grawl Ulodyte	Mk	3	12	Plague Signet	Heal Other	St.G.D.Ar
Grawl Ulodyte	N	22	66	Ltng -20	Plague Signet	Chilblains	Signet of Agony	St.R.F.D.Ar
Hurzag	E	3	12	Fireball	Lava Font	Conjure Flame	Aura of Restoration	G.Ar
Ipillo Wupwup •B•	Mk	24	71	Ltng -20	Unyield. Aura	Healing Seed	Healing Touch	Mend Condition	R.F.D.Ar
Karobo Dimdim •B•	N	24	71	Ltng -20	Plague Signet	Chilblains	Signet of Agony	Life Siphon	R.F.D.Ar
Makani Ookook •B•	Mk	2	9	Orison of Healing	Symbol of Wrath	Vital Blessing	St.G.D
Mok Waagwaag •B•	E	2	9	Fireball	Lava Font	Conjure Flame	Aura of Restoration	G.Ar
Mono Ookook •B•	Mk	2	9	Shielding Hands	Live Vicariously	Smite	St.G.Ar
Murg •B•	R	3	32	Dmg 8-15 (R-Prc)	Dual Shot	Penetr. Attack	Favorable Winds	Troll Ung.	B.G.Ar
Onaona Kubkub •B•	W	2	29	Phy +20, Blt -40, Cold -20	Counter Blow	Mighty Blow	"Watch Yourself!"	Healing Signet	H.G.D
Palila Uggugg •B•	N	2	9	Deathly Swarm	Shadow of Fear	Soul Feast	Life Siphon	St.G.Ar
Sakalo Yawpyawl •B•	W	24	–	Phy +20, Ltng -20	"Victory is Mine!"	Belly Smash	Hammer Bash	Healing Signet	Sw.Sh.Ar.D
Salani Pippip •B•	R	24	81	Ltng -40, Elem +30	Poison Arrow	Hunter's Shot	Lightning Reflexes	B.Ar.D
Turzag	E	3	12	Fireball	Lava Font	Conjure Flame	Aura of Restoration	G.Ar

Griffon

Foe	Prof	Lvl	AL	Description
Blessed Griffon	Mk	24	81	Dmg 7-20 (M-Sla)	Ltng -20, Prc -20	Spell Breaker	Holy Strike	Smite Hex	G.D
Desert Griffon	Mk	21	63	Dmg 10-16 (M-Sla)	G.D
Featherclaw •B•	Ms	24	–	Mantra of Recall	Diversion	Shatter Hex	Ether Feast
Griffon •B•	N	10	32	Dmg 10-16 (M-Sla)	Weaken Armor	Mark of Pain	Shadow of Fear	Lingering Curse	Life Siphon	G.D
Old Red Claw •B•	E	24	–	Mind Shock	Windborne Speed	Shock	Aura of Restoration	G.D
Raptorhawk •B•	Mk	24	81	Dmg 19-29 (M-Sla)	Ltng -20, Prc -20	Spell Breaker	Holy Strike	Smite Hex	Divine Healing	G.D

Human

Foe	Prof	Lvl	AL	Description
Agnar the Foot	W	5	37	Dmg 4-6 (M-Blt)	Health 100	Healing Breeze	D
Alain	W	3	15	Dmg 6-10 (M-Blt)	D.Ar
Bandit	W	11	54	Phy +20	Healing Signet	Sw.Ax.Sh.G.D
Bandit Blood Sworn	W	3	15	Dmg 2-3 (M-Blt)	D.Ar
Bandit Firestarter	E	1	2	Dmg 1-3 (R-Fire)	Flare	D.St.R.F.Ar
Bandit Raider	W	2	11	Dmg 2-3 (M-Blt)	D.Ar
Bonetti •B•	W	2	29	Phy +20	Hundr. Blades	Bonetti's Def.	"Watch Yourself!"	Heal. Signt	Sw.Sh.G.D
Garr the Merciful •B•	Mk	16	49	Divine Intervention	Judge's Insight	Shielding Hands	Convert Hexes	Restore Life	St.R.F.Ar.D
(Guild) Archer	R	20	80	Dmg 11-29 (R-Prc)
(Guild) Footman	W	20	80	Dmg 6-17 (M-Sla)	Phy +20
Irwyn the Severe •B•	Ms	16	49	Guilt	Shame	Shatter Enchantment	Ether Feast	St.R.F.G.Ar.D
Marnta Doomspeaker •B•	Ms	24	–	Fire +80	Peace and Harmony	Balthazar's Aura	Zealot's Fire	Blessed Aura	Reversal of Fortune
Maxine Coldstone •B•	R	24	–	Quick Shot	Kindle Arrows	Favorable Winds	Quickening Zephyr	Troll Unguent
Monk Deserter	Mk	7	43	Phy +20	Vigor. Spirit	Heal. Breeze	Purge Condition	Mend Ailment	St.R.F.Ar.G
Oberan the Reviled	N	6	20	Dmg 4-7 (R-Dark)	Life Siphon	Animate Bone Horror	St.G.D
Oberan's Minion	N	4	20	Dmg 1-30 (M-Blt)
Ranger Deserter	R	7	43	Phy +20	Dual Shot	B.Ar.G
Renegade	W	3	32	Dmg 5-7 (M-Blt)	Phy +20	G.D.Ar

See page 187 for table guidelines.

character uses elite Word of Healing and other Healing and Protection skills to assist the team. Warrior's Sprint quickly takes him to problem spots and equally as quickly away from harm. He can also heal the other Monks.

- **Killer/anti-tank:** Any strong anti-Warrior character. It is usually best if this character is a Warrior, but there are a number of other specialized professions that will work as well.

- **Killer/anti-caster:** Any character who can effectively intercept the enemy's spells. Warriors with interruption skills are excellent, as are Rangers and Mesmers. In particular, Ranger/Mesmers can combine long-range Interruption skills with Domination Magic such as Backfire, and a Mesmer/Monk can use Domination combined with Smiting skills like Scourge Healing.

- **Killer/area-damage:** An Elementalist who is destroying packed formations of opponents with area damage. Certain Mesmers and Rangers can also be effective in this role.

- **Meddler/decoy:** Warrior/Monk using a sword and shield and plenty of defensive skills (Healing Hands, Stances, Riposte, and so forth). This character's role is to take a beating for the team. This is often the best character to perform battlefield resurrections.

- **Meddler/snarer:** A character who helps control mobility and slow down opponents' movements. Elementalists with Earth or Water are good in this role, as are Rangers with Pin Down and various Traps.

Now you should have the basics for creating a good, general-purpose team. However, the best teams have an overall strategy that takes advantage of stacked skills across the different characters. When you look at the skill combinations that can make an individual character more powerful, you'll realize that these synergies are even stronger when applied to team play.

The following is an example of a team that takes advantage of various cross-character synergies.

The "Smackdown" Team

This team makes heavy use of knockdowns and snares to dominate a battlefield.

- Monk/Warrior with Healing Prayers, Divine Favor, Smiting Prayers, and the elite Shield of Judgment. This character takes the frontline, healing the team as needed, and activating Shield of Judgment to cause unwise opponents to fall when attacking.

- Monk/Elementalist with Healing Prayers, Divine Favor, and Earth Magic. This is the primary healer, (with Word of Healing) but he also snares opponents with Earth's Ward Against Foes.

- Warrior/Elementalist with Hammer, Strength, and Earth Magic. This character uses Hammer attacks with knockdowns, and opportunistically uses Aftershock to deliver high damage to anyone unfortunate enough to be on the ground.

Foe	Prof	Lvl	AL	Description
Renegade Elementalist	E	3	15	Dmg 3-4 (R-Fire)	Lightning Orb	Fire Storm	Inferno	G.D.Ar
Tachi Forvent •B•	Ms	20	80	Arcane Conundrum	Ineptitude	Phantom Pain	Mantra of Persistence	D
Torin	W	4	34	Phy +20	Wild Blow	Bonetti's Def.	"Watch Yourself!"	Heal. Signet	Sw.Sh.G.D
Warrior Deserter	W	7	43	Phy +20	Hammer Bash	H.Ar.G

Hydra

Foe	Prof	Lvl	AL	Description
Hydra	E	11/22	60	Dmg 9-12/14-22 (M-Prc)	Fireball	Inferno (22)	Meteor	G.D
Mahgo Hydra	E	24	–	Blt -40	Glyph of Renewal	Meteor Shower	Inferno	Phoenix	Fire Attunement
Nayl Klaw Tuthan •B•	E	24	–	Glyph of Renewal	Meteor Shower	Inferno	Phoenix	Aura of Restoration
Rwek Khawl Mawl •B•	Ms	24	–	Echo	Energy Burn	Power Drain	Cry of Frustration

Ice Elemental

Foe	Prof	Lvl	AL	Description
Hail Blackice •B•	W	24	91	Dmg 26-38 (M-Blt)	Phy +20	Skull Crack	Irresistible Blow	Crushing Blow	G.D.
Ice Elemental	E	3	10	Dmg 7-9 (M-Cold)	Fire -40	Elemental Attunement	D
Ice Elemental	E	24	71	Dmg 20-38 (R-Blt)	Elemental Attune.	Swirling Aura	Deep Freeze	Aura of Restor.
Ice Elemental Shard	E	1	4	Dmg 3-4 (M-Cold)	Health 80	D
Ice Lord	Mk	24	71	Dmg 20-38 (R-Blt)	Elemental Attune.	Swirling Aura	Deep Freeze	Aura of Restor.
Rock Ice	W	22	86	Dmg 20-33 (M-Blt)	Phy +20	Skull Crack	Irresistible Blow	Crushing Blow	G.D.
Rune Ethercrash •B•	Ms	24	–	Keystone Signet	Leech Signet	Signet of Weariness	Signet of Humility

Imp

Foe	Prof	Lvl	AL	Description
Fire Imp	E	11	29	Dmg 8-13 (R-Fire)	Fire +30	Inferno	Immolate	G.D
Hops Flameinator •B•	E	18	54	Dmg 8-21 (R-Holy)	Phoenix	Mark of Rodgort	Lava Font	Aura of Restor.	G.D
Ice Imp	E	22	66	Dmg 7-18 (R-Cold)	Cold +40	Mind Fr.	Ice Spear	Maelstr.	Water Attune.	G.D
Inferno Imp	E	13	36	Dmg 8-13 (R-Fire)	Fire +80	Incendiary Bonds	Immolate	Aura of Restor.	G.D
Lava Imp	E	20	–	Fire +80	Mind Burn	Immolate
Maak Frostfriend •B•	E	24	–	Fire -10	Mind Freeze	Ice Spear	Maelstrom	Aura of Restor.	G.D
Sniik Hungrymind •B•	Ms	24	–	Energy Drain	Spirit of Failure	Diversion	Energy Burn	Ether Feast

Minotaur

Foe	Prof	Lvl	AL	Description
Forest Minotaur	W	19	77	Dmg 13-36 (M-Blt)	Phy +20	Wary Stance	Flurry	Rush	G.D.Ar
Minotaur	W	10	52	Dmg 11-19 (M-Blt)	Phy +20	Wary Stance	Bull's Strike	Rush	G.D.Ar
Minotaur	W	20	100	Dmg 15-42 (M-Blt)	Wary Stance	Frenzy	Skull Crack	G.D.Ar
Minotaur •B•	W	9	49	Dmg 11-19 (M-Blt)	Phy +20	Wary Stance	Bull's Strike	Rush	Heal. Signet	G.D.Ar
Muu Swifthorn •B•	W	18	74	Dmg 15-42 (M-Blt)	Phy +20	Wary Stance	Flurry	Rush	Heal. Signet	G.D.Ar
Rage Maulhoof •B•	W	24	91	Dmg 25-46 (M-Cold)	Phy +20	Bull's Charge	Wild Blow	Distracting Blow	Healing Signet	D.Ar

Mursaat

Foe	Prof	Lvl	AL	Description
Argyris the Scoundrel •B•	N	24	139	Life Transfer	Insidious Parasite	Blood Renewal	Life Siphon	St.R.F.D.Ar
Chrysos the Magnetic •B•	E	24	139	Thunderclap	Enervating Charge	Chain Lightning	Aura of Restoration	Glyph of Concentration	St.R.F.D.Ar
Demetrios the Enduring •B•	Mk	24	139	Contemplation of Purity	Draw Cond.	Aura of Faith	Orison of Heal.	St.R.F.D.Ar
Jade Armor	W	24	91	Phy +20	Devastating Hammer	Wild Blow	Crushing Blow	H.G.D.Ar
Jade Bow	R	24	91	Phy +20	Oath Shot	Whirling Defense	Determined Shot	B.G.D.Ar
Mursaat Elementalist	E	24	71	Thunderclap	Enervating Charge	Chain Ltng	Glyph of Concent.	St.R.F.G.D.Ar
Mursaat Mesmer	Ms	24	71	Power Leak	Energy Surge	Physical Resistance	Ether Feast	St.R.F.D.Ar
Mursaat Monk	Mk	24	71	Contemplat. of Purity	Draw Cond.	Aura of Faith	Orison of Heal.	St.R.F.G.D.Ar
Mursaat Necromancer	N	24	71	Life Transfer	Insidious Parasite	Blood Renewal	St.R.F.G.D.Ar
Pantheras the Deceiver •B•	Ms	24	139	Power Leak	Energy Surge	Physical Resistance	Ether Feast	St.R.F.D.Ar
Perfected Armor •B•	W	24	139	Devastating Hammer	Wild Blow	Crushing Blow	H.D.Ar
Perfected Cloak •B•	R	24	139	Oath Shot	Whirling Defense	Determined Shot	Healing Spring	B.D.Ar

Nightmare

Foe	Prof	Lvl	AL	Description
Abyssal	W	24	–	Earth Shaker	Endure Pain
Azure shadow	Mk	22	104	Dmg 20-46 (M-Cold)	Signet of Judgm.	Retribut.	Holy Wrath	Order of Pain	D
Bladed Aatxe	W	23	89	Dmg 68-100 (M-Blt)	Health 940	Savage Slash	Deadly Riposte	Sever Artery	Riposte	Gash	G.D
Brrrr Windburn •B•	E	24	71	Dmg 19-29 (M-Cold)	Elem -20	Mist Form	Conjure Frost	Frozen Burst	Aura of Restoration	G.D
Charged Blackness	E	23	71	Dmg 14-28 (R-Ltng)	Phy +40	Glimmering Mark	Chain Lightning	Shock	Lightning Orb	Whirlwind	Aura of Restoration	G.D
Coldfire Night	E	22	70	Dmg 14-28 (R-Ltng)	Ward Against Harm	Maelstrom	Frozen Burst	Shard Storm	Rust	Aura of Restoration	G.D
Cry Darkday •B•	N	24	–	Blood is Power	Dark Aura	Touch of Agony	Unholy Feast	Life Siphon
Crypt Fiend	N	3	11	Dmg 6-8 (M-Cold)	Chilblains	D.T
Dread Nightstalk •B•	N	18	54	Dmg 15-42 (M-Cold)	Phy +40	Dark Aura	Touch of Agony	Mark of Subversion	Life Siphon	D
Fog Nightmare	N	20	60	Dmg 13-36 (M-Cold)	Phy +40	Dark Aura	Touch of Agony	Mark of Subvers.	D
Frostbite •B•	Mk	24	71	Dmg 28-54 (M-Cold)	Elem -20	Signet of Judgment	Retribut.	Holy Wrath	G.D
Grasping Darkness	W	22	71	Dmg 16-22 (M-Sla)	Phy +40	Distract. Blow	Skull Crack	Flurry	"Fear Me!"	G.D
Murk Darkshriek •B•	N	24	72	Dmg 25-46 (M-Cold)	Blt +20, Fire -20	Dark Aura	Touch of Agony	Mark of Subversion	Life Transfer	H.G.D
Nighh SpineChill •B•	N	24	71	Dmg 28-54 (M-Cold)	Elem -20	Spiteful Spirit	Spinal Shivers	Weaken Armor	Life Siphon	G.D
Nightmare	N	24	–	Well of Bld.	Dark Aura	Touch of Ag.	Strip Enchant.	Plague Touch	Order of Pain
Seear Windlash •B•	Ms	24	71	Dmg 19-29 (M-Cold)	Elem -20	Illus. Weapon.	Clumsin.	Illus. of Weakness	G.D

See page 187 for table guidelines.

Foe	Prof	Lvl	AL	Description
Shadow Beast	N	24	–	Mark of Pain | Spiteful Spirit | Consume Corpse | Dark Pact
Shadow Elemental	E	24	–	Fire Storm | Fireball | Incendiary Bonds | Aura of Restoration
Shadow Mesmer	Ms	24	–	Channeling | Shatter Enchantment | Empathy | Illusion of Haste
Shadow Monk	Mk	24	–	Orison of Healing | Heal Other | Healing Breeze | Heal Area | Restore Life
Shadow of Death •B•	N	24	72	Dmg 25-46 (M-Cold) | Phy +40 | Dark Aura | Touch of Agony | Mark of Subversion | Life Transfer | D
Shadow Ranger	R	24	–	Elem +30 | Barrage | Power Shot | Dual Shot | Troll Unguent
Shadow Warrior	W	24	–	Phy +20 | Healing Signet | Hundred Blades | Griffon's Sweep | "I Will Avenge You!" | Final Thrust
Stalking Night	E	22	90	Dmg 14-28 (R-Ltng) | Counter Blow | Earthquake | Aftershock | Earth Attunement | Aura of Restoration | G.D
Stalking Night	W	22	90	Dmg 24-45 (M-Dark) | Counter Blow | Bull's Charge | G.D
Terror	N	20	60	Dmg 13-36 (M-Cold) | Life Transfer | Dark Aura | Touch of Agony | Dark Pact
Tomb Nightmare	N	4	14	Dmg 8-10 (M-Cold) | Health 120 | Chilblains | D.T
Vengeful Aatxe	W	24	91	Dmg 68-100 (M-Blt) | Protector's Strike | G.D

Plant

Foe	Prof	Lvl	AL	Description
Afrhul Deeproot •B•	R	24	91	Dmg 19-35 (R-Blt) | Fire -40, Sla -40 | Muddy Terrain | Barbed Trap | Determined Shot | Troll Unguent | D
Aloe Husk	Mk	0	3	Fire -40, Sla -40 | Shielding Hands | Healing Breeze | D
Aloe Seed	W	0	3	Orison of Healing | D
Ancient Oakheart	Mk	17	71	Dmg 16-29 (R-Blt) | Fire -40, Sla -40 | Balthazar's Aura | Retribution | Healing Breeze | D
Arkhel Havenwood •B•	E	24	91	Dmg 19-35 (R-Blt) | Fire -40, Sla -40 | Ward Against Harm | Blurred Vision | Ice Prison | Aura of Restoration | D
Crown of Thorns	Mk	5	22	Dmg 2-5 (R-Fire) | Fire -40, Sla -40 | Orison of Healing | Mend Condition | Heal Other | Holy Wrath | D
Entangling Root	R	18	83	Dmg 12-34 (M-Blt) | Fire -40, Sla -40 | Muddy Terrain | Penetrating Attack | G.D
Esnhal Hardwood •B•	Mk	24	91	Dmg 19-35 (R-Blt) | Fire -40, Sla -40 | Life Barrier | Pacifism | Reversal of Fortune | D
Harth Mendbranch •B•	Mk	18	54	Dmg 8-21 (R-Holy) | Protective Spirit | Vengeance | Holy Strike | Heal. Breeze | D
Juniper Bark	Mk	7	30	Dmg 6-10 (R-Holy) | Men. | Holy Veil | Rev. of Fortune | Pacif. | D
Large Aloe Seed	W	3	15	Dmg 3-9 (R-Holy) | Fire -40, Sla -40 | Shielding Hands | D
Life Pod	Mk	15	61	Dmg 9-15 (R-Holy) | Fire -40, Sla -40 | Orison of Healing | Mend Condition | Heal Other | Holy Wrath | G.D
Oakheart	Mk	5	17	Dmg 4-6 (R-Blt) | Fire -40, Sla -40 | Power Shot | D
Oakheart	R	13	60	Dmg 12-23 (R-Blt) | Fire -40, Sla -40 | Power Shot | Barb. Trap | Energiz. Wind | G.D
Obrhit Barkwood •B•	W	24	91	Dmg 19-35 (M-Blt) | Fire -40, Sla -40 | Defy Pain | Hammer Bash | Belly Smash | Healing Signet | D
Pinesoul	R	24	112	Dmg 13-33 (R-Blt) | Fire -40, Sla -40 | Muddy Terrain | Barb. Trap | Determ. Shot | D
Psion Tanglebranch •B•	Ms	18	54	Dmg 8-21 (R-Holy) | Sympathetic Visage | Clumsiness | Shatter Delusions | Soothing Images | Ether Feast | D
Redwood Shepherd	R	19	87	Dmg 13-35 (M-Blt) | Fire -40, Sla -40 | Primal Echoes | Debilitating Shot | G.D
Reed Stalker	Ms	17	51	Dmg 10-17 (R-Chaos) | Sympathetic Visage | Clumsiness | Wastrel's Worry | D
Salving Cactus	Mk	20	60	Dmg 7-18 (R-Holy) | Orison of Healing | Mend Cond. | Heal Other | Holy Wrath | D
Singed Oak	R	10	42	Dmg 13-20 (R-Blt) | Fire -40, Sla -40 | D
Snarling Driftwood	W	17	–	Fire -40, Sla -40 | Hamstring | Protector's Strike | "Victory is Mine!" | Flourish | Warrior's Cunning
Spined Aloe	Mk	11	45	Dmg 9-14 (R-Holy) | Fire -40, Sla -40 | Orison of Healing | Mend Condition | Heal Other | Holy Wrath | D
Spirit Shepherd	E	17	–	Fire -40, Sla -40 | Iron Mist | Chain Ltng | Ltng Touch | Ltng Strike | Aura of Restor.
Spirit Wood	R	10	–	Fire -40, Sla -40 | Edge of Extinction | Primal Echoes | Nature's Renewal | Troll Unguent | Choking Gas
Succulent Junniper	Mk	7	30	Dmg 6-10 (R-Holy) | Fire -40, Sla -40 | Mend. | Holy Veil | Rev.l of Fortune | Pacif. | D
Thorn Stalker	E	17	68	Dmg 6-16 (R-Holy) | Fire -40, Sla -40 | Whirlwind | Aftershock | Glyph of Renewal | Stoning | G.D
Thorn Stalker Sprout	E	13	53	Dmg 6-16 (R-Holy) | Fire -40, Sla -40 | Whirlwind | Aftershock | Glyph of Renewal | Stoning | G.D
Thornwrath •B•	E	16	69	Dmg 6-15 (R-Earth) | Fire -40, Sla -40 | Earthquake | Aftershock | Stoning | Aura of Restoration | Earth Attunement | G.Ar
Tree of Autumn •B•	R	18	74	Dmg 13-39 (R-Blt) | Nature's Renewal | Debilitat. Shot | Dust Trap | Heal. Spring | G.D
Tree of Judgment •B•	Mk	24	71	Dmg 25-46 (M-Cold) | Balthazar's Aura | Signet of Judgment | Scourge Healing | Healing Breeze | Convert Hexes | D
Tree of Life •B•	Mk	16	69	Dmg 13-36 (M-Blt) | Fire -40, Sla -40 | Watchful Spirit | Guardian | Holy Wrath | Rebirth | Scourge Sacrifice | D
Tree of Renewal •B•	R	13	60	Dmg 16-29 (R-Blt) | Power Shot | Barbed Trap | Energizing Wind | Troll Ung. | G.D
Tree of Vitality •B•	Mk	14	62	Dmg 17-30 (M-Blt) | Fire -40, Sla -40 | Blessed Signet | Guardian | Protective Bond | Orison of Healing | Restore Life | D
Tree of Winds •B•	R	16	69	Dmg 12-30 (R-Prc) | Fire -40, Sla -40 | D
Unthet Rotwood •B•	N	24	91	Dmg 19-29 (M-Blt) | Fire -40, Sla -40 | Virulence | Plague Sending | Chilblains | D

Rift

Foe	Prof	Lvl	AL	Description
Chained Soul	N	22	1	Rend Enchantments | Blood is Power | St.R.F
Rift Warden	E	24	91	Dmg 27-40 (M-Cold) | Ice Spikes | Maelstrom | Deep Freeze | Aura of Restoration | Glyph of Lesser Energy | Glyph of Concentration

Scarab

Foe	Prof	Lvl	AL	Description
Grech Trundle •B•	N	14	43	Dmg 12-17 (M-Prc) | Deathly Swarm | Mark of Subversion | Soul Feast | Life Siphon | G.D
Jade Scarab	N	20	60	Dmg 7-20 (M-Prc) | Vile Touch | Parasitic Bond | G.D
Moss Scarab	N	12/16	36/48	Dmg 9-15 (M-Prc) | Vampiric Touch | G.D
Rock Eater Scarab	N	20	60	Dmg 7-20 (M-Prc) | Vile Touch | Parasitic Bond | G.D

- Warrior/Elementalist with Hammer, Strength, and Water Magic. This character uses Hammer attacks with knockdowns and knockdown-followup attacks like Belly Smash. Other useful skills include Water for close-range snaring and Water Trident to knock down runners.

- Elementalist/Mesmer with the majority of his points in Earth Magic and Fire Magic, and any extra points devoted to Inspiration Magic and Energy Storage. This character uses spells like Meteor from a distance and Earthquake followed by Aftershock when up close to demolish snared opponents. The Mesmer's Inspiration Magic offers Energy Tap to help fuel the expensive spells.

- Mesmer/Monk with Domination Magic, Inspiration Magic, and Smiting Prayers. This character fills the normal anti-caster role with Domination Magic. He can use Scourge Healing to harm enemy Monks, and Signet of Judgment for knockdowns. Mantra of Inscriptions speeds the recharge time on the Signet.

- Warrior/Monk with Hammer and Smiting. This character does high damage with a hammer, especially when enhanced with Judge's Insight. He uses Signet of Judgment for extra knockdown attacks and, coupled with Holy Strike, causes extra damage.

The best strategies are those that your opponent does not expect. Consider these teams just a starting point for your exploration of the myriad of options available in *Guild Wars*.

See page 187 for table guidelines.

Communication

Even if you have a great team, you won't win unless everyone knows what to do and when to do it.

Every team needs a captain. This person is responsible for designating targets, leading charges, and directing movement. Of course, your team may have multiple people capable of taking on this responsibility, but only one person should hold this position at a time. The rest of the team should refrain from inserting contradictory instructions. Listening to your captain and reacting quickly will increase your chances of survival.

As a leader, directing focus-fire is easy. Press Shift+double-click on an enemy, and everyone in your group is told whom you are targeting. They can then select the same target by pressing their targeting hot key (which defaults to T).

For other communication, the built-in chat is a start. Unfortunately, people tend to miss out on the information there because they focus on other parts of the screen. The most successful teams use voice conferencing software like Ventrilo or Teamspeak.

Foe	Prof	Lvl	AL	Description
Shining Blade				
Evennia	Mk	15	150	Heal Area | Heal Other
Markis	W	15	150	Concussion Shot
Shining Blade Elementalist	E	15	46	Flare | Aura of Restoration
Shining Blade Mesmer	Ms	15	46	Ether Feast
Shining Blade Monk	Mk	15	46	Healing Hands
Shining Blade Necromancer	N	15	46	Life Siphon
Shining Blade Ranger	R	15	65/120	Troll Unguent
Shining Blade Scout	R	15	150	–
Shining Blade Warrior	W	15	66/120	Phy +20 | Healing Signet
Shock				
Lamaan Wickedwail •B•	E	17	–	Phy +40 | Chain Ltng | Conj. Ltng | Enervat. Charge | Aura of Restor. | Chaos Storm
Smoke Phantom	E	17/18	–	Phy +40 | Chain Ltng | Conjure Ltng | Enervating Charge | Aura of Restoration
Zeki Lament •B•	E	17	–	Phy +40 | Chain Ltng | Conjure Lightning | Enervating Charge | Aura of Restoration
Skale				
Ancient Skale	N	24	–	Life Transfer | Life Siphon | Rend Enchantments | Blood Ritual | Grenth's Balance
Bog Skale	N	11	29	Dmg 8-13 (R-Dark) | Cold +30 | Demonic Flesh | (Soul Barbs) | (Parasitic Bond) | Price of Failure | (Life Siphon) | G.D
Bog Skale Blighter	N	18	45	Dmg 8-13 (R-Dark) | Cold +30 | Putrid Explosion | (Chilblains) | (Soul Barbs) | Price of Failure | Life Siphon | G.D
Cella the Hooded •B•	R	11	54	Dmg 12-17 (R-Dark) | Choking Gas | Spike Trap | Energizing Wind | Troll Ung. | G.D
Frash the Cold •B•	E	24	71	Dmg 19-27 (M-Sla) | Mist Form | Frozen Burst | Phoenix | Aura of Restoration | D
Gack the Mindwrecker •B•	Ms	24	71	Dmg 19-27 (M-Sla) | Clumsiness | Illusionary Weaponry | Arcane Conundrum | Ether Feast | Shatter Hex | D
Geck the Coldblooded •B•	N	11	34	Dmg 12-17 (R-Dark) | Demon. Flesh | Soul Barbs | Price of Failure | Life Siphon | G.D
Jungle Skale	E	19	57	Dmg 7-17 (R-Dark) | Defile Flesh | Rotting Flesh | Weaken Armor | G.D
Laris the Meateater •B•	E	11	34	Dmg 12-17 (R-Dark) | Rust | Armor of Mist | Ltng Javelin | Aura of Restor. | G.D
Rago the Scaled •B•	E	13	40	Dmg 12-17 (R-Dark) | Deep Freeze | Glyph of Lesser Energy | Grasping Earth | Aura of Restoration | G.D
River Skale	E	1	4	Dmg 3-5 (R-Cold) | Health 70 | G.D
River Skale Brood	E	4	40	Dmg 3-5 (R-Cold) | Health 100 | Ice Spear | Aura of Restoration | G.D
River Skale Tad	E	0	1	Dmg 3-5 (R-Cold) | G.D
Skale Broodcaller	E	2	7	Dmg 3-5 (R-Cold) | G.D
Skigg the Tongue •B•	N	13	40	Dmg 12-17 (R-Dark) | Demon. Flesh | Soul Barbs | Price of Failure | Life Siphon | G.D
Skeleton				
Abijah the Decayed •B•	R	12	–	Prc +30, Blt -10 | Concussion Shot | Edge of Extinction | Debilitat. Shot | Troll Ung.
Archer	R	20	–	–
Bija Gravewailer •B•	Ms	13	–	Phy +40 | Fragility | Spirit of Failure | Phantom Pain | Ether Feast
Blood Fanatic	N	2	29	Vile Touch | D
Captain	W	20	–	Phy +20 | Sever Artery
Cleric	Mk	20	–	Fire -10 | Heal Other | Restore Life | Orison of Healing | Healing Breeze | Divine Spirit | Divine Boon | Mend Ailment | Glyph of Concentration
Elite Guard	W	20	–	Phy +20 | Sever Artery
Footman	W	20	–	Fire -60
Gezna Shadowstalker •B•	E	12	–	Prc +20, Blt -20 | Lightning Touch | Blinding Flash | Earthquake | Aura of Restor.
Ghita Bonz •B•	R	12	–	Prc +20, Blt -20 | Concussion Shot | Edge of Extinction | Debilitat. Shot | Troll Ung.
Hellfire Mage	E	20	60	Meteor Shower | Flare | Sear. Heat | Glyph of Elemental Power | Glyph of Sacrifice
Hellhound	W	20	80	Dmg 7-20 (M-Sla) | Phy +20 | Frenzy | Sever Artery | Endure Pain
Ijan the Cursed •B•	Mk	11	–	Prc +20, Blt -20 | Scourge Healing | Smite Hex | Vengeance | Healing Breeze
Kemal the Deadened •B•	Mk	12	–	Prc +20, Blt -20 | Symbol of Wrath | Smite Hex | Vengeance | Healing Breeze
Najja Doombringer •B•	E	13	–	Prc +20, Blt -20 | Lightning Touch | Blinding Flash | Earthquake | Aura of Restor.
Nazeem the Damned •B•	E	11	–	Prc +20, Blt -20 | Lightning Touch | Blinding Flash | Earthquake | Aura of Restor.
Onan the Spiritless •B•	Ms	11	–	Prc +30, Blt -10 | Fragility | Spirit of Failure | Phantom Pain | Ether Feast
Raging Cadaver	N	3	32	D
Raja Crux •B•	Mk	13	–	Prc +20, Blt -20 | Scourge Healing | Smite Hex | Vengeance | Healing Breeze
Restless Corpse	W	1	26	Health 80 | D
Savage Sniper	R	20	73	Apply Poison | Distracting Shot | Savage Shot
Sayad the Bloodless •B•	R	10	–	Prc +20, Blt -20 | Concussion Shot | Edge of Extinction | Debilitat. Shot | Troll Ung.
Skeletal Berserker	W	24	–	Dismember | Axe Rake | Axe Twist | Cyclone Axe | "Victory is Mine!" | Wild Blow
Skeletal Bond	Mk	24	–	Prc +20, Blt -20 | Infuse Health | Live Vicariously | Life Bond | Spell Breaker
Skeletal Ether Breaker	Ms	24	–	Prc +20, Blt -20 | Shatter Enchantment | Cry of Frustration | Chaos Storm | Energy Surge | Sympathetic Visage
Skeletal Icehand	E	24	–	Prc +20, Blt -20 | Blurred Vision | Maelstrom | Deep Freeze | Lightning Touch | Windborne Speed | Glyph of Energy
Skeletal Impaler	R	24	–	Prc +20, Blt -20 | Dust Trap | Spike Trap | Flame Trap | Barbed Trap | Distract. Shot
Skeleton Bowmaster	R	17	–	Prc +20, Blt -20 | Apply Poison | Pin Down
Skeleton Mesmer	Ms	13	–	Prc +20, Blt -20 | Fragility | Phantom Pain | Shatter Hex
Skeleton Monk	Mk	12/18/20	-/-/60	Prc +20, Blt -20 (L12, L18) | Healing Breeze | Smite Hex | Infuse Health
Skeleton Raider	W	1	26	Health 80 | D
Skeleton Ranger	R	13/18	–	Prc +20, Blt -20 | Apply Poison
Skeleton Sorcerer	E	13	–	Prc +20, Blt -20 | Lightning Touch | Blinding Flash | Earthquake
Skeleton Torturer	Ms	20	73	Fragility | Phantom Pain | Backfire | Ineptitude | Energy Tap
Ziyad Soulreaper •B•	Ms	12	–	Prc +20, Blt -20 | Fragility | Spirit of Failure | Phantom Pain | Ether Feast

See page 187 for table guidelines.

Foe	Prof	Lvl	AL	Description
Tengu				
Avicara Ardent	Mk	24	71	Ltng -20 | Shield of Judgment | Dwayna's Kiss | Healing Touch | R.F.D.Ar
Avicara Brave	W	24	91	Phy +20, Ltng -20 | Flourish | Pure Strike | Savage Slash | Sw.Sh.Ar.D.
Avicara Fierce	R	24	81	Ltng -40, Elem +30 | Practiced Stance | Ignite Arrows | Dual Shot | B.Ar.D
Avicara Guile	N	24	71	Well of Power | Strip Enchantment | Deathly Swarm | R.F.D.Ar
Avicara Wise	Ms	24	71	Ltng -20 | Ineptitude | Phantom Pain | Fragility | R.F.D.Ar
Caromi Tengu Brave	W	12/13	57/60	Phy +20, Ltng -20 | Seeking Blade | Def. Stance (L12) | Riposte (L13) | Sw.Ax.Sh.Ar.D.
Caromi Tengu Elite	W	18	74	Phy +20, Ltng -20 | Swift Chop | (Riposte) | (Defensive Stance) | Ax.Sw.Sh.Ar.D.
Caromi Tengu Fierce	R	13	50	Dmg 9-21 (R-Prc) | Ltng -40, Elem +30 | Tiger's Fury | Point Blank Shot | Read the Wind | B.Ar.D
Caromi Tengu Wild	Ms	12	37	Ltng -20 | Conjure Phantasm | Cry of Frustration | Shatter Enchantment | R.F.D.Ar
Chuff Quickbeak •B•	E	11	34	Incendiary Bonds | Flame Burst | Immolate | Aura of Restoration | St.R.F.Ar.D
Dyv Cloudclaw •B•	R	14	63	Dmg 10-26 (R-Prc) | Dual Shot | Penetrat. Attack | Favor. Winds | Troll Ung. | B.D.Ar
Glyd Swiftwing •B•	N	14	43	Suffering | Mark of Subversion | Soul Feast | Life Siphon | R.St.F.Ar.D
Hyl Thunderwing •B•	E	24	71	Ltng -20 | Glyph of Energy | Ltng Orb | Iron Mist | Aura of Restoration | R.F.D.Ar
Myd Springclaw •B•	Mk	24	71	Ltng -20 | Shield of Judgm. | Dwayna's Kiss | Heal. Touch | Scourge Heal. | R.F.D.Ar
Nav Sharpquill •B•	W	11	54	Phy +20 | Swift Chop | Seek. Blade | Heal. Signt | Riposte | Ax.Sw.Sh.Ar.D
Nhy Darkclaw •B•	N	24	71	Ltng -20 | Well of Power | Strip Enchantment | Deathly Swarm | R.F.D.Ar
Pello Agileclaw •B•	Ms	11	34	Drain Enchantment | Power Drain | Wastrel's Worry | Ether Feast | St.R.F.Ar.D
Rawr Wildeye •B•	N	11	34	Suffering | Mark of Subversion | Soul Feast | Life Siphon | R.St.F.Ar.D
Ryk Arrowwing •B•	R	24	81	Ltng -40, Elem +30 | Practiced Stance | Ignite Arrows | Dual Shot | Troll Ung. | B.Ar.D
Sky Quickfeather •B•	W	14	63	Phy +20 | Swift Chop | Def. Stance | Seek. Blade | Heal. Sigt | Riposte | Ax.Sw.Sh.Ar.D
Squaw Nimblecrest •B•	R	11	54	Tiger's Fury | Point Blank Shot | Read the Wind | Troll Unguent | B.G.D.Ar
Swoop Needlegrip •B•	Mk	11	34	Vigorous Spirit | Holy Strike | Smite | Healing Breeze | Mend Ailment | Purge Conditions | St.R.F.Ar.D
Syr Honorcrest •B•	W	24	91	Phy +20, Ltng -20 | Flourish | Pure Strike | Savage Slash | Heal. Signet | Sw.Sh.Ar.D.
Winglord Caromi •B•	R	24	91	Whirling Defense | Distracting Shot | Read the Wind | Troll Unguent | B.D.Ar
Wyt Sharpfeather •B•	Ms	24	71	Ltng -20 | Ineptitude | Phantom Pain | Fragility | Ether Feast | R.F.D.Ar
Titan				
Burning Titan	W	24	–	Phy +20 | Healing Signet | (Irresistible Blow) | (Wild Blow)
Fist of the Titans	W	24	–	Phy +20 | Hundred Blades | Final Thrust | Deadly Riposte
Hand of the Titans	W	24	–	Phy +20 | Eviscerate | Axe Twist | Axe Rake | Swift Chop
Maligo Libens •B•	N	24	–	Aura of the Lich | Shadow of Fear | Shadow Strike | Strip Enchantment | Life Siphon
Moles Quibus •B•	Ms	24	–	Panic | Spirit of Failure | Cry of Frustration | Mantra of Flame | Ether Feast
Risen Ashen Hulk	N	24	–	Aura of the Lich | Unholy Feast | Shadow Strike
Scelus Prosum •B•	E	24	–	Mind Burn | Rodgort's Invocat. | Inferno | Glyph of Lesser Energy | Aura of Restor.
Spark of the Titans	E	24	–	Mind Burn | Meteor Shower | Inferno | Glyph of Lesser Energy | Aura of Restor.
Tortitudo Probo •B•	W	24	–	Eviscerate | Axe Twist | Axe Rake | Swift Chop | Healing Signet
Valetudo Rubor •B•	R	24	–	Greater Conflagration | Flame Trap | Troll Unguent
Troll				
Fen Troll	W	20	112	Dmg 13-36 (M-Blt) | Troll Unguent | Endure Pain | D
Grook Plugalug •B•	W	14	63	Phy +20 | Gash | Sever Artery | Seeking Blade | Troll Ung. | D
Jungle Troll	W	18	74	Dmg 15-26 (M-Blt) | Phy +20 | Troll Unguent | Endure Pain | Power Attack | G.D
Krogg Shmush •B•	W	22	86	Dmg 33-42 (M-Blt) | Phy +20 | Battle Rage | Mighty Blow | Disrupting Chop | D
Mountain Troll	W	24	91	Dmg 28-35 (M-Blt) | Phy +20 | Battle Rage | Mighty Blow | Disrupting Chop | D
Whuup Buumbuul •B•	R	22	86	Dmg 33-42 (M-Blt) | Phy +20 | Escape | Frozen Soil | Troll Unguent | D
Undead				
Hellhound	W	16	–	Fire -60 | Frenzy | Sever Artery | Endure Pain
Undead Lich •B•	W	24	–	Deathly Swarm
Vizier Khilbron	N	20	–	—
Verata & Followers				
Apprentice of Verata	N	20	80	Phy +20 | Verata's Gaze | Taste of Death | Animate Bone Fiend | R.St.F.Ar
Eyes of Verata	R	20	80	Phy +20 | Barbed Trap | Choking Gas | Flame Trap | B.Ar.D
Sage of Verata	Ms	20	80	Phy +20 | Arcane Conundrum | Inept. | Phantom Pain | Mantra of Persist. | R.St.F.Ar
Shepherd of Verata	Mk	20	80	Phy +20 | Mending | Healing Breeze | R.St.F.Ar
Verata •B•	N	20	60	Dmg 15-42 (M-Cold) | Phy +40 | Verata's Gaze | Verata's Aura | Verata's Sacrifice | Taste of Death | Animate Bone Fiend | D
Verata's Fiend	R	6	20	Dmg 1-30 (R-Prc)
Verata's Horror	N	6	28	Dmg 1-30 (M-Blt)
White Mantle				
Bairn the Sinless •B•	Ms	16	49	Guilt | Shame | Shatter Enchantment | Ether Feast | St.R.F.Ar.D
Bearn the Implacable •B•	N	16	49	Well of the Profane | Mark of Subversion | Order of Pain | Vamp. Gaze | St.R.F.Ar.D
Braima the Callous •B•	E	16	49	Searing Heat | Glyph of Elemental Power | Ward Against Elements | Aura of Restoration | St.R.F.Ar.D
Confessor Dorian	Mk	20	60	Heal Area | Banish
Corbin the Upright •B•	Mk	16	69	Div. Interv. | Judge's Insight | Shield. Hands | Convert Hexes | Restore Life | St.R.F.Ar.D
Cuthbert the Chaste •B•	R	16	69	Savage Shot | Dryder's Defenses | Antidote Signet | Troll Unguent | B.Ar.D
Cyrus the Unflattering •B•	W	16	69	Phy +20 | "Watch Yourself!" | "I Will Avenge You!" | Executioner's Strike | Galrath Slash | Sw.Ax.Sh.Ar.D.
Darwym the Spiteful •B•	R	16	69	Savage Shot | Dryder's Defenses | Antidote Signet | Troll Unguent | B.Ar.D
Edgar the Iron Fist •B•	R	16	69	Savage Shot | Dryder's Defenses | Antidote Signet | Troll Unguent | B.Ar.D
Holt the Iron Boot Heel •B•	W	16	69	Phy +20 | "Watch Yourself!" | "I Will Avenge You!" | Executioner's Strike | Galrath Slash | Sw.Ax.Sh.Ar.D.
Irwin the Severe •B•	Ms	16	49	Phy +20 | Guilt | Shame | Shatter Enchantment | Ether Feast | Sw.Ax.Sh.Ar.D
Justiciar Hablion	W	18	74	Phy +20 | Sever Artery | Cyclone Axe | Dismember | Healing Signet | Axe Rake
Justiciar Hablion •B•	W	16	69	Dmg 4-22 (M-Sla) | Phy +20 | Sever Artery | Cyclone Axe | Dismember | Healing Signet | Ax.Sh.Ar.D.

See page 187 for table guidelines.

Coordination

Communication is key, but practiced group tactics will win even more battles. Here are a few tactics and techniques to consider:

- **Define Your Kill Order:** Sometimes the targeting system is not fast enough for the split decisions of battle. Let everyone know what the kill priority is in advance. There's no hard and fast rule when deciding upon the kill order. However, the general principle is to kill healers first, followed by soft-caster targets (Elementalists, Mesmers, and Necromancers), and then the rest.

- **Use Decoys:** Characters with strong defense can sometimes rush the front lines, when supported by healers, soaking up vast amounts of damage. If they become subject to a focus-firing effort, you may win by wasting the enemy's Energy.

- **Feint:** Focus-fire on a particular target to get the enemy healers to concentrate on them, then quickly switch to another target (such as one of the healers) before they anticipate the targeting change.

- **False Retreat:** Have people fighting at the front-line break away in a retreat. If your opponent takes the bait, it can be a great opportunity to drop snares and area damage on them.

- **Disciplined Charges:** The order to charge a position shouldn't be made lightly, but once made, must be completed without hesitation. Half-hearted charges are quickly routed. It's okay to lose a

couple of people in a charge if it means the overall objective (displacing or killing the opponent) is accomplished.

- **Hold Formation:** People have a natural tendency to chase individual opponents, seeking an easy kill. Sometimes this works, but more often than not it ends badly: either they are led into a trap and killed, or the rest of their team is attacked while the distraction is taking place. Everyone in the group should refrain from breaking formation unnecessarily.

Movement Is Key

The importance of movement on the battlefield can not be stressed enough. With the possibility of battles coming to you as well as you moving toward battles, it becomes very important to be constantly aware of where your allies and enemies are located. When matches start, use good communication skills to prevent your group from becoming spread out and separated. Also keep in mind that *Guild Wars* uses a collision detection system, which makes it impossible to move your character through objects or other characters.

Conclusion

Winning is a combination of knowing the maps, creating teams with complementary skills, communicating well, and executing coordinated tactics.

Keep all these things in mind, practice them often, and your team will take these arenas by storm.

FOE	PROF	LVL	AL	DESCRIPTION
Kenric the Believer •B•	N	16	49	Well of the Profane | Mark of Subversion | Order of Pain | Vamp. Gaze | St.R.F.Ar.D
Lars the Obeisant •B•	Ms	16	49	Guilt | Shame | Shatter Enchantment | Ether Feast | St.R.F.Ar.D
Manton the Indulgent •B•	E	16	49	Sear. Heat | Glyph of Elem. Power | Ward Against Elem. | Aura of Restor. | St.R.F.Ar.D
Markis	R	20	150	Concussion Shot | Barrage | Troll Unguent | B.Ar.D.G
Nyle the Compassion. •B•	Ms	16	49	Guilt | Shame | Shatter Enchantment | Ether Feast | St.R.F.Ar.D
Oswald the Amiable •B•	N	16	49	Well of the Profane | Mark of Subversion | Order of Pain | Vamp. Gaze | St.R.F.Ar.D
Pleoh the Ugly •B•	E	16	49	Sear. Heat | Glyph of Elem. Power | Ward Against Elem. | Aura of Restor. | St.R.F.Ar.D
Ramm the Benevolent •B•	Mk	16	49	Div. Interv. | Judge's Insight | Shield. Hands | Convert Hexes | Restore Life | St.R.F.Ar.D
Selwin the Fervent •B•	Mk	16	49	Div. Interv. | Judge's Insight | Shield. Hands | Conv. Hexes | Restore Life | St.R.F.G.Ar.D
Torr the Relentless •B•	R	16	69	Savage Shot | Dryder's Defenses | Antidote Signet | Troll Unguent | B.Ar.D
White Mantle Abbot	Mk	15	46	Divine Intervention | Heal Other | Infuse Health
White Mantle Abbot	Mk	18	54	Divine Intervention | Judge's Insight | Shielding Hands | Convert Hexes | St.R.F.Ar.D
White Mantle Justiciar	W	18	74	Phy +20 | "Watch Yourself!" | "I Will Avenge You!" | Executioner's Strike | Galrath Slash | Sw.Ax.Sh.Ar.D
White Mantle Knight	W	15/16	66/69	Phy +20 | "Watch Yourself!" | "I Will Avenge You!" (L16) | Executioner's Strike (L16) | Galrath Slash (L16) | Sw.Ax.Sh.Ar.D
White Mantle Priest	Mk	24	71	Divine Intervention | Judge's Insight | Shielding Hands | Convert Hexes | St.R.F.Ar.D
White Mantle Ritualist	N	15/16	46/49	Well of the Profane | Barbs | Rotting Flesh (15) | Mark of Subversion (15) | Order of Pain (16) | Vampiric Gaze (16) | St.R.F.Ar.D
White Mantle Savant	E	15/16	46/49	Searing Heat | Lightning Orb (15) | Glyph of Elemental Power (16) | Ward Against Elements (16) | St.R.F.Ar.D
White Mantle Seeker	R	12/16	57/69	Savage Shot | Barrage (12) | Dryder's Def. (16) | Antidote Signet (16) | B.Ar.D.G
White Mantle Seeker	R	20	80	Savage Shot | Dryder's Def. | Antidote Signet | Troll Unguent | Pin Down | B.Ar.D.G
White Mantle Sycophant	Ms	15/16	46/49	Guilt | En. Burn (15) | Shame (16) | Shatter Enchant. (16) | Empathy (16) | St.R.F.Ar.D
White Mantle Zealot	W	24	91	Phy +20 | Sever Artery | Gash | Dismember | Heal. Signet | Axe Rake | Sw.Ax.Sh.Ar.D

Windrider

FOE	PROF	LVL	AL	DESCRIPTION
Breeze Keeper	Ms	24	–	Migraine | Energy Drain | Shatter Enchantment | Mind Wrack
Chott Stormsinger •B•	Ms	14	43	Dmg 10-16 (R-Chaos) | Hex Breaker | Cry of Frustration | Shatter Enchantment | Ether Feast | Empathy | G.Ar
Grenn Mindvenom •B•	Ms	5	20	Dmg 4-8 (R-Ltng) | Backfire | Shatter Hex | Energy Tap | Ether Feast | D
Grun Galesurge •B•	Mk	24	–	Shield of Deflec. | Essence Bond | Scourge Heal. | Balthazar's Aura | Rev. of Fortune
Hepp Bilespitter •B•	Ms	16	49	Dmg 6-15 (R-Chaos) | Hex Break. | Cry of Frust. | Shat. Ench. | Ether Feast | Emp. | G.Ar
Jyth Sprayburst •B•	E	24	–	Ether Prodigy | Stoning | Enervating Change | Kinetic Armor | Aura of Restoration
Larrk Etherburn •B•	Ms	5	20	Dmg 4-8 (R-Ltng) | Backfire | Shatter Hex | Energy Tap | Ether Feast | D
Pytt Spitespew •B•	Ms	24	–	Migraine | Power Spike | Wastrel's Worry
Smoke Walker	Mk	24	–	Healing Touch | Heal Area | Healing Breeze | Mend Condition | Healing Seed
Storm Kin	Ms	20	60	Dmg 12-46 (R-Fire) | Conj. Phant. | Cripp. Anguish | Drain Enchant. | Ether Feast | D
Storm Rider	Ms	7	20	Dmg 4-8 (R-Ltng) | Backfire | Shatter Hex | Energy Tap | D
Wind Rider	Ms	17	51	Dmg 8-13 (R-Chaos) | Conjure Phant. | Cry of Frustration | Shatter Enchant. | G.D
Wydd Kindlerun •B•	E	14	43	Dmg 10-16 (R-Chaos) | Maelst. | Glyph of Less. En. | Ice Spikes | Aura of Restor. | G.Ar

Worm

FOE	PROF	LVL	AL	DESCRIPTION
Maw The Mtn. Heart •B•	N	24	–	Feast of Corruption | Suffering
Plague Worm	W	0	1	Dmg 1 (R-Blt) | G.D
Plague Worm	W	1	24	Dmg 3-5 (R-Blt) | Health 80 | G.D
Rock Borer Worm	R	20	–	Concussion Shot | Pin Down | Choking Gas | Throw Dirt | Lightning Reflexes
Worm	W	0	1	Dmg 1 (R-Blt) | G.D
Worm Queen	W	2	27	Dmg 5-7 (R-Blt) | G.D
Infernal Wurm	W	24	–	–
Sand Wurm	W	20	160	Dmg 13-36 (M-Blt) | G.D

Zombie

FOE	PROF	LVL	AL	DESCRIPTION
Bakkir the Forsaken •B•	N	11	–	Animate Bone Minions | Death Nova | Dark Bond | Life Siphon
Bane Darkfist •B•	N	12	–	Animate Bone Minions | Death Nova | Dark Bond | Life Siphon
Bone Dragon	R	18/20	–/100	Dmg 13-35 (R-Prc) (L20) | Dodge | Choking Gas
Damis the Malignant •B•	N	17	–	Barbs | Desecrate Enchantments | Animate Bone Fiend | Life Siphon
Damned Cleric	Mk	17	–	Bane Signet | Infuse Health | Reversal of Fortune | Draw Conditions
Dracul Cadava •B•	Mk	17	–	Reversal of Fortune | Draw Conditions | Bane Signet
Dragon Lich	W	24	100	Dmg 68-100 (M-Blt) | Barrage | G.D
Essam Festerskull •B•	W	17	–	Phy +20 | Heavy Blow | Irresistible Blow | Warrior's Cunning | Healing Signet
Executioner	W	18	–	Phy +20 | Hammer Bash | (Staggering Blow) | (Warrior's Cunning) | ("I Will Avenge You!") | (Skull Crack)
Fareed the Unworthy •B•	W	17	–	Phy +20 | Heavy Blow | Irresistible Blow | Warrior's Cunning | Healing Signet
Fariq Earthturner •B•	Mk	17	–	Reversal of Fortune | Draw Conditions | Bane Signet
Ghazal the Corrupter •B•	N	17	–	Barbs | Desecrate Enchantments | Animate Bone Fiend | Life Siphon
Judgments Disciple	Mk	20	60	Shield of Judgment | Holy Strike | Balthazar's Aura | Reversal of Fortune
Necrid Horseman	N	18	–	Barbs | Animate Bone Fiend | Desecrate Enchantments
Nizza the Sickle •B•	W	12	–	Phy +20 | "I Will Survive!" | Irresistible Blow | Deflect Arrows | Healing Signet
Prince Rurik •B•	W	24	–	Hundred Blades | Final Thrust | Thrill of Victory | Deadly Riposte
Rotscale •B•	R	17	–	Primal Echoes | Choking Gas | Troll Unguent
Rotscale •B•	N	24	–	Prc +40, Blt -10, Lgt -30 | Heal Area | Life Attunement
Ruinwing •B•	R	17	–	Dodge | Primal Echoes | Choking Gas | Troll Unguent
Undertaker	W	20	80	Phy +20 | Earth Shaker | Irresistible Blow | Warrior's Cunning
Underworld Lord	N	20	60	Feast of Corruption | Feast of Corruption | Desecrate Enchant. | Well of Suffering
Zameel Dirge •B•	W	13	–	Phy +20 | "I Will Survive!" | Irresistible Blow | Deflect Arrows | Healing Signet
Zombie Captain	N	18	–	Barbs | Animate Bone Fiend | Desecrate Enchantments
Zombie Warlock	N	14/20	–/60	Death Nova | Animate Bone Minions | Rend Enchantments (20) | Dark Bond (14)
Zukra Cadava •B•	N	13	–	Animate Bone Minions | Death Nova | Dark Bond | Life Siphon

See page 187 for table guidelines.

The Spoils of Victory

The following table contains all the quests available in the game at release time, along with their rewards. Each skill listing pertains to a given profession, e.g., if a Mesmer completes the The Lost Princess Quest, she is rewarded with the Mesmer skill Blackout. Expect to see additional quests and rewards over time.

Quest Rewards

Quest Name	EXP	Item 1	Item 2	Mesmer Skill	Necromancer Skill	Elementalist Skill	Monk Skill	Warrior Skill	Ranger Skill
The Ascalon Settlement	500	–	–	Wastrel's Worry	Enfeeble	Lightning Orb	Heal Other	Final Thrust	Throw Dirt
The Villainy of Galrath	500	Smiting Staff	Long Sword	–	–	–	–	–	–
Bandit Trouble	500	Tall Shield	–	–	–	–	–	–	–
The Weaver of Nebo	500	–	–	–	–	–	–	–	–
To Kryta: Journey's End	500	–	–	–	–	–	–	–	–
Graven Images	600	–	–	Mantra of Lightning	Dark Aura	Inferno	Dwayna's Kiss	Axe Twist	Determined Shot
The Hot Springs Murders	500	–	–	Illusion of Weakness	Blood of the Master	Grasping Earth	Mend Ailment	Counter Blow	Bestial Pounce
The Last Hog	500	–	–	Leech Signet	Blood Ritual	Gale	Life Attunement	Staggering Blow	Otyugh's Cry
The Lost Princess	500	–	–	Blackout	Price of Failure	Earthquake	Balthazar's Aura	Balanced Stance	Edge of Extinction
Duties of a Lionguard	500	–	–	–	–	–	–	–	–
The Royal Papers	750	–	–	Mantra of Earth	Animate Bone Minions	Fire Attunement	Scourge Healing	Savage Slash	Concussion Shot
Blankets for the Settlers	500	Longbow	–	–	–	–	–	–	–
Orrian Excavation	400	–	–	–	–	–	–	–	–
Malaquire's Test	500	–	–	Signet of Capture	–	–	–	–	–
Reversing the Skales	500	Protective Icon	Smiting Rod	–	–	–	–	–	–
The Undead Hordes	500	–	–	Inspired Enchantment	Plague Touch	Water Attunement	Holy Veil	Griffon's Sweep	Symbiosis
Lagaan's Ordeal	500	Protective Icon	–	–	–	–	–	–	–
Lagaan's Gratitude	500	Protective Icon	–	–	–	–	–	–	–
Report to the White Mantle	500	Smiting Rod	–	–	–	–	–	–	–
A Belated Betrothal	1000	–	–	Ether Lord	Signet of Agony	Windborne Speed	Mend Condition	Bull's Strike	Tiger's Fury
Ancient Secrets	1000	–	–	–	–	–	–	–	–
The Forgotten Ones	1000	–	–	Elemental Resistance	Animate Bone Fiend	Incendiary Bonds	Vengeance	Defensive Stance	Precision Shot
Forgotten Wisdom	1500	–	–	–	–	–	–	–	–
Ghostly Vengeance	1000	–	–	Mantra of Persistence	Malaise	Obsidian Flame	Blessed Aura	Shield Bash	Dust Trap
Into the Unknown	1000	–	–	Arcane Conundrum	Chilblains	Swirling Aura	Zealot's Fire	"Fear me!"	Winnowing
The Misplaced Sword	1000	–	–	Guilt	Well of the Profane	Flame Burst	Healing Touch	"Shields Up!"	Flame Trap
Sands Of Souls	500	–	–	–	–	–	–	–	–
The Mesmer's Path	1000	–	–	–	–	–	–	–	–
The Necromancer's Path	1000	–	–	–	–	–	–	–	–
The Elementalist's Path	1000	–	–	–	–	–	–	–	–
The Monk's Path	1000	–	–	–	–	–	–	–	–
The Warrior's Path	1000	–	–	–	–	–	–	–	–
The Ranger's Path	1000	–	–	–	–	–	–	–	–
War Preparations	250	–	–	–	–	–	–	–	–
The Hunter's Horn	500	Longbow	–	–	–	–	–	–	–
The Supremacy of Air	250	–	–	–	–	–	–	–	–
Rites of Remembrance	250	Protective Icon	–	–	–	–	–	–	–
Little Thom's Big Cloak	250	Battle Axe	Smiting Rod	–	–	–	–	–	–
The Vineyard Problem	250	–	–	–	–	–	–	–	–
Bandit Raid	250	Protective Icon	Tall Shield	–	–	–	–	–	–
A Test of Marksmanship	250	–	–	–	–	–	–	–	–
The Power of Blood	250	–	–	–	–	–	–	–	–
The Rogue's Replacement	250	Smiting Staff	–	–	–	–	–	–	–
Charr in the Catacombs	250	–	–	–	–	–	–	–	–
Charr at the Gate	200	Long Sword	–	–	–	–	–	–	–
The Accursed Path	500	–	–	–	–	–	–	–	–
The Poison Devourer	250	Protective Icon	–	–	–	–	–	–	–
Domination Magic	250	–	–	–	–	–	–	–	–
The True King	750	Protective Icon	War Hammer	–	–	–	–	–	–
The Egg Hunter	150	–	–	–	–	–	–	–	–
The Worm Problem	250	Smiting Rod	–	–	–	–	–	–	–
The Prize Moa Bird	250	Smiting Staff	Long Sword	–	–	–	–	–	–
Further Adventures	250	–	–	–	–	–	–	–	–
The Wayward Wizard	250	Smiting Staff	–	–	–	–	–	–	–
Adventure with an Ally	100	–	–	Resurrection Signet	–	–	–	–	–
The Orchard	250	Battle Axe	Protective Icon	–	–	–	–	–	–
A Gift for Althea	250	Protective Icon	–	–	–	–	–	–	–
Gwen's Flute	250	–	–	–	–	–	–	–	–
Warrior's Challenge	250	–	–	–	–	–	–	–	–

Quest Rewards cont.

Quest Name	EXP	Item 1	Item 2	Mesmer Skill	Necromancer Skill	Elementalist Skill	Monk Skill	Warrior Skill	Ranger Skill
Tithe for Ashford Abbey	250	–	–	–	–	–	–	–	–
The Charr Threat	250	Tall Shield	–	–	–	–	–	–	–
A New Mesmer Trainer	250	–	–	–	–	–	–	–	–
A New Necromancer Trainer	250	–	–	–	–	–	–	–	–
A New Elementalist Trainer	250	–	–	–	–	–	–	–	–
A New Monk Trainer	250	–	–	–	–	–	–	–	–
A New Warrior Trainer	250	–	–	–	–	–	–	–	–
A New Ranger Trainer	250	–	–	–	–	–	–	–	–
Across the Wall	250	Longbow	Smiting Rod	–	–	–	–	–	–
Poor Tenant	500	Protective Icon	–	–	–	–	–	–	–
A Mesmer's Burden	250	–	–	–	–	–	–	–	–
The Necromancer's Novice	250	–	–	–	–	–	–	–	–
The Elementalist Experiment	250	–	–	–	–	–	–	–	–
A Monk's Mission	250	–	–	–	–	–	–	–	–
Grawl Invasion	250	–	–	–	–	–	–	–	–
The Ranger's Companion	250	–	–	–	–	–	–	–	–
Protection Prayers	250	–	–	–	–	–	–	–	–
Opposition to the King	500	–	–	–	–	–	–	–	–
A Second Profession	250	–	–	–	–	–	–	–	–
Message from a Friend	100	–	–	–	–	–	–	–	–
Mesmer Test	500	–	–	Empathy	Ether Feast	–	–	–	–
Necromancer Test	500	–	–	Vampiric Gaze	Deathly Swarm	–	–	–	–
Elementalist Test	500	–	–	Flare	Aura of Restoration	–	–	–	–
Monk Test	500	–	–	Healing Breeze	Banish	–	–	–	–
Warrior Test	500	–	–	Frenzy	Healing Signet	–	–	–	–
Ranger Test	500	–	–	Power Shot	Troll Unguent	–	–	–	–
The Blessings of Balthazar	250	–	–	–	–	–	–	–	–
Unnatural Growths	250	–	–	–	–	–	–	–	–
Trouble in the Woods	500	War Hammer	–	–	–	–	–	–	–
White Mantle Wrath: A Helping Hand	500	Protective Icon	–	–	–	–	–	–	–
Urgent Warning	500	Battle Axe	Smiting Staff	–	–	–	–	–	–
Blood And Smoke	500	–	–	Spirit Shackles	Barbed Signet	Meteor	Protective Spirit	"I Will Survive!"	Savage Shot
Dropping Eaves	500	–	–	Spirit of Failure	Death Nova	Iron Mist	Rebirth	Shield Stance	Predatory Season
A Brother's Fury	500	Longbow	Smiting Rod	–	–	–	–	–	–
Eye for Profit	500	–	–	Hex Breaker	Dark Bond	Air Attunement	Smite Hex	Axe Rake	Antidote Signet
Mysterious Message	500	–	–	Ethereal Burden	Well of Suffering	Stone Daggers	Healing Seed	Pure Strike	Storm Chaser
The Price of Steel	500	–	–	Arcane Thievery	Rend Enchantments	Conjure Frost	Contemplation of Purity	Crushing Blow	Barbed Trap
White Mantle Wrath: Demagogue's Vanguard	500	Smiting Rod	–	–	–	–	–	–	–
Passage Through the Dark River	500	Protective Icon	–	–	–	–	–	–	–
Servants of Grenth	5000	–	–	–	–	–	–	–	–
Demon Assassin	5000	–	–	–	–	–	–	–	–
Imprisoned Spirits	5000	–	–	–	–	–	–	–	–
The Four Horsemen	5000	–	–	–	–	–	–	–	–
Terrorweb Queen	5000	–	–	–	–	–	–	–	–
Wrathful Spirits	5000	–	–	–	–	–	–	–	–
Charr Reinforcements	500	–	–	Distracting Shot	Call of Haste	–	–	–	–
Symon's History of Ascalon	2000	–	–	–	–	–	–	–	–
Experimental Elixir	500	–	–	Shatter Hex	–	–	–	–	–
Trying Times	300	–	–	Chaos Storm	Mantra of Flame	–	–	–	–
Unnatural Creatures	250	–	–	Diversion	–	–	–	–	–
The Charr Patrol	250	–	–	Feral Lunge	Favorable Winds	–	–	–	–
The Charr Staging Area	300	–	–	Dodge	Quickening Zephyr	–	–	–	–
A Cure for Ralena	300	–	–	Illusion of Haste	Energy Burn	–	–	–	–
Casualty Report	150	–	–	Shadow Strike	–	–	–	–	–
Death in the Ruins	250	–	–	Dark Pact	Mark of Pain	–	–	–	–
Fallen Soldiers	250	–	–	Soul Feast	–	–	–	–	–
Oberan's Rage	350	–	–	Parasitic Bond	Putrid Explosion	–	–	–	–
Althea's Ashes	2000	–	–	–	–	–	–	–	–
Hammer and Anvil	500	Tall Shield	–	–	–	–	–	–	–
The Geomancer's Test	500	–	–	Magnetic Aura	Earth Attunement	–	–	–	–
The Way of the Geomancer	500	–	–	–	–	–	–	–	–
Shalev's Task	300	–	–	Eruption	Shard Storm	–	–	–	–
Elemental Knowledge	250	–	–	Armor of Earth	Frozen Burst	–	–	–	–
The Duke's Daughter	2000	–	–	–	–	–	–	–	–
Barradin's Advance	250	–	–	–	–	–	–	–	–
Fires in the East	500	Smiting Staff	Long Sword	–	–	–	–	–	–

Quest Rewards cont.

Quest Name	EXP	Item 1	Item 2	Mesmer Skill	Necromancer Skill	Elementalist Skill	Monk Skill	Warrior Skill	Ranger Skill
Fires in the North	1000	Smiting Rod	–	–	–	–	–	–	–
Frontier Gate Fugitives	1000	Longbow	Protective Icon	–	–	–	–	–	–
Helping the People of Ascalon	200	–	–	Energy Tap	Vile Touch	Lava Font	Mending	"For Great Justice!"	Penetrating Attack
Cities of Ascalon	1000	Protective Icon	Protective Icon	–	–	–	–	–	–
Counting the Fallen	500	Protective Icon	Protective Icon	–	–	–	–	–	–
Scavengers in Old Ascalon	500	Battle Axe	–	–	–	–	–	–	–
Garfazz Bloodfang	500	Smiting Rod	Long Sword	–	–	–	–	–	–
The King's Message	100	War Hammer	–	–	–	–	–	–	–
In Memory of Paulus	300	–	–	Resurrect	Live Vicariously	–	–	–	–
Protecting Ascalon	300	–	–	Heal Area	Vital Blessing	–	–	–	–
The Ambassador's Quandary	500	Battle Axe	Smiting Staff	–	–	–	–	–	–
Rastin's Ritual	500	–	–	–	–	–	–	–	–
A Mission of Peace	250	Protective Icon	–	–	–	–	–	–	–
The Troublesome Artifact	500	Protective Icon	–	–	–	–	–	–	–
Barradin's Stand	500	Tall Shield	–	–	–	–	–	–	–
Army Life	250	–	–	Mighty Blow	Dismember	–	–	–	–
Into the Breach	300	–	–	Penetrating Blow	Endure Pain	–	–	–	–
Military Matters	250	–	–	Power Attack	Sprint	–	–	–	–
The Red-Cloaked Deserter	1000	Longbow	Protective Icon	–	–	–	–	–	–
The Siege of Piken Square	500	Smiting Staff	War Hammer	–	–	–	–	–	–
Replacement Healers	500	–	–	Infuse Health	Strength of Honor	–	–	–	–
Regent Valley Defense	500	Longbow	–	–	–	–	–	–	–
Mesmerizing the Enemy	200	–	–	Power Leak	Conjure Phantasm	Ether Feast	Imagined Burden	–	–
The Stolen Artifact	200	–	–	Insidious Parasite	Life Siphon	Deathly Swarm	Animate Bone Horror	–	–
Scorched Earth	200	–	–	Ward Against Elements	–	–	–	–	–
Sowing Seeds	200	–	–	Heal Party	Bane Signet	Orison of Healing	–	–	–
Gargoyle Trouble	200	–	–	Wild Blow	Sever Artery	Gash	Healing Signet	–	–
Endangered Species	200	–	–	Hunter's Shot	Comfort Animal	Troll Unguent	Charm Animal	–	–
Supplies for the Duke	300	–	–	Weaken Armor	Distortion	Purge Conditions	"Watch Yourself!"	Called Shot	Ice Spikes
Ruins of Surmia	500	Smiting Rod	–	–	–	–	–	–	–
Vanguard Equipment	500	Protective Icon	–	–	–	–	–	–	–
Deliver a Message to My Wife	500	–	–	–	–	–	–	–	–
Recruits for Hollis	500	Protective Icon	–	–	–	–	–	–	–
The Krytan Ambassador	500	–	–	–	–	–	–	–	–
Defend the Wall	500	–	–	–	–	–	–	–	–
The Road to Borlis Pass	500	Protective Icon	–	–	–	–	–	–	–
To Kryta: The Ice Cave	500	–	–	–	–	–	–	–	–
The Stone Summit Champion	350	–	–	Fragility	Power Spike	Channeling	–	–	–
Renegade Necromancer	350	–	–	Necrotic Traversal	Defile Flesh	Well of Blood	–	–	–
The Deserters	500	–	–	Inspired Hex	Strip Enchantment	Ice Spear	Balthazar's Spirit	Bonetti's Defense	Serpent's Quickness
A Heart of Ice	350	–	–	Whirlwind	Ward Against Foes	Ice Prison	–	–	–
The Missing Artisan	500	–	–	–	–	–	–	–	–
Helping the Dwarves	250	–	–	Mantra of Frost	Suffering	Gale	Remove Hex	Protector's Strike	Debilitating Shot
Hungry Devourer	400	–	–	Shatter Enchantment	Rotting Flesh	Lightning Strike	Divine Spirit	Flurry	Pin Down
Oswalt's Epitaph	500	Protective Icon	–	–	–	–	–	–	–
Securing the Vale	500	–	–	Swift Chop	Irresistible Blow	Seeking Blade	–	–	–
Minaar's Trouble	500	Tall Shield	Protective Icon	–	–	–	–	–	–
Iron Horse War Machine	500	Smiting Staff	Longbow	–	–	–	–	–	–
Minaar's Worry	500	Battle Axe	–	–	–	–	–	–	–
Stone Summit Beastmasters	350	–	–	Whirling Defense	Winter	Call of Protection	–	–	–
The Hero's Journey	500	–	–	–	–	–	–	–	–
The Hero's Challenge	5000	–	–	–	–	–	–	–	–
Seeking the Seer	500	–	–	–	–	–	–	–	–
Shiverpeak Stragglers	500	Smiting Rod	War Hammer	–	–	–	–	–	–
The Way is Blocked	500	–	–	–	–	–	–	–	–
To Kryta: Refugees	500	–	–	–	–	–	–	–	–
The Wayward Monk	350	–	–	Vigorous Spirit	Pacifism	Divine Boon	–	–	–
Final Blow	500	–	–	–	–	–	–	–	–

PRIMA OFFICIAL GAME GUIDE

The Armory

Herein you'll find all the armor available in *Guild Wars* at release time, broken down into material costs and effects. Expect to see more armor items over time.

Armor

Name	Type	Gold	Material 1	Material 2	Material 3	Material 4	Armor Level	Effect 1	Effect 2	Effect 3
MESMER BOOTS										
Courtly Footwear	BOOTS	150	4 Bolts of Cloth	1 Bolt of Linen	0	0	30	+ 1 Energy Regen	+15 Armor while casting	–
Courtly Footwear	BOOTS	250	6 Bolts of Cloth	1 Bolt of Linen	0	0	39	+ 1 Energy Regen	+15 Armor while casting	–
Courtly Footwear	BOOTS	400	8 Bolts of Cloth	2 Bolts of Linen	0	0	45	+ 1 Energy Regen	+15 Armor while casting	–
Courtly Footwear	BOOTS	700	9 Bolts of Cloth	3 Bolts of Linen	0	0	51	+ 1 Energy Regen	+15 Armor while casting	–
Courtly Footwear	BOOTS	1,000	11 Bolts of Cloth	3 Bolts of Linen	0	0	57	+ 1 Energy Regen	+15 Armor while casting	–
Courtly Footwear	BOOTS	1,500	25 Bolts of Cloth	4 Bolts of Linen	0	0	60	+ 1 Energy Regen	+15 Armor while casting	–
Noble Footwear	BOOTS	15,000	50 Bolts of Cloth	5 Bolts of Damask	0	0	60	+ 1 Energy Regen	+15 Armor while casting	–
Noble Footwear	BOOTS	15,000	50 Bolts of Cloth	5 Bolts of Damask	15 Globs of Ectoplasm	15 Obsidian Shards	60	+ 1 Energy Regen	+15 Armor while casting	–
Enchanter's Footwear	BOOTS	150	4 Bolts of Cloth	1 Pile of Glittering Dust	0	0	30	+ 1 Energy Regen	Max Energy +1	–
Enchanter's Footwear	BOOTS	250	6 Bolts of Cloth	1 Pile of Glittering Dust	0	0	39	+ 1 Energy Regen	Max Energy +1	–
Enchanter's Footwear	BOOTS	400	8 Bolts of Cloth	2 Piles of Glittering Dust	0	0	45	+ 1 Energy Regen	Max Energy +1	–
Enchanter's Footwear	BOOTS	700	9 Bolts of Cloth	3 Piles of Glittering Dust	0	0	51	+ 1 Energy Regen	Max Energy +1	–
Enchanter's Footwear	BOOTS	1,000	11 Bolts of Cloth	3 Piles of Glittering Dust	0	0	57	+ 1 Energy Regen	Max Energy +1	–
Enchanter's Footwear	BOOTS	1,500	25 Bolts of Cloth	4 Piles of Glittering Dust	0	0	60	+ 1 Energy Regen	Max Energy +1	–
Enchanter's Footwear	BOOTS	15,000	50 Bolts of Cloth	5 Piles of Glittering Dust	0	0	60	+ 1 Energy Regen	Max Energy +1	–
Enchanter's Footwear	BOOTS	15,000	50 Bolts of Cloth	5 Piles of Glittering Dust	15 Globs of Ectoplasm	15 Obsidian Shards	60	+ 1 Energy Regen	Max Energy +1	–
Performer's Footwear	BOOTS	150	4 Bolts of Cloth	1 Silk	0	0	30	+ 1 Energy Regen	+15 Armor while casting	–
Performer's Footwear	BOOTS	250	6 Bolts of Cloth	1 Silk	0	0	39	+ 1 Energy Regen	+15 Armor while casting	–
Performer's Footwear	BOOTS	400	8 Bolts of Cloth	2 Silk	0	0	45	+ 1 Energy Regen	+15 Armor while casting	–
Performer's Footwear	BOOTS	700	9 Bolts of Cloth	3 Silk	0	0	51	+ 1 Energy Regen	+15 Armor while casting	–
Performer's Footwear	BOOTS	1,000	11 Bolts of Cloth	3 Silk	0	0	57	+ 1 Energy Regen	+15 Armor while casting	–
Performer's Footwear	BOOTS	1,500	25 Bolts of Cloth	4 Silk	0	0	60	+ 1 Energy Regen	+15 Armor while casting	–
Virtuoso's Footwear	BOOTS	15,000	50 Bolts of Cloth	5 Silk	0	0	60	+ 1 Energy Regen	+15 Armor while casting	–
Virtuoso's Footwear	BOOTS	15,000	50 Bolts of Cloth	5 Silk	15 Globs of Ectoplasm	15 Obsidian Shards	60	+ 1 Energy Regen	+15 Armor while casting	–
Rogue's Footwear	BOOTS	50	2 Bolts of Cloth	0	0	0	15	+ 1 Energy Regen	Armor vs. Physical +10	Max Energy -1
Rogue's Footwear	BOOTS	150	4 Bolts of Cloth	1 Leather Square	0	0	30	+ 1 Energy Regen	Armor vs. Physical +10	Max Energy -1
Rogue's Footwear	BOOTS	250	6 Bolts of Cloth	1 Leather Square	0	0	39	+ 1 Energy Regen	Armor vs. Physical +10	Max Energy -1
Rogue's Footwear	BOOTS	400	8 Bolts of Cloth	2 Leather Squares	0	0	45	+ 1 Energy Regen	Armor vs. Physical +10	Max Energy -1
Rogue's Footwear	BOOTS	700	9 Bolts of Cloth	3 Leather Squares	0	0	51	+ 1 Energy Regen	Armor vs. Physical +10	Max Energy -1
Rogue's Footwear	BOOTS	1,000	11 Bolts of Cloth	3 Leather Squares	0	0	57	+ 1 Energy Regen	Armor vs. Physical +10	Max Energy -1
Rogue's Footwear	BOOTS	1,500	25 Bolts of Cloth	4 Leather Squares	0	0	60	+ 1 Energy Regen	Armor vs. Physical +10	Max Energy -1
Rogue's Footwear	BOOTS	15,000	50 Bolts of Cloth	5 Elonian Leather Squares	0	0	60	+ 1 Energy Regen	Armor vs. Physical +10	Max Energy -1
Rogue's Footwear	BOOTS	15,000	50 Bolts of Cloth	5 Elonian Leather Squares	15 Globs of Ectoplasm	15 Obsidian Shards	60	+ 1 Energy Regen	Armor vs. Physical +10	Max Energy -1
Regal Footwear	BOOTS	150	4 Bolts of Cloth	1 Silk	0	0	35	+ 1 Energy Regen	Armor vs. Earth -5	–
Regal Footwear	BOOTS	250	6 Bolts of Cloth	1 Silk	0	0	44	+ 1 Energy Regen	Armor vs. Earth -5	–
Regal Footwear	BOOTS	400	8 Bolts of Cloth	2 Silk	0	0	50	+ 1 Energy Regen	Armor vs. Earth -5	–
Regal Footwear	BOOTS	700	9 Bolts of Cloth	3 Silk	0	0	56	+ 1 Energy Regen	Armor vs. Earth -5	–
Regal Footwear	BOOTS	1,000	11 Bolts of Cloth	3 Silk	0	0	62	+ 1 Energy Regen	Armor vs. Earth -5	–
Regal Footwear	BOOTS	1,500	25 Bolts of Cloth	4 Silk	0	0	65	+ 1 Energy Regen	Armor vs. Earth -5	–
Regal Footwear	BOOTS	15,000	50 Bolts of Cloth	5 Silk	0	0	65	+ 1 Energy Regen	Armor vs. Earth -5	–
Regal Footwear	BOOTS	15,000	50 Bolts of Cloth	5 Silk	15 Globs of Ectoplasm	15 Obsidian Shards	65	+ 1 Energy Regen	Armor vs. Earth -5	–
Stylish Footwear	BOOTS	10	1 Bolt of Cloth	0	0	0	5	+ 1 Energy Regen	–	–
Stylish Footwear	BOOTS	50	1 Bolt of Cloth	0	0	0	15	+ 1 Energy Regen	–	–
Stylish Footwear	BOOTS	150	2 Bolts of Cloth	0	0	0	30	+ 1 Energy Regen	–	–
Stylish Footwear	BOOTS	250	3 Bolts of Cloth	0	0	0	39	+ 1 Energy Regen	–	–
Stylish Footwear	BOOTS	400	4 Bolts of Cloth	0	0	0	45	+ 1 Energy Regen	–	–
Stylish Footwear	BOOTS	700	8 Bolts of Cloth	0	0	0	51	+ 1 Energy Regen	–	–
Stylish Footwear	BOOTS	1,000	9 Bolts of Cloth	0	0	0	57	+ 1 Energy Regen	–	–
Stylish Footwear	BOOTS	1,500	11 Bolts of Cloth	0	0	0	60	+ 1 Energy Regen	–	–
NECROMANCER BOOTS										
Bonelace Boots	BOOTS	50	2 Tanned Hide Squares	0	0	0	15	+ 1 Energy Regen	Armor vs. Piercing +15	–
Bonelace Boots	BOOTS	150	4 Tanned Hide Squares	4 Bone	0	0	30	+ 1 Energy Regen	Armor vs. Piercing +15	–
Bonelace Boots	BOOTS	250	6 Tanned Hide Squares	4 Bone	0	0	39	+ 1 Energy Regen	Armor vs. Piercing +15	–
Bonelace Boots	BOOTS	400	8 Tanned Hide Squares	8 Bone	0	0	45	+ 1 Energy Regen	Armor vs. Piercing +15	–
Bonelace Boots	BOOTS	700	9 Tanned Hide Squares	9 Bone	0	0	51	+ 1 Energy Regen	Armor vs. Piercing +15	–
Bonelace Boots	BOOTS	1,000	11 Tanned Hide Squares	11 Bone	0	0	57	+ 1 Energy Regen	Armor vs. Piercing +15	–
Bonelace Boots	BOOTS	1,500	25 Tanned Hide Squares	25 Bone	0	0	60	+ 1 Energy Regen	Armor vs. Piercing +15	–

Armor cont.

Name	Type	Gold	Material 1	Material 2	Material 3	Material 4	Armor Level	Effect 1	Effect 2	Effect 3
Bonelace Boots	BOOTS	15,000	50 Tanned Hide Squares	50 Bone	0	0	60	+ 1 Energy Regen	Armor vs. Piercing +15	–
Bonelace Boots	BOOTS	15,000	50 Tanned Hide Squares	50 Bone	15 Globs of Ectoplasm	15 Obsidian Shards	60	+ 1 Energy Regen	Armor vs. Piercing +15	–
Tormentor's Boots	BOOTS	150	4 Tanned Hide Squares	1 Steel Ingot	0	0	40	+ 1 Energy Regen	Increased damage vs. Holy	–
Tormentor's Boots	BOOTS	250	6 Tanned Hide Squares	1 Steel Ingot	0	0	49	+ 1 Energy Regen	Increased damage vs. Holy	–
Tormentor's Boots	BOOTS	400	8 Tanned Hide Squares	2 Steel Ingots	0	0	55	+ 1 Energy Regen	Increased damage vs. Holy	–
Tormentor's Boots	BOOTS	700	9 Tanned Hide Squares	3 Steel Ingots	0	0	61	+ 1 Energy Regen	Increased damage vs. Holy	–
Tormentor's Boots	BOOTS	1,000	11 Tanned Hide Squares	3 Steel Ingots	0	0	67	+ 1 Energy Regen	Increased damage vs. Holy	–
Tormentor's Boots	BOOTS	1,500	25 Tanned Hide Squares	4 Steel Ingots	0	0	70	+ 1 Energy Regen	Increased damage vs. Holy	–
Tormentor's Boots	BOOTS	15,000	50 Tanned Hide Squares	5 Deldrimor Steel Ingots	0	0	70	+ 1 Energy Regen	Increased damage vs. Holy	–
Tormentor's Boots	BOOTS	15,000	50 Tanned Hide Squares	5 Deldrimor Steel Ingots	15 Globs of Ectoplasm	15 Obsidian Shards	70	+ 1 Energy Regen	Increased damage vs. Holy	–
Fanatic's Boots	BOOTS	150	4 Tanned Hide Squares	1 Leather Square	0	0	30	+ 1 Energy Regen	Armor vs. Piercing +15	–
Fanatic's Boots	BOOTS	250	6 Tanned Hide Squares	1 Leather Square	0	0	39	+ 1 Energy Regen	Armor vs. Piercing +15	–
Fanatic's Boots	BOOTS	400	8 Tanned Hide Squares	2 Leather Squares	0	0	45	+ 1 Energy Regen	Armor vs. Piercing +15	–
Fanatic's Boots	BOOTS	700	9 Tanned Hide Squares	3 Leather Squares	0	0	51	+ 1 Energy Regen	Armor vs. Piercing +15	–
Fanatic's Boots	BOOTS	1,000	11 Tanned Hide Squares	3 Leather Squares	0	0	57	+ 1 Energy Regen	Armor vs. Piercing +15	–
Fanatic's Boots	BOOTS	1,500	25 Tanned Hide Squares	4 Leather Squares	0	0	60	+ 1 Energy Regen	Armor vs. Piercing +15	–
Cultist's Boots	BOOTS	15,000	50 Tanned Hide Squares	5 Elonian Leather Squares	0	0	60	+ 1 Energy Regen	Armor vs. Piercing +15	–
Cultist's Boots	BOOTS	15,000	50 Tanned Hide Squares	5 Elonian Leather Squares	15 Globs of Ectoplasm	15 Obsidian Shards	60	+ 1 Energy Regen	Armor vs. Piercing +15	–
Necrotic Boots	BOOTS	150	4 Tanned Hide Squares	1 Shell	0	0	40	+ 1 Energy Regen	Increased damage vs. Holy	–
Necrotic Boots	BOOTS	250	6 Tanned Hide Squares	1 Shell	0	0	49	+ 1 Energy Regen	Increased damage vs. Holy	–
Necrotic Boots	BOOTS	400	8 Tanned Hide Squares	2 Shells	0	0	55	+ 1 Energy Regen	Increased damage vs. Holy	–
Necrotic Boots	BOOTS	700	9 Tanned Hide Squares	3 Shells	0	0	61	+ 1 Energy Regen	Increased damage vs. Holy	–
Necrotic Boots	BOOTS	1,000	11 Tanned Hide Squares	3 Shells	0	0	67	+ 1 Energy Regen	Increased damage vs. Holy	–
Necrotic Boots	BOOTS	1,500	25 Tanned Hide Squares	4 Shells	0	0	70	+ 1 Energy Regen	Increased damage vs. Holy	–
Necrotic Boots	BOOTS	15,000	50 Tanned Hide Squares	5 Shells	0	0	70	+ 1 Energy Regen	Increased damage vs. Holy	–
Necrotic Boots	BOOTS	15,000	50 Tanned Hide Squares	5 Shells	15 Globs of Ectoplasm	15 Obsidian Shards	70	+ 1 Energy Regen	Increased damage vs. Holy	–
Foot Scar Pattern	BOOTS	150	4 Rolls of Parchment	0	0	0	30	+ 1 Energy Regen	Max Energy +1	–
Foot Scar Pattern	BOOTS	200	6 Rolls of Parchment	1 Feather	0	0	39	+ 1 Energy Regen	Max Energy +1	–
Foot Scar Pattern	BOOTS	300	8 Rolls of Parchment	2 Feathers	0	0	45	+ 1 Energy Regen	Max Energy +1	–
Foot Scar Pattern	BOOTS	400	9 Rolls of Parchment	3 Feathers	0	0	51	+ 1 Energy Regen	Max Energy +1	–
Foot Scar Pattern	BOOTS	600	11 Rolls of Parchment	3 Feathers	0	0	57	+ 1 Energy Regen	Max Energy +1	–
Foot Scar Pattern	BOOTS	800	25 Rolls of Parchment	4 Feathers	0	0	60	+ 1 Energy Regen	Max Energy +1	–
Foot Scar Pattern	BOOTS	8,000	50 Rolls of Vellum	5 Feathers	0	0	60	+ 1 Energy Regen	Max Energy +1	–
Foot Scar Pattern	BOOTS	8,000	50 Rolls of Vellum	5 Feathers	15 Globs of Ectoplasm	0	60	+ 1 Energy Regen	Max Energy +1	–
Bloodstained Boots	BOOTS	400	8 Tanned Hide Squares	2 Scales	0	0	45	+ 1 Energy Regen	Increased casting speed with Corpse spells	–
Bloodstained Boots	BOOTS	700	9 Tanned Hide Squares	3 Scales	0	0	51	+ 1 Energy Regen	Increased casting speed with Corpse spells	–
Bloodstained Boots	BOOTS	1,000	11 Tanned Hide Squares	3 Scales	0	0	57	+ 1 Energy Regen	Increased casting speed with Corpse spells	–
Bloodstained Boots	BOOTS	1,500	25 Tanned Hide Squares	4 Scales	0	0	60	+ 1 Energy Regen	Increased casting speed with Corpse spells	–
Necromancer's Boots	BOOTS	50	1 Tanned Hide Square	0	0	0	15	+ 1 Energy Regen	–	–
Necromancer's Boots	BOOTS	150	2 Tanned Hide Squares	0	0	0	30	+ 1 Energy Regen	–	–
Necromancer's Boots	BOOTS	250	3 Tanned Hide Squares	0	0	0	39	+ 1 Energy Regen	–	–
Necromancer's Boots	BOOTS	400	4 Tanned Hide Squares	0	0	0	45	+ 1 Energy Regen	–	–
Necromancer's Boots	BOOTS	700	8 Tanned Hide Squares	0	0	0	51	+ 1 Energy Regen	–	–
Necromancer's Boots	BOOTS	1,000	9 Tanned Hide Squares	0	0	0	57	+ 1 Energy Regen	–	–
Necromancer's Boots	BOOTS	1,500	11 Tanned Hide Squares	0	0	0	60	+ 1 Energy Regen	–	–
Pagan Boots	BOOTS	150	4 Tanned Hide Squares	1 Granite Slab	0	0	40	+ 1 Energy Regen	Increased damage vs. Holy	–
Pagan Boots	BOOTS	250	6 Tanned Hide Squares	1 Granite Slab	0	0	49	+ 1 Energy Regen	Increased damage vs. Holy	–
Pagan Boots	BOOTS	400	8 Tanned Hide Squares	2 Granite Slabs	0	0	55	+ 1 Energy Regen	Increased damage vs. Holy	–
Pagan Boots	BOOTS	700	9 Tanned Hide Squares	3 Granite Slabs	0	0	61	+ 1 Energy Regen	Increased damage vs. Holy	–
Pagan Boots	BOOTS	1,000	11 Tanned Hide Squares	3 Granite Slabs	0	0	67	+ 1 Energy Regen	Increased damage vs. Holy	–
Pagan Boots	BOOTS	1,500	25 Tanned Hide Squares	4 Granite Slabs	0	0	70	+ 1 Energy Regen	Increased damage vs. Holy	–
Blasphemer's Boots	BOOTS	15,000	50 Tanned Hide Squares	5 Granite Slabs	0	0	70	+ 1 Energy Regen	Increased damage vs. Holy	–

ELEMENTALIST BOOTS

Name	Type	Gold	Material 1	Material 2	Material 3	Material 4	Armor Level	Effect 1	Effect 2	Effect 3
Aeromancer's Shoes	BOOTS	150	4 Bolts of Cloth	1 Bolt of Linen	0	0	30	+ 1 Energy Regen	Armor vs. Lightning +15	–
Aeromancer's Shoes	BOOTS	250	6 Bolts of Cloth	1 Bolt of Linen	0	0	39	+ 1 Energy Regen	Armor vs. Lightning +15	–
Aeromancer's Shoes	BOOTS	400	8 Bolts of Cloth	2 Bolts of Linen	0	0	45	+ 1 Energy Regen	Armor vs. Lightning +15	–
Aeromancer's Shoes	BOOTS	700	9 Bolts of Cloth	3 Bolts of Linen	0	0	51	+ 1 Energy Regen	Armor vs. Lightning +15	–
Aeromancer's Shoes	BOOTS	1,000	11 Bolts of Cloth	3 Bolts of Linen	0	0	57	+ 1 Energy Regen	Armor vs. Lightning +15	–
Aeromancer's Shoes	BOOTS	1,500	25 Bolts of Cloth	4 Bolts of Linen	0	0	60	+ 1 Energy Regen	Armor vs. Lightning +15	–
Aeromancer's Shoes	BOOTS	15,000	50 Bolts of Cloth	5 Bolts of Damask	0	0	60	+ 1 Energy Regen	Armor vs. Lightning +15	–
Aeromancer's Shoes	BOOTS	15,000	50 Bolts of Cloth	5 Bolts of Damask	15 Globs of Ectoplasm	15 Obsidian Shards	60	+ 1 Energy Regen	Armor vs. Lightning +15	–
Geomancer's Shoes	BOOTS	150	4 Bolts of Cloth	1 Granite Slab	0	0	30	+ 1 Energy Regen	Armor vs. Earth +15	–
Geomancer's Shoes	BOOTS	250	6 Bolts of Cloth	1 Granite Slab	0	0	39	+ 1 Energy Regen	Armor vs. Earth +15	–

Armor cont.

Name	Type	Gold	Material 1	Material 2	Material 3	Material 4	Armor Level	Effect 1	Effect 2	Effect 3
Geomancer's Shoes	BOOTS	400	8 Bolts of Cloth	2 Granite Slabs	0	0	45	+ 1 Energy Regen	Armor vs. Earth +15	–
Geomancer's Shoes	BOOTS	700	9 Bolts of Cloth	3 Granite Slabs	0	0	51	+ 1 Energy Regen	Armor vs. Earth +15	–
Geomancer's Shoes	BOOTS	1,000	11 Bolts of Cloth	3 Granite Slabs	0	0	57	+ 1 Energy Regen	Armor vs. Earth +15	–
Geomancer's Shoes	BOOTS	1,500	25 Bolts of Cloth	4 Granite Slabs	0	0	60	+ 1 Energy Regen	Armor vs. Earth +15	–
Geomancer's Shoes	BOOTS	15,000	50 Bolts of Cloth	5 Granite Slabs	0	0	60	+ 1 Energy Regen	Armor vs. Earth +15	–
Geomancer's Shoes	BOOTS	15,000	50 Bolts of Cloth	5 Granite Slabs	15 Globs of Ectoplasm	15 Obsidian Shards	60	+ 1 Energy Regen	Armor vs. Earth +15	–
Pyromancer's Shoes	BOOTS	50	2 Bolts of Cloth	0	0	0	15	+ 1 Energy Regen	Armor vs. Fire +15	–
Pyromancer's Shoes	BOOTS	150	4 Bolts of Cloth	1 Scale	0	0	30	+ 1 Energy Regen	Armor vs. Fire +15	–
Pyromancer's Shoes	BOOTS	250	6 Bolts of Cloth	1 Scale	0	0	39	+ 1 Energy Regen	Armor vs. Fire +15	–
Pyromancer's Shoes	BOOTS	400	8 Bolts of Cloth	2 Scales	0	0	45	+ 1 Energy Regen	Armor vs. Fire +15	–
Pyromancer's Shoes	BOOTS	700	9 Bolts of Cloth	3 Scales	0	0	51	+ 1 Energy Regen	Armor vs. Fire +15	–
Pyromancer's Shoes	BOOTS	1,000	11 Bolts of Cloth	3 Scales	0	0	57	+ 1 Energy Regen	Armor vs. Fire +15	–
Pyromancer's Shoes	BOOTS	1,500	25 Bolts of Cloth	4 Scales	0	0	60	+ 1 Energy Regen	Armor vs. Fire +15	–
Pyromancer's Shoes	BOOTS	15,000	50 Bolts of Cloth	5 Scales	0	0	60	+ 1 Energy Regen	Armor vs. Fire +15	–
Pyromancer's Shoes	BOOTS	15,000	50 Bolts of Cloth	5 Scales	15 Globs of Ectoplasm	15 Obsidian Shards	60	+ 1 Energy Regen	Armor vs. Fire +15	–
Adept's Shoes	BOOTS	1,000	11 Bolts of Cloth	3 Silk	0	0	57	+ 1 Energy Regen	Armor vs. Elemental +5	–
Adept's Shoes	BOOTS	1,500	25 Bolts of Cloth	4 Silk	0	0	60	+ 1 Energy Regen	Armor vs. Elemental +5	–
Master's Shoes	BOOTS	15,000	50 Bolts of Cloth	5 Silk	0	0	60	+ 1 Energy Regen	Armor vs. Elemental +5	–
Elementalist's Shoes	BOOTS	50	1 Bolt of Cloth	0	0	0	15	+ 1 Energy Regen	–	–
Elementalist's Shoes	BOOTS	150	2 Bolts of Cloth	0	0	0	30	+ 1 Energy Regen	–	–
Elementalist's Shoes	BOOTS	250	3 Bolts of Cloth	0	0	0	39	+ 1 Energy Regen	–	–
Elementalist's Shoes	BOOTS	400	4 Bolts of Cloth	0	0	0	45	+ 1 Energy Regen	–	–
Elementalist's Shoes	BOOTS	700	8 Bolts of Cloth	0	0	0	51	+ 1 Energy Regen	–	–
Elementalist's Shoes	BOOTS	1,000	9 Bolts of Cloth	0	0	0	57	+ 1 Energy Regen	–	–
Elementalist's Shoes	BOOTS	1,500	11 Bolts of Cloth	0	0	0	60	+ 1 Energy Regen	–	–
Hydromancer's Shoes	BOOTS	150	4 Bolts of Cloth	1 Shell	0	0	30	+ 1 Energy Regen	Armor vs. Cold +15	–
Hydromancer's Shoes	BOOTS	250	6 Bolts of Cloth	1 Shell	0	0	39	+ 1 Energy Regen	Armor vs. Cold +15	–
Hydromancer's Shoes	BOOTS	400	8 Bolts of Cloth	2 Shells	0	0	45	+ 1 Energy Regen	Armor vs. Cold +15	–
Hydromancer's Shoes	BOOTS	700	9 Bolts of Cloth	3 Shells	0	0	51	+ 1 Energy Regen	Armor vs. Cold +15	–
Hydromancer's Shoes	BOOTS	1,000	11 Bolts of Cloth	3 Shells	0	0	57	+ 1 Energy Regen	Armor vs. Cold +15	–
Hydromancer's Shoes	BOOTS	1,500	25 Bolts of Cloth	4 Shells	0	0	60	+ 1 Energy Regen	Armor vs. Cold +15	–
Hydromancer's Shoes	BOOTS	15,000	50 Bolts of Cloth	5 Shells	0	0	60	+ 1 Energy Regen	Armor vs. Cold +15	–
Hydromancer's Shoes	BOOTS	15,000	50 Bolts of Cloth	5 Shells	15 Globs of Ectoplasm	15 Obsidian Shards	60	+ 1 Energy Regen	Armor vs. Cold +15	–

MONK BOOTS

Name	Type	Gold	Material 1	Material 2	Material 3	Material 4	Armor Level	Effect 1	Effect 2	Effect 3
Silk-Laced Sandals	BOOTS	150	4 Bolts of Cloth	1 Silk	0	0	35	+ 1 Energy Regen	Armor vs. Cold -5	–
Silk-Laced Sandals	BOOTS	250	6 Bolts of Cloth	1 Silk	0	0	44	+ 1 Energy Regen	Armor vs. Cold -5	–
Silk-Laced Sandals	BOOTS	400	8 Bolts of Cloth	2 Silk	0	0	50	+ 1 Energy Regen	Armor vs. Cold -5	–
Silk-Laced Sandals	BOOTS	700	9 Bolts of Cloth	3 Silk	0	0	56	+ 1 Energy Regen	Armor vs. Cold -5	–
Silk-Laced Sandals	BOOTS	1,000	11 Bolts of Cloth	3 Silk	0	0	62	+ 1 Energy Regen	Armor vs. Cold -5	–
Silk-Laced Sandals	BOOTS	1,500	25 Bolts of Cloth	4 Silk	0	0	65	+ 1 Energy Regen	Armor vs. Cold -5	–
Silk-Laced Sandals	BOOTS	15,000	50 Bolts of Cloth	5 Silk	0	0	65	+ 1 Energy Regen	Armor vs. Cold -5	–
Silk-Laced Sandals	BOOTS	15,000	50 Bolts of Cloth	5 Silk	15 Globs of Ectoplasm	15 Obsidian Shards	65	+ 1 Energy Regen	Armor vs. Cold -5	–
Sacred Sandals	BOOTS	150	4 Bolts of Cloth	1 Bolt of Linen	0	0	30	+ 1 Energy Regen	Armor vs. Elemental +5	–
Sacred Sandals	BOOTS	250	6 Bolts of Cloth	1 Bolt of Linen	0	0	39	+ 1 Energy Regen	Armor vs. Elemental +5	–
Sacred Sandals	BOOTS	400	8 Bolts of Cloth	2 Bolts of Linen	0	0	45	+ 1 Energy Regen	Armor vs. Elemental +5	–
Sacred Sandals	BOOTS	700	9 Bolts of Cloth	3 Bolts of Linen	0	0	51	+ 1 Energy Regen	Armor vs. Elemental +5	–
Sacred Sandals	BOOTS	1,000	11 Bolts of Cloth	3 Bolts of Linen	0	0	57	+ 1 Energy Regen	Armor vs. Elemental +5	–
Sacred Sandals	BOOTS	1,500	25 Bolts of Cloth	4 Bolts of Linen	0	0	60	+ 1 Energy Regen	Armor vs. Elemental +5	–
Saintly Sandals	BOOTS	15,000	50 Bolts of Cloth	5 Bolts of Damask	0	0	60	+ 1 Energy Regen	Armor vs. Elemental +5	–
Saintly Sandals	BOOTS	15,000	50 Bolts of Cloth	5 Bolts of Damask	15 Globs of Ectoplasm	15 Obsidian Shards	60	+ 1 Energy Regen	Armor vs. Elemental +5	–
Ascetic's Foot Design	BOOTS	150	4 Rolls of Parchment	0	0	0	30	+ 1 Energy Regen	Max Energy +1	–
Ascetic's Foot Design	BOOTS	200	6 Rolls of Parchment	1 Feather	0	0	39	+ 1 Energy Regen	Max Energy +1	–
Ascetic's Foot Design	BOOTS	300	8 Rolls of Parchment	2 Feathers	0	0	45	+ 1 Energy Regen	Max Energy +1	–
Ascetic's Foot Design	BOOTS	400	9 Rolls of Parchment	3 Feathers	0	0	51	+ 1 Energy Regen	Max Energy +1	–
Ascetic's Foot Design	BOOTS	600	11 Rolls of Parchment	3 Feathers	0	0	57	+ 1 Energy Regen	Max Energy +1	–
Ascetic's Foot Design	BOOTS	800	25 Rolls of Parchment	4 Feathers	0	0	60	+ 1 Energy Regen	Max Energy +1	–
Ascetic's Foot Design	BOOTS	800	25 Rolls of Parchment	4 Feathers	0	0	60	+ 1 Energy Regen	Max Energy +1	–
Ascetic's Foot Design	BOOTS	800	25 Rolls of Parchment	4 Feathers	0	0	60	+ 1 Energy Regen	Max Energy +1	–
Monk Sandals	BOOTS	50	1 Bolt of Cloth	0	0	0	15	+ 1 Energy Regen	–	–
Monk Sandals	BOOTS	150	2 Bolts of Cloth	0	0	0	30	+ 1 Energy Regen	–	–
Monk Sandals	BOOTS	250	3 Bolts of Cloth	0	0	0	39	+ 1 Energy Regen	–	–
Monk Sandals	BOOTS	400	4 Bolts of Cloth	0	0	0	45	+ 1 Energy Regen	–	–
Monk Sandals	BOOTS	700	8 Bolts of Cloth	0	0	0	51	+ 1 Energy Regen	–	–

Armor cont.

Name	Type	Gold	Material 1	Material 2	Material 3	Material 4	Armor Level	Effect 1	Effect 2	Effect 3
Monk Sandals	BOOTS	1,000	9 Bolts of Cloth	0	0	0	57	+ 1 Energy Regen	–	–
Monk Sandals	BOOTS	1,500	11 Bolts of Cloth	0	0	0	60	+ 1 Energy Regen	–	–
Wanderer's Sandals	BOOTS	50	2 Bolts of Cloth	0	0	0	15	+ 1 Energy Regen	Armor vs. Elemental +5	–
Wanderer's Sandals	BOOTS	150	4 Bolts of Cloth	1 Tanned Hide Square	0	0	30	+ 1 Energy Regen	Armor vs. Elemental +5	–
Wanderer's Sandals	BOOTS	250	6 Bolts of Cloth	1 Tanned Hide Square	0	0	39	+ 1 Energy Regen	Armor vs. Elemental +5	–
Wanderer's Sandals	BOOTS	400	8 Bolts of Cloth	2 Tanned Hide Squares	0	0	45	+ 1 Energy Regen	Armor vs. Elemental +5	–
Wanderer's Sandals	BOOTS	700	9 Bolts of Cloth	3 Tanned Hide Squares	0	0	51	+ 1 Energy Regen	Armor vs. Elemental +5	–
Wanderer's Sandals	BOOTS	1,000	11 Bolts of Cloth	3 Tanned Hide Squares	0	0	57	+ 1 Energy Regen	Armor vs. Elemental +5	–
Wanderer's Sandals	BOOTS	1,500	25 Bolts of Cloth	4 Tanned Hide Squares	0	0	60	+ 1 Energy Regen	Armor vs. Elemental +5	–
Wanderer's Sandals	BOOTS	15,000	50 Bolts of Cloth	5 Tanned Hide Squares	0	0	60	+ 1 Energy Regen	Armor vs. Elemental +5	–
Wanderer's Sandals	BOOTS	15,000	50 Bolts of Cloth	5 Tanned Hide Squares	15 Globs of Ectoplasm	15 Obsidian Shards	60	+ 1 Energy Regen	Armor vs. Elemental +5	–
Censor's Sandals	BOOTS	150	4 Bolts of Cloth	1 Steel Ingot	0	0	30	+ 1 Energy Regen	Armor vs. Physical +10	Max Energy -1
Censor's Sandals	BOOTS	250	6 Bolts of Cloth	1 Steel Ingot	0	0	39	+ 1 Energy Regen	Armor vs. Physical +10	Max Energy -1
Censor's Sandals	BOOTS	400	8 Bolts of Cloth	2 Steel Ingots	0	0	45	+ 1 Energy Regen	Armor vs. Physical +10	Max Energy -1
Censor's Sandals	BOOTS	700	9 Bolts of Cloth	3 Steel Ingots	0	0	51	+ 1 Energy Regen	Armor vs. Physical +10	Max Energy -1
Censor's Sandals	BOOTS	1,000	11 Bolts of Cloth	3 Steel Ingots	0	0	57	+ 1 Energy Regen	Armor vs. Physical +10	Max Energy -1
Censor's Sandals	BOOTS	1,500	25 Bolts of Cloth	4 Steel Ingots	0	0	60	+ 1 Energy Regen	Armor vs. Physical +10	Max Energy -1
Judge's Sandals	BOOTS	15,000	50 Bolts of Cloth	5 Deldrimor Steel Ingots	0	0	60	+ 1 Energy Regen	Armor vs. Physical +10	Max Energy -1
Judge's Sandals	BOOTS	15,000	50 Bolts of Cloth	5 Deldrimor Steel Ingots	15 Globs of Ectoplasm	15 Obsidian Shards	60	+ 1 Energy Regen	Armor vs. Physical +10	Max Energy -1
Ascetic's Foot Design	BOOTS	150	4 Rolls of Parchment	0	0	0	30	+ 1 Energy Regen	Max Energy +1	–
Ascetic's Foot Design	BOOTS	200	6 Rolls of Parchment	1 Feather	0	0	39	+ 1 Energy Regen	Max Energy +1	–
Ascetic's Foot Design	BOOTS	300	8 Rolls of Parchment	2 Feathers	0	0	45	+ 1 Energy Regen	Max Energy +1	–
Ascetic's Foot Design	BOOTS	400	9 Rolls of Parchment	3 Feathers	0	0	51	+ 1 Energy Regen	Max Energy +1	–
Ascetic's Foot Design	BOOTS	600	11 Rolls of Parchment	3 Feathers	0	0	57	+ 1 Energy Regen	Max Energy +1	–
Ascetic's Foot Design	BOOTS	800	25 Rolls of Parchment	4 Feathers	0	0	60	+ 1 Energy Regen	Max Energy +1	–

WARRIOR BOOTS

Name	Type	Gold	Material 1	Material 2	Material 3	Material 4	Armor Level	Effect 1	Effect 2	Effect 3
Ascalon Boots	BOOTS	50	2 Iron Ingots	0	0	0	35	Armor vs. Physical + 10	Damage -1	–
Ascalon Boots	BOOTS	150	4 Iron Ingots	1 Fur Square	0	0	50	Armor vs. Physical + 10	Damage -1	–
Ascalon Boots	BOOTS	250	6 Iron Ingots	1 Fur Square	0	0	59	Armor vs. Physical + 10	Damage -1	–
Ascalon Boots	BOOTS	400	8 Iron Ingots	2 Fur Squares	0	0	65	Armor vs. Physical + 10	Damage -1	–
Ascalon Boots	BOOTS	700	9 Iron Ingots	3 Fur Squares	0	0	71	Armor vs. Physical + 10	Damage -1	–
Ascalon Boots	BOOTS	1,000	11 Iron Ingots	3 Fur Squares	0	0	77	Armor vs. Physical + 10	Damage -1	–
Ascalon Boots	BOOTS	1,500	25 Iron Ingots	4 Fur Squares	0	0	80	Armor vs. Physical + 10	Damage -1	–
Ascalon Boots	BOOTS	15,000	50 Iron Ingots	5 Fur Squares	0	0	80	Armor vs. Physical + 10	Damage -1	–
Ascalon Boots	BOOTS	15,000	50 Iron Ingots	5 Fur Squares	15 Globs of Ectoplasm	15 Obsidian Shards	80	Armor vs. Physical + 10	Damage -1	–
Chainmail Boots	BOOTS	400	4 Iron Ingots	0	0	0	65	Armor vs. Physical + 20	–	–
Chainmail Boots	BOOTS	700	8 Iron Ingots	0	0	0	71	Armor vs. Physical + 20	–	–
Chainmail Boots	BOOTS	1,000	9 Iron Ingots	0	0	0	77	Armor vs. Physical + 20	–	–
Wyvern Boots	BOOTS	150	4 Iron Ingots	1 Scale	0	0	55	Armor vs. Physical + 10	–	–
Wyvern Boots	BOOTS	250	6 Iron Ingots	1 Scale	0	0	64	Armor vs. Physical + 10	–	–
Wyvern Boots	BOOTS	400	8 Iron Ingots	2 Scales	0	0	70	Armor vs. Physical + 10	–	–
Wyvern Boots	BOOTS	700	9 Iron Ingots	3 Scales	0	0	76	Armor vs. Physical + 10	–	–
Wyvern Boots	BOOTS	1,000	11 Iron Ingots	3 Scales	0	0	82	Armor vs. Physical + 10	–	–
Wyvern Boots	BOOTS	1,500	25 Iron Ingots	4 Scales	0	0	85	Armor vs. Physical + 10	–	–
Dragon Boots	BOOTS	15,000	50 Iron Ingots	5 Scales	0	0	85	Armor vs. Physical + 10	–	–
Dragon Boots	BOOTS	15,000	50 Iron Ingots	5 Scales	15 Globs of Ectoplasm	15 Obsidian Shards	85	Armor vs. Physical + 10	–	–
Gladiator's Boots	BOOTS	150	4 Iron Ingots	4 Tanned Hide Squares	0	0	50	Max Energy +1	Armor vs. Physical +20	–
Gladiator's Boots	BOOTS	250	6 Iron Ingots	6 Tanned Hide Squares	0	0	59	Max Energy +1	Armor vs. Physical +20	–
Gladiator's Boots	BOOTS	400	8 Iron Ingots	8 Tanned Hide Squares	0	0	65	Max Energy +1	Armor vs. Physical +20	–
Gladiator's Boots	BOOTS	700	9 Iron Ingots	9 Tanned Hide Squares	0	0	71	Max Energy +1	Armor vs. Physical +20	–
Gladiator's Boots	BOOTS	1,000	11 Iron Ingots	11 Tanned Hide Squares	0	0	77	Max Energy +1	Armor vs. Physical +20	–
Gladiator's Boots	BOOTS	1,500	25 Iron Ingots	16 Tanned Hide Squares	0	0	80	Max Energy +1	Armor vs. Physical +20	–
Gladiator's Boots	BOOTS	15,000	50 Iron Ingots	16 Tanned Hide Squares	0	0	80	Max Energy +1	Armor vs. Physical +20	–
Gladiator's Boots	BOOTS	15,000	50 Iron Ingots	16 Tanned Hide Squares	15 Globs of Ectoplasm	15 Obsidian Shards	80	Max Energy +1	Armor vs. Physical +20	–
Knight's Boots	BOOTS	1,000	11 Iron Ingots	3 Leather Squares	0	0	77	Armor vs. Physical + 10	Damage -1	–
Knight's Boots	BOOTS	1,500	25 Iron Ingots	4 Leather Squares	0	0	80	Armor vs. Physical + 10	Damage -1	–
Knight's Boots	BOOTS	1,500	25 Iron Ingots	4 Leather Squares	0	0	80	Armor vs. Physical + 10	Damage -1	–
Soldier's Boots	BOOTS	700	9 Iron Ingots	3 Steel Ingots	0	0	71	Armor vs. Physical + 20	–	–
Soldier's Boots	BOOTS	1,000	11 Iron Ingots	3 Steel Ingots	0	0	77	Armor vs. Physical + 20	–	–
Platemail Boots	BOOTS	1,000	11 Iron Ingots	3 Steel Ingots	0	0	77	Armor vs. Physical + 20	–	–
Platemail Boots	BOOTS	1,500	25 Iron Ingots	4 Steel Ingots	0	0	80	Armor vs. Physical + 20	–	–
Platemail Boots	BOOTS	15,000	50 Iron Ingots	5 Deldrimor Steel Ingots	0	0	80	Armor vs. Physical + 20	–	–
Platemail Boots	BOOTS	15,000	50 Iron Ingots	5 Deldrimor Steel Ingots	15 Globs of Ectoplasm	15 Obsidian Shards	80	Armor vs. Physical + 20	–	–

Armor cont.

Name	Type	Gold	Material 1	Material 2	Material 3	Material 4	Armor Level	Effect 1	Effect 2	Effect 3
Ringmail Boots	BOOTS	50	1 Iron Ingot	0	0	0	35	Armor vs. Physical + 20	–	–
Ringmail Boots	BOOTS	150	2 Iron Ingots	0	0	0	50	Armor vs. Physical + 20	–	–
Ringmail Boots	BOOTS	250	3 Iron Ingots	0	0	0	59	Armor vs. Physical + 20	–	–

RANGER BOOTS

Name	Type	Gold	Material 1	Material 2	Material 3	Material 4	Armor Level	Effect 1	Effect 2	Effect 3
Hunter's Boots	BOOTS	150	4 Tanned Hide Squares	4 Bone	0	0	40	Armor vs. Elemental +30	Armor vs. Piercing +15	–
Hunter's Boots	BOOTS	250	6 Tanned Hide Squares	4 Bone	0	0	49	Armor vs. Elemental +30	Armor vs. Piercing +15	–
Hunter's Boots	BOOTS	400	8 Tanned Hide Squares	8 Bone	0	0	55	Armor vs. Elemental +30	Armor vs. Piercing +15	–
Hunter's Boots	BOOTS	700	9 Tanned Hide Squares	9 Bone	0	0	61	Armor vs. Elemental +30	Armor vs. Piercing +15	–
Hunter's Boots	BOOTS	1,000	11 Tanned Hide Squares	11 Bone	0	0	67	Armor vs. Elemental +30	Armor vs. Piercing +15	–
Hunter's Boots	BOOTS	1,500	25 Tanned Hide Squares	25 Bone	0	0	70	Armor vs. Elemental +30	Armor vs. Piercing +15	–
Hunter's Boots	BOOTS	15,000	50 Tanned Hide Squares	50 Bone	0	0	70	Armor vs. Elemental +30	Armor vs. Piercing +15	–
Hunter's Boots	BOOTS	15,000	50 Tanned Hide Squares	50 Bone	15 Globs of Ectoplasm	15 Obsidian Shards	70	Armor vs. Elemental +30	Armor vs. Piercing +15	–
Druid's Boots	BOOTS	150	4 Tanned Hide Squares	4 Wood Planks	0	0	40	Max Energy +1	Armor vs. Elemental +30	–
Druid's Boots	BOOTS	250	6 Tanned Hide Squares	4 Wood Planks	0	0	49	Max Energy +1	Armor vs. Elemental +30	–
Druid's Boots	BOOTS	400	8 Tanned Hide Squares	8 Wood Planks	0	0	55	Max Energy +1	Armor vs. Elemental +30	–
Druid's Boots	BOOTS	700	9 Tanned Hide Squares	9 Wood Planks	0	0	61	Max Energy +1	Armor vs. Elemental +30	–
Druid's Boots	BOOTS	1,000	11 Tanned Hide Squares	11 Wood Planks	0	0	67	Max Energy +1	Armor vs. Elemental +30	–
Druid's Boots	BOOTS	1,500	25 Tanned Hide Squares	25 Wood Planks	0	0	70	Max Energy +1	Armor vs. Elemental +30	–
Druid's Boots	BOOTS	15,000	50 Tanned Hide Squares	50 Wood Planks	0	0	70	Max Energy +1	Armor vs. Elemental +30	–
Druid's Boots	BOOTS	15,000	50 Tanned Hide Squares	50 Wood Planks	15 Globs of Ectoplasm	15 Obsidian Shards	70	Max Energy +1	Armor vs. Elemental +30	–
Fur-Lined Boots	BOOTS	50	2 Tanned Hide Squares	0	0	0	25	Armor vs. Elemental +30	Armor vs. Cold +15	–
Fur-Lined Boots	BOOTS	150	4 Tanned Hide Squares	1 Fur Square	0	0	40	Armor vs. Elemental +30	Armor vs. Cold +15	–
Fur-Lined Boots	BOOTS	250	6 Tanned Hide Squares	1 Fur Square	0	0	49	Armor vs. Elemental +30	Armor vs. Cold +15	–
Fur-Lined Boots	BOOTS	400	8 Tanned Hide Squares	2 Fur Squares	0	0	55	Armor vs. Elemental +30	Armor vs. Cold +15	–
Fur-Lined Boots	BOOTS	700	9 Tanned Hide Squares	3 Fur Squares	0	0	61	Armor vs. Elemental +30	Armor vs. Cold +15	–
Fur-Lined Boots	BOOTS	1,000	11 Tanned Hide Squares	3 Fur Squares	0	0	67	Armor vs. Elemental +30	Armor vs. Cold +15	–
Fur-Lined Boots	BOOTS	1,500	25 Tanned Hide Squares	4 Fur Squares	0	0	70	Armor vs. Elemental +30	Armor vs. Cold +15	–
Frostbound Boots	BOOTS	15,000	50 Tanned Hide Squares	5 Fur Squares	0	0	70	Armor vs. Elemental +30	Armor vs. Cold +15	–
Frostbound Boots	BOOTS	15,000	50 Tanned Hide Squares	5 Fur Squares	15 Globs of Ectoplasm	15 Obsidian Shards	70	Armor vs. Elemental +30	Armor vs. Cold +15	–
Studded Leather Boots	BOOTS	150	4 Tanned Hide Squares	1 Steel Ingot	0	0	40	Armor vs. Elemental +30	Armor vs. Lightning +15	–
Studded Leather Boots	BOOTS	250	6 Tanned Hide Squares	1 Steel Ingot	0	0	49	Armor vs. Elemental +30	Armor vs. Lightning +15	–
Studded Leather Boots	BOOTS	400	8 Tanned Hide Squares	2 Steel Ingots	0	0	55	Armor vs. Elemental +30	Armor vs. Lightning +15	–
Studded Leather Boots	BOOTS	700	9 Tanned Hide Squares	3 Steel Ingots	0	0	61	Armor vs. Elemental +30	Armor vs. Lightning +15	–
Studded Leather Boots	BOOTS	1,000	11 Tanned Hide Squares	3 Steel Ingots	0	0	67	Armor vs. Elemental +30	Armor vs. Lightning +15	–
Studded Leather Boots	BOOTS	1,500	25 Tanned Hide Squares	4 Steel Ingots	0	0	70	Armor vs. Elemental +30	Armor vs. Lightning +15	–
Studded Leather Boots	BOOTS	15,000	50 Tanned Hide Squares	5 Deldrimor Steel Ingots	0	0	70	Armor vs. Elemental +30	Armor vs. Lightning +15	–
Studded Leather Boots	BOOTS	15,000	50 Tanned Hide Squares	5 Deldrimor Steel Ingots	15 Globs of Ectoplasm	15 Obsidian Shards	70	Armor vs. Elemental +30	Armor vs. Lightning +15	–
Drakescale Boots	BOOTS	150	4 Tanned Hide Squares	1 Scale	0	0	40	Armor vs. Elemental +30	Armor vs. Fire +15	–
Drakescale Boots	BOOTS	250	6 Tanned Hide Squares	1 Scale	0	0	49	Armor vs. Elemental +30	Armor vs. Fire +15	–
Drakescale Boots	BOOTS	400	8 Tanned Hide Squares	2 Scales	0	0	55	Armor vs. Elemental +30	Armor vs. Fire +15	–
Drakescale Boots	BOOTS	700	9 Tanned Hide Squares	3 Scales	0	0	61	Armor vs. Elemental +30	Armor vs. Fire +15	–
Drakescale Boots	BOOTS	1,000	11 Tanned Hide Squares	3 Scales	0	0	67	Armor vs. Elemental +30	Armor vs. Fire +15	–
Drakescale Boots	BOOTS	1,500	25 Tanned Hide Squares	4 Scales	0	0	70	Armor vs. Elemental +30	Armor vs. Fire +15	–
Drakescale Boots	BOOTS	15,000	50 Tanned Hide Squares	5 Scales	0	0	70	Armor vs. Elemental +30	Armor vs. Fire +15	–
Drakescale Boots	BOOTS	15,000	50 Tanned Hide Squares	5 Scales	15 Globs of Ectoplasm	15 Obsidian Shards	70	Armor vs. Elemental +30	Armor vs. Fire +15	–
Leather Boots	BOOTS	50	1 Tanned Hide Square	0	0	0	25	Armor vs. Elemental +30	–	–
Leather Boots	BOOTS	150	2 Tanned Hide Squares	0	0	0	40	Armor vs. Elemental +30	–	–
Leather Boots	BOOTS	250	3 Tanned Hide Squares	0	0	0	49	Armor vs. Elemental +30	–	–
Leather Boots	BOOTS	400	4 Tanned Hide Squares	0	0	0	55	Armor vs. Elemental +30	–	–
Leather Boots	BOOTS	700	8 Tanned Hide Squares	0	0	0	61	Armor vs. Elemental +30	–	–
Leather Boots	BOOTS	1,000	9 Tanned Hide Squares	0	0	0	67	Armor vs. Elemental +30	–	–
Leather Boots	BOOTS	1,500	11 Tanned Hide Squares	0	0	0	70	Armor vs. Elemental +30	–	–

MESMER COATS

Name	Type	Gold	Material 1	Material 2	Material 3	Material 4	Armor Level	Effect 1	Effect 2	Effect 3
Courtly Attire	COAT	150	12 Bolts of Cloth	3 Bolts of Linen	0	0	30	Max Energy +5	+15 Armor while Casting	–
Courtly Attire	COAT	250	18 Bolts of Cloth	3 Bolts of Linen	0	0	39	Max Energy +5	+15 Armor while Casting	–
Courtly Attire	COAT	400	24 Bolts of Cloth	6 Bolts of Linen	0	0	45	Max Energy +5	+15 Armor while Casting	–
Courtly Attire	COAT	700	27 Bolts of Cloth	9 Bolts of Linen	0	0	51	Max Energy +5	+15 Armor while Casting	–
Courtly Attire	COAT	1,000	33 Bolts of Cloth	9 Bolts of Linen	0	0	57	Max Energy +5	+15 Armor while Casting	–
Courtly Attire	COAT	1,500	75 Bolts of Cloth	12 Bolts of Linen	0	0	60	Max Energy +5	+15 Armor while Casting	–
Noble Attire	COAT	15,000	150 Bolts of Cloth	15 Bolts of Damask	0	0	60	Max Energy +5	+15 Armor while Casting	–
Noble Attire	COAT	15,000	150 Bolts of Cloth	15 Bolts of Damask	45 Globs of Ectoplasm	45 Obsidian Shards	60	Max Energy +5	+15 Armor while Casting	–
Enchanter's Attire	COAT	150	12 Bolts of Cloth	3 Piles of Glittering Dust	0	0	30	Max Energy +8	–	–
Enchanter's Attire	COAT	250	18 Bolts of Cloth	3 Piles of Glittering Dust	0	0	39	Max Energy +8	–	–

Armor cont.

Name	Type	Gold	Material 1	Material 2	Material 3	Material 4	Armor Level	Effect 1	Effect 2	Effect 3
Enchanter's Attire	COAT	400	24 Bolts of Cloth	6 Piles of Glittering Dust	0	0	45	Max Energy +8	–	–
Enchanter's Attire	COAT	700	27 Bolts of Cloth	9 Piles of Glittering Dust	0	0	51	Max Energy +8	–	–
Enchanter's Attire	COAT	1,000	33 Bolts of Cloth	9 Piles of Glittering Dust	0	0	57	Max Energy +8	–	–
Enchanter's Attire	COAT	1,500	75 Bolts of Cloth	12 Piles of Glittering Dust	0	0	60	Max Energy +8	–	–
Enchanter's Attire	COAT	15,000	150 Bolts of Cloth	15 Piles of Glittering Dust	0	0	60	Max Energy +8	–	–
Enchanter's Attire	COAT	15,000	150 Bolts of Cloth	15 Piles of Glittering Dust	45 Globs of Ectoplasm	45 Obsidian Shards	60	Max Energy +8	–	–
Performer's Attire	COAT	150	12 Bolts of Cloth	3 Silk	0	0	30	Max Energy +5	+15 Armor while casting	–
Performer's Attire	COAT	250	18 Bolts of Cloth	3 Silk	0	0	39	Max Energy +5	+15 Armor while casting	–
Performer's Attire	COAT	400	24 Bolts of Cloth	6 Silk	0	0	45	Max Energy +5	+15 Armor while casting	–
Performer's Attire	COAT	700	27 Bolts of Cloth	9 Silk	0	0	51	Max Energy +5	+15 Armor while casting	–
Performer's Attire	COAT	1,000	33 Bolts of Cloth	9 Silk	0	0	57	Max Energy +5	+15 Armor while casting	–
Performer's Attire	COAT	1,500	75 Bolts of Cloth	12 Silk	0	0	60	Max Energy +5	+15 Armor while casting	–
Virtuoso's Attire	COAT	15,000	150 Bolts of Cloth	15 Silk	0	0	60	Max Energy +5	+15 Armor while casting	–
Virtuoso's Attire	COAT	15,000	150 Bolts of Cloth	15 Silk	45 Globs of Ectoplasm	45 Obsidian Shards	60	Max Energy +5	+15 Armor while casting	–
Rogue's Attire	COAT	50	6 Bolts of Cloth	0	0	0	15	Max Energy +4	Armor vs. Physical +10	–
Rogue's Attire	COAT	150	12 Bolts of Cloth	3 Leather Squares	0	0	30	Max Energy +4	Armor vs. Physical +10	–
Rogue's Attire	COAT	250	18 Bolts of Cloth	3 Leather Squares	0	0	39	Max Energy +4	Armor vs. Physical +10	–
Rogue's Attire	COAT	400	24 Bolts of Cloth	6 Leather Squares	0	0	45	Max Energy +4	Armor vs. Physical +10	–
Rogue's Attire	COAT	700	27 Bolts of Cloth	9 Leather Squares	0	0	51	Max Energy +4	Armor vs. Physical +10	–
Rogue's Attire	COAT	1,000	33 Bolts of Cloth	9 Leather Squares	0	0	57	Max Energy +4	Armor vs. Physical +10	–
Rogue's Attire	COAT	1,500	75 Bolts of Cloth	12 Leather Squares	0	0	60	Max Energy +4	Armor vs. Physical +10	–
Rogue's Attire	COAT	15,000	150 Bolts of Cloth	15 Elonian Leather Squares	0	0	60	Max Energy +4	Armor vs. Physical +10	–
Rogue's Attire	COAT	15,000	150 Bolts of Cloth	15 Elonian Leather Squares	45 Globs of Ectoplasm	45 Obsidian Shards	60	Max Energy +4	Armor vs. Physical +10	–
Regal Attire	COAT	150	12 Bolts of Cloth	3 Silk	0	0	35	Max Energy +5	Armor vs. Earth -5	–
Regal Attire	COAT	250	18 Bolts of Cloth	3 Silk	0	0	44	Max Energy +5	Armor vs. Earth -5	–
Regal Attire	COAT	400	24 Bolts of Cloth	6 Silk	0	0	50	Max Energy +5	Armor vs. Earth -5	–
Regal Attire	COAT	700	27 Bolts of Cloth	9 Silk	0	0	56	Max Energy +5	Armor vs. Earth -5	–
Regal Attire	COAT	1,000	33 Bolts of Cloth	9 Silk	0	0	62	Max Energy +5	Armor vs. Earth -5	–
Regal Attire	COAT	1,500	75 Bolts of Cloth	12 Silk	0	0	65	Max Energy +5	Armor vs. Earth -5	–
Regal Attire	COAT	15,000	150 Bolts of Cloth	15 Silk	0	0	65	Max Energy +5	Armor vs. Earth -5	–
Stylish Attire	COAT	50	3 Bolts of Cloth	0	0	0	15	Max Energy +5	–	–
Stylish Attire	COAT	150	6 Bolts of Cloth	0	0	0	30	Max Energy +5	–	–
Stylish Attire	COAT	250	9 Bolts of Cloth	0	0	0	39	Max Energy +5	–	–
Stylish Attire	COAT	400	12 Bolts of Cloth	0	0	0	45	Max Energy +5	–	–
Stylish Attire	COAT	700	24 Bolts of Cloth	0	0	0	51	Max Energy +5	–	–
Stylish Attire	COAT	1,000	27 Bolts of Cloth	0	0	0	57	Max Energy +5	–	–
Stylish Attire	COAT	1,500	33 Bolts of Cloth	0	0	0	60	Max Energy +5	–	–

NECROMANCER COATS

Name	Type	Gold	Material 1	Material 2	Material 3	Material 4	Armor Level	Effect 1	Effect 2	Effect 3
Bonelace Tunic	COAT	50	6 Tanned Hide Squares	0	0	0	15	Max Energy +5	Armor vs. Piercing +15	–
Bonelace Tunic	COAT	150	12 Tanned Hide Squares	12 Bone	0	0	30	Max Energy +5	Armor vs. Piercing +15	–
Bonelace Tunic	COAT	250	18 Tanned Hide Squares	12 Bone	0	0	39	Max Energy +5	Armor vs. Piercing +15	–
Bonelace Tunic	COAT	400	24 Tanned Hide Squares	24 Bone	0	0	45	Max Energy +5	Armor vs. Piercing +15	–
Bonelace Tunic	COAT	700	27 Tanned Hide Squares	27 Bone	0	0	51	Max Energy +5	Armor vs. Piercing +15	–
Bonelace Tunic	COAT	1,000	33 Tanned Hide Squares	33 Bone	0	0	57	Max Energy +5	Armor vs. Piercing +15	–
Bonelace Tunic	COAT	1,500	75 Tanned Hide Squares	75 Bone	0	0	60	Max Energy +5	Armor vs. Piercing +15	–
Bonelace Tunic	COAT	15,000	150 Tanned Hide Squares	150 Bone	0	0	60	Max Energy +5	Armor vs. Piercing +15	–
Bonelace Tunic	COAT	15,000	150 Tanned Hide Squares	150 Bone	45 Globs of Ectoplasm	45 Obsidian Shards	60	Max Energy +5	Armor vs. Piercing +15	–
Tormentor's Tunic	COAT	150	12 Tanned Hide Squares	3 Steel Ingots	0	0	40	Max Energy +5	Increased damage vs. Holy	–
Tormentor's Tunic	COAT	250	18 Tanned Hide Squares	3 Steel Ingots	0	0	49	Max Energy +5	Increased damage vs. Holy	–
Tormentor's Tunic	COAT	400	24 Tanned Hide Squares	6 Steel Ingots	0	0	55	Max Energy +5	Increased damage vs. Holy	–
Tormentor's Tunic	COAT	700	27 Tanned Hide Squares	9 Steel Ingots	0	0	61	Max Energy +5	Increased damage vs. Holy	–
Tormentor's Tunic	COAT	1,000	33 Tanned Hide Squares	9 Steel Ingots	0	0	67	Max Energy +5	Increased damage vs. Holy	–
Tormentor's Tunic	COAT	1,500	75 Tanned Hide Squares	12 Steel Ingots	0	0	70	Max Energy +5	Increased damage vs. Holy	–
Tormentor's Tunic	COAT	15,000	150 Tanned Hide Squares	15 Deldrimor Steel Ingots	0	0	70	Max Energy +5	Increased damage vs. Holy	–
Tormentor's Tunic	COAT	15,000	150 Tanned Hide Squares	15 Deldrimor Steel Ingots	45 Globs of Ectoplasm	45 Obsidian Shards	70	Max Energy +5	Increased damage vs. Holy	–
Fanatic's Tunic	COAT	150	12 Tanned Hide Squares	3 Leather Squares	0	0	30	Max Energy +5	Armor vs. Piercing +15	–
Fanatic's Tunic	COAT	250	18 Tanned Hide Squares	3 Leather Squares	0	0	39	Max Energy +5	Armor vs. Piercing +15	–
Fanatic's Tunic	COAT	400	24 Tanned Hide Squares	6 Leather Squares	0	0	45	Max Energy +5	Armor vs. Piercing +15	–
Fanatic's Tunic	COAT	700	27 Tanned Hide Squares	9 Leather Squares	0	0	51	Max Energy +5	Armor vs. Piercing +15	–
Fanatic's Tunic	COAT	1,000	33 Tanned Hide Squares	9 Leather Squares	0	0	57	Max Energy +5	Armor vs. Piercing +15	–
Fanatic's Tunic	COAT	1,500	75 Tanned Hide Squares	12 Leather Squares	0	0	60	Max Energy +5	Armor vs. Piercing +15	–
Cultist's Tunic	COAT	15,000	150 Tanned Hide Squares	15 Elonian Leather Squares	0	0	60	Max Energy +5	Armor vs. Piercing +15	–
Cultist's Tunic	COAT	15,000	150 Tanned Hide Squares	15 Elonian Leather Squares	45 Globs of Ectoplasm	45 Obsidian Shards	60	Max Energy +5	Armor vs. Piercing +15	–

Armor cont.

Name	Type	Gold	Material 1	Material 2	Material 3	Material 4	Armor Level	Effect 1	Effect 2	Effect 3
Necrotic Tunic	COAT	150	12 Tanned Hide Squares	3 Shells	0	0	40	Max Energy +5	Increased damage vs. Holy	–
Necrotic Tunic	COAT	250	18 Tanned Hide Squares	3 Shells	0	0	49	Max Energy +5	Increased damage vs. Holy	–
Necrotic Tunic	COAT	400	24 Tanned Hide Squares	6 Shells	0	0	55	Max Energy +5	Increased damage vs. Holy	–
Necrotic Tunic	COAT	700	27 Tanned Hide Squares	9 Shells	0	0	61	Max Energy +5	Increased damage vs. Holy	–
Necrotic Tunic	COAT	1,000	33 Tanned Hide Squares	9 Shells	0	0	67	Max Energy +5	Increased damage vs. Holy	–
Necrotic Tunic	COAT	1,500	75 Tanned Hide Squares	12 Shells	0	0	70	Max Energy +5	Increased damage vs. Holy	–
Necrotic Tunic	COAT	15,000	150 Tanned Hide Squares	15 Shells	0	0	70	Max Energy +5	Increased damage vs. Holy	–
Necrotic Tunic	COAT	15,000	150 Tanned Hide Squares	15 Shells	45 Globs of Ectoplasm	45 Obsidian Shards	70	Max Energy +5	Increased damage vs. Holy	–
Chest Scar Pattern	COAT	150	12 Rolls of Parchment	0	0	0	30	Max Energy +8	–	–
Chest Scar Pattern	COAT	200	18 Rolls of Parchment	3 Feathers	0	0	39	Max Energy +8	–	–
Chest Scar Pattern	COAT	300	24 Rolls of Parchment	6 Feathers	0	0	45	Max Energy +8	–	–
Chest Scar Pattern	COAT	400	27 Rolls of Parchment	9 Feathers	0	0	51	Max Energy +8	–	–
Chest Scar Pattern	COAT	400	27 Rolls of Parchment	9 Feathers	0	0	57	Max Energy +8	–	–
Chest Scar Pattern	COAT	800	75 Rolls of Parchment	12 Feathers	0	0	60	Max Energy +8	–	–
Chest Scar Pattern	COAT	8,000	150 Rolls of Vellum	15 Feathers	0	0	60	Max Energy +8	–	–
Chest Scar Pattern	COAT	8,000	150 Rolls of Vellum	15 Feathers	45 Globs of Ectoplasm	0	60	Max Energy +8	–	–
Pagan Tunic	COAT	400	24 Tanned Hide Squares	6 Steel Ingots	0	0	40	Max Energy +5	–	–
Pagan Tunic	COAT	700	27 Tanned Hide Squares	9 Steel Ingots	0	0	46	Max Energy +5	–	–
Pagan Tunic	COAT	1,000	33 Tanned Hide Squares	9 Steel Ingots	0	0	52	Max Energy +5	–	–
Pagan Tunic	COAT	1,500	75 Tanned Hide Squares	12 Steel Ingots	0	0	55	Max Energy +5	–	–
Necromancer's Tunic	COAT	50	3 Tanned Hide Squares	0	0	0	15	Max Energy +5	–	–
Necromancer's Tunic	COAT	150	6 Tanned Hide Squares	0	0	0	30	Max Energy +5	–	–
Necromancer's Tunic	COAT	250	9 Tanned Hide Squares	0	0	0	39	Max Energy +5	–	–
Necromancer's Tunic	COAT	400	12 Tanned Hide Squares	0	0	0	45	Max Energy +5	–	–
Necromancer's Tunic	COAT	700	24 Tanned Hide Squares	0	0	0	51	Max Energy +5	–	–
Necromancer's Tunic	COAT	1,000	27 Tanned Hide Squares	0	0	0	57	Max Energy +5	–	–
Necromancer's Tunic	COAT	1,500	33 Tanned Hide Squares	0	0	0	60	Max Energy +5	–	–
Pagan Tunic	COAT	150	12 Tanned Hide Squares	3 Granite Slabs	0	0	40	Max Energy +5	Increased damage vs. Holy	–
Pagan Tunic	COAT	250	18 Tanned Hide Squares	3 Granite Slabs	0	0	49	Max Energy +5	Increased damage vs. Holy	–
Pagan Tunic	COAT	400	24 Tanned Hide Squares	6 Granite Slabs	0	0	55	Max Energy +5	Increased damage vs. Holy	–
Pagan Tunic	COAT	700	27 Tanned Hide Squares	9 Granite Slabs	0	0	61	Max Energy +5	Increased damage vs. Holy	–
Pagan Tunic	COAT	1,000	33 Tanned Hide Squares	9 Granite Slabs	0	0	67	Max Energy +5	Increased damage vs. Holy	–
Pagan Tunic	COAT	1,500	75 Tanned Hide Squares	12 Granite Slabs	0	0	70	Max Energy +5	Increased damage vs. Holy	–
Blasphemer's Tunic	COAT	15,000	150 Tanned Hide Squares	15 Granite Slabs	0	0	70	Max Energy +5	Increased damage vs. Holy	–

ELEMENTALIST COATS

Name	Type	Gold	Material 1	Material 2	Material 3	Material 4	Armor Level	Effect 1	Effect 2	Effect 3
Aeromancer's Robes	COAT	150	12 Bolts of Cloth	3 Bolts of Linen	0	0	30	Max Energy +5	Armor vs. Lightning +15	–
Aeromancer's Robes	COAT	250	18 Bolts of Cloth	3 Bolts of Linen	0	0	39	Max Energy +5	Armor vs. Lightning +15	–
Aeromancer's Robes	COAT	400	24 Bolts of Cloth	6 Bolts of Linen	0	0	45	Max Energy +5	Armor vs. Lightning +15	–
Aeromancer's Robes	COAT	700	27 Bolts of Cloth	9 Bolts of Linen	0	0	51	Max Energy +5	Armor vs. Lightning +15	–
Aeromancer's Robes	COAT	1,000	33 Bolts of Cloth	9 Bolts of Linen	0	0	57	Max Energy +5	Armor vs. Lightning +15	–
Aeromancer's Robes	COAT	1,500	75 Bolts of Cloth	12 Bolts of Linen	0	0	60	Max Energy +5	Armor vs. Lightning +15	–
Aeromancer's Robes	COAT	15,000	150 Bolts of Cloth	15 Bolts of Damask	0	0	60	Max Energy +5	Armor vs. Lightning +15	–
Aeromancer's Robes	COAT	15,000	150 Bolts of Cloth	15 Bolts of Damask	45 Globs of Ectoplasm	45 Obsidian Shards	60	Max Energy +5	Armor vs. Lightning +15	–
Geomancer's Robes	COAT	150	12 Bolts of Cloth	3 Granite Slabs	0	0	30	Max Energy +5	Armor vs. Earth +15	–
Geomancer's Robes	COAT	250	18 Bolts of Cloth	3 Granite Slabs	0	0	39	Max Energy +5	Armor vs. Earth +15	–
Geomancer's Robes	COAT	400	24 Bolts of Cloth	6 Granite Slabs	0	0	45	Max Energy +5	Armor vs. Earth +15	–
Geomancer's Robes	COAT	700	27 Bolts of Cloth	9 Granite Slabs	0	0	51	Max Energy +5	Armor vs. Earth +15	–
Geomancer's Robes	COAT	1,000	33 Bolts of Cloth	9 Granite Slabs	0	0	57	Max Energy +5	Armor vs. Earth +15	–
Geomancer's Robes	COAT	1,500	75 Bolts of Cloth	12 Granite Slabs	0	0	60	Max Energy +5	Armor vs. Earth +15	–
Geomancer's Robes	COAT	15,000	150 Bolts of Cloth	15 Granite Slabs	0	0	60	Max Energy +5	Armor vs. Earth +15	–
Geomancer's Robes	COAT	15,000	150 Bolts of Cloth	15 Granite Slabs	45 Globs of Ectoplasm	45 Obsidian Shards	60	Max Energy +5	Armor vs. Earth +15	–
Pyromancer's Robes	COAT	50	6 Bolts of Cloth	0	0	0	15	Max Energy +5	Armor vs. Fire +15	–
Pyromancer's Robes	COAT	150	12 Bolts of Cloth	3 Scales	0	0	30	Max Energy +5	Armor vs. Fire +15	–
Pyromancer's Robes	COAT	250	18 Bolts of Cloth	3 Scales	0	0	39	Max Energy +5	Armor vs. Fire +15	–
Pyromancer's Robes	COAT	400	24 Bolts of Cloth	6 Scales	0	0	45	Max Energy +5	Armor vs. Fire +15	–
Pyromancer's Robes	COAT	700	27 Bolts of Cloth	9 Scales	0	0	51	Max Energy +5	Armor vs. Fire +15	–
Pyromancer's Robes	COAT	1,000	33 Bolts of Cloth	9 Scales	0	0	57	Max Energy +5	Armor vs. Fire +15	–
Pyromancer's Robes	COAT	1,500	75 Bolts of Cloth	12 Scales	0	0	60	Max Energy +5	Armor vs. Fire +15	–
Pyromancer's Robes	COAT	15,000	150 Bolts of Cloth	15 Scales	0	0	60	Max Energy +5	Armor vs. Fire +15	–
Pyromancer's Robes	COAT	15,000	150 Bolts of Cloth	15 Scales	45 Globs of Ectoplasm	45 Obsidian Shards	60	Max Energy +5	Armor vs. Fire +15	–
Adept's Robes	COAT	1,000	33 Bolts of Cloth	9 Silk	0	0	57	Max Energy +5	Armor vs. Elemental +5	–
Adept's Robes	COAT	1,500	75 Bolts of Cloth	12 Silk	0	0	60	Max Energy +5	Armor vs. Elemental +5	–
Adept's Robes	COAT	15,000	150 Bolts of Cloth	15 Silk	0	0	60	Max Energy +5	Armor vs. Elemental +5	–

Armor cont.

Name	Type	Gold	Material 1	Material 2	Material 3	Material 4	Armor Level	Effect 1	Effect 2	Effect 3
Elementalist's Robes	COAT	50	3 Bolts of Cloth	0	0	0	15	Max Energy +5	–	–
Elementalist's Robes	COAT	150	6 Bolts of Cloth	0	0	0	30	Max Energy +5	–	–
Elementalist's Robes	COAT	250	9 Bolts of Cloth	0	0	0	39	Max Energy +5	–	–
Elementalist's Robes	COAT	400	12 Bolts of Cloth	0	0	0	45	Max Energy +5	–	–
Elementalist's Robes	COAT	700	24 Bolts of Cloth	0	0	0	51	Max Energy +5	–	–
Elementalist's Robes	COAT	1,000	27 Bolts of Cloth	0	0	0	57	Max Energy +5	–	–
Elementalist's Robes	COAT	1,500	33 Bolts of Cloth	0	0	0	60	Max Energy +5	–	–
Hydromancer's Robes	COAT	150	12 Bolts of Cloth	3 Shells	0	0	30	Max Energy +5	Armor vs. Cold +15	–
Hydromancer's Robes	COAT	250	18 Bolts of Cloth	3 Shells	0	0	39	Max Energy +5	Armor vs. Cold +15	–
Hydromancer's Robes	COAT	400	24 Bolts of Cloth	6 Shells	0	0	45	Max Energy +5	Armor vs. Cold +15	–
Hydromancer's Robes	COAT	700	27 Bolts of Cloth	9 Shells	0	0	51	Max Energy +5	Armor vs. Cold +15	–
Hydromancer's Robes	COAT	1,000	33 Bolts of Cloth	9 Shells	0	0	57	Max Energy +5	Armor vs. Cold +15	–
Hydromancer's Robes	COAT	1,500	75 Bolts of Cloth	12 Shells	0	0	60	Max Energy +5	Armor vs. Cold +15	–
Hydromancer's Robes	COAT	15,000	150 Bolts of Cloth	15 Shells	0	0	60	Max Energy +5	Armor vs. Cold +15	–
Hydromancer's Robes	COAT	15,000	150 Bolts of Cloth	15 Shells	45 Globs of Ectoplasm	45 Obsidian Shards	60	Max Energy +5	Armor vs. Cold +15	–

MONK COATS

Name	Type	Gold	Material 1	Material 2	Material 3	Material 4	Armor Level	Effect 1	Effect 2	Effect 3
Silk Raiment	COAT	150	12 Bolts of Cloth	3 Silk	0	0	35	Max Energy +5	Armor vs. Cold -5	–
Silk Raiment	COAT	250	18 Bolts of Cloth	3 Silk	0	0	44	Max Energy +5	Armor vs. Cold -5	–
Silk Raiment	COAT	400	24 Bolts of Cloth	6 Silk	0	0	50	Max Energy +5	Armor vs. Cold -5	–
Silk Raiment	COAT	700	27 Bolts of Cloth	9 Silk	0	0	56	Max Energy +5	Armor vs. Cold -5	–
Silk Raiment	COAT	1,000	33 Bolts of Cloth	9 Silk	0	0	61	Max Energy +5	Armor vs. Cold -5	–
Silk Raiment	COAT	1,500	75 Bolts of Cloth	12 Silk	0	0	65	Max Energy +5	Armor vs. Cold -5	–
Silk Raiment	COAT	15,000	150 Bolts of Cloth	15 Silk	0	0	65	Max Energy +5	Armor vs. Cold -5	–
Silk Raiment	COAT	15,000	150 Bolts of Cloth	15 Silk	45 Globs of Ectoplasm	45 Obsidian Shards	65	Max Energy +5	Armor vs. Cold -5	–
Sacred Raiment	COAT	150	12 Bolts of Cloth	3 Bolts of Linen	0	0	30	Max Energy +5	Armor vs. Elemental +5	–
Sacred Raiment	COAT	250	18 Bolts of Cloth	3 Bolts of Linen	0	0	39	Max Energy +5	Armor vs. Elemental +5	–
Sacred Raiment	COAT	400	24 Bolts of Cloth	6 Bolts of Linen	0	0	45	Max Energy +5	Armor vs. Elemental +5	–
Sacred Raiment	COAT	700	27 Bolts of Cloth	9 Bolts of Linen	0	0	51	Max Energy +5	Armor vs. Elemental +5	–
Sacred Raiment	COAT	1,000	33 Bolts of Cloth	9 Bolts of Linen	0	0	57	Max Energy +5	Armor vs. Elemental +5	–
Sacred Raiment	COAT	1,500	75 Bolts of Cloth	12 Bolts of Linen	0	0	60	Max Energy +5	Armor vs. Elemental +5	–
Saintly Raiment	COAT	15,000	150 Bolts of Cloth	15 Bolts of Damask	0	0	60	Max Energy +5	Armor vs. Elemental +5	–
Saintly Raiment	COAT	15,000	150 Bolts of Cloth	15 Bolts of Damask	45 Globs of Ectoplasm	45 Obsidian Shards	60	Max Energy +5	Armor vs. Elemental +5	–
Ascetic's Chest Design	COAT	150	12 Rolls of Parchment	0	0	0	30	Max Energy +8	–	–
Ascetic's Chest Design	COAT	200	18 Rolls of Parchment	3 Feathers	0	0	39	Max Energy +8	–	–
Ascetic's Chest Design	COAT	300	24 Rolls of Parchment	6 Feathers	0	0	45	Max Energy +8	–	–
Ascetic's Chest Design	COAT	400	27 Rolls of Parchment	9 Feathers	0	0	51	Max Energy +8	–	–
Ascetic's Chest Design	COAT	600	33 Rolls of Parchment	9 Feathers	0	0	57	Max Energy +8	–	–
Ascetic's Chest Design	COAT	800	75 Rolls of Parchment	12 Feathers	0	0	60	Max Energy +8	–	–
Ascetic's Chest Design	COAT	8,000	150 Rolls of Vellum	15 Feathers	0	0	60	Max Energy +8	–	–
Ascetic's Chest Design	COAT	8,000	150 Rolls of Vellum	15 Feathers	45 Globs of Ectoplasm	0	60	Max Energy +8	–	–
Monk Raiment	COAT	50	3 Bolts of Cloth	0	0	0	15	Max Energy +5	–	–
Monk Raiment	COAT	150	6 Bolts of Cloth	0	0	0	30	Max Energy +5	–	–
Monk Raiment	COAT	250	9 Bolts of Cloth	0	0	0	39	Max Energy +5	–	–
Monk Raiment	COAT	400	12 Bolts of Cloth	0	0	0	45	Max Energy +5	–	–
Monk Raiment	COAT	700	24 Bolts of Cloth	0	0	0	45	Max Energy +5	–	–
Monk Raiment	COAT	1,000	27 Bolts of Cloth	0	0	0	57	Max Energy +5	–	–
Monk Raiment	COAT	1,500	33 Bolts of Cloth	0	0	0	60	Max Energy +5	–	–
Wanderer's Vestments	COAT	50	6 Bolts of Cloth	0	0	0	15	Max Energy +5	Armor vs. Elemental +5	–
Wanderer's Vestments	COAT	150	12 Bolts of Cloth	3 Tanned Hide Squares	0	0	30	Max Energy +5	Armor vs. Elemental +5	–
Wanderer's Vestments	COAT	250	18 Bolts of Cloth	3 Tanned Hide Squares	0	0	39	Max Energy +5	Armor vs. Elemental +5	–
Wanderer's Vestments	COAT	400	24 Bolts of Cloth	6 Tanned Hide Squares	0	0	45	Max Energy +5	Armor vs. Elemental +5	–
Wanderer's Vestments	COAT	700	27 Bolts of Cloth	9 Tanned Hide Squares	0	0	51	Max Energy +5	Armor vs. Elemental +5	–
Wanderer's Vestments	COAT	1,000	33 Bolts of Cloth	9 Tanned Hide Squares	0	0	57	Max Energy +5	Armor vs. Elemental +5	–
Wanderer's Vestments	COAT	1,500	75 Bolts of Cloth	12 Tanned Hide Squares	0	0	60	Max Energy +5	Armor vs. Elemental +5	–
Wanderer's Vestments	COAT	15,000	150 Bolts of Cloth	15 Tanned Hide Squares	0	0	60	Max Energy +5	Armor vs. Elemental +5	–
Wanderer's Vestments	COAT	15,000	150 Bolts of Cloth	15 Tanned Hide Squares	45 Globs of Ectoplasm	45 Obsidian Shards	60	Max Energy +5	Armor vs. Elemental +5	–
Censor's Vestments	COAT	150	12 Bolts of Cloth	3 Steel Ingots	0	0	30	Max Energy +4	Armor vs. Physical +10	–
Censor's Vestments	COAT	250	18 Bolts of Cloth	3 Steel Ingots	0	0	39	Max Energy +4	Armor vs. Physical +10	–
Censor's Vestments	COAT	400	24 Bolts of Cloth	6 Steel Ingots	0	0	45	Max Energy +4	Armor vs. Physical +10	–
Censor's Vestments	COAT	700	27 Bolts of Cloth	9 Steel Ingots	0	0	51	Max Energy +4	Armor vs. Physical +10	–
Censor's Vestments	COAT	1,000	33 Bolts of Cloth	9 Steel Ingots	0	0	57	Max Energy +4	Armor vs. Physical +10	–
Censor's Vestments	COAT	1,500	75 Bolts of Cloth	12 Steel Ingots	0	0	60	Max Energy +4	Armor vs. Physical +10	–
Judge's Vestments	COAT	15,000	150 Bolts of Cloth	15 Deldrimor Steel Ingots	0	0	60	Max Energy +4	Armor vs. Physical +10	–

Armor cont.

Name	Type	Gold	Material 1	Material 2	Material 3	Material 4	Armor Level	Effect 1	Effect 2	Effect 3
Judge's Vestments	COAT	15,000	150 Bolts of Cloth	15 Deldrimor Steel Ingots	45 Globs of Ectoplasm	45 Obsidian Shards	60	Max Energy +4	Armor vs. Physical +10	–
Ascetic's Chest Design	COAT	150	12 Rolls of Parchment	0	0	0	30	Max Energy +8	–	–
Ascetic's Chest Design	COAT	200	18 Rolls of Parchment	3 Feathers	0	0	39	Max Energy +8	–	–
Ascetic's Chest Design	COAT	300	24 Rolls of Parchment	6 Feathers	0	0	45	Max Energy +8	–	–
Ascetic's Chest Design	COAT	400	27 Rolls of Parchment	9 Feathers	0	0	51	Max Energy +8	–	–
Ascetic's Chest Design	COAT	600	33 Rolls of Parchment	9 Feathers	0	0	57	Max Energy +8	–	–
Ascetic's Chest Design	COAT	800	75 Rolls of Parchment	12 Feathers	0	0	60	Max Energy +8	–	–
Ascetic's Chest Design	COAT	8,000	150 Rolls of Vellum	15 Feathers	0	0	60	Max Energy +8	–	–

WARRIOR COATS

Name	Type	Gold	Material 1	Material 2	Material 3	Material 4	Armor Level	Effect 1	Effect 2	Effect 3
Ascalon Cuirass	COAT	50	6 Iron Ingots	0	0	0	35	Armor vs. Physical + 10	Damage -1	–
Ascalon Cuirass	COAT	150	12 Iron Ingots	3 Fur Squares	0	0	50	Armor vs. Physical + 10	Damage -1	–
Ascalon Cuirass	COAT	250	18 Iron Ingots	3 Fur Squares	0	0	59	Armor vs. Physical + 10	Damage -1	–
Ascalon Cuirass	COAT	400	24 Iron Ingots	6 Fur Squares	0	0	65	Armor vs. Physical + 10	Damage -1	–
Ascalon Cuirass	COAT	700	27 Iron Ingots	9 Fur Squares	0	0	71	Armor vs. Physical + 10	Damage -1	–
Ascalon Cuirass	COAT	1,000	33 Iron Ingots	9 Fur Squares	0	0	77	Armor vs. Physical + 10	Damage -1	–
Ascalon Cuirass	COAT	1,500	75 Iron Ingots	12 Fur Squares	0	0	80	Armor vs. Physical + 10	Damage -1	–
Ascalon Cuirass	COAT	15,000	150 Iron Ingots	15 Fur Squares	0	0	80	Armor vs. Physical + 10	Damage -1	–
Ascalon Cuirass	COAT	15,000	150 Iron Ingots	15 Fur Squares	45 Globs of Ectoplasm	45 Obsidian Shards	80	Armor vs. Physical + 10	Damage -1	–
Chainmail Hauberk	COAT	400	12 Iron Ingots	0	0	0	65	Armor vs. Physical + 20	–	–
Chainmail Hauberk	COAT	700	24 Iron Ingots	0	0	0	71	Armor vs. Physical + 20	–	–
Chainmail Hauberk	COAT	1,000	27 Iron Ingots	0	0	0	77	Armor vs. Physical + 20	–	–
Wyvern Hauberk	COAT	150	12 Iron Ingots	3 Scales	0	0	55	Armor vs. Physical + 10	–	–
Wyvern Hauberk	COAT	250	18 Iron Ingots	3 Scales	0	0	64	Armor vs. Physical + 10	–	–
Wyvern Hauberk	COAT	400	24 Iron Ingots	6 Scales	0	0	70	Armor vs. Physical + 10	–	–
Wyvern Hauberk	COAT	700	27 Iron Ingots	9 Scales	0	0	76	Armor vs. Physical + 10	–	–
Wyvern Hauberk	COAT	1,000	33 Iron Ingots	9 Scales	0	0	82	Armor vs. Physical + 10	–	–
Wyvern Hauberk	COAT	1,500	75 Iron Ingots	12 Scales	0	0	85	Armor vs. Physical + 10	–	–
Dragon Hauberk	COAT	15,000	150 Iron Ingots	15 Scales	0	0	85	Armor vs. Physical + 10	–	–
Dragon Hauberk	COAT	15,000	150 Iron Ingots	15 Scales	45 Globs of Ectoplasm	45 Obsidian Shards	85	Armor vs. Physical + 10	–	–
Gladiator Hauberk	COAT	150	12 Iron Ingots	12 Tanned Hide Squares	0	0	50	Max Energy +3	Armor vs. Physical +20	–
Gladiator Hauberk	COAT	250	18 Iron Ingots	18 Tanned Hide Squares	0	0	59	Max Energy +3	Armor vs. Physical +20	–
Gladiator Hauberk	COAT	400	24 Iron Ingots	24 Tanned Hide Squares	0	0	65	Max Energy +3	Armor vs. Physical +20	–
Gladiator Hauberk	COAT	700	27 Iron Ingots	27 Tanned Hide Squares	0	0	71	Max Energy +3	Armor vs. Physical +20	–
Gladiator Hauberk	COAT	1,000	33 Iron Ingots	33 Tanned Hide Squares	0	0	77	Max Energy +3	Armor vs. Physical +20	–
Gladiator Hauberk	COAT	1,500	75 Iron Ingots	48 Tanned Hide Squares	0	0	80	Max Energy +3	Armor vs. Physical +20	–
Gladiator Hauberk	COAT	15,000	150 Iron Ingots	48 Tanned Hide Squares	0	0	80	Max Energy +3	Armor vs. Physical +20	–
Gladiator Hauberk	COAT	15,000	150 Iron Ingots	48 Tanned Hide Squares	45 Globs of Ectoplasm	45 Obsidian Shards	80	Max Energy +3	Armor vs. Physical +20	–
Knight's Cuirass	COAT	1,000	33 Iron Ingots	9 Leather Squares	0	0	77	Armor vs. Physical + 10	Damage -1	–
Knight's Cuirass	COAT	1,500	75 Iron Ingots	12 Leather Squares	0	0	80	Armor vs. Physical + 10	Damage -1	–
Knight's Cuirass	COAT	1,500	75 Iron Ingots	12 Leather Squares	0	0	80	Armor vs. Physical + 10	Damage -1	–
Soldier's Cuirass	COAT	700	27 Iron Ingots	9 Steel Ingots	0	0	71	Armor vs. Physical + 20	–	–
Soldier's Cuirass	COAT	1,000	33 Iron Ingots	9 Steel Ingots	0	0	77	Armor vs. Physical + 20	–	–
Platemail Cuirass	COAT	1,000	33 Iron Ingots	9 Steel Ingots	0	0	77	Armor vs. Physical + 20	–	–
Platemail Cuirass	COAT	1,500	75 Iron Ingots	12 Steel Ingots	0	0	80	Armor vs. Physical + 20	–	–
Platemail Cuirass	COAT	15,000	150 Iron Ingots	15 Deldrimor Steel Ingots	0	0	80	Armor vs. Physical + 20	–	–
Platemail Cuirass	COAT	15,000	150 Iron Ingots	15 Deldrimor Steel Ingots	45 Globs of Ectoplasm	45 Obsidian Shards	80	Armor vs. Physical + 20	–	–
Ringmail Hauberk	COAT	50	3 Iron Ingots	0	0	0	35	Armor vs. Physical + 20	–	–
Ringmail Hauberk	COAT	150	6 Iron Ingots	0	0	0	50	Armor vs. Physical + 20	–	–
Ringmail Hauberk	COAT	250	9 Iron Ingots	0	0	0	59	Armor vs. Physical + 20	–	–

RANGER COATS

Name	Type	Gold	Material 1	Material 2	Material 3	Material 4	Armor Level	Effect 1	Effect 2	Effect 3
Rawhide Vest	COAT	150	12 Tanned Hide Squares	12 Bone	0	0	40	Max Energy +5	Armor vs. Elemental +30	Armor vs. Piercing +15
Rawhide Vest	COAT	250	18 Tanned Hide Squares	12 Bone	0	0	49	Max Energy +5	Armor vs. Elemental +30	Armor vs. Piercing +15
Rawhide Vest	COAT	400	24 Tanned Hide Squares	24 Bone	0	0	55	Max Energy +5	Armor vs. Elemental +30	Armor vs. Piercing +15
Rawhide Vest	COAT	700	27 Tanned Hide Squares	27 Bone	0	0	61	Max Energy +5	Armor vs. Elemental +30	Armor vs. Piercing +15
Rawhide Vest	COAT	1,000	33 Tanned Hide Squares	33 Bone	0	0	67	Max Energy +5	Armor vs. Elemental +30	Armor vs. Piercing +15
Rawhide Vest	COAT	1,500	75 Tanned Hide Squares	75 Bone	0	0	70	Max Energy +5	Armor vs. Elemental +30	Armor vs. Piercing +15
Rawhide Vest	COAT	15,000	150 Tanned Hide Squares	150 Bone	0	0	70	Max Energy +5	Armor vs. Elemental +30	Armor vs. Piercing +15
Rawhide Vest	COAT	15,000	150 Tanned Hide Squares	150 Bone	45 Globs of Ectoplasm	45 Obsidian Shards	70	Max Energy +5	Armor vs. Elemental +30	Armor vs. Piercing +15
Druid's Vest	COAT	150	12 Tanned Hide Squares	12 Wood Planks	0	0	40	Max Energy +8	Armor vs. Elemental +30	–
Druid's Vest	COAT	250	18 Tanned Hide Squares	12 Wood Planks	0	0	49	Max Energy +8	Armor vs. Elemental +30	–
Druid's Vest	COAT	400	24 Tanned Hide Squares	24 Wood Planks	0	0	55	Max Energy +8	Armor vs. Elemental +30	–
Druid's Vest	COAT	700	27 Tanned Hide Squares	27 Wood Planks	0	0	61	Max Energy +8	Armor vs. Elemental +30	–

Armor cont.

Name	Type	Gold	Material 1	Material 2	Material 3	Material 4	Armor Level	Effect 1	Effect 2	Effect 3
Druid's Vest	COAT	1,000	33 Tanned Hide Squares	33 Wood Planks	0	0	67	Max Energy +8	Armor vs. Elemental +30	–
Druid's Vest	COAT	1,500	75 Tanned Hide Squares	75 Wood Planks	0	0	70	Max Energy +8	Armor vs. Elemental +30	–
Druid's Vest	COAT	15,000	150 Tanned Hide Squares	150 Wood Planks	0	0	70	Max Energy +8	Armor vs. Elemental +30	–
Druid's Vest	COAT	15,000	150 Tanned Hide Squares	150 Wood Planks	45 Globs of Ectoplasm	45 Obsidian Shards	70	Max Energy +8	Armor vs. Elemental +30	–
Fur-Lined Vest	COAT	50	6 Tanned Hide Squares	0	0	0	25	Max Energy +5	Armor vs. Elemental +30	Armor vs. Cold +15
Fur-Lined Vest	COAT	150	12 Tanned Hide Squares	3 Fur Squares	0	0	40	Max Energy +5	Armor vs. Elemental +30	Armor vs. Cold +15
Fur-Lined Vest	COAT	250	18 Tanned Hide Squares	3 Fur Squares	0	0	49	Max Energy +5	Armor vs. Elemental +30	Armor vs. Cold +15
Fur-Lined Vest	COAT	400	24 Tanned Hide Squares	6 Fur Squares	0	0	55	Max Energy +5	Armor vs. Elemental +30	Armor vs. Cold +15
Fur-Lined Vest	COAT	700	27 Tanned Hide Squares	9 Fur Squares	0	0	61	Max Energy +5	Armor vs. Elemental +30	Armor vs. Cold +15
Fur-Lined Vest	COAT	1,000	33 Tanned Hide Squares	9 Fur Squares	0	0	67	Max Energy +5	Armor vs. Elemental +30	Armor vs. Cold +15
Fur-Lined Vest	COAT	1,500	75 Tanned Hide Squares	12 Fur Squares	0	0	70	Max Energy +5	Armor vs. Elemental +30	Armor vs. Cold +15
Frostbound Vest	COAT	15,000	150 Tanned Hide Squares	15 Fur Squares	0	0	70	Max Energy +5	Armor vs. Elemental +30	Armor vs. Cold +15
Frostbound Vest	COAT	15,000	150 Tanned Hide Squares	15 Fur Squares	45 Globs of Ectoplasm	45 Obsidian Shards	70	Max Energy +5	Armor vs. Elemental +30	Armor vs. Cold +15
Studded Leather Vest	COAT	150	12 Tanned Hide Squares	3 Steel Ingots	0	0	40	Max Energy +5	Armor vs. Elemental +30	Armor vs. Lightning +15
Studded Leather Vest	COAT	250	18 Tanned Hide Squares	3 Steel Ingots	0	0	49	Max Energy +5	Armor vs. Elemental +30	Armor vs. Lightning +15
Studded Leather Vest	COAT	400	24 Tanned Hide Squares	6 Steel Ingots	0	0	55	Max Energy +5	Armor vs. Elemental +30	Armor vs. Lightning +15
Studded Leather Vest	COAT	700	27 Tanned Hide Squares	9 Steel Ingots	0	0	61	Max Energy +5	Armor vs. Elemental +30	Armor vs. Lightning +15
Studded Leather Vest	COAT	1,000	33 Tanned Hide Squares	9 Steel Ingots	0	0	67	Max Energy +5	Armor vs. Elemental +30	Armor vs. Lightning +15
Studded Leather Vest	COAT	1,500	75 Tanned Hide Squares	12 Steel Ingots	0	0	70	Max Energy +5	Armor vs. Elemental +30	Armor vs. Lightning +15
Studded Leather Vest	COAT	15,000	150 Tanned Hide Squares	15 Deldrimor Steel Ingots	0	0	70	Max Energy +5	Armor vs. Elemental +30	Armor vs. Lightning +15
Studded Leather Vest	COAT	15,000	150 Tanned Hide Squares	15 Deldrimor Steel Ingots	45 Globs of Ectoplasm	45 Obsidian Shards	70	Max Energy +5	Armor vs. Elemental +30	Armor vs. Lightning +15
Drakescale Vest	COAT	150	12 Tanned Hide Squares	3 Scales	0	0	40	Armor vs. Elemental +30	Armor vs. Fire +15	Max Energy +5
Drakescale Vest	COAT	250	18 Tanned Hide Squares	3 Scales	0	0	49	Armor vs. Elemental +30	Armor vs. Fire +15	Max Energy +5
Drakescale Vest	COAT	400	24 Tanned Hide Squares	6 Scales	0	0	55	Armor vs. Elemental +30	Armor vs. Fire +15	Max Energy +5
Drakescale Vest	COAT	700	27 Tanned Hide Squares	9 Scales	0	0	61	Armor vs. Elemental +30	Armor vs. Fire +15	Max Energy +5
Drakescale Vest	COAT	1,000	33 Tanned Hide Squares	9 Scales	0	0	67	Armor vs. Elemental +30	Armor vs. Fire +15	Max Energy +5
Drakescale Vest	COAT	1,500	75 Tanned Hide Squares	12 Scales	0	0	70	Armor vs. Elemental +30	Armor vs. Fire +15	Max Energy +5
Drakescale Vest	COAT	15,000	150 Tanned Hide Squares	15 Scales	0	0	70	Armor vs. Elemental +30	Armor vs. Fire +15	Max Energy +5
Drakescale Vest	COAT	15,000	150 Tanned Hide Squares	15 Scales	45 Globs of Ectoplasm	45 Obsidian Shards	70	Armor vs. Elemental +30	Armor vs. Fire +15	Max Energy +5
Leather Vest	COAT	50	3 Tanned Hide Squares	0	0	0	25	Armor vs. Elemental +30	Max Energy +5	–
Leather Vest	COAT	150	6 Tanned Hide Squares	0	0	0	40	Armor vs. Elemental +30	Max Energy +5	–
Leather Vest	COAT	250	9 Tanned Hide Squares	0	0	0	49	Armor vs. Elemental +30	Max Energy +5	–
Leather Vest	COAT	400	12 Tanned Hide Squares	0	0	0	55	Armor vs. Elemental +30	Max Energy +5	–
Leather Vest	COAT	700	24 Tanned Hide Squares	0	0	0	61	Armor vs. Elemental +30	Max Energy +5	–
Leather Vest	COAT	1,000	27 Tanned Hide Squares	0	0	0	67	Armor vs. Elemental +30	Max Energy +5	–
Leather Vest	COAT	1,500	33 Tanned Hide Squares	0	0	0	70	Armor vs. Elemental +30	Max Energy +5	–
Courtly Gloves	GLOVES	50	2 Bolts of Cloth	0	0	0	15	Max Energy +5	–	–
Courtly Gloves	GLOVES	150	4 Bolts of Cloth	1 Bolt of Linen	0	0	30	Max Energy +5	+15 Armor while casting	–
Courtly Gloves	GLOVES	250	6 Bolts of Cloth	1 Bolt of Linen	0	0	39	Max Energy +5	+15 Armor while casting	–
Courtly Gloves	GLOVES	400	8 Bolts of Cloth	2 Bolts of Linen	0	0	45	Max Energy +5	+15 Armor while casting	–
Courtly Gloves	GLOVES	700	9 Bolts of Cloth	3 Bolts of Linen	0	0	51	Max Energy +5	+15 Armor while casting	–
Courtly Gloves	GLOVES	1,000	11 Bolts of Cloth	3 Bolts of Linen	0	0	57	Max Energy +5	+15 Armor while casting	–
Courtly Gloves	GLOVES	1,500	25 Bolts of Cloth	4 Bolts of Linen	0	0	60	Max Energy +5	+15 Armor while casting	–
Noble Gloves	GLOVES	15,000	50 Bolts of Cloth	5 Bolts of Damask	0	0	60	Max Energy +5	+15 Armor while casting	–
Noble Gloves	GLOVES	15,000	50 Bolts of Cloth	5 Bolts of Damask	15 Globs of Ectoplasm	15 Obsidian Shards	60	Max Energy +5	+15 Armor while casting	–

MESMER GLOVES

Name	Type	Gold	Material 1	Material 2	Material 3	Material 4	Armor Level	Effect 1	Effect 2	Effect 3
Enchanter's Gloves	GLOVES	150	4 Bolts of Cloth	1 Pile of Glittering Dust	0	0	30	Max Energy +6	–	–
Enchanter's Gloves	GLOVES	250	6 Bolts of Cloth	1 Pile of Glittering Dust	0	0	39	Max Energy +6	–	–
Enchanter's Gloves	GLOVES	400	8 Bolts of Cloth	2 Piles of Glittering Dust	0	0	45	Max Energy +6	–	–
Enchanter's Gloves	GLOVES	700	9 Bolts of Cloth	3 Piles of Glittering Dust	0	0	51	Max Energy +6	–	–
Enchanter's Gloves	GLOVES	1,000	11 Bolts of Cloth	3 Piles of Glittering Dust	0	0	57	Max Energy +6	–	–
Enchanter's Gloves	GLOVES	1,500	25 Bolts of Cloth	4 Piles of Glittering Dust	0	0	60	Max Energy +6	–	–
Enchanter's Gloves	GLOVES	15,000	50 Bolts of Cloth	5 Piles of Glittering Dust	0	0	60	Max Energy +6	–	–
Enchanter's Gloves	GLOVES	15,000	50 Bolts of Cloth	5 Piles of Glittering Dust	15 Globs of Ectoplasm	15 Obsidian Shards	60	Max Energy +6	–	–
Performer's Gloves	GLOVES	150	4 Bolts of Cloth	1 Silk	0	0	30	Max Energy +5	+15 Armor while casting	–
Performer's Gloves	GLOVES	250	6 Bolts of Cloth	1 Silk	0	0	39	Max Energy +5	+15 Armor while casting	–
Performer's Gloves	GLOVES	400	8 Bolts of Cloth	2 Silk	0	0	45	Max Energy +5	+15 Armor while casting	–
Performer's Gloves	GLOVES	700	9 Bolts of Cloth	3 Silk	0	0	51	Max Energy +5	+15 Armor while casting	–
Performer's Gloves	GLOVES	1,000	11 Bolts of Cloth	3 Silk	0	0	57	Max Energy +5	+15 Armor while casting	–
Performer's Gloves	GLOVES	1,500	25 Bolts of Cloth	4 Silk	0	0	60	Max Energy +5	+15 Armor while casting	–
Virtuoso's Gloves	GLOVES	15,000	50 Bolts of Cloth	5 Silk	0	0	60	Max Energy +5	+15 Armor while casting	–
Virtuoso's Gloves	GLOVES	15,000	50 Bolts of Cloth	5 Silk	15 Globs of Ectoplasm	15 Obsidian Shards	60	Max Energy +5	+15 Armor while casting	–
Rogue's Gloves	GLOVES	50	2 Bolts of Cloth	0	0	0	15	Max Energy +4	Armor vs. Physical +10	–

Armor cont.

Name	Type	Gold	Material 1	Material 2	Material 3	Material 4	Armor Level	Effect 1	Effect 2	Effect 3
Rogue's Gloves	GLOVES	150	4 Bolts of Cloth	1 Leather Square	0	0	30	Max Energy +4	Armor vs. Physical +10	–
Rogue's Gloves	GLOVES	250	6 Bolts of Cloth	1 Leather Square	0	0	39	Max Energy +4	Armor vs. Physical +10	–
Rogue's Gloves	GLOVES	400	8 Bolts of Cloth	2 Leather Squares	0	0	45	Max Energy +4	Armor vs. Physical +10	–
Rogue's Gloves	GLOVES	700	9 Bolts of Cloth	3 Leather Squares	0	0	51	Max Energy +4	Armor vs. Physical +10	–
Rogue's Gloves	GLOVES	1,000	11 Bolts of Cloth	3 Leather Squares	0	0	57	Max Energy +4	Armor vs. Physical +10	–
Rogue's Gloves	GLOVES	1,500	25 Bolts of Cloth	4 Leather Squares	0	0	60	Max Energy +4	Armor vs. Physical +10	–
Rogue's Gloves	GLOVES	15,000	50 Bolts of Cloth	5 Elonian Leather Squares	0	0	60	Max Energy +4	Armor vs. Physical +10	–
Rogue's Gloves	GLOVES	15,000	50 Bolts of Cloth	5 Elonian Leather Squares	15 Globs of Ectoplasm	15 Obsidian Shards	60	Max Energy +4	Armor vs. Physical +10	–
Regal Gloves	GLOVES	150	4 Bolts of Cloth	1 Silk	0	0	35	Max Energy +5	Armor vs. Earth -5	–
Regal Gloves	GLOVES	250	6 Bolts of Cloth	1 Silk	0	0	44	Max Energy +5	Armor vs. Earth -5	–
Regal Gloves	GLOVES	400	8 Bolts of Cloth	2 Silk	0	0	50	Max Energy +5	Armor vs. Earth -5	–
Regal Gloves	GLOVES	700	9 Bolts of Cloth	3 Silk	0	0	56	Max Energy +5	Armor vs. Earth -5	–
Regal Gloves	GLOVES	1,000	11 Bolts of Cloth	3 Silk	0	0	62	Max Energy +5	Armor vs. Earth -5	–
Regal Gloves	GLOVES	1,500	25 Bolts of Cloth	4 Silk	0	0	65	Max Energy +5	Armor vs. Earth -5	–
Regal Gloves	GLOVES	15,000	50 Bolts of Cloth	5 Silk	0	0	65	Max Energy +5	Armor vs. Earth -5	–
Stylish Gloves	GLOVES	50	1 Bolt of Cloth	0	0	0	15	Max Energy +5	–	–
Stylish Gloves	GLOVES	150	2 Bolts of Cloth	0	0	0	30	Max Energy +5	–	–
Stylish Gloves	GLOVES	250	3 Bolts of Cloth	0	0	0	39	Max Energy +5	–	–
Stylish Gloves	GLOVES	400	4 Bolts of Cloth	0	0	0	45	Max Energy +5	–	–
Stylish Gloves	GLOVES	700	8 Bolts of Cloth	0	0	0	51	Max Energy +5	–	–
Stylish Gloves	GLOVES	1,000	9 Bolts of Cloth	0	0	0	57	Max Energy +5	–	–
Stylish Gloves	GLOVES	1,500	11 Bolts of Cloth	0	0	0	60	Max Energy +5	–	–

NECROMANCER GLOVES

Name	Type	Gold	Material 1	Material 2	Material 3	Material 4	Armor Level	Effect 1	Effect 2	Effect 3
Bonelace Gloves	GLOVES	50	2 Tanned Hide Squares	0	0	0	15	Max Energy +5	Armor vs. Piercing +15	–
Bonelace Gloves	GLOVES	150	4 Tanned Hide Squares	4 Bone	0	0	30	Max Energy +5	Armor vs. Piercing +15	–
Bonelace Gloves	GLOVES	250	6 Tanned Hide Squares	4 Bone	0	0	39	Max Energy +5	Armor vs. Piercing +15	–
Bonelace Gloves	GLOVES	400	8 Tanned Hide Squares	8 Bone	0	0	45	Max Energy +5	Armor vs. Piercing +15	–
Bonelace Gloves	GLOVES	700	9 Tanned Hide Squares	9 Bone	0	0	51	Max Energy +5	Armor vs. Piercing +15	–
Bonelace Gloves	GLOVES	1,000	11 Tanned Hide Squares	11 Bone	0	0	57	Max Energy +5	Armor vs. Piercing +15	–
Bonelace Gloves	GLOVES	1,500	25 Tanned Hide Squares	25 Bone	0	0	60	Max Energy +5	Armor vs. Piercing +15	–
Bonelace Gloves	GLOVES	15,000	50 Tanned Hide Squares	50 Bone	0	0	60	Max Energy +5	Armor vs. Piercing +15	–
Bonelace Gloves	GLOVES	15,000	50 Tanned Hide Squares	50 Bone	15 Globs of Ectoplasm	15 Obsidian Shards	60	Max Energy +5	Armor vs. Piercing +15	–
Tormentor's Gloves	GLOVES	150	4 Tanned Hide Squares	1 Steel Ingot	0	0	40	Max Energy +5	Increased damage vs. Holy	–
Tormentor's Gloves	GLOVES	250	6 Tanned Hide Squares	1 Steel Ingot	0	0	49	Max Energy +5	Increased damage vs. Holy	–
Tormentor's Gloves	GLOVES	400	8 Tanned Hide Squares	2 Steel Ingots	0	0	55	Max Energy +5	Increased damage vs. Holy	–
Tormentor's Gloves	GLOVES	700	9 Tanned Hide Squares	3 Steel Ingots	0	0	61	Max Energy +5	Increased damage vs. Holy	–
Tormentor's Gloves	GLOVES	1,000	11 Tanned Hide Squares	3 Steel Ingots	0	0	67	Max Energy +5	Increased damage vs. Holy	–
Tormentor's Gloves	GLOVES	1,500	25 Tanned Hide Squares	4 Steel Ingots	0	0	70	Max Energy +5	Increased damage vs. Holy	–
Tormentor's Gloves	GLOVES	15,000	50 Tanned Hide Squares	5 Deldrimor Steel Ingots	0	0	70	Max Energy +5	Increased damage vs. Holy	–
Tormentor's Gloves	GLOVES	15,000	50 Tanned Hide Squares	5 Deldrimor Steel Ingots	15 Globs of Ectoplasm	15 Obsidian Shards	70	Max Energy +5	Increased damage vs. Holy	–
Fanatic's Gloves	GLOVES	150	4 Tanned Hide Squares	1 Leather Square	0	0	30	Max Energy +5	Armor vs. Piercing +15	–
Fanatic's Gloves	GLOVES	250	6 Tanned Hide Squares	1 Leather Square	0	0	39	Max Energy +5	Armor vs. Piercing +15	–
Fanatic's Gloves	GLOVES	400	8 Tanned Hide Squares	2 Leather Squares	0	0	45	Max Energy +5	Armor vs. Piercing +15	–
Fanatic's Gloves	GLOVES	700	9 Tanned Hide Squares	3 Leather Squares	0	0	51	Max Energy +5	Armor vs. Piercing +15	–
Fanatic's Gloves	GLOVES	1,000	11 Tanned Hide Squares	3 Leather Squares	0	0	57	Max Energy +5	Armor vs. Piercing +15	–
Fanatic's Gloves	GLOVES	1,500	25 Tanned Hide Squares	4 Leather Squares	0	0	60	Max Energy +5	Armor vs. Piercing +15	–
Cultist's Gloves	GLOVES	15,000	50 Tanned Hide Squares	5 Elonian Leather Squares	0	0	60	Max Energy +5	Armor vs. Piercing +15	–
Cultist's Gloves	GLOVES	15,000	50 Tanned Hide Squares	5 Elonian Leather Squares	15 Globs of Ectoplasm	15 Obsidian Shards	60	Max Energy +5	Armor vs. Piercing +15	–
Necrotic Gloves	GLOVES	150	4 Tanned Hide Squares	1 Shell	0	0	40	Max Energy +5	Increased damage vs. Holy	–
Necrotic Gloves	GLOVES	250	6 Tanned Hide Squares	1 Shell	0	0	49	Max Energy +5	Increased damage vs. Holy	–
Necrotic Gloves	GLOVES	400	8 Tanned Hide Squares	2 Shells	0	0	55	Max Energy +5	Increased damage vs. Holy	–
Necrotic Gloves	GLOVES	700	9 Tanned Hide Squares	3 Shells	0	0	61	Max Energy +5	Increased damage vs. Holy	–
Necrotic Gloves	GLOVES	1,000	11 Tanned Hide Squares	3 Shells	0	0	67	Max Energy +5	Increased damage vs. Holy	–
Necrotic Gloves	GLOVES	1,500	25 Tanned Hide Squares	4 Shells	0	0	70	Max Energy +5	Increased damage vs. Holy	–
Necrotic Gloves	GLOVES	15,000	50 Tanned Hide Squares	5 Shells	0	0	70	Max Energy +5	Increased damage vs. Holy	–
Necrotic Gloves	GLOVES	15,000	50 Tanned Hide Squares	5 Shells	15 Globs of Ectoplasm	15 Obsidian Shards	70	Max Energy +5	Increased damage vs. Holy	–
Arm Scar Pattern	GLOVES	150	4 Rolls of Parchment	0	0	0	30	Max Energy +6	–	–
Arm Scar Pattern	GLOVES	200	6 Rolls of Parchment	1 Feather	0	0	39	Max Energy +6	–	–
Arm Scar Pattern	GLOVES	300	8 Rolls of Parchment	2 Feathers	0	0	45	Max Energy +6	–	–
Arm Scar Pattern	GLOVES	400	9 Rolls of Parchment	3 Feathers	0	0	51	Max Energy +6	–	–
Arm Scar Pattern	GLOVES	600	11 Rolls of Parchment	3 Feathers	0	0	57	Max Energy +6	–	–
Arm Scar Pattern	GLOVES	800	25 Rolls of Parchment	4 Feathers	0	0	60	Max Energy +6	–	–
Arm Scar Pattern	GLOVES	8,000	50 Rolls of Vellum	5 Feathers	0	0	60	Max Energy +6	–	–

Armor cont.

Name	Type	Gold	Material 1	Material 2	Material 3	Material 4	Armor Level	Effect 1	Effect 2	Effect 3
Arm Scar Pattern	GLOVES	8,000	50 Rolls of Vellum	5 Feathers	15 Globs of Ectoplasm	0	60	Max Energy +6	–	–
Necromancer's Gloves	GLOVES	50	1 Tanned Hide Square	0	0	0	15	Max Energy +5	–	–
Necromancer's Gloves	GLOVES	150	2 Tanned Hide Squares	0	0	0	30	Max Energy +5	–	–
Necromancer's Gloves	GLOVES	250	3 Tanned Hide Squares	0	0	0	39	Max Energy +5	–	–
Necromancer's Gloves	GLOVES	400	4 Tanned Hide Squares	0	0	0	45	Max Energy +5	–	–
Necromancer's Gloves	GLOVES	700	8 Tanned Hide Squares	0	0	0	51	Max Energy +5	–	–
Necromancer's Gloves	GLOVES	1,000	9 Tanned Hide Squares	0	0	0	57	Max Energy +5	–	–
Necromancer's Gloves	GLOVES	1,500	11 Tanned Hide Squares	0	0	0	60	Max Energy +5	–	–
Pagan Gloves	GLOVES	150	4 Tanned Hide Squares	1 Granite Slab	0	0	40	Max Energy +5	Increased damage vs. Holy	–
Pagan Gloves	GLOVES	250	6 Tanned Hide Squares	1 Granite Slab	0	0	49	Max Energy +5	Increased damage vs. Holy	–
Pagan Gloves	GLOVES	400	8 Tanned Hide Squares	2 Granite Slabs	0	0	55	Max Energy +5	Increased damage vs. Holy	–
Pagan Gloves	GLOVES	700	9 Tanned Hide Squares	3 Granite Slabs	0	0	61	Max Energy +5	Increased damage vs. Holy	–
Pagan Gloves	GLOVES	1,000	11 Tanned Hide Squares	3 Granite Slabs	0	0	67	Max Energy +5	Increased damage vs. Holy	–
Pagan Gloves	GLOVES	1,500	25 Tanned Hide Squares	4 Granite Slabs	0	0	70	Max Energy +5	Increased damage vs. Holy	–
Blasphemer's Gloves	GLOVES	15,000	50 Tanned Hide Squares	5 Granite Slabs	0	0	70	Max Energy +5	Increased damage vs. Holy	–

ELEMENTALIST GLOVES

Name	Type	Gold	Material 1	Material 2	Material 3	Material 4	Armor Level	Effect 1	Effect 2	Effect 3
Aeromancer's Gloves	GLOVES	150	4 Bolts of Cloth	1 Bolt of Linen	0	0	30	Max Energy +5	Armor vs. Lightning +15	–
Aeromancer's Gloves	GLOVES	250	6 Bolts of Cloth	1 Bolt of Linen	0	0	39	Max Energy +5	Armor vs. Lightning +15	–
Aeromancer's Gloves	GLOVES	400	8 Bolts of Cloth	2 Bolts of Linen	0	0	45	Max Energy +5	Armor vs. Lightning +15	–
Aeromancer's Gloves	GLOVES	700	9 Bolts of Cloth	3 Bolts of Linen	0	0	51	Max Energy +5	Armor vs. Lightning +15	–
Aeromancer's Gloves	GLOVES	1,000	11 Bolts of Cloth	3 Bolts of Linen	0	0	57	Max Energy +5	Armor vs. Lightning +15	–
Aeromancer's Gloves	GLOVES	1,500	25 Bolts of Cloth	4 Bolts of Linen	0	0	60	Max Energy +5	Armor vs. Lightning +15	–
Aeromancer's Gloves	GLOVES	15,000	50 Bolts of Cloth	5 Bolts of Damask	0	0	60	Max Energy +5	Armor vs. Lightning +15	–
Aeromancer's Gloves	GLOVES	15,000	50 Bolts of Cloth	5 Bolts of Damask	15 Globs of Ectoplasm	15 Obsidian Shards	60	Max Energy +5	Armor vs. Lightning +15	–
Geomancer's Gloves	GLOVES	150	4 Bolts of Cloth	1 Granite Slab	0	0	30	Max Energy +5	Armor vs. Earth +15	–
Geomancer's Gloves	GLOVES	250	6 Bolts of Cloth	1 Granite Slab	0	0	39	Max Energy +5	Armor vs. Earth +15	–
Geomancer's Gloves	GLOVES	400	8 Bolts of Cloth	2 Granite Slabs	0	0	45	Max Energy +5	Armor vs. Earth +15	–
Geomancer's Gloves	GLOVES	700	9 Bolts of Cloth	3 Granite Slabs	0	0	51	Max Energy +5	Armor vs. Earth +15	–
Geomancer's Gloves	GLOVES	1,000	11 Bolts of Cloth	3 Granite Slabs	0	0	57	Max Energy +5	Armor vs. Earth +15	–
Geomancer's Gloves	GLOVES	1,500	25 Bolts of Cloth	4 Granite Slabs	0	0	60	Max Energy +5	Armor vs. Earth +15	–
Geomancer's Gloves	GLOVES	15,000	50 Bolts of Cloth	5 Granite Slabs	0	0	60	Max Energy +5	Armor vs. Earth +15	–
Geomancer's Gloves	GLOVES	15,000	50 Bolts of Cloth	5 Granite Slabs	15 Globs of Ectoplasm	15 Obsidian Shards	60	Max Energy +5	Armor vs. Earth +15	–
Pyromancer's Gloves	GLOVES	50	2 Bolts of Cloth	0	0	0	15	Max Energy +5	Armor vs. Fire +15	–
Pyromancer's Gloves	GLOVES	150	4 Bolts of Cloth	1 Scale	0	0	30	Max Energy +5	Armor vs. Fire +15	–
Pyromancer's Gloves	GLOVES	250	6 Bolts of Cloth	1 Scale	0	0	39	Max Energy +5	Armor vs. Fire +15	–
Pyromancer's Gloves	GLOVES	400	8 Bolts of Cloth	2 Scales	0	0	45	Max Energy +5	Armor vs. Fire +15	–
Pyromancer's Gloves	GLOVES	700	9 Bolts of Cloth	3 Scales	0	0	51	Max Energy +5	Armor vs. Fire +15	–
Pyromancer's Gloves	GLOVES	1,000	11 Bolts of Cloth	3 Scales	0	0	57	Max Energy +5	Armor vs. Fire +15	–
Pyromancer's Gloves	GLOVES	1,500	25 Bolts of Cloth	4 Scales	0	0	60	Max Energy +5	Armor vs. Fire +15	–
Pyromancer's Gloves	GLOVES	15,000	50 Bolts of Cloth	5 Scales	0	0	60	Max Energy +5	Armor vs. Fire +15	–
Pyromancer's Gloves	GLOVES	15,000	50 Bolts of Cloth	5 Scales	15 Globs of Ectoplasm	15 Obsidian Shards	60	Max Energy +5	Armor vs. Fire +15	–
Adept's Gloves	GLOVES	1,000	11 Bolts of Cloth	3 Silk	0	0	57	Max Energy +5	Armor vs. Elemental +5	–
Adept's Gloves	GLOVES	1,500	25 Bolts of Cloth	4 Silk	0	0	60	Max Energy +5	Armor vs. Elemental +5	–
Master's Gloves	GLOVES	15,000	50 Bolts of Cloth	5 Silk	0	0	60	Max Energy +5	Armor vs. Elemental +5	–
Elementalist's Gloves	GLOVES	50	1 Bolt of Cloth	0	0	0	15	Max Energy +5	–	–
Elementalist's Gloves	GLOVES	150	2 Bolts of Cloth	0	0	0	30	Max Energy +5	–	–
Elementalist's Gloves	GLOVES	250	3 Bolts of Cloth	0	0	0	39	Max Energy +5	–	–
Elementalist's Gloves	GLOVES	400	4 Bolts of Cloth	0	0	0	45	Max Energy +5	–	–
Elementalist's Gloves	GLOVES	700	8 Bolts of Cloth	0	0	0	51	Max Energy +5	–	–
Elementalist's Gloves	GLOVES	1,000	9 Bolts of Cloth	0	0	0	57	Max Energy +5	–	–
Elementalist's Gloves	GLOVES	1,500	11 Bolts of Cloth	0	0	0	60	Max Energy +5	–	–
Hydromancer's Gloves	GLOVES	150	4 Bolts of Cloth	1 Shell	0	0	30	Max Energy +5	Armor vs. Cold +15	–
Hydromancer's Gloves	GLOVES	250	6 Bolts of Cloth	1 Shell	0	0	39	Max Energy +5	Armor vs. Cold +15	–
Hydromancer's Gloves	GLOVES	400	8 Bolts of Cloth	2 Shells	0	0	45	Max Energy +5	Armor vs. Cold +15	–
Hydromancer's Gloves	GLOVES	700	9 Bolts of Cloth	3 Shells	0	0	51	Max Energy +5	Armor vs. Cold +15	–
Hydromancer's Gloves	GLOVES	1,000	11 Bolts of Cloth	3 Shells	0	0	57	Max Energy +5	Armor vs. Cold +15	–
Hydromancer's Gloves	GLOVES	1,500	25 Bolts of Cloth	4 Shells	0	0	60	Max Energy +5	Armor vs. Cold +15	–
Hydromancer's Gloves	GLOVES	15,000	50 Bolts of Cloth	5 Shells	0	0	60	Max Energy +5	Armor vs. Cold +15	–
Hydromancer's Gloves	GLOVES	15,000	50 Bolts of Cloth	5 Shells	15 Globs of Ectoplasm	15 Obsidian Shards	60	Max Energy +5	Armor vs. Cold +15	–

MONK GLOVES

Name	Type	Gold	Material 1	Material 2	Material 3	Material 4	Armor Level	Effect 1	Effect 2	Effect 3
Silk Handwraps	GLOVES	150	4 Bolts of Cloth	1 Silk	0	0	35	Max Energy +5	Armor vs. Cold -5	–
Silk Handwraps	GLOVES	250	6 Bolts of Cloth	1 Silk	0	0	44	Max Energy +5	Armor vs. Cold -5	–

Armor cont.

Name	Type	Gold	Material 1	Material 2	Material 3	Material 4	Armor Level	Effect 1	Effect 2	Effect 3
Silk Handwraps	GLOVES	400	8 Bolts of Cloth	2 Silk	0	0	50	Max Energy +5	Armor vs. Cold -5	–
Silk Handwraps	GLOVES	700	9 Bolts of Cloth	3 Silk	0	0	56	Max Energy +5	Armor vs. Cold -5	–
Silk Handwraps	GLOVES	1,000	11 Bolts of Cloth	3 Silk	0	0	61	Max Energy +5	Armor vs. Cold -5	–
Silk Handwraps	GLOVES	1,500	25 Bolts of Cloth	4 Silk	0	0	65	Max Energy +5	Armor vs. Cold -5	–
Silk Handwraps	GLOVES	15,000	50 Bolts of Cloth	5 Silk	0	0	65	Max Energy +5	Armor vs. Cold -5	–
Silk Handwraps	GLOVES	15,000	50 Bolts of Cloth	5 Silk	15 Globs of Ectoplasm	15 Obsidian Shards	65	Max Energy +5	Armor vs. Cold -5	–
Sacred Handwraps	GLOVES	150	4 Bolts of Cloth	1 Bolt of Linen	0	0	30	Max Energy +5	Armor vs. Elemental +5	–
Sacred Handwraps	GLOVES	250	6 Bolts of Cloth	1 Bolt of Linen	0	0	39	Max Energy +5	Armor vs. Elemental +5	–
Sacred Handwraps	GLOVES	400	8 Bolts of Cloth	2 Bolts of Linen	0	0	45	Max Energy +5	Armor vs. Elemental +5	–
Sacred Handwraps	GLOVES	700	9 Bolts of Cloth	3 Bolts of Linen	0	0	51	Max Energy +5	Armor vs. Elemental +5	–
Sacred Handwraps	GLOVES	1,000	11 Bolts of Cloth	3 Bolts of Linen	0	0	57	Max Energy +5	Armor vs. Elemental +5	–
Sacred Handwraps	GLOVES	1,500	25 Bolts of Cloth	4 Bolts of Linen	0	0	60	Max Energy +5	Armor vs. Elemental +5	–
Saintly Handwraps	GLOVES	15,000	50 Bolts of Cloth	5 Bolts of Damask	0	0	60	Max Energy +5	Armor vs. Elemental +5	–
Saintly Handwraps	GLOVES	15,000	50 Bolts of Cloth	5 Bolts of Damask	15 Globs of Ectoplasm	15 Obsidian Shards	60	Max Energy +5	Armor vs. Elemental +5	–
Ascetic's Arm Design	GLOVES	150	4 Rolls of Parchment	0	0	0	30	Max Energy +6	–	–
Ascetic's Arm Design	GLOVES	200	6 Rolls of Parchment	1 Feather	0	0	39	Max Energy +6	–	–
Ascetic's Arm Design	GLOVES	300	8 Rolls of Parchment	2 Feathers	0	0	45	Max Energy +6	–	–
Ascetic's Arm Design	GLOVES	400	9 Rolls of Parchment	3 Feathers	0	0	51	Max Energy +6	–	–
Ascetic's Arm Design	GLOVES	600	11 Rolls of Parchment	3 Feathers	0	0	57	Max Energy +6	–	–
Ascetic's Arm Design	GLOVES	800	25 Rolls of Parchment	4 Feathers	0	0	60	Max Energy +6	–	–
Ascetic's Arm Design	GLOVES	8,000	50 Rolls of Vellum	5 Feathers	0	0	60	Max Energy +6	–	–
Ascetic's Arm Design	GLOVES	8,000	50 Rolls of Vellum	5 Feathers	15 Globs of Ectoplasm	0	60	Max Energy +6	–	–
Monk Handwraps	GLOVES	50	1 Bolt of Cloth	0	0	0	15	Max Energy +5	–	–
Monk Handwraps	GLOVES	150	2 Bolts of Cloth	0	0	0	30	Max Energy +5	–	–
Monk Handwraps	GLOVES	250	3 Bolts of Cloth	0	0	0	39	Max Energy +5	–	–
Monk Handwraps	GLOVES	400	4 Bolts of Cloth	0	0	0	45	Max Energy +5	–	–
Monk Handwraps	GLOVES	700	8 Bolts of Cloth	0	0	0	51	Max Energy +5	–	–
Monk Handwraps	GLOVES	1,000	9 Bolts of Cloth	0	0	0	57	Max Energy +5	–	–
Monk Handwraps	GLOVES	1,500	11 Bolts of Cloth	0	0	0	60	Max Energy +5	–	–
Wanderer's Handwraps	GLOVES	50	2 Bolts of Cloth	0	0	0	15	Max Energy +5	Armor vs. Elemental +5	–
Wanderer's Handwraps	GLOVES	150	4 Bolts of Cloth	1 Tanned Hide Square	0	0	30	Max Energy +5	Armor vs. Elemental +5	–
Wanderer's Handwraps	GLOVES	250	6 Bolts of Cloth	1 Tanned Hide Square	0	0	39	Max Energy +5	Armor vs. Elemental +5	–
Wanderer's Handwraps	GLOVES	400	8 Bolts of Cloth	2 Tanned Hide Squares	0	0	45	Max Energy +5	Armor vs. Elemental +5	–
Wanderer's Handwraps	GLOVES	700	9 Bolts of Cloth	3 Tanned Hide Squares	0	0	51	Max Energy +5	Armor vs. Elemental +5	–
Wanderer's Handwraps	GLOVES	1,000	11 Bolts of Cloth	3 Tanned Hide Squares	0	0	57	Max Energy +5	Armor vs. Elemental +5	–
Wanderer's Handwraps	GLOVES	1,500	25 Bolts of Cloth	4 Tanned Hide Squares	0	0	60	Max Energy +5	Armor vs. Elemental +5	–
Wanderer's Handwraps	GLOVES	15,000	50 Bolts of Cloth	5 Tanned Hide Squares	0	0	60	Max Energy +5	Armor vs. Elemental +5	–
Wanderer's Handwraps	GLOVES	15,000	50 Bolts of Cloth	5 Tanned Hide Squares	15 Globs of Ectoplasm	15 Obsidian Shards	60	Max Energy +5	Armor vs. Elemental +5	–
Censor's Handwraps	GLOVES	150	4 Bolts of Cloth	1 Steel Ingot	0	0	30	Max Energy +4	Armor vs. Physical +10	–
Censor's Handwraps	GLOVES	250	6 Bolts of Cloth	1 Steel Ingot	0	0	39	Max Energy +4	Armor vs. Physical +10	–
Censor's Handwraps	GLOVES	400	8 Bolts of Cloth	2 Steel Ingots	0	0	45	Max Energy +4	Armor vs. Physical +10	–
Censor's Handwraps	GLOVES	700	9 Bolts of Cloth	3 Steel Ingots	0	0	51	Max Energy +4	Armor vs. Physical +10	–
Censor's Handwraps	GLOVES	1,000	11 Bolts of Cloth	3 Steel Ingots	0	0	57	Max Energy +4	Armor vs. Physical +10	–
Censor's Handwraps	GLOVES	1,500	25 Bolts of Cloth	4 Steel Ingots	0	0	60	Max Energy +4	Armor vs. Physical +10	–
Judge's Handwraps	GLOVES	15,000	50 Bolts of Cloth	5 Deldrimor Steel Ingots	0	0	60	Max Energy +4	Armor vs. Physical +10	–
Judge's Handwraps	GLOVES	15,000	50 Bolts of Cloth	5 Deldrimor Steel Ingots	15 Globs of Ectoplasm	15 Obsidian Shards	60	Max Energy +4	Armor vs. Physical +10	–
Ascetic's Arm Design	GLOVES	150	4 Rolls of Parchment	0	0	0	30	Max Energy +6	–	–
Ascetic's Arm Design	GLOVES	200	6 Rolls of Parchment	1 Feather	0	0	39	Max Energy +6	–	–
Ascetic's Arm Design	GLOVES	300	8 Rolls of Parchment	2 Feathers	0	0	45	Max Energy +6	–	–
Ascetic's Arm Design	GLOVES	400	9 Rolls of Parchment	3 Feathers	0	0	51	Max Energy +6	–	–
Ascetic's Arm Design	GLOVES	600	11 Rolls of Parchment	3 Feathers	0	0	57	Max Energy +6	–	–
Ascetic's Arm Design	GLOVES	800	25 Rolls of Parchment	4 Feathers	0	0	60	Max Energy +6	–	–
Ascetic's Arm Design	GLOVES	8,000	50 Rolls of Vellum	5 Feathers	0	0	60	Max Energy +6	–	–

WARRIOR GLOVES

Name	Type	Gold	Material 1	Material 2	Material 3	Material 4	Armor Level	Effect 1	Effect 2	Effect 3
Ascalon Gauntlets	GLOVES	50	2 Iron Ingots	0	0	0	35	Armor vs. Physical + 10	Damage -1	–
Ascalon Gauntlets	GLOVES	150	4 Iron Ingots	1 Fur Square	0	0	50	Armor vs. Physical + 10	Damage -1	–
Ascalon Gauntlets	GLOVES	250	6 Iron Ingots	1 Fur Square	0	0	59	Armor vs. Physical + 10	Damage -1	–
Ascalon Gauntlets	GLOVES	400	8 Iron Ingots	2 Fur Squares	0	0	65	Armor vs. Physical + 10	Damage -1	–
Ascalon Gauntlets	GLOVES	700	9 Iron Ingots	3 Fur Squares	0	0	71	Armor vs. Physical + 10	Damage -1	–
Ascalon Gauntlets	GLOVES	1,000	11 Iron Ingots	3 Fur Squares	0	0	77	Armor vs. Physical + 10	Damage -1	–
Ascalon Gauntlets	GLOVES	1,500	25 Iron Ingots	4 Fur Squares	0	0	80	Armor vs. Physical + 10	Damage -1	–
Ascalon Gauntlets	GLOVES	15,000	50 Iron Ingots	5 Fur Squares	0	0	80	Armor vs. Physical + 10	Damage -1	–
Ascalon Gauntlets	GLOVES	15,000	50 Iron Ingots	5 Fur Squares	15 Globs of Ectoplasm	15 Obsidian Shards	80	Armor vs. Physical + 10	Damage -1	–

Armor cont.

Name	Type	Gold	Material 1	Material 2	Material 3	Material 4	Armor Level	Effect 1	Effect 2	Effect 3
Chainmail Gauntlets	GLOVES	400	4 Iron Ingots	0	0	0	65	Armor vs. Physical + 20	–	–
Chainmail Gauntlets	GLOVES	700	8 Iron Ingots	0	0	0	71	Armor vs. Physical + 20	–	–
Chainmail Gauntlets	GLOVES	1,000	9 Iron Ingots	0	0	0	77	Armor vs. Physical + 20	–	–
Wyvern Gauntlets	GLOVES	150	4 Iron Ingots	1 Scale	0	0	55	Armor vs. Physical + 10	–	–
Wyvern Gauntlets	GLOVES	250	6 Iron Ingots	1 Scale	0	0	61	Armor vs. Physical + 10	–	–
Wyvern Gauntlets	GLOVES	400	8 Iron Ingots	2 Scales	0	0	70	Armor vs. Physical + 10	–	–
Wyvern Gauntlets	GLOVES	700	9 Iron Ingots	3 Scales	0	0	76	Armor vs. Physical + 10	–	–
Wyvern Gauntlets	GLOVES	1,000	11 Iron Ingots	3 Scales	0	0	82	Armor vs. Physical + 10	–	–
Wyvern Gauntlets	GLOVES	1,500	25 Iron Ingots	4 Scales	0	0	85	Armor vs. Physical + 10	–	–
Dragon Gauntlets	GLOVES	15,000	50 Iron Ingots	5 Scales	0	0	85	Armor vs. Physical + 10	–	–
Dragon Gauntlets	GLOVES	15,000	50 Iron Ingots	5 Scales	15 Globs of Ectoplasm	15 Obsidian Shards	85	Armor vs. Physical + 10	–	–
Gladiator's Gauntlets	GLOVES	150	4 Iron Ingots	4 Tanned Hide Squares	0	0	50	Max Energy +1	Armor vs. Physical +20	–
Gladiator's Gauntlets	GLOVES	250	6 Iron Ingots	6 Tanned Hide Squares	0	0	59	Max Energy +1	Armor vs. Physical +20	–
Gladiator's Gauntlets	GLOVES	400	8 Iron Ingots	8 Tanned Hide Squares	0	0	65	Max Energy +1	Armor vs. Physical +20	–
Gladiator's Gauntlets	GLOVES	700	9 Iron Ingots	9 Tanned Hide Squares	0	0	71	Max Energy +1	Armor vs. Physical +20	–
Gladiator's Gauntlets	GLOVES	1,000	11 Iron Ingots	11 Tanned Hide Squares	0	0	77	Max Energy +1	Armor vs. Physical +20	–
Gladiator's Gauntlets	GLOVES	1,500	25 Iron Ingots	16 Tanned Hide Squares	0	0	80	Max Energy +1	Armor vs. Physical +20	–
Gladiator's Gauntlets	GLOVES	15,000	50 Iron Ingots	16 Tanned Hide Squares	0	0	80	Max Energy +1	Armor vs. Physical +20	–
Gladiator's Gauntlets	GLOVES	15,000	50 Iron Ingots	16 Tanned Hide Squares	15 Globs of Ectoplasm	15 Obsidian Shards	80	Max Energy +1	Armor vs. Physical +20	–
Knight's Gauntlets	GLOVES	1,000	11 Iron Ingots	3 Leather Squares	0	0	77	Armor vs. Physical + 10	Damage -1	–
Knight's Gauntlets	GLOVES	1,500	25 Iron Ingots	4 Leather Squares	0	0	80	Armor vs. Physical + 10	Damage -1	–
Knight's Gauntlets	GLOVES	1,500	25 Iron Ingots	4 Leather Squares	0	0	80	Armor vs. Physical + 10	Damage -1	–
Soldier's Gauntlets	GLOVES	700	9 Iron Ingots	3 Steel Ingots	0	0	71	Armor vs. Physical + 20	–	–
Soldier's Gauntlets	GLOVES	1,000	11 Iron Ingots	3 Steel Ingots	0	0	77	Armor vs. Physical + 20	–	–
Platemail Gauntlets	GLOVES	1,000	11 Iron Ingots	3 Steel Ingots	0	0	77	Armor vs. Physical + 20	–	–
Platemail Gauntlets	GLOVES	1,500	25 Iron Ingots	4 Steel Ingots	0	0	80	Armor vs. Physical + 20	–	–
Platemail Gauntlets	GLOVES	15,000	50 Iron Ingots	5 Deldrimor Steel Ingots	0	0	80	Armor vs. Physical + 20	–	–
Platemail Gauntlets	GLOVES	15,000	50 Iron Ingots	5 Deldrimor Steel Ingots	15 Globs of Ectoplasm	15 Obsidian Shards	80	Armor vs. Physical + 20	–	–
Ringmail Gauntlets	GLOVES	50	1 Iron Ingot	0	0	0	35	Armor vs. Physical + 20	–	–
Ringmail Gauntlets	GLOVES	150	2 Iron Ingots	0	0	0	50	Armor vs. Physical + 20	–	–
Ringmail Gauntlets	GLOVES	250	3 Iron Ingots	0	0	0	59	Armor vs. Physical + 20	–	–
Stonefist Gauntlets	GLOVES	400	8 Iron Ingots	2 Granite Slabs	0	0	60	Armor vs. Physical + 20	Increased knockdown duration	–
Stonefist Gauntlets	GLOVES	700	9 Iron Ingots	3 Granite Slabs	0	0	66	Armor vs. Physical + 20	Increased knockdown duration	–
Stonefist Gauntlets	GLOVES	1,000	11 Iron Ingots	3 Granite Slabs	0	0	72	Armor vs. Physical + 20	Increased knockdown duration	–
Stonefist Gauntlets	GLOVES	1,500	25 Iron Ingots	4 Granite Slabs	0	0	75	Armor vs. Physical + 20	Increased knockdown duration	–

RANGER GLOVES

Name	Type	Gold	Material 1	Material 2	Material 3	Material 4	Armor Level	Effect 1	Effect 2	Effect 3
Hunter's Gloves	GLOVES	150	4 Tanned Hide Squares	4 Bone	0	0	40	Armor vs. Elemental +30	Armor vs. Piercing +15	–
Hunter's Gloves	GLOVES	250	6 Tanned Hide Squares	4 Bone	0	0	49	Armor vs. Elemental +30	Armor vs. Piercing +15	–
Hunter's Gloves	GLOVES	400	8 Tanned Hide Squares	8 Bone	0	0	55	Armor vs. Elemental +30	Armor vs. Piercing +15	–
Hunter's Gloves	GLOVES	700	9 Tanned Hide Squares	9 Bone	0	0	61	Armor vs. Elemental +30	Armor vs. Piercing +15	–
Hunter's Gloves	GLOVES	1,000	11 Tanned Hide Squares	11 Bone	0	0	67	Armor vs. Elemental +30	Armor vs. Piercing +15	–
Hunter's Gloves	GLOVES	1,500	25 Tanned Hide Squares	25 Bone	0	0	70	Armor vs. Elemental +30	Armor vs. Piercing +15	–
Hunter's Gloves	GLOVES	15,000	50 Tanned Hide Squares	50 Bone	0	0	70	Armor vs. Elemental +30	Armor vs. Piercing +15	–
Hunter's Gloves	GLOVES	15,000	50 Tanned Hide Squares	50 Bone	15 Globs of Ectoplasm	15 Obsidian Shards	70	Armor vs. Elemental +30	Armor vs. Piercing +15	–
Druid's Gloves	GLOVES	150	4 Tanned Hide Squares	4 Wood Planks	0	0	40	Max Energy +1	Armor vs. Elemental +30	–
Druid's Gloves	GLOVES	250	6 Tanned Hide Squares	4 Wood Planks	0	0	49	Max Energy +1	Armor vs. Elemental +30	–
Druid's Gloves	GLOVES	400	8 Tanned Hide Squares	8 Wood Planks	0	0	55	Max Energy +1	Armor vs. Elemental +30	–
Druid's Gloves	GLOVES	700	9 Tanned Hide Squares	9 Wood Planks	0	0	61	Max Energy +1	Armor vs. Elemental +30	–
Druid's Gloves	GLOVES	1,000	11 Tanned Hide Squares	11 Wood Planks	0	0	67	Max Energy +1	Armor vs. Elemental +30	–
Druid's Gloves	GLOVES	1,500	25 Tanned Hide Squares	25 Wood Planks	0	0	70	Max Energy +1	Armor vs. Elemental +30	–
Druid's Gloves	GLOVES	15,000	50 Tanned Hide Squares	50 Wood Planks	0	0	70	Max Energy +1	Armor vs. Elemental +30	–
Druid's Gloves	GLOVES	15,000	50 Tanned Hide Squares	50 Wood Planks	15 Globs of Ectoplasm	15 Obsidian Shards	70	Max Energy +1	Armor vs. Elemental +30	–
Fur-Lined Gloves	GLOVES	50	2 Tanned Hide Squares	0	0	0	25	Armor vs. Elemental +30	Armor vs. Cold +15	–
Fur-Lined Gloves	GLOVES	150	4 Tanned Hide Squares	1 Fur Square	0	0	40	Armor vs. Elemental +30	Armor vs. Cold +15	–
Fur-Lined Gloves	GLOVES	250	6 Tanned Hide Squares	1 Fur Square	0	0	49	Armor vs. Elemental +30	Armor vs. Cold +15	–
Fur-Lined Gloves	GLOVES	400	8 Tanned Hide Squares	2 Fur Squares	0	0	55	Armor vs. Elemental +30	Armor vs. Cold +15	–
Fur-Lined Gloves	GLOVES	700	9 Tanned Hide Squares	3 Fur Squares	0	0	61	Armor vs. Elemental +30	Armor vs. Cold +15	–
Fur-Lined Gloves	GLOVES	1,000	11 Tanned Hide Squares	3 Fur Squares	0	0	67	Armor vs. Elemental +30	Armor vs. Cold +15	–
Fur-Lined Gloves	GLOVES	1,500	25 Tanned Hide Squares	4 Fur Squares	0	0	70	Armor vs. Elemental +30	Armor vs. Cold +15	–
Frostbound Gloves	GLOVES	15,000	50 Tanned Hide Squares	5 Fur Squares	0	0	70	Armor vs. Elemental +30	Armor vs. Cold +15	–
Frostbound Gloves	GLOVES	15,000	50 Tanned Hide Squares	5 Fur Squares	15 Globs of Ectoplasm	15 Obsidian Shards	70	Armor vs. Elemental +30	Armor vs. Cold +15	–
Studded Leather Gloves	GLOVES	150	4 Tanned Hide Squares	1 Steel Ingot	0	0	40	Armor vs. Elemental +30	Armor vs. Lightning +15	–
Studded Leather Gloves	GLOVES	250	6 Tanned Hide Squares	1 Steel Ingot	0	0	49	Armor vs. Elemental +30	Armor vs. Lightning +15	–

Armor cont.

Name	Type	Gold	Material 1	Material 2	Material 3	Material 4	Armor Level	Effect 1	Effect 2	Effect 3
Studded Leather Gloves	GLOVES	400	8 Tanned Hide Squares	2 Steel Ingots	0	0	55	Armor vs. Elemental +30	Armor vs. Lightning +15	–
Studded Leather Gloves	GLOVES	700	9 Tanned Hide Squares	3 Steel Ingots	0	0	61	Armor vs. Elemental +30	Armor vs. Lightning +15	–
Studded Leather Gloves	GLOVES	1,000	11 Tanned Hide Squares	3 Steel Ingots	0	0	67	Armor vs. Elemental +30	Armor vs. Lightning +15	–
Studded Leather Gloves	GLOVES	1,500	25 Tanned Hide Squares	4 Steel Ingots	0	0	70	Armor vs. Elemental +30	Armor vs. Lightning +15	–
Studded Leather Gloves	GLOVES	15,000	50 Tanned Hide Squares	5 Deldrimor Steel Ingots	0	0	70	Armor vs. Elemental +30	Armor vs. Lightning +15	–
Studded Leather Gloves	GLOVES	15,000	50 Tanned Hide Squares	5 Deldrimor Steel Ingots	15 Globs of Ectoplasm	15 Obsidian Shards	70	Armor vs. Elemental +30	Armor vs. Lightning +15	–
Drakescale Gloves	GLOVES	150	4 Tanned Hide Squares	1 Scale	0	0	40	Armor vs. Elemental +30	Armor vs. Fire +15	–
Drakescale Gloves	GLOVES	250	6 Tanned Hide Squares	1 Scale	0	0	49	Armor vs. Elemental +30	Armor vs. Fire +15	–
Drakescale Gloves	GLOVES	400	8 Tanned Hide Squares	2 Scales	0	0	55	Armor vs. Elemental +30	Armor vs. Fire +15	–
Drakescale Gloves	GLOVES	700	9 Tanned Hide Squares	3 Scales	0	0	61	Armor vs. Elemental +30	Armor vs. Fire +15	–
Drakescale Gloves	GLOVES	1,000	11 Tanned Hide Squares	3 Scales	0	0	67	Armor vs. Elemental +30	Armor vs. Fire +15	–
Drakescale Gloves	GLOVES	1,500	25 Tanned Hide Squares	4 Scales	0	0	70	Armor vs. Elemental +30	Armor vs. Fire +15	–
Drakescale Gloves	GLOVES	15,000	50 Tanned Hide Squares	5 Scales	0	0	70	Armor vs. Elemental +30	Armor vs. Fire +15	–
Drakescale Gloves	GLOVES	15,000	50 Tanned Hide Squares	5 Scales	15 Globs of Ectoplasm	15 Obsidian Shards	70	Armor vs. Elemental +30	Armor vs. Fire +15	–
Leather Gloves	GLOVES	50	1 Tanned Hide Square	0	0	0	25	Armor vs. Elemental +30	–	–
Leather Gloves	GLOVES	150	2 Tanned Hide Squares	0	0	0	40	Armor vs. Elemental +30	–	–
Leather Gloves	GLOVES	250	3 Tanned Hide Squares	0	0	0	49	Armor vs. Elemental +30	–	–
Leather Gloves	GLOVES	400	4 Tanned Hide Squares	0	0	0	55	Armor vs. Elemental +30	–	–
Leather Gloves	GLOVES	700	8 Tanned Hide Squares	0	0	0	61	Armor vs. Elemental +30	–	–
Leather Gloves	GLOVES	1,000	9 Tanned Hide Squares	0	0	0	67	Armor vs. Elemental +30	–	–
Leather Gloves	GLOVES	1,500	11 Tanned Hide Squares	0	0	0	70	Armor vs. Elemental +30	–	–

MESMER HELMS

Name	Type	Gold	Material 1	Material 2	Material 3	Material 4	Armor Level	Effect 1	Effect 2	Effect 3
Imposing Mask	HELM	150	4 Bolts of Cloth	1 Steel Ingot	0	0	30	+1 Domination Magic	–	–
Imposing Mask	HELM	250	6 Bolts of Cloth	1 Steel Ingot	0	0	39	+1 Domination Magic	–	–
Imposing Mask	HELM	400	8 Bolts of Cloth	2 Steel Ingots	0	0	45	+1 Domination Magic	–	–
Imposing Mask	HELM	700	9 Bolts of Cloth	3 Steel Ingots	0	0	51	+1 Domination Magic	–	–
Imposing Mask	HELM	1,000	11 Bolts of Cloth	3 Steel Ingots	0	0	57	+1 Domination Magic	–	–
Imposing Mask	HELM	1,500	25 Bolts of Cloth	4 Steel Ingots	0	0	60	+1 Domination Magic	–	–
Sleek Mask	HELM	150	4 Bolts of Cloth	1 Bolt of Linen	0	0	30	+1 Fastcasting	–	–
Sleek Mask	HELM	250	6 Bolts of Cloth	1 Bolt of Linen	0	0	39	+1 Fastcasting	–	–
Sleek Mask	HELM	400	8 Bolts of Cloth	2 Bolts of Linen	0	0	45	+1 Fastcasting	–	–
Sleek Mask	HELM	700	9 Bolts of Cloth	3 Bolts of Linen	0	0	51	+1 Fastcasting	–	–
Sleek Mask	HELM	1,000	11 Bolts of Cloth	3 Bolts of Linen	0	0	57	+1 Fastcasting	–	–
Sleek Mask	HELM	1,500	25 Bolts of Cloth	4 Bolts of Linen	0	0	60	+1 Fastcasting	–	–
Costume Mask	HELM	150	4 Bolts of Cloth	1 Feather	0	0	30	+1 Illusion Magic	–	–
Costume Mask	HELM	250	6 Bolts of Cloth	1 Feather	0	0	39	+1 Illusion Magic	–	–
Costume Mask	HELM	400	8 Bolts of Cloth	2 Feathers	0	0	45	+1 Illusion Magic	–	–
Costume Mask	HELM	700	9 Bolts of Cloth	3 Feathers	0	0	51	+1 Illusion Magic	–	–
Costume Mask	HELM	1,000	11 Bolts of Cloth	3 Feathers	0	0	57	+1 Illusion Magic	–	–
Costume Mask	HELM	1,500	25 Bolts of Cloth	4 Feathers	0	0	60	+1 Illusion Magic	–	–
Animal Mask	HELM	150	4 Bolts of Cloth	1 Tanned Hide Square	0	0	30	+1 Inspiration Magic	–	–
Animal Mask	HELM	250	6 Bolts of Cloth	1 Tanned Hide Square	0	0	39	+1 Inspiration Magic	–	–
Animal Mask	HELM	400	8 Bolts of Cloth	2 Tanned Hide Squares	0	0	45	+1 Inspiration Magic	–	–
Animal Mask	HELM	700	9 Bolts of Cloth	3 Tanned Hide Squares	0	0	51	+1 Inspiration Magic	–	–
Animal Mask	HELM	1,000	11 Bolts of Cloth	3 Tanned Hide Squares	0	0	57	+1 Inspiration Magic	–	–
Animal Mask	HELM	1,500	25 Bolts of Cloth	4 Tanned Hide Squares	0	0	60	+1 Inspiration Magic	–	–
Discreet Mask	HELM	10	1 Pile of Glittering Dust	0	0	0	5	–	–	–
Discreet Mask	HELM	50	1 Pile of Glittering Dust	0	0	0	15	–	–	–
Discreet Mask	HELM	150	2 Piles of Glittering Dust	0	0	0	30	–	–	–
Discreet Mask	HELM	250	3 Piles of Glittering Dust	0	0	0	39	–	–	–
Discreet Mask	HELM	400	4 Piles of Glittering Dust	0	0	0	45	–	–	–
Discreet Mask	HELM	700	8 Piles of Glittering Dust	0	0	0	51	–	–	–
Discreet Mask	HELM	1,000	9 Piles of Glittering Dust	0	0	0	57	–	–	–
Discreet Mask	HELM	1,500	11 Piles of Glittering Dust	0	0	0	60	–	–	–

NECROMANCER HELMS

Name	Type	Gold	Material 1	Material 2	Material 3	Material 4	Armor Level	Effect 1	Effect 2	Effect 3
Ragged Scar Pattern	HELM	150	4 Rolls of Parchment	0	0	0	30	+1 Blood Magic	–	–
Ragged Scar Pattern	HELM	200	6 Rolls of Parchment	1 Feather	0	0	39	+1 Blood Magic	–	–
Ragged Scar Pattern	HELM	300	8 Rolls of Parchment	2 Feathers	0	0	45	+1 Blood Magic	–	–
Ragged Scar Pattern	HELM	400	9 Rolls of Parchment	3 Feathers	0	0	51	+1 Blood Magic	–	–
Ragged Scar Pattern	HELM	600	11 Rolls of Parchment	3 Feathers	0	0	57	+1 Blood Magic	–	–
Ragged Scar Pattern	HELM	800	25 Rolls of Parchment	4 Feathers	0	0	60	+1 Blood Magic	–	–
Wicked Scar Pattern	HELM	150	4 Rolls of Parchment	0	0	0	30	+1 Curses	–	–

Armor cont.

Name	Type	Gold	Material 1	Material 2	Material 3	Material 4	Armor Level	Effect 1	Effect 2	Effect 3
Wicked Scar Pattern	HELM	200	6 Rolls of Parchment	1 Feather	0	0	39	+1 Curses	–	–
Wicked Scar Pattern	HELM	300	8 Rolls of Parchment	2 Feathers	0	0	45	+1 Curses	–	–
Wicked Scar Pattern	HELM	400	9 Rolls of Parchment	3 Feathers	0	0	51	+1 Curses	–	–
Wicked Scar Pattern	HELM	600	11 Rolls of Parchment	3 Feathers	0	0	57	+1 Curses	–	–
Wicked Scar Pattern	HELM	800	25 Rolls of Parchment	4 Feathers	0	0	60	+1 Curses	–	–
Vile Scar Pattern	HELM	150	4 Rolls of Parchment	0	0	0	30	+1 Death Magic	–	–
Vile Scar Pattern	HELM	200	6 Rolls of Parchment	1 Feather	0	0	39	+1 Death Magic	–	–
Vile Scar Pattern	HELM	300	8 Rolls of Parchment	2 Feathers	0	0	45	+1 Death Magic	–	–
Vile Scar Pattern	HELM	400	9 Rolls of Parchment	3 Feathers	0	0	51	+1 Death Magic	–	–
Vile Scar Pattern	HELM	600	11 Rolls of Parchment	3 Feathers	0	0	57	+1 Death Magic	–	–
Vile Scar Pattern	HELM	800	25 Rolls of Parchment	4 Feathers	0	0	60	+1 Death Magic	–	–
Devilish Scar Pattern	HELM	150	4 Rolls of Parchment	0	0	0	30	+1 Soul Reaping	–	–
Devilish Scar Pattern	HELM	200	6 Rolls of Parchment	1 Feather	0	0	39	+1 Soul Reaping	–	–
Devilish Scar Pattern	HELM	300	8 Rolls of Parchment	2 Feathers	0	0	45	+1 Soul Reaping	–	–
Devilish Scar Pattern	HELM	400	9 Rolls of Parchment	3 Feathers	0	0	51	+1 Soul Reaping	–	–
Devilish Scar Pattern	HELM	600	11 Rolls of Parchment	3 Feathers	0	0	57	+1 Soul Reaping	–	–
Devilish Scar Pattern	HELM	800	25 Rolls of Parchment	4 Feathers	0	0	60	+1 Soul Reaping	–	–
Crude Scar Pattern	HELM	10	1 Roll of Parchment	0	0	0	5	–	–	–
Crude Scar Pattern	HELM	50	2 Rolls of Parchment	0	0	0	15	–	–	–
Crude Scar Pattern	HELM	150	4 Rolls of Parchment	0	0	0	30	–	–	–
Crude Scar Pattern	HELM	200	6 Rolls of Parchment	1 Feather	0	0	39	–	–	–
Crude Scar Pattern	HELM	300	8 Rolls of Parchment	2 Feathers	0	0	45	–	–	–
Crude Scar Pattern	HELM	400	9 Rolls of Parchment	3 Feathers	0	0	51	–	–	–
Crude Scar Pattern	HELM	600	11 Rolls of Parchment	3 Feathers	0	0	57	–	–	–
Crude Scar Pattern	HELM	800	25 Rolls of Parchment	4 Feathers	0	0	60	–	–	–

ELEMENTALIST HELMS

Name	Type	Gold	Material 1	Material 2	Material 3	Material 4	Armor Level	Effect 1	Effect 2	Effect 3
Storm's Eye	HELM	150	4 Piles of Glittering Dust	4 Iron Ingots	0	0	30	+1 Air Magic	–	–
Storm's Eye	HELM	250	6 Piles of Glittering Dust	6 Iron Ingots	0	0	39	+1 Air Magic	–	–
Storm's Eye	HELM	400	8 Piles of Glittering Dust	8 Iron Ingots	0	0	45	+1 Air Magic	–	–
Storm's Eye	HELM	700	9 Piles of Glittering Dust	9 Iron Ingots	0	0	51	+1 Air Magic	–	–
Storm's Eye	HELM	1,000	11 Piles of Glittering Dust	11 Iron Ingots	0	0	57	+1 Air Magic	–	–
Storm's Eye	HELM	1,500	25 Piles of Glittering Dust	25 Iron Ingots	0	0	60	+1 Air Magic	–	–
Stone's Eye	HELM	150	4 Piles of Glittering Dust	1 Granite Slab	0	0	30	+1 Earth Magic	–	–
Stone's Eye	HELM	250	6 Piles of Glittering Dust	1 Granite Slab	0	0	39	+1 Earth Magic	–	–
Stone's Eye	HELM	400	8 Piles of Glittering Dust	2 Granite Slabs	0	0	45	+1 Earth Magic	–	–
Stone's Eye	HELM	700	9 Piles of Glittering Dust	3 Granite Slabs	0	0	51	+1 Earth Magic	–	–
Stone's Eye	HELM	1,000	11 Piles of Glittering Dust	3 Granite Slabs	0	0	57	+1 Earth Magic	–	–
Stone's Eye	HELM	1,500	25 Piles of Glittering Dust	4 Granite Slabs	0	0	60	+1 Earth Magic	–	–
All-Seeing Eye	HELM	150	4 Piles of Glittering Dust	4 Iron Ingots	0	0	30	+1 Energy Storage	–	–
All-Seeing Eye	HELM	250	6 Piles of Glittering Dust	6 Iron Ingots	0	0	39	+1 Energy Storage	–	–
All-Seeing Eye	HELM	400	8 Piles of Glittering Dust	8 Iron Ingots	0	0	45	+1 Energy Storage	–	–
All-Seeing Eye	HELM	700	9 Piles of Glittering Dust	9 Iron Ingots	0	0	51	+1 Energy Storage	–	–
All-Seeing Eye	HELM	1,000	11 Piles of Glittering Dust	11 Iron Ingots	0	0	57	+1 Energy Storage	–	–
All-Seeing Eye	HELM	1,500	25 Piles of Glittering Dust	25 Iron Ingots	0	0	60	+1 Energy Storage	–	–
Flame's Eye	HELM	150	4 Piles of Glittering Dust	4 Iron Ingots	0	0	30	+1 Fire Magic	–	–
Flame's Eye	HELM	250	6 Piles of Glittering Dust	6 Iron Ingots	0	0	39	+1 Fire Magic	–	–
Flame's Eye	HELM	400	8 Piles of Glittering Dust	8 Iron Ingots	0	0	45	+1 Fire Magic	–	–
Flame's Eye	HELM	700	9 Piles of Glittering Dust	9 Iron Ingots	0	0	51	+1 Fire Magic	–	–
Flame's Eye	HELM	1,000	11 Piles of Glittering Dust	11 Iron Ingots	0	0	57	+1 Fire Magic	–	–
Flame's Eye	HELM	1,500	25 Piles of Glittering Dust	25 Iron Ingots	0	0	60	+1 Fire Magic	–	–
Third Eye	HELM	10	1 Pile of Glittering Dust	0	0	0	5	–	–	–
Third Eye	HELM	50	1 Pile of Glittering Dust	0	0	0	15	–	–	–
Third Eye	HELM	150	2 Piles of Glittering Dust	0	0	0	30	–	–	–
Third Eye	HELM	250	3 Piles of Glittering Dust	0	0	0	30	–	–	–
Third Eye	HELM	400	4 Piles of Glittering Dust	0	0	0	45	–	–	–
Third Eye	HELM	700	8 Piles of Glittering Dust	0	0	0	51	–	–	–
Third Eye	HELM	1,000	9 Piles of Glittering Dust	0	0	0	57	–	–	–
Third Eye	HELM	1,500	11 Piles of Glittering Dust	0	0	0	60	–	–	–
Glacier's Eye	HELM	150	4 Piles of Glittering Dust	4 Iron Ingots	0	0	30	+1 Water Magic	–	–
Glacier's Eye	HELM	250	6 Piles of Glittering Dust	6 Iron Ingots	0	0	39	+1 Water Magic	–	–
Glacier's Eye	HELM	400	8 Piles of Glittering Dust	8 Iron Ingots	0	0	35	+1 Water Magic	–	–
Glacier's Eye	HELM	700	9 Piles of Glittering Dust	9 Iron Ingots	0	0	51	+1 Water Magic	–	–
Glacier's Eye	HELM	1,000	11 Piles of Glittering Dust	11 Iron Ingots	0	0	57	+1 Water Magic	–	–
Glacier's Eye	HELM	1,500	25 Piles of Glittering Dust	25 Iron Ingots	0	0	60	+1 Water Magic	–	–

Armor cont.

Name	Type	Gold	Material 1	Material 2	Material 3	Material 4	Armor Level	Effect 1	Effect 2	Effect 3
MONK HELMS										
Prophet's Scalp Design	HELM	150	4 Rolls of Parchment	0	0	0	30	+1 Divine Favor	–	–
Prophet's Scalp Design	HELM	200	6 Rolls of Parchment	1 Feather	0	0	39	+1 Divine Favor	–	–
Prophet's Scalp Design	HELM	300	8 Rolls of Parchment	2 Feathers	0	0	45	+1 Divine Favor	–	–
Prophet's Scalp Design	HELM	400	9 Rolls of Parchment	3 Feathers	0	0	51	+1 Divine Favor	–	–
Prophet's Scalp Design	HELM	600	11 Rolls of Parchment	3 Feathers	0	0	57	+1 Divine Favor	–	–
Prophet's Scalp Design	HELM	800	25 Rolls of Parchment	4 Feathers	0	0	60	+1 Divine Favor	–	–
Servant's Scalp Design	HELM	150	4 Rolls of Parchment	0	0	0	30	+1 Healing Prayers	–	–
Servant's Scalp Design	HELM	200	6 Rolls of Parchment	1 Feather	0	0	39	+1 Healing Prayers	–	–
Servant's Scalp Design	HELM	300	8 Rolls of Parchment	2 Feathers	0	0	45	+1 Healing Prayers	–	–
Servant's Scalp Design	HELM	400	9 Rolls of Parchment	3 Feathers	0	0	51	+1 Healing Prayers	–	–
Servant's Scalp Design	HELM	600	11 Rolls of Parchment	3 Feathers	0	0	57	+1 Healing Prayers	–	–
Servant's Scalp Design	HELM	800	25 Rolls of Parchment	4 Feathers	0	0	60	+1 Healing Prayers	–	–
Scalp Design	HELM	150	4 Rolls of Parchment	0	0	0	30	Max Energy +1	–	–
Scalp Design	HELM	200	6 Rolls of Parchment	1 Feather	0	0	39	Max Energy +1	–	–
Scalp Design	HELM	300	8 Rolls of Parchment	2 Feathers	0	0	45	Max Energy +1	–	–
Scalp Design	HELM	400	9 Rolls of Parchment	3 Feathers	0	0	51	Max Energy +1	–	–
Scalp Design	HELM	600	11 Rolls of Parchment	3 Feathers	0	0	57	Max Energy +1	–	–
Scalp Design	HELM	800	25 Rolls of Parchment	4 Feathers	0	0	60	Max Energy +1	–	–
Defender's Scalp Design	HELM	150	4 Rolls of Parchment	0	0	0	30	+1 Protection Prayers	–	–
Defender's Scalp Design	HELM	200	6 Rolls of Parchment	1 Feather	0	0	39	+1 Protection Prayers	–	–
Defender's Scalp Design	HELM	300	8 Rolls of Parchment	2 Feathers	0	0	45	+1 Protection Prayers	–	–
Defender's Scalp Design	HELM	400	9 Rolls of Parchment	3 Feathers	0	0	51	+1 Protection Prayers	–	–
Defender's Scalp Design	HELM	600	11 Rolls of Parchment	3 Feathers	0	0	57	+1 Protection Prayers	–	–
Defender's Scalp Design	HELM	800	25 Rolls of Parchment	4 Feathers	0	0	60	+1 Protection Prayers	–	–
Defender's Scalp Design	HELM	150	4 Rolls of Parchment	0	0	0	30	+1 Smiting	–	–
Defender's Scalp Design	HELM	200	6 Rolls of Parchment	1 Feather	0	0	39	+1 Smiting	–	–
Defender's Scalp Design	HELM	300	8 Rolls of Parchment	2 Feathers	0	0	45	+1 Smiting	–	–
Defender's Scalp Design	HELM	400	9 Rolls of Parchment	3 Feathers	0	0	51	+1 Smiting	–	–
Defender's Scalp Design	HELM	600	11 Rolls of Parchment	3 Feathers	0	0	57	+1 Smiting	–	–
Defender's Scalp Design	HELM	800	25 Rolls of Parchment	4 Feathers	0	0	60	+1 Smiting	–	–
Believer's Scalp Design	HELM	10	1 Roll of Parchment	0	0	0	5	–	–	–
Believer's Scalp Design	HELM	50	2 Rolls of Parchment	0	0	0	15	–	–	–
Believer's Scalp Design	HELM	150	4 Rolls of Parchment	0	0	0	30	–	–	–
Believer's Scalp Design	HELM	200	6 Rolls of Parchment	1 Feather	0	0	39	–	–	–
Believer's Scalp Design	HELM	300	8 Rolls of Parchment	2 Feathers	0	0	45	–	–	–
Believer's Scalp Design	HELM	400	9 Rolls of Parchment	3 Feathers	0	0	51	–	–	–
Believer's Scalp Design	HELM	600	11 Rolls of Parchment	3 Feathers	0	0	57	–	–	–
Believer's Scalp Design	HELM	800	25 Rolls of Parchment	4 Feathers	0	0	60	–	–	–
Ascetic's Scalp Design	HELM	150	4 Rolls of Parchment	0	0	0	30	Max Energy +1	–	–
Ascetic's Scalp Design	HELM	200	6 Rolls of Parchment	1 Feather	0	0	39	Max Energy +1	–	–
Ascetic's Scalp Design	HELM	300	8 Rolls of Parchment	2 Feathers	0	0	45	Max Energy +1	–	–
Ascetic's Scalp Design	HELM	400	9 Rolls of Parchment	3 Feathers	0	0	51	Max Energy +1	–	–
Ascetic's Scalp Design	HELM	600	11 Rolls of Parchment	3 Feathers	0	0	57	Max Energy +1	–	–
Ascetic's Scalp Design	HELM	800	25 Rolls of Parchment	4 Feathers	0	0	60	Max Energy +1	–	–
WARRIOR HELMS										
Ascalon Helm	HELM	50	2 Iron Ingots	0	0	0	35	Armor vs. Physical + 20	–	–
Ascalon Helm	HELM	150	4 Iron Ingots	1 Fur Square	0	0	50	Armor vs. Physical + 20	+1 Tactics	–
Ascalon Helm	HELM	250	6 Iron Ingots	1 Fur Square	0	0	59	Armor vs. Physical + 20	+1 Tactics	–
Ascalon Helm	HELM	400	8 Iron Ingots	2 Fur Squares	0	0	65	Armor vs. Physical + 20	+1 Tactics	–
Ascalon Helm	HELM	700	9 Iron Ingots	3 Fur Squares	0	0	71	Armor vs. Physical + 20	+1 Tactics	–
Ascalon Helm	HELM	1,000	11 Iron Ingots	3 Fur Squares	0	0	77	Armor vs. Physical + 20	+1 Tactics	–
Ascalon Helm	HELM	1,500	25 Iron Ingots	4 Fur Squares	0	0	80	Armor vs. Physical + 10	Damage -1	–
Ascalon Helm	HELM	15,000	50 Iron Ingots	5 Fur Squares	0	0	80	Armor vs. Physical + 10	Damage -1	–
Ascalon Helm	HELM	15,000	50 Iron Ingots	5 Fur Squares	15 Globs of Ectoplasm	15 Obsidian Shards	80	Armor vs. Physical + 10	Damage -1	–
Executioner's Helm	HELM	150	4 Iron Ingots	1 Steel Ingot	0	0	50	Armor vs. Physical + 20	+1 Axe Mastery	–
Executioner's Helm	HELM	250	6 Iron Ingots	1 Steel Ingot	0	0	59	Armor vs. Physical + 20	+1 Axe Mastery	–
Executioner's Helm	HELM	400	8 Iron Ingots	2 Steel Ingots	0	0	65	Armor vs. Physical + 20	+1 Axe Mastery	–
Executioner's Helm	HELM	700	9 Iron Ingots	3 Steel Ingots	0	0	71	Armor vs. Physical + 20	+1 Axe Mastery	–
Executioner's Helm	HELM	1,000	11 Iron Ingots	3 Steel Ingots	0	0	77	Armor vs. Physical + 20	+1 Axe Mastery	–
Executioner's Helm	HELM	1,500	25 Iron Ingots	4 Steel Ingots	0	0	80	Armor vs. Physical + 20	+1 Axe Mastery	–
Captain's Helm	HELM	1,500	25 Iron Ingots	4 Silk	0	0	75	Armor vs. Physical + 10	–	–
Chainmail Helm	HELM	400	4 Iron Ingots	0	0	0	65	–	–	–

Armor cont.

Name	Type	Gold	Material 1	Material 2	Material 3	Material 4	Armor Level	Effect 1	Effect 2	Effect 3
Chainmail Helm	HELM	700	8 Iron Ingots	0	0	0	71	–	–	–
Chainmail Helm	HELM	1,000	9 Iron Ingots	0	0	0	77	–	–	–
Wyvern Helm	HELM	150	4 Iron Ingots	1 Scale	0	0	55	Armor vs. Physical + 10	+1 Strength	–
Wyvern Helm	HELM	250	6 Iron Ingots	1 Scale	0	0	64	Armor vs. Physical + 10	+1 Strength	–
Wyvern Helm	HELM	400	8 Iron Ingots	2 Scales	0	0	70	Armor vs. Physical + 10	+1 Strength	–
Wyvern Helm	HELM	700	9 Iron Ingots	3 Scales	0	0	76	Armor vs. Physical + 10	+1 Strength	–
Wyvern Helm	HELM	1,000	11 Iron Ingots	3 Scales	0	0	82	Armor vs. Physical + 10	+1 Strength	–
Wyvern Helm	HELM	1,500	25 Iron Ingots	4 Scales	0	0	85	Armor vs. Physical + 10	+1 Strength	–
Dragon Helm	HELM	15,000	50 Iron Ingots	5 Scales	0	0	85	Armor vs. Physical + 10	+1 Strength	–
Wyvern Helm	HELM	15,000	50 Iron Ingots	5 Scales	15 Globs of Ectoplasm	15 Obsidian Shards	85	Armor vs. Physical + 10	+1 Strength	–
Gladiator's Helm	HELM	150	4 Iron Ingots	4 Tanned Hide Squares	0	0	50	Max Energy +1	Armor vs. Physical +20	+1 Tactics
Gladiator's Helm	HELM	250	6 Iron Ingots	6 Tanned Hide Squares	0	0	59	Max Energy +1	Armor vs. Physical +20	+1 Tactics
Gladiator's Helm	HELM	400	8 Iron Ingots	8 Tanned Hide Squares	0	0	65	Max Energy +1	Armor vs. Physical +20	+1 Tactics
Gladiator's Helm	HELM	700	9 Iron Ingots	9 Tanned Hide Squares	0	0	71	Max Energy +1	Armor vs. Physical +20	+1 Tactics
Gladiator's Helm	HELM	1,000	11 Iron Ingots	11 Tanned Hide Squares	0	0	77	Max Energy +1	Armor vs. Physical +20	+1 Tactics
Gladiator's Helm	HELM	1,500	25 Iron Ingots	16 Tanned Hide Squares	0	0	80	Max Energy +1	Armor vs. Physical +20	+1 Tactics
Dwarven Helm	HELM	150	4 Iron Ingots	1 Steel Ingot	0	0	50	Armor vs. Physical + 20	+1 Hammer Mastery	–
Dwarven Helm	HELM	250	6 Iron Ingots	1 Steel Ingot	0	0	59	Armor vs. Physical + 20	+1 Hammer Mastery	–
Dwarven Helm	HELM	400	8 Iron Ingots	2 Steel Ingots	0	0	65	Armor vs. Physical + 20	+1 Hammer Mastery	–
Dwarven Helm	HELM	700	9 Iron Ingots	3 Steel Ingots	0	0	71	Armor vs. Physical + 20	+1 Hammer Mastery	–
Dwarven Helm	HELM	1,000	11 Iron Ingots	3 Steel Ingots	0	0	77	Armor vs. Physical + 20	+1 Hammer Mastery	–
Dwarven Helm	HELM	1,500	25 Iron Ingots	4 Steel Ingots	0	0	80	Armor vs. Physical + 20	+1 Hammer Mastery	–
Knight's Helm	HELM	1,000	11 Iron Ingots	3 Steel Ingots	0	0	77	Armor vs. Physical + 20	–	–
Knight's Helm	HELM	1,500	25 Iron Ingots	4 Steel Ingots	0	0	80	Armor vs. Physical + 20	+1 Strength	–
Soldier's Helm	HELM	700	9 Iron Ingots	3 Steel Ingots	0	0	71	Armor vs. Physical + 20	–	–
Soldier's Helm	HELM	1,000	11 Iron Ingots	3 Steel Ingots	0	0	77	Armor vs. Physical + 20	–	–
Platemail Helm	HELM	1,000	11 Iron Ingots	3 Steel Ingots	0	0	77	Armor vs. Physical + 20	–	–
Platemail Helm	HELM	1,500	25 Iron Ingots	4 Steel Ingots	0	0	80	Armor vs. Physical + 20	–	–
Platemail Helm	HELM	15,000	50 Iron Ingots	5 Deldrimor Steel Ingots	0	0	80	Armor vs. Physical + 20	+1 Strength	–
Lieutenant's Helm	HELM	400	8 Iron Ingots	2 Silk	0	0	60	Armor vs. Physical + 10	–	–
Recruit's Cap	HELM	50	1 Iron Ingot	0	0	0	35	Armor vs. Physical + 20	–	–
Recruit's Cap	HELM	150	2 Iron Ingots	0	0	0	50	Armor vs. Physical + 20	–	–
Recruit's Cap	HELM	250	3 Iron Ingots	0	0	0	59	Armor vs. Physical + 20	–	–
Duelist's Helm	HELM	150	4 Iron Ingots	1 Steel Ingot	0	0	50	Armor vs. Physical + 20	+1 Swordsmanship	–
Duelist's Helm	HELM	250	6 Iron Ingots	1 Steel Ingot	0	0	59	Armor vs. Physical + 20	+1 Swordsmanship	–
Duelist's Helm	HELM	400	8 Iron Ingots	2 Steel Ingots	0	0	65	Armor vs. Physical + 20	+1 Swordsmanship	–
Duelist's Helm	HELM	700	9 Iron Ingots	3 Steel Ingots	0	0	71	Armor vs. Physical + 20	+1 Swordsmanship	–
Duelist's Helm	HELM	1,000	11 Iron Ingots	3 Steel Ingots	0	0	77	Armor vs. Physical + 20	+1 Swordsmanship	–
Duelist's Helm	HELM	1,500	25 Iron Ingots	4 Steel Ingots	0	0	80	Armor vs. Physical + 20	+1 Swordsmanship	–
Brute's Helm	HELM	150	4 Iron Ingots	1 Steel Ingot	0	0	50	Armor vs. Physical + 20	+1 Strength	–
Brute's Helm	HELM	250	6 Iron Ingots	1 Steel Ingot	0	0	59	Armor vs. Physical + 20	+1 Strength	–
Brute's Helm	HELM	400	8 Iron Ingots	2 Steel Ingots	0	0	65	Armor vs. Physical + 20	+1 Strength	–
Brute's Helm	HELM	700	9 Iron Ingots	3 Steel Ingots	0	0	71	Armor vs. Physical + 20	+1 Strength	–
Brute's Helm	HELM	1,000	11 Iron Ingots	3 Steel Ingots	0	0	77	Armor vs. Physical + 20	+1 Strength	–
Brute's Helm	HELM	1,500	25 Iron Ingots	4 Steel Ingots	0	0	80	Armor vs. Physical + 20	+1 Strength	–
Tactician's Helm	HELM	150	4 Iron Ingots	1 Steel Ingot	0	0	50	Armor vs. Physical + 20	+1 Tactics	–
Tactician's Helm	HELM	250	6 Iron Ingots	1 Steel Ingot	0	0	59	Armor vs. Physical + 20	+1 Tactics	–
Tactician's Helm	HELM	400	8 Iron Ingots	2 Steel Ingots	0	0	65	Armor vs. Physical + 20	+1 Tactics	–
Tactician's Helm	HELM	700	9 Iron Ingots	3 Steel Ingots	0	0	71	Armor vs. Physical + 20	+1 Tactics	–
Tactician's Helm	HELM	1,000	11 Iron Ingots	3 Steel Ingots	0	0	77	Armor vs. Physical + 20	+1 Tactics	–
Tactician's Helm	HELM	1,500	25 Iron Ingots	4 Steel Ingots	0	0	80	Armor vs. Physical + 20	+1 Tactics	–

RANGER HELMS

Name	Type	Gold	Material 1	Material 2	Material 3	Material 4	Armor Level	Effect 1	Effect 2	Effect 3
Tamer's Mask	HELM	150	4 Bolts of Cloth	1 Fur Square	0	0	40	+1 Beast Mastery	–	Armor vs. Elemental +30
Tamer's Mask	HELM	250	6 Bolts of Cloth	1 Fur Square	0	0	49	+1 Beast Mastery	–	Armor vs. Elemental +30
Tamer's Mask	HELM	400	8 Bolts of Cloth	2 Fur Squares	0	0	55	+1 Beast Mastery	–	Armor vs. Elemental +30
Tamer's Mask	HELM	700	9 Bolts of Cloth	3 Fur Squares	0	0	61	+1 Beast Mastery	–	Armor vs. Elemental +30
Tamer's Mask	HELM	1,000	11 Bolts of Cloth	3 Fur Squares	0	0	67	+1 Beast Mastery	–	Armor vs. Elemental +30
Tamer's Mask	HELM	1,500	25 Bolts of Cloth	4 Fur Squares	0	0	70	+1 Beast Mastery	–	Armor vs. Elemental +30
Archer's Mask	HELM	150	4 Bolts of Cloth	1 Bolt of Linen	0	0	40	+1 Marksmanship	–	Armor vs. Elemental +30
Archer's Mask	HELM	250	6 Bolts of Cloth	1 Bolt of Linen	0	0	49	+1 Marksmanship	–	Armor vs. Elemental +30
Archer's Mask	HELM	400	8 Bolts of Cloth	2 Bolts of Linen	0	0	55	+1 Marksmanship	–	Armor vs. Elemental +30
Archer's Mask	HELM	700	9 Bolts of Cloth	3 Bolts of Linen	0	0	61	+1 Marksmanship	–	Armor vs. Elemental +30
Archer's Mask	HELM	1,000	11 Bolts of Cloth	3 Bolts of Linen	0	0	67	+1 Marksmanship	–	Armor vs. Elemental +30

Armor cont.

Name	Type	Gold	Material 1	Material 2	Material 3	Material 4	Armor Level	Effect 1	Effect 2	Effect 3
Archer's Mask	HELM	1,500	25 Bolts of Cloth	4 Bolts of Linen	0	0	70	+1 Marksmanship	–	Armor vs. Elemental +30
Hunter's Mask	HELM	150	4 Bolts of Cloth	1 Silk	0	0	40	+1 Expertise	–	Armor vs. Elemental +30
Hunter's Mask	HELM	250	6 Bolts of Cloth	1 Silk	0	0	49	+1 Expertise	–	Armor vs. Elemental +30
Hunter's Mask	HELM	400	8 Bolts of Cloth	2 Silk	0	0	55	+1 Expertise	–	Armor vs. Elemental +30
Hunter's Mask	HELM	700	9 Bolts of Cloth	3 Silk	0	0	61	+1 Expertise	–	Armor vs. Elemental +30
Hunter's Mask	HELM	1,000	11 Bolts of Cloth	3 Silk	0	0	67	+1 Expertise	–	Armor vs. Elemental +30
Hunter's Mask	HELM	1,500	25 Bolts of Cloth	4 Silk	0	0	70	+1 Expertise	–	Armor vs. Elemental +30
Simple Mask	HELM	10	1 Bolt of Cloth	0	0	0	10	Armor vs. Elemental +30	–	–
Simple Mask	HELM	50	1 Bolt of Cloth	0	0	0	25	Armor vs. Elemental +30	–	–
Simple Mask	HELM	150	2 Bolts of Cloth	0	0	0	40	Armor vs. Elemental +30	–	–
Simple Mask	HELM	250	3 Bolts of Cloth	0	0	0	49	Armor vs. Elemental +30	–	–
Simple Mask	HELM	400	4 Bolts of Cloth	0	0	0	55	Armor vs. Elemental +30	–	–
Simple Mask	HELM	700	8 Bolts of Cloth	0	0	0	61	Armor vs. Elemental +30	–	–
Simple Mask	HELM	1,000	9 Bolts of Cloth	0	0	0	67	Armor vs. Elemental +30	–	–
Simple Mask	HELM	1,500	11 Bolts of Cloth	0	0	0	70	Armor vs. Elemental +30	–	–
Traveler's Mask	HELM	150	4 Bolts of Cloth	1 Scale	0	0	40	+1 Wilderness Survival	–	Armor vs. Elemental +30
Traveler's Mask	HELM	250	6 Bolts of Cloth	1 Scale	0	0	49	+1 Wilderness Survival	–	Armor vs. Elemental +30
Traveler's Mask	HELM	400	8 Bolts of Cloth	2 Scales	0	0	55	+1 Wilderness Survival	–	Armor vs. Elemental +30
Traveler's Mask	HELM	700	9 Bolts of Cloth	3 Scales	0	0	61	+1 Wilderness Survival	–	Armor vs. Elemental +30
Traveler's Mask	HELM	1,000	11 Bolts of Cloth	3 Scales	0	0	67	+1 Wilderness Survival	–	Armor vs. Elemental +30
Traveler's Mask	HELM	1,500	25 Bolts of Cloth	4 Scales	0	0	70	+1 Wilderness Survival	–	Armor vs. Elemental +30

MESMER LEGGINGS

Name	Type	Gold	Material 1	Material 2	Material 3	Material 4	Armor Level	Effect 1	Effect 2	Effect 3
Courtly Hose	LEGGINGS	50	4 Bolts of Cloth	0	0	0	15	+ 1 Energy Regen	+15 Armor while casting	–
Courtly Hose	LEGGINGS	150	8 Bolts of Cloth	2 Bolts of Linen	0	0	30	+ 1 Energy Regen	+15 Armor while casting	–
Courtly Hose	LEGGINGS	250	12 Bolts of Cloth	2 Bolts of Linen	0	0	39	+ 1 Energy Regen	+15 Armor while casting	–
Courtly Hose	LEGGINGS	400	16 Bolts of Cloth	4 Bolts of Linen	0	0	45	+ 1 Energy Regen	+15 Armor while casting	–
Courtly Hose	LEGGINGS	700	18 Bolts of Cloth	6 Bolts of Linen	0	0	51	+ 1 Energy Regen	+15 Armor while casting	–
Courtly Hose	LEGGINGS	1,000	22 Bolts of Cloth	6 Bolts of Linen	0	0	57	+ 1 Energy Regen	+15 Armor while casting	–
Courtly Hose	LEGGINGS	1,500	50 Bolts of Cloth	8 Bolts of Linen	0	0	60	+ 1 Energy Regen	+15 Armor while casting	–
Noble Hose	LEGGINGS	15,000	100 Bolts of Cloth	10 Bolts of Damask	0	0	60	+ 1 Energy Regen	+15 Armor while casting	–
Noble Hose	LEGGINGS	15,000	100 Bolts of Cloth	10 Bolts of Damask	30 Globs of Ectoplasm	30 Obsidian Shards	60	+ 1 Energy Regen	+15 Armor while casting	–
Enchanter's Hose	LEGGINGS	150	8 Bolts of Cloth	2 Piles of Glittering Dust	0	0	30	+ 1 Energy Regen	Max Energy +2	–
Enchanter's Hose	LEGGINGS	250	12 Bolts of Cloth	2 Piles of Glittering Dust	0	0	39	+ 1 Energy Regen	Max Energy +2	–
Enchanter's Hose	LEGGINGS	400	16 Bolts of Cloth	4 Piles of Glittering Dust	0	0	45	+ 1 Energy Regen	Max Energy +2	–
Enchanter's Hose	LEGGINGS	700	18 Bolts of Cloth	6 Piles of Glittering Dust	0	0	51	+ 1 Energy Regen	Max Energy +2	–
Enchanter's Hose	LEGGINGS	1,000	22 Bolts of Cloth	6 Piles of Glittering Dust	0	0	57	+ 1 Energy Regen	Max Energy +2	–
Enchanter's Hose	LEGGINGS	1,500	50 Bolts of Cloth	8 Piles of Glittering Dust	0	0	60	+ 1 Energy Regen	Max Energy +2	–
Enchanter's Hose	LEGGINGS	15,000	100 Bolts of Cloth	10 Piles of Glittering Dust	0	0	60	+ 1 Energy Regen	Max Energy +2	–
Enchanter's Hose	LEGGINGS	15,000	100 Bolts of Cloth	10 Piles of Glittering Dust	30 Globs of Ectoplasm	30 Obsidian Shards	60	+ 1 Energy Regen	Max Energy +2	–
Performer's Hose	LEGGINGS	150	8 Bolts of Cloth	2 Silk	0	0	30	+ 1 Energy Regen	+15 Armor while casting	–
Performer's Hose	LEGGINGS	250	12 Bolts of Cloth	2 Silk	0	0	39	+ 1 Energy Regen	+15 Armor while casting	–
Performer's Hose	LEGGINGS	400	16 Bolts of Cloth	4 Silk	0	0	45	+ 1 Energy Regen	+15 Armor while casting	–
Performer's Hose	LEGGINGS	700	18 Bolts of Cloth	6 Silk	0	0	51	+ 1 Energy Regen	+15 Armor while casting	–
Performer's Hose	LEGGINGS	1,000	22 Bolts of Cloth	6 Silk	0	0	57	+ 1 Energy Regen	+15 Armor while casting	–
Performer's Hose	LEGGINGS	1,500	50 Bolts of Cloth	8 Silk	0	0	60	+ 1 Energy Regen	+15 Armor while casting	–
Virtuoso's Hose	LEGGINGS	15,000	100 Bolts of Cloth	10 Silk	0	0	60	+ 1 Energy Regen	+15 Armor while casting	–
Virtuoso's Hose	LEGGINGS	15,000	100 Bolts of Cloth	10 Silk	30 Globs of Ectoplasm	30 Obsidian Shards	60	+ 1 Energy Regen	+15 Armor while casting	–
Rogue's Hose	LEGGINGS	50	4 Bolts of Cloth	0	0	0	15	+ 1 Energy Regen	Armor vs. Physical +10	Max Energy -1
Rogue's Hose	LEGGINGS	150	8 Bolts of Cloth	2 Leather Squares	0	0	30	+ 1 Energy Regen	Armor vs. Physical +10	Max Energy -1
Rogue's Hose	LEGGINGS	250	12 Bolts of Cloth	2 Leather Squares	0	0	39	+ 1 Energy Regen	Armor vs. Physical +10	Max Energy -1
Rogue's Hose	LEGGINGS	400	16 Bolts of Cloth	4 Leather Squares	0	0	45	+ 1 Energy Regen	Armor vs. Physical +10	Max Energy -1
Rogue's Hose	LEGGINGS	700	18 Bolts of Cloth	6 Leather Squares	0	0	51	+ 1 Energy Regen	Armor vs. Physical +10	Max Energy -1
Rogue's Hose	LEGGINGS	1,000	22 Bolts of Cloth	6 Leather Squares	0	0	57	+ 1 Energy Regen	Armor vs. Physical +10	Max Energy -1
Rogue's Hose	LEGGINGS	1,500	50 Bolts of Cloth	8 Leather Squares	0	0	60	+ 1 Energy Regen	Armor vs. Physical +10	Max Energy -1
Rogue's Hose	LEGGINGS	15,000	100 Bolts of Cloth	10 Elonian Leather Squares	0	0	60	+ 1 Energy Regen	Armor vs. Physical +10	Max Energy -1
Rogue's Hose	LEGGINGS	15,000	100 Bolts of Cloth	10 Elonian Leather Squares	30 Globs of Ectoplasm	30 Obsidian Shards	60	+ 1 Energy Regen	Armor vs. Physical +10	Max Energy -1
Regal Hose	LEGGINGS	150	8 Bolts of Cloth	2 Silk	0	0	35	+ 1 Energy Regen	Armor vs. Earth -5	–
Regal Hose	LEGGINGS	250	12 Bolts of Cloth	2 Silk	0	0	44	+ 1 Energy Regen	Armor vs. Earth -5	–
Regal Hose	LEGGINGS	400	16 Bolts of Cloth	4 Silk	0	0	50	+ 1 Energy Regen	Armor vs. Earth -5	–
Regal Hose	LEGGINGS	700	18 Bolts of Cloth	6 Silk	0	0	56	+ 1 Energy Regen	Armor vs. Earth -5	–
Regal Hose	LEGGINGS	1,000	22 Bolts of Cloth	6 Silk	0	0	62	+ 1 Energy Regen	Armor vs. Earth -5	–
Regal Hose	LEGGINGS	1,500	50 Bolts of Cloth	8 Silk	0	0	65	+ 1 Energy Regen	Armor vs. Earth -5	–
Regal Hose	LEGGINGS	15,000	100 Bolts of Cloth	10 Silk	0	0	65	+ 1 Energy Regen	Armor vs. Earth -5	–

Armor cont.

Name	Type	Gold	Material 1	Material 2	Material 3	Material 4	Armor Level	Effect 1	Effect 2	Effect 3
Regal Hose	LEGGINGS	15,000	100 Bolts of Cloth	10 Silk	30 Globs of Ectoplasm	30 Obsidian Shards	65	+ 1 Energy Regen	Armor vs. Earth -5	–
Stylish Hose	LEGGINGS	50	2 Bolts of Cloth	0	0	0	15	+ 1 Energy Regen	–	–
Stylish Hose	LEGGINGS	150	4 Bolts of Cloth	0	0	0	30	+ 1 Energy Regen	–	–
Stylish Hose	LEGGINGS	250	6 Bolts of Cloth	0	0	0	39	+ 1 Energy Regen	–	–
Stylish Hose	LEGGINGS	400	8 Bolts of Cloth	0	0	0	45	+ 1 Energy Regen	–	–
Stylish Hose	LEGGINGS	700	16 Bolts of Cloth	0	0	0	51	+ 1 Energy Regen	–	–
Stylish Hose	LEGGINGS	1,000	18 Bolts of Cloth	0	0	0	57	+ 1 Energy Regen	–	–
Stylish Hose	LEGGINGS	1,500	22 Bolts of Cloth	0	0	0	60	+ 1 Energy Regen	–	–

NECROMANCER LEGGINGS

Name	Type	Gold	Material 1	Material 2	Material 3	Material 4	Armor Level	Effect 1	Effect 2	Effect 3
Bonelace Leggings	LEGGINGS	50	4 Tanned Hide Squares	0	0	0	15	+ 1 Energy Regen	Armor vs. Piercing +15	–
Bonelace Leggings	LEGGINGS	150	8 Tanned Hide Squares	8 Bone	0	0	30	+ 1 Energy Regen	Armor vs. Piercing +15	–
Bonelace Leggings	LEGGINGS	250	12 Tanned Hide Squares	8 Bone	0	0	39	+ 1 Energy Regen	Armor vs. Piercing +15	–
Bonelace Leggings	LEGGINGS	400	16 Tanned Hide Squares	16 Bone	0	0	45	+ 1 Energy Regen	Armor vs. Piercing +15	–
Bonelace Leggings	LEGGINGS	700	18 Tanned Hide Squares	18 Bone	0	0	51	+ 1 Energy Regen	Armor vs. Piercing +15	–
Bonelace Leggings	LEGGINGS	1,000	22 Tanned Hide Squares	22 Bone	0	0	57	+ 1 Energy Regen	Armor vs. Piercing +15	–
Bonelace Leggings	LEGGINGS	1,500	50 Tanned Hide Squares	50 Bone	0	0	60	+ 1 Energy Regen	Armor vs. Piercing +15	–
Bonelace Leggings	LEGGINGS	15,000	100 Tanned Hide Squares	100 Bone	0	0	60	+ 1 Energy Regen	Armor vs. Piercing +15	–
Bonelace Leggings	LEGGINGS	15,000	100 Tanned Hide Squares	100 Bone	30 Globs of Ectoplasm	30 Obsidian Shards	60	+ 1 Energy Regen	Armor vs. Piercing +15	–
Tormentor's Leggings	LEGGINGS	150	8 Tanned Hide Squares	2 Steel Ingots	0	0	40	+ 1 Energy Regen	Increased damage vs. Holy	–
Tormentor's Leggings	LEGGINGS	250	12 Tanned Hide Squares	2 Steel Ingots	0	0	49	+ 1 Energy Regen	Increased damage vs. Holy	–
Tormentor's Leggings	LEGGINGS	400	16 Tanned Hide Squares	4 Steel Ingots	0	0	55	+ 1 Energy Regen	Increased damage vs. Holy	–
Tormentor's Leggings	LEGGINGS	700	18 Tanned Hide Squares	6 Steel Ingots	0	0	61	+ 1 Energy Regen	Increased damage vs. Holy	–
Tormentor's Leggings	LEGGINGS	1,000	22 Tanned Hide Squares	6 Steel Ingots	0	0	67	+ 1 Energy Regen	Increased damage vs. Holy	–
Tormentor's Leggings	LEGGINGS	1,500	50 Tanned Hide Squares	8 Steel Ingots	0	0	70	+ 1 Energy Regen	Increased damage vs. Holy	–
Tormentor's Leggings	LEGGINGS	15,000	100 Tanned Hide Squares	10 Deldrimor Steel Ingots	0	0	70	+ 1 Energy Regen	Increased damage vs. Holy	–
Tormentor's Leggings	LEGGINGS	15,000	100 Tanned Hide Squares	10 Deldrimor Steel Ingots	30 Globs of Ectoplasm	30 Obsidian Shards	70	+ 1 Energy Regen	Increased damage vs. Holy	–
Fanatic's Leggings	LEGGINGS	150	8 Tanned Hide Squares	2 Leather Squares	0	0	30	+ 1 Energy Regen	Armor vs. Piercing +15	–
Fanatic's Leggings	LEGGINGS	250	12 Tanned Hide Squares	2 Leather Squares	0	0	39	+ 1 Energy Regen	Armor vs. Piercing +15	–
Fanatic's Leggings	LEGGINGS	400	16 Tanned Hide Squares	4 Leather Squares	0	0	45	+ 1 Energy Regen	Armor vs. Piercing +15	–
Fanatic's Leggings	LEGGINGS	700	18 Tanned Hide Squares	6 Leather Squares	0	0	51	+ 1 Energy Regen	Armor vs. Piercing +15	–
Fanatic's Leggings	LEGGINGS	1,000	22 Tanned Hide Squares	6 Leather Squares	0	0	57	+ 1 Energy Regen	Armor vs. Piercing +15	–
Fanatic's Leggings	LEGGINGS	1,500	50 Tanned Hide Squares	8 Leather Squares	0	0	60	+ 1 Energy Regen	Armor vs. Piercing +15	–
Cultist's Leggings	LEGGINGS	15,000	100 Tanned Hide Squares	10 Elonian Leather Squares	0	0	60	+ 1 Energy Regen	Armor vs. Piercing +15	–
Cultist's Leggings	LEGGINGS	15,000	100 Tanned Hide Squares	10 Elonian Leather Squares	30 Globs of Ectoplasm	30 Obsidian Shards	60	+ 1 Energy Regen	Armor vs. Piercing +15	–
Necrotic Leggings	LEGGINGS	150	8 Tanned Hide Squares	2 Shells	0	0	40	+ 1 Energy Regen	Increased damage vs. Holy	–
Necrotic Leggings	LEGGINGS	250	12 Tanned Hide Squares	2 Shells	0	0	49	+ 1 Energy Regen	Increased damage vs. Holy	–
Necrotic Leggings	LEGGINGS	400	16 Tanned Hide Squares	4 Shells	0	0	55	+ 1 Energy Regen	Increased damage vs. Holy	–
Necrotic Leggings	LEGGINGS	700	18 Tanned Hide Squares	6 Shells	0	0	61	+ 1 Energy Regen	Increased damage vs. Holy	–
Necrotic Leggings	LEGGINGS	1,000	22 Tanned Hide Squares	6 Shells	0	0	67	+ 1 Energy Regen	Increased damage vs. Holy	–
Necrotic Leggings	LEGGINGS	1,500	50 Tanned Hide Squares	8 Shells	0	0	70	+ 1 Energy Regen	Increased damage vs. Holy	–
Necrotic Leggings	LEGGINGS	15,000	100 Tanned Hide Squares	10 Shells	0	0	70	+ 1 Energy Regen	Increased damage vs. Holy	–
Necrotic Leggings	LEGGINGS	15,000	100 Tanned Hide Squares	10 Shells	30 Globs of Ectoplasm	30 Obsidian Shards	70	+ 1 Energy Regen	Increased damage vs. Holy	–
Leg Scar Pattern	LEGGINGS	150	8 Rolls of Parchment	0	0	0	30	+ 1 Energy Regen	Max Energy +2	–
Leg Scar Pattern	LEGGINGS	200	12 Rolls of Parchment	2 Feathers	0	0	39	+ 1 Energy Regen	Max Energy +2	–
Leg Scar Pattern	LEGGINGS	300	16 Rolls of Parchment	4 Feathers	0	0	45	+ 1 Energy Regen	Max Energy +2	–
Leg Scar Pattern	LEGGINGS	400	18 Rolls of Parchment	6 Feathers	0	0	51	+ 1 Energy Regen	Max Energy +2	–
Leg Scar Pattern	LEGGINGS	600	22 Rolls of Parchment	6 Feathers	0	0	57	+ 1 Energy Regen	Max Energy +2	–
Leg Scar Pattern	LEGGINGS	800	50 Rolls of Parchment	8 Feathers	0	0	60	+ 1 Energy Regen	Max Energy +2	–
Leg Scar Pattern	LEGGINGS	8,000	100 Rolls of Vellum	10 Feathers	0	0	60	+ 1 Energy Regen	Max Energy +2	–
Leg Scar Pattern	LEGGINGS	8,000	100 Rolls of Vellum	10 Feathers	30 Globs of Ectoplasm	0	60	+ 1 Energy Regen	Max Energy +2	–
Necromancer's Leggings	LEGGINGS	50	2 Tanned Hide Squares	0	0	0	15	+ 1 Energy Regen	–	–
Necromancer's Leggings	LEGGINGS	150	4 Tanned Hide Squares	0	0	0	30	+ 1 Energy Regen	–	–
Necromancer's Leggings	LEGGINGS	250	6 Tanned Hide Squares	0	0	0	39	+ 1 Energy Regen	–	–
Necromancer's Leggings	LEGGINGS	400	8 Tanned Hide Squares	0	0	0	45	+ 1 Energy Regen	–	–
Necromancer's Leggings	LEGGINGS	1,000	18 Tanned Hide Squares	0	0	0	57	+ 1 Energy Regen	–	–
Necromancer's Leggings	LEGGINGS	1,500	22 Tanned Hide Squares	0	0	0	60	+ 1 Energy Regen	–	–
Pagan Leggings	LEGGINGS	150	8 Tanned Hide Squares	2 Granite Slabs	0	0	40	+ 1 Energy Regen	Increased damage vs. Holy	–
Pagan Leggings	LEGGINGS	250	12 Tanned Hide Squares	2 Granite Slabs	0	0	49	+ 1 Energy Regen	Increased damage vs. Holy	–
Pagan Leggings	LEGGINGS	400	16 Tanned Hide Squares	4 Granite Slabs	0	0	55	+ 1 Energy Regen	Increased damage vs. Holy	–
Pagan Leggings	LEGGINGS	700	18 Tanned Hide Squares	6 Granite Slabs	0	0	61	+ 1 Energy Regen	Increased damage vs. Holy	–
Pagan Leggings	LEGGINGS	1,000	22 Tanned Hide Squares	6 Granite Slabs	0	0	67	+ 1 Energy Regen	Increased damage vs. Holy	–
Pagan Leggings	LEGGINGS	1,500	50 Tanned Hide Squares	8 Granite Slabs	0	0	70	+ 1 Energy Regen	Increased damage vs. Holy	–
Blasphemer's Leggings	LEGGINGS	15,000	100 Tanned Hide Squares	10 Granite Slabs	0	0	70	+ 1 Energy Regen	Increased damage vs. Holy	–

Armor cont.

Name	Type	Gold	Material 1	Material 2	Material 3	Material 4	Armor Level	Effect 1	Effect 2	Effect 3
ELEMENTALIST LEGGINGS										
Aeromancer's Leggings	LEGGINGS	150	8 Bolts of Cloth	2 Bolts of Linen	0	0	30	+ 1 Energy Regen	Armor vs. Lightning +15	–
Aeromancer's Leggings	LEGGINGS	250	12 Bolts of Cloth	2 Bolts of Linen	0	0	39	+ 1 Energy Regen	Armor vs. Lightning +15	–
Aeromancer's Leggings	LEGGINGS	400	16 Bolts of Cloth	4 Bolts of Linen	0	0	45	+ 1 Energy Regen	Armor vs. Lightning +15	–
Aeromancer's Leggings	LEGGINGS	700	18 Bolts of Cloth	6 Bolts of Linen	0	0	51	+ 1 Energy Regen	Armor vs. Lightning +15	–
Aeromancer's Leggings	LEGGINGS	1,000	22 Bolts of Cloth	6 Bolts of Linen	0	0	57	+ 1 Energy Regen	Armor vs. Lightning +15	–
Aeromancer's Leggings	LEGGINGS	1,500	50 Bolts of Cloth	8 Bolts of Linen	0	0	60	+ 1 Energy Regen	Armor vs. Lightning +15	–
Aeromancer's Leggings	LEGGINGS	15,000	100 Bolts of Cloth	10 Bolts of Damask	0	0	60	+ 1 Energy Regen	Armor vs. Lightning +15	–
Aeromancer's Leggings	LEGGINGS	15,000	100 Bolts of Cloth	10 Bolts of Damask	30 Globs of Ectoplasm	30 Obsidian Shards	60	+ 1 Energy Regen	Armor vs. Lightning +15	–
Geomancer's Leggings	LEGGINGS	150	8 Bolts of Cloth	2 Granite Slabs	0	0	30	+ 1 Energy Regen	Armor vs. Earth +15	–
Geomancer's Leggings	LEGGINGS	250	12 Bolts of Cloth	2 Granite Slabs	0	0	39	+ 1 Energy Regen	Armor vs. Earth +15	–
Geomancer's Leggings	LEGGINGS	400	16 Bolts of Cloth	4 Granite Slabs	0	0	45	+ 1 Energy Regen	Armor vs. Earth +15	–
Geomancer's Leggings	LEGGINGS	700	18 Bolts of Cloth	6 Granite Slabs	0	0	51	+ 1 Energy Regen	Armor vs. Earth +15	–
Geomancer's Leggings	LEGGINGS	1,000	22 Bolts of Cloth	6 Granite Slabs	0	0	57	+ 1 Energy Regen	Armor vs. Earth +15	–
Geomancer's Leggings	LEGGINGS	1,500	50 Bolts of Cloth	8 Granite Slabs	0	0	60	+ 1 Energy Regen	Armor vs. Earth +15	–
Geomancer's Leggings	LEGGINGS	15,000	100 Bolts of Cloth	10 Granite Slabs	0	0	60	+ 1 Energy Regen	Armor vs. Earth +15	–
Geomancer's Leggings	LEGGINGS	15,000	100 Bolts of Cloth	10 Granite Slabs	30 Globs of Ectoplasm	30 Obsidian Shards	60	+ 1 Energy Regen	Armor vs. Earth +15	–
Pyromancer's Leggings	LEGGINGS	50	4 Bolts of Cloth	0	0	0	15	+ 1 Energy Regen	Armor vs. Fire +15	–
Pyromancer's Leggings	LEGGINGS	150	8 Bolts of Cloth	2 Scales	0	0	30	+ 1 Energy Regen	Armor vs. Fire +15	–
Pyromancer's Leggings	LEGGINGS	250	12 Bolts of Cloth	2 Scales	0	0	39	+ 1 Energy Regen	Armor vs. Fire +15	–
Pyromancer's Leggings	LEGGINGS	400	16 Bolts of Cloth	4 Scales	0	0	45	+ 1 Energy Regen	Armor vs. Fire +15	–
Pyromancer's Leggings	LEGGINGS	700	18 Bolts of Cloth	6 Scales	0	0	51	+ 1 Energy Regen	Armor vs. Fire +15	–
Pyromancer's Leggings	LEGGINGS	1,000	22 Bolts of Cloth	6 Scales	0	0	57	+ 1 Energy Regen	Armor vs. Fire +15	–
Pyromancer's Leggings	LEGGINGS	1,500	50 Bolts of Cloth	8 Scales	0	0	60	+ 1 Energy Regen	Armor vs. Fire +15	–
Pyromancer's Leggings	LEGGINGS	15,000	100 Bolts of Cloth	10 Scales	0	0	60	+ 1 Energy Regen	Armor vs. Fire +15	–
Pyromancer's Leggings	LEGGINGS	15,000	100 Bolts of Cloth	10 Scales	30 Globs of Ectoplasm	30 Obsidian Shards	60	+ 1 Energy Regen	Armor vs. Fire +15	–
Master's Leggings	LEGGINGS	1,000	22 Bolts of Cloth	6 Silk	0	0	57	+ 1 Energy Regen	Armor vs. Elemental +5	–
Master's Leggings	LEGGINGS	1,500	50 Bolts of Cloth	8 Silk	0	0	60	+ 1 Energy Regen	Armor vs. Elemental +5	–
Master's Leggings	LEGGINGS	15,000	100 Bolts of Cloth	10 Silk	0	0	60	+ 1 Energy Regen	Armor vs. Elemental +5	–
Elementalist's Leggings	LEGGINGS	50	2 Bolts of Cloth	0	0	0	15	+ 1 Energy Regen	–	–
Elementalist's Leggings	LEGGINGS	150	4 Bolts of Cloth	0	0	0	30	+ 1 Energy Regen	–	–
Elementalist's Leggings	LEGGINGS	250	6 Bolts of Cloth	0	0	0	30	+ 1 Energy Regen	–	–
Elementalist's Leggings	LEGGINGS	400	8 Bolts of Cloth	0	0	0	45	+ 1 Energy Regen	–	–
Elementalist's Leggings	LEGGINGS	700	16 Bolts of Cloth	0	0	0	51	+ 1 Energy Regen	–	–
Elementalist's Leggings	LEGGINGS	1,000	18 Bolts of Cloth	0	0	0	57	+ 1 Energy Regen	–	–
Elementalist's Leggings	LEGGINGS	1,500	22 Bolts of Cloth	0	0	0	60	+ 1 Energy Regen	–	–
Hydromancer's Leggings	LEGGINGS	150	8 Bolts of Cloth	2 Shells	0	0	30	+ 1 Energy Regen	Armor vs. Cold +15	–
Hydromancer's Leggings	LEGGINGS	250	12 Bolts of Cloth	2 Shells	0	0	39	+ 1 Energy Regen	Armor vs. Cold +15	–
Hydromancer's Leggings	LEGGINGS	400	16 Bolts of Cloth	4 Shells	0	0	45	+ 1 Energy Regen	Armor vs. Cold +15	–
Hydromancer's Leggings	LEGGINGS	700	18 Bolts of Cloth	6 Shells	0	0	51	+ 1 Energy Regen	Armor vs. Cold +15	–
Hydromancer's Leggings	LEGGINGS	1,000	22 Bolts of Cloth	6 Shells	0	0	57	+ 1 Energy Regen	Armor vs. Cold +15	–
Hydromancer's Leggings	LEGGINGS	1,500	50 Bolts of Cloth	8 Shells	0	0	60	+ 1 Energy Regen	Armor vs. Cold +15	–
Hydromancer's Leggings	LEGGINGS	15,000	100 Bolts of Cloth	10 Shells	0	0	60	+ 1 Energy Regen	Armor vs. Cold +15	–
Hydromancer's Leggings	LEGGINGS	15,000	100 Bolts of Cloth	10 Shells	30 Globs of Ectoplasm	30 Obsidian Shards	60	+ 1 Energy Regen	Armor vs. Cold +15	–
MONK LEGGINGS										
Silk Pants	LEGGINGS	150	8 Bolts of Cloth	2 Silk	0	0	35	+ 1 Energy Regen	Armor vs. Cold -5	–
Silk Pants	LEGGINGS	250	12 Bolts of Cloth	2 Silk	0	0	44	+ 1 Energy Regen	Armor vs. Cold -5	–
Silk Pants	LEGGINGS	400	16 Bolts of Cloth	4 Silk	0	0	50	+ 1 Energy Regen	Armor vs. Cold -5	–
Silk Pants	LEGGINGS	700	18 Bolts of Cloth	6 Silk	0	0	56	+ 1 Energy Regen	Armor vs. Cold -5	–
Silk Pants	LEGGINGS	1,000	22 Bolts of Cloth	6 Silk	0	0	62	+ 1 Energy Regen	Armor vs. Cold -5	–
Silk Pants	LEGGINGS	1,500	50 Bolts of Cloth	8 Silk	0	0	65	+ 1 Energy Regen	Armor vs. Cold -5	–
Silk Pants	LEGGINGS	15,000	100 Bolts of Cloth	10 Silk	0	0	65	+ 1 Energy Regen	Armor vs. Cold -5	–
Silk Pants	LEGGINGS	15,000	100 Bolts of Cloth	10 Silk	30 Globs of Ectoplasm	30 Obsidian Shards	65	+ 1 Energy Regen	Armor vs. Cold -5	–
Sacred Pants	LEGGINGS	150	8 Bolts of Cloth	2 Bolts of Linen	0	0	30	+ 1 Energy Regen	Armor vs. Elemental +5	–
Sacred Pants	LEGGINGS	250	12 Bolts of Cloth	2 Bolts of Linen	0	0	39	+ 1 Energy Regen	Armor vs. Elemental +5	–
Sacred Pants	LEGGINGS	400	16 Bolts of Cloth	4 Bolts of Linen	0	0	45	+ 1 Energy Regen	Armor vs. Elemental +5	–
Sacred Pants	LEGGINGS	700	18 Bolts of Cloth	6 Bolts of Linen	0	0	51	+ 1 Energy Regen	Armor vs. Elemental +5	–
Sacred Pants	LEGGINGS	1,000	22 Bolts of Cloth	6 Bolts of Linen	0	0	57	+ 1 Energy Regen	Armor vs. Elemental +5	–
Sacred Pants	LEGGINGS	1,500	50 Bolts of Cloth	8 Bolts of Linen	0	0	60	+ 1 Energy Regen	Armor vs. Elemental +5	–
Saintly Pants	LEGGINGS	15,000	100 Bolts of Cloth	10 Bolts of Damask	0	0	60	+ 1 Energy Regen	Armor vs. Elemental +5	–
Saintly Pants	LEGGINGS	15,000	100 Bolts of Cloth	10 Bolts of Damask	30 Globs of Ectoplasm	30 Obsidian Shards	60	+ 1 Energy Regen	Armor vs. Elemental +5	–
Ascetic's Leg Design	LEGGINGS	150	8 Rolls of Parchment	0	0	0	30	+ 1 Energy Regen	Max Energy +2	–
Ascetic's Leg Design	LEGGINGS	200	12 Rolls of Parchment	2 Feathers	0	0	39	+ 1 Energy Regen	Max Energy +2	–

Armor cont.

Name	Type	Gold	Material 1	Material 2	Material 3	Material 4	Armor Level	Effect 1	Effect 2	Effect 3
Ascetic's Leg Design	LEGGINGS	300	16 Rolls of Parchment	4 Feathers	0	0	45	+ 1 Energy Regen	Max Energy +2	–
Ascetic's Leg Design	LEGGINGS	400	18 Rolls of Parchment	6 Feathers	0	0	51	+ 1 Energy Regen	Max Energy +2	–
Ascetic's Leg Design	LEGGINGS	600	22 Rolls of Parchment	6 Feathers	0	0	57	+ 1 Energy Regen	Max Energy +2	–
Ascetic's Leg Design	LEGGINGS	800	50 Rolls of Parchment	8 Feathers	0	0	60	+ 1 Energy Regen	Max Energy +2	–
Ascetic's Leg Design	LEGGINGS	8,000	100 Rolls of Vellum	10 Feathers	0	0	60	+ 1 Energy Regen	Max Energy +2	–
Ascetic's Leg Design	LEGGINGS	8,000	100 Rolls of Vellum	10 Feathers	30 Globs of Ectoplasm	0	60	+ 1 Energy Regen	Max Energy +2	–
Monk Pants	LEGGINGS	50	2 Bolts of Cloth	0	0	0	15	+ 1 Energy Regen	–	–
Monk Pants	LEGGINGS	150	4 Bolts of Cloth	0	0	0	30	+ 1 Energy Regen	–	–
Monk Pants	LEGGINGS	250	6 Bolts of Cloth	0	0	0	39	+ 1 Energy Regen	–	–
Monk Pants	LEGGINGS	400	8 Bolts of Cloth	0	0	0	45	+ 1 Energy Regen	–	–
Monk Pants	LEGGINGS	1,000	18 Bolts of Cloth	0	0	0	57	+ 1 Energy Regen	–	–
Monk Pants	LEGGINGS	1,500	22 Bolts of Cloth	0	0	0	60	+ 1 Energy Regen	–	–
Wanderer's Pants	LEGGINGS	50	4 Bolts of Cloth	0	0	0	15	+ 1 Energy Regen	Armor vs. Elemental +5	–
Wanderer's Pants	LEGGINGS	150	8 Bolts of Cloth	2 Tanned Hide Squares	0	0	30	+ 1 Energy Regen	Armor vs. Elemental +5	–
Wanderer's Pants	LEGGINGS	250	12 Bolts of Cloth	2 Tanned Hide Squares	0	0	39	+ 1 Energy Regen	Armor vs. Elemental +5	–
Wanderer's Pants	LEGGINGS	400	16 Bolts of Cloth	4 Tanned Hide Squares	0	0	45	+ 1 Energy Regen	Armor vs. Elemental +5	–
Wanderer's Pants	LEGGINGS	700	18 Bolts of Cloth	6 Tanned Hide Squares	0	0	51	+ 1 Energy Regen	Armor vs. Elemental +5	–
Wanderer's Pants	LEGGINGS	1,000	22 Bolts of Cloth	6 Tanned Hide Squares	0	0	57	+ 1 Energy Regen	Armor vs. Elemental +5	–
Wanderer's Pants	LEGGINGS	1,500	50 Bolts of Cloth	8 Tanned Hide Squares	0	0	60	+ 1 Energy Regen	Armor vs. Elemental +5	–
Wanderer's Pants	LEGGINGS	15,000	100 Bolts of Cloth	10 Tanned Hide Squares	0	0	60	+ 1 Energy Regen	Armor vs. Elemental +5	–
Wanderer's Pants	LEGGINGS	15,000	100 Bolts of Cloth	10 Tanned Hide Squares	30 Globs of Ectoplasm	30 Obsidian Shards	60	+ 1 Energy Regen	Armor vs. Elemental +5	–
Censor's Pants	LEGGINGS	150	8 Bolts of Cloth	2 Steel Ingots	0	0	30	+ 1 Energy Regen	Armor vs. Physical +10	Max Energy -1
Censor's Pants	LEGGINGS	250	12 Bolts of Cloth	2 Steel Ingots	0	0	39	+ 1 Energy Regen	Armor vs. Physical +10	Max Energy -1
Censor's Pants	LEGGINGS	400	16 Bolts of Cloth	4 Steel Ingots	0	0	45	+ 1 Energy Regen	Armor vs. Physical +10	Max Energy -1
Censor's Pants	LEGGINGS	700	18 Bolts of Cloth	6 Steel Ingots	0	0	51	+ 1 Energy Regen	Armor vs. Physical +10	Max Energy -1
Censor's Pants	LEGGINGS	1,000	22 Bolts of Cloth	6 Steel Ingots	0	0	57	+ 1 Energy Regen	Armor vs. Physical +10	Max Energy -1
Censor's Pants	LEGGINGS	1,500	50 Bolts of Cloth	8 Steel Ingots	0	0	60	+ 1 Energy Regen	Armor vs. Physical +10	Max Energy -1
Judge's Pants	LEGGINGS	15,000	100 Bolts of Cloth	10 Deldrimor Steel Ingots	0	0	60	+ 1 Energy Regen	Armor vs. Physical +10	Max Energy -1
Judge's Pants	LEGGINGS	15,000	100 Bolts of Cloth	10 Deldrimor Steel Ingots	30 Globs of Ectoplasm	30 Obsidian Shards	60	+ 1 Energy Regen	Armor vs. Physical +10	Max Energy -1
Ascetic's Leg Design	LEGGINGS	150	8 Rolls of Parchment	0	0	0	30	+ 1 Energy Regen	Max Energy +2	–
Ascetic's Leg Design	LEGGINGS	200	12 Rolls of Parchment	2 Feathers	0	0	39	+ 1 Energy Regen	Max Energy +2	–
Ascetic's Leg Design	LEGGINGS	300	16 Rolls of Parchment	4 Feathers	0	0	45	+ 1 Energy Regen	Max Energy +2	–
Ascetic's Leg Design	LEGGINGS	400	18 Rolls of Parchment	6 Feathers	0	0	51	+ 1 Energy Regen	Max Energy +2	–
Ascetic's Leg Design	LEGGINGS	600	22 Rolls of Parchment	6 Feathers	0	0	57	+ 1 Energy Regen	Max Energy +2	–
Ascetic's Leg Design	LEGGINGS	800	50 Rolls of Parchment	8 Feathers	0	0	60	+ 1 Energy Regen	Max Energy +2	–
Ascetic's Leg Design	LEGGINGS	8,000	100 Rolls of Vellum	10 Feathers	0	0	60	+ 1 Energy Regen	Max Energy +2	–

WARRIOR LEGGINGS

Name	Type	Gold	Material 1	Material 2	Material 3	Material 4	Armor Level	Effect 1	Effect 2	Effect 3
Ascalon Leggings	LEGGINGS	50	4 Iron Ingots	0	0	0	35	Armor vs. Physical + 10	Damage -1	–
Ascalon Leggings	LEGGINGS	150	8 Iron Ingots	2 Fur Squares	0	0	50	Armor vs. Physical + 10	Damage -1	–
Ascalon Leggings	LEGGINGS	250	12 Iron Ingots	2 Fur Squares	0	0	59	Armor vs. Physical + 10	Damage -1	–
Ascalon Leggings	LEGGINGS	400	16 Iron Ingots	4 Fur Squares	0	0	65	Armor vs. Physical + 10	Damage -1	–
Ascalon Leggings	LEGGINGS	700	18 Iron Ingots	6 Fur Squares	0	0	71	Armor vs. Physical + 10	Damage -1	–
Ascalon Leggings	LEGGINGS	1,000	22 Iron Ingots	6 Fur Squares	0	0	77	Armor vs. Physical + 10	Damage -1	–
Ascalon Leggings	LEGGINGS	1,500	50 Iron Ingots	8 Fur Squares	0	0	80	Armor vs. Physical + 10	Damage -1	–
Ascalon Leggings	LEGGINGS	15,000	100 Iron Ingots	10 Fur Squares	0	0	80	Armor vs. Physical + 10	Damage -1	–
Ascalon Leggings	LEGGINGS	15,000	100 Iron Ingots	10 Fur Squares	30 Globs of Ectoplasm	30 Obsidian Shards	80	Armor vs. Physical + 10	Damage -1	–
Chainmail Leggings	LEGGINGS	400	8 Iron Ingots	0	0	0	65	Armor vs. Physical + 20	–	–
Chainmail Leggings	LEGGINGS	700	16 Iron Ingots	0	0	0	71	Armor vs. Physical + 20	–	–
Chainmail Leggings	LEGGINGS	1,000	18 Iron Ingots	0	0	0	77	Armor vs. Physical + 20	–	–
Wyvern Leggings	LEGGINGS	150	8 Iron Ingots	2 Scales	0	0	55	Armor vs. Physical + 10	–	–
Wyvern Leggings	LEGGINGS	250	12 Iron Ingots	2 Scales	0	0	61	Armor vs. Physical + 10	–	–
Wyvern Leggings	LEGGINGS	400	16 Iron Ingots	4 Scales	0	0	70	Armor vs. Physical + 10	–	–
Wyvern Leggings	LEGGINGS	700	18 Iron Ingots	6 Scales	0	0	76	Armor vs. Physical + 10	–	–
Wyvern Leggings	LEGGINGS	1,000	22 Iron Ingots	6 Scales	0	0	82	Armor vs. Physical + 10	–	–
Wyvern Leggings	LEGGINGS	1,500	50 Iron Ingots	8 Scales	0	0	85	Armor vs. Physical + 10	–	–
Dragon Leggings	LEGGINGS	15,000	100 Iron Ingots	10 Scales	0	0	85	Armor vs. Physical + 10	–	–
Dragon Leggings	LEGGINGS	15,000	100 Iron Ingots	10 Scales	30 Globs of Ectoplasm	30 Obsidian Shards	85	Armor vs. Physical + 10	–	–
Gladiator's Leggings	LEGGINGS	150	8 Iron Ingots	8 Tanned Hide Squares	0	0	50	Max Energy +2	Armor vs. Physical +20	–
Gladiator's Leggings	LEGGINGS	250	12 Iron Ingots	12 Tanned Hide Squares	0	0	59	Max Energy +2	Armor vs. Physical +20	–
Gladiator's Leggings	LEGGINGS	400	16 Iron Ingots	16 Tanned Hide Squares	0	0	65	Max Energy +2	Armor vs. Physical +20	–
Gladiator's Leggings	LEGGINGS	700	18 Iron Ingots	18 Tanned Hide Squares	0	0	71	Max Energy +2	Armor vs. Physical +20	–
Gladiator's Leggings	LEGGINGS	1,000	22 Iron Ingots	22 Tanned Hide Squares	0	0	77	Max Energy +2	Armor vs. Physical +20	–
Gladiator's Leggings	LEGGINGS	1,500	50 Iron Ingots	32 Tanned Hide Squares	0	0	80	Max Energy +2	Armor vs. Physical +20	–

Armor cont.

Name	Type	Gold	Material 1	Material 2	Material 3	Material 4	Armor Level	Effect 1	Effect 2	Effect 3
Gladiator's Leggings	LEGGINGS	15,000	100 Iron Ingots	32 Tanned Hide Squares	0	0	80	Max Energy +2	Armor vs. Physical +20	–
Gladiator's Leggings	LEGGINGS	15,000	100 Iron Ingots	32 Tanned Hide Squares	30 Globs of Ectoplasm	30 Obsidian Shards	80	Max Energy +2	Armor vs. Physical +20	–
Knight's Leggings	LEGGINGS	1,000	22 Iron Ingots	6 Leather Squares	0	0	77	Armor vs. Physical + 10	Damage -1	–
Knight's Leggings	LEGGINGS	1,500	50 Iron Ingots	8 Leather Squares	0	0	80	Armor vs. Physical + 10	Damage -1	–
Knight's Leggings	LEGGINGS	15,000	100 Iron Ingots	10 Elonian Leather Squares	0	0	80	Armor vs. Physical + 10	Damage -1	–
Knight's Leggings	LEGGINGS	1,500	50 Iron Ingots	8 Leather Squares	0	0	80	Armor vs. Physical + 10	Damage -1	–
Soldier's Leggings	LEGGINGS	700	18 Iron Ingots	6 Steel Ingots	0	0	71	Armor vs. Physical + 20	–	–
Soldier's Leggings	LEGGINGS	1,000	22 Iron Ingots	6 Steel Ingots	0	0	77	Armor vs. Physical + 20	–	–
Platemail Leggings	LEGGINGS	1,000	22 Iron Ingots	6 Steel Ingots	0	0	77	Armor vs. Physical + 20	–	–
Platemail Leggings	LEGGINGS	1,500	50 Iron Ingots	8 Steel Ingots	0	0	80	Armor vs. Physical + 20	–	–
Platemail Leggings	LEGGINGS	15,000	100 Iron Ingots	10 Deldrimor Steel Ingots	0	0	80	Armor vs. Physical + 20	–	–
Platemail Leggings	LEGGINGS	15,000	100 Iron Ingots	10 Deldrimor Steel Ingots	30 Globs of Ectoplasm	30 Obsidian Shards	80	Armor vs. Physical + 20	–	–
Ringmail Leggings	LEGGINGS	50	2 Iron Ingots	0	0	0	35	Armor vs. Physical + 20	–	–
Ringmail Leggings	LEGGINGS	150	4 Iron Ingots	0	0	0	50	Armor vs. Physical + 20	–	–
Ringmail Leggings	LEGGINGS	250	6 Iron Ingots	0	0	0	59	Armor vs. Physical + 20	–	–

RANGER LEGGINGS

Name	Type	Gold	Material 1	Material 2	Material 3	Material 4	Armor Level	Effect 1	Effect 2	Effect 3
Hunter's Leggings	LEGGINGS	150	8 Tanned Hide Squares	8 Bone	0	0	40	+ 1 Energy Regen	Armor vs. Elemental +30	Armor vs. Piercing +15
Hunter's Leggings	LEGGINGS	250	12 Tanned Hide Squares	8 Bone	0	0	49	+ 1 Energy Regen	Armor vs. Elemental +30	Armor vs. Piercing +15
Hunter's Leggings	LEGGINGS	400	16 Tanned Hide Squares	16 Bone	0	0	55	+ 1 Energy Regen	Armor vs. Elemental +30	Armor vs. Piercing +15
Hunter's Leggings	LEGGINGS	700	18 Tanned Hide Squares	18 Bone	0	0	61	+ 1 Energy Regen	Armor vs. Elemental +30	Armor vs. Piercing +15
Hunter's Leggings	LEGGINGS	1,000	22 Tanned Hide Squares	22 Bone	0	0	67	+ 1 Energy Regen	Armor vs. Elemental +30	Armor vs. Piercing +15
Hunter's Leggings	LEGGINGS	1,500	50 Tanned Hide Squares	50 Bone	0	0	70	+ 1 Energy Regen	Armor vs. Elemental +30	Armor vs. Piercing +15
Hunter's Leggings	LEGGINGS	15,000	100 Tanned Hide Squares	100 Bone	0	0	70	+ 1 Energy Regen	Armor vs. Elemental +30	Armor vs. Piercing +15
Hunter's Leggings	LEGGINGS	15,000	100 Tanned Hide Squares	100 Bone	30 Globs of Ectoplasm	30 Obsidian Shards	70	+ 1 Energy Regen	Armor vs. Elemental +30	Armor vs. Piercing +15
Druid's Leggings	LEGGINGS	150	8 Tanned Hide Squares	8 Wood Planks	0	0	40	+ 1 Energy Regen	Max Energy +1	Armor vs. Elemental +30
Druid's Leggings	LEGGINGS	250	12 Tanned Hide Squares	8 Wood Planks	0	0	49	+ 1 Energy Regen	Max Energy +1	Armor vs. Elemental +30
Druid's Leggings	LEGGINGS	400	16 Tanned Hide Squares	16 Wood Planks	0	0	55	+ 1 Energy Regen	Max Energy +1	Armor vs. Elemental +30
Druid's Leggings	LEGGINGS	700	18 Tanned Hide Squares	18 Wood Planks	0	0	61	+ 1 Energy Regen	Max Energy +1	Armor vs. Elemental +30
Druid's Leggings	LEGGINGS	1,000	22 Tanned Hide Squares	22 Wood Planks	0	0	67	+ 1 Energy Regen	Max Energy +1	Armor vs. Elemental +30
Druid's Leggings	LEGGINGS	1,500	50 Tanned Hide Squares	50 Wood Planks	0	0	70	+ 1 Energy Regen	Max Energy +1	Armor vs. Elemental +30
Druid's Leggings	LEGGINGS	15,000	100 Tanned Hide Squares	100 Wood Planks	0	0	70	+ 1 Energy Regen	Max Energy +1	Armor vs. Elemental +30
Druid's Leggings	LEGGINGS	15,000	100 Tanned Hide Squares	100 Wood Planks	30 Globs of Ectoplasm	30 Obsidian Shards	70	+ 1 Energy Regen	Max Energy +1	Armor vs. Elemental +30
Fur-Lined Leggings	LEGGINGS	50	4 Tanned Hide Squares	0	0	0	25	+ 1 Energy Regen	Armor vs. Elemental +30	Armor vs. Cold +15
Fur-Lined Leggings	LEGGINGS	150	8 Tanned Hide Squares	2 Fur Squares	0	0	40	+ 1 Energy Regen	Armor vs. Elemental +30	Armor vs. Cold +15
Fur-Lined Leggings	LEGGINGS	250	12 Tanned Hide Squares	2 Fur Squares	0	0	49	+ 1 Energy Regen	Armor vs. Elemental +30	Armor vs. Cold +15
Fur-Lined Leggings	LEGGINGS	400	16 Tanned Hide Squares	4 Fur Squares	0	0	55	+ 1 Energy Regen	Armor vs. Elemental +30	Armor vs. Cold +15
Fur-Lined Leggings	LEGGINGS	700	18 Tanned Hide Squares	6 Fur Squares	0	0	61	+ 1 Energy Regen	Armor vs. Elemental +30	Armor vs. Cold +15
Fur-Lined Leggings	LEGGINGS	1,000	22 Tanned Hide Squares	6 Fur Squares	0	0	67	+ 1 Energy Regen	Armor vs. Elemental +30	Armor vs. Cold +15
Fur-Lined Leggings	LEGGINGS	1,500	50 Tanned Hide Squares	8 Fur Squares	0	0	70	+ 1 Energy Regen	Armor vs. Elemental +30	Armor vs. Cold +15
Frostbound Leggings	LEGGINGS	15,000	100 Tanned Hide Squares	10 Fur Squares	0	0	70	+ 1 Energy Regen	Armor vs. Elemental +30	Armor vs. Cold +15
Frostbound Leggings	LEGGINGS	15,000	100 Tanned Hide Squares	10 Fur Squares	30 Globs of Ectoplasm	30 Obsidian Shards	70	+ 1 Energy Regen	Armor vs. Elemental +30	Armor vs. Cold +15
Studded Leather Leggings	LEGGINGS	150	8 Tanned Hide Squares	2 Steel Ingots	0	0	40	+ 1 Energy Regen	Armor vs. Elemental +30	Armor vs. Lightning +15
Studded Leather Leggings	LEGGINGS	250	12 Tanned Hide Squares	2 Steel Ingots	0	0	49	+ 1 Energy Regen	Armor vs. Elemental +30	Armor vs. Lightning +15
Studded Leather Leggings	LEGGINGS	400	16 Tanned Hide Squares	4 Steel Ingots	0	0	55	+ 1 Energy Regen	Armor vs. Elemental +30	Armor vs. Lightning +15
Studded Leather Leggings	LEGGINGS	700	18 Tanned Hide Squares	6 Steel Ingots	0	0	61	+ 1 Energy Regen	Armor vs. Elemental +30	Armor vs. Lightning +15
Studded Leather Leggings	LEGGINGS	1,000	22 Tanned Hide Squares	6 Steel Ingots	0	0	67	+ 1 Energy Regen	Armor vs. Elemental +30	Armor vs. Lightning +15
Studded Leather Leggings	LEGGINGS	1,500	50 Tanned Hide Squares	8 Steel Ingots	0	0	70	+ 1 Energy Regen	Armor vs. Elemental +30	Armor vs. Lightning +15
Studded Leather Leggings	LEGGINGS	15,000	100 Tanned Hide Squares	10 Deldrimor Steel Ingots	0	0	70	+ 1 Energy Regen	Armor vs. Elemental +30	Armor vs. Lightning +15
Studded Leather Leggings	LEGGINGS	15,000	100 Tanned Hide Squares	10 Deldrimor Steel Ingots	30 Globs of Ectoplasm	30 Obsidian Shards	70	+ 1 Energy Regen	Armor vs. Elemental +30	Armor vs. Lightning +15
Drakescale Leggings	LEGGINGS	150	8 Tanned Hide Squares	2 Scales	0	0	40	Armor vs. Elemental +30	Armor vs. Fire +15	+1 Energy Regen
Drakescale Leggings	LEGGINGS	250	12 Tanned Hide Squares	2 Scales	0	0	49	Armor vs. Elemental +30	Armor vs. Fire +15	+1 Energy Regen
Drakescale Leggings	LEGGINGS	400	16 Tanned Hide Squares	4 Scales	0	0	55	Armor vs. Elemental +30	Armor vs. Fire +15	+1 Energy Regen
Drakescale Leggings	LEGGINGS	700	18 Tanned Hide Squares	6 Scales	0	0	61	Armor vs. Elemental +30	Armor vs. Fire +15	+1 Energy Regen
Drakescale Leggings	LEGGINGS	1,000	22 Tanned Hide Squares	6 Scales	0	0	67	Armor vs. Elemental +30	Armor vs. Fire +15	+1 Energy Regen
Drakescale Leggings	LEGGINGS	1,500	50 Tanned Hide Squares	8 Scales	0	0	70	Armor vs. Elemental +30	Armor vs. Fire +15	+1 Energy Regen
Drakescale Leggings	LEGGINGS	15,000	100 Tanned Hide Squares	10 Scales	0	0	70	Armor vs. Elemental +30	Armor vs. Fire +15	+1 Energy Regen
Drakescale Leggings	LEGGINGS	15,000	100 Tanned Hide Squares	10 Scales	30 Globs of Ectoplasm	30 Obsidian Shards	70	Armor vs. Elemental +30	Armor vs. Fire +15	+1 Energy Regen
Leather Leggings	LEGGINGS	50	2 Tanned Hide Squares	0	0	0	25	Armor vs. Elemental +30	+1 Energy Regen	–
Leather Leggings	LEGGINGS	150	4 Tanned Hide Squares	0	0	0	40	Armor vs. Elemental +30	+1 Energy Regen	–
Leather Leggings	LEGGINGS	250	6 Tanned Hide Squares	0	0	0	49	Armor vs. Elemental +30	+1 Energy Regen	–
Leather Leggings	LEGGINGS	400	8 Tanned Hide Squares	0	0	0	55	Armor vs. Elemental +30	+1 Energy Regen	–
Leather Leggings	LEGGINGS	700	16 Tanned Hide Squares	0	0	0	61	Armor vs. Elemental +30	+1 Energy Regen	–
Leather Leggings	LEGGINGS	1,000	18 Tanned Hide Squares	0	0	0	67	Armor vs. Elemental +30	+1 Energy Regen	–
Leather Leggings	LEGGINGS	1,500	22 Tanned Hide Squares	0	0	0	70	Armor vs. Elemental +30	+1 Energy Regen	–